Set
2 vers

The Letters of
Alfred Lord Tennyson

1851–1870

THE LETTERS OF
—ALFRED—
LORD TENNYSON

Edited by
Cecil Y. Lang and Edgar F. Shannon, Jr.

VOLUME II · 1851–1870

CLARENDON PRESS · OXFORD
1987

Oxford University Press, Walton Street, Oxford OX2 6DP
*Oxford New York Toronto
Delhi Bombay Calcutta Madras Karachi
Petaling Jaya Singapore Hong Kong Tokyo
Nairobi Dar es Salaam Cape Town
Melbourne Auckland
and associated companies in
Beirut Berlin Ibadan Nicosia*

Oxford is a trade mark of Oxford University Press

© *Cecil Y. Lang and Edgar F. Shannon Jr. 1987*

All rights reserved. No part of this publication may be reproduced, stored in a retrieval system, or transmitted, in any form or by any means, electronic, mechanical, photocopying, recording, or otherwise, without the prior permission of Oxford University Press

*British Library Cataloguing in Publication Data
Tennyson, Alfred Tennyson, Baron
The letters of Alfred Lord Tennyson.
Vol. 2: 1851–1870
1. Tennyson, Alfred Tennyson, Baron—Biography
2. Poets, English—19th century—Biography
I. Title II. Lang, Cecil Y. III. Shannon, Edgar F.
821'.8 PR5581.A2
ISBN 0-19-812691-3*

*Library of Congress Cataloging in Publication Data
(Revised for volume 2)
Tennyson, Alfred Tennyson, Baron, 1809–1892.
The letters of Alfred Lord Tennyson.
Includes bibliographical references and indexes.
Contents: v. 1. 1821–1850—v. 2. 1851–1870.
1. Tennyson, Alfred Tennyson, Baron, 1809–1892—
Correspondence. 2. Poets, English—19th century—
Correspondence. I. Lang, Cecil Y. II. Shannon,
Edgar Finley, 1918– . III. Title.
PR5581.A4 1981   821'.8   80-49924
ISBN 0-19-812569-0 (Oxford University Press: v. 1)
ISBN 0-19-812691-3*

*Set by Hope Services, Abingdon
Printed at the Oxford University Printing House, Oxford
by David Stanford
Printer to the University*

ACKNOWLEDGEMENTS

IN preparing Volume Two of these letters we have accrued many more debts. To those already mentioned in Volume One we reaffirm our thanks, and with equal gratitude for permission to publish letters or for other assistance we add to the roster the following names: W. Baker, Mary Anne Bonney, Lord Boyne, Gordon Braden, T. A. J. Burnett, Sidney Burris, Herbert Cahoon, Nancy Coffin, Betty Coley, Michael Darling, Pauline Dower, Hoyt Duggan, Angus Easson, Ray English, Roger Evans, Richard Garnett, Philip Gaskell, Susan Gates, Lesley Gordon, Anne S. Gwyn, Walter E. Houghton, Jr., Derek Hudson, Kathleen Hughes, Ian Jack, Walter C. Johnson, Trevor Kaye, J. C. Levenson, Kenneth A. Lohf, William H. Loos, Roger G. L. Lushington, R. B. MacCarthy, Terry Meyers, Leonée Ormond, Mark Scowcroft, Arthur Sherbo, Jerry N. Showalter, Margaret Stetz, Robert H. Super, Lola Szladits, Kathleen Tillotson, J. B. Trapp, Patrick Waddington, John O. Waller, Patricia C. Willis, and Viola Winner.

Charlottesville, Virginia

C.Y.L.
E.F.S., Jr.

CONTENTS

Editorial Principles	ix
Abbreviations	xi
Text of the Letters (1851–1870)	1
Appendices	559
Index of Correspondents	569
Index	573

EDITORIAL PRINCIPLES

1. In all letters, the date, address, salutation, and closing have been normalized; square brackets indicate that an *essential* part of the date is an editorial addition.

2. Most abbreviations have been expanded, superior numbers and letters lowered.

3. Punctuation has occasionally been silently adjusted.

4. A few cancellations have been retained in angle brackets ⟨ ⟩.

5. Hallam Tennyson's *Memoir* in its various forms is the primary source of many letters and much information. The 1897 edition is more common than the one-volume issue in 1899 and has therefore been preferred when feasible. *Materials for a Life of A. T.* has been used only when the *Memoir* is inferior or deficient, and 'draft *Materials*', *postremus inter pares*, only when for some reason no other will serve.

6. Previous publication, in whole or in part, has not been recorded. No earlier collection of Tennyson letters exists, but so many extracts have been published in so many memoirs and biographies and critical studies that any fair accounting would be otiose, overwhelming, and, finally, ridiculous.

7. Postmarks, addresses, and watermarks have been recorded when conceivably useful in any way.

ABBREVIATIONS

Allibone	S. Austin Allibone, *A Critical Dictionary of English Literature and British and American Authors*
Background	Charles Tennyson and Hope Dyson, *The Tennysons: Background to Genius* (Macmillan, 1974)
Boase	Frederic Boase, *Modern English Biography*
BL	British Library
CBEL	*Cambridge Bibliography of English Literature*
Charles Tennyson	*Alfred Tennyson* by His Grandson Charles Tennyson (Macmillan, 1949; reissued, with alterations, 1968)
DNB	*The Dictionary of National Biography*
draft *Materials*	Manuscript of *Materials for a Life of A. T.* in Tennyson Reseearch Centre (TRC)
Foster	*Alumni Oxonienses*
Journal	*Emily Tennyson's Journal*, ed. James O. Hoge (Charlottesville: University Press of Virginia, 1981)
Journal	The manuscript of Emily Tennyson's Journal in the Tennyson Research Centre
LAO	Lincolnshire Archives Office, The Castle, Lincoln
The Letters of Arthur Henry Hallam	*The Letters of Arthur Henry Hallam*, ed. Jack Kolb (Ohio State University Press, 1981)
The Letters of Edward FitzGerald	*The Letters of Edward FitzGerald*, ed. Alfred McKinley Terhune and Annabelle Burdick Terhune (4 vols., Princeton University Press, 1980)
Materials	[Hallam Tennyson] *Materials for a Life of A.T. Collected for My Children* (4 vols., privately printed, 1895)
Memoir	[Hallam Tennyson] *Alfred Lord Tennyson: A Memoir By His Son* (2 vols., Macmillan, 1897)
Memoir, 1899	[Hallam Tennyson] *Alfred Lord Tennyson: A Memoir By His Son* (Macmillan, 1899)
Motter	T. H. Vail Motter (ed.), *The Writings of Arthur Henry Hallam* (New York: Modern Language Association of America; London: Oxford University Press, 1943)
OED	*The Oxford English Dictionary*
Rader	Ralph Rader, *Tennyson's Maud: The Biographical Genesis* (Berkeley and Los Angeles: University of California Press, 1963)

Abbreviations

Ricks	Christopher Ricks (ed.), *The Poems of Tennyson* (Longmans, 1969)
Sanders	Charles R. Sanders, *Carlyle's Friendships and Other Studies* (Durham, N.C.: Duke University Press, 1977)
Trinity College	Trinity College, University of Cambridge
TRC	Tennyson Research Centre, Central Library, Lincoln
Venn	John Venn and J. A. Venn, *Alumni Cantabrigienses*

THE LETTERS

To EDWARD MOXON
MS. Harvard.

PARK HOUSE, MAIDSTONE, Tuesday, [?c. 7 January 1851]

Dear Moxon

Your tailor wanted ready money and I had none so I sent him to you.

In the new stanza to Lady Clare[1] I hope the Printers did not print the word 'dropp*ed*' I always writing 'dropt.' Correct it if there is time, if so printed—not that it matters much—

Ever yours
A. Tennyson

To EMILY SELLWOOD TENNYSON
MS. Tennyson Research Centre.

[? early January 1851]

The Twickenham house is a very good one with lots of room. The only objection I have to it is its nearness to London: which is rather a horror to me. I will tell thee all about it tomorrow and other things.

Thine
A.

I shall come by one of the afternoon trains.

To EDWARD MOXON
MS. Historical Society of Pennsylvania.

[*c.* 12 or 13 January 1851]

My dear Moxon

Will you be kind enough to send these papers to Rogers's Bank, viz. four Treasury receipt stamps and the E. C. Railway papers and the cheque on Prescott for £40, as soon as you can. I don't know if any harm could be done if the papers were stolen but the parcel seems less likely to be violated if directed to a publisher than to a Banker.

With respect to the Princess you shall have her in a day or two but as I have inserted two or three passages[1] which in my opinion very greatly improve the work though they alter the paging it may be as well for you to delay printing the remainder till you get the first sheets back. I shall then

---

[1] Lines 61–4.

[1] 'The Seizure-Cataleptic alterations' (*Journal*, p. 23), added to *The Princess*, 4th edn. (1851).

want them back once more to see that all is right before they go to press, *not to keep*, so mind you send them.

We are moving tomorrow to the Talbot Hotel, Cuckfield, having taken a house near that town and I suppose we shall be at the inn for a week or ten days. Our new house is called Buckingham hall in the parish of Slaugham. I will write again but be so good as to acknowledge this per return of post by a note directed to the Talbot Hotel as before stated.

Ever yours
A. Tennyson

To SOPHIA (RAWNSLEY) ELMHIRST

MS. Duke.

PARK HOUSE, MAIDSTONE, [mid-January 1851]

My dear Sophy

I have been for more than a fortnight very unwell and latterly quite knocked up with an excruciating face-ache agreeably varied with nervous headache like a hammer in the temples; but even were I quite well I could not come at present being just about to move into our new house near Cuckfield and having to be on the spot to superintend unpacking furniture etc. I am grieved that I cannot come but *really and truly* I cannot.

Ever yours affectionately
A. Tennyson

To JOHN FORSTER

MS. Tennyson Research Centre.

THE HALL, WARNINGLID, CRAWLEY, [21 January 1851]

My dear Forster

You might have written a week ago or a month for aught I knew. I have left Park House and been living at an Hotel in Cuckfield, an Hotel at Horsham and in this place, Warninglid, from which again I am going to move as soon as I possibly can: indeed I am going today in two hours perhaps to Twickenham to look for a house.

I am in such a peck of troubles that you might get figs from thistles as soon as sense from me. I honour M.[1] as much as you or any man can but I cannot write indeed. My own affairs are too urgent and harassing. I am

Not less yours in great haste
A. Tennyson

[1] W. C. Macready (see i. 278 n.).

To EMILY SELLWOOD TENNYSON

MS. Yale; Tennyson Research Centre.

CASTLE HOTEL, TWICKENHAM, [22 January 1851][1]

Dearest

I wonder whether thou hast seen the fat man[2] and had any talk with him. I came on here last night driving from the Brighton terminus. Highshot House is still to be let and Mr. Cain talks of spending 30 to 40£ on it. I went all over it this morning. Every room is out of repair but he declares that 30 or 40 would set it for the most part to right. But O dear how grieved am I that I did not look at Chapel House when I was here before. The most lovely house with a beautiful view in every room at top and all over the rooms are so high that you may put up your beds. A large staircase with great statues and carved and all rooms splendidly papered—with a kind *gentlemanly* old man as proprietor—and all in for 50 guineas. A lady has taken it. I cursed my stars! I think it doubtful whether your beds will get into the rooms at High Shot House. The glory has gone from it[3] since I saw the other: however I have seen Mr. Cain and he is going to correspond with me on the subject. It *would* be a nice house if in good order. But there are some things about it not at all to be wished and I am so afraid of being choused again.

I hope thou hast had a good night. I will write you from the town.

Ever thine
A.

O dear how I groan over Chapel House—*every* room bright and light and lofty and gay. Quite a joy to look at and the proprietor certainly an educated gentleman—no *fat knave* and all for 50 guineas[4] the most (as book [?] says) hateful conjunction. Οι μοι![5] Is it not enough to make one rage?

Is the little mouth pretty quiet? did M[6] sleep in your room? direct to me at C. Weld's.

The old gentleman regretted when I told my name that he had missed me. He told me he had a rage for poetry in his youth but married a poetical wife and they neutralised each other—in conclusion begged me to call on him: [*wd. illeg.*] and certainly *wished* to have me for a tenant. O dear! O dear! O dear! can't be helped: but I assure thee I would sooner give £100 for Chapel than £20 for Highshot. O dear! O dear! O dear!

I was wicked enough to want him (as he said the agreement was not settled) to let me have the house but he said sharply My word's my bond! I said this to him though because he said the Lady who had taken it had been

---

[1] Addressed: Mrs. Tennyson | The Hill | Warninglid | by Crawley | Sussex. Postmarked: Richmond and Crawley, 23 January.

[2] Apparently, Edward Stanford (see below, pp. 8, 12).

[3] A witty allusion to 1 Samuel 4:21 [?].

[4] The placing of 'No *fat* . . . guineas', written above the line, is conjectural.

[5] Alas! (etc.)

[6] Possibly Mrs. Milnes (see i. 177 n. and *Journal*, p. 23), but probably either Matilda or Martha Millar (from Lincolnshire), identified by Charles Tennyson in 'Tennyson and Twickenham', *TRB*, ii. No. 3 (Nov. 1973), 78–81, which includes a description of Chapel House and some of the circumstances mentioned in these letters.

wavering very much because her Doctor had wanted to keep her near *him*. In fact he said she had *not* taken it and he was waiting to hear from her today: but I did not dare to tell thee this at first, and Cain too says that after having inspected Highshot for several days she *decided* on the other. I feel *sure* she has taken it. Thou wilt think me a Harnet Wright[7] but I write big on purpose.

What makes it worse is that I was (when here before) on the point of looking at Chapel House but Weld[8] said we must go home and I yielded to the indolence of the moment and went with him. I am half crazed at missing it I assure thee.[9]

It is now one. The post does not go till 5 ½. It is just possible I may write again when I get to town tonight. But I won't promise.

I am to hear from Mr. Clifton (his name) tomorrow but it is gone no doubt.[10]

To SOPHIA (RAWNSLEY) ELMHIRST
MS. Duke.

[22 February 1851][1]

My dear Sophy

Emily fell down a step at Reigate and sprained her ancle and has ever since suffered a good deal of pain.[2] I have had in other ways a great deal of trouble and perplexity and am yet (though paying £85 a year for a house) without a house to live in. If she were not one of the sweetest and *justest* natures in the world I should be almost at my wits' end (as the saying is) but she bears with me and with her troubles and mine. Now I feel hurt at the letter you have written me. You ought to have known me better than to have accused me of expressing myself as annoyed at your invitation. I was really annoyed at your accusation and took some pains to inquire what you could mean. At last I find out that Emily said to Kate[3] that I was annoyed that I could not come or annoyed that you wouldn't believe that I couldn't. Is being annoyed that I couldn't come or being annoyed that you wouldn't believe me the same thing as being annoyed that I was asked? is it not just the contrary? Sophy, Sophy, how could you? Under whose influences are you acting so unhappily? I had really fancied that you did know a little more of me and that I am not the weathercock of change you would make me. Really your note is not kind and to sign yourself 'Yours etc. etc.' makes it worse. I do not like unkind things to be thought, said or done, and least of all did I expect it of *you*. Pray, reconsider, and see if you be not the party in fault: as for me I am (as I have always been)

Yours not etc. etc. etc. but affectionately
A.

---

[7] Unidentified.   [8] See below, p. 13 n.   [9] See below, pp. 5–8.
[10] This last sentence is on the envelope flap.

[1] Postmark.   [2] See *Journal*, p. 24.
[3] Catherine Rawnsley (see next letter).

EMILY SELLWOOD TENNYSON
to SOPHIA (RAWNSLEY) ELMHIRST

MS. Duke (on envelope flap of letter preceding).

[22 February 1851]

My dear Sophy

I told Kate that he was annoyed you did not take him at his word that he could not come but repeated the invitation immediately, as if not believing him that he could not.

Yours affectionately
Emily Tennyson

To EMILY SELLWOOD TENNYSON

MS. Yale.

[26 February 1851]

Dearest

I am not going to the Levee today not being able to meet with any court clothes. Rogers sent a message offering his—but I do not fancy they will fit. However I shall have to call there and try.[1]

I went with Taylor[2] over both houses yesterday. I have written to appoint an interview with Mr. Clifton. People at Twickenham seem to think him a hard man to drive a bargain but I do not know.

I believe I am going to Lady John's tonight.[3] Venables has offered me a waistcoat.

Very glad to hear thou art a little better.

I shall most probably be back the day after tomorrow.

Thine ever
A.

---

[1] 'Man recommended by Mr. Rawnsley but could not find him and so had to give up the Levee on the 26th.

'[Samuel] Rogers hearing of this kindly sent for him and offered him his own dress which had been worn also by Wordsworth. . . . The coat did well enough but about other parts of the dress there was some anxiety (for the Levee on March 6th) as they had not been tried on' (*Journal*, p. 24; *Memoir*, i. 338). See below, p. 8. It was the end of November 1850 (not February or March 1851, as Robert Martin has it) when Thackeray wrote to William Allingham that Tennyson 'has just been here much excited about his court dress and sword (he says his legs are very good but we know what the Psalms say on that subject) and as much pleased and innocent about it as a girl or a page' (Thackeray's *Letters*, ed. Ray, ii. 710–1).

[2] Henry Taylor, who lived nearby at Ladon House, Mortlake, on the Thames.

[3] 'Alfred went again to London and stayed at Sir Alexander Duff-Gordon's. He went in the evening to Lord John Russell's party put off from last week by the change of ministry and was introduced to [Baron von] Bunsen [the Prussian Ambassador] and the Duke of Argyll' (*Journal*, 3 March, p. 25).

To MR CLIFTON

MS. Brotherton Collection.

TEMPLE, [27 February 1851]

My dear Sir

Many thanks for the pleasant evening you gave me yesterday.

I think I may as well say at once that I agree to your terms, though it may be that a more *formal* document will be necessary: but that we may consider afterwards. I expect therefore to enter in the house in about a week from this time.

> Ever yours, dear sir
> A. Tennyson

To EMILY SELLWOOD TENNYSON

MS. Tennyson Research Centre.[1]

[? 2 MITRE COURT BUILDINGS, TEMPLE] [*c.* 28 February 1851]

Dearest

Please send me one line here if thou canst.

> Thine
> A.

Open Venables' letter to me, take out the auctioneer's draft, the copy of Stanford's and my note about the fixtures and direct them all to Cuthbert Ellison Esq., 3 Figtree Court, Temple, London.[2] He can get me the best legal advice gratis. Venables was just sending off a pretty box of ornaments for our drawing-room table; but finding how matters stood he has kept them till we get another house.

ALFRED TENNYSON AND EMILY SELLWOOD TENNYSON to MR CLIFTON

MS. National Library of Scotland.

Sunday Evening [2 March 1851]

My dear Sir

Would you oblige me by a line directed to me at

> Sir Alexander Gordon's
> 8 Queen Square
> Westminster

---

[1] Written at the end of a letter from Anne Weld to Emily Tennyson: 'message to you, he will be with you in a day or two. All that can be done about a house will be done. He seems very anxious. I am scribbling in a hurry as I have to go out walking with Charlie.'

[2] Cuthbert Edward Ellison (1817–83). Trinity College, BA 1840. He was a barrister ('He and Tom Taylor used to live in the Temple together, and had my name on the door,' Thackeray's *Letters*, ed. Ray, iv. 22) and equity draftsman and conveyancer and, later, stipendiary magistrate in Newcstle and Manchester, and police magistrate (1864–83) in London. (Boase, Venn). See below, p. 433.

and say whether you have received my note which I left with a friend to put into the Post when I left town on Thursday? We think of entering upon your House on Monday week. The note was simply an acceptance of the terms proposed.

Perhaps you would kindly give us a recommendation to a Twickenham or Richmond coal merchant as coals must be ordered in before we arrive, or rather I should say my servants* who are now packing up the furniture at my rashly taken house which I could not live in. But I enter Chapel House, I hope, with happier auspices.

Ever yours sincerely
A. Tennyson

My wife begs that I will petition of you to send her some little plan of the disposition of the rooms at C. H. for I myself (who have what the Philosophers might call a deficient locality) could not tell her very distinctly about this. Any little scratch upon paper would serve the purpose. She only wants to know where her servants are to put up her beds. She is a little afraid too that you may not be stringent enough with the tenants of the cottage about keeping their drains and sewers in order. If they should take a fancy to keep a dung heap by their door they might annoy me.

Farewell. I hope your little one is recovered from her influenza.

*who will be there in a very few days to put things in order for us.

Will Mr. Clifton be so kind as to send the plan of the rooms in Chapel House here to me at Park House, Maidstone. I am almost ashamed to make so troublesome a request; a few words however will answer the purpose.

To MR CLIFTON

MS. Mitchell Library.

[? 3 March 1851]

My dear Sir

Don't call tomorrow as I am obliged to be out nearly the whole day, and I dine out too. Could you come and dine with me on Wednesday somewhere at 6 o'clock in this neighbourhood. The Rainbow is a good place close by the Temple. Just send me word if you can and I will hold myself unengaged.

Ever yours
A. Tennyson

Peach's words are very gratifying.[1] He is a kind, good-hearted fellow.

---

[1] Charles Peach (see i. 290, 325; vol. iii, letter to Peach, 16 March 1886).

To EMILY SELLWOOD TENNYSON

MS. Yale.

[6 March 1851][1]

The levee went off very well and the inexpressibles were not hopelessly tight. Lord Monte[a]gle introduced me to Sir George Grey and Lord Stanley has written 'My dear Mr. Tennyson come and dine with me' so that you see I am in danger of being spoilt.[1] I have signed the final arrangement with Mr. Clifton: he seems to me a mighty good fellow. I shall be down tomorrow morning.

To EDWARD STANFORD

Text. draft Materials, iv. 11[v]

[c. 7 March 1851]

Dear Sir

I am anxious to have done with the house at Warninglid[1] and with the business connected with it, and I presume you will have no objection to resume possession on payment of whatever sums may be due from me. I understand that one half year's rates and taxes will not under present circumstances be payable and I understand from you that the whole amount will be 20£. I should be glad however to know what your claims upon me may be on the understanding that I now wish to give up the premises and that I shall in any case determine the tenancy at the earliest possible period. It appears to me that your interest is the same as my own and I hope you will also concur in my wish to settle the matter finally.

Yours truly
A. Tennyson

To MR COX[1]

MS. Yale.

March 7, [1851]

Sir

Not having been lately or indeed except for a few days at all at Warninglid,

---

[1] Postmark.

[2] See above, p. 5 n. For Lord Monteagle, see i. 96 n., 282. Sir George Grey (1799–1882), 2nd Baronet, statesman, was Russell's (and later Palmerston's) Home Secretary. Edward John Stanley (1802–69), created Baron Eddisbury of Winnington in 1848, succeeded as 2nd Baron Stanley of Alderley in 1850. He 'was, like his father, a man of some ability and also married a remarkable woman. He held various posts in various Whig Governments, and ended in a burst of glory as Postmaster-General with a seat in the Cabinet. He was known in London as Benjamin Backbite and was . . . a very disagreeable character. [It is said] that on his deathbed he apologized to his wife and children for his great nastiness to them at all times' (*The Ladies of Alderley*, ed. Nancy Mitford, 1938, pp. xxi–xxii).

[1] See above, p. 3 n.

[1] Unidentified, but see below, p. 11.

and wandering about the country in search of another house I have neglected to answer your letter. This however is of the less importance as I should in any case have declined to sign the agreement which you sent me. There were terms included in it, which it is not now necessary to discuss, but which were not a part of my original agreement with Mr. Stanford.

I have now succeeded in finding another house and I have proposed to Mr. Stanford to take Warninglid off my hands on such terms as might be agreed upon by both parties: he refers me to yourself. This plan seems to me the best for both, though of course if Mr. Stanford refuses to take the house off my hands upon some compromise, I shall be necessitated to find a tenant elsewhere; and in that case I should be glad to know your terms both in the event of your succeeding or failing to succeed in the finding such a tenant.

I am on the move and shall not be settled down in one locality for some days. Would you be kind enough to direct your answer to the chambers of Mr. G. S. Venables, 2 Mitre Court Buildings, Temple. I am Sir
Your obedient servant
A. Tennyson

To SOPHIA (RAWNSLEY) ELMHIRST

MS. Duke.

PARK HOUSE, MAIDSTONE, [8 March 1851]

My dear Sophy

You might have found out that I had totally forgiven you for listening to idle rumours by my signing myself as I did: pray do not suffer yourself to be so swayed again by tongues. Things in this foolish world of ours do get so distorted by heat and misapprehension and sometimes by downright lies that I have long made it a rule to believe in what I know, not what I hear. I *know* my friends. I do not mean chance companions; and knowing them shall I credit on dits and malicious hints of that wide-mouthed fool, society. No, I will stick by them and bear them out till the end, whatever talk I hear. Gossip is my total abhorrence. I wish it were some living crawling thing that I might tread it out for ever.

So again exhorting you, dear Sophy, to believe me because you have known me from your cradle and because you *know* me incapable of saying unkind things—and with Emily's love, I am
Yours affectionately
A. Tennyson

I would have answered your last before but I only arrived here last night from town and found your letters. I have not said a syllable to Kate nor intend [to]. Nor will Emily.

To THOMAS WOOLNER

Text. Amy Woolner, *Thomas Woolner*, p. 13.

March 10, [1851]

My dear Woolner

I had rather let Dr. Davy[1] have his own way but since he and you require an opinion, look here is an epitaph on the Duke of Wellington.

>To the memory
>of the Duke of
>Wellington

who by a singular calling and through the special foresight of Almighty God was [raised] up to be the safeguard of the greatest people in the world—who possessing the greatest military genius which the world etc. won the battles of Waterloo etc. etc. etc. etc.—who was equally great in statesmanship as he was etc. Now look here, do not the very words

>Duke of Wellington

involve all this?

Is Wordsworth a great poet? Well then don't let us talk of him as if he were half known.

>To the Memory
>of
>William Wordsworth
>The Great Poet.

Even that seems too much but certainly is much better than the other, far nobler in its simplicity.[2]

My dear Woolner, I would have answered you sooner but your letter did not know where to find me.

>Ever yours
>A. Tennyson

I am leaving this place to-day and going if I can to a house in Twickenham. I am very glad to hear that you have got work to do. My wife desires her kindest regards.

To ?

Text. William Harris Arnold, *Ventures in Book Collecting*, p. 244.

[*c.* 10 March 1851]

You will have seen that I kissed the Queen's hand on the sixth. Rogers lent

---

[1] John Davy (see i. 338 n.).
[2] Woolner's medallion for the Grasmere church. 'In the end a lengthy passage from Keble was chosen' (Leonée Ormond, *Tennyson and Thomas Woolner*, The Tennyson Society, 1981, p. 7).

me his court dress, the very same that poor Wordsworth had worn. I hate all publicities and so was a little bit nervous but got through very creditably.[1]

EMILY SELLWOOD TENNYSON
to GEORGE STOVIN VENABLES

MS. National Library of Wales.

[12 March 1851]

My dear Mr. Venables
One of the first things we did on arriving was to unpack your little box and certainly the very next to admire its contents extremely and to think and say how very very kind in you to give us such a beautiful present.[1]

I hope we shall soon see you. Meanwhile believe me
Very sincerely yours
Emily Tennyson

To GEORGE STOVIN VENABLES

MS. National Library of Wales.

CHAPEL HOUSE, TWICKENHAM, [12 March 1851]

My dear Venables
I don't know whether you have any letter from Cox.[1] I am quite in the mind to pay the blackguard his rent. He refused to take the key of the house when my servants came away and refused to let his bailiff and said that the windows would be broken and all kinds of damage done by boys and tramps for which he should make me answerable. So the key was left with the village carpenter and it is likely enough if the man be malicious as well as a rogue that he will cause damage to be done for which I shall have a great bill to pay. Under these circumstances (and considering that the whole village are his creatures) would it not be better to pay him at once and let the business end?

Ever yours
A. Tennyson

We arrived yesterday. Send an answer by Grigsby,[2] please.

To JOHN FORSTER

MS. Tennyson Research Centre.

Monday, [? *c.* 17 March 1851]

My dear Forster
I waited for you all Sunday but you came not. Let me see you some time

---
[1] See above, p. 5.
[1] See above, p. 6.
[1] See above, p. 8   [2] The Park House coachman (*Journal*, p. 25).

this week. I shall be back in town on Wednesday. I am going to Chapel House, Twickenham, today.

Ever yours
A. Tennyson

To SAMUEL SHARPE[1]

MS. University College, London.

March 26, [1851]

Dear Sir

I sent a note to your Bank the other day requesting that £85 might be paid to Mr. Edward Stanford of Slaugham[2] by Crawley, Sussex. By the enclosed from him you will see that he has not received it. I sent the note to your Bank by the clerk of my friend Mr. Venables of 2 Mitre Court Buildings, Temple. Will you be so good as to see whether the money has been paid to Mr. Stanford? And if the clerk did not, as he had orders to do, take away my Banking book would you have the kindness to send it by post to me at Chapel House, Twickenham. Believe me,

Yours truly
A. Tennyson

Samuel Sharpe Esq.

To HENRY TAYLOR

MS. Dr. W. Baker.

[? March or April 1851][1]

My dear Taylor

I had intended to call upon you and thank you in person for your kindness in sending the powders—something has always occurred to prevent me—take then my thanks by letter and believe me

Ever yours
A. Tennyson

To MARY A. MARSHALL[1]

MS. Duke.

CHAPEL HOUSE, TWICKENHAM, [? April 1851]

My dear M. A. M.

If you will: so be it. I would be very loth to cause you any uneasiness but your mode of operation was a little crafty and perhaps I shall be on my guard another time. Now will you do another thing for me, you or James— go into my little smoking room at No. 1. and pull open the drawer of the table and

---

[1] See i. 299 n.   [2] See above, p. 8–9.
[1] The handwriting seems to belong to this period.
[1] Mrs. James Garth Marshall (see i. 96 and n., 330).

take out what letters may be possibly left there for in the hurry of getting off I quite forgot to look into it and if you find any send them on here. Another thing—you see I am putting you to use—I only gave the two servants in my house 5s apiece and I rather think I should have given them each half a sovereign. Will you pay them 5s each over and above, i.e. if you think they were underpaid? And that shall be my debt to you instead of the £6 you have enclosed. You needn't tell Dofo [?] this as maybe she would despise me for mal-economy. Love to her and to James and the bairnies

Ever affectionately yours
A. Tennyson

To ANNE WELD[1]

MS. Tennyson Research Centre.

Monday Evening [21–2 April 1851]

My dear Anne

Mrs. Marshall was kind enough to undertake to write to you yesterday. I did not know your direction, so could only tell her Somerset House. You will be grieved to hear of our misfortune. The child got suffocated in being born. He was as grand looking [a] little fellow as ever I saw as large as if he had been three months old at least, and the Doctor said he would have been very hefty if he could have escaped this accident of birth.

Well God orders all. She is going on well I am glad to say. Kindest regards to Weld. I have only seen Emily for a moment and did not ask her where you were. I know it is somewhere in Glo[uce]stershire, Frocester or some such place—but not being certain of it I send this to S. H.

Ever yours
A. Tennyson

Tuesday morning

The Doctor has just been and says she is going on as well as can be. So that I hope you will make yourself easy.

To JOHN FORSTER

Text. Materials, iv. 473.

CHAPEL HOUSE, TWICKENHAM, April 22, 1851

My dear Forster

My poor boy died in being born. My wife is safe as yet, but I rather dread

---

[1] Anne Sellwood (d. 1894), 'Nanny', Emily Sellwood Tennyson's younger sister, married in 1842 Charles Richard Weld (1813–69: *DNB*), who became Assistant Secretary and Librarian to the Royal Society, 1845–61. Although he studied at the Middle Temple and was called to the bar in 1844, his true interest lay in science. He was of primary assistance to Sir John Franklin, his wife's uncle, in organizing his polar explorations. Weld had a significant administrative role in the International Exhibition of 1862, and represented Great Britain as an assistant commissioner at the Exhibition in Paris in 1867. Highly regarded for his *History of the Royal Society* (2 vols., 1848), he wrote a number of travel books, as will be seen below. See also i. xx, 144 n.

the third day. The nurse drest up the little body in pure white. He was a grand, massive, manchild, noble brow, and hands, which he had clenched as in his determination to be born. Had he lived the doctor said he would have been lusty and healthy; but somehow he got strangled.[1]

I kissed his poor, pale hands and came away, and they buried him last night in Twickenham church-yard. She has borne all with the utmost fortitude. I thought you would sympathize with me. I am foolish enough to be affected with all this. The doctor says it is not likely to occur again if God gives us another.

Ever yours truly
A. Tennyson

To EMILY AUGUSTA PATMORE

MS. Boston College.

CHAPEL HOUSE, TWICKENHAM, [late April 1851]

My dear Mrs. Patmore

It has pleased God that my boy should not be born alive. The whole night before he was born he was vigourously alive, but in being born he died. I suspect it was that severe fall my wife got some weeks ago, which shook him out of his place. The nurse drest him up in a white frock. I thought I had never seen a finer child. He looked three or four months old. She weighed him poor fellow and he was some pounds heavier than the average child. He looked, I thought, as if he had had a battle for his life. I am glad to say that she is going on very well.

Ever yours
A. Tennyson

To EDMUND LUSHINGTON [?]

Text. Memoir, i. 340.

[late April 1851]

It was Easter Sunday and at his birth I heard the great roll of the organ, of the uplifted psalm (in the Chapel adjoining the house).... Dead as he was I felt proud of him. To-day when I write this down, the remembrance of it rather overcomes me; but I am glad that I have seen him, dear little nameless one that hast lived though thou hast never breathed, I, thy father, love thee and weep over thee, though thou hast no place in the Universe. Who knows? It may be that thou hast.... God's Will be done.

---

[1] See 'Little bosom not yet cold' (Ricks, p. 992).

To ROBERT MONTEITH

MS. Richard L. Purdy.

[*c.* 24 April 1851]

My dear Robert

I am quite sure you will feel with me. My poor little boy got strangled in being born. I would not send the notice of my misfortune to the Times and I have had to write some 60 letters. If you desire to know about it ask Edmund Lushington to show you that letter which I wrote to him. My wife has been going on very well since; but last night she lost her voice and I thought I should lose *her*: she is however free from all danger this morning according to my medical man. I have suffered more than ever I thought I could have done for a child still born: I fancy I should not have cared so much if he had been a seven months spindling, but he was the grandest-looking child I had ever seen. Pardon my saying this. I do not speak only as a father but as an Artist—if you do not despise the word from German associations. I mean as a man who has eyes and can judge from seeing.

I refused to see the little body at first, fearing to find some pallid abortion which would have haunted me all my life—but he looked (if it be not absurd to call a newborn babe so) even majestic in his mysterious silence after all the turmoil of the night before.

He was—not born, I cannot call it born for he never breathed—but he was released from the prison where he moved for nine months—on Easter Sunday. Awful day! We live close upon an English-church chapel. The organ rolled—the psalm sounded—and the wail of a woman in her travail—of a true and tender nature suffering, as it seemed intolerable wrong, rose ever and anon.

But ask Edmund for the account and God bless you and your wife, dear Robert,

For ever and ever
A. Tennyson

I sent part of your note (I mean about the Novel) to Moxon but he has taken no notice of it.

I look over this note and I find I have written so obscurely that it is a chance whether you ever make it out: and perhaps it does not matter; I think that other written to Edmund is clearer. Ask for it. I don't remember what it was but I am sure there was more of me in it.

To ANNE WELD

MS. Tennyson Research Centre.

[late April 1851]

My dear Anne

Emily after some little relapses and goings back now and then is I hope now quite out of danger. I have not let her see any letters fearing to excite her. She is now lying on the sofa and much better than she has been since her accouchement though as yet quite incapable of seeing anybody except perhaps for a minute but as yet she has seen nobody. I hope that by next week she may be able to meet you.

I am much grieved to hear of poor Catherine's illness. I used to fancy her so strong. Thank her and Drummond (if you please) for their very kind letters. And believe me (with Emily's best love to all at Shiplake),

Yours affectionately
A. Tennyson

To JOHN FORSTER

MS. Tennyson Research Centre.

[24 April 1851]

My dear Forster

Many thanks for your very kind note. I am happy to say that she is going on very well, and that I am less moved than I was at first. I do not wish to have any record of it in any paper.

If at any time you can run over by the train and see me I shall be grateful. Any one will tell you where Montpelier Row is, and mine is the last house in it by the Chapel.

I flatter myself with the hope that the next birth (if another child be granted to us) will be more fortunate and indeed the Doctor gives it as his opinion. Mrs. Marshall who saw the poor little fellow says he was nobly made and she having had a family ought to know; but that perhaps makes it all the sadder. Perhaps if he had been a sickly 7-months spindling, I should have minded it less—but I don't know: and they tell me that if had not been so large a child he would have had a chance for his life. Ever yours, my dear F,

Most truly
A. Tennyson

To LORD MONTEAGLE

MS. Duke.

May 7, [1851]

Dear Lord Monteagle

I am much obliged to you for your kind letter but it really does so happen today that I am too unwell to go. I got your letter (though marked immediate) only at four o'clock today. I sent to James Marshall a note to be despatched to the Lord Chamberlain begging him (if necessary) to make my excuses but I know so little about court forms that I did not venture to send it direct to the Lord Chamberlain, fearing to do something out of course in this land of repectabilities. The sum of all is this: I would have gone today if I could but I can't: and I can't write a note to the Queen as I would to Mrs. Wilson excusing myself. What then is to be done except writing to the Lord Chamberlain? or are court balls like levees where you can go to which you like?

I am very grieved for poor Stephen:[1] at the same time I do not believe it will have any lasting effects. I have a cousin who broke a blood vessel with over exertion and after lying by for a short time was as well as ever and is now hale and hearty.

I should have very much liked to have gone with yourself and the Marshalls. There is small doubt of that: but my Fates have been against me. In the meantime I intend to go on the 19th. Believe me,

Ever yours
A. Tennyson

To SAMUEL ROGERS

Text. Morgan Library.

May 7, [1851]

My dear Mr. Rogers

I had intended today to have availed myself of your kindness—to have dined with you if I had found you disengaged—to have borrowed the old Laureate suit and to have gone to the Queen's Ball from under your hospitable roof; and I told Moxon to call on you and say all this.

But these good purposes are all frustrated. I am really thoroughly unwell today and cannot come. I can only hope that I have put you, my dear sir, to no inconvenience, and that the Fates will be more prosperous to me on the 19th—the next Queen's Ball.

I send my boy[1] with this to your door. Believe me.

Yours always
A. Tennyson

To JOHN REUBEN THOMPSON[1]

MS. University of Virginia.

[? May or June 1851]

My dear Sir

I received your note some weeks after date and have to thank you for it, for your criticism and for your poem. I hate writing and hate usque ad nauseam writing out my own poems particularly after they have been printed, so you really must be content with one of the pieces specified. Are you coming over to see the great Glass House in Hyde Park? If so I shall be glad to see you if I

---

[1] Stephen Spring Rice, his son.

[1] Thomas Metcalf, errand-boy, from Lincolnshire (*TRB*, ii, No. 2 [Nov. 1973], 80).

[1] John Reuben Thompson (1823–73). Born in Richmond, Va., he was well educated, having attended the University of Virginia, and, for better or worse, became a southern gentleman. He was a poet, critic, essayist, and, from 1847, owner and editor of the *Southern Literary Messenger* (which brought him in touch with Edgar Allan Poe), and later, under William Cullen Bryant, literary editor of the New York *Evening Post*. See below, pp. 385, 425 n., 432, 439. Gerald M. Garmon's book *John Reuben Thompson* (Twayne, 1979), from which these notes are derived, is (*faute de mieux*) the best source of information. (The poem cannot be identified in *The Poems of John Reuben Thompson*, ed. J. S. Patton, 1920.)

am in the way. I live at Twickenham about 10 miles from London. Believe me with every good wish

Yours very truly
A. Tennyson

To MATILDA JESSE[1]

Text. Tennyson Research Centre (transcript by Charles Tennyson).

June 11, 1851

My dear Mattie

I am much obliged to you for your letter and Richard's, which I return. Dora[2] (as you say) is not much changed, only a little staider than of old, which is as it should be. I grieve for poor Mrs. Shiel, but there is hardly any misfortune that cannot be borne by a heart that looks to God as the doer of all. So be it with her. Forgive my brevity and believe me, dear Mattie,

Ever yours
A. Tennyson

Kindest regards to all yours

To WILLIAM ALLINGHAM[1]

MS. University of Kansas.

TWICKENHAM, July 1 [1851]

My dear Sir

My wife requests me to present to you her best thanks for the graceful little bracelet you have been kind enough to give her—to which I beg to add mine, and my regrets that as we are so soon to leave England I shall scarce have the pleasure of seeing you again at this time. Believe me, my dear Sir,

[A. Tennyson]

---

[1] See i. 296 and n.
[2] Identified by Charles Tennyson as 'Dora MacGillicuddy, afterwards Mrs. Leader'. Mrs Shiel remains unidentified.

[1] William Allingham (1824–89: *DNB*), the Irish poet, is an important figure in these volumes because he came close to being Tennyson's Boswell. His *Diary*, edited by Helen Allingham, his wife, and D. Radford, published in 1907, is admirable and indispensable. Through Coventry Patmore, whom he had met at the British Museum, he sent Tennyson his *Poems* (see i. 336–7), and this led to their first meeting, 28 June 1851 (*Diary*, pp. 60–3). Their second meeting was in November 1853, and they saw each other occasionally thereafter (he visited the Tennysons at Coniston in 1857). But the intimacy began early in 1863, when Allingham was transferred to the custom-house at Lymington. *Day and Night Songs* (1854), his best-known volume, was reissued (revised and enlarged) as *The Music Master* in 1855. In June 1874 he became editor of *Fraser's Magazine*, and in August married Helen Paterson (1848–1926), a water-colour painter.

WILLIAM MAKEPEACE THACKERAY
to EMILY SELLWOOD TENNYSON

Text. draft *Materials,* iv. 24.

[? *c.* 6 July 1851]

My dear Mrs. Tennyson

I will come to you on Tuesday with a great deal of pleasure; and I wonder whether I might bring my two girls? If you have a party, that of course won't be right: but if only a friend or two—those young women might have their dinner at home, and would sit quietly upstairs while we had ours. You will please not be displeased at this proposal, will you? but I get so hampered with engagements in London that I see the children very little; and had arranged to spend part of that evening with them.

And do you know that there is a feud between me and F[orster]? I say this lest a pleasant evening should be made unpleasant by our scowling at each other, across the table. Here are a many conditions about accepting an invitation to dinner! If the coming of the young ones is in the least inconvenient do tell me and believe me

Most sincerely yours
W. M. Thackeray

(P.S. My dear Mrs. Tennyson: for though I don't see Alfred a very great deal yet there are no friends like youthful friends and though we are 40, we were young once and though I've seen you but once I consider you a friend too.)

To WILLIAM HENRY BROOKFIELD

MS. Yale.

[? 15 July 1851]

My dear WB

Can't indeed. I am this morning starting for Italy[1]—very sorry not to be able to oblige your friend—but can't if I would being in a stew. I trust that you are getting better. I had some hopes of your travelling with us, but it seems to be no go.

Excuse conventionalisms. Kind regards from my wife to you and yours.

A.

To WILLIAM HENRY AND JANE OCTAVIA BROOKFIELD

MS. Yale.

[October or early November, 1851]

My dear William and Jane

I have only just got back to England and heard of you in calling on Mrs. Taylor at Mortlake. Grieved I was to hear that I may not see you again for a

---

[1] For the *italienische Reise* (which included neither Rome nor Venice), see 'The Daisy' (Ricks, p. 1019) and, less enchantingly, *Memoir,* i. 340–2, and below, p. 000.

20   12 *January* 1852

long time; yet I do not know what I should write except to tell you that my sympathies go with you and to wish that you, William, may soon be better, and that God's blessing may be with you on the waste seas, and in the fair island which I have so often longed to see.[1] If my wife could stand the sea nothing would please me better than to have accompanied you thither, but I hear that one friend at least has preceded you, and is there now—Stephen Spring Rice: that we may soon see you back in renewed health is this wish and prayer of

Yours affectionately
A. Tennyson

My wife joins me in all kind wishes to you both.

To EMILY SELLWOOD TENNYSON [?]
Text. Materials, ii. 64–5.

CHELTENHAM, January 12, 1852

Count D'Orsay is a friend of mine, co-godfather to Dickens' child with me. He is Louis Napoleon's intimate friend and secretary, and moreover I am told a man who has wept over my poems.[1] See how strangely things are connected. Just put the things together. Wonderful are these times and no one knows what may arise from the smallest things. I the poet [laureate] of England with the secretary of Louis Napoleon whom I have abused.

To COVENTRY PATMORE
MS. Berg Collection.

[mid-January 1852]

Rifle-Clubs!!!^[1]

  Riflemen, form in town and in shire
   From John O'Groat's house to the wild land's end!
  Practice and fire, practice and fire
   God, He knows what an hour may send.
    Ready be ready to meet the storm!
    Riflemen, form! Riflemen, form!
    Riflemen, riflemen, riflemen, form!

---

[1] 'It became evident from Mr Brookfield's state of health that he would not be able to winter in England, and therefore arrangements were made for an early departure to Madeira'. They returned to England in late June of the following year (*Mrs. Brookfield and Her Circle*, ii. 352–78).

[1] Alfred Guillaume Gabriel Count D'Orsay (1801–52: *DNB*), wit, dandy. See i. 253 n., and *Memoir*, i. 347 n. On Louis Napoleon, see below, p. 47 and n.

[1] Published in *The Times* in a muted adaptation as 'The War' in 1859 and, signed 'T.', mistaken by many for Martin Tupper's work (similar in subject and tone, at least). See Derek Hudson, *Martin Tupper, His Rise and Fall*, pp. 191–2. See also Ricks, pp. 1778–9, 996–7, 1110–11, and below p. 233 and n.

> We thought them friends and we had them here,
>   But now the traitor and tyrant rules!
> And Waterloo from year to year
>   Has rankled in the hearts of the fools.
>   We love peace but the French love storm,
>   Riflemen, form! Riflemen, form!
>   Riflemen, riflemen, Riflemen, form!
>
> Ready, be ready! they mean no good,
>   Ready, be ready! the times are wild!
> Bearded monkeys of lust and blood
>   Coming to violate woman and child!
>   We love liberty: they love storm:
>   Riflemen, form! Riflemen, form!
>   Riflemen, Riflemen, Riflemen, form!
>
> Workmen, workmen, away with your strikes!
>   Close with your masters! sound an alarm!
> Get your weapons, muskets and pikes!
>   Close with your masters and arm and arm!
>   You love freedom, the French love storm
>   Riflemen, form! Riflemen, form!
>   Riflemen, Riflemen, Riflemen, form!

Very wild but I think too savage! Written in about 2 minutes! The authorship a most deep secret! mind, Mr. P.

Really I think on writing it out it's enough to make a war of itself.

My wife thinks it too insulting to the F. and too inflaming to the English. Better not make a broadsheet of it, say I.

To EMILY SELLWOOD TENNYSON

Text. Memoir, i. 347.

CHELTENHAM, January 18, 1852

Alan Ker has taken four copies of my Ode 'My Lords'[1] to send to papers here and there. Mother was delighted beyond measure to see me, making me remorseful that I had not been here before. Alan and Mary seem well and hopeful: they say it is only a fortnight's steam to Jamaica (where he is appointed a judge), and they will not take a large outfit because at any time they can have things from England. Dobson says we could live here much better and cheaper than at Twickenham. I find the air much fresher.

[1] 'The Third of February, 1852' (see Ricks, p. 1000), written in December 1851. Alan Ker (1819–85), barrister and, later, judge of the High Court of Jamaica, married Mary Tennyson 7 July 1851. For Tennyson's friendship with Ker's brother at Cheltenham, Dr Buchanan Ker (1821–98), see *Memoir*, i. 263–5, and *Materials*, i. 341–4. See also below, pp. 24, 70, and *Landed Gentry*.

To THE EDITOR OF THE *MORNING CHRONICLE*

Text. Ricks, p. 994.

[*c.* 20 January 1852]

Sir

If you please, insert the inclosed.[1] My name is known well enough in the literary world, though I have rather chosen to subscribe myself,

A Scorner of the Penny-Wise.

To RICHARD MONCKTON MILNES

MS. Trinity College.

CHELTENHAM, Wednesday, [21 January 1852]

My dear Richard

I am at Cheltenham on a visit and go home on Saturday. I should like very well to come on to you, but I cannot again so soon leave my wife alone—nor can she at present travel. I have given you perhaps but a sheepish reason for not coming, but let it serve.

Poor E. W.[1] I grieve for those that loved him. I knew him not, but have always heard of him as a good fellow.

Ever yours both
Compts to Mrs. Milnes
A. Tennyson

To CHARLES RICHARD WELD

MS. Indiana University.

Thursday, [22 January 1852]

My dear Weld

*The Poem of Arm etc.[1] is public property. I might have made some £5 of it but I give it to the people. Let it be published and spread as widely as may be. If the Times won't put it in, send it to the Morning Chronicle, the Athenaeum, anywhere. It is too long a time to wait for Fraser. The little squib must be Fraser's sole property as you have sent it thither. I had wished to retract it as it is not overgood, but let it stand. I have put a title, not a good one but I can think of no other.

Ever yours
A. Tennyson

*It has already been sent to some Scotch papers.

---

[1] See below.

[1] Eliot Warburton (1801–52: *DNB*), writer, died 'in the steamer *Amazon*, which on the 4th of January was destroyed by fire at sea' (Reid, *Richard Monckton Milnes*, i. 467–8).

[1] 'The Penny-Wise' (see Ricks, p. 994). See above.

To EMILY SELLWOOD TENNYSON

Text. Memoir, i. 348

CHELTENHAM, January 22, [1852]

A note from Charles Weld this morning. He sent my poem to the *Times*, but the *Times* ignores it. Alan Ker says it is not their custom to put in poems except they are allowed to subscribe the author's name. I have told him to try the *Morning Chronicle*: he seems for *Fraser*, though it is so long before *Fraser* comes out that my poem will be half superannuated like the musket. I see that here and there people are really beginning to be awake to their danger. . . . In this horrible age of blab I can scarce trust aright.

To EMILY SELLWOOD TENNYSON

MS. Tennyson Research Centre.

[CHELTENHAM] [23 January 1852]

Dearest

Canst thou not hold on till Monday evening without me. I shall barely have time to select what books I want by Monday. Yet I fear thou wilt be bothered by my not coming—particularly as thou callest thyself unwell. The Kers and Cissy[1] are *not* coming back with me so do not plague thyself about them. They do not go till the 16th (I think) of February. Ker will come up to buy a law-library and I have offered to give him £5 worth of his books when he comes. I have been out every day dining nearly and I am going out again today so that my reason for stopping is partly that I may spend *one* day alone with my family. And on Sunday all trains are so slow that I should be hours on the road. So rest thee perturbed spirit[2] till Monday afternoon and sleep sound upon the *certainty* that I shall come then. Did I say Forster would peach? No I am not sure, indeed if you had his word that he would not, he would not. My poem is public property. I wish every paper to have it. Though readers of the Examiner would no doubt guess the authorship from knowing his friendship for me. Never mind. The Times is a fool. Hast thou read it every day? The military letters are very interesting.[3] The hills here have very fine lights on them as seen from my windows. I wish thou couldst see them. Now bear up! be jolly—for to think of thee sad spoils me here for enjoyment of most things. If C. R. W.[4] comes on Sunday couldst thou get him to undertake the conveyance of the railway paper and Treasury receipt stamps to town? or hast thou already sent them? or forgotten them altogether? Milnes[5] needn't be in any fright about our coming to Cheltenham. John

---

[1] Tennyson's sister Cecilia (Mrs Edmund Lushington).
[2] *Hamlet*, I. v. 83.
[3] Letters by Patmore and others about a Volunteer Rifle Corps.
[4] Charles Richard Weld.
[5] Mrs Milnes, the cook.

Rashdall[6] wants us to go and spend 3 weeks with him at Malvern, which I think will be nice when thou canst move.

Thine, darling,
A. T.

Ker has borrowed Mary's principal for a start in life—a bad enough look out—be jolly *be jolly*. × × × ×

To MR AND MRS THOMAS HARDWICKE RAWNSLEY

MS. Harvard.

January 27 [1852]

My dear Mr. and Mrs. Rawnsley

I have returned from Cheltenham where I have been on a visit to see my mother and Mary Ker née Tennyson before she starts for the hot little isle, Antigua: and coming home I find your very kind present of fowl, sausages, etc. which are so much better than anything of the kind we have here. Thank you much. I believe I owed you a letter before I went abroad, and the debt rather lay upon my conscience when I was among the Appennines [*sic*] but I know how it is. I get few letters to my friends written nowadays, not that I care for my friends less, but that I really have so many to write and have always had a hatred of letter writing. Give my love to Edward and his wife, and believe me, with my wife's to you both,

Yours affectionately
A. Tennyson

EMILY SELLWOOD TENNYSON *to* COVENTRY PATMORE

MS. Boston College.

CHAPEL HOUSE, January 28 [1852]

Dear Mr. Patmore

Alfred did not come till tea time on Monday. Since, he has been busy but he would have written to you this evening had not a friend come in. We have distributed all the notices except two.[1] It is really refreshing to see such earnestness of energy as yours. Who knows but when the secrets of all things are known you may in this instance be proved to have mainly contributed to the safety of your country.

Will you not come on Saturday, Mrs. Patmore and yourself, and then you and Alfred can talk things over together. It seems to me he can be no more than an honorary member of your club (and an honorary member of such a club seems an absurdity) as you know we are trying to get a house in the country as soon as we can. Indeed we have heard of one extremely likely to

---

[6] See i. 115 n., 287 n., and below, p. 29

[1] For the Volunteer Rifle Corps—printed in Champneys, *Memoirs and Correspondence of Coventry Patmore*, i. 74-6. See below, p. 26.

suit. At all events do not speak of him as an 'agitator' for any cause whatsoever. Neither him nor yourself if I might be so bold as to say so. The word has come to have so evil a meaning, a sort of hysterical lady meaning if nothing worse. I know you will be disappointed at not getting an answer from Alfred but I thought these hasty lines would be better than nothing.

Let us hear that you and Mrs. Patmore come to stay over Sunday. We can dine when convenient to you on Saturday. Let us know the hour. Kindest remembrances to her.

Yours very sincerely
Emily Tennyson

JAMES SPEDDING to EMILY SELLWOOD TENNYSON

MS. Tennyson Research Centre.

4 February 1852

Dear Mrs. Tennyson

I shall be very glad to dine with you on Tuesday next at 5 ½. And if the author of the seasons can afford no more than one fine day out of every two, I may perhaps see you before. In the mean time I will send £5 to Coventry Patmore for the Rifles, thinking that the more noise we make in that way the better, and the more we practise the less likely are we to be called upon to perform. I answered your summons to the Thatched House[1] and found a room full of people not one of whom I knew; all sufficiently zealous, and at the same time rational, and (so far as the preliminaries went) of one mind. I suppose they knew one another, or some knew some; and as there seemed to be no want of volunteers for the Committee and Sub-committee to arrange details, I thought I might, without abandoning my country in her extremity, leave that part of the business to them and join some club when it is organized. I think I could hit a Frenchman at 100 yards, if he did not frighten me.

Forster sent for me yesterday to look at the new poem,[2] which I highly approve, and by no means allow of the objection suggested against the last stanza. America is our daughter but the men of America are our sons. Forster wants a name for the Poet, which I think very desirable; and no great matter what name is chosen so it be short and pronounceable, Alfred, Arthur, Merlin Tyrtaeus, Edward Bull, Britannicus, Honved, Hylax, anything. Amyntor would sound well, is not hackneyed, and is good Greek for defender or protector.

Yours very truly
James Spedding

Your note though dated the 2nd did not arrive yesterday till I had gone out.

---

[1] 'O knowledge ill-inhabited, worse than Jove in a thatch'd house' (*As You Like It*, II. iii. 11).
[2] 'Hands All Round', ll. 49–60, published in the *Examiner*, 7 February 1852, signed 'Merlin' (Ricks, p. 1002).

FRANKLIN LUSHINGTON
to WILLIAM HENRY BROOKFIELD (extract)

Text. Mrs. Brookfield and Her Circle, ii. 370.

February 8, 1852

... I suppose you are aware of the National panic, and how we are all on the point of becoming riflemen to resist the invasion which the French are going to try on. Among the most enthusiastic national defenders are Alfred Tennyson and Mrs. A. T. At least they have been induced by Coventry Patmore to subscribe five pounds apiece for the purchase of rifles to teach the world to shoot—which appears to me a rather exaggerated quota for the laureate to contribute out of his official income, his duty being clearly confined to the howling of patriotic staves. A great damper has been thrown on the volunteering spirit generally by Nicol's advertising 'Volunteer outfit, inclusive of rifle, powder horn, etc., dark green rifle frock with epaulettes, etc., for £8. Cheaper description of ditto, £5'. Alfred Tennyson is naturally in a restless state of mind which impels him to quit Twickenham and get a house in some remote part of the country, from which of course he would be equally anxious to return again into the neighbourhood of London. It was very stupid of him not to stay the winter in Italy while he was about it. The chief motive of his return appears to have been the want of English tobacco, but the immediate cause of his starting northwards from Florence was his having made up his mind to go southward to Rome or Naples on a particular day and packed his trunks accordingly. When the day came it happened to blow too hard for them to go by the Leghorn steamer southward, so instead of waiting with Christian patience till the weather was better, they immediately started northwards.

To THE EDITOR OF THE EXAMINER

Text. Ricks, p. 1004.

February [c. 9], 1852

Sir

I have read with much itnerest the poems by *Merlin*.[1] The enclosed is longer than either of those, and certainly not so good; yet as I flatter myself that it has a smack of Merlin's style in it, and as I feel that it expresses forcibly enough some of the feelings of our time, perhaps you may be induced to admit it.[2]

Taliessin

---

[1] 'The Third of February, 1852' and 'Hands All Round' (see above, pp. 21, 25).
[2] 'Suggested by Reading an Article in a Newspaper' (Ricks, p. 1004), signed 'Taliessin'.

JOHN FORSTER to EMILY SELLWOOD TENNYSON

Text. draft *Materials,* iv. 24.

58 LINCOLN'S INN FIELDS, February 9, 1852

My dear Mrs. Tennyson

Praise of the poems pours in upon me from all sides—and Alfred's name is sometimes suggested, but I say nothing—not to friends the most intimate. But I must send you (though I am greatly pressed with the necessity of leaving town tomorrow) what Landor says in a note this morning. ' "Hands All Round" is incomparably the best lyric poem in the language—though Dryden's "Drinking Song" is fine.' I shall send Abbott Lawrence (the American Minister) slips of all for direct transmission to America. Love to Alfred.

Yours ever truly
John Forster

To FRANCIS TURNER PALGRAVE[1]

MS. British Library.[2]

CHAPEL HOUSE, February 19, 1852

My dear Palgrave

There was a knife and fork for you on Tuesday at Chapel House and we waited till 4 ½. Why didn't you come?

Ever yours
A. Tennyson

To MARTIN FARQUHAR TUPPER[1]

MS. University of Illinois.

CHELTENHAM, February 19, 1852

My dear Sir

I could not answer you before for a reason which you will acknowledge to

---

[1] Francis Turner Palgrave (1824–97: *DNB*), poet, critic, and perhaps, after Emily and Hallam Tennyson, the Laureate's most faithful attendant and friend. (See i. xvii, xix, 298 n.) He was the son of Sir Francis Palgrave (1788–1861: *DNB*), 'the greatest of all the historians of early England, the only one who was un-English; and the reason of his superiority lay in his name, which was Cohen, and his mind which was Cohen also, or at least not English. He changed his name to Palgrave to please his wife', according to *The Education of Henry Adams* (ch. 14). Francis Turner (Frank) Palgrave may be remembered now mostly for the *Golden Treasury* anthology (1861), of which Tennyson was the *éminence grise*, but as art critic for the *Saturday Review* 'he may perhaps have had a right to claim the much-disputed rank of being the most unpopular man in London', as Adams wrote. He was Professor of Poetry at Oxford, 1885–95.

[2] We have seen two forgeries of this letter, which was reproduced in facsimile in J. Holt Schooling's article, 'The Handwriting of Alfred Lord Tennyson', *Strand Magazine,* vii (1894), 599–608.

[1] Martin Farquhar Tupper (1810–89: *DNB*) poetaster, author of one of the most popular books in the nineteenth century, *Proverbial Philosophy* (1838 and after). He attended Christ Church, Oxford (BA 1832), and became a Lincoln's Inn barrister. He published a great many other books, including *The Rifle Movement Foreshewn in Prose and Verse, from 1858 to the Present Time*

be satisfactory—I had not received your letter. Moxon generally lets my letters wait till they grow to a parcel and then forwards them, or I call at his shop and get them altogether. Here then is my hand likewise—on paper—as you say—and I shake yours ideally and wish we may be friends.

Your verses have a good hearty smack of the right feeling in them and I doubt not have done much good. For my part I have not been wanting to the good cause, though I never contemplated my own or wife's appearance in the isolation of a newspaper paragraph. Nor was it altogether pleasing. Yet if [it] did any good why should I regret it?

Hoping some time to know you better (though I know much of you through your books) believe me

Truly yours
A. Tennyson

JANE WELSH CARLYLE to EMILY SELLWOOD TENNYSON

Text. Sanders, pp. 109–10.

CHEYNE ROW, Monday, [? 22 March 1852]

Dear Mrs. Tennyson

In the flutter of coming away last night, after a day so unusually *white*; I left, on the toilet of Mrs. Ker's room, a great black cross of jet—important to me enough to have a special message about it; for it was given to me once at parting, by my Mother—who is dead. If it be given into *your* hands, will you take good care of it, till we meet, or till some safe opportunity offer of sending it. I would rather be without it a long while than run any risk of having it lost or broken in any public transit.

Thank you much for being so good to me yesterday, and thanks to your husband for letting me *smoke* with him, and talking to me 'all to myself' (as the children say). I hope to hear you do not find the Gloucestershire house feasible, and that you have made peace with the one you are in. Mrs. Ker, I suppose is off by this time.[1] God prosper them, poor souls—uprooting at that time of life is a sorrowful business.

Most truly yours
Jane Carlyle

(1859), of which the fifth edition (1864), inscribed, is in the Tennyson Research Centre (*Tennyson in Lincoln*, i, No. 2233). See Derek Hudson, *Martin Tupper, His Rise and Fall*, pp. 190–1, where the verses mentioned here are identified as 'Englishmen, up! make ready your rifles!' or 'Reply to sundry who object to "Arm"' and the like (the like sometimes confused with Tennyson's—see above, p. 20.

[1] Alan and Mary Tennyson Ker's move to the West Indies (see below, p. 70).

To SOPHIA (RAWNSLEY) ELMHIRST

MS. Duke.

MALVERN, REVD J. RASHDALL'S,[1] Saturday, [27 March 1852]

My dear Sophy

I am much obliged to you for your remembering me in connection with Franklin Willingham's house at Lutterworth, but though it is true that I do not much approve of Twickenham as a place of residence and desire if possible to let my house there and take another still I am not sufficiently opulent to give more for any other house than I do for my Twickenham one and my rent for that is little more than fifty guineas per annum, so that you see Franklin's is considerably beyond my means and moreover I should desire an unfurnished house. My letter 'without a beginning' as you say was simply a joke in answer to Elmhirst's 'without a beginning.' Don't be so sensitive, particularly as Catherine says you are getting quite plump and in good condition. So there is the less excuse for you. Emily and myself have both been considerably unwell and I am still so. I trust Elmhirst is well. Give my best remembrances to him and believe me, dear Sophy,

Ever yours affectionately
A. Tennyson

We are both here at present having come last [night] from Cheltenham.

To JAMES SPEDDING

MS. Jack Kolb.

GT. MALVERN, April 22, [1852]

My dear James

Send this[1] (if you please) to F. Pollock's for I have forgotten his direction and have no Court Guide.

Ever yours
A. Tennyson

To FREDERICK POLLOCK[1]

MS. University of Kentucky.

MALVERN, April 22, [1852]

My dear Pollock

I am sorry that we are not at present, nor likely for some time to be, at

---

[1] See above, p. 24 n. 6.

[1] The next letter.

[1] William Frederick Pollock (1815–88: *DNB*), Queen's Remembrancer (of which the duties are described in his *Personal Remembrances*, 1887, ii. 268), author, friend of the great, and dispenser of charm. Like his father, Sir Frederick Pollock (1783–1870: *DNB*), 1st Baronet, and eldest son, Sir Frederick Pollock (1845–1937: *DNB*), 3rd Baronet, all three distinguished jurists (and each more distinguished than his father), he attended Trinity College (BA 1836) and, like his eldest son, was an Apostle. In 1844 he married Juliet Creed, and in 1870 succeeded as 2nd Baronet.

Twickenham. Had we been at home it would have given us great pleasure to have received you and Mrs. Pollock. We are now in the Vicarage of Great Malvern near Worcester. If you will send your cousin's music either to us here or to Moxon's we shall be very glad to have it.

With mine and my wife's best thanks,

Ever yours
A. Tennyson

I send this to Spedding's to forward as I have mislaid your letter and forgotten the direction.

To MR BARNAND[1]

MS. Bodleian.

GREAT MALVERN, April 29 [1852]

My dear Sir
My wife is much obliged. Let it be Peach.

Ever yours
A. Tennyson

To CHARLES RICHARD WELD

MS. Yale.

MALVERN, Monday, [? 31 May 1852]

My dear Weld
I am for free trade in the bookselling question as in other things, yet I can scarcely think that my opinion is of much value for I have neither read those discussions in the paper nor have I of myself carefully examined it. Perhaps you would say this to Parker for me.[1]

Many thanks for Lord Rosse's [?] card. We shall most likely in a few days be at home. Love to Anne from both and to Missie.[2]

Ever yours
A. Tennyson

I am very sorry that I know no Tory Lords or great men who might help you out of Somerset House. Most of my friends are Whigs or Radicals.

To JAMES SPEDDING

MS. Tennyson Research Centre.

[mid-June 1852]

My dear James
Thanks for your letter. It was very good and suggestive. If I haven't acted

---

[1] Unidentified. (A pencilled note reads: 'gift from Mr. Barnand to whom it was written'.)

[1] John William Parker (1792–1870: *DNB*), printer and publisher (see below, p. 80).
[2] William Parsons (1800–67), 3rd Earl of Rosse, astronomer, Chancellor of the University of Dublin, President of the Royal Society; Agnes Grace, Weld's daughter?

upon it the more the pity. But that isn't what I was going to say. Go to see (and having seen, if you can interest yourself in) Thomas Woolner's design for the William Wordsworth Westminster monument.[1] I am told it is good and I promised to say a good word for him.

Ever yours
A. Tennyson

To EMILY SELLWOOD TENNYSON
Text. Memoir, i. 348–9.

YORK, July 7, 1852

Slept at Spedding's where I found they expected me. Started this morning 11 a.m. Hay fever atrocious with irritation of railway, nearly drove me crazed, but could not complain, the only other occupant of the carriage having a curiously split shoe for his better ease, and his eyes and teeth in a glare at me with pain of gout the whole way, and finally helped out by his servant, going to drink Harrogate waters. Came here to the Black Swan, ordered dinner, went out and bought weed, having left mine at Spedding's with gloves (ay me!). Enquired of tobacconist state of parties here, 'Never was anything so satisfactory, all purity of Election, no row, no drunkenness, Mr. Vincent will come in without any bother.' While he was yet speaking arose a row, innumerable mob raging, housekeepers all down the street rushed out with window-shutters to prevent windows being broken. My dinner waiting for me, I having to plunge through mob to get at it, essayed the fringes of the crowd, very dense nucleus of enormous brawl somewhere within. Presently the glazed hats of policemen, like sunshine striking here and there at the breaking up of a storm, showed me an issue of hope. I plunged through in the wake of the bluecoats and got home. To-morrow to Whitby. Vincent after all not returned.[1] When I got to Waterloo the roses had snapt off short and lay at the bottom of the carriage. The porter opened the door, picked up one snuffed at it with vast satisfaction, and never so much as 'by your leave.'

To EMILY SELLWOOD TENNYSON
Text. Memoir, i. 349–50

5 NORTH TERRACE, WEST CLIFF, WHITBY, July 8, 1852

I am set down here for a week at least in lodgings. It is rather a fine place, a

---

[1] 'A seated figure of the poet with a bas-relief of Peter Bell and the ass set in the pedestal, and a group of two figures on either side: The Father admonishing his son; the Mother guiding her daughter to the beauties of nature. And although this design was very highly praised Woolner failed to gain the commission, and he was so disappointed he determined to leave England' (Amy Woolner, *Thomas Woolner*, p. 14; reproduction facing p. 28). Woolner sailed for Australia on 24 July.

[1] Henry Vincent (1813–78: *DNB*), political agitator and Chartist.

river running into the sea between precipices, on one side new buildings and a very handsome royal hotel belonging to Hudson the railway king,[1] on the other at the very top a gaunt old Abbey, and older parish Church hanging over the town amid hundreds of white gravestones that looked to my eye something like clothes laid out to dry. Moreover there is the crackiness of an election going on and lots of pink and blue flags, and insane northland boatmen of Danish breed, who meet and hang each other for the love of liberty, foolish fellows. In the midst of the row yesterday came a funeral followed by weeping mourners, a great hearse, plumes nodding and mourning coach, and the gaunt old Abbey looked down with its hollow eyes on life and death, the drunkenness and the political fury, rather ironically as it seemed to me, only that it was too old to have much feeling left about anything. No bathing men were to be had, so I e'en walked into the sea by myself and had a very decent bathe. Hay fever was much better yesterday and is bad again this morning. I could not write yesterday for I came in after the post had started by a very pretty rail which curves like a common road between great wolds, the Esk, which is the stream that debouches here, running below. Then we really went down a considerable hill with a rope. The same thing I think occurs at Liège, but this seemed to me much steeper. I am told there are very fine views in the neighbourhood, though most probably shall not get out far enough to see them as it is pestilent hot.

To EMILY SELLWOOD TENNYSON

Text. *Materials*, ii. 69–70.

WHITBY, July 13 [1852]

I want to go to Redcliffe Scar which old Wordsworth once told me of, or perhaps to Bolton Abbey. If I go through Leeds, I should like to see James Marshall if he be there still. It is a pity you did not see Owen,[1] you called him Mr. (do you mean the bone man, the professor?) and old Mr. Jesse.[2] Either of these would have told you about the bird. I suppose if the young ones have

---

[1] George Hudson (1800–71: *DNB*). Carlyle wrote about him in 'Hudson's Statue', *Latter-Day Pamphlets*, no. 7 (July 1850), and he may have contributed something to the portrait of Mr Merdle in Dickens's *Little Dorrit* (1857–8).

[1] Richard Owen (1804–82: *DNB*), naturalist and anatomist, Hunterian Professor of Comparative Anatomy and Physiology at the Royal College of Surgeons (1835–56). He was a distinguished scientist and a man of broad culture (music, poetry, theatre, chess), who seems to have been friends with everyone (including the royal family), except perhaps—being also a fearsome ('adroit', 'acrimonious') controversialist—many fellow-scientists.

On 6 August he wrote: 'To-day we had a visit from Alfred Tennyson. His wife sat in the carriage, being in a delicate state of health. Miss Tennyson came in with her brother, who struck me as being a care-marked, dark-eyed, rather bilious-looking young man, with spectacles; middle height, and rather thin' (Richard Owen, *The Life of Richard Owen*, ii. 388–9). Owen himself was 'tall and ungainly in figure, with massive head, lofty forehead . . . long, lank, dark hair' (*DNB*). Leslie Ward's caricature of Owen in *Vanity Fair*, 1 March 1773, was captioned 'Old Bones' for two reasons. See below, p. 36.

[2] Edward Jesse (1780–1868), writer on natural history (*DNB*). His *Gleanings in Natural History* (7th edn., 1849) was in Tennyson's library (*Tennyson in Lincoln*, i, No. 1260).

come out of the nest, they were going to fly and have all gone by this. You can send a sovereign if you like to the sapper and miner, but I think it is very hard that I am obliged to subscribe to all the bad poets, and I am indignant that I should be aidant in filling the world with more trash than there is at present. Besides this kind of demand (if it be found out that I respond to such claims) is likely to increase, and I do not believe that old Wordey paid any attention to such. He was far too canny. Tom Taylor I will answer, though I think it a great pity that your 'Sweet and low' hadn't the start of Mrs. Taylor's and all these. I have had two very good days coasting, I mean walking along on and under the cliffs. Very singular they are with great bivalve shells sticking out of them. They are made of a great dark slate coloured shale (is it to be called) that comes showering down ever and anon from a great height; and on the hard flat rock which makes the beach on one side of the town (for on the other side are sands), you see beautiful little ammonites which you stoop to pick up but find them part of the solid rock. You know these are the snakes which St. Hilda drove over the cliff and falling they lost their heads, and she changed them into stone. I found a strange fish on the shore with rainbows about its wild staring eyes, enclosed in a sort of sack with long tentacula beautifully coloured, quite dead, but when I took it up by the tail spotted all the sand underneath with great drops of ink, so I suppose a kind of cuttle fish. I found too a pale pink orchis on the sea bank and a pink vetch, a low sort of shrub with here and there a thorn. I am reading lots of novels. The worst is they do not last longer than the day. I am such a fierce reader I think I have had pretty well my quantum suff: Venables' anecdotes are very interesting indeed one cannot help wishing that such a man as Gladstone may come to sit on the top branch of the tree.

To TOM TAYLOR

MS. Robert Taylor.

WHITBY, July 16, [1852]

My dear Tom

I send the permission trusting that Miss L. B.[1] will not serve me as some do i. e. transpose all the stanzas and alter some of the words and then put in the titlepage 'by express permission of A. T. the P. L.'

I am here at Whitby killed with hay fever.

Ever yours affectionately
A. Tennyson

My wife has long since set sweet and low and very prettily too.[2]

---

[1] Unidentified, but conceivably Mrs. J. Worthington Bliss, née M. Lindsay (see *Tennyson in Lincoln*, ii, No. 5278).

[2] The familiar music is by Charles Albert Stebbins. For Laura Barker Taylor's setting, see below, p. 456.

To EMILY SELLWOOD TENNYSON

Text. Memoir, i. 351–3.

WHITBY, July 19, [1852]

I have ordered a carriage and am going to see Lord Normanby's park near here,[1] though I am half afraid of it, a carriage so excites my hay fever. I met an old smuggler on the coast yesterday who had been in Lord N's service (not as smuggler of course!), and he took me for Lord Normanby at first, a likeness I have been told of more than once before. I got into conversation with him and I am going to call for him to-day and he is to show me the caves and holes in the coast where they used to land their kegs. I am going from here to-morrow, and I think I shall go by the Scarborough packet but I am not certain. I shall most likely pop down on Charles at Grasby, but if I go to Scarborough I hardly think I shall go out of my way again to Leeds. I shall like much to see the Brownings again, Mrs. B particularly. I suppose when I come back the Lushingtons will want me to spend some days at Park House. I have seen no houses here to be sold, but then I have not looked out for them. A tailor who sewed me on some buttons, told me Whitby was remarkable for longevity, the healthiest place in England except some place (he said) near Cheltenham, he had forgotten the name. I dare say he meant Malvern.

GRASBY, July 22, [1852]

I came by the packet boat to Scarborough where I stopt the night and came on here yesterday. The train only stopt at Moortown, and I was obliged to walk through the fields to Grasby when I admired the deep long-stemmed Lincolnshire wheat which I had not seen for many a day.

I find Charles and Louisa very well, only Charles rather low as it seems to me. It is a nice little place they have and the country really looks pretty at this time of year. I shall stop a few days.

GRASBY, July 27, [1852]

Pray take drives every day. The school children have a feast here to-morrow for which I am going to stay. They run in sacks and do all manner of queer things. Our parson-party went off well. Agnes[2] I suppose will be triumphant to-morrow. I think when I leave here I shall go round by Grimsby to see the new docks and perhaps get a bathe at Cleethorpes.

We went over to drink tea the other afternoon with Mr. Maclean,[3] the Vicar of Caistor, where I made fun for the children, and saw a young cuckoo which a boy had found in a sparrow's nest, a rather rare circumstance so late

---

[1] Mulgrave Castle, seat of the 2nd Marquis of Normanby (1819–90: *DNB*), in a park near the coast.

[2] Agnes Grace Weld?

[3] The Revd Hippisley Maclean (1807 or 1808–95), vicar, rural dean, chaplain to the Union, Caistor Union, 1844–86 (Venn, White's *Lincolnshire*).

27 *July* 1852   35

in July; but the boy had had him for three weeks and fed him with worms. He was a good deal duskier than the adult cuckoo, and with a white band on his head and very voracious, would have swallowed anything.

HULL, July 31, [1852]

I am going out of the way to see Crowland Abbey and maybe I shall stop a day or so there. I write this in vast at haste the Mason Arms, Louth, Daddy[4] drove me over last night to Grimsby to see the new dock, truly a great work.

To FREDERIC WILLIAM FARRAR[1]

MS. Gordon Ray.

August 9, [1852]

Dear Sir

I have just received your Prize-poem for which I return my best thanks. I believe, it is true that mine was the first written in blank verse which obtained the Chancellor's Medal. Nevertheless (and though you assure me that reading it gave you 'the deepest pleasure') I could wish that it had never been written. Believe me, dear Sir,

Yours very truly
A. Tennyson

---

[4] Henry Sellwood.

[1] Frederic William Farrar (1831–1903: *DNB*), Dean of Canterbury, 1895–1903. In his youth he attended King William's College, Isle of Man. Later he came under the influence of F. D. Maurice's disciples at King's College, London, and continued his own discipleship as an Apostle at Trinity College (winning the Chancellor's Gold Medal in 1852). Master at Marlborough, 1853–5, and at Harrow, 1855–70, he succeeded George Granville Bradley as headmaster of the former in 1871, and five years later became a canon of Westminster and Rector of St Margaret's (see Tennyson's 'Epitaph on Caxton', Ricks, p. 1316). In 1878, Dean Stanley being ill, Farrar married Lionel Tennyson and Eleanor Locker in Westminster Abbey (see below, vol. iii, February, 1878). He was also a novelist of no distinction, a philologist of some (see below, p. 400), and, as a theologian, variously of none, some, and much. Of his novels the best-known is certainly *Eric: or, Little by Little*, the hero of which is said to have been based on Cyril Flower (later Lord Battersea), himself of Harrow and Trinity (Penelope Fitzgerald, *Edward Burne-Jones*, pp. 183–4; Richard Tobias, *T. E. Brown*, pp. 71–2). He also wrote (among other things) a novel of college life (Trinity: *Julian Home*) and two historical fictions. His *Life of Christ* (1874) was prodigiously popular and influential; his *Seekers after God* (1868)—on Seneca, Epictetus, Marcus Aurelius—may have influenced Pater. Tennyson has pride of place in Farrar's *Men I Have Known* (1897), which is virtually a *Who's Who* of late Victorian England (and America), with the tactful (pointed?) omission of Bradley.

It was not easy to succeed Bradley, temperamentally his opposite and very popular at Marlborough. 'I remember the shock which the contrast between Bradley and Farrar produced on veteran pupils of Bradley. One of them indeed . . . wrote to his late Head-master on a postcard . . .: "Dear Dr. Bradley, | we miss you sadly, | And wish Dr. Farra' | Would go back to Harra"' (Reginald Farrar, *The Life of Frederic William Farrar*, p. 149).

EMILY SELLWOOD TENNYSON
to ELIZABETH BARRETT BROWNING

Text. University of Virginia (microfilm).

CHAPEL HOUSE, August 9, [1852]

My dear Mrs. Browning

Right welcome will you be. I wish we could put off the time to a day more convenient to you than Friday but my Doctor names the 25th as the latest day on which I may have to turn.[1] If it were not so I would say pray come here for several days and see all that is pleasant around us. As it is I am obliged to talk about dinner. Half past five is the hour our friends generally choose because of the quicker train which brings them down for that hour. Will this suit you? I will not give you the trouble of writing again if it do but if it do not, if you fear the night air or if any other cause make you wish to fix another hour do, we beg.

Most sincerely yours
Emily Tennyson

To CATHERINE RAWNSLEY

MS. University of British Colombia.

CHAPEL HOUSE, August 11, [1852]
half past nine a.m.

Dear Catherine

Emily is *just* delivered of a fine boy.[1] We had two doctors but both were out of the way, but she got on very well with a nurse. Both she and the child are at present likely to do well. She *does* look so pleased!

Ever yours in haste
A. Tennyson

To ELIZABETH RUSSELL

MS. Viscount Boyne.

CHAPEL HOUSE, TWICKENHAM, August 11, [1852]

Dearest Aunt

Emily was delivered of a fine boy at 9 ½ a.m. this morning rather before her time but mother and child are both doing well. A great London doctor

---

[1] See the next letter.

[1] Hallam Tennyson, 2nd Baron Tennyson, who died in 1928, after a career more or less divided between filial duty (1874–97), culminating in the *Memoir*, and public service (Governor and Commander-in-Chief of South Australia, 1899–1902; Acting Governor-General of the Commonwealth of Australia, 1902; and Governor-General, 1902–4). In 1884 he married Audrey Boyle (see vol. iii, Allingham, *A Diary*, and Hallam Tennyson's Journal, both 25 June 1884), who died in 1916, and in 1918 Mary Emily Hichens (née Prinsep). See *Who Was Who, 1916–28*, and i. xvii–xviii.

had just left her thinking it would not come off till the afternoon. The nurse managed it all. God bless you. Love to Emma¹ if with you.

Ever yours affectionately, in vast haste
A. Tennyson

To JULIA MARGARET CAMERON[1]

Text. Tennyson Research Centre (transcript).

CHAPEL HOUSE, TWICKENHAM, August 11, 1852

My dear Mrs. Cameron

Mrs Taylor's servant says he is going by your house so I write this scrap to tell you that all is going well with Mother and Child and that I shall never till the hour of my death forget your great kindness in rushing off to Town as you did in the hour of my trouble. God bless you ever.

A. Tennyson

To JOHN FORSTER

Text. Memoir, i. 356.

August 11, 1852

My dear John Forster

I did not tell you of my marriage which you rather took in dudgeon.[1] Now I will tell you of the birth of a little son this day. I have seen beautiful things in my life, but I never saw anything more beautiful than the mother's face as she lay by the young child an hour or two after, or heard anything sweeter than the little lamblike bleat of the young one. I had fancied that children after birth had been all shriek and roar; but he gave out a little note of satisfaction every now and then, as he lay by his mother, which was the most pathetic sound in its helplessness I ever listened to. You see I talk almost like a bachelor, yet unused to these things: but you—I don't hear good reports of you. You should have been better by this. Get better quickly if you would have me be as I always am,

Yours most truly
A. Tennyson

To ELIZABETH BARRETT BROWNING

MS. Berg Collection.

CHAPEL HOUSE, TWICKENHAM, August 11, [1852]

My dear Mrs. Browning

I wrote to you once before this morning. I now write again to tell you what I am sure your woman's and poet's heart will rejoice in that my wife was delivered of a fine boy at 9 ½ a.m. this day and that both she and the child

---

[1] Her daughter (see i. 23 n.)
[1] See Appendix A.
[1] See i. 331.

are doing well. I never saw any face so radiant with all high and sweet expression as hers, when I saw her some time after.

Ever yours truly
A. Tennyson

To EMILY AUGUSTA PATMORE

Text. Basil Champneys, *Memoirs and Correspondence of Coventry Patmore,* i. 304.

[12 August 1852]

My dear Mrs. Patmore

I know that your kind womanly heart, will rejoice in hearing that it is all safely over. She had a very easy confinement, and was delivered of what the nurse calls 'a fine boy' yesterday. We are keeping her very quiet according to advice, but, as soon as she can see anybody, she would be glad to see you. She was so anxious that the little godson[1] should have the cup on his birthday (for it was her thought, not mine), that there was no time to write and enquire the exact initials and get them engraved.

Ever yours, in great haste,
A. Tennyson

To EDMUND LUSHINGTON ET AL.

MS. Yale.

[12 August 1852]

My dear Edmund, Cissy, Harry, Frank

My best thanks for your kind letters to each and to all not forgetting Venables. I have no doubt of his *sincere* gratulations. Never man was less untrue. I cannot see you Harry on Wednesday for I dine with our parson Dr. Parish[1] on that day. All is going on well. I have just been down to see the little brickfaced monkey sucking in his muslin cap. Every now and then he gives a little lamblike bleat of satisfaction only much lower and sweeter than any lamb's bleat. The great London accoucheur, Dr. Anderson,[2] yesterday called him 'a splendid child' so that I trust all is well.

Yours ever affectionately
A. Tennyson

---

[1] Tennyson Patmore (see i. 333 and n.).

[1] Henry Parish (1791?–1873), 'minister of Montpellier Chapel, Twickenham' (Foster; *Journal,* p. 28).

[2] Unidentified.

? 14 August 1852

To ELIZABETH BARRETT BROWNING

MS. University of Virginia.

Saturday, [? 14 August 1852]

My dear Mrs. Browning

Here is one word of bulletin as you desired. All is going on as well as can be.

To this one word let me add another—that is how very grateful your little note and Browning's epilogue made me. I began to read it to my wife but could not get on with it so I put it away by her bedside and she shall read it as soon as she reads anything.

Ever yours and your husband's
A. Tennyson

To HENRY HALLAM

MS. Robert Taylor.

CHAPEL HOUSE, TWICKENHAM, August 16 [1852]

My dear Sir

You may perhaps have heard through the Brookfields of the birth of my boy. My wife will have him called Alfred; but we intend his second name to be, with your permission, Hallam. Will you grant my request and be my child's Godfather? I am sure you will feel that such a request is by no means a mere compliment or piece of civility nor without reference to times now remote but never to be by me forgotten.

My love to Julia[1] and remembrances to her husband. I send this to your house in Wilton Crescent not knowing your direction. Believe me to be, my dear Sir,

Always yours
A. Tennyson

To SOPHIA (RAWNSLEY) ELMHIRST

MS. Duke.

TWICKENHAM, [16 August 1852]

My dear Sophy

I write to ask after Catherine whether she be unwell or whether my letter announcing the birth of a son and that the mother and child were going on well had been forwarded to Shawell. I directed Shiplake and learning afterwards that she was on a visit at Shawell,[1] I thought that you would communicate together and that (as I had about 60 letters to write) the omission of a particular dispatch to you would be forgiven. Now both I and Emily are rather alarmed about her, knowing her to be near her time.[2] Pray write and

---

[1] Julia Hallam Cator (later, Lennard: see i. 195 n.) For Hallam's acceptance, see *Memoir*, i. 359.

[1] See above, p. 36.   [2] Alfred Edward Rawnsley (1852–98).

let us know as soon as may be. We were rejoiced to hear that you had got over your trouble happily. With best remembrances to Elmhirst,

Ever yours affectionately
A. Tennyson

To AUBREY DE VERE
MS. Duke.

[*c.* 17 August 1852]

My dear Aubrey

I have been through the whole narration so often in the week (having written I should think—a strange matter to me—about sixty letters) that I really cannot go through it again this morning to you, sick as I am with last night's watchings and trying to soothe the mother to sleep while the young unconscientious monsterling kept wailing his hard fate which was yet not so hard as his mother's who suffers from an almost total want of sleep. The doctor says it does not matter but it keeps her very nervous. As to who the babe is like no one knows. His poor little silent elder brother was very like me, Mrs. Marshall said; and certainly a larger finer child to look on than this. My cook I believe cannot bring herself to look with patience on this second. She thinks he looks so much less like the son of a king. Nevertheless Dr. Anderson pronounced him 'a splendid baby' and what more can be wished for; though if one go by the adage of 'handsome is that handsome does' he could scarce be called pretty. Such a roar he sets up if he cannot get the milk in a moment out of the breast, such a lamentation if his little demi-bald sconce has to be brushed with a brush that would not bruise a midge. Strange too that the nurse calls him a very quiet child as children go. I was rather awestruck by him on his third day of life. I went into the nursery to look at him as he was lying alone and while I was regarding him I found that he was earnestly regarding me with wide open eyes in perfect silence. I felt as if I had seen a spirit; but the little incubus gets more carnal every day. I see by the mouths he makes when he is meditating that he is always dreaming of his dinner. You ask what his name is to be. My wife sticks out for Alfred to which (though I am an enemy to polyonomy as interfering with a man's sense of personal identity and causing him double trouble in signatures etc. all through his life) to which I cannot resist my desire to add the name of my old friend Hallam.

There now I have told you some little bits of news.

Leave me, leave me to repose.[1] However to repose I am not to be left having plenty more epistles to indite this blessed morning. Goodby therefore. I shall take no notice of your 'tapestries' and 'pulling of loose threads' but leave you at least for the present to settle all that with your conscience and your priest but I will say I am grieved that we did not get to Rome. You see we fancied at that time that there was a probability of another little one and

---

[1] Thomas Gray, 'Descent of Odin', ll. 50, 58, 72.

I did not wish her to be confined in Italy. My love to Vere,[2] to your dear mother and all whom I know who may be with you. God bless you.

Ever yours
A. Tennyson

To RICHARD MONCKTON MILNES

MS. Trinity College.

August 17, [1852]

My dear Richard

I will come if I can. I cannot absolutely promise. My wife has not been so well these last two days suffering from an almost total want of sleep and the little sensual wretch roaring day and night for ailment lets her have no quiet. I was rather wishing for a little girl you I doubt not for a little boy.[1]

Well we will take the goods the gods provide us[2] and be grateful.

Ever yours
A. Tennyson

To JOHN FORSTER

MS. Yale.

Wednesday, [18 August 1852]

My dear John Forster

I have only time for one word of bulletin. Everything I believe is going on well though the mother suffers from an almost total want of sleep and the little monster does anything but what Hamlet says Osric did in his nursery days.[1] I found him lying alone on the 3d day of his life and while I was looking at him I saw him looking at me with such apparently earnest wide open eyes I felt as awestruck as if I had seen a spirit. I hope you are mending.

God bless you
A. Tennyson

To MISS HAYWARD[1]

MS. Boston University.

CHAPEL HOUSE, TWICKENHAM, 28 [August 1852]

My dear Miss Hayward

You may have heard of my wife's safe delivery of a fine boy, but if you have

---

[2] Sir Vere Edmond de Vere (see i. 283 n., 321 n.).

[1] Amicia Henrietta Milnes (later, Lady FitzGerald), born 3 August 1852.
[2] Dryden, 'Alexander's Feast', l. 106 (see below, p. 59)

[1] 'He did comply with his dug before he sucked it' (*Hamlet*, v. ii. 195).

[1] Unidentified, but perhaps one of the nameless sisters of Abraham Hayward (1801–84: *DNB*), journalist, critic, essayist, and man about town, who, though his name does not crop up in books on Tennyson, knew everyone that Tennyson knew (and others), and whose influential prose translation of *Faust* was published by Moxon in 1833. See Abraham Hayward, *A Selection from the Correspondence*, ed. H. E. Carlisle (2 vols., 1886).

not I have to pray your forgiveness as she has been constantly urging me to write to you ever since, and I as constantly intending but as I have an irrational dislike to putting events of this kind in the paper, I really have had near a hundred letters to write in all directions and the work has been rather hard: nevertheless not at the eleventh hour but past the eleventh day I write to tell you and to thank you for your innumerable kindnesses in the matter of househunting, nay even to beg yet another good office of you which is that if you happen to know of a good honest practical nursemaid in your country, you would send her to us, as our nurse leaves us in a short time. Neither she nor our doctor nor any one else to whom we have applied knows of one. If you can provide us with such a friend in need you will add another to our many obligations. My wife's best love. She will write as soon as she can hold a pen. The boy appears sound and healthy and as yet all goes on well.

Ever yours most truly
A. Tennyson

To MISS HAYWARD

Text. *Materials*, ii. 76.

[early September 1852]

My dear Miss Hayward

I thank you very much for so immediately attending to my request. We have of course a nurse still here, but E. J.[1] may come this week in fact as soon as she likes. My wife lays stress on her being healthy, but I suppose from your not touching on her health she may be considered so, also she says that if she were not in such absolute need of a nursemaid immediately she would have liked to ascertain whether she were a good needlewoman, and could occasionally help to get up and iron the baby's linen. I think that this is all I have been commissioned to ask. With Emily's best love, believe me dear Miss H.

Yours ever truly
A. Tennyson

To JOHN FORSTER

MS. Gordon Ray.

HOTEL, BLACKGANG CHINE,[1] ISLE OF WIGHT, Saturday, [? 4 September 1852]

My dear John Forster

I am very glad to learn from yourself that you are at last somewhat better, and able to go to Brighton. I got yours just now at White's[2] where I was on a

---

[1] Unidentified.

[1] 'On the romantic Cliffs, near the water fall, is *Blackgang Chine Hotel*, a large and handsome building, commanding extensive marine views, in which the Bill of Portland may be seen in fine weather' (William White, *History, Gazetteer, and Directory of Hampshire and the Isle of Wight*, 1859, p. 653).

[2] James White (see i. 257 n.).

visit. All was well at home—when I left—with wife and child, though she still continues very weak and unable to move without assistance. However I trust another week will set her right or nearly so.

Ever yours most truly
A. Tennyson

To DRUMMOND RAWNSLEY

MS. Harvard.

September 8, [1852]

Dear Drummond

I wrote to Moultrie[1] and he answers he cannot let me have the papers without leave given by W[alker]'s executor: which no doubt may without difficulty be obtained.

I have just come from the Isle of Wight. Emily is getting on well and the boy is sound and plump. Send us news of Catherine. We received your round robin in which the paternal and regal style was barely distinguishable.

Ever yours
A. Tennyson

To RICHARD MONCKTON MILNES

MS. Trinity College.

CHAPEL HOUSE, ⟨Wedn⟩ Thursday [? 16 September 1852]

My dear M

Thanks for your inquiries. The little one flourishes but the Mother, I regret to say, is still very weak. Her having been stung by a wasp this morning has not improved her condition. We have not yet fixt on the time of our christening. Of course we are not irrational enough to expect that any of our friends to [*sic*] attend except those who may be in or near town. I will write again when we have fixed the time. It is Mrs. Marshall[1] the Godmother who keeps us in uncertainty. She has exprest a wish to be present at the ceremony. She is coming from Germany to London and then (after a few days interval) going to Italy with an ailing child; but we do not as yet know when she will be here.

An interesting anecdote, that of your Aunt and the Duke![2] My wife desires her best remembrances to you. Give mine to yours and believe me

Yours always
A. Tennyson

---

[1] John Moultrie: see i. 343 n.; below, p. 44; and Ricks, p. 1239.

[1] Mrs James Garth Marshall (see i. 96 n., 330, 332).

[2] 'Will you think "The Duke" worth writing about? That is a kind of royalty you need not disdain to commemorate. An old aunt of mine called on Lady Mornington over a pastry-cook's in Bond St., and found a lean youth leaning on the edge of a sofa. "That," said his mother, "is Arthur. He wants to go into the army, but we will buy him a commission." "I don't want that," said the boy. "I want to *walk* to Germany and learn fortification."' (Milnes to Tennyson, *c*. 15 September 1852, TRC). The Duke of Wellington died 14 September.

To JOHN MOULTRIE

MS. Stephen Wilson.

CHAPEL HOUSE, TWICKENHAM, September 18, [1852]

My dear Sir

I am sure I am very much obliged to you for collecting and sending me these poetic scraps of my old days from Sydney Walker's MSS.[1] I trust that whenever you come to town you will (if not prest for time) come over here and dine with me. I am only half an hour from Waterloo Station by the quick trains. Meantime believe me

Ever yours
A. Tennyson

To RICHARD MONCKTON MILNES

MS. Trinity College.

Monday, September 22 [for 20?, 1852]

Small déjeuner (or some such thing) at 3 o'clock October 5th our christening-day, when I don't expect you—though ever yours

A. Tennyson

To JOHN FORSTER

MS. Tennyson Research Centre.

September 22, 1852

My dear Forster

If you are at all in better health and in town on the 5 Oct. I need not say how glad I and my wife would be to see you at our christening collation about 3 o'clock.

Ever yours
A. Tennyson

To HENRY HALLAM

MS. Robert Taylor.

Sunday, [? 26 September 1852]

My dear Sir

We have fixed on the 5th of October for the boy's christening. I need not

---

[1] William Sydney Walker (1795–1846: *DNB*), critic, poet, scholar, and eccentric. After Eton, he went to Trinity College (BA 1819) and was elected next year to a fellowship, which he resigned in 1829. In London 'He lived entirely alone, and a painful hallucination that he was possessed by a "demon" gradually clouded his reason. He neglected his dress and person, and social intercourse with him grew impossible. . . . He died of the stone . . . on 15 Oct. 1846.' See also *CBEL*, iii. 1028.

say how glad we should be to see you at our small déjeuner at 3 o'clock if you happen to be in town at that time.

Ever affectionately yours
A. Tennyson

To DRUMMOND RAWNSLEY

MS. Harvard.

[27 September 1852]

My dear Drummond

There is a small déjeuner at 3 o'clock on October 5th our christening-day. Come if you can and taste your own venison. I hope Catherine is hopeful. Guter hoffnung in German I know she is[1]—but I trust she is in better spirits than some weeks ago.

Ever yours
A. Tennyson

To ELIZABETH RUSSELL

MS. Tennyson Research Centre.

TWICKENHAM, September 28, [1852]

Dearest Aunt

I have had so much trouble and anxiety for these many days and such heaps of correspondence to go through that I must be forgiven for not having sent you a line before now. The trouble was in great measure about the state of things at Cheltenham and latterly about Emily and the boy. The first does not seem to get well at all. Perhaps she will have to give up nursing which will be a great grief to her and the child from having been walked out (the 2d time in his bit of a life) on a dampish coldish day, has had what seems to us (fearful ones) a very bad cold. Nose stopt up so that he could scarce suck and mightily indignant he was against the whole order of things in this unjust world. Then that past away and he got a rattling in his throat making us afraid of croup and all kinds of horrors. Today I hope he is better but I hope you may easily conceive how all this has acted upon the mother and then her state reacts on the child. Ah well, we shall get on somehow. I trust you are not suffering so much from those hateful heart attacks though I hear that you complain of a bruised foot—and Emma too I hope is well.

As for myself I am full of trouble and shall be for a long time and by way of helping me out of it the 200,000,000 poets of Great Britain deluge me daily with volumes of poems—truly the Laureateship is no sinecure. If any good soul would just by way of a diversion send me a tome of prose. O the shoals of trash!

---

[1] Pregnant.

Our christening on the fifth. I wish I could [see] your dear face at it, but I shan't. So goodbye and God bless you, dearest Aunt.

Your affectionate
A. Tennyson

Emily's best love.

To HENRY HALLAM

MS. John Rylands Library.

September 30 [1852]

My dear Sir
The ceremony will be performed at half past one o'clock. If you cannot be in time to assist at it we can easily light upon a proxy. I shall be very glad to see Julia Lennard and her husband if they can come and likewise the Brookfields but where they are I know not: for my last letter to Mrs. Brookfield was unanswered. Will you be kind enough to forward the enclosed to her if you know where she is.

Ever yours
A. Tennyson

To JANE OCTAVIA BROOKFIELD

MS. Gordon Ray.

[September 30, 1852]

Dear Jane
Come with William to our little Christening déjeuner on the 5th October at 3 o'clock.

Ever affectionately yours
A. Tennyson

To JOHN FORSTER

MS. Columbia.

September 30, [1852]

My dear F.
I am very sorry indeed that you cannot come and the more so that it is your invalid state which prevents you. I have written to Carlyle and Mrs. C. but from them I have no answer. To Dickens too I wrote but neither have I heard from him.[1] I wrote to Tavistock House No. 59[?]. If you know where he is I wish you would tell him that it would give me all manner of delight to see him on the fifth and any of his he would like to bring. What you say about

---

[1] See Dickens's answer in *Memoir*, i. 360.

30 *September* 1852   47

that French Dutch pseudo-Corsican-bastard-blackleg kite-eaglet chimes in too terribly with my own surmises.[2]

Ever yours, dear J. F.
A. Tennyson

To LADY FRANKLIN[1]

MS. Syracuse University.

September 30, [1852]

Dear Lady Franklin

Might we hope to see you at our little christening déjeuner on the 5 October with your niece Sophy? I hardly dare expect you as we cannot offer you beds, yet my wife would be so glad to see you both. I send this to Somerset House to C. Weld as I do not know your direction.

Ever yours truly
A. Tennyson

HALLAM TENNYSON'S CHRISTENING, 5 October 1852.

Text. Journal.

He was christened at Twickenham, 5 October. There was some question as to the name. A. with a loud voice said 'Hallam', and Mr. Hallam looked pleased though jokingly he said afterwards in London they were afraid he might be a fool so they would not call him Alfred but they called him Hallam. The guests were: Mr. Hallam, Mr. Maurice,[1] Mr. and Mrs. Brookfield, Mr.

---

[2] Louis Napoleon (1808–73) seized dictatorial powers in a *coup d'état* on 1 December 1851, and exactly a year later declared himself Emperor of the French under the name of Napoleon III. In mid-September he had begun a public tour of the south of France and (Tennyson's 'surmises') was becoming more and more forthright about his imperial designs.

The epithets are resonant. Louis Napoleon was the son, certainly, of Hortense de Beauharnais, legally of her husband, Louis Bonaparte, King of Holland and brother of Napoleon, putatively of the Dutch Admiral Verhuel—in which case he was a 'pseudo-Corsican bastard'. The eagle was of course the emblem of Napoleon I, and 'eaglet' implies the same as Hugo's famous 'Napoleon le petit', with 'blackleg' making him a swindler.

[1] Lady Jane Franklin (1792–1875), née Griffin, widow of Sir John Franklin (see i. 190 n., 144 n.) and aunt by marriage of Emily Sellwood Tennyson. Sophia Cracroft was the daughter of Isabella Franklin and Thomas Cracroft (*DNB*; *Landed Gentry*).

[1] John Frederick Denison Maurice (1805–72: *DNB*), clergyman, founding father (with John Sterling) of the Apostles, and professor. 'I hope to be in London on Tuesday. Alfred Tennyson has done me the high honour of asking me to be godfather to his son, who is to be baptized on that day. I accept the office with real thankfulness and fear. It was to please his wife he asked me' (Maurice to Charles Kingsley, 29 September, in Frederick Maurice, *Frederick Denison Maurice*, ii, 143). See Tennyson's charming poem 'To the Rev. F. D. Maurice' and the editor's head-note in Ricks, p. 1022, and, as a counterweight, Una Pope-Hennessy, *Canon Charles Kingsley*, p. 72. In 1853 he parted company with King's College, London, on charges of heterodoxy, and in 1854 inaugurated the Working Men's College.

and Mrs. James Marshall and Victor,[2] Mr. Henry Taylor and Aubrey [de Vere], Mr. and Mrs. Cameron, Mr. Venables, Sir Alexander and Lady Duff Gordon, Mr. Palgrave, Mr. Morier,[3] Edmund Lushington, Charles and Louisa Turner, Charles, Anne, and Agnes Weld, Matilda Tennyson, Drummond Rawnsley, Stephen Spring Rice, Mr. Browning, Mr. and Miss Bolton,[4] Mr. Archibald and Miss Peel. Mr. James Marshall, Mr. Hallam and Mr. Maurice were sponsors. Mrs. Browning too ill to come though they had stayed in England on purpose. Mr. Carlyle's letter got thrown aside in the hurry of moving. Mr. Tom Taylor came next day by mistake. Mr. Charles Spring Rice[5] did not come through another mistake. Mrs. Henry Taylor and Catherine Rawnsley kept at home by their babies. Mr. Scoones[6] performed the service. Drummond Rawnsley gave the haunch of Venison, the best I had ever tasted. There were flowers and beautiful peaches and other fruit and the best champagne we could get. Milnes made so perfect a breakfast that it was thought to have come from Gunters[7] and we were proud.

EDWARD MOXON to ALFRED TENNYSON

MS. Morgan Library.

PUTNEY HEATH, November 6, 1852

My dear Tennyson

For an edition of 10,000 copies of your Ode on the death of the Duke of Wellington[1] I beg to offer you two hundred pounds, the amount to be paid at Christmas, or, should you wish it, on the day of publication.

Faithfully yours
Edward Moxon

The selling price to be 1s/−

---

[2] Victor Marshall (1841–1928), their oldest child.
[3] Robert Burnet David Morier (1826–93: *DNB*; knighted, 1882), diplomat and nephew of James Justinian Morier, the author of *Hajji Baba* and also a diplomat. Morier's account of the christening is worth reading (*Memoirs and Letters of the Rt. Hon. Sir Robert Morier*, ed. Mrs Rosslyn Wemyss, 2 vols., 1911, i. 116–17). See below, p. 67 n. In 1861 he married Alice Peel, daughter of General Jonathan Peel, Baronet, of Marble Hall, Twickenham, father of five sons, including Archibald Peel (1828–1910) and three daughters. See *DNB* and Burke's *Peerage*, *sub* Peel of Drayton Manor.
[4] The Boltons were Twickenham neighbours.
[5] Charles Spring Rice (1819–70), younger brother of Stephen, in 1855 married Elizabeth Margaret Marshall, the niece of two of his brothers-in-law and of his stepmother (see i. 96 n.).
[6] Probably the Rev. William Dalton Scoones (*c.* 1821–?), from 1856 Vicar of Langley Marish, Bucks. (Foster, Allibone). He called on the Tennysons at Farringford in April 1860 (*Journal*, p. 144).
[7] Thomas Gunter and Sons, 7 and 8 Berkeley Square, confectioners.

[1] Ricks, p. 1007. See E. F. Shannon, Jr., 'The History of a Poem: Tennyson's *Ode on the Death of the Duke of Wellington*', *Studies in Bibliography*, xiii (1960), 149–77, and *idem* and Christopher Ricks, 'A Further History of Tennyson's *Ode* . . . ,' *Studies in Bibliography*, xxxii (1979), 125–57.

To JOHN FORSTER [?]

MS. Morgan Library.[1]

[*c*. 8 November 1852]

I have written to accept. Tell P. I tell Moxon that I shall want the same for all other 10,000. Come down here if you can.

A. Tennyson

To EMILY SELLWOOD TENNYSON

MS. Tennyson Research Centre.

[11 November 1852][1]

Dearest

Can't possibly be back till tomorrow—working like a Turk in Franklin Lushington's rooms, 5 Paper Building, Temple. Venables here suggests various things. Forster triumphant about it. Kiss babe. Thine ever.

A.T.

Written at Dick's Tavern by Temple Bar where I dine. I trust I *shall* be able to be with you by tomorrow night.

To ?

MS. Yale (transcript).

SEAFORD HOUSE, SEAFORD, SUSSEX, [? mid-November 1852]

Sir

The silver horns of the mountain range before which the shepherd stands are simply the snowy peaks. You know there is a Silberhorn in Switzerland so called from its beautifully shaped snow peak. Silver (by the bye) ought not to be spelt as it is with a capital letter in that passage. The Shepherd personifying Love personifies likewise the lifelessness of those high places where not a lichen grows—as Death and as to[1] Morning which is personified too. No doubt he has for years seen its earliest light moving on the mountains when all the valleys were in shade. He says figuratively Love cannot live in those snowy heights, where all is lifeless in the cold lights of Morning. I have expressed myself clumsily, but I hope you see what I mean. I am, Sir,

Yours truly
A. Tennyson

---

[1] Written across the top of page 1 of the letter from Moxon preceding. 'P.' is probably Palgrave.

[1] Addressed to his wife at Seaford and postmarked twice: London, 11 November, and LEWES | NO 12 | 1852 | A. 'The river is so much out that we are afraid of damp for our little Hallam and take him to Lord Howard de Walden's house at Seaford'. (*Journal*, p. 29). See below, pp. 50, 53–4. Charles Augustus Ellis (1799–1868), 6th Baron Howard de Walden and 2nd Baron Seaford, diplomat, was minister plenipotentiary at Brussels 1846–68.

[1] *Sic* ('also Morning'?). The letter explicates *The Princess*, vii. 189: 'Come Down, O Maid'.

To MRS FITZGERALD[1]

MS. Brotherton Collection.

Monday, November 15, [1852]

Mrs. Fitzgerald

Have a fire lighted in Mr. Lushington's rooms by one o'clock tomorrow Tuesday as I shall most likely come up.

A. Tennyson

Tell Mr. Venables that I am coming up.

To ELIZABETH RUSSELL

MS. Viscount Boyne.

SEAFORD HOUSE, SEAFORD, SUSSEX, November 16, [1852]

Dearest Aunt

We have only just heard in a letter from Tilly[1] sent on to us here from Twickenham that you had been so unwell. It was very bad news though the antidote of good news came along with it viz. that you were now recovered. I think most people I know have suffered more or less this season of floods and earthquakes. I am going up to London today in order to get some place from which to see the Duke's funeral. I ordered Moxon to send you a copy of my ode which I hope you will have received before this. I have made some improvements since it was printed. It is not so good as I could wish it to be. Then, you see, I wrote it because it was expected of me to write: you will be glad to hear that Moxon has paid me £200 for the first 10,000 copies and at that rate for more, if more are wanted. Accept my kindest love from Emily and myself. The babe is very fat and healthy and would send his love too if he could.

The drains (that curse of houses now-a-days) have driven us from Twickenham and we are here at a house of Lord Howard's by the sea, let, out of the season, at £2 a week which seems reasonable enough as it is a large good house.[2]

Let us know please either by your own hand or some amanuensis how you are progressing and believe me

Ever affectionately yours
A. Tennyson

---

[1] Addressed to her at 8 Hemlock Court | Strand | London.
[1] Matilda Tennyson.
[2] See above, p. 49.

To EMILY SELLWOOD TENNYSON [?]

Text. Memoir, i. 362.

November 18, [1852]

Have seen the procession at the Duke of Wellington's funeral: very fine; hope to see the interior of St. Paul's before I leave.[1]

To TOM TAYLOR

MS. Indiana University.

SHIPLAKE VICARAGE, OXON.,[1] November 21, [1852]

My dear Tom

Your letter having been first to Twickenham then sent on to Seaford where I have hired a house till Christmas reached me here just now, quite too late, you see, for Mrs. Stirling.[2] I should have been glad enough to avail myself of her vocal powers if I had heard of this in time. Now, I take it, it would be of no, or small, use. Don't bother yourself with what happened at Chapel House. Any man (as I told you at the time) might be overset with shag upon port who was not used to the mixture. I shall be glad to see you at Seaford House where I am any time you like to run down to Newhaven four miles off from me—a fly thence will bring you in ¾ of an hour.

Ever yours affectionately
A. Tennyson

I go back on Tuesday night.

To HENRY TAYLOR

Text. Memoir, i. 362–3.

SEAFORD HOUSE, SEAFORD, November 23, 1852

Thanks, Thanks! I have just returned from Reading and found your letter. In the all but universal depreciation of my ode by the Press, the prompt and

---

[1] 'To Edward Fitzgerald he observed: "At the funeral I was struck with the look of sober manhood in the British soldier"' (*Memoir*, i. 362; *Tennyson and His Friends*, p. 144). '"In the midst of the solemn silence", said my father, "Magdalene Brookfield whispered to her mother when she saw the Duke's boots carried by his charger, 'Mama, when I am dead shall I be that?' meaning the boots"' (*Memoir*, i. 362).

[1] At the Drummond Rawnsleys (see below, p. 53). A charming anecdote about this visit is related in a letter to Tennyson in 1884 from Maria Volckmann Bonewitz, who, 'a child of sixteen summers, all tremulous how she should be received, not speaking a word of English', arrived 'to teach music to Mrs. Rawnsley's children' (*Materials*, iv. 484–5).

[2] Mary Ann (Fanny) Stirling (1815–95: *DNB*), actress, with some singing ability. In 1850 she played Olivia in Taylor's adaptation of 'The Vicar of Wakefield', and later appeared in two more of Taylor's plays.

hearty appreciation of it by a man as true as the Duke himself is doubly grateful.

Ever, my dear Taylor, yours
A. Tennyson

To LUDOVIC COLQUHOUN

Text. The Sussex County Magazine, February, 1929, p. 126.

SEAFORD HOUSE, SEAFORD, SUSSEX, November 27, [1852]

My dear Colquhoun

Many thanks for your note received here where myself, wife and babe have been for some weeks and shall he till Christmas or perhaps a little [longer]. I am distressed to hear of your 'maiden' fit of gout though perhaps I ought rather to be glad. Doctors have more than once told me that a fit of gout would be the making of me. For all that I say to it walk your chalks O podagre. Apage![1] I will not have to do with thee! I trust, my dear fellow, however, that you will arise from your couch of torment a stronger man than you have been for years—nay, that ere this you are already risen for I see your date is 2 and to-day is 27. I am very glad too that you like my Civic Ode; it was expected of me so I wrote it. I intend to put in a passage or two if it gets into another edition. Moxon gave me £200 for the first 10,000 copies which was handsome, I think. Now goodbye and believe me, dear Colquhoun,

Ever yours
A. Tennyson

Best regards from my wife. The bairn is very stout and healthy.

To EDWARD MOXON

MS. Robert Taylor.

December 8, [1852]

My dear Moxon

If you lose by the Ode I will not consent to accept the whole sum of £200 which you offered me. I consider it as quite a sufficient bore to you if you do not gain by it.

I see a mistake in the Dying Swan p. 48, silver for silvery—a small mistake yet an important one as regards the metre. I wish this to be as near as may be a perfect edition[1] and I hope that if I am not to see the sheets except in cases of alteration yourself or your brother will be very careful in collating the proofs with the book which I sent you. Probably this proof had not yet been looked over when sent.

---

[1] 'Go away, O gout in the feet. Begone!'

[1] *Poems*, 8th edn.

Your friend Philips[2] of the Times has not behaved well to you in the matter of reviewing. I consider his notice the most damaging one I have seen to your sale. I continue to receive letters from those who really are authorities on literary matters full of admiration for the Ode. Henry Taylor among others has written me a letter which I intend to keep and show my son in after years if he live.[3] This judgement of Henry Taylor makes the whole hodiernal press kick the beam, to my mind at least.

Ever yours
A. Tennyson

To ?

MS. Princeton.

SEAFORD HOUSE, SEAFORD, SUSSEX, December 9, [1852]

My dear Sir

Many thanks for the Book you have sent me which I find very interesting. With respect to your corrections I agree with Professor Aytoun that the alliteration in that line about the vine is excessive. 'Fast-clinging' to my mind would be better than 'Close-clinging climbs'. As to the variations in that distich about the night I cannot pronounce so securely not having the Italian by me but it seems to me that I like the first better than the second as easier and not liable to the objection of the imperfect rhyme glad and shade with the further objection of the perfect rhyme 'made' occurring just before the imperfect. I have only received your letter just now, being not at Twickenham but at this place where we have hired a house and stay till Christmas. Ever, my dear Sir,

Yours
A. Tennyson

ALFRED AND EMILY SELLWOOD TENNYSON *to* FREDERICK TENNYSON (incomplete)

MS. Harvard.

December 9, 1852

. . . was lowered into the vault. After the funeral[1] Ally went to Shiplake to stand for Drummond Rawnsley's last child Alfred Edward. What would Mama say to three babies in one year, three all in arms together? Drummond and Kate seem quite jovial.

We have been here, that is at Seaford, a lonely sea-place between Beachy Head and Brighton as I dare say you know, these six or seven weeks. We

---

[2] Samuel Philips (1814–54: *DNB*), literary reviewer for *The Times* from about 1845 till his death. His influential notice of Tennyson's Ode appeared on 15 November, p. 8 (his 'Memoir of the Duke of Wellington' was in *The Times* on 15 and 16 September).

[3] For Tennyson's response to this letter, see above, p. 51.

[1] The funeral of the Duke of Wellington.

have a comfortable house, one that belongs to Lord Howard and so far from Skeggie bareness and desolation. It has a garden moreover with a high ivy-covered arched wall dividing it and with urns and vases and balustrades besides. It was only last week the scarlet geraniums were taken out of the ground to be housed, so it must be a mild place. It looks pleasantly on sea and down, which has been fortunate for us since I, at least, have scarcely left the garden the weather has been so stormy. The sea therefore of course fine. Great white-headed waves leaping up every moment from behind the shingle-bank and looking at us. Twickenham is still our home though, for we were disappointed in our hope to get a house which we should like to buy at Malvern, and we have not been able to find one yet elsewhere.

But two or three days ago Dunbar Heath's book was sent to me by Mr. Peel of Bonchurch. I have not yet had time to look into it.[2] Of a book which we have purchased and which arrived at the same time Ally has read me a little. It is Hengstenberg's Christology of the Old Testament;—we like much what we have seen of it. We have also got his Psalms.[3]

A little pamphlet, a collection of letters on Mesmerism from Edinburgh papers by Dr. Gregory would interest you, I think.[4] Strange stories too we have heard lately of a house in London said to be haunted and now deserted by all except an old Porter who does not fear the spirits, and who is paid to live there because the spirits have twice foretold it is to be burned down, and there is a fear some not altogether spirits may take the realisation of the prophecy into their own hands if the house be left unguarded.

This is a huge volume, I will add no more except kind love from us both to you all. Has Arthur's book of sketches progressed? and how does Giulio get on at school? Mr. Garden seems very fond of him.[5]

Your affectionate sister
Emily Tennyson

Charles and Louie have been staying with us two or three weeks. Tilly four months or more. She likes our neighbours very much.

---

[2] Dunbar Isidore Heath (1816–88), younger brother of John Moore and Douglas Denon Heath (see i. 348–9) and least as well as last of the three. Like them, he went to Trinity. He was ordained, and, like John Moore and in the same year (1859) but for perhaps opposite reasons, got 'involved in doctrinal troubles'—and was in fact 'deprived of the vicarage of Brading', Isle of Wight (*DNB*). The book sent by Peel was *The Future Human Kingdom of Christ* (2 vols., 1852–3).

[3] Ernest Wilhelm Hengstenberg's books are *Christology of the Old Testament and Commentary on the Messianic Predictions of the Prophets*, abridged from the translation of Reuel Keith by The Revd Thomas Kerchever Arnold (1847) and his *Commentary on the Psalms*, translated by The Revd P. Fairbairn (2 vols., Edinburgh, 1844–5).

[4] William Gregory (1803–58), Professor of Medicine, University of Edinburgh, *Letters to a Candid Inquirer on Animal Magnetism* (1851); second edition, *Animal Magnetism, or Mesmerism and Its Phenomena*, 1877 (*DNB*).

[5] Arthur Tennyson (brother) and Frederick's son Giulio (or Julius). Frederick Tennyson 'in 1839 married Maria Giuliotti, daughter of the chief magistrate of Siena, and settled in Florence'. Julius, his eldest son, 'reputed the strongest man in the British Army, inherited the paternal temper and tendency to fits of violence' (*Background*, pp. 100, 104). Frederick lived with Julius in Kensington from 1896 to 1898. For Francis Garden, see i. 347–8.

Baby is very huge with a beautiful face for a mere babe. His leg and arm I attempted to delineate on a blank part of the letter which alas I find is the place left for the direction. What if your Italians take the delineations to be political. P. S. I have spoilt the leg and arm (as well as I could) with the direction. I wish you could hear him shout. Love to Arthur and all of yours.
Your affectionate
Alfred

Captain Inglefield has called an Arctic promontory Cape Tennyson after me which makes me as proud as Lucifer.[6] So don't let your major-domo look down upon *me*!
A. T.

To WILLIAM ALLINGHAM

MS. University of Kansas.

SEAFORD HOUSE, SEAFORD, SUSSEX [12 December 1852]

My dear Sir

You are welcome to the medallion if you wish for it. There is a fault in it which Woolner himself acknowledged when he was visiting me just before he went off to Australia—a fault which my friend James Spedding had previously pointed out. The face and forehead are not in their proper relation to one another. The face is too forward. Woolner, poor fellow, said he would alter it when he came back. It certainly needs this alteration.[1] I trust that you are teaching your 'dumb words'[2] to speak. Believe me, with kind remembrances from my wife,
Yours very truly
A. Tennyson

[6] Edward Augustus Inglefield (1820–94), RN (promoted Admiral, 1879; knighted, 1887). Early on, he served under Sir Graham Eden Hamond (1771–1862), a neighbour of the Tennysons on the Isle of Wight. 'In 1852 he commanded Lady Franklin's private steamer, Isabella, in a summer expedition to the Arctic' (*DNB*). His book *A Summer Search for Sir John Franklin* (1853) was in Tennyson's library inscribed: 'To the Poet Laureate from his humble admirer the Author, July 1871' (*Tennyson in Lincoln*, i, No. 1327). The Arctic promontory has not been identified.

[1] It got it. On his return from Australia, Woolner began a second medallion. See Leonée Ormond, *Tennyson and Thomas Woolner*, pp. 1–10, and Richard Ormond, *Early Victorian Portraits* (1973), i. 451–3.

[2] Unidentified.

29 December 1852

EDWARD FITZGERALD *to* ELIZABETH COWELL[1] (extract)

Text. *The Letters of Edward FitzGerald*, ii. 82–3.

29 December 1852

Having just returned from visiting Mr. and Mrs. A. Tennyson at Seaford,[2] I must tell you that I talked of my visit to you, and also of the wishes you had exprssed that they should one day go and visit you at Oxford. . . . You had best address to her at Chapel House | Twickenham | Middlesex | though they may not be back there for some days. I admired the Baby greatly and sincerely: and Alfred nurses him with humour and majesty. He told me I had not seen him in his full glory however—'sitting high and smiling' as he called it. We had two long talks and smokes over the Ode: which he has altered and enlarged quite successfully, I think. He is disappointed that people in general care so little for it—but I tell him they will learn to understand it by degrees: and that it will outlive all ignorance. He is full of *Invasion*; and I believe truly is more wise and grave about it than any of our Ministers. He also wrote some very fine songs on the Subject—but he says nobody listens or cares. I told A.T. he was to learn Persian at Oxford; and follow the example of yours truly. . . .

To GEORGE HERBERT REPTON[1]

MS. Tennyson Research Centre.

CHAPEL HOUSE, TWICKENHAM, [? early January 1853]

My dear Sir

I cannot but think that this woman whom you mentioned to me yesterday must simply be an infamous swindler, who has invented a story to raise a subscription; for if as you supposed she had been deceived by some one assuming my name she would at any rate have endeavoured to find out me: this it does not appear that she has attempted to do. It is only one of the many fraudulent schemes for raising the wind which rogues and harlots have resort to and instead of being elected matron of an emigrant ship she ought rather to be chucked overboard. If you know any of the parties she is

---

[1] Elizabeth Cowell, née Charlesworth (*c.* 1812–99), married (1847) Edward Byles Cowell (1826–1903: *DNB*), FitzGerald's tutor in Spanish and Persian and 'discoverer' of the manuscript of Omar Khayyám's *Rubáiyát*. Both were long-time friends of FitzGerald's. Cowell seems to have met Tennyson (who studied Persian with him) in 1848 or thereabouts, and he and his wife, with Fitzgerald, dined with the Tennyson's at Chapel House on 27 December 1851. 'Alfred the Great was very genial and kind,' Cowell wrote, 'and talked very finely about many things, and altogether it was a memorable day' (*The Letters of Edward FitzGerald*, i. 623; ii. 46 n.). See also *Journal*, p. 47, and George Cowell, *Life and Letters of Edward Byles Cowell*, pp. 97, 103, 101–2, 373–4. The Cowells went to Calcutta in June 1856, and returned in 1864. In 1867 he became Professor of Sanskrit at Cambridge.

[2] See *Tennyson and His Friends*, p. 144.

[1] George Herbert Repton (*c.* 1804–60), 'a minor canon of Westminster and priest in ordinary to the Queen' (Foster).

deceiving I think it is your duty to write and inform them what I think of her proceedings. Believe me to be

Yours truly
A. Tennyson

P. S. Since writing this I have thought it *my* duty to myself to write to Mrs. Chisholm who is interested about all these matters. As I do not know her direction and possibly you do I send it to you to forward.[2]

To MRS CAROLINE CHISHOLM[1]

MS. Tennyson Research Centre.

CHAPEL HOUSE, TWICKENHAM, [? early January 1853]

Madam

I make no apology for intruding upon your time with this letter, for your time and your heart have long been consecrated to the matter on which this note touches.

The Rev. G. H. Repton of Richmond called on me yesterday and told me that a woman who calls herself Gillies or Gillian went to him and stated that she had been married to me at a Wesleyan Chapel at Cheltenham and requested him to perform the residue of the ceremony according to the Church of England. I do not recognize even the name of the woman. She represented herself as having applied for or having applied for and obtained the place of matron in an emigrant ship. She is either a swindler or insane, in either case an unfit subject I should think to have the care of female emigrants.

Mr. R. fancied that someone might have deceived her using my name. I that case I should have fancied she would [have] tried to find me out. She has been, I am told, getting benevolent persons to subscribe for her. I am sure that you will see what I mean in telling you this. I am quite ready to meet the woman any day you may appoint, disagreeable as it is to a shy man like myself. But that she cannot be a fit person to be the matron of an emigrant ship (except in the case of her having been deceived by someone using my name) I feel quite sure. I am told that she writes verses on pink paper. I repeat that she is to me an utter stranger. I thought it right to give this information to yourself who feel so deeply on the subject of the comforts of emigrants. I am, Madam, with the greatest respect,

Yours
A. Tennyson

---

[2] See the next letter.

[1] Caroline Chisholm (1808–77: *DNB*), 'the emigrant's friend', was a social worker, first in India, then in Australia, and from 1846 to 1854 (when she returned to Australia) in England.

17 January 1853

To EMILY SELLWOOD TENNYSON

MS. Tennyson Research Centre.

Monday [17 January 1853]

Dearest

Very sorry. Barrett[1] *must* have another day. I should not like to come to you with three or four teeth prematurely stopt and therefore aching.

There are only about 6000 of the Ode sold I am sorry to say. I shall go to hear Flowers's chorus perform the first part tonight which I refused to do—to him last night thinking I should be at home.[2] I think I may say *for certain* that I shall be back tomorrow by the 5 o'clock express which arrives at 6.15. Love to Tilly and M[arshall?]s.

Ever thine
A. Tennyson

I got thine this morning.

To GEORGE FRENCH FLOWERS[1]

MS. Indiana University.

82 MARINE PARADE, BRIGHTON, [early February 1853]

My dear Flowers

If you *will* direct Sleaford instead of Seaford you can scarce expect an answer in wholesome time. I am coming to town in a couple of days or so and will bring you my corrections. I approve of your scheme as to the W[ellington?] Testimonial.

Ever yours
A. Tennyson

To HENRY HALLAM

MS. Robert Taylor.

February 11, [1853]

My dear Sir

Many thanks for your costly gift to my boy. I hope that he will live to appreciate your books and learn from them to be as just and impartial in his views of men and history as his great Godfather. But at present when a volume is offered to him he seems more inclined to put the contents into his mouth than into his head.

My wife and I were delighted to hear the good news* of Julia.[1] She begins promisingly—twins at the first accouchement—though, perhaps, you might think that one boy would make the two girls kick the beam: but we must take

---

[1] Henry John Barrett (see i. xxxiii).   [2] See the next letter.

[1] George French Flowers (1811–72), composer and theorist (born in Boston, Lincs.), who set the Wellington Ode to music (*Grove's Dictionary of Music and Musicians*, 1880, 1904; *DNB*). See previous letter.

[1] Julia Hallam Cator had twin girls, Julia and Eleanor.

the goods the Gods provide us:[2] like enough the young gentleman as Martin Tupper says, is even now waiting in the anteroom of unclad ghosts.[3]

I am glad to learn that you are reprinting the Remains[4] inadequate evidences as they must always appear to me of the greatness of the man. Perhaps you could spare me half a dozen or even a dozen copies.

Give mine and my wife's most cordial congratulations to Julia and take them likewise on your own account and believe me,
Affectionately yours
A. Tennyson

*now first heard from yourself.

I saw, breakfasted and dined with Rogers at Brighton from whence we are just returned: he seemed to me wonderfully well and clear in all his faculties.

ALFRED AND EMILY SELLWOOD TENNYSON to BENEDICT LAWRENCE CHAPMAN

MS. Boston Public Library.

TWICKENHAM, February 13, [?1853]

My dear Sir

We have had friends with us and now my husband must have his pipe so he bids me write to thank you for your kind invitation and to say he thinks he had better not dine with you on **Thursday also he wishes me to say he is obliged to go to London to-morrow* and he would therefore be very glad if you could fix some earlier time for seeing him, were it only for five minutes.
Yours sincerely
Emily Tennyson

Note by myself having descended from my smoking-attic.

*and to stop there two or three days; and any day from Monday to Thursday I should like to see you if you can (without inconvenience to yourself in your professional avocations) appoint me a few minutes. Direct to me at Mr. F. Lushington's, 5 Paper Buildings, Temple, and believe me,
Yours ever
A. Tennyson

**2d note by me after my descent.

Charles Weld told me yesterday that he couldn't go to you on Thursday and that he understood (i.e. if *I* understood him rightly) that your party would be put off.

---

[2] Dryden, 'Alexander's Feast', l. 106 (see above, p. 41).
[3] 'Of Truth in Things False', l. 25, in *Proverbial Philosophy* (Auburn and Geneva, NY, 1847), p. 13: 'The waiting-room for unclad ghosts'.
[4] Arthur Henry Hallam's *Remains in Verse and Prose* (1834; see i. 106–9), reissued in 1853. See vol. iii, letter to W. J. Smith, 16 December 1874.

To EMILY SELLWOOD TENNYSON

MS. Tennyson Research Centre.

Tuesday, [15 February 1853], 6 o'cl.

Dearest

I called on Hallam yesterday. The 1st twin is not expected to live.[1] He, I thought, rather agitated. No disease, but want of vitality, the doctors said: the other had got it, a not uncommon thing with twins. I am on the point of coming home tonight but suppose I shan't.

Saw Barrett and since have been eating dinner with new teeth. Queer—seems as if I never could get accustomed to it. I sent Daddy[2] down to thee yesterday. Hope he went. I have asked only Morris[3] for Sunday. Such a good fellow as he is, I couldn't help it.

Thine
A.T.

Thy account of Mrs. C's nurse very good! pen very bad! don't know whether this will be readable—haven't been after the bed yet. Going to dine with Weld tomorrow and with Barrett on Friday. But perhaps shall be home between whiles.

To RICHARD MONCKTON MILNES

MS. Trinity College.

CHAPEL HOUSE, February 23, [1853]

My dear M.

I cannot dine with you on Monday as I expect my wife's father to dine with me on that day.

Hallam's love to Amicia[1]—and my best remembrances to Mrs. Milnes.

Ever yours
A. Tennyson

To APPLEBY STEPHENSON, MD[1]

Text. Memoir, i. 363.

LONDON, March 1, 1853

Sir

Your letter of the twenty-fourth of February has reached me only this

---

[1] See above, p. 58.   [2] Henry Sellwood.
[3] Probably Mowbray Morris (1819–74), Eton, Trinity, manager of *The Times*, 1847–73. He was a friend of Dickens and Thackeray (see Dickens's *Letters*, Pilgrim Edition, v. 291 n.; Thackeray's *Letters*, ii. 390). His health began to fail in 1869. 'In July [1873] he was for a period placed under restraint, and on April 27 of the following year, 1874, he died, aged 56, having served the paper with great versatility, extreme ability, perfect conscientiousness, and complete loyalty for twenty-seven years' (*The History of The Times*, ii. 503; a portrait by George Richmond faces p. 64). See also Venn, Boase.

[1] See above, p. 41 n.

[1] Unidentified. 'At the beginning of next year (1853) my father was asked whether he would allow himself to be nominated as Rector of the University of Edinboro' ' (*Memoir*, i. 363). See below, p. 75.

morning. I trust that yourself and those other gentlemen, whom you speak of as being willing to give their vote for me as President of your University, will forgive me when I say that however gratefully sensible of the honour intended me, I must beg leave with many thanks to decline it. I could neither undertake to come to Edinboro' nor to deliver an inaugural address at the time specified. You will doubtless find another and worthier than myself to fill this office. I am, Sir,

Your obliged and obedient servant
A. Tennyson

EMILY SELLWOOD TENNYSON *to* MRS SCHOLFIELD

MS. Huntington Library.

CHAPEL HOUSE, TWICKENHAM, MIDDLESEX, March 15, [1853]

Mrs. Alfred Tennyson presents her compliments to Mrs. Scholfield[1] and requests that she will do her the favour to say if she considers her late nurse Gandy capable of undertaking the entire management of a child seven months old. Mrs. Tennyson also begs to be informed if she left Mrs. Scholfield for any fault, whether she is perfectly cleanly, good-tempered, honest, truthful and in every respect well-principled.

To GEORGE STOVIN VENABLES

MS. National Library of Wales.

CHAPEL HOUSE, March 17, [1853]

My dear Venables

I send you Stanford's letter. I thought he would not let me off under £85. I send likewise a check on Rogers for that sum to be paid him.[1] If you think it ought to go have the kindness to send it for me by your clerk and let him get at the same time my banking book from them which you can keep till I call or you bring it over here. We shall be very glad to see you any day you like to come. We dine at 5. Should I not write to Stanford and get from him in writing an assurance that he has no further claims upon me. I shall not write to him till I hear from you.

Ever yours
A. Tennyson

I pay the whole sum at once rather than quarterly not for any love to Stanford but to wish my mind clear of the whole abomination at once.

I don't believe that he is at all right as to the year and a half and if I had put in a tenant he would have been by the terms of his own letter bound to have made considerable repairs.

---

[1] Unidentified. Nurse Gandy was hired, and (later) perhaps fired (see below, p. 174).

[1] Edward Stanford, and Rogers' Bank (see above, p. 12).

To EMILY SELLWOOD TENNYSON

MS. Tennyson Research Centre.

[5 April 1853][1]

Dearest

Venables is coming and I have asked Brookfield and Garden but have not heard the issue. I dined yesterday with Hallam and after went to the Geographical Society where I saw Captain Inglefield who can't come. Lear's picture I thought very good.[2]

Ever thine
A. Tennyson

Julia Cator I have asked to come over and call in the morning on Thursday which she promised to do.

To SOPHIA (RAWNSLEY) ELMHIRST

MS. Duke.

FARNHAM, SURREY, April 23, [1853]

My dear Sophy

I am sorry that I cannot come being engaged to go to my brother-in-law's Edmund Lushington. We have been here some time looking after houses and shall be here some days longer, and then we go into Kent, having been invited months ago by a letter sent from Glasgow. I am thus specific because you wrote me a letter which contained a grain of what seemed to me injustice and made me rather angry. You ought to know your old friends better. If I had asked you and Elmhirst a hundred times and you had not come I should never have reproached you with coldness. Pray remember me most kindly to him and believe me also yourself,

Yours affectionately
A. Tennyson

Emily sends her love.

To EMILY SELLWOOD TENNYSON

Text. Memoir, i. 363-4.

FARNHAM, [early May 1853]

I saw Elstead Lodge yesterday, dry soil but quite flat, with view of distant hills, and one hill very near; splendid lawn but house looking north. The park here is delicious and the little house to be sold has a large garden.... As for the house, you would find the rooms too low. If I buy, there is plenty of room for building two good additional rooms. I saw the lawyer here and he has

---

[1] Postmark. On 6 April the Cosmopolitan Club, according to Henry Reeve (*Memoirs*, ed. Laughton, i. 299), 'was very brilliant. Tennyson there, Higgins, Milnes, Spedding, Stirling, Hodgson, etc. I don't know any other room in London which could contain such a force of men.'

[2] See below, p. 64.

given me the refusal. It is quite retired, just under the Bishop's palace. What an air after Twickenham! I walked over to Hale and looked into the old premises.[1]

To CHARLES KINGLSEY

Text. Memoir, i. 366-7.

[? early May 1853]

My dear Kingsley

I hope your wife got my books which mine ordered Moxon to send.[1] In the conclusion of the 'Princess' the compositors have made a slight mistake.

> Grey halls alone among their massive groves.[2]

They have printed 'their' 'the' which somewhat weakens the line.

Hypatia[3] never came; but I cannot afford to be without it. Part of the conclusion seems to me particularly valuable. I mean the talk of the Christianized Jew to the classic boy. Hypatia's mistreatment by the Alexandrians I found almost too horrible. It is very powerful and tragic; but I objected to the word 'naked.' Pelagia's nakedness has nothing which revolts one . . . but I really was hurt at having Hypatia stript, though I see that it adds to the tragic, and the picture as well as the moral is a fine one.

Will you lay your hand on my Adam Smith and send it per post?[4] I enclose you six Queen's heads for that purpose. Believe me, dear Kingsley,

Ever yours
A. Tennyson

To RICHARD CHENEVIX TRENCH

MS. Free Library of Philadelphia.

PARK HOUSE, MAIDSTONE, May 12 [1853]

My dear Trench

I am sorry that I only received your letter yesterday morning (Wednesday) when we had already gone from Farnham and been here more than a week. It would have given myself and my wife great pleasure to have visited you. I am now at my brother-in-law's house, Edmund Lushington. I trust that you and Mrs. Trench and all yours are well and flourishing. Believe me,

Ever yours
A. Tennyson

---

[1] Where she had lived with her father from 1848 till her marriage.

[1] At Farnham they were visited by Kingsley 'whose talk was as ever interesting' (*Journal*, p. 30), 'as fresh and vivacious as ever' (*Memoir*, i. 363).
[2] Line 43 (Ricks, p. 842).
[3] Kingsley's novel (serialized in *Fraser's Magazine*, January 1852–April 1853).
[4] *An Enquiry into the Nature and Causes of the Wealth of Nations* (3 vols., 1822). See *Tennyson in Lincoln*, i, No. 315.

? 30 June 1853

To RICHARD MONCKTON MILNES

MS. Yale.

Thursday, [? 30 June 1853]

My dear Milnes

I have never dined in town (except once with Hallam en famille, when I met him by chance in Lear the painter's rooms looking at his pictures of the Syracusan quarries and once or twice with my brother-in-law en famille also) since I dined with you, Heaven knows how long ago, and met Doyle[1] and others. I have given up dining out and am about to retire in utter solitude in some country house but if you feel yourself aggrieved at sending one invitation after another to me, unaccepted, I will come. You have not mentioned your hour, 6? 7? 8? let me know. Don't bother yourself about giving me a bed. I can get one—(and my own way too in the matter of smoke, better) at Spedding's. Really I am very unwell and though hay fever sometimes lets me alone for a whole day together yet it sometimes makes me quite unfit to sit at table. Send me a line to say what your hour is and what Maurice's hour is and I will see if I can come in time for Maurice.

Ever yours
A. Tennyson

To JAMES SPEDDING

Text. Materials, ii. 73; *Memoir*, i. 354.

[? *c.* 30 June 1853]

Dear J. S.

Can you let me have your attic next Saturday night and Sunday. I am going to dine with Milnes on Sunday, he has offered me a bed but I am more at mine ease in mine inn (smoking-room I should say) with you.

Ever yours
A. Tennyson

To ROBERT MONTEITH

MS. Richard L. Purdy.

[? June 1853]

My dear Robert

I should like very well to come and see you but the journey is too expensive and too extensive: self-wife, child and nurse—if I *did* come (as I have often thought of doing) when should I come? How long will you remain at

---

[1] Richard ('Dicky') Doyle (1824–83), artist, illustrator, and caricaturist, was on the staff of *Punch*, for which he designed the classic cover of Mr. Punch and Toby, from 1843 to 1850, when he resigned in protest against the 'attacks made by "Punch" at this time upon papal aggression' (*DNB*). Thackeray, his colleague at *Punch*, modelled J. J. Ridley in *The Newcomes* at least in part on Doyle, who illustrated the monthly parts 1854–5. See the fine article by Viola Hopkins Winner 'Thackeray and Richard Doyle, the "wayward artist" of *The Newcomes*', *Harvard Library Bulletin*, xxvi (Apr. 1978), 193–211. See below pp. 146, 168–9.

Carstairs? I scarce know what to send the young Quillinans.[1] I thought at first you meant original verse and really I do not know that I have any such gear by me. I will write out a poem for them which very likely they have not seen as it is only published in my eighth edition.[2] Best love to Mrs. Monteith. And pardon my brevity for I have the twenty million poets of Young England always sucking at my time and leisure. Yours, dear Robert, though in haste,

Affectionately
A. Tennyson

To RICHARD HILL[1]

MS. Brotherton Collection.

July 4, 1853

My dear Sir

A thousand thanks for your kind present. I was not the person in whose behalf my wife was making enquiries, neither am I much subject to headaches, but I have found the Aromatic water efficacious in Hayfever to which I *am* subject. Miss Gully (the sister of the Malvern Water doctor)[2] suffers much from headaches and my wife commissioned Mrs. Stephenson[3] (whom I dare say you know) to procure her a case of Aromatic plants which arrived here directed to me and have been forwarded to his conservatory at Malvern. But I am not the less bound to you for your kindness in thinking of me. I did not receive either your note or the case of bottles till long after the date prefixed to the former (May 10th) or I would have thanked you earlier. Believe me now

Yours very gratefuly
A. Tennyson

To BENEDICT LAWRENCE CHAPMAN

MS. Yale.

RICHMOND, YORKSHIRE, July 25, 1853

My dear Chapman

I expect to be in Edinburgh Wednesday night by the express 8.20. Will you send the deed to Ludovic Colquhoun's, 18 George Sq., Edinburgh and

---

[1] Unidentified.
[2] 'To E. L. on His Travels in Greece' (Ricks, p. 993).

[1] Richard Hill (1795–1872), of Spanish Town, Jamaica, assisted Philip Henry Gosse in the preparation of *The Birds of Jamaica* (1847) and *A Naturalist's Sojourn in Jamaica* (1851), and wrote a number of things himself, including *A Week at Port Royal* (1855) and *Lights and Shadows of Jamaica History* (1859). Frank Cundall (*History of Jamaica*, 1915, p. 351) refers to him as 'one of Jamaica's most talented sons'. (Hill was identified as addressee by Dr T. E. Harvey, of Leeds, who presented this letter to the Brotherton Collection.)
[2] Anne Gully (see i. 280 n.).
[3] Unidentified (but see above, p. 60).

I will there sign it—before witnesses of course—and remit it to you immediately. I suppose this arrangement will do. Believe me,

Always yours
A. Tennyson

I guess that I was not at Twickenham when you called. I cannot tell you when we shall return Southward.

To EMILY SELLWOOD TENNYSON
MS. Tennyson Research Centre.

TAIT'S HOTEL, [EDINBURGH,] [27 July 1853]

Dearest

We arrived here about 8.40 very dusty and rather fatigued—the journey I am sure would have been too much for thee. I shall hope to hear sooner or later of thy safe arrival and the amendment of the boy. I have not yet called on L. Colquhoun but I am going immediately. So no more at present from

Thy loving husband
A. Tennyson

Love to Charles and Louie. One of the guards at York spoke to me commiserating you and your looks at parting.

A Roman epitaph in the Museum at York

I [*four short lines cut out*] touched me

D. M.

Simpliciae Florentinae
  animae innocentissimae
  quae vixit menses decem
Simplicius Felix
  pater fecit.
Leg. VI. V.

To the Gods of the Ghosts.

To or for Simplicia Florentina
  a most innocent soul
  who lived 10 months
Simplicius Felix her father
of the 6th conquering legion
(built or) made (this).

To EMILY SELLWOOD TENNYSON

MS. Tennyson Research Centre.

CARSTAIRS HOUSE, CARSTAIRS, LANARK, [29 July 1853][1]

Dearest

I came on tonight to R. Monteith's, Carstairs. He and she were *delighted* to see me and so grieved not to see you that I am grieved you did not come even if you had made three days of the journey. Such large lofty rooms for the babe and sweet outlooks through trees of the Clyde would have charmed you. There was no deed waiting for me at Colquhoun's and Colquhoun himself was in London so here till I hear from Chapman I am stationary. I may for aught I know have to go to London to sign the deed and in that case I should give up my tour. Palgrave poor fellow I have left at Edinburgh—he accused me at parting of a Goethe like coldness and indifference to friends and I told him that this would apply to him rather than me, but I really believe that he has a liking for me which he thinks is not fully returned. I send this by express man and horse to Lanark tomorrow not to miss a letter of thine.

Ever thine lovingly
A. Tennyson

To EMILY SELLWOOD TENNYSON

Text. Materials, ii. 84.

OBAN, August 5 [for 2, 1853]

Palgrave is going over to his friend Sellar[1] to-morrow across the water. I think I must go to Iona to-morrow as it will be the sole new thing that I shall have seen in this tour.

To EMILY SELLWOOD TENNYSON

MS. Tennyson Research Centre.

OBAN, August 4, [1853]

Dearest

By great good luck I got thy last on my return from Staffa and Iona, and am delighted to hear of the little boy's being better and therefore possibly may not come back at once as I was intending to do. Thou canst not conceive the stew and bore of this little hotel crammed to suffocation, dinners, teas, suppers going on altogether which makes it impossible to write. I do believe I missed out the initial Dearest in my last night's note not liking to write it

---

[1] Postmark.

[1] William Young Sellar (1825–90) studied at Glasgow under Edmund Lushington (see the next letter) and at Balliol, where, along with Alexander Grant, Palgrave, Robert Morier, and others, he was one of Jowett's coterie of idolaters. A couple of months after Tennyson's visit (see the next letters) he was transferred from Glasgow to St. Andrews (1853–63), and then became Professor of Latin at Edinburgh. See *DNB*; *Memoir* (1899 and later), pp. 304–7; E. M. Sellar, *Recollections and Impressions*; and J. M. Barrie, *An Edinburgh Eleven.*

with people looking over one's shoulder and intending to add it afterwards. Perhaps it has hurt thee and if so I am vext at myself.

Sellar, P's friend and a friend of E. L. L, a very nice good fellow has been with us to Staffa. The cave is very remarkable not so grand as I expected, and Iona as interesting as it could be with people chatting and 40 minutes to see it in. I am grieved to hear of the death of Mrs. H[enry] M[arshall][1] for the effect it will have on her sister. Kisses to Babe. My note to that nincompoop[2] will I think do very well. The deed has arrived at last here to me in Oban. If thou would'st like to come on to Carstairs do but I fear the journey may be injurious.

I conclude in haste. I write this in my little stuffy bedroom the coffeeroom being intolerable.

Ever thine affectionate
A. Tennyson

(Over) Palgrave has been very kindly and good to me. I think he improves as one knows him better.

To EMILY SELLWOOD TENNYSON

MS. Tennyson Research Centre.

August 6, [1853]

Dearest

I am here at Ardtornish*[1] where they only get letters twice a week so there is a man dispatched over lock and frith and fall to carry this and to see if perchance there may be anything for me in the Oban P. O. I have nothing to tell except my trust that the Child is improving and that thou art pretty well and that I shall in all probability be at Grasby if nothing occurs to hinder me at the latter end of next week. This is my birthday—and the 11th is baby's—they come very close together. Their babe here (3 months old)[2] is a very pretty one not however near so pretty as ours was at his age.

Ever thine affectionately
A. Tennyson

*Sellar's house by the Sound of Mull all rock and sea about it—the meaning is the Point of the 3 waterfalls. Kisses for Baby. Love to Grandp. and C[harles] and L[ouy].

---

[1] See i. 96 n. She died 23 July 1853.
[2] Unidentified (but see below, p. 72).

[1] The visit is described in *Memoir*, 1899, pp. 304–7. In the first of Tennyson's improvised verses (p. 304, 'Dennistoun's daughter' is Sellar's wife, Eleanor (married 1 June 1852), on whose name no Tennysonian jingle is preserved; 'Crosskin' (for 'Crossling'?) is her cousin (see below, p. 000. For Ardtornish, see also Philip Gaskell's fine book *Morvern Transformed* (Cambridge, 1968).

[2] 'Our eldest child [unnamed] . . . was then about six months old' (*Memoir*, 1899, p. 307).

To EMILY SELLWOOD TENNYSON

Text. *Materials*, ii. 84.

August 11, [1853]

Sellar is a man I quite 'tackle' to[1] and his wife is a very nice creature, enthusiastic and joyous.

To WILLIAM YOUNG SELLAR

Text. *Materials*, ii. 85.

EDINBURGH, August [13], 1853

My dear Sellar
I am here still under your friend Syme's[1] care who thinks I may move again on Monday. Now today is Saturday and you told me to give you a week's notice if you were to join me at Inverness. I will be at Inverness next Saturday. I will stay over Sunday to give you some time to join me (only I am afraid nobody travels on Sunday in Scotland). I hope this will arrive in time and that you are not from home, and that you will be at liberty to run through Sutherland with me. I shall then have only a fortnight left before I return to England but a great deal may be done in that time. In case you cannot come pray send a note to me at the Post Office Inverness, and believe me,

Ever yours
A. Tennyson

I never enjoyed a visit much more than the short one I paid to you at Ardtornish. Will you thank Mrs. Sellar for her kind note (by the by I ought to have written to her rather than to you) and tell her that the keys were mine though I only received these and her note quite lately. They were sent to me from Carstairs whither I have not yet been.[2] Give my best remembrances to her and likewise to Crossling,[3] and say that I hope soon to see them both again. My wife and child are not well able to join me at present.

If you find any letter for me at the Oban Post Office be so kind (i. e. if you can) to bring it with you: but it does not much matter as I have later news from home than can be contained in any letter lying there.

---

[1] *Sic* ('take to'?).

[1] James Syme (1799–1870: *DNB*), Professor of Clinical Surgery at Edinburgh University and a noted surgeon (he operated on Carlyle in 1868).

[2] For his second visit (see above, p. 67).

[3] Elizabeth Dennistoun Cross ('Zibbie'), Eleanor Sellar's cousin, married Wiliam Henry Bullock (later Hall), and was the sister of John W. Cross, who married George Eliot. See E. M. Sellar, *Recollections and Impressions*, pp. 219–20, 290–2; *The George Eliot Letters*, ed. Gordon Haight, *passim*.

To EMILY SELLWOOD TENNYSON

Text. Materials, ii. 85.

29, ST. ANDREW'S SQUARE, EDINBURGH, August 15, [1853]

Shall be here till Thursday. On Thursday start on a three weeks or a month's tour which I expect will do me a great deal of good.

To EMILY SELLWOOD TENNYSON

Text. Materials, ii. 85.

August 18, [1853]

Colquhoun I see every day, poor fellow suffering much from rheumatic twitches, I want three weeks of fresh air in the Highlands.

To HENRY HALLAM

MS. Rosenbach Foundation.

EDINBORO', August 26, 1853

My dear Sir

I do not know whether you are in town nor when this may reach you nor whether it will be in your power to assist me: if it be not I shall only have given you the trouble of reading this note.

I go at once in medias res. I have a brother-in-law who married my elder sister Mary as perhaps you may have heard, a very honest fellow, worthy but poor, not without talent, but for years (as is the case with so many nowadays) an unsuccessful and briefless London barrister. He is Scotch, by name Alan Ker. Immediately after his marriage he and she went out to Antigua as there seemed to be a good prospect of his making a livelihood as *the* lawyer in that island. A relation of his, Mr. Macintosh,[1] was then Governor. Things went on pretty prosperously at first though not so well as in the days before free trade and free niggers. He now writes to me begging me to use whatever influence I may have with the Duke of Newcastle[2] (which is none at all) to get him the post of Colonial Secretary there which is vacant. I was in the Highlands when the letter arrived and time pressing my wife wrote to the Duke and received a letter from Henry Robert Sec. stating that no claims could be attended to except they came through the Governor of the Island. It seems that the *ex*-Governor (Macintosh) had in a measure promised him this place if it fell vacant during his Governorship, but it did not. Macintosh has however spoken in his behalf in London. I am sorry to say that both Ker and his wife and their child have all lately had yellow fever though in a mild form

---

[1] Apparently, Robert James Mackintosh. (See David P. Henige, *Colonial Governors from the Fifteenth Century to the Present*.)

[2] Henry Pelham Fiennes Pelham Clinton (1811–64), 5th Duke of Newcastle, was Colonial Secretary under Lord Aberdeen.

and the resultant debility adds greatly to his present distress and anxiety.[3]

Believe me I am sorry to trouble you in this. I do not [know] whether you could do anything in this matter but I am sure that you will if you can. I am at present in Edinburgh but I expect next week to be at Grasby Vicarage, Brigg, Lincolnsh. where a line from you will find me. I trust that all yours are well and sound.

Ever affectionately yours
A. Tennyson

P. S. By the by I think I may as well send you the poor fellow's letter.

To EMILY SELLWOOD TENNYSON

Text. Materials, ii. 85.

August 28, [1853]

Circumstances over which I have no control have kept me here tourless.

To ROBERT MONTEITH

MS. Richard L. Purdy.

29 ST. ANDREWS SQUARE, [c. 30 August 1853]

My dear Robert

I intended to have been with you before but going to consult a doctor about a matter which seemed trifling enough I found that I had two surgical operations to undergo which have left me horizontal. Mr. Inglis[1] (out of Edinburg[h]) has lent me his house where I be and am ever yours

Without lying
A. Tennyson

---

[3] 'Alan Ker remained for over thirty years in the Judicial Service of the West Indies. In 1853 he was acting Attorney General of Antigua, from 1854 to 1856 Chief Justice of Nevis; after that he was appointed Chief Justice of Dominica, and later be became a puisne judge of the Supreme Court of Jamaica. This office he continued to hold until the end of December 1884 when he retired because of ill-health. He died at Kingston, Jamaica, on 20th March 1885, just under a year after his wife' (*Background*, p. 161).

[1] Henry Inglis (1806–85), of Torsonce, senior partner in the Edinburgh law firm Messrs H. and A. Inglis, author of *The Briar of Threave and the Lily of Barholm* (1855), translator of German ballads, later a very prominent Mason, and a director of the City of Glasgow Bank, of which the collapse cut short his public career (*Edinburgh Post Office Directory, History of the Society of Writers to His Majesty's Signet*, and obituary in a cutting from an unidentified newspaper).

To ?[1]

MS. University of Virginia.

[? LONDON] Sunday, [? September, 1853]

Dear Sir

The letter *was* written and dispatched on the 6th August, so that I cannot conceive how it has happened that you have only just received it. Tomorrow is my last day here and I shall be obliged to you, if you can (for I have much to do in Town), to call not later than 11 o'clock.

Yours faithfully
A. Tennyson

To GEORGE FRENCH FLOWERS (extract)

Text. *The Collector*, viii (Mar. 1895), 71.[1]

[? September 1853]

I am so engaged in flying about the country in this wretched house hunting business—now in Kent—now in Surrey—now in Gloucestershire—now in Yorkshire—that I can never be sure of my whereabouts a day beforehand.

To EMILY SELLWOOD TENNYSON

MS. Yale.

[ISLE OF WIGHT] [? October 1853][1]

You have done quite right I think in respect to Mother. I believe I told her myself at Twickenham that I was afraid if she came to live with us the rest would flock there and that this was the sole objection to the plan of her living with us.

With respect to Merwood's[2] request really the land not being mine, I must not be appealed to at all. The land may never be mine, nor should I particularly wish to purchase that bit of land opposite the gate. And possibly for all Merwood says Seymour[3] may *not* wish to have that piece ploughed: so

---

[1] Perhaps the nincompoop referred to above, p. 68.

[1] Published later in 'My Tennysons', *Scribner's Magazine*, lxxi (Jan.–June 1922), 597, and also in *Ventures in Book Collecting*, pp. 244–5, both by William Harris Arnold, who dated it 1853 and named Flowers as addressee.

[1] Written while house-hunting. 'Later, he went to Bonchurch to his friends the James Whites, Edmund Peels, and Feildens. From them he heard of Farringford as a place that might possibly do for us. He went and found it rather wretched with wet leaves trampled into the downs' (*Journal*, pp. 32–3).

[2] [Jeremiah?] Merwood, a tenant occupying a farmhouse on the Farringford property, could neither read nor write, but, as Emily Tennyson's *Journal* reveals, he could do everything else. See also *The Letters of Emily Lady Tennyson*, p. 104, and below, p. 194.

[3] The Revd George Turner Seymour (1792–1880), owner of Farringford, attended Eton and then (1809) Oriel College (Foster; Montague Charles Owen, *The Sewells of the Isle of Wright* [privately printed], p. 115).

that all the answer to be given is that I must not be asked at all: he must not say if S. rows about having that bit ploughed that *I* gave him leave.

I send you a diagram of Orion which we looked at last night. It is drawn for you by Dr. Mann.[4] Look out at Orion at a faintish star under the lowest star of the belt. That is really 8 stars all moving in connection with one another a system by themselves, a most lovely object through the glass. I saw also the famous nebula which is in the 2d star of the sword and is amazing. Rigel one of the bright stars in Gemini is double two brilliant suns. I hope we shall have another peep tonight.

I don't think I should much object to live in one of the houses on this Terrace except it were for poor Peel.[5] Mann says if you would come and live here he would live here too and he says you would have for yourself and your children a 'most careful' physician always at hand and ready to serve you. I think him a most excellent and pure-minded man—from whose society everyone must reap advantage.

You have a bright view of the sea underneath your windows and a little town close at hand. Altogether we might do worse I think. There is never a house to be let or sold.

To CHARLES ELLIS[1]

MS. Rowland L. Collins.

Monday morning, [? 3 October 1853][2]

Dear Sir

I was from home when your present arrived or I would have thanked you by the messenger you sent. The wine was pronounced 'superb' by two guests who dined with me. I cannot repay you in kind but if you will do me the favour to accept what St. Jerome called Vinum Demonum,[3] a volume of Poems, you will make me happy. I have not a copy by me at present but I will forward one tomorrow. Believe me

Yours very truly
A. Tennyson

[4] Robert James Mann (1817–86), scientific writer and popularizer (on and of a wide variety of subjects), medical doctor, and in general exactly the sort of picker-up of learning's crumbs who would have attracted and been attracted to Tennyson. 'In 1857, on the invitation of Bishop Colenso, he left England for Natal, where he resided for nine years' (*DNB*; see below, pp. 182, 193. For his essay on *Maud*, see below, p. 145. See also below, p. 141.

[5] Edmund Peel (though the meaning is not entirely clear).

[1] Charles Ellis (1824–1908), the 'poetic wine dealer' (Charles Tennyson, p. 366), was proprietor of the Star and Garter Hotel, Richmond (see i. 74) and of Charles Ellis and Co., Wine Merchants, Brickhill Lane, London. For many years he purveyed wines to Dickens, vastly more knowledgeable and discriminating than Tennyson, but, himself a poet (*Richmond and Other Poems*, 1845), he seems, as a number of letters and Emily Tennyson's *Journal* suggest, to have presented them to Tennyson, perhaps annually, as a sort of oblation. See N. C. Peyrouton, 'When the Wine Merchant Wrote to Dickens', *The Dickensian*, lvii (1961), 105–11 (cited in Dickens's *Letters*, Pilgrim Edition, v. 490 n.

[2] So docketed in an unidentified hand; a different unidentified hand inscribed 'Chapel House, Montpelier Row, Twickenham'.

[3] Quoted by Bacon, *Advancement of Learning*, II, xxii. 13.

ALFRED AND EMILY SELLWOOD TENNYSON
to HENRY LUSHINGTON

MS. University of Virginia.

November 8, [1853] (night)[1]

My dear Henry

I wish that I had seen you before even if you had but made a morning call as you once did. Here I am at Plum[b]ley's Hotel, Freshwater, with Emily close upon concluding what seems a perilous bargain and having to return an answer by Friday and very possibly having to go to Lyme Regis in the interval to see another house which *may* be preferable to this. I *may* come to see you before the end of this week but it is problematical. If I go home tomorrow instead of to Lyme I shall come on. I should like to bring Emily too but I fear there is no room. It seems odd to me that I have seen nothing of you all this time, but I suppose it could not well be helped.

Ever yours
A. Tennyson

If I brought Emily and you had no room would any of you be vexed if we went to sleep at Maidstone? for we should take it quite easily if you did.

There are greater probabilities Alfred will be down with you on Thursday or Friday now. Do not expect me, for I think it is really settled we take Farringford for three years with the option of purchasing it at the end of the term or at any period of the term, and we shall come to it probably in a week or ten days. So I shall have a great deal to do. I should like very much to see you all but as I say I do not think I can. Kindest love to all. (I say *think* because the owner seemed changeable while we have settled the matter as far as we are concerned.)

To EMILY SELLWOOD TENNYSON

Text. Memoir, i. 365.

November 14, 1853

I wrote on Friday to accept the house (Farringford), I also wrote to-day to Moxon to advance one thousand pounds, four hundred pounds he owes me, the odd six hundred to be paid if he will in March when I get my moneys in. Why I did it? Because by buying safe debentures in the East Lincolnshire Line for two thousand five hundred pounds, with that and five hundred a year I think we ought to get on. . . . Venables and Chapman agree in the propriety of the investment. Seymour has sent no papers yet. I don't know what is to be done with Laurence: it would be in the highest degree inconvenient for me to come back from the Isle of Wight to sit for him. Fitz would, I have no doubt, let him have his old sketch of me.[1]

---

[1] William Allingham's visit at Twickenham, exactly a week later, is worth reading (*Diary,* pp. 63–5).

[1] See i. 235–6 n., and below, p. 341.

To APPLEBY STEPHENSON [?][1]

MS. Tennyson Research Centre.

Saturday, November 18 [for 19], 1853

Dear Sir

I have just arrived at home from a visit in Kent and received yours of the 16th wherein you state that the Earl of Eglinton has been reelected Lord Rector of your University.[2]

Pray present my warmest thanks to all those of your brother students who have given me their votes. I am sure I do not err in asserting that there is no man on British ground whom you could have pitched upon as a candidate for your Lord Rectorship, who would have been more grateful than I am to yourself and your party for your kindness in proposing me for that office, and your subsequent exertions in my favour. However, and though I am aware that it will seem a little strange to you, I cannot but confess that I feel a kind of relief in learning that the college has adhered to its custom of reelecting the Rector of the former year; and though it may seem still stranger, I would fain request you (if I could hope that my wish as to this matter might have any weight among you) not to repropose me next year but to pass by one who is so essentially not a public man in character, whatever he may chance to be in name, and to raise to the honour of your Lord Rectorship some other who would not only gratify you by his personal appearance but possibly instruct you with his oratory. Renewing my thanks to all, I am, my dear sir,

Yours obligedly
A. Tennyson

To ALAN KER

Text. draft *Materials*, iv. 90.

[November 1853]

We are going to buy this house and little estate here, only I rather shake under the fear of being ruined. If we buy it I need not say how glad we should be to see you here some happy day when you return.

---

[1] See above, p. 60. This letter is a rough draft with many deletions.

[2] Archibald Wilson Montgomerie (1812–61), 13th Earl of Eglinton, had been elected Lord Rector of the University of Glasgow in 1852. He 'was a high-minded nobleman and a thorough sportsman, with frank and genial manners and no particular ability. In August 1839 he held the famous tournament at Eglinton Castle, described by Disraeli in "Endymion". . . . This remarkable entertainment, which created an immense sensation at the time, is said to have cost him between 30,000£ and 40,000£, and to have made him the most poplar nobleman in Scotland' (*DNB*). The Eglinton Tournament may also have been significant in the background of *The Princess* (see John Killham, *Tennyson and the Princess*, pp. 272–5). See also Mark Girouard, *The Return to Camelot*, pp. 87–110.

To CHARLES KINGSLEY

Text. William Harris Arnold Sale Catalogue, 10–11 Nov. 1924, Lot 982.
FARRINGFORD, ISLE OF WIGHT, December 13, 1853

I have considered and reconsidered the proposal made to me through yourself from your friend Mr. Ludlow, and I have this morning finally determined not to lend my name to this business.[1] . . . In the meantime the result is what you and your friend are more immediately concerned with. I will only add that the veneration for Maurice which induced me to pass by all my family claims and select him as Godfather to my child remains unabated—I may say increased.

To GEORGE STOVIN VENABLES

MS. National Library of Wales.
FARRINGFORD, FRESHWATER, December 23, [1853]

My dear Venables

I do not know where you are, at P. H. or M. C. B.[1] Eitherwhere you will be sure to get this. I have watched the East Lincolnshire shares for three weeks and I see that business is again done at 143. I think you told the broker to buy at 142. There seems little chance of that. They have been at 146. Will you write to your broker and tell him to do so and then be kind enough to write to me and state precisely the kind of thing I am to do and the form thereof.

My best love to all Lushingtons, whether going, gone, or resident.

Ever yours
A. Tennyson

This is a very fresh and pretty place and a good house though I can scarce promise you [*2 wds. illeg.*][2] but come whenever you will we shall *really* be most glad to see you.

To EDWARD MOXON

MS. Harvard.
FARRINGFORD, FRESHWATER, ISLE OF WIGHT, January 9, 1854

My dear Moxon

My wife wrote to you a fortnight ago requesting you to send as you have

---

[1] Evidently a protest (to be signed by eminent sympathizers) against Maurice's dismissal from King's College, London, because of *Theological Essays*. The 'result' was that upon the founding of the Working Men's College (1854), Maurice became Principal. John Malcolm Forbes Ludlow (1821–1911), friend of Maurice, Kingsley, and Tom Hughes, was a social reformer, and, like them, a Christian Socialist. See N. C. Masterman's *John Malcolm Ludlow, The Founder of Christian Socialism* (Cambridge, 1963), and, for a different point of view, *The Swinburne Letters*, i. 32–3. See below, p. 79.

[1] Park House or Mitre Court Buildings.
[2] Two words smudged (Millns-dishes? Millais-shades?).

always done the Christmas account. That you have not done so makes me apprehend that you are unwell. Pray let us know what is the matter. I find that one of your letters to her states that you would have to pay me £650 at the end of the year. Believe me I am not the less anxious to know the position of my affairs because you have advanced me money. We have taken a house here (where by the bye we shall be very glad to see you whenever you like to come as I think my wife told you) with the option of buying it any time in the next three years at £4350 which I certainly mean to do if I can get the money together and this makes it all the more imperative that I should know how I stand with respect to you. I see that you advertise the book as before at 9s: I suppose you know best what price to affix; but why not advertise In Memoriam? though not under my name it might easily come in after the other two volumes divided from them by a little line in the advertisement.[1]

Remember me kindly to Mrs. Moxon and your sister and believe me,

Ever yours truly
A. Tennyson

To GEORGE STOVIN VENABLES

MS. National Library of Wales (incomplete).

FARRINGFORD, FRESHWATER, ISLE OF WIGHT, January 11, [1854]

My dear Venables

'Striving to better oft we mar what's well.'[1] The E. L. shares are down at 140 and the fees are £25 so (the fees in selling out being I suppose the same) if I were to sell out tomorrow I should lose £100—the per centage on the shares.[2] Now who knows how far when war is declared (as I think it must needs be) the shares may fall and whether it would not be better at once to lose £100 and sell out again: for you see I wished to buy this house and 45 acres which I can never do if these shares go down considerably. Catch me at rails again. Baines[3] in a letter to me says that war is very uncertain and that the shares will rise enormously if there be no war. But I cannot help thinking that war is all but certain [*top two-thirds of page two cut out*].[4]

I sent Chapman a volume of my poems as a New Year's gift, through Palgrave, which I hope he received safely.

Is Harry gone?[5] if not, love

---

[1] Moxon replied: 'As you have an idea of purchasing your house if you can get together the requisite amount, you cannot in my opinion do better than allow me to bring out an illustrated edition of your poems. I could by this means I am almost sure, within a very short time too, put into your pocket at least a couple of thousand pounds . . . (June Steffensen Hagen, *Tennyson and His Publishers*, p. 100). See below, p. 79.

[1] *King Lear*, I. iv. 369.   [2] See above, p. 76, and below, p. 99.

[3] Benjamin Baines, Stock and Shares Broker, 2 Copthallet, Throgmorton Street (*P.O. London Directory*).

[4] War was declared on 29 March (see below, p. 82 n.).   [5] Henry Lushington.

To FRANKLIN LUSHINGTON

MS. University of Virginia.

FARRINGFORD, FRESHWATER, I.W., January 28, 1854

My dear Frank

It is about a week since I signed the last of four Transfer Deeds and despatched it to your friend Baines, but I have yet received no Registration Certificate: now I don't like to write to Baines for fear of seeming to mistrust him, and hurting his broker-heart, but I want to know from you whether it is usual for the registration to be so long a-doing, lest, as brokers are not immaculate, Mr. B. may have flitted to America and I in my solitude be none the wiser. I dare say it is all right but I cannot help feeling slightly anxious; which anxiety do you, as you can, by one word dissipate.

I have almost given up the hope of purchasing this place since my shares fell. It is a very pretty place nevertheless and one which I hope you will sooner or later illustrate by your presence.

Chapman tells me in a note that your Maltese are off at last.[1] I hope they parted in good health and heart. Thank C. when you see him for his kind acknowledgement of my book.

We expect another bairn in March.[2] I pray God it be not twins.

Love to all at Park House.

Ever yours
A. Tennyson

To WILLIAM BODHAM DONNE

Text. Materials, ii. 181.

[? February 1854]

My dear Donne

My wife has a great fancy for books about King Arthur, so oblige her as far as you can.[1] She thinks I can write about the old king. I don't think books can help me to it, nevertheless oblige her. Where is Fitz? We have been expecting him down ever so long.

Ever yours
A. Tennyson

---

[1] Henry Lushington, Home from Malta, where he was Chief Secretary to the Government, and his sister Louisa Sophia (Louy).

[2] See below, p. 81.

---

[1] Donne was librarian of the London Library. See below, pp. 171–2.

To BENJAMIN BAINES

MS. Rosenbach Foundation.

February 1, 1854

Sir

I have this day received the Registration Certificate for £1700. East Lincolnshire Railway Stock purchased by me and remain, Sir,

Yours faithfully
A. Tennyson

To FREDERICK JAMES FURNIVALL[1]

MS. Huntington Library.

FRESHWATER, I. W., February 2, [185]4

Sir

I beg to thank you for the Address to Maurice from the Members of Lincoln's Inn, and his reply thereto. This paper (though your letter is dated Jan 12th) has, in consequence I suppose of a misdirection, only just reached me. Some time ago I signed an address sent to me by the Revd C. Kingsley and transmitted it to my friend the Hon. F. Garden at the Cambridge and Oxford Club, but I have originated none as your phrase of 'put in circulation' almost seems to imply.[2] I do not suppose that the address which I signed can have been *materially* altered since I signed it or a copy of it with the alterations would have been sent me. The address when I saw it was such as people (not members of the Church) might subscribe. I am, Sir,

Yours faithfully,
A. Tennyson

I have not seen Prof. Trench's letter and should be much obliged if you would send it.

To EDWARD MOXON

Text. A. M. Broadley, *Chats on Autographs*, facsimile, p. 217.

February 28, [1854]

My dear Moxon

I am glad you give me so good a prospect of the Illustrated Edition.[1]

---

[1] Frederick James Furnivall (1825–1910: *DNB*), enthusiastic and intemperate scholar, sculler, editor, antiquary, teacher (Working Men's College), Christian Socialist (for a while), and polemicist (all his life). Tennyson's 'Morte d'Arthur', in 1842, 'first kindled in him the flame of his enthusiasm for the older literature' (*Frederick James Furnivall, A Volume of Personal Record*, p. 11). He founded the Early English Text, Chaucer, Ballad, New Shakespere, and Wiclif (as well as Shelley and Browning) societies, and was influential in the creation of the *OED*. His virtues, though numerous and conspicuous, did not include moderation or modesty, self-restraint or self-doubt.

[2] See above, p. 76.

[1] The famous 'Moxon Tennyson', published in 1857. See Hagen, *Tennyson and His Publishers*, pp. 100–6, and below, pp. 89, 180 and n.

It was rather a cruel disappointment to me that my Telescope came back *without* a night-glass, only cleaned, which I could have done myself. In this lovely place one has nothing to look at but sea and stars and a night-glass would have been very welcome, but you must have forgotten to deliver my message, I fear.

Ever yours
A. Tennyson

To JOHN WILLIAM PARKER[1]

MS. Historical Society of Pennsylvania.

FRESHWATER, March 15, 1854

My dear Parker

A Mrs. Davey* (a friend of mine many years ago) has been living at Cagliari in Sardinia and has written a tale illustrative of Sardinian customs.[2] Her friends want her to publish. She thinks that would be a troublesome and expensive proceeding and prefers insertion in a Magazine and applies to me thinking a word of mine will be sufficient to procure the admission of her story into any Magazine whatsoever; but I am not so sanguine. You are the only Magazine Editor I am personally acquainted with. I have told her to forward her papers to you and assured her you will give them all due consideration.

The proofs shall be forwarded as soon as I have got through them. Believe me in haste,

Yours very truly
A. Tennyson

*direction. Britonferry, Neath, Glamorganshire.

---

[1] John William Parker (1792–1870: *DNB*), publisher and printer, established his own business in London in 1832, after superintending Cambridge University Press from 1829. Publisher for the Christian Knowledge Society and of the *Saturday Magazine*, he was also printer to the University of Cambridge, 1836–54. He and his son of the same name (see i. 323 n.), who had been at King's College, London, with Charles Kingsley, were both (like Tennyson) tentatively drawn towards and finally repelled by Chartism and then Christian Socialism. At the time of this letter, he was the proprietor of *Fraser's Magazine* and the publisher of such authors as John Stuart Mill, George Henry Lewes, William Whewell, Julius Hare, Frederick Denison Maurice, Charles Kingsley, and James Anthony Froude. Parker sold his firm to Messrs Longman in 1863.

[2] Mary Davey, author of *Icnusa; or Pleasant Reminiscences of Two Years' Residence in the Island of Sardinia*, 325 pp., published in Bath and London in 1860; an adaptation, with plates, 128 pp., was published in 1874 by the Christian Knowledge Society. (An article entitled 'The Kingdom of Sardinia', signed 'M. E. M.' [? Marian E. Martin], appeared in *Fraser's* in September 1853.)

To CATHERINE RAWNSLEY

MS. Harvard.

March 17, 1854

My dear Catherine
There was a fine big boy born last night about 9.[1] All is well. Love to Drummond and a kiss for my Godson.[2]

Affectionately yours
A. Tennyson

To ANNE WELD (fragment)

MS. Tennyson Research Centre.

March [17, 1854]

My dear Anne
A fine lusty boy born about 9 p.m. last night. All well. I have written to Grasby and to Catherine R[awnsley].

To MARY ANNE FYTCHE

MS. Tennyson Research Centre.

FARRINGFORD HOUSE, FRESHWATER, ISLE OF WIGHT, March 17, 1854

Dearest Aunt
A strong and stout young fellow came into the world, abusing it loudly, last night at 9. The mother is doing exceedingly well. Thank Lewis[1] for his amusing note received some time back.

Affectionately yours
A. Tennyson

To ELIZABETH COWELL

MS. Trinity College.

March 17, 1854

Dear Mrs. Cowell
A boy was born last night. A stout little fellow. Mars was culminating in the Lion. Does that mean soldiership? All is quite right. Kind regards to your husband and to E. F. G.

Yours ever
A. Tennyson

---

[1] Lionel, christened on 6 June but not referred to by name in these letters until mid-August (see below, p. 95). See below and *Journal*, p. 33.
[2] Probably Alfred Edward Rawnsley (see above, p. 39 n.).

[1] Her nephew (see i. 170).

To ANNE WELD

MS. Tennyson Research Centre; Harvard.[1]

Monday morning, [20 March 1854]

My dear Anne

Everything is going on very well. Emily has had a good deal of pain but no more I believe than is very common on such occasions.* Little Hallam's behaviour to his small brother was very enchanting: he kissed him very reverently, then began to bleat in imitation of his cries; and once looking at him he began to weep, Heaven knows why: children are such mysterious things. I don't think the younger one will turn out such a noble child as Hallam but who can tell.

Thank Weld for his lesson about the ships. Would I had been there.[2]

Ever affectionately yours
A. Tennyson

*and she is much better this morning.

To JULIA MARGARET CAMERON

Text. Tennyson Research Centre (transcript).

FARRINGFORD LODGE, FRESHWATER, ISLE OF WIGHT, March 22, 1854

My dear Mrs. Cameron

In my first batch of letters, sent off in all directions, when the new babe was born, I omitted to write to you, not willingly but of necessity, not knowing your 'Terrace,' and my wife, who did know it, not being [able] to be spoken to, and Mrs. Sellway[1] employed about her and not to be come at. Therefore in my notelet to Mrs. Taylor[2] I begged her to let you know: then I thought better to wait a day or two till I could give you a further account. Up to this morning and even this morning Emily has been, and is, suffering, I believe more pain than is common in these cases, so as rather to annoy her Vectian Doctor, but I hope that this day (the 6th from her confinement) will, ere it fade (a very brilliant one over cape and sea) see her well, except for weakness. I have been mesmerizing her, which, she says, has done her a great deal of good. If she could but get a sleepful night, I have no doubt it would be all right by the morrow. As for the little fellow, he is as jolly as can be, and hardly cries at all yet. Little Hallam watches him, awe-struck, cannot make him out, and occasionally wails over him. I daresay these are phenomena which you have often tenderly watched in your own family. You have not written which I would far rather impute to the fact of my not having written than to the possibility of your being unwell. Pray heaven the last be

---

[1] The TRC folio ends with 'children are such', Harvard's begins with 'mysterious things'.

[2] Spithead, where the Baltic Fleet, over a thousand guns, had assembled. It sailed on 11 March to blockade Russian ports, and reached the Baltic Sea on the 25th. England declared war on Russia on the 29th (*Annual Register*). See below, p. 87.

---

[1] Unidentified.   [2] Mrs Henry Taylor, who also lived at East Sheen, IW.

not the case with you; neither has Mary Marshall answered, which makes me anxious about her. God bless you, dear Julia Cameron, and believe me,

Affectionately yours
A. Tennyson

To ELIZABETH RUSSELL

MS. Viscount Boyne.

Thursday, [23 March 1854]

Dearest Aunt

Received your first half of the £50 cheque. *Very much obliged!*

I will write to you tomorrow. The post only gives one a couple of hours and I have—oh so many unimportant notelets to answer: and so many bulletins of Emily's health to issue this morning. She has suffered a good deal and 7 days of after pains—but there has been no danger. Tomorrow, dearest Aunt, I will write again.

Yours most affectionately
A. Tennyson

No green paper nothing but white chalk.

To ELIZABETH RUSSELL

MS. Viscount Boyne.

FARRINGFORD LODGE, FRESHWATER, I OF W., Friday, [24 March 18]54

Dearest Aunt

I told you I would write again today but even today I am so hurried with having both my own and my wife's correspondence to manage that I cannot give you a letter, only a note, in reply to yours which was not at all 'tedious' as you are pleased to malign it.

It was very kind in you to think of me and my expenses at this juncture. Your cheque was most welcome, however someone (I know not who, perhaps that cackling fellow, Jesse)[1] may have been dilating to you about my 'elegant sufficiency.'[2] If I were to die tomorrow I could only leave my wife and now two sons £150 per ann. in railway shares: that is surely no great matter: meantime my books make money but who can guarantee that they will continue to do so. A new name, and such must arise sooner or later, may throw me out of the market: even a Russian war (for books are nearly as sensitive as the funds) may go far to knock my profits on the head.

I am grieved to hear about your eyes and must again regret that I have nothing to write on of the cool verdant kind nor could I procure it I suppose nearer than at Southampton. One cannot live without bore and bother of all kinds, daily frettings, which of course affect all the nerves, optic and others.

Since I came here my house-troubles have been so great (servant-troubles I mean, these all quarrelling among themselves and unkindly to their

---

[1] Richard Jesse, his brother-in-law.   [2] James Thomson, *The Seasons* ('Spring', l. 1161).

mistress who wanted great kindness in her then-condition) that in spite of pure air and frequent outings I have got some 15 *new* specks in my right eye: these all occur together, like a group of dark Pleiads something in this position

.*. .
*. *..
...* *.

not pleasant, rolling round as the eye rolls and damaging these splendid sea-views considerably. I cannot help thinking that these have resulted solely from house-bother and from having been put out, as they say, 3 or 4 times a day for at least 4 months. 'Muscae volitantes' I believe do not lead to amaurosis, which if true is a comfort. The only advice I can give you or I believe that any Doctor could give is 'Keep your mind easy' but it is just that advice which is the hardest to follow. Whewell's Plurality of Worlds[3] I bought but I would not wish you to waste your eyes over it: it is to me anything but a satisfactory book. That quotation in your letter about the space occupied by men and animals is I fancy founded on facts. The post, confound it, is just starting. Emily is better and has less pain today. She has had 8 or 9 days of pain which has kept her very weak. More pain than most women have.

Would Emma be Godmother if I asked her?[4] Farewell. God bless you, dearest Aunt.

Yours ever affectionately
A. Tennyson

To WILLIAM ALLINGHAM

Text. *Letters to William Allingham*, ed. H. Allingham and E. Baumer Williams, p. 276.

March 27, 1854

My dear Sir

I got your note some days ago and this morning came the 'two publications.'[1] Some of them I see are my old friends and favourites—slightly altered. With the new ones I have not yet had time to make acquaintance.

I trust that your perilous-seeming experiment of living by literary labour

---

[3] Published in 1853. 'It is inconceivable that the whole Universe was merely created for us who live in this third-rate planet of a third-rate sun' (*Memoir*, i. 379).

[4] The answer was yes (see below, p. 88).

[1] 'Peace and War', an ode printed in the *Daily News*, 20 February 1854, and separately (with reset type) as a pamphlet about the same time. *Day and Night Songs* appeared in late February (received by the British Library, 23 February).

will turn out well. All is not rash that seems so; and you were certainly thrown away at Ballyshannon.[2]

Yours truly in haste
A. Tennyson

To JOHN FORSTER

Text. Memoir, i. 373-4.

FARRINGFORD HOUSE, ISLE OF WIGHT, March 29, 1854

My dear Forster

I understand from Archibald Peel[1] that you are aggrieved at my not writing to you: that is wrong, morbid I think. I almost never write except in answer. Why, if you wished to know of me did you not write to me and you would have heard? Pray don't be distrustful. I love you all the same, though I should not write for 100 years.

Now it happens that a letter was half written to you partly to condole with you on the loss of dear good genial Talfourd,[2] partly to announce the birth of another son of mine. I had dozens of letters to indite at that time to female cousins, etc., and I put this by to finish another day, and I cannot find it, or I would send it to prove that you are not forgotten, but you *must* be more trustful of me, or how can we get on? You must at any rate try the effect of a small note addrest to *me* before you find fault with me.

A reason for my not writing much is the bad condition of my right eye which quite suddenly came on as I was reading or trying to read small Persian text. You know perhaps how very minute in some of those Eastern tongues are the differences of letters: a little dot more or less: in a moment, after a three hours' hanging over this scratchy text, my right eye became filled with great masses of floating blackness, and the other eye similarly affected though not so badly. I am in great fear about them, and think of coming up to town about them, for (whatever you may conjecture) I have not been in town for many months, not ever since I came here—did not even pass through town on my way here but went by Kingston.

I beseech your and all my friends' most charitable interpretation of whatever I do or may be said to do.

Our post only allows us from 11 o'clock to 1 o'clock to receive and answer letters which is (I think) another reason why I write so few.

---

[2] 'Early in 1854 Allingham gave up the Customs [at Coleraine, after Ballyshannon], determined to try literary life in London' (*Diary*, p. 69).

[1] Archibald Peel (see above, p. 48 n.), nephew of Sir Robert Peel, the statesman, after Eton and Trinity College, Oxford, was JP (Denbigh and Herts.) and DL (Denbigh). In 1857 he married Mary Ellen Palmer (d. 1863), whom he had met in the Crimea, and in 1867 Lady Georgiana Adelaide, daughter of 1st Earl Russell. He 'was a most faithful friend from 1851 onwards', and Tennyson and Hallam stayed 'with the Archibald Peels at Wrexham' on their Welsh tour in August 1871 (*Memoir*, ii. 108 and n.). Peel's name turns up frequently in Emily Tennyson's Journal. The best source of information on him (and a good one) is *Recollections of Lady Georgiana Peel*, ed. Ethel Peel.

[2] See i. 324 n.

I have been correcting my brother Frederick's proofs.[3] I dare say you may have seen notice of their approaching publication. He is a true poet, though his book (I think) ought to have been a shorter one.

Farewell, my dear fellow, God bless you and keep you.

Yours affectionately and unchangingly
A. Tennyson

My wife's kind regards to you: she has been in a great state of suffering and sleeplessness for nine days, but at last I set her right by mesmerizing,—the effect was really wonderful.

To MARY DAVEY [?][1]

Text. Materials, ii. 100–1.

[? April 1854]

You will not often see anything so sweet as my little, not quite two years old boy, who is toddling up and down the room, and saying, 'Da, date, and dada,' meaning 'give' in a very respectable Italian lingo, pointing to everything that strikes his fancy. Singularly enough the very day when I despatched my note to you, another boy was born at 9 p.m., a lusty young fellow, who strikes the elder one with awe, sometimes into sympathetic tears, sometimes into a kind of mimic bleating, when he hears the younger one's inarticulate cooings. I dare say all these things are perfectly familiar to you in your own household; but you asked about my children. The first we had was born dead (a great grief to us), really the finest boy of the three; and I nearly broke my heart with going to look at him. He lay like a little warrior, having fought the fight and failed, with his hands clenched, and a frown on his brow. . . . If my latest born were to die to-night, I do not think that I should suffer so much as I did, looking on that noble fellow who had never seen the light. My wife, who had a most terrible time lasting near the whole of one Easter Sunday, never saw him. Well for her.

Yours sincerely
A. Tennyson

To COVENTRY PATMORE

MS. Yale.

FARRINGFORD, FRESHWATER, I. OF W., [April 1854]

My dear Patmore

Many thanks for your congratulations if the births of babes to poor men are matters of congratulation. When you call me such a happy man you lie.

---

[3] *Days and Hours*, published by John William Parker in April or May, a selection from a volume privately printed in Italy in 1853. (See *The Letters of Edward FitzGerald*, ii. 116–17, 128.)

[1] See above, p. 80. In *Materials* the addressee is identified as Mrs Cameron; in *Memoir*, i. 375, as 'a friend'.

I have had vexations enough since I came here to break my back. These I will not transfer to paper though I can yet scarcely repeat with satisfaction the proverb of let bygones be bygones: for most of these troubles have not gone by. My wife though now a full month from her confinement is still so weak as not to be able to walk, nor even to read or write; or she would have answered a letter from Mrs. Patmore which came round to us from Bonchurch on the other side of the island, where a friend of ours saw it lying in the Post Office. So you have made acquaintance with Aubrey de Vere whom I have not seen since he went over to Rome. I wish, as he likes this place so much he would pay me a visit here. We have hardly seen a human face since we came here except the members of our household. Happy I certainly have not been. I entirely disagree with the saying you quote of happy men not writing poetry. Vexation (particularly long vexation of a petty kind) is much more destructive of the 'gay science' as the Troubadours (I believe) called it. I am glad to hear you have been busy. The Baltic fleet I never saw! Not a vessel. Not a line have I written about it or the war. Some battle things I have done I think successfully. End of my paper. Goodbye. Love to Mrs. P.

Ever yours
A. Tennyson

To GERALD MASSEY[1]

MS. National Library of Scotland.

FRESHWATER, I. OF WIGHT, April 1, 1854

My dear Sir

In consequence of my change of residence I did not receive your captivating volume till yesterday. I am no reader of papers and reviews; I had not seen, nor even heard of any of your poems; my joy was all the fresher and the greater in thus suddenly coming on a poet of such fine lyrical impulse, and of so rich, half-oriental an imagination. It must be granted that you make our good old English tongue crack and sweat for it occasionally; but Time will chasten all that. Go on and prosper and believe me grateful for your gift and

Yours most truly
A. Tennyson

---

[1] Gerald Massey (1828–1907: *DNB*), poet and journalist, of Chartist, Christian Socialist, and, in general, liberal political sympathies, with a list toward spiritualism, mesmerism, and identifying the author of Shakespeare's sonnets. 'Massey fully established his position as a poet of liberty, labour, and the people with . . . *The Ballad of Babe Christabel and Other Poems*, which appeared in February 1854 [London: Bogue], . . . passed through five editions within a year, and was reprinted in New York. See *Tennyson in Lincoln*, i, Nos. 1528–31.

To ELIZABETH RUSSELL
MS. Viscount Boyne.

FARRINGFORD HOUSE, FRESHWATER, ISLE OF WIGHT, April 10, [1854]

Dearest Aunt

Let me not be despised for ever for carelessness! One half of your cheque has been missing ever since the day it came. I have looked high and low till I am weary. I have no doubt it is the fault of a housemaid I have who puts everything out of the way.

I am *really* grieved to give you the trouble of writing the cheque over again. I send you the first half.

I do not know whether you are aware that when you live more than 15 miles from your London Banker you ought to send a cheque with a penny draft stamp and a part of your writing over the stamp or you will subject yourself to a fine of, I think, £10 or so. I send you an old cheque of my own to show you the manner of it.

Do not trouble yourself to write any answer to me but just send the cheque with the penny stamp upon it which I enclose.

I write large not to bother your eyes. My own right eye, the other day, suddenly became alarmingly worse in consequence of my trying to read Persian which is a very small scratchy type.

My wife sends her best love. She is still very weak. Emma has kindly consented to be Godmother.

Ever your affectionate nephew
A. Tennyson

To ELIZABETH RUSSELL
MS. Viscount Boyne.

FARRINGFORD, FRESHWATER, ISLE OF WIGHT, April 13, [18]54

Dearest Aunt—received!

I am most glad to hear from you though grieved that you have given yourself the fatigue of writing.

In my hurry of writing (and having the whole of my own and my wife's correspondence on my hands) I find that I must have neglected enclosing what I told you I had enclosed—a draft stamp. You speak of a *blue* stamp. Now the blue are receipt stamps. I have never seen any cheques (with the new stamp) written on a leaf of a Banker's cheque-book, but I suppose that if you were to scratch out the printed 'London' and put Cheltenham it would pass or if you clapt the stamp on over the 'London' and wrote over it; for your own handwriting is essential on the stamp. Probably Emma who is with you as I understand from your note will know all about these new regulations.

My best love to her and believe me dearest Aunt,

Ever affectionately yours
A. Tennyson

I am most sorry to give you all this bother but I am so afraid of your incurring a heavy fine if you neglect the regulations. Don't please part with my cheque on Rogers for an autograph, if anyone should happen to ask you: it *might* be unsafe so to do.

My right eye continues nearly as bad as before. Emily is slightly stronger.

To EMILY SELLWOOD TENNYSON

Text. *Materials*, ii. 101.

LINCOLN'S INN FIELDS, May [16 or 17], 1854

I have done nothing as yet but call on Moxon and the Marshalls which last were not at home.

To EMILY SELLWOOD TENNYSON

Text. draft *Materials*, iv. 50–1.

[60 LINCOLN'S INN FIELDS], May 18, [1854]

I called on Moxon and we went round to the artist Creswick, a capital broad genial fellow; Mulready, an old man who was full of vivacity and showed me lots of his drawings and one or two of his pictures. Then on to Horsley who was likewise very amiable and said that I was the painter's poet, etc., then on to Millais, who has agreed to come down in a month's time and take little Hallam as an illustration of 'Dora'. Sir E. Landseer I did not call upon and Holman Hunt was out of town.[1]

I called on Forster who wants me to dine with him on Saturday. I am going now to dine with Spedding somewhere, and then going to the Exhibition.[2]

---

[1] Of these well-known painters, Thomas Creswick (1811–69) had six illustrations in the 'Moxon Tennyson'; William Mulready (1786–1863) three; John Callcott Horsley (1817–1903) six; John Everett Millais (1829–96, created Baronet 1895) eighteen; William Holman Hunt (1827–1910) seven; Sir Edwin Landseer (1802–73) none. The illustrators *not* named here were Dante Gabriel Rossetti (1828–82) with five contributions; Clarkson Stanfield (1793–1867) six; Daniel Maclise (1806–70) two. All but Rossetti and Hunt were Academicians (Millais and Horsley were Associates at this time), and all are pictured in Jeremy Maas, *The Victorian Art World in Photographs* (London: Barrie and Jenkins, 1984). Thomas Woolner's second medallion portrait of Tennyson was used as a frontispiece.

Financially, the edition was a failure, historically a triumph, artistically a toss-up. Martin Hardie, who called it 'a landmark in the history of book illustration', described the contributions of Hunt, Millais, and Rossetti as the 'crowning glory' of the volume, and of the remainder said (quoting Samuel Johnson) 'Some are worse than others'. See 'The Moxon Tennyson: 1857', *Book-Lover's Magazine*, viii (1907–8), 45–51; *Lady Tennyson's Journal*, ed. Hoge, pp. 40, 125 n.; J. G. Millais, *The Life and Letters of John Everett Millais*, ii. 143. See also below, p. 210.

[2] At the Royal Academy.

To EMILY SELLWOOD TENNYSON

MS. Tennyson Research Centre.

Saturday, [20 May 1854]

Dearest

I went to the Crystal Palace yesterday with Weld. Certainly a marvellous place but yet all in confusion. I do not think it will be worth while to go up on the 10th for the opening as it will be by no means so striking an affair as the last opening.[1] I was much pleased with the Pompeii house and with the Iguanadons and Ic[h]thyosaurs. I dined with Franklin Lushington at the Oxford and Cambridge Club afterwards. Horatio dined with us. Tom Taylor came to Spedding's in the evening and gave me a book of Breton ballads[2] which I will bring, exceedingly beautiful, many of them. I think it will be better to put off the Christening till the 6th of June if the child has the thrush. Thinking this, I have not sent the letter to Mr. H. H.,[3] but I shall still as far as I see be back on Thursday. Altogether this little outing has done me good.

Thine ever
A. Tennyson

To EMILY SELLWOOD TENNYSON

Text. *Memoir*, i. 376.

May 23, [1854]

I called on Hallam yesterday, he looks very well.

To CLARA (TENNYSON D'EYNCOURT) PALMER[1]

MS. Huntington Library.

FARRINGFORD, FRESHWATER, ISLE OF WIGHT, May 24, 1854

My dear Clara

You told me Emma's London direction, but I suppose the racket of that

---

[1] The Crystal Palace had been bought by a private company, and moved from Hyde Park (where it had opened in 1851) to Sydenham.

[2] Theodore Hersart, Vicomte de la Villemarqué, *Barzas-Breis, chants populaires de la Bretagne, recueillis et publiés avec une traduction française, des éclaircissements, des notes et les mélodies originales* (Paris: Charpentier, 1839; 4th edn., 1846). It was translated by Tom Taylor as *Ballads and Songs of Brittany*, . . . with some of the original melodies harmonized by Mrs Tom Taylor and with illustrations by Tissot, Millais, C. Keene, E. Corbould, and H. K. Browne, published by Macmillan in 1865. In December 1856 the Tennysons were reading La Villemarqué's *Poèmes des Bardes Bretons* (*Journal*, p. 79). 'Le *Barzaz-Breiz* est, aujourd'hui encore, le livre aimé des bretonnants. C'est indubitablement à son rayonnement que nous devons la vocation des tous ceux qui, par la suite, écrivirent en breton' (*Encyclopédie de la Pléiade, Histoires des littératures*, iii. 1521). See below, p. 131, 430.

[3] Henry Hallam.

[1] Clara d'Eyncourt Palmer (d. 1863), daughter of Tennyson's uncle Charles Tennyson d'Eyncourt (see i. 62 n.). In 1849 she married John Hinde Palmer (d. 1884), a barrister, who was returned as liberal MP for Lincoln in 1868. (See Francis Hill, *Victorian Lincoln*, pp. 32–4, 36.) He was savagely caricatured by Spy in *Vanity Fair*, 28 July 1883.

Cosmopolitan club drove it out of my head, for I could not remember it next morning and as Monday was my last day in town, and I had many commissions to execute I had no time to call on you again and enquire. Will you be so good as to forward the enclosed to her? I hope some time to renew my brief but pleasant acquaintance with Mr. Palmer. In the meantime with my best regards to him. Believe me,

Affectionately yours
A. Tennyson

To THE SECRETARY, GLASGOW UNIVERSITY

MS. University of British Columbia.

FARRINGFORD, FRESHWATER, I. W., May 26, 1854

Dear Sir

I was in town two days ago and calling on Moxon found your note. The College Album had not arrived: but I suppose it will in due time.[1] Meantime I request yourself and your fellow students to accept my best thanks and to believe me

Yours very truly
A. Tennyson

To GEORGE GROVE[1]

Text. University of Texas (photocopy).

FARRINGFORD, FRESHWATER, I. W., June 7, 1854

My dear Sir

I cannot, I am sorry to say, be present at the opening of the Crystal Palace. Many thanks nevertheless for the invitation. Will you thank the Directors in mine and my wife's name for their kindness and believe me to be

Yours truly
A. Tennyson

---

[1] The *Glasgow University College Album*, a student literary publication, dedicated to Tennyson, according to a cutting from a bookseller's catalogue preserved with the letter.

[2] George Grove (1820–1900: *DNB*; knighted 1883), an engineer by profession, is remembered as a music historian and first director of the Royal College of Music (1883–94) and also, as later letters will show, as editor of *Macmillan's Magazine*. In 1854 he was secretary to the Crystal Palace Company, and in this capacity tried to induce Tennyson (whom he had met through his brother-in-law, George Granville Bradley) to compose an inaugural ode for the grand opening on 10 June. 'Tennyson was very kind and good to me,' Grove said later. 'He received me [at Farringford] with the greatest cordiality, but he could not see his way to writing the poem; and the net result of my visit was the beginning of a truly delightful and valuable friendship' (Charles L. Graves, *The Life and Letters of Sir George Grove*, pp. 44–5.

To SOPHIA (RAWNSLEY) ELMHIRST

MS. Duke.

June 8, 1854

My dear Sophy

As the lady's request comes through you, it must be granted; but my name will do her small good if her volume be not worthy in itself.

You ask after Emily—she has been very weak ever since her last confinement and not able to walk; but the young one (with the exception of a long-continuing thrush) is lusty enough and the merriest babe I ever came across, always laughing. He was christened the day before yesterday and very sorry we were not to see Drummond at our christening but it seems that his friends the Prices[1] proposed a visit to him just at that time.

I did not know that Rosa[2] was at Ryde. I hope that you will be coming to see her and if so that you will come on here. This is by far in my opinion the most noteworthy part of the island with an air on the downs 'worth' as somebody said 'sixpence a pint.'[3] Your father made some sort of promise of a visit to us, but whether he means to keep it, I know not.

Why did neither you nor Elmhirst ever let me know the price of that book I seem to have left unpaid for at Rugby? Kindest remembrances to him and believe me, with my wife's love always,

Yours affectionately
A. Tennyson

EMILY SELLWOOD TENNYSON *to* JOHN FORSTER

MS. Tennyson Research Centre.

FARRINGFORD, June 9, [1854]

Dear Mr. Forster

I am so unwell I fear I shall not write intelligibly but I must nevertheless write to-day full of regret that I could not yesterday to say that in spite of all his grumbling at the age he has not lost his trust in true and generous and loving hearts and assuredly among these yours cannot stand last.[1] What he has said about letters, as far as you are concerned, has been a joke born of a painfully earned feeling of the pervading evil of social faithlessness. Some,

---

[1] Unidentified.

[2] Conceivably Rosa Chawner (see i. 296 and n.) but more probably, as one hopes, Rosa (Baring) Shafto, with whom Tennyson had been in love in the thirties. About this time Tennyson 'took some very long walks in the great heat. To Bonchurch once and back (sometimes he walked) over the shingly shore. Other walks almost as long to Newport and back and to Newtown. He knocked himself up but did not tell me.' (See *Journal*, p. 35.) Newport and Bonchurch are about halfway to Ryde. In early September he recited to Palgrave the poem (Ricks, 634–5) beginning 'June on many a flower reposes | Many a blossom May discloses | But in Autumn unto me | Blooms a rose the rose of roses.' (See Rader, pp. 31–2.)

[3] Keats (speaking of Winchester) in a letter to John Taylor, 5 September 1819 (see below, p. 98).

---

[1] See above, pp. 85–6.

I am sure you have done well to destroy if, as I think, they were some which cast blame, however well deserved, on a living man.

He is very sorry to have forgotten his promise about Ninnie.[2] That other of coming again to see you, he had not time to perform. People bother him so that he doubts whether he will publish at all now. His love.

Most truly yours
Emily Tennyson

It was not our wedding-day but your affectionate wishes were not the less welcome. The 13th is our day of days. I fear this will seem cold and lifeless. Believe me it is but seeming if it be so. I am parting from the nurse who has been with me almost ever since Hallam was born and we are in the midst of other household troubles which have upset me and almost worst of all we are kept at home while he is pining for mountains.

To LEWIS FYTCHE

MS. Trinity College.

June 13, 1854

My dear Lewis

Inclosed you will find a couple of autographs. I could not see you in town as I was obliged (having many commissions to do and only 6 days to do them in) to be out and about almost all day long.

Yours affectionately
A. Tennyson

To HENRY WADSWORTH LONGFELLOW[1]

MS. Harvard.

LONDON, July 16, 1854

My dear Sir

I do not know you except as you are known by Europe and America, so that my address may possibly look a little strange to you particularly as it is accompanied with a request that you will see my brother-in-law Mr. Charles Weld Secretary of the Royal Society, who desires much to make your acquaintance.

---

[2] Unidentified.

[1] Henry Wadsworth Longfellow (1807–82), who had just resigned the professorship of French and Spanish at Harvard, was probably the only poet writing in English whose international reputation at this time outstripped Tennyson's. He had already published more than half a dozen volumes of verse, with his two most popular, *Hiawatha* (1855) and (pre-eminently) *The Courtship of Miles Standish* (1858) yet to come. This letter would seem to prove that the two poets had *not* met at Dickens's house in the autumn of 1842 (Charles Tennyson, p. 213).

Weld's book *A Vacation Tour in the United States and Canada* shows that his North American tour, beginning and ending in Boston, included Quebec, Toronto, Chicago, Richmond and Norfolk, Baltimore, Philadelphia, and New York. In (and near) Boston he met Longfellow, as well as Louis Agassiz, W. H. Prescott, Edward Everett, Abbott Lawrence, and Laura Bridgman (see i. 239 and n.). In Washington he met (and next day dined with) President Franklin Pierce.

Is there so much freemasonry extant among literary men as will lead you not only to pardon me but to grant mine and Mr. Weld's petition. Believe me,

Yours truly
A. Tennyson

To EDMUND LUSHINGTON

MS. Roger G. L. Lushington.

July 26, 1854

Dearest Edmund

It is indeed very terrible news which your letter of this morning conveys.¹ The loss of one who seemed almost—, as far as humanity can be,—perfection must needs tell upon you all. What can be said in such a case? What comfort suggested? The blow must be borne. It is some satisfaction at least in the midst of such grief to find that you are not quite prostrated by it, but capable of writing. I had had hopes of going down to the Pyrenees and spending some weeks there with them in the same places where I spent some of the happiest d[a]ys of my life with Arthur Hallam 25 years ago. But you see, that which rules over us will not have it be. Kiss dear Cissy for me and tell her to be of good cheer: the mother of a family must not give way. I would write to her as you suggest only this note is as much to her as to you. Poor Emmy is writing and weeping at once. Who but must weep to miss for ever so sweet and gentle a creature? but it is exactly in and through these hopes that the human expectation of another life for the individual in a nobler world rises into a passionate assurance that will not be gainsaid. We shall meet again if we be worthy to meet her. Meantime we must bear.

Perhaps Henry will not now continue in his office at Malta but return to us which will be some gain in the midst of so vast a loss. I dread to think of the effect of this news upon him and poor Maria,² so far off from home.

Pray forgive and accept this most imperfect expression of my sympathy with you all and believe me ever,

Affectionately yours in sorrow as in joy
A. Tennyson

To EMILY SELLWOOD TENNYSON

Text. draft *Materials*, 51–2; *Memoir*, i. 376–7.

[15–16 August 1854]

I went into Wokey Hole this morning,¹ a cave; it was not quite what I wanted to see, though very grim.

---

¹ The death of his sister Louisa, at Avignon on 19 July, not 17 (Journal).
² See below, p. 116 n.

¹ A fragment (TRC) postmarked Glastonbury and then Bath, 15 August 1854, reads: 'Dearest | I went into Wok[ey Hole] this m[orning . . .].'

I came to Glastonbury after parting from Grant,[2] then to Yeovil in a fly, 17 miles which rather jarred against my paternity when I thought that little Hallam and Lionel had to be educated. I went to the Abbey. As soon as I got there, there rose an awful thunderstorm, and I took shelter over Arimathean Joseph's bones in the crypt of his chapel for they say (credat Judaeus) he lies there.

Glastonbury. Walked over to Wells this morning. Am at Swan hotel, shall go over to Cheddar tomorrow. In the crypt here, one arch of which was left, I stood during a thunderstorm.

I arrived at Cheddar today and have just seen a stalactite cavern, a thing I had never seen before.

To EMILY SELLWOOD TENNYSON (fragment)

MS. Tennyson Research Centre.

August 16, 1854

Dearest

[P. S.] in the crypt (one arch, which was left) of this chapel I stood out the thunder storm.

To EMILY SELLWOOD TENNYSON

Text. Memoir, i. 377.

August 17, [1854][1]

Corfe Castle, Christchurch, very well worth seeing: Bournemouth fashionable, not at all a place to buy a house in. We found an old Waterloo soldier on the coast.

To CHARLES JOHN HENRY [MASSINGBERD-]MUNDY

MS. Society of Genealogists, London.

FARRINGFORD, August 25, 1854

My dear Mundy

I shall be very glad to see you but you will find me in bad trim, recumbent,

---

[2] Alexander Grant (1826–84: *DNB*), Harrow, Oxford, succeeded as 10th Baronet of Dalvey, 1856, and was a fellow of Oriel College, Oxford, 1859–60. He went to India in 1859, and in 1863 became Vice-Chancellor of the University of Bombay. His edition of the *Ethics* of Aristotle (2 vols., 1857–8; *Tennyson in Lincoln*, i, No. 438—see also Nos. 1035–9) was standard for years. In 1859 he married Susan Ferrier, daughter of James Frederick Ferrier (see below, p. 103 and n.). Grant probably met Tennyson through Palgrave, his friend from Balliol days, when both were among the Jowett-worshippers (see above, p. 67 and n.). 'Of all the men of his time he was most generally looked upon as having made Jowett his ideal' (Evelyn Abbott and Lewis Campbell, *Life and Letters of Benjamin Jowett*, 2nd edn., i. 126–7). Grant ('my most agreeable and affectionate companion, came with me from Marseilles to Genoa') was abroad with Palgrave in July 1854 (Gwenllian Palgrave, *Francis Turner Palgrave*, p. 47).

[1] So dated, but see *Journal*, p. 36, which suggests 12 August.

suffering from one of those fashionable boils—nevertheless very glad to see you, and capable of giving you a frugal dinner and a bed.

Ever yours
A. Tennyson

Our kindest remembrances to Mrs. Mundy.

To JOHN SAUNDERS[1]

MS. Huntington Library.

FARRINGFORD, FRESHWATER, September 15, 1854

Dear Sir

Though my eyes will scarcely allow me to read much I have read your play, and though I cannot be considered as a good judge of how a play might tell in being acted, I think I may conscientiously congratulate our time in possessing in you a man of true dramatical genius. I intend to read it again and reconsider it, but I do not suppose that I shall have any other verdict to deliver. You will pardon me for not answering you sooner and you will I have no doubt easily forgive me for not having done so. I have so many books of poems etc. sent me [that] not only have I no time to read them all, but some that I do look over, wearying me 'out of all cess'[2] make me sometimes undertake a new book with a sigh of exceeding weariness. From your book I really got refreshment and pleasure. May you go on in your work and prosper!

Yours truly
A. Tennyson

AUBREY DE VERE *to* ISABELLA FENWICK[1] (extract)

Text. Wilfred Ward, *Aubrey de Vere*, pp. 227–8.

September 24, 1854

I passed some ten days . . . with the Tennysons; and it was a real pleasure to me to be under their roof. Certainly A. Tennyson has been very greatly blessed in his marriage; and he deserved it; for he seems to have been guided by the highest motives, and to have followed the true wisdom of the heart, in his choice. He is much happier and proportionately less morbid than he used

---

[1] John Saunders (1810–85), novelist, dramatist, and magazine editor. The bland sentence in *DNB* about his professional relations with the Howitts should be supplemented by the account in C. R. Woodring, *Victorian Samplers: William and Mary Howitt*, pp. 127–9. The TRC copy of his drama *Love's Martyrdom* (printed 1854), with a Lincoln setting, is inscribed 'To Alfred Tennyson, Esq. with the author's earnest respects' (*Tennyson in Lincoln*, i, No. 1942). The play was produced at the Haymarket in June 1855.

[2] *1 Henry IV*, II. i. 8.

[1] See i. 339–40. Isabella Fenwick (1783–1856) is remembered generally as the friend and neighbour of Wordsworth, and specifically as the midwife of his Fenwick notes. Aubrey de Vere became a Roman Catholic 15 November 1851.

to be; and in all respects improved. I never saw anyone richer in the humanities than he is, or more full of that cordiality and simplicity which are apt to accompany real genius, and which mere talents, or cleverness, seem to repel. My friends, Sir J. Simeon and the Baron de Schroeter,[2] who have been seeing them several times, have, I think, a deeper appreciation of him than anyone else whom I have seen; and, much as they like him, they like his wife not less. I can hardly say how deeply interesting she is to me. She is a woman full of soul as well as mind, and in all her affections, it seems to me that it is in the soul, and for the soul, that she loves those dear to her. She would, I have no doubt, make any imaginable sacrifice of her happiness to promote the real and interior good of her husband, and not of her happiness only, but of his also. In the same way she looks on her two beautiful children, with an affection so deeply *human* and religious, that there seems in it nothing of the alloy that so often sophisticates the most sacred ties, causing them rather to lead from God than to Him. I regard her as one of the 'few noble' whom it has been my lot to meet in life; and with a nature so generous, and so religious a use of the high qualities God has given her, I cannot but hope that the happiness accorded to her after so many years of trial, may be more and more blessed to her as the days go by. She is a person to whom you will be greatly drawn whenever you are near her. . . .

To JOHN FORSTER

MS. Tennyson Research Centre.

FARRINGFORD, FRESHWATER, I. W., October 23, 1854

My dear John Forster

You were kind enough to say that you would come and see us this year. Now, I fear, that you have quite forgotten your promise and I write this to 'whet your blunted purpose'[1] and likewise to inform you that the steamer

---

[2] Sir John Simeon (1815–70), 3rd Baronet, 'Roman Catholic squire of Swainston Hall near Newport, eight miles to the east. Simeon was a fine type of country gentleman; a good scholar, an excellent landlord and Master of the Isle of Wight Foxhounds, he had represented the island in Parliament a few years before [1847–51], and was to do so again in ten years' time [1865–70]. Fresh, cultivated, humorous, simple and sincere, he gave an impression of goodness, candour, and human sympathy' (Charles Tennyson, pp. 280–1). Tennyson first met Simeon, through Carlyle, at Bath House, the Ashburtons' London residence, perhaps in January 1850, but the memorable friendship began on 6 June, the day of Lionel's christening: 'On returning from Church we found Sir John Simeon. This was my first introduction to a friend who was to be so much to us both as long as he lived' (*Journal*, p. 35). He is of course the 'Prince of courtesy' of the elegy 'In the Garden at Swainston' (Ricks, p. 1219). See Louisa E. Ward (Simeon's eldest daughter), 'Tennyson and Sir John Simeon', *Tennyson and His Friends*, pp. 306–21, and Boase.

Gottlieb Heinrich von Schroeter (1802–?), like his friends Simeon, de Vere, W. G. Ward, and Newman (who broke with him), was a convert to Roman Catholicism and by no means the least enthusiastic among them. See *Memoir*, i. 377, and *Journal*, pp. 36–8. A proselytizing letter from Schroeter to the Tennysons is in *Materials*, ii. 1034. The best source of information on him is in *The Letters and Diaries of John Henry Newman*, ed. Charles Stephen Dessain, vols. 13 and 14.

[1] *Hamlet*, III. iv. 111.

between Lymington and Yarmouth in a week or two will cease running and it will not then be so easy to come at us.

Affectionately yours
A. Tennyson

I assure you this place is well worth seeing and the air on the downs 'worth' (as Keats says) 'sixpence a pint'.[2]

To FREDERICK JAMES FURNIVALL

MS. Huntington Library.

October 23, 1854

Dear Sir

You are welcome to any of my books you may think desirable. If you will write a line to Moxon he will forward them to your establishment. Believe me

Yours truly
A. Tennyson

F. J. Furnivall Esq.
(Working Men's College)
31 Red Lion Square
London

To EDWARD MOXON

MS. Berg Collection.

FARRINGFORD, FRESHWATER, October 23, 1854

My dear Moxon

One of the Teachers of the Working Men's college, 31 Red Lion Square, has written to me to petition that I will present one or more of my volumes to that establishment. I have desired him to state to you which volumes he wanted and I have told him you will forward them or it.

I should like to know how my books are going on or off rather, and whether the Russian war has interfered with their sale. Are we likely to see you here for a day or two as we did last year? I need not say how welcome you would be. Believe me,

Ever yours
A. Tennyson

---

[2] See above, p. 92.

To COVENTRY PATMORE

MS. Wellesley.

FARRINGFORD, October 30, 1854

My dear Patmore

Many thanks for your volume.[1] I still hold that you have written a poem which has a fair chance of immortality; though I have praised (Landorlike) so many poems that perhaps my praise may not be thought much of: but such as it is, accept it, for it is quite sincere. There are passages [that] want smoothing here and there; such as

> Her power makes not defeats but pacts,

a line that seems to me hammered up out of old nail-heads. Others want correcting on another score, such as

> 'I slid
> My curtain,'

which is not English. You mean I made my curtains slide and that (even so exprest) would not be good. There is nothing for it but

> I drew my curtain.

Little objections of this calibre, I could make, but as for the whole, I admire it exceedingly and trust that it will do our age good, and not ours only. The women ought to subscribe for a statue to you.

Ever yours
A. Tennyson

To JOHN WILLIAM PARKER

MS. University of Virginia.

FARRINGFORD, I. W., November 23, 1854

My dear Parker

I enclose you a letter from Mrs. Davey, the authoress of the Sard[inian] tale.[1] I have promised to let her hear from me. It may be a difficult matter for you to answer if you have made up your mind to reject the contributions. However write me a note which I may send on to her if you prefer communicating with me.

Ever yours
A. Tennyson

If Drake's Eumenides[2] is a book which can come by post I wish you would send it me. Pray come and see us whenever you have a little leisure.

---

[1] *The Angel in the House: The Betrothal* (see *Tennyson in Lincoln*, i, No. 1752). Patmore revised the lines cited to 'Defeats from her all tender pacts' and 'My curtains slid'.

[1] See above, p. 80.

[2] *Aeschyli Eumenides*. The Greek Text, with English notes . . . an English verse translation; and an introduction, containing an analysis of the dissertations of C. O. Muller, ed. by Bernard Drake (1853). Drake, a fellow of King's College, Cambridge, died on 29 May, age 29 (Boase).

EMILY SELLWOOD TENNYSON to JOHN FORSTER

MS. Tennyson Research Centre.

FARRINGFORD, FRESHWATER, I. W., December 6, [1854]

Dear Mr. Forster

Will you kindly put this into the Examiner for Alfred?[1] It was written yesterday on a recollection of the first report of 'the Times' which gave the number as 607. He prefers 'six hundred' on account of the metre but if you think it should be altered to 700 which from later accounts seems to have been the number he says you are to alter it.[2]

What dreary news! How one wishes to be some bird of fabulous size and power to carry warm clothing and nourishing food to the poor soldiers and death and destruction to the enemy.[3]

We hope you are well; brave we know you are to do that part of the fighting that has to be done at home, and how much this is! Alfred's love to you and to Mr. Spedding also if within reach.

Very sincerely yours
Emily Tennyson

---

[1] 'The Charge of the Light Brigade' (Ricks, p. 1034), printed in the *Examiner* on 9 December, signed 'A. T.' (see below, p. 104 n.). Although this letter and the next both refer to an enclosure, only one manuscript seems to have been sent to Forster on 6 December.

[2] In a leader on 13 November, *The Times* said that the Light Brigade had 'entered into action about 700 strong' (p. 6). The account on 14 November twice (in the text and in a table) put the number at 607 (p. 8). According to E. L. Woodward, 'of the 673 horsemen who had begun the charge 113 were killed and wounded; 475 of the horses were killed and 42 wounded.' Only 196 men 'answered at the first muster after the charge'—the reason why two-thirds of the brigade are often reported to have been killed and wounded—'but the unwounded men who had lost their horses, and a good many stragglers, would not have been present at this muster' (*The Age of Reform, 1815–1872* [reprint with corrections, 1946], p. 272 and n.).

For a full analysis of the manuscripts, proofs, and textual variants of the poem discussed in the next few letters, see E. F. Shannon, Jr. and Christopher Ricks's article ' "The Charge of the Light Brigade": The Creation of a Poem', *Studies in Bibliography*, xxviii (1985), 1–44. See also Jerome J. McGann, 'Tennyson and the Histories of Criticism', *Review*, iv (1982), 221–2, 235–50.

[3] An unusually violent storm in the Crimea on 14 November had wrecked thirty-two English transport vessels. 'Many of these were burnt to prevent their contents falling into the hands of the Cossacks, who thronged down to the shore, and are said to have deliberately shot down the wrecked seamen as they clung to the rigging.... The destruction of the *Prince* and her cargo was an incalculable mischief to the British army; and much of the intense suffering of the troops during the winter was caused by the loss of clothing, blanketing, and other provisions.... The armies on shore suffered frightfully from the effects of the storm. The tents were torn up from their fastenings, the huts blown down, and the men exposed, naked and half-starved, to the full severity of the gale and the bitter cold.... Many soldiers were found dead in the trenches or on the heights; the horses died of cold and starvation; and the whole sanitary condition of the army became seriously deteriorated' (*Annual Register*, 1854, pp. 200–1). See also *Journal*, p. 40.

ALFRED AND EMILY SELLWOOD TENNYSON
to JOHN FORSTER

MS. Tennyson Research Centre.

December 6, 1854

My dear Forster

If you like to put this in your paper put only A. T. at the foot. Six is much better than seven hundred (as I think) metrically so keep it and put the note I have made at the bottom.[1]

I have no time to add more, the post just going. Only if you do not put it in this week let me know as I may alter it for the next.

Ever yours with love
A. Tennyson

If you think that Stanza crossed out 'Half a league, half a league' would begin the poem better than the present beginning will you put it [in] please? Make it begin

'Half a league, half a league'—

as a separate stanza. If not omit the stanza altogether.[2]

ALFRED AND EMILY SELLWOOD TENNYSON
to JOHN FORSTER[1]

MS. Tennyson Research Centre.

FARRINGFORD, FRESHWATER, I. W., December 7, 1854

My dear Forster

You will get this amended copy in time for your paper.[2] If you print it print it exactly as written. I have only retained 'valley of Death' in one instance when the ear has got accustomed to the metre, and whatever other alterations there may be, believe that I have good reasons for them and print as I said exactly what is sent *last*. There is no objection to your keeping it another week if you have any suggestion to make.

You would have been amazed at our notes yesterday. They were written in such a scuffle. A caller came and sat talking in our last 10 minutes before the letters went. Our boy has to run a mile to the Post Office in the village and then the postman has to walk 5 miles to the post-town and he won't wait for the boy.

Ever yours
A. Tennyson

---

[1] The manuscript (TRC) is largely in Emily Tennyson's hand, but with the title, the last six lines, the signature, and the note in Tennyson's. It also bears Forster's directions to the printer.

[2] The postscript is in Emily Tennyson's hand. Tennyson had crossed out the third stanza; Forster transposed it by a guideline to be the opening four lines.

[1] The date, address, and postscript are in Emily Tennyson's hand.

[2] Except for the title, in Tennyson's autograph, this new manuscript is in Emily Tennyson's hand (TRC).

Alfred has just bid me say he begs you will by no means put the ballad in if you do not think it good. Then the fact of the numbers—we don't know what it is—would it be well to add a note and say this ballad was written on the computation first made by the Times? Forgive all this trouble we have given you.

To JOHN FORSTER

MS. Tennyson Research Centre.

FRESHWATER, I. W., Friday, December 9 [for 8], 1854

My dear F.

On receiving the *printed* ballad I wished that *my* 'order' (my last) had been 'blundered' and that the first edition had stood—never mind—I have corrected

> Flash'd all their
> Flash'd all at once —

which you can adopt if you have time, and if you approve it. I send back the proof but I should like it back again.

Ever yours affectionately
A. Tennyson

JOHN FORSTER *to* ALFRED TENNYSON

MS. Yale.

58 LINCOLN'S INN FIELDS, December 9, 1854

My dear Alfred Tennyson

That you may see how determined I was to carry out your order without a blunder—though I may say I disapproved of its suggestions, which, if you had persisted in them, I would *not* have said—I enclose you the proof which was before me this morning when your letter arrived.

But by a sharp effort there *was* time to try back again—and here you see it is done. I am particularly glad that Mrs. Tennyson thinks with you, with all of us, the original version the best.

I will send her a dozen slips of the ballad printed on good paper either on Tuesday or Wednesday next. (It is not until one of those days that the types are 'released' from the forms of the paper, and available for separate working.) By tonight's post I send you two *Examiners*.

How I value this noble ballad, I need not say—how proud I am to print it first, and that my old friend sent it to me, I *must* say. I hear little of you, but again and again I think of you, and never have I done it so often as of late—never, with a throbbing heart, have read of those fights of heroes at Alma, Balaklava, and Inkermann, that I have not been eager for *you* to celebrate them—the only man that can do it up to their own pitch—the only 'muse of fire'[1] now left to us that can of right ascend to the level of such deeds. And now you have done it—have at any rate begun!

[1] *Henry V*, Prologue, l. 1.

What more I have to say I must say when I send the slips to Mrs. Tennyson. Hold me in your love and remembrance, my dear A. T., for you and she are much in mine. In the midst of this whirling life I lead here I have sense enough to feel how much better is the life that you lead, and thoroughly to rejoice in the happiness which the wisest and joyous life has secured to you.

Most affectionately yours
John Forster

To JAMES FREDERICK FERRIER[1]

MS. University of Virginia.

FRESHWATER, ISLE OF WIGHT, December 14, 1854

Sir

A day or two since Moxon sent me your Institutes of Metaphysics,[2] a book which I intend to read carefully. At present I have only had time to admire the form of it. I have always said that this ought to be the form of a book of Metaphysics, Euclidlike, leading from proposition to proposition, and that if I ever had the good fortune to light upon such a book I would read it. Pray accept my best thanks and believe me (may I not say Dear Sir?)

Yours very truly
A. Tennyson

To SIR JOHN SIMEON

MS. Bryn Mawr College.

FARRINGFORD, January 11, 1855

My dear Simeon

I was truly sorry for your accident both for itself and because it was the occasion of my missing you. We were only pacing the down and descended immediately on the nursemaid's information that you had arrived, Hallam calling out all the way 'Sambul Sambul' till at last it fell into a piping note 'Sambul gone'! Well, we shall meet again. I would willingly walk over but I am not up to long walks as in the summer. Mine and my wife's best regards to Lady S. and your b[air]n.

Ever yours
A. Tennyson

---

[1] James Frederick Ferrier (1808–64: *DNB*), metaphysician and moral philosopher. He was a nephew of Susan Ferrier (1782–1854: *DNB*) the novelist, and also of John Wilson, 'Christopher North' (see i. 109 n.), and later, father-in-law of Alexander Grant (see above, p. 95 n.), who, with Edmund Lushington, edited Ferrier's *Lectures on Greek Philosophy, and Other Philosophical Remains* in 1866 (*Tennyson in Lincoln*, i, No. 930). See E. M. Sellar, *Recollections and Impressions*, pp. 64–70, and *Journal*, pp. 41, 137, 279. Ferrier's reply to this letter is in *Memoir*, i. 381.

[2] *Institutes of Metaphysics: The Theory of Metaphysics* (1854).

To [1]

Text. William Harris Arnold Sale Catalogue, 10–11 Nov. 1924, Lot 983.

January 23 [or 29?], 1855

I can sympathize with your genius but not at this hour with any song of triumph when my heart almost bursts with indignation at the accursed mismanagement of our noble little army, that flower of men.

FREDERICK GODDARD TUCKERMAN[1]
to ALFRED TENNYSON

MS. Tennyson Research Centre.

WINDSOR, January 31, 1855

Alfred Tennyson, Esq.,

My dear Sir

On the eve of departure, I cannot leave England without once more again expressing to you my deep sense of your hospitality and kindness. Three days, so delightful, so memorable, I never remember to have experienced as those passed in your society and beneath your roof and only now come 'the bitter of the sweet' and the feeling that I have rather lost a friend, than gained one. This conviction indeed though prospective, was felt before we parted and I have no doubt made me feel dull and insensible to the surpassing beauty of your *Idyl*, or of Maud, scraps of which are floating through my head like 'fragments of the golden day'. (I can hear you drily remark 'O I *dare*say' but you need not fear that I shall ever deserve the punishment of Prometheus by reaching after them.) Besides one dares not speak inadequately of such creations even in words of praise. I may now say, however, that portions of these poems have come back to me with a power and beauty unexampled and that I only wait until the curves come full circle to do justice to the perfection of the whole, in regard too, to your manner of reading or chanting,

---

[1] Conceivably Martin Tupper (see above, p. 27), but probably Sydney Dobell (see i. 246 n., 297 n.), whose volume (with Alexander Smith) *Sonnets on the War* appeared in early January 1855. Both Smith and Dobell had already presented volumes to Tennyson (*Tennyson in Lincoln*, i, Nos. 866, 2056). A letter (TRC) from Dobell, 7 February [1855], apologizes for not thanking Tennyson 'long ago' for his 'kind note of criticism'. 'I am sorry to infer from something you say', he goes on, 'that the Edinburgh rumour is correct which denies to you the Authorship of the "Charge of the six hundred". I feel rather humiliated; for I could have staked whatever poetical acumen I possess on the position that no man living but yourself could have written the first verse and the "cannon" verse.'

[1] Frederick Goddard Tuckerman (1821–73), American poet, who, with his brother, Samuel Tuckerman (see below, p. 109), had called on the Tennysons on 12 January and dined with them several times. See *Journal*, p. 42. 'It is interesting to see how they cling to the thought of the old English home', Emily Tennyson wrote. 'They have been to see that of some of their ancestors. A family some of which are my own near relatives' (Journal).

A less discreet account of Tuckerman's first visit is recorded by a cousin, Charles K. Tuckerman, in *Personal Recollections of Notable People at Home and Abroad*, pp. 21–6.

I feel that it must be the true one; at all events I cannot recite your lines—the exquisite ones for instance—

> 'Came glimmering through the laurels
> In the quiet evenfall,'

in any other way. The Locksley Hall, your most valued gift, contains also a part of the Golden Year; I should return this as perhaps not designed to be given me, but the other side of the leaf is written upon.[2] In reading this fragment I have discovered a curious substitution of sound for sense. You remember the line, 'Yet seas that daily gain upon the shore'[;] in the American editions this is printed, 'Yet seize the daily gain upon the shore'; almost as bad as the 'costly tales,' regarding which latter misprint I will give you a remarkable illustration when we meet again. You will I trust yet see America, for where else can I repay you? or even attempt to do so. Should the Russians overrun Europe, or the 'auri sacra fames' of publishers become insatiable you will there find one (among many) who will proudly serve you to the extent of his influence and fortune. May this feeling, the growth of many years, the flowering of a few days, yet bear fruit. In regard to your unpublished poems, which you did me the honour to read me, rest assured that I will never repeat a single word until I see them printed. Once more, with a full sense of your favours and with grateful expression, in which my brother desires to join, I bid you farewell. Assure Mrs. Tennyson of my warm recollection of her many graceful acts of courtesy and kindness and believe me, dear Sir, with the highest respect and regard,

Ever your servant and friend
F. G. Tuckerman

Perhaps you will favour me by accepting a book that I send—a copy of Webster's Dictionary. I only regret that it is not quite a new one, which is not to be obtained here; I think that you will find it in spite of imperfections a valuable addition to your library. If the volumes of Poe are not to be had here, I will send them from America. My address is Greenfield, Mass., U. S. America. If I can ever be of service in procuring you books, or otherwise, do not hesitate to inform me. Any communication through Ticknor Reed and Fields will reach me (the Boston publishers).

To GEORGE STOVIN VENABLES

MS. National Library of Wales.

January 31, 1855

My dear Venables

The day here is frightful, bitter wind and driving snow. I dare not think of starting with this pain in the face and perhaps shall not be in town for some days if the weather does not mitigate.

Ever yours
A. Tennyson

[2] The manuscript is now at Yale.

To FREDERICK GODDARD TUCKERMAN[1]

MS. Harvard.

FARRINGFORD, FRESHWATER, ISLE OF WIGHT, *February 6, 1855*

My dear Sir

The pleasure which I received from reading your kind letter (and trust me that it *was* a pleasure) was rather qualified by the ferocious character of the weather here on the day when the letter came to hand. The wind blew 'as 'twad blawn its last' as wild as the wind in Tam O'Shanter[2] and the thin snow blew in a white powder past our windows for twelve hours till I almost shuddered to think of you tossing on the homeless Atlantic and indeed shall not be easy about you till I hear that you have safely arrived at your pleasant-sounding Greenfield, Mass.

That you past your three days here happily is another satisfaction to me: for the place is dull enough; indeed, during winter it is called by everyone who comes the dullest of the dull: so your happiness must have been derived from talks with myself over my little fire in my wind-shaken attic, except indeed, so much of your happiness as may have been drawn from a central fund of it in your own heart to mingle with the former and make it a 'tertium quid.' I perceive this last sentence is very clumsy but let it be pardoned.

Now let me thank you for the costly pipe you sent me in return for my two clays: you have not been wise in the matter any more than old Glaucus in the Iliad who made that exchange of his gold for the other's brass,[3] nor wise either in the sense of carrying coals to Newcastle: nevertheless the bowl has already acquired a mellow autumn brown which will no doubt deepen for many a long month as I sit and smoke to your memory. But Webster is really a superb gift for which I can scarce thank you adequately.[4] I will only say that I thank you much, and hope that if ever you come back to us you will put up at no hotel but in my house and I if I come to you will likewise find you out and we will be as happy together as two friends may on either side the Atlantic: meantime believe me

Ever yours
A. Tennyson

My wife desires her kind remembrances. Little Hallam recollected you for three days as was to be gathered from his two expressions of

Where's gempleum (gentleman)
and
Melliky (America)

Then you faded and past out of his horizon.

---

[1] See above, p. 104.
[2] Line 73 in Burns's poem.
[3] *Iliad,* vi. 236.
[4] *Webster's Dictionary* (see above, p. 105: below, p. 113; and *Tennyson in Lincoln,* i, No. 2312).

EMILY SELLWOOD TENNYSON
to FREDERICK GODDARD TUCKERMAN

MS. Harvard.

FARRINGFORD, FRESHWATER, ISLE OF WIGHT, February 8, [1855]

My dear Sir

My husband bids me write without delay to tell you he has received the volumes of Poe you so kindly promised him and strange to say from the last guest who preceded yourself in our house, Mr. Palgrave. We hope this may be in time to spare you the trouble of looking after the books.[1] Perhaps his letter and mine will reach you by the same packet for he wrote to you two days ago and I cannot refrain from adding my assurance to his of the great pleasure your letter and your gifts have afforded him. The bright Iris berries[2] you put up in the card rack are there still, so you see you have a kind of visible presence by our hearth still, a pledge, I hope, that you will be there yourself in your actual presence before very long.

If you at all feel as we do, and I cannot but think you do so feel, of the brotherhood of America and England, as of the bond never to be broken, you will grieve for us in our present state. The one comfort we have is in the heroic endurance of our soldiers and I cannot rate this low, but how sad it is words cannot tell.

Sometimes however I dare to hope when I think of 'the cloudy porch,'[3] yes hope even for our officials.

My husband joins me in all kind remembrances. We see ships did not leave port that stormy day so we hope you have escaped the worst of what we feared you had had to encounter and that you will very soon be safe and happy with your little ones.

Most truly yours
Emily Tennyson

To WILLIAM ALLINGHAM

Text. Letters to William Allingham, ed. H. Allingham and E. Baumer Williams, p. 277.

FARRINGFORD, I. W., February 17, 1855

Dear Mr. Allingham

My thanks for your 'Happy New Year' though it is yet so unhappily cold that I can scarcely hold the pen in my hand as some of those poor officers say

---

[1] It wasn't. See *Tennyson in Lincoln,* i, No. 1805, and below, p. 113.

[2] Probably Iris *foetidissima* (Gladwin iris), of which the 'capsules remain on the plant in winter, bursting open and displaying rows of orange-red berries' (L. H. Bailey, *Standard Cyclopedia of Horticulture*), 'prized for dried arrangements' (*Wyman's Gardening Encyclopedia*).

[3] 'Love and Duty', l. 9 (Ricks, p. 727). Parliament, reassembled on 23 January, immediately faced motions of inquiry into the conduct of the war. Aberdeen's Coalition Ministry resigned on 1 February. A week later Palmerston formed a new ministry, and after much debate reluctantly agreed on 23 February to the formation of a Sebastopol committee of inquiry of ten members. The commissioners went to the Crimea in March, and their report, in mid-July, laid the blame on Aberdeen's cabinet, especially the Duke of Newcastle, Secretary for War (*Annual Register*).

who write from the Crimea. One has no right to complain when one reflects on them in their thin tents. . . .

Could I hope to describe my part of the world as picturesquely as you have done yours I might be tempted to paint the corner of this 'nookshotten isle'[1] for you: then it is so well-known and so cockney that perhaps it would scarce be worth while.

With respect to your request I cannot grant it by myself, Moxon having a share of my profits, but I do not at all suppose that he would start any objection. I have known him do so indeed, but only when extracts are very long. I cannot say that I like much your choice of poems, three at least out of the seven[teen] are to my mind totally worthless.[2] Believe me dear sir,

Yours very truly
A. Tennyson

Have you seen Patmore's new Poem? It promises (I think) very well. I am glad that you too promise us something more.

FREDERICK GODDARD TUCKERMAN
to ALFRED TENNYSON (extract)

MS. Tennyson Research Centre.

GREENFIELD, [MASSACHUSETTS,] February 22, 1855

Do you remember my quoting some lines one evening from a newspaper and objecting to the rhymes 'blunder'd' and 'hundred,' thinking it should read 'blund*ered*'?[1] I had then seen exactly *three* lines, and knew nothing of the connexion. Judge then of my surprise at discovering the whole poem in an American paper, with your name attached. I read it with a mixture of astonishment and delight and think it a most noble performance, the finest irregular Ode ever written upon the grandest subject. The repetitions too are wonderfully effective and I cannot help hoping that this poem will not receive any alteration. (Of course I refer to your general habit of retouching your poems and not to any remarks of mine.) Yet your poetry is so suggestive that every student of it must find not only 'a meaning suited to his mind'[2] but something more. I have been reading the 'In Memoriam' since my return

---

[1] *Henry V*, III. v. 14.

[2] Allingham's anthology *Nightingale Valley: A Collection including a Great Number of the Choicest Lyrics and Short Poems in the English Language*, edited by 'Giraldus' (Bell and Daldy, 1860; 1862, signed). Five of the selections were from *Poems, Chiefly Lyrical* (1830): 'Claribel', 'Song—The Owl', 'Circumstance', 'Song' ['A spirit haunts the year's last hours'], and '[Leonine] Elegiacs'.

[1] In response to criticism (including Tuckerman's) of the rhyme, Tennyson omitted lines 5–12 from 'The Charge of the Light Brigade' in *Maud, and Other Poems* (July 1855) but restored them thereafter. See Shannon and Ricks, *Studies in Bibliography*, xxxviii (1985), 6–10. See also below, pp. 114, 117, 119, 132–3.

[2] 'Moral', l. 12, in 'The Day-Dream' (Ricks, p. 624).

and never has its solemn music affected me so deeply, for how could I help hearing a

> voice the richest-toned that sings

chanting these strains,

> > From point to point with power and grace
> > And music in the bounds of law.[3]

Your reading in truth made a deep impression upon me, though I am so slow at 'taking in' as often to seem insensible. I am almost ashamed to ask the meaning of the last line in the last quoted poem,[4] but I have been ransacking my memories of Italy in vain.

To SOPHIA MAY TUCKERMAN[1]

MS. University of Virginia.

FARRINGFORD, FRESHWATER, I. W., February 23, 1855

Madam

I do not wonder that you are pleased with your son's poem[2] but I cannot think of retaining it as it seems to have been so carefully treasured amongst you. I rejoice that he was not disappointed in his visit to Farringford. For myself I can assure you that I have seldom met any man whom I should be more glad to meet again. My house is always open to him whenever he chooses to revisit England. Since he left it, I have dispatched a letter in acknowledgement of a handsomely-bound Webster's Dictionary which he gave me and which both for itself and for the manner of the gift I esteem very highly. It was accompanied by a meerschaum from himself and two cherry-wood pipesticks from your son Dr. Tuckerman, to whom I ought also to have written my thanks but I do not know his address and I will therefore request that you will do me the favour to thank him for me. Believe me, dear Madam,
Yours truly
A. Tennyson

---

[3] *In Memoriam*, 75. 7; 87. 33–4.
[4] 'The bar of Michael Angelo'.

[1] Mother of Frederick Goddard Tuckerman and of (Dr) Samuel Tuckerman (1819–90), distinguished organist and musicologist (awarded a Lambeth Mus.D. 1851), who had familiarized himself with the practices at St. George's Chapel, Windsor (see above, p. 104 n.), Canterbury, and elsewhere. See *New Grove Dictionary of Music and Musicians*.
[2] Unidentifiable in *The Complete Poems of Frederick Goddard Tuckerman*, ed. N. Scott Momaday.

110   *c. 8 April* 1855

To EMILY SELLWOOD TENNYSON

Text. *Memoir*, i. 383–4.

[BONCHURCH, I. W.] [*c.* 8 April 1855][1]

If I stop another day here, I may have a chance of seeing double stars through a telescope of Dr. Mann's,[2] a very clever interesting doctor with whom I spent two hours this morning. He showed me things through his microscope.

To CATHERINE RAWNSLEY

Text. Yale (transcript).

FARRINGFORD, FRESHWATER, May 2, 1855

Dear Catherine

Thanks for your letter. After what you have said I shall not trouble you with this document. I shall leave it sealed with the rest of the memoir in the hands of my brother-in-law Edmund Lushington to be by him published after my death—unless indeed I should see some good cause to change my mind.[1] Emily's love. Believe me,

Very truly yours
A. Tennyson

To EMILY SELLWOOD TENNYSON

MS. Tennyson Research Centre.

[6 June 1855]

Dearest

I have strangely enough accepted the Oxford Doctorship. Friends told me that I ought to accept so I did: but it is not as you might have seen by Temple's letter certain whether it will be conferred, as he talks of byelaws which they have which may interfere.[1] If I go I should like you to go likewise. I went to Barrett[2] this morning and shall have to go again next Tuesday. I

---

[1] 'We drive to Newport, he on his way to Bonchurch whence he returns on the 9th and tells the wonderful facts of which he has heard from Dr. Mann' (Journal).

[2] See above, p. 73.

[1] A puzzler—but possibly relevant to the 'Painful tidings of the Arctic Expedition' mentioned in *Journal*, p. 39, since Catherine Rawnsley (like Emily Tennyson) was a niece of Sir John Franklin (see i. 190 n.). 'The startling intelligence . . . of the corpses of a great part of Sir John Franklin's crews having been found by the Esquimeaux on a river bank—made certain by the surrender of a great quantity of articles known to have belonged to the unfortunate adventurers —probably brings the Arctic Expeditions to a close' (*Annual Register*). See below, p. 251 n.

[1] See below, p. 112. Frederick Temple (1821–1902), later Archbishop of Canterbury, was at this time Principal of Kneller Hall, a training college of schoolmasters and very close to Chapel House. F. T. Palgrave had followed him at Balliol.

[2] Henry John Barrett, dental surgeon (see i. xxxiii).

6 *June* 1855

shall be with you on Friday night or Saturday morning. I went and got measured yesterday at Buckmaster's.[3]

Thine
A. T.

Lear has sent Hallam his funny book which I am to bring down.[4]

To EDWARD LEAR[1]

MS. Tennyson Research Centre.

Thursday, June 7, 1855

My dear Lear

Many thanks for your nonsense book[2] with which Hallam will be delighted. As to your question Spedding would be very glad to come some time next week; the others I have not spoken with. I of course should be happy to make friends with the Nile.[3] I go to Park House on Friday evening and shall have to come up to a dentist next Tuesday. Meanwhile

Yours ever
A. Tennyson

To EDWARD LEAR

MS. Tennyson Research Centre.

[8 June 1855]

My dear Lear

I ought to have told you that I am engaged for Wednesday and Thursday next week. Don't bore yourself to give a dinner. I love you all, as well undined.

I was engaged before I wrote to Weld for Wednesday and I called on

---

[3] Tailors and Army Clothiers, 3 Burlington Street.   [4] See the next letter.

[1] Edward Lear (1812–88), the water-colourist, author of nonsense verse and travel books, and amateur musician, first met Tennyson at 'Park House, and probably in [? early July] 1849', according to Vivian Noakes (*Edward Lear, the Life of a Wanderer*, p. 104). He had travelled to Greece in March–April 1849 with Franklin Lushington, whom he had met in Malta and for whom he came to have an intense affection. They complemented each other like the Scarecrow and the Tin Woodman: Lear was ugly, affectionate, chatty, diffident, emotional; Lushington handsome, stern, silent, self-assured, intellectual. 'If Lushington had loved and encouraged him, theirs might have developed into a full homosexual relationship' (Noakes, p. 134). Lushington later married and had seven children. Lear's relationship with Emily Tennyson, which brought out the best in her (including her best letters), was in its own way almost equally intense. He had called on the Tennysons on their honeymoon (see i. 332 n.), but eighteen months and a wedding present later he was still 'my dear Sir' to her (see *The Letters of Emily Lady Tennyson*, ed. Hoge, pp. 56–7). This changed soon, but his relationship with Tennyson was never altogether comfortable.

[2] Lear's *A Book of Nonsense*, by Derry Down Derry (2 vols., 1847; signed, 3rd edn., 1861).

[3] In a letter of 6 June (TRC), Lear spoke of inviting Venables, Chapman, Spedding, and Tennyson to dine and see his Nile drawings.

Carlyle last night and gave him (as perhaps I ought not to have done) a promise to dine with him on Thursday. If wrong, pray let me be forgiven and

Yours always
A. Tennyson

I am going to Park House today.

To ROBERT SCOTT[1]

MS. Pusey House, Oxford.

June 11, 1855

Dear Sir

I beg to assure you that I am very sensible of the honour done me in offering me an Honorary Degree,[2] an offer which I accepted through Mr. Temple of Kneller Hall[3] but it seems by a note from him this day inclosing your own that he has by some chance never received my letter.

I have much pleasure in accepting your hospitality, and I trust that my wife will be able to accompany me but she fears that even if she should then be well enough to travel it might not be good for Mrs. Scott to receive her.[4] As for gaiety neither I nor my wife care for anything.

Your letter of the 8th only reached me just now at my brother's home near Maidstone. With our united thanks to yourself and Mrs. Scott, believe me, dear Sir,

Yours very truly
A. Tennyson

---

[1] In reply to an invitation (8 June, TRC) to come to Oxford on 19 June from Robert Scott (1811–87: *DNB*), lexicographer, Master of Balliol (1854–70), and Dean of Rochester (1870–87). Posterity has not been kind to Scott. Of the great *Greek-English Lexicon* a contemporary quatrain said:

> Two men wrote a lexicon, Liddell and Scott;
> One half was clever, one half was not.
> Give me the answer, boys, quick, to this riddle:
> Which was by Scott, and which was by Liddell?

And it is clear that he was elected Master of Balliol in a raw power play to block Jowett, who then had to wait sixteen years until, in another political manœuvre, just as raw but far more subtle, Scott was shunted off to Rochester in order to make room for Jowett. See Geoffrey Faber, *Jowett, A Portrait with a Background*, pp. 109–10, 349–51.

[2] DCL, awarded on 20 June to Tennyson and two Crimean commanders (just a month before the publication of *Maud*): 'It was very interesting to see the old soldiers Sir de Lacy Evans and Sir John Burgoyne,' Emily Tennyson wrote (*Journal*). 'A. had met Sir de Lacy before and had a long talk with him now, also with Montalembert, a fine stately looking man. A. sat down on the steps nearly under Lord Derby [the Chancellor].' See the account in *Journal*, pp. 46–8, and *Memoir*, i. 384–5.

[3] See above, p. 110 n.

[4] A daughter was born to Mrs Scott on 12 July.

To EDMUND LUSHINGTON[1]

MS. National Library of Wales.

[? Oxford, late June 1855]

My dear Edmund

Many thanks for your very kind note. I would come willingly this week but I find that I cannot—tiring, I find it—so shuffling. I shall hope to come to Park House afterwards. Love to you all.

Affectionately yours
A. Tennyson

To JANE OCTAVIA BROOKFIELD

MS. Gordon Ray.

[? early July 1855]

My dear Job

Very kind in you to ask me: but I can't come. Why? I go to dine with my poor old mother at Twickenham. Love to B.

Affectionately yours
A. Tennyson

To FREDERICK GODDARD TUCKERMAN

MS. Harvard.

[8 July 1855]

Dear Mr. Tuckerman

I have just returned home[1] (i.e. to Farringford) from a visit to London during which I called on Moxon and found your kind present of books waiting for me.[2] I fear that you must have thought me ungrateful in not immediately acknowledging them: and so I should have done had I not been waiting to send along with my thanks a small volume of my own, containing some of the things which I repeated to you in my little smoking-attic here. And those poems when printed I found needed considerable elision, and so the book has hung in Limbo. It will now be ready I suppose in a week or so and I have ordered Moxon to send you a copy.[3]

When I arrived here I found that my small smoking room did not smell of smoke at all, nay was even fragrant. I could not at first make it out: at last I perceived it was owing to the Russian leather on your Webster which you made mine even so (as someone says)

> The actions of the just
> Smell sweet and blossom in the dust[4]

---

[1] This letter begins 'My dear Venables', but the message to him has been completely cut out. The watermark is 1855.

[1] They returned home on 7 July (*Memoir*, i. 385; *Journal*, p. 48).
[2] The three volumes of Poe (see above, p. 107, and *Tennyson in Lincoln*, i, No. 1805).
[3] *Maud, and Other Poems*, published 28 July.
[4] James Shirley, *The Contention of Ajax and Ulysses*, iii. 23-4. See below, p. 282.

and there was dust enough on the table almost to justify the application.

You will find in my little volume 'The Charge of the Light Brigade' with the 'blunder'd' that offended you and others, omitted. It is not a poem on which I pique myself but I cannot help fancying that, such as it is, I have improved it.

Farewell and forgive my silence hitherto. I shall always remember with pleasure your coming to see me in the frost and our pleasant talks together. Did you see in your papers that the Oxford University would make me a doctor the other day, and how the young ones shouted? I am, dear Mr. Tuckerman,

Ever yours
A. Tennyson

To GERALD MASSEY

MS. National Library of Scotland.

FARRINGFORD, FRESHWATER, I. W., July 11, 1855

Dear Mr. Massey

Will you accept a little volume from me of my own poems? I have ordered Moxon to forward one to you. My mother now between 70 and 80, one who takes far more interest in the next world than in this, and not generally given to the reading of literature, was quite delighted with your paper in Hogg's Instructor.[1] Believe me, dear Mr Massey,

Yours very truly
A. Tennyson

To LEWIS FYTCHE

MS. Tennyson Research Centre.

July 18, 1855

My dear Lewis

I was much grieved to hear of the death of your dear Father:[1] it was entirely unsuspected by me even that he had been unwell: I live here so far out of the world and my family write so seldom. He was a good, just and honest man such as there are few in our varnished days. God help you all in your affliction and support the spirits of your poor Mother. You have been severely visited, two losses following each other so closely. I write in haste. Let me hear again from you, how you are and particularly how your Mother bears up against her afflictions and believe me

Ever your affectionate cousin (with my wife's love)
A. Tennyson

---

[1] 'The Poetry of Alfred Tennyson', *Hogg's Instructor*, v (July 1855), 1–14. Emily Tennyson, however, was less than 'quite delighted' (see *The Letters of Emily Tennyson*, ed. Hoge, pp. 76–7).

[1] John Fytche (see i. 21 n.).

July 1855

To CHARLES RICHARD WELD

MS. Tennyson Research Centre.

FARRINGFORD, July 1855

My dear Weld

I don't much wonder at your complaining that you waste your sweetness on the desert air[1] when you write to me: but this time I have had some little excuse. I have been writing letters which must be attended to since I received yours. Then, you know, what have I got to tell you from this place. You wouldn't care to hear about the wildflowers which we gather and anatomize daily, nor to be told that we sit listening to the cry of the seamews and hardly ever see a human face not of our household. But you in the heart of London society with something new everyday almost occurring of course must needs be full of matter to talk or to write of. I set to work on your brother's[2] epigram yesterday and made about 20 translations—none of them good. These translations are no easy thing to manage neatly and if not done neatly, I don't see why they should be done at all. Here is one of mine

> The doctor's draught and the surgeon's knife
> And the rope of the hangman, all take life.
> Of the three executioners (who can doubt it)
> The hangman is best: he is quicker about it.

Your brother missed out a word in his Latin which omission spoils the pentameter.

> quod *facit* ille cito

it ought to be. Another

> I hate to be slowly killed by the draught or the Surgeon's knife:
> The Devil take Doctor and Surgeon both, for they both take life!
> Does honest Jack Ketch do more: nay (I think we can hardly doubt it)
> Jack Ketch is the best of the three: he is scarcely a minute about it.

They are neither of them what they ought to be, and not worth preserving: the first is the best where bad's the best.

I have heard nothing of Mayall's photographs.[3] Whenever you or he will tell me what I owe him, I will send him a cheque for the amount.

I have ordered Moxon to send you a copy of my new book. He is going to print 5000 copies, having already orders for 3000.

Love to Anne and the little Irlandaise.[4]

Ever yours
A. Tennyson

[1] Gray's 'Elegy', l. 56. [2] Isaac Weld (1774–1856: *DNB*), a half-brother.
[3] John Jabez Edwin Mayall (1810–1901), the Regent Street photographer. One of these, engraved after a drawing, was reproduced in the *National Magazine*, November 1856. (The Mayall photograph used as a frontispiece for the *Memoir* was taken in 1864.) See Richard Ormond, *Early Victorian Portraits*, i. 454–5.
[4] His daughter, Agnes Grace Weld, author of *Glimpses of Tennyson* (1902). See her long letter about Tennyson in Henry J. Jennings, *Lord Tennyson, a Biographical Sketch* (1884), pp. 200–15, and *Tennyson in Lincoln*, i, Nos. 3200, 3403.

EMILY SELLWOOD TENNYSON to EDWARD MOXON

MS. Harvard.

[1 August 1855]

p. 37 (11th line from the top)
stuff'd for stuft

p. 98 dele comma after throat
5th line from the top

; instead of :   on p. 153 (2d line)[1]

Many thanks dear Mr. Moxon for your kind note.[2] We did not know Mr. Browning was in England. We want him to come here. Is Mrs. Browning with him?

Mr. Henry Taylor has also written very kindly about the poem[3] but I am prepared for a different tone of criticism from the many. It will take, I think, some time before they understand either the metres or the thoughts but in the end I should not wonder at its being popular.[4] So much for my prophecy!

Are you likely to be coming within reach of us this autumn? You know how glad we shall be to see you if it be so.

Very sincerely yours
Emily Tennyson

Will you be so kind as to send us ⟨two⟩ four more Mauds.

BENEDICT LAWRENCE CHAPMAN to ALFRED TENNYSON

Text. Materials, ii. 149.

3 STONE BUILDINGS, LINCOLN'S INN, August 3, 1855

My dear Tennyson

I say now what I ought to have said before, that I was very much gratified with the acceptable gift of an early copy of 'Maud' 'from the author,' and that I am much obliged to you for it. One reason of the delay was, as you may have heard, a good deal of trouble about Harry Lushington.[1] Matters at present are that he, Venables and Edmund, Miss Heathcote and Maria are

---

[1] *Maud*, I. 371; III. 27; 'The Charge of the Light Brigade', l. 35. All the changes were made in the next printing (1855), but in 1859 'stuff'd' became 'crammed'.

[2] 'Browning has just been here. "Maud" he says "is a great poem. He has read it four times. ... I sent him an *early* copy' (Moxon to Emily Tennyson, 31 July, in *Materials*, ii. 148).

[3] See *Memoir*, i. 399–400.

[4] It was widely reviewed and roundly (and also, according to Tennyson, narrowly) abused, though from the first it had sympathetic readers and critics, and it *was* popular (10,000 copies printed by December). The reception brought him pain, but it bought him Farringford. See E. F. Shannon, Jr., 'The Critical Reception of Tennyson's "Maud"', *PMLA*, lxvii (1953), 397–417.

[1] See below, pp. 123–4. Margaret Heathcote was an old family friend of the Lushingtons and semi-permanent resident of Park House. Maria (d. 1891), Emily (d. 1893), and Ellen (d. 1886) were Lushington sisters.

still at Paris, that the last accounts, from Monday, are more favourable than any that have been received, but leaving the stay there and the prospect of restoration in great obscurity and that Emily or Ellen wishes to go in which case I shall accompany her to Paris.

In the absence of any criticism of my own I mention what an acquaintance of mine in the department of the S. P. G., as he calls it, Society for Propagation of the Gospel, was saying, how a Chaplain in the Crimea sent by the Society writes to the Society (neither he nor the Society being suspected of any Tennysonian prejudices), 'The greatest service you can do just now is to send out on printed slips Mr. A. T.'s 'Charge at Balaclava.' It is the greatest favourite of the soldiers, half are singing it and all want to have it in black and white, so as to *read* what has so much taken them!'[2] Believe me,

Yours sincerely
B. L. Chapman

To JOHN FORSTER

MS. Tennyson Research Centre.

[6 August 1855][1]

My dear Forster

In the first place thanks for your critique,[2] which seems to me good and judicious—many thanks—my wife will write to you about it: but what I am writing to you now about is a matter which interests me very much.

My friend Chapman of 3 Stone Buildings, Lincoln's Inn writes to me thus:

'An acquaintance of mine in the department of the S. P. G. as he calls it—Society for the Propagation of the Gospel—was saying how a chaplain in the Crimea sent by the Society writes to the Society (neither he nor the Society being suspected of any Tennysonian prejudices)

"*the* greatest service you can do* just now is to send out on printed slips Mr. A. T.'s Charge at Balaclava. It is the greatest favourite of the soldiers—half are singing it and all want to have it on black and white—so as to read—what has so taken them."'

Now my dear Forster you see I cannot possibly be deaf to such an appeal. I wish to send out about 1000 slips; but I don't at all want the S. P. G. or any one else to send out the *version last printed*: it would, I believe, quite disappoint the soldiers. Don't you live quite close to the S. P. G.? Could you not send Henry[3] over to say that *I* am sending over the soldier's version of my ballad and beg them not to stir in the matter? The soldiers are the best critics in what pleases them. I send you a copy which retains 'the light Brigade' and the 'blunder'd' and I declare I believe it is the best of the two and that the criticism of two or three London friends (not yours) induced me to spoil it.[4] For Heaven's sake get *this* copy fairly printed at once at once [*sic*]—and sent out. I have sent it by this post likewise to Moxon but you are closer to your

---

[2] Nothing could have gratified him more, as the letters following attest.
[1] *Journal*, p. 49.   [2] *Examiner*, 4 August 1855, pp. 483–4.
[3] Unidentified, but doubtless an errand-boy or clerk.   [4] See above, p. 108.

printer's. Concoct with him how it is all to be managed; I am so sorry that I was not in town to have it done at once. I have written a little note to the soldiers which need not be sent—just as you like—it might be merely printed from A. Tennyson.[5]

Please see to all this: and see that there *are no mistakes*; and I will be bound to you for evermore, and more than ever—

Yours in great haste
A. Tennyson

*thus underscored in the original.

P. S. I am convinced now after writing it out—that this *is* the best version. I have told Moxon to call on you.

EMILY SELLWOOD TENNYSON to JOHN FORSTER

MS. Tennyson Research Centre.

[6 August 1855]

Dear Mr. Forster

My best thanks for the kind and admirable critique which we received yesterday. It is peoples' own fault or misfortune if they do not understand what manner of man the hero is and read the story of his life now that you have made it a whole for them out of the many poems.

I am particularly glad you feel as I do about the picture one gets of the scene and the actors without a word of direct description. But I am not taking upon me to review your review speaking thus for which you will have no cause to thank me.

Once more thanks and all kind remembrances from

Yours most sincerely
Emily Tennyson

When you write, will you tell us when you think you can come that Alfred may arrange his tour accordingly.[1]

---

[5] Tennyson's autograph draft of his note reads: 'Brave Soldiers | whom I am proud to call my countrymen, I have heard that you have a liking for my ballad on the Charge of the Light Brigade at Balaclava. No writing of mine can add to the glory you have acquired in the Crimea; but I send you a thousand copies of my ballad because I am told that you like it and that you may know that those who sit at home love and honour you. | . A. Tennyson.'

Emily Tennyson wrote across the top: 'It would be pleasant to write to the soldiers only one is afraid it looks too regal to do so.' Forster agreed: see his revised version in *Memoir*, i. 386.

[1] See below, pp. 125–6.

BENEDICT LAWRENCE CHAPMAN
to EMILY SELLWOOD TENNYSON (extract)

MS. Yale.

3 STONE BUILDINGS, LINCOLN'S INN, Tuesday, [7 August 1855]

My dear Mrs. Tennyson

It will be [but] civil to acknowledge your two notes, though I have nothing to say that Moxon will not have said better than I can say it. It was quite right to have the Newspaper version—or as near as may be. We were very much afraid that the 'blundered' would have been omitted in your copy. Moxon called on me today on the way to the printers. He seemed quite to go with the spirit of the thing and take it up quite hearty—would see that everything is done by Thursday. He is to send it to the SPG, and the SPG would send it on—why not 2000 says the sanguine and sanguinary Moxon? It is very kind of you and Mr. A. T. to take so much trouble about these low fellows.

To JOHN FORSTER

MS. Tennyson Research Centre.

[8 August 1855]

My dear Forster

Moxon reports that you are out but I suppose the duties of your Examinership have recalled you to town before this. I write to tell you that I think the letter should not go along with the Poem: let that be despatched by itself.

In case the letter be already printed on the same slip[1] as the Poem then of course it had better go as time I think would be lost in rearranging the printed form; and my desire is that the soldiers should have it as soon as possible.

I enclose you a letter received this morning.[2] Anonymous, as you see, but if

---

[1] Thus it was, and thus it went.

[2] 'One of his never ended stories was about an anonymous letter running thus (received since *Maud* came out)—"Sir, I used to worship you, but now I hate you. I loathe and detest you. You beast! So you've taken to imitating Longfellow. Yours in aversion, ———" and no name, says Alfred, scoring the table with an indignant thumb, and glaring round with suspended pipe, while his auditors look as sympathising as their view of the matter permits. He has an irreconcilable grudge against a poor moke of a fellow called Archer Gurney, who he swears must be the author of the letter, having treated him before to titbits something in the same taste.' (Rossetti to William Allingham, 25 November 1855, describing an evening with the Brownings on 27 September (see below, p. 128, printed in *Letters of Dante Gabriel Rossetti*, ed. Oswald Doughty and John Robert Wahl, i. 282.

Archer Thompson Gurney (1820–87: *DNB*), though called to the bar in 1846, became, rather, a theologian and a poet. From 1851 to 1854 he was at St. Mary's, Crown Street, Soho, and then moved to the senior curacy at Buckingham (*DNB*). He was a fervent, even excessive, admirer of Grillparzer, some of whose works he translated (*CBEL*, iii. 32), or adapted (*Turandot, Princess of China*). He also wrote *Love's Legends* (poems, 1845), *King Charles the First* (a dramatic poem, 1846), *Poems, Spring* (1853), *A Satire for the Age, The Transcendentalists* (1853; 2nd edn., 1855: see below, Appendix II), and some theological works. He was on friendly terms with Arnold, Browning, Kingsley, and Maurice, among others. Augustus Gurney wrote an 'extensive apologia' of his brother, now owned by his grandson, parts of which have been communicated to us by Gerald Gurney, whose generosity we gratefully acknowledge. See below, pp. 124, 127, 137–8.

I subscribed Archer Gurney at the foot of it I believe I should be right. I wonder at him. How can men and clergymen reconcile themselves to the doing such mean things. A year or two back he wrote me a letter telling me I ought to speak out publicly and tell the world he was a poet. The letter was too full of insult for me to answer it: altogether he seems to me the most unmagnanimous literary man I have ever known—if you know him and see him you may tell him that I am amazed at him.

Ever yours, my dear F.
A. Tennyson

To ROBERT STEPHEN HAWKER

MS. Exeter City Library.

FARRINGFORD, FRESHWATER, ISLE OF WIGHT, August 8, 1855

Dear Mr. Hawker

I send you a copy of Maud with my autograph as requested: I ought to have sent one to you without being requested; but you must forgive me.

I found in moving my books before I left my last domicile those two Lectures which you once lent me; and if you still want them I will send them to you.[1] Believe me

Yours very truly
A. Tennyson

To EDWARD MOXON

MS. Richard Garnett.

August 8, 1855

My dear Moxon

Chapman reports that you said 'why not 2000 slips?' another 1000 or more let be sent afterwards if the Secretary thinks they are wanted: they might be sent now if the printing another 1000 did not delay the sending of the first; but I am anxious that the soldiers should have it at once.

I have sent a copy of Maud to Mr. Hawker as requested. You may send a few slips down here.

Ever yours
A. Tennyson

Thanks for the Bennett verses.[1]

---

[1] See i. 304.
[1] See below, p. 129.

EMILY SELLWOOD TENNYSON to JOHN FORSTER

MS. Tennyson Research Centre.

FARRINGFORD, August 9, [1855]

Dear Mr. Forster

Thank you very heartily for your kindness in looking after Alfred's affairs when you had scarcely time enough for your own. He wrote yesterday to Moxon saying another 1000 copies might be printed or more even. I am glad you have not sent the letter.

September will, as far as we foresee, be perfectly convenient to us and we hope nothing will rob us of the pleasure of seeing you then. I know how precious your time is so I will only add Alfred's love and our best thanks.

Very sincerely yours
Emily Tennyson

We suppose Mr. Spedding has left London.

To GERALD MASSEY

MS. Johns Hopkins.

11 August 1855

Dear Mr. Massey

Many thanks for the Critique in the Edinburgh paper which I suppose you sent me.[1] You have done wisely in not attempting, as most other of the periodical writers have done, a full explanation of the poem. Men should read and ponder over a work before they judge it: to prejudge it is ten to one to misjudge it.

I trust that you got a copy of a Maud which I sent you, inscribed.[2] I believe you are quite right as to the conclusion of the Charge. I send you a copy of that version of it which I have just transmitted to the Crimea. The Secretary of the Society for the Propagation of the Gospel out there told a friend of mine that the ballad had in some strange way taken the fancy of the soldiers: that half of them were singing it but that they only knew it in fragments and that *all* of them wanted it in black and white. The chaplain of the Society wrote to the Society. '*You can do no greater service* just now than to send out copies of the Charge on slips for the army to sing.' Who could resist such an appeal? This is the soldier's version and I dare say they are the best critics.

I trust my dear sir that you are by this time somewhat reconciled to the loss of your child. Believe me,

Yours most truly
A. Tennyson

---

[1] *Edinburgh News and Literary Chronicle*, 28 July, p. 7 (anonymous); reprinted (signed) in the *Dundee, Perth, and Cupar Advertiser*, 31 July, p. 2: the first review of *Maud*.

[2] 'One of the accompanying copies of Maud is for Mr. Gerald Massey, who has requested me to forward it to you for Mr. Tennyson's autograph' (Moxon to Emily Tennyson, [25 July 1855]) (TRC).

GEORGE GRANVILLE BRADLEY[1]
to WILLIAM B. PHILPOT (extract)

Text. Edith Nicholl Ellison, *A Child's Recollections of Tennyson* (New York: E. P. Dutton, 1906), pp. 12–14.

[THE WARREN, IW] [c. 12 August 1855]

... I've seen a good deal of Tennyson. I made bold to call: found him at dinner: so left my card with a line of apology and an appeal to the name of Franklin Lushington. A genial note next day, and an invite to meet Lear, the artist. Two days after another dinner—five o'clock, with long evenings—and since then sundry talks, culminating in a whole day yesterday spent tête-à-tête with him, except just at dinner, etc. We walked early to see the Wealden strata five miles off, and spent all the day walking and sitting. I found I could talk to him as to an old friend on all subjects, high and low, and I believe that even if he had never written a line I should think him one of the finest of the *genus humanum*.

I wish I could see you, my dear fellow, to talk it all over. He explained to me sundry *cruces* in 'Maud,' and read or chanted me a good deal of it. Don't you form an opinion about it until you've read it over and over. We talked a great deal on religious questions. A grand fellow, sir! I implored him to come to Rugby, but that is not likely. However, please God, we return here next year, and for a longer time. His house is two miles off, and he walked back with me towards midnight, so I am still under the spell of a great man.

I've read right through the Odyssey here: but not much else, except Jowett's Essays and some geology—you see how it has entered into the Tennysonian brain. . . . The last three nights I've excited myself talking to the poet over much—but I've had little enough of that in this place. . . .

---

[1] George Granville Bradley (1821–1903: *DNB*) first met Tennyson in 1841 or 1842, while still an undergraduate (see i. 193 n.), but 'the beginning of our acquaintance with this good and affectionate friend' (*Journal*, p. 49) dated from early August 1855, when Bradley, on holiday, called on Tennyson at Farringford. As a master at Rugby (1845–58) he helped to 'save the school from disaster' (*DNB*), and he performed a similar service at Marlborough (of which he became headmaster in 1858), where Tennyson sent his elder son in 1866 ('I am not sending my son to Marlborough—I am sending him to Bradley'). In 1870 he became Master of University College, Oxford, which he also reformed, and in 1881 succeeded A. P. Stanley as Dean of Westminster and there, once more ('Stanley was no man of business'—*DNB*), exercised his genius in combining organization, administration, restoration, and even (having taken orders in 1858) salvation.

On 6 August, the forty-sixth birthday of Tennyson and the third of Edith Bradley, four Tennysons (with nurse) came upon the Bradleys picnicking, and this meeting apparently cemented the friendship, for Emily Tennyson and Marian Bradley (née Philpot) also became fast friends. See *Memoir*, i. 467–8; *Tennyson and His Friends*, pp. 175–85; and Edith Nicholl [Bradley] Ellison, *A Child's Recollections of Tennyson*, pp. 1–10, all three based on Marian Bradley's 'Diaries', British Library.

Bradley and Tennyson must have been a conspicuous pair. Tennyson was tall, Bradley short, as the Ape and Spy cartoons in *Vanity Fair* (22 July 1871, 29 September 1888) and numerous references reveal. Bradley was 'vivacious, curt, plain-spoken, ubiquitous, restlessly energetic', and, in addition, 'sunny, sensible, and wide-awake' (Reginald Farrar, *The Life of Frederic William Farrar*, pp. 160, 180).

To LEWIS FYTCHE

MS. Tennyson Research Centre.

[August 13, 1855]

Dearest Lewis

I have received your letter of the fourth and am glad that you are able to give so fair an account of your poor Mother. 'To bow like the willow before the storm'[1] is far better than to break like the oak as strong and powerful men sometimes do under great and sudden loss. I trust that as days and years go on, all this suffering will be mellowed more and more to her and to all of you.

There is another sorrow come to me lately: a very dear friend of mine, Cissy's brother-in-law, Henry Lushington, a man of great intellect and genius, is now either dying or dead at Paris and all the Lushingtons are in the greatest affliction. A sister died last year[2]—two losses coming in one house so closely together, as in your own, are hard to bear: 'God tempers the wind to the shorn lamb' is a pretty adage:[3] I hope that it may apply sooner or later both to your case and theirs. Believe me,

Affectionately yours
A. Tennyson

ALFRED AND EMILY SELLWOOD TENNYSON *to* EDMUND LAW LUSHINGTON

MS. Betty N. Lushington.

FARRINGFORD, August 14, [1855]

My dear Edmund

There is indeed no need to ask for our sympathy, it must come unbidden. Little did we, who were looking to his remaining in England and hoping for that more intimate communion of past years which had in a measure been broken by his residence in Malta, little did we think how it would be and now one of the thoughts which is uppermost is, why did we not make more of our opportunities while we had them. For you Edmund who have lost the brother and companion from infancy what comfort is left but the memory of the unbroken unsullied love of your lives, now, we humbly hope sealed for eternity. When you can write we shall be very grateful for news of you all. God bless you.

Your loving sister
Emily Tennyson

Dear Edmund, take this as from me too: to me too it is an unspeakable loss and if Edward Lear's letters had not prepared us for the event would have been still harder to be borne: but he has been very kind in giving us almost daily bulletins, so that the shock was in a great measure broken. The after-grief is what I fear for most in the case of all of you; particularly poor Ellen:

---

[1] Unidentified. [2] Louisa Sophia Lushington.
[3] Proverbial, of course, and originally French, but in this form from Sterne's *A Sentimental Journey*.

but you must not be conquered by it nor let her (if by any means you can hinder it) be conquered.

Ever your affectionate brother
A: Tennyson

To GEORGE GRANVILLE BRADLEY

Text. Memoir, i. 410.

FARRINGFORD, August 25, 1855

Dear Mr. Bradley

Many thanks for the Arnold:[1] nobody can deny that he is a poet. 'The Merman' was an old favourite of mine, and I like him as well as ever. 'The Scholar Gipsy' is quite new to me, and I have already an affection for him, which I think will increase. There are several others which seem very good, so that altogether I may say that you have conferred a great boon upon me. I have received a Scotch paper, in which it is stated that poor 'Maud' is to be slashed all to pieces by that mighty man, that pompholygous, broad-blown Apollodorus, the gifted X.[2] Her best friends do not expect her to survive it! I am

Yours very truly
A. Tennyson

To JOHN ALFRED LANGFORD[1]

MS. Historical Society of Pennsylvania.

FRESHWATER, ISLE OF WIGHT, Monday, August 26 [for 27], 1855

Dear Sir

I am much obliged to you for sending me your critique on my Poem; and happy to find that you approve of it and unlike most of the critics (so called) have taken some pains to look into it and see what it means. There has been from many quarters a torrent of abuse against it; and I have even had insulting anonymous letters: indeed I am quite at a loss to account for the bitterness of feeling which this poor little work of mine has excited. Yesterday

---

[1] *Poems*, Second Series (1855). Arnold and Bradley (both of whom entered Rugby in August 1847) were old friends.

[2] The meaning of the invective (cited in *OED*) is not altogether clear: 'broad-blown' (*Maud*, I. 450) must mean plump; 'pompholygous'—which could refer to slag, blisters (erysipelas), or bubbles ('puffed up')—apparently means self-important; 'Apollodorus' in this context remains enigmatic. See Appendix B.

[1] This letter was published (surprisingly) in Henry J. Jennings, *Lord Tennyson, A Biographical Sketch* (1884), pp. 163–4.

John Alfred Langford (1823–1903: *DNB*), antiquary and journalist, whose highly favourable critique of *Maud* (not before identified) in the *Birmingham Daily Press* (3 August, p. 4) is almost Tennysonian in some of its resonance and cadences: 'Out of personal sorrow and grief rises a nobler and finer life—unselfish, corporate, and grand. . . . National love, national life, and national duties, these are what a man must turn to who wishes to build up, amid the wreck of youthful passion and of fallen hopes, a true, a noble, and a glorious life.'

with your kind letter came also the notice in the Times by the Rev. Robert Aris Wilmott (I believe).[2] I suppose you have seen it; to make any comment on it whatsoever were waste of ink. Thanking you again, believe me, dear Sir,
Yours truly
A. Tennyson

To EMILY SELLWOOD TENNYSON
Text. Memoir, i. 389.

August 31, [1855]

Haven't the heart to get further than Winchester and Salisbury. I am going to-day to take a gig across country to Lyndhurst.[1]

To EMILY SELLWOOD TENNYSON
MS. Tennyson Research Centre.

CROWN HOTEL, LYNDHURST, Friday night, 8.30 o'clock, [31 August 1855]

Though I have lost my umbrella today in the Forest and my tobacco-case (which Simeon gave me), lost them at two separate sessions, twice sitting down to read a novel which I carried in my pocket to lighten the way (and indeed one of Bulwer's (and that indeed on the recommendation of Sir John Herschel[1] who is reported to have said that everyone should read it)—whose novels since he fell foul of me in the New Timon had I not sworn never to read again?[2] (what a long clause!)—though I had these two losses, though I had said that the New Forest (for didn't I expect that it was *dis*forested) would not do again—though when I started this morning, I got on a wrong track for four miles, or so, out of the way of the great timber—yet at last I struck in among the great timber—the vast solemn beeches—and my soul

---

[2] Robert Aris Willmott (1809–63: *DNB*) was a prolific reviewer and compiler of anthologies (BA Trinity College, Cambridge, 1841; ordained priest 1843). *The Times* had been unenthusiastic about *The Princess* and *In Memoriam*, and Tennyson perhaps suspected Willmott because of his association with John Walter (1776–1847: *DNB*), proprietor of *The Times* (who had built St. Catherine's Church, Bearwood, Berks., and appointed Willmott first incumbent), as well as with the third John Walter (1818–94), who succeeded his father as proprietor. See below, p. 127, and *Tennyson in Lincoln*, i, Nos. 2351, 2613.

The reviewer was in fact Eneas Sweetland Dallas (1828–79: *DNB*), a Scot, who had just joined *The Times* staff (see *The History of the Times*, ii. 471, 482), and no doubt wanted to make his presence felt. Later, Dallas edited *Once a Week* and wrote two notable books, *The Gay Science* (1866: see J. H. Buckley, *The Victorian Temper*, ch. 8) and, more important, *Kettner's Book of the Table, A Manual of Cookery* (1877).

[1] See above, p. 118.

[1] John Frederick William Herschel (1792–1871; created baronet 1838), the astronomer, no doubt met Tennyson through the Camerons. See Colin Ford, *The Cameron Collection, An Album of Photographs by Julia Margaret Cameron Presented to Sir John Herschel* (1975).

[2] See i. 251 and n.

was not *satisfied*, for I did not meet with any so very large beech as I had met with before—but I, the man, I, myself, rejoiced, in spite of past I's, in the beeches and have resolved to stay till Monday and see them twice again. Wherefore do you (if you can) on Monday meet me in a Plumley fly, for I shall come by the five o'clock boat from Lymington on Monday.

Thine always
A. T.

I am grieved to lose the tobacco-case but it was so like the colour of last year's beech leaves that I did not see it as I turned to leave the spot where I had smoked.

I may (in spite of what I have written) come tomorrow: then I should come before this letter:* and I am a fool for suggesting that I shall come tomorrow! never mind!

*I believe so at least—may be wrong.

I had gathered a lovely bit of forget-me-not to send to you in a letter— gathered it by the side of that lovely clear river that runs from Winchester— and put it in my waistcoat pocket—it is gone! What beautiful water that Itchen is!

This is very blotty. Inn-ink, inn pens, haste, I writing obliquely, on sofa, recumbently, with half-palsied elbow.

Mind, meet me (if you can) Monday evening, in time for the arrival of the five o'clock packet. *Don't* have dinner for me! for what can I do at Lymington but dine?

To EMILY SELLWOOD TENNYSON

MS. Tennyson Research Centre.

CROWN HOTEL, LYNDHURST, [1 September 1855]

I lost my way in the Forest today and have walked I don't know how many miles. I found a way back to Lyndhurst by *resolutely* following a track which brought me at last to a turnpike: on this I went a mile in the wrong direction i.e. to Christchurch, then met a surly fellow who grudgingly told me I was 4 miles from Lyndhurst whereupon I turned and walked to Lyndhurst. My admiration of the forest is great. It (the forest) is true old wild English Nature—and then the fresh heath-sweetened air is so delicious. The Forest is grand. Monday evening, please send or meet

Thine ever
A.

P. S. I think it will be better to dine with thee after all and to w[h]ile away my two hours at Lymington as I may—so have dinner ready—at 6 ½ or thereabouts.

To ROBERT JAMES MANN

Text. Materials, ii. 136–7.

[September 1855]

My dear Sir

I am glad that you like poor 'Maud', she has been beaten as black and blue by the penny-a-liners as the 'trampled wife' by the drunken ruffian in the opening poem.[1] I always calculated on a certain quantity of anonymous insolence but I have had more than my share this time and it goes on still. I one day got an anonymous letter, such a thing, signed pleasantly, 'Yours in aversion, a former admirer.'[2] The best notices I have seen are first that in the *Examiner* (but then that I expected). My friend Forster would speak justly and honestly about it; the next are in two Edinburgh papers *The Daily Express* and another,[3] I forget the name, and last comes your letter, so that poor 'Maud' begins to believe that if she can by any means get clear of the political *mob* and general calcitration she may yet have a chance for her life.

A. T.

To ROBERT JAMES MANN

Text. draft *Materials*, iv. 74.

[September 1855]

My dear Sir

The prestige of Shakespeare is great: else Hamlet (if it came out now) would be treated in just the same way, so that one ought not to care for their cackling—not that I am comparing poor little Maud to the Prince except as—what's the old quotation out of Virgil? sic parvis componere.[1] Would it not be better that all literary criticisms should be signed with the name or at least the initials of the writer. Then such a foolish spiteful article as that in the Times being subscribed R. A. W. would point it out as the work of a certain clergyman living in the same village as one of the editors and it would be to the world just the opinion of this chuckling little Mr. [Willmott] for without the backing of the Times the article would never have been written in that fashion.[2] To sign political articles would be perhaps unadvisable and inconvenient, but my opinion is that we never shall have a good school of criticism in England while the writer is anonymous and irresponsible. Your account of our friend is interesting and likewise the jotting down of the lady's remarks. What shall I say touching the kind offer of the telescope? No doubt I should like to have it, but my great fear is that it might be damaged either here or in the transit hither; and that thought chills my desire; so I think that I will decide not to have it but to come on to you at Ventnor. Thank you all the same as the phrase is, and believe me,

A. T.

---

[1] '*Maud*', I. 37–8.   [2] See *Memoir*, i. 400 n., and below, p. 137).
[3] *Daily Express*, 1 August, p. 4, and Massey's review (see above, p. 121).

[1] [. . . magna solebam]: 'Thus used I to compare great things with small' (*Eclogues*, i. 23).
[2] See above, p. ooo and n.

To JEAN BAPTISTE FRANÇOIS ERNEST, CHEVALIER DE CHATELAIN[1]

Text. Materials, ii. 110.

[c. 20 September 1855]

Sir

I beg you will accept my thanks for the *Fables Nouvelles*, which you have sent me and for the copies of 'Mariana' and 'Sonnez Cloches Sonnez,' which you have done me the honour to translate. I am, Sir,

Your obedient servant
A. Tennyson

To EMILY SELLWOOD TENNYSON

MS. Tennyson Research Centre.

Thursday, September 27, [1855]

Dearest

I dined yesteday with the Brownings and had a very pleasant evening—both of them are great admirers of poor little Maud—made very kind enquiries after thee.[1] Frederic and his wife are still at 16 Regent's Villas,

---

[1] Chevalier de Chatelain (1801–81: *DNB*), journalist, translator, and republican, was naturalized a British subject in 1848. For his *Fables Nouvelles, suivies de poésies diverses*, inscribed, see *Tennyson in Lincoln*, i, No. 743. See also *Memoir*, i. 385, and below, p. 195. (The manuscript of 'Sonnez, Cloches, Sonnez' is in TRC.)

[1] 'It was on 27 September 1855 that the Brownings, being then for a while in London, invited two or three friends to the house they were occupying, 13 Dorset Street, to meet Tennyson, who had undertaken to read aloud his poem of *Maud*, recently published. The audience was a small one . . .: Mr. and Mrs. Browning, Miss Browning, my brother [D. G. Rossetti], and myself, and I think there was one more—either Madox Brown, or else Hunt or Woolner. . . . Tennyson seated on a sofa in a characteristic attitude, and holding the volume near his eyes . . . read *Maud* right through. My brother made two pen-and-ink sketches of him, and gave one of them to Browning. So far as I remember, the Poet Laureate neither saw what Dante was doing, nor knew of it afterwards. His deep grand voice, with slightly chanting intonation, was a noble vehicle for the perusal of mighty verse. On it rolled, sonorous and emotional. Rossetti, according to Mr. Hall Caine, spoke of the incident in these terms: "I once heard Tennyson read *Maud*; and, whilst the fiery passages were delivered with a voice and vehemence which he alone of living men can compass, the softer passages and the songs made the tears course down his cheeks"' (*Dante Gabriel Rossetti, His Family-Letters with a Memoir*, ed. W. M. Rossetti, i. 190–1). Rossetti gave the original sketch, of which he made two copies, to Browning. See Virginia Surtees, *The Paintings and Drawings of Dante Gabriel Rossetti, A Catalogue Raisonné*, i. 198–9.
'I was never more amused in my life than by Tennyson's groanings and horrors over the reviews of *Maud*, which poem he read through to us, spouting also several sections to be introduced in a new edition. I made a sketch of him reading, which I gave to Browning, and afterwards duplicated for Miss S[iddall]. His conversation was really one perpetual groan, and I am sure, during two long evenings I spent in his company, he repeated the same stories about anonymous letters he gets, etc.—at the very least six or eight times in my hearing, besides an odd time or two as I afterwards found, that he told them over to members of the company in private. He also repeated them to me again, walking home together' (Rossetti to Allingham, 25 November 1855, in *Letters of Dante Gabriel Rossetti*, ed. Doughty and Wahl, i. 281–2. See above, p. 119 n.

Avenue Road, Regents Park (the Ormes[2] still) and means to be there till he goes from London to us: but I have not seen him. The two Ros[s]ettis came in in the evening. Edmund is coming up today to carry me off to Park House, but I cannot go. I shall be back I suppose on Monday. The watch is come.
                                       Thine ever
                                         A.T.

I have got both thine. The book is [?] tops. Barrett[3] wants the Welds' Paris direction. Send it him if thou knowest it.

To EMILY SELLWOOD TENNYSON

Text. Memoir, i. 390.

October 1, [1855]

I dined at Twickenham, my mother looking very well and intending to keep the house on another year. I also dined with the Camerons last night, she is more wonderful than ever I think in her wild-beaming benevolence. I read 'Maud' to five or six people at the Brownings.

To WILLIAM COX BENNETT[1]

MS. McGill.

FARRINGFORD, FRESHWATER, I. W., October 4, 1855

Dear Sir

I was in London two days ago and received from Moxon your volume of warsongs.[2] Your letter is dated July I am sorry to see. I ought while I thank you for these to thank you too for a generous little poem on my poem of Maud—which Moxon sent me. I am, dear Sir,
                                       Yours truly
                                       A. Tennyson

EMILY SELLWOOD TENNYSON
to GEORGE STOVIN VENABLES

MS. National Library of Wales.

FARRINGFORD, October 5, [1855]

Blame you, dear Mr. Venables, No, trust me, I owe you real gratitude for

---

[2] Charles E. Orme (*P.O. London Directory*), probably a Lincolnshire connection (headmaster at Louth School in 1800 was a Mr Orme). For Frederick Tennyson's wife, Maria Giuliotti (d. 1884), see above, p. 54 n.

[3] Henry John Barrett, the dental surgeon.

[1] William Cox Bennett (1820–95: *DNB*), writer and poet.

[2] *War Songs* (1855). Bennett's poem on 'Maud' is mentioned above, p. 120.

speaking out to me if ever so little of what is in your heart.[1] I only wish there were the smallest chance of my being able to comfort you in any way. I had thought of writing to you before your note come this morning. Because I had heard from Maria[2] and I felt you would like me to tell you what she says about your being away from them though you, of course, know it all in substance. Yet for my own part I can never hear too often what I love to hear and so I judge you so far by myself when I quote Maria's letter. 'Mr. Venables is in Wales. We feel a great blank without him, the great gulf between the present and the past hardly seems to impassable while he is here and he helps everybody to bear the burthen which is so peculiarly heavy for himself'.

Then there is a word wiped out which makes part of the next sentence obscure as it stands though one can easily supply that which renders it quite clear, then it continues, 'though he gives us all the comfort he can in his letter. There is no one with whom we have so much in common now.'

She tells me Emily's attendance on Eddy,[3] though unremitting, is not so laborious as it was. Frank speaks on the whole cheerfully about her and Maria when compared with his tone when he mentions Ellen. We hope to see him here in the course of a few days and we will not give up the hope of welcoming you to our home again before very long. I would believe your inexorable loss has left you a fresh bond to Alfred in your memory of the past. At all events I am sure you are right in your resolution not to shut yourself up in yourself however hard it may be to do otherwise.

Thanks many for those precious assurances of the love and admiration of him so highly prized and dearly loved. I suppose we all must have our jealousies where there is much love and much separation also and yet not no not all—but of late[4] we sometimes thought he did not care for him as he used but what you say and what Maria says quite removes any such painful thought. That In Memoriam should have been a comfort to even one so noble and loving and self-devoting is enough I do think.

Alfred's tooth is cured thank you. Hallam and Lionel quite well. Thanks for your kind remembrance of them. I have no time to add more as the post is going.

Very sincerely yours
Emily Tennyson

---

[1] Venables's letter (TRC) of 2 October spoke of his relationship with Henry Lushington, confessing that he had been 'in some degree jealous and dissatisfied with a feeling less warm' than his own and that he did not 'think that any other man [besides Tennyson] exercised so strong an attachment' upon Lushington. He added: 'I am sure you will not blame me for dwelling on myself to you and on him'.

[2] Maria Lushington.

[3] Edmund Henry Lushington (1843–56), son of Cecilia and Edmund Law Lushington.

[4] 'and yet . . . of late' added above the line.

early October 1855

To CHARLES RICHARD WELD

MS. Tennyson Research Centre.

FARRINGFORD, FRESHWATER, [early] October 1855

My dear Weld

Many thanks for the Asylum review[1] for which believe me not the less grateful because it had been forwarded to me some two or three days previously. The testimony borne by the Doctor to the truth of the delineation is more valuable to me than that of the mere literary critic. Indeed the last seems I think from all I have read (with the exception of one Scotch paper[2] and the British Quarterly) to have set himself foolishly and stupidly enough against it. I can wait; I have generally almost (always when I published, I believe) had to run the gauntlet of much stupidity and some spite; and this time there has been rather more of both than usual. I have been thrice be-Wilmotted[3] in the Times, yet I survive. You do not say whether the Edinburgh proofs were favourable;[4] and by your silence I suppose not: can't help it: meantime it sells.

I will look up the Breton Ballads for you and send them:[5] some time let me have them again. I do not know whether they are a gift or a loan to me. I grieve to hear that you have not yet recovered from your fall. Is the Greek book you mention a new edition of the Arundines Cami or something in Romaic.[6]

Ever yours
A. Tennyson

To ROBERT JAMES MANN

Text. draft *Materials,* iv. 74.

October 9, 1855

My dear Sir

I have just returned from town and found your letter here. Many thanks,

---

[1] In the *Asylum Journal of Mental Science,* ii (Oct. 1855), 95–104, by John Charles Bucknill (1817–97: *DNB*; knighted, 1894), who reviewed *Maud* not as literature but as a case history and vouched for the accuracy of the mental pathology of the protagonist. Bucknill was editor of the *Asylum Journal* (afterwards, *Journal of Mental Science*), head of the Devon County Lunatic Asylum, and later, along with Tennyson, an FRS and a member of the Metaphysical Society.

[2] See above, p. 127; *British Quarterly Review,* xxii (Oct. 1855), 467–98.

[3] See above, p. 125.

[4] Proofs of the anonymous critique of *In Memoriam* and *Maud, and Other Poems* in the *Edinburgh Review,* cii (Oct. 1855), 498–519. The authorship of Coventry Patmore was first revealed by Frederick Page in his collection of Patmore's uncollected articles, *Courage in Politics and Other Essays* (1921), p. 205. Patmore questioned the popular dictum—to which *Maud* seemed a response—that a great poet must reflect the age, complained of the 'fever of politics' in the poem, and objected to the 'war passages'. It is tempting to speculate that Tennyson's belated discovery of the authorship of this critique was the reason, or part of the reason, for the inexplicable rift in their friendship. See below, p. 312–13.

[5] See above, p. 90 and n.

[6] *Arundines Cami, siue, Musarum Cantabrigiensium Lusus Canori,* ed. Henry Drury, Cambridge, 1841: 'A collection of translations into Latin and Greek verse by different Cambridge men', in six editions 1841–65 (*National Union Catalogue*; *DNB,* s.v. 'Drury').

but it is a loan that I shall accept with fear and trembling.[1] It appears that my landlord here, Mr. Seymour,[2] had a large telescope and the gardener, who still remains here, says he knows how to put a telescope together and take it to pieces. Still I should be sorry to trust him with it. I am curious to hear your 'plan' touching Maud.[3] I seem to have the Doctors on my side if no one else. I have just received an article by a madhouse Doctor giving his testimony as to the truth to nature in the delineation of the hero's madness. Valuable testimony it seems to me.

A. T.

ALFRED AND EMILY SELLWOOD TENNYSON
to FREDERICK GODDARD TUCKERMAN

MS. Harvard.

FARRINGFORD, October 17, 1855

My dear Sir

I cannot refrain from telling you how much your poet's review of my husband has rejoiced my heart.[1] The freshness of nature breathed into your words from your virgin forests and untrodden Savannahs fits you better for bearing the stern voice of truth in hand, gives you more vigour to wrestle with her great if morbid lover than can be gathered from our ordered parks and cultivated fields or our crowded cities and dingy factories save by the very few who wax in every limb under all circumstances. But are even all these poets? I think not but Christians they must be if not. Well, after all you know I do not wish to disparage England, you know I am English and very English. I have not the remotest sympathy with those who talk of the decrepitude of age, of dotage when they speak of England. The worst I say of her is that she has lost her Arab sensitiveness[2] for the purest spring.

I enclose you the soldier's copy of 'The Charge'. I think you will like to hear two thousand of it have been printed for my husband and sent out by

---

[1] Probably not *Much Ado about Nothing*, II. iii. 203, or *2 Henry IV*, IV. iii. 15–16, or even Psalm 55:5.

[2] See above, p. 72 and n.

[3] The plan resulted in Mann's pamphlet *Tennyson's 'Maud' Vindicated: An Explanatory Essay* (London, 1856). See below, p. 145.

[1] Not hitherto identified, but pretty certainly the review in *Putnam's Monthly Magazine*, vi (October 1855), 382–92, which dealt primarily with *Maud* and 'The Charge of the Light Brigade', but touched on many of the earlier poems. (A brief notice in September, p. 318, which said that 'The Charge' had 'been changed' and 'not for the better', and promised a 'detailed consideration' of Tennyson's poetry in the next number was also presumably by Tuckerman.)

The Tennysons' letter seems to reply to one from Tuckerman to Tennyson (in draft *Materials and Materials*, ii. 152–3), dated 22 October 1855, from the Clarendon Hotel, New York, apparently enclosing the review and beginning: 'I remember once saying to you that I was no poet. The remark perhaps should have been that in your presence I dared not claim such a title, for it seems to me that only poets can fully appreciate and enjoy "the singular beauty of Maud".' It seems to us (since only editors can fully appreciate and enjoy the impossibility of this date) that it was mistranscribed from *2* October. (In Eidson, *Tennyson in America*, p. 246, the original, still untraced, is incorrectly said to be at Harvard.)

[2] Apparently an allusion to 'Maud', I. 551: 'the delicate Arab arch of her feet'.

him to our Army in the East because the senior chaplain wrote that half the men were singing it and all wished to possess what they so much admired. We often think and speak of you and we hope the time is not far distant when we may also speak to you.

Hallam has grown a big brown boy. Lionel runs alone and some people admire him more than Hallam. I hope you and yours are well and happy. You have from time to time given us such kind proof of your rem[em]brance that I need not also add I hope you sometimes think of us. Believe me, my dear Sir,

Very truly yours
Emily Tennyson

My father, if all be well is at this time a guest at Hackthorne.[3]

Dear Mr. Tuckerman
Many thanks for your critique of Maud. She has been very roughly treated on this side of the water. I sent you out an early copy which I should like much to know whether you received and the accompanying letter. Some other day I will write more fully to you. Believe me now,

Ever yours
A. Tennyson

You are right about the Charge. I was overpersuaded to spoil it.

To WILLIAM DAVIS TICKNOR

MS. Harvard.

FRESHWATER, ISLE OF WIGHT, October 24, 1855

Dear Mr. Ticknor
I have this morning received your draft for £30 for which I request yourself and Mr. Fields to accept my thanks.[1] The English Press has (as you remark) being [*sic*] stupid enough: but I have, as far as I know, always been attacked in a similar fashion whenever I put forth a fresh publication: this time the assault has been a little ruder than usual. As it is a new form of Poem altogether, the critic not being able to make it out, went at it: why not? he is anonymous: his credit would not suffer from a bad criticism; nor I suppose did mine. Believe me,

Yours very truly
A. Tennyson

---

[3] In Lincolnshire, where he was presumably visiting his deceased wife's sister and her husband, the Thomas Cracrofts, or Cracroft's older brother, Col. Robert Cracroft-Amcotts (1783–1862). See i. 310.

[1] Ticknor and Fields (as Ticknor's firm had become in 1854), who had received advance proof-sheets of *Maud, and Other Poems*, published its edition on 15 August, and by this date had issued 7,400 copies (Eidson, *Tennyson in America*, pp. 128–9, 245).

To WILLIAM JOHNSON FOX[1]

MS. Harvard.

FARRINGFORD, October 25, 1855

Dear Sir

Your friend has my full permission to publish her music with my words. She can put likewise to the Charge 'by permission' if she will.[2] Indeed I have never yet that I know refused a request of this kind. Believe me, dear Sir,

Yours very truly
A. Tennyson

The Charge I was overpersuaded to spoil. I send you a copy of that which I sent to the Crimean army at the soldiers' own request.

To CHARLES RICHARD WELD

MS. Robert Taylor.

FARRINGFORD, November 21, 1855.

My dear Weld

I was grieved that I had no books to refer to here whereby I might have enlightened you as to Teutates. Now you quote it, I remember that half-line in Lucan.[1] I do not believe in his being Mercury any more than I believe that Woden and Thor are Mars and Jupiter but in the old unlearned days when men thought themselves most learned and knew but little Latin and less Greek they used to confuse and transubstantiate the Classic and Barbaric Divinities at pleasure.

That is very singular, your account of Notre Dame de la Haine[2]—how many unconsciously or half consciously worship in her Temple still.

I received the other day a most flattering letter from Ruskin, touching poor little Maud.[3] I am glad that you too find something in her. It is a poem

---

[1] William Johnson Fox (1786–1864: *DNB*), preacher, politician, writer, editor and proprietor of the *Monthly Repository* (1831–77). See i. 220 n. He reviewed (anonymously) Tennyson's *Poems, Chiefly Lyrical*, in the *Westminster Review*, xiv (Jan. 1831).

[2] 'Half a league' (1855), by Mrs. W. H. Owen, listed in Brian N. S. Gooch and David S. Thatcher, *Musical Settings of Early and Mid-Victorian Literature, A Catalogue* (Garland Publishing Co., 1979), p. 520.

[1] *Pharsalia*, i. 455.

[2] 'Tennyson always took a great interest in Brittany, and after my father's tour there it formed a frequent topic of conversation. My uncle was somewhat startled to learn that there was a church in that part of France dedicated to Our Lady of Hatred' (Agnes Grace Weld, *Glimpses of Tennyson*, p. 33).

'It is a strange fact that Treguier, with its magnificent church and large ecclesiastical establishment, should possess a chapel dedicated to Notre Dame de la Haine. This stands on a bleak unlovely hill near the town. Superstitious peasants imagine that three *Aves* repeated with particular fervour in this building will infallibly cause the death of the hated being within a year; and to this day, when night darkens the scene, the malignant peasant skulks to the chapel and offers up prayers against the object of his hatred. This is truly a relic of paganism, and especially of the belief entertained by the ancient worshippers of Teutates that a prayer offered to that God was more powerful than the sword' (Weld, *A Vacation in Brittany* [1856], pp. 131–2).

[3] *Memoir*, i. 411.

written in an *entirely new form*, as far as I know. I think that properly to appreciate it you ought to hear the author read it, and this I say not in vanity, but that to give full effect to the long sweeps of metre, you must have a reader who not only reads somewhat dramatically, but likewise has a full voice and ample lungs.

If you write a book on Brittany I am sure that it will be, as all yours are, pleasant, picturesque and graceful. The subject is, to me at least, most captivating, but Heaven help you, if you intend to dive *deeply* into Celtic antiquities! You ought not, in that case, to be 'wasting clerk's blood' in the service of the Royal Society but to have all your time to yourself.

We are both happy in learning that dear little Agnes[4] is recovering.

You know that whenever you wish to shake off London smut you are welcome here: and if you see Forster pray tell him; I have been expecting him every Saturday since I left town: he *promised* to come and doesn't.

Ever yours
A. Tennyson

On Saturday I walked seven miles back from Sir John Simeon's hoping to find him arrived—so if you see him you may row him.

I see that my East Lincolnshire shares which I bought at 145 are again fallen to 128–132. Should I sell out do you think? Will they fall yet lower?[5] I take it the war will go on in spite of Cobden, Bright, and Co.[6]

To ?

Text. *T. P.'s Weekly*, ii (Oct. 1903), 570.

November 24, 1855

Dear Sir

I owe you many thanks for your kind letter. I have been of late half-deafened with the abuse of anonymous, therefore irresponsible, writers condemning what they do not or will not understand. All the more grateful to me is your affectionate greeting, proving, in despite of their vituperation, that words of mine have had power to speak here and there to suffering hearts. Believe me, my dear sir,

Yours truly
A. Tennyson

---

[4] Agnes Grace Weld.
[5] See above, p. 77.
[6] Richard Cobden (1804–65: *DNB*) and John Bright (1811–89: *DNB*) were the leaders of the peace party; 'and Co.' had included Gladstone since his great speech in the House on 3 August: 'His case against the Govt. going on with the war irresistible, and felt to be so' (*The Diaries of John Bright*, ed. R. A. J. Walling, p. 201). Tennyson denied that the 'broad-brimmed hawker of holy things' ('Maud', I. 370) referred to Bright (*Memoir*, i. 403.).

To GEORGE BRIMLEY[1]

Text. Memoir, i. 408–9.

FRESHWATER, I. W., November 28, 1855

Sir

I wish to assure you that I quite close with your commentary on 'Maud'.[2] I may have agreed with portions of other critiques on the same poem, which have been sent to me; but when I saw your notice I laid my finger upon it and said, 'There, that is my meaning.' Poor little 'Maud,' after having run the gauntlet of so much brainless abuse and anonymous spite, has found a critic. Therefore believe her father (not the gray old wolf)[3] to be

Yours not unthankfully
A. Tennyson

P. S. But there are two or three points in your comment to which I should take exception, e.g. 'The writer of the fragments, etc.,' surely the speaker or thinker rather than the writer;[4] again, as to the character of the love, do any of the expressions 'rapturous,' 'painful' [*for* fanciful], 'childish,' however they may apply to some of the poems, fully characterize the 18th?[5] is it not something deeper? but perhaps some day I may discuss these things with you, and therefore I will say no more here, except that I shall be very glad to see you if ever you come to the Isle of Wight.

---

[1] Ill health prevented George Brimley (1819–57: *DNB*), a scholar of Trinity College, Cambridge, 1841 (BA 1845), from competing for university honours or a fellowship; but his conspicuous ability led to his appointment as Librarian of the College (2 June 1845), a post that he held until shortly before his death. Brother-in-law of the publisher Alexander Macmillan, he contributed anonymously to the *Spectator* and *Fraser's Magazine* (Preface to *Essays by the Late George Brimley*, ed. William G. Clark, 1858; *DNB*). See below, p. 243.

[2] Brimley defended 'Maud' as a tragedy of character and the poet as free from the imputations of having the same personal attributes as his protagonist in 'Alfred Tennyson's Poems' (in *Cambridge Essays, Contributed by Members of the University*, [4 vols., 1855–8], i. 226–81; reprinted in Brimley's *Essays*, pp. 1–103)—a survey of the canon, showing that Tennyson's admirers had solid grounds for their 'faith' in him as 'a poet of large compass, of profound insight, of finished skill'. The commentary on 'Maud' is reprinted in *Tennyson: The Critical Heritage*, ed. J. D. Jump, pp. 191–6.

[3] The speaker, in his madness, uses the 'gray old wolf' as an image for Maud's father (II. 293).

[4] Brimley had written: 'It may be at once conceded that the writer of the fragments of a life which tell the story of *Maud*, is not in a comfortable state of mind when he begins his record; and that if a gentleman were to utter such sentiments at a board of railway directors, or at a marriage breakfast, he might not improperly be called hysterical.'

[5] In justification of Tennyson's intention, Brimley had written: 'We . . . are prepared that the love should be of a kind corresponding to the character [of the speaker],—rapturous, fanciful, childish, fitted more for a Southern woman like Juliet . . . than for an Englishman.' Lyric 18 became I, xviii. 599–683.

To ARCHER THOMPSON GURNEY

Text. Transcript by Augustus Gurney.

December 6, 1855

Dear Sir

I have this morning received your Ode.[1] Many thanks for what (though perhaps here and there I might suggest an alteration, as to inversions for instance which though made use of by poets of the highest name, are never pleasing to me), for what appears to me well executed, noble in sentiment and rolling in sound. Long ago I ought to have thanked you for much that was well done and to be admired in another volume of yours, but when it reached me I did not know who was the author—nor for long after, for I see no literary people here and scarce ever a review: and when I did learn, it seemed so ungracefully late to acknowledge it that I let it be, not to mention that my desire so to do was a little chilled by the recollection of a very angry letter you had written me years ago. And now let me take this occasion of writing to you to express my sorrow that anything like a tiff has past between us. I wrote to you a little curt note (as I generally to friends write as curtly as may be, hating letter writing) certainly not intending to be ironical: one cannot always measure the effect of one's own written words on the mind of the reader; the tone, the glance of the eye, the good-humoured smile are wanting. It was some time after this, when I was in the Scotch Highlands—I had not acknowledged as soon as I ought to have done the receipt of your *Spring*[2]—and you wrote me so angry a letter that I could not answer it, for it made me angry too. Surely *I* too believe that Love is the great law of the world and would fain neither be bitter with any man nor have any man bitter with me for want of a little explanation. 'The noblest strife is Love's.'[3]

Now let me confess to you a sin which I have sinned against you, and do you grant me your forgiveness. Shortly after the publication of *Maud* I received a most bitter anonymous letter accompanied by a printed abusive notice out of some paper, and signed 'Yours with aversion.'[4] A strange fancy came into my head that possibly you might be [the] author of it, but after reading your Ode I feel quite convinced that I wronged you greatly, though but by a fancy. Cursed is he that smiteth his neighbour secretly.[5] I am sure you are not he—and as I am remorseful for having imagined so, do you as good man and Christian priest grant me absolution.

So I have sung my palinode; and now I wish to say one word about *Maud* which you and others so strangely misinterpret. I have had Peace party papers sent to me claiming me as being on their side because I had put the cry for war into the mouth of a madman. Surely that is not half so wrong a criticism as some I have seen. Strictly speaking I do not see how from the poem I could be pronounced with certainty either peace man or war man. I wonder that you and others did not find out that all along the man was intended to have an hereditary vein of insanity, and that he falls foul on the

---

[1] *The Ode of Peace*, 1855.   [2] *Poems, Spring*, 1853.   [3] See above, pp. 119–20.
[4] Printed in *Memoir*, i. 400 n. See above, pp. 119, 127, 128 n.   [5] Deuteronomy 27:24.

swindling, on the times, because he feels that his father has been killed by the work of the lie, and that all through he fears the coming madness. How could you or anyone suppose that if I had had to speak in my own person my own opinion of this war or war generally I should have spoken with so little moderation. The whole was intended to be a new form of dramatic composition. I took a man constitutionally diseased and dipt him into the circumstances of the time and took him out on fire.[6] I shall show this better in a second edition and shall be happy if you will accept a copy from me and judge it more leniently and take it as a proof that if there were any little shadow of a quarrel between us, we have shaken hands.[7]

Yours truly
A. Tennyson

I do not mean that my madman does not speak truths too: witness this extract from the letter of an enlightened German, quoted in one of our papers about the state of England, and then think if he is all wrong when he calls our peace a war, and worse in some respects than an open civil war—'Every day a murder or two or three—every day a wife beaten to death by her husband —every day a father or mother starving their children, or pinching, knocking, and kicking them into a state of torture and living putrefaction.' Then he asks, 'Has this *always* been so? or is it so only of late?'

'Is not the true war that of evil and good?'[8]

To LADY ASHBURTON[1]

Text. The Autographic Mirror, iii (July 1865), Plate 6 (facsimile).
FARRINGFORD, FRESHWATER, ISLE OF WIGHT, December 21, 1855
Dear Lady Ashburton
I have my house at present full of visitors, but before you leave the Grange I will, if possible, come.[2]

Yours very truly
A. Tennyson

---

[6] Perhaps an allusion (unconscious?) to the 'Baphometic Fire-baptism' of *Sartor Resartus*, ch. 7, 8; in *Memoir*, i. 396, Tennyson changes the metaphor to 'passed through the fiery furnace' (Daniel 3:6, etc.).

[7] The second edition added ten pages that, among other things, attempted to clear the poet himself of the invective of the speaker, to show the latter's inclination to rave as inherited from a father who had committed suicide, to mitigate the suddenness and severity of the satire against the peace orator, and to clarify, in a six-line conclusion, Tennyson's attitudes toward the war.

The edition that contains these alterations—A New Edition, 1856—is erroneously designated the third edition by T. J. Wise, who alleges a second edition in 1855 (*Bibliography of Tennyson*, i. 131–2). In fact, a new (i.e. second) edition was not needed until late in 1856. 'I get A. to read me a good part of "Maud" before it goes for a second edition' (*Journal*, p. 76).

[8] Unidentified. See below, p. 146.

[1] See i. 212 n. 'Lord Ashburton was a man of intellect and culture, and by no means a social cipher, though a less important figure than his wife. Lady Ashburton was a great lady, perhaps the nearest counterpart that England could produce to the queen of a French *salon* before the Revolution. In person, though not beautiful, she was majestic. Her wit was of the very brightest and dearly she loved to give it play' (Goldwin Smith, *Reminiscences*, ed. Arnold Haultain, 1910,

To ROBERT JAMES MANN

Text. Materials, ii. 138–9.

[? 23 December 1855]

Dear Dr. Mann

I would have come ere now but I could not and now my house is filled with visitors whom I cannot leave. They will go at the end of the year and then I must myself depart on a visit to Lady Ashburton, who has asked me at Christmas almost every year since I married. This time not to seem ungracious I must accept, but I hope nevertheless in January to come over to you. You may be certain that I desire to do so.

To GEORGE STOVIN VENABLES

MS. Harvard.

[*c.* 23 December 1855]

My dear Venables

I will meet you at the Grange if possible on the 31st. At present my house is full of visitors.

Ever yours
A. Tennyson

To EMILY SELLWOOD TENNYSON

MS. Tennyson Research Centre.

[31 December 1855]

Dearest

I have just got to South[ampto]n and lunched at ye Refreshment rooms too well on some capital un-I.W. boil'd beef, 'alike but O how different.'[1] So now I send back J[owett]'s letter.[2] I fear C[harles] W[eld] will not stay till I come back. I wish he w[oul]d but the place must be dull for a London man with no fishing. I am a little nervous, at the Ashburton meeting, but I dare say it will go off well enough.

Ever thine
A. Tennyson

---

p. 140). See below, p. 000.

'Lady Ashburton was an ideal hostess, for she knew how to make each of her guests happy in his own way. She knew how and when to use the best, the most appreciative or the most encouraging word. She never intruded herself, in fact, she skilfully and cleverly occasionally made herself missed. She would dine in her own apartments an hour or so before a big dinner in order that she might have all her powers to devote to her guests; she made it a rule that she should talk with all, that none should be neglected (*Mrs. Brookfield and Her Circle*, ii. 437).

[2] As a lion-hunter, Lady Ashburton had no peer—but she had a pedagogue: 'Mr. Jowett has gone to visit the Alfred Tennyson's with a note from Lady A. begging Alfred to come back with him here about Saturday for a few days, but I suppose he will, as usual, decline' (Jane Brookfield to her husband, 19 December 1855, in *Mrs. Brookfield and Her Circle*, ii. 425–6).

[1] Wordsworth, 'Yes, it was the mountain echo', l. 8.

[2] This note is written at the top of the first page of a letter from Jowett to Tennyson, dated 29 December, postmarked 31, expressing admiration of *Maud*. (A short word at the end is illegible.)

1 *January* 1856

To EMILY SELLWOOD TENNYSON

MS. Tennyson Research Centre.

[1 January 1856]

Dearest

I arrived in time for dinner having stayed at Winchester to buy sundry things. There are here Carlyles, Brookfields, Venables, Tom Taylor and wife and among others Mister Golding Smith who wrote that article in the Saturday Review[1] but I cannot say I find his presence particularly annoying. Lord Ashburton very tender mannered and amiable, Lady Ashburton exceedingly agreeable[2]—altogether it seems a house not uneasy to live in—only I regret my little fumatory at Farringford. Here they smoke among the oranges and lemons and camellias. That sounds pleasant but isn't. My love to Weld and regret that he should as I fear he does find it dull being at Farringford. Another time (tell him) I will make no such engagement if duly forewarned. Kisses to the little ones.

Thine ever
A. Tennyson

Venables talks of coming before the winter is over.

To EMILY SELLWOOD TENNYSON

MS. Tennyson Research Centre.

(I don't know the date) 2d of the Year I think. [2 January 1856]

Dearest

I have just been driving over to call on Trench who lives 4 miles off with

---

[1] Goldwin Smith (1823–1910: *DNB*), critic, historian, polemicist, was at this time a tutor and fellow of University College, Oxford. In 1858 he was appointed Regius Professor of History at Oxford, and ten years later, on the opening of Cornell University, was appointed Professor of English and Constitutional History. After 1872 he settled in Toronto, where he wrote widely, wisely, and therefore controversially on political issues in Great Britain, Canada, and the United States. On the staff of the *Saturday Review* from the beginning, he published in the opening number (13 November 1855) 'The War Passages in "Maud"' (reprinted in *The Critical Heritage*, pp. 186–90), in which he tended to identify the opinions of the protagonist and the author. 'To wage "war with a thousand battles and shaking a hundred thrones," in order to cure a hypochondriac and get rid of the chicory in coffee,' he wrote, 'is a bathos. . . . A painful impression has been created . . . by that which appears to be bloodthirstiness because it is unconnected with . . . political or social aspirations. In Milton, Byron, Shelley, Wordsworth, a passionate cry for a just war would have seemed like the foam on the wave—in Mr. Tennyson it seems a little like the foam without the wave.'

Goldwin Smith's very readable *Reminiscences*, ed. Arnold Haultain (1910) show that he was a wit as well as a connoisseur of wit. Of Herbert Spencer's 'famous definition of Evolution— "While an aggregate evolves, not only the matter composing it, but also the motion of that matter, passes from an indefinite incoherent homogeneity to a definite coherent heterogeneity"' —Smith remarked that 'the universe may well have heaved a sigh of relief when through the cerebrations of an eminent thinker, it had been delivered of this account of itself' (p. 140 n.). Smith has an interesting page (142) on Tennyson during this visit. See also Justin McCarthy, *Portraits of the Sixties*, pp. 266–77.

[2] For the Ashburtons, see above, p. 000. The best accounts of the visit are in the *Correspondence of Henry Taylor*, ed. Dowden, pp. 210–15, and *Mrs. Brookfield and Her Circle*, ii. 424–37. See also Sanders, pp. 212–14, and D. A. Wilson, *Carlyle at Threescore and Ten* (1929), pp. 197–207.

Mrs. Brookfield and Miss Baring, Lady Ashburton's sister,[1] and this morning I had to read Maud to a circle of (I think) admirers. I was a little nervous but got through it very well on the whole.[2] Mrs. Brookfield seems to have a great respect for you and says that she loved you as an old friend from the first time she saw you. Is Charles Weld yet with you? my love again to him. If you can find the sheets of the new poem in the st[u]d[y] enclose them to me here as Venables wants to see them.[3] Eddy[4] is rather better I believe.

Ever thine
A. T.

I admire Lady Ashburton and shall do so more I dare say. She is very lively.

To EMILY SELLWOOD TENNYSON

Text. Materials, ii. 158.

January 3, [1856]

We looked at Orion last night, the faintest star under the lowest star of the belt is really eight stars all moving in connection with one another, a system by themselves, a most lovely object through the glass. I saw also the famous nebula which is in the second star of the sword, and is amazing. Rigel too I saw, but am uncertain whether I saw its minute companion.[1]

January 4, [1856]

Hallam is good on the kite, I hope he won't live to be hanged, which 'going to heaven with a string' seems to imply.[2]

January 5, [1856]

Lady Ashburton seemed I fancy to muse upon it when I said to her that

---

[1] Louisa Baring (d. 1888), the elder of Lord Ashburton's two surviving sisters; it was her sister Emily (d. 1868) whom Venables adroitly managed not to marry (see Virginia Surtees, *The Ludovisi Goddess, The Life of Louisa Lady Ashburton*, 1984, p. 107.

[2] 'They asked Tennyson to read some of his own poetry aloud. This he was understood to enjoy. But to the general disappointment he refused. At his side was sitting Carlyle, who had been publishing his contempt of poetry. Immolating myself to the public cause, I went over to Carlyle and asked him to come for a walk in the grounds. While we were gone, the reading came off' (Goldwin Smith, *Reminiscences*, p. 142).
William Thomson (later Archbishop of York but at this time Provost of Queen's College, Oxford) was another guest, and his wife's account is worth reading: 'At dinner that night I asked my neighbour, Mr. Brookfield, "Who is that brigand-like man opposite?" He said, "It is the great Tennyson." I was struck by his white face and black hair.... After dinner, on coming down from my room where I went for my work, I met our hostess, who said, "Good night, my dear, I am not coming down again until that man is gone." I said, "What man?" She answered, "Tennyson; I asked him to recite, and he has refused...."" I gained by her absence in the evening as Tennyson talked to me the whole time about Greece, and my recollections of it. Next day we all went to Winchester, where Tennyson took me over the Cathedral, and talked in the most interesting way about it.' (E. C. Richards, *Zoe Thomson of Bishopthorpe and Her Friends*, 1916, pp. 62–7, with Doyle's sketch of Tennyson—also in Martin, *Tennyson*.

[3] Probably the additions to *Maud*. [4] See above, p. 130 n.

---

[1] See above, p. 73. [2] See *Journal*, p. 59.

I wished some rich man would buy the little Farringford estate to prevent its being brick-box-dotted. I wish he would buy it but I don't fancy that he will. There is here a garrulous old Whig, once Secretary of War in Lord Grey's time,[3] a jolly fellow swearing by Whigdom, and continually bantered by the hostess. I cannot see in the least a touch of the haughtiness which Fame attributes to her, she is most perfectly natural though like enough she sometimes snubs her own grade now and then, when she sees presumption or folly. But as Brookfield said this morning, 'She is very loyal to her "printers." '[4]

January 6, [1856]

The Tom Taylors have gone this morning and the Carlyles go next Monday. Spedding came here last night and looks as mild and wise as usual.

January 6, [1856]

There has come a summons to Windsor Castle from the Queen to Lady Ashburton and she is, may be, going to-morrow and we the guests are all to take care of one another as well as we can.

To WILLIAM FULFORD[1] (extract)

Text. J. W. Mackail, *The Life of William Morris*, i. 90.

[January 1856]

I find, in such of the articles as I have read, a truthfulness and earnestness very refreshing to me: very refreshing likewise is the use of the plain 'I' in lieu of the old hackneyed unconscientious editorial 'we.' May you go on and prosper. As to your essay on myself, you may easily see that I have some difficulty in speaking; to praise it, seeming too much like self-praise.

EMILY SELLWOOD TENNYSON to JOHN FORSTER

MS. Tennyson Research Centre.

FARRINGFORD, January 18, [1856]

Dear Mr. Forster

We don't know whether it is a matter of congratulation to you, this

---

[3] Edward Ellice (1781–1863: *DNB*), who had been Secretary to the Treasury and Whip in 1832, was Secretary for War in the cabinet in 1833–4, under Grey and Melbourne (*DNB*). Brookfield described him as 'very kindly and universally liked and liking' (*Mrs. Brookfield and Her Circle*, ii. 433).

[4] A coterie joke—'printers' was Lady Jersey's contemptuous name for Lady Ashburton's literary friends (*Mrs. Brookfield and Her Circle*, ii. 433).

[1] William Fulford (1832–97), friend of Edward [Burne-]Jones and William Morris at Oxford, was the author of 'Alfred Tennyson: An Essay in Three Parts', devoted to Tennyson's work from 1842 on, in *The Oxford and Cambridge Magazine* (of which he succeeded Morris as editor) in January–March 1856. Fulford took orders, and also published several volumes of poetry. See Foster, Allibone, J. W. Mackail, *The Life of William Morris*, and *The Letters of William Morris*, ed. Norman Kelvin, i. 14.

appointment, but we are sure it is matter of congratulation to the appointment and so since you have identified yourself in a measure with it you are at all events doomed to a portion of congratulation greater or less. But we hope it is really pleasant to you, that so we may be glad for you without any drawback. We hope too you are not suffering from this damp but that the new year has begun in this and in all things happily with you and so will go on and close too.

It is rather an important time for us, we are in treaty for this place, being obliged either to buy it or leave it in November next, and being rather anxious to know which it is to be. When shall we have the gratification of seeing you here? We flatter ourselves the way hither will now be made easier by a railway to Lymington.

This Russian acceptance seems too good to be true. Ungrateful wretch that I am to write such a faithless sentence.

Alfred and the boys are pretty well. He sends his love. Believe me
Most sincerely yours
Emily Tennyson

To EMILY SELLWOOD TENNYSON

MS. Tennyson Research Centre.

[29 January 1856]

Dearest

I did not write yesterday for I went over to Ventnor and got back late having bought Hallam a big top and a trumpet. I saw Saturn pretty well the night before last but I could not see the division of the rings—it only seemed one big ring flaking off into thinness towards the edges but I saw a bit of the dark ring at the base of the planet.

[*drawing of Saturn*]   [*larger drawing*]
   dark ring   dark ring

The dark ring is the most interior and I only saw it where it crost the bright part but others saw it slatecolour pulsing within the other rings.

I shall go to Swainston next Monday—if I meet you there well and good if not on Tuesday I shall return. I saw Mrs. Peel[2] and had a talk with her. She looked rather wan but otherwise for the time seemed comfortable and without pain.

Thine
A. T.

---

[1] Postmark.
[2] Maria Peel (née Brown), wife of Edmund Peel of Underrock, IW (see i. 245 n.).

1 *February* 1856

To EMILY SELLWOOD TENNYSON

MS. Tennyson Research Centre.

[1 February 1856]

Dearest

I am glad Maud has made so much: the other vols have not sold so well as usual on account of the war I presume.[1]

Stephens' Central America I should like to have and also Spencer's Circassia and I shall be obliged to take Milman if nobody else wants them: but I'd as lief be without them.[2]

Tomorrow I go to Swainston.

To EMILY SELLWOOD TENNYSON

MS. Tennyson Research Centre.

SWAINSTON, ISLE OF WIGHT, Sunday [3 February 1856]

Dearest

We (i.e. Simeon and Lady (perhaps) and Milnes and Mrs. Milnes.[1] are coming to lunch tomorrow at about ½ or 2 o'clock—if you have nothing in the house it can't be helped—so let it be.

Thine
A.

They are going afterwards to Alum Bay.

EMILY SELLWOOD TENNYSON *to* GEORGE STOVIN VENABLES

MS. National Library of Wales.

FARRINGFORD, March 10, [1856]

Dear Mr. Venables

You will be right welcome whatever you may talk about when you come. Mr. and Mrs. Tom Taylor and Mr. FitzGerald have said they will visit us about the time you mention. If they come we could not give you the room we reserved for you in February. We should have to ask you to put up with a small room for we are very badly off for bedrooms.

---

[1] According to a statement headed 'Receipts from Messrs. Moxon, Publisher, by A. Tennyson' (TRC), in 1855 he received £445, in 1856 £2058. (For the record: 1851, £749; 1852; £757; 1853, £1658; 1854 and 1857, no figures; 1858, £1299; 1859, £928; 1860, £4542; 1861, £1876.)

[2] Since the five-year lease on Chapel House was expiring, Elizabeth Tennyson, who had lived there since 1853, was moving to Hampstead. The books are John Lloyd Stephens, *Incidents of Travel in Central America, Chiapas, and Yucatan* (2 vols., 1841; revised, 1854); Edmund Spencer, *Travels in Circassia, Krim Tartary, etc.*, including a Steam Voyage from Vienna to Constantinople and around the Black Sea (2 vols., 1837, 1838), or his *Turkey, Rumania, the Black Sea, and Circassia* (1854); and Henry Hart Milman, either *The History of the Jews* (3 vols., 1829); or *The History of Christianity from the Birth of Christ to the Abolition of Paganism* (3 vols., 1840).

[1] Milnes had married Annabella Hungerford Crewe (d. 1874; see vol. iii, letter to Houghton, 6 March 1874), daughter of 2nd Baron Crewe, 30 July 1851.

I will say no more in hoping so soon to speak to you. Alfred's love. The children are well. I am very glad those two names are joined.[1]

Most sincerely yours
Emily Tennyson

The post-boy goes on Sunday even before we have read the letters it brings so I could not answer you by return of post.

ROBERT JAMES MANN to ALFRED TENNYSON

MS. Yale.

VENTNOR, March 13, [1856]

My dear Friend

I expect you will to-day have received the first proof sheets of my Maud vindication.[1] When you have looked through them will you send them on *to me* with any emendations you would wish. I shall, of course, also give them a very careful revision and reconsideration myself.

I have been amongst the Quakers and to my utter surprize I find that they really think you have made an attack upon their principles, and a personal onslaught upon Bright. I have been having some great fun among some of them about it. I shall add something on this question—and will send you the Sketch in MSS of what I incline to say in a day or two.[2]

Please always to send on to me the proofs that come to you, after you have considered them. If the proof has not duly been transmitted to you please let me know.

Ever truly yours
Robert James Mann

Let me know if you like the type and style.

To ROBERT JAMES MANN

Text. Materials, ii. 139.

March 15, 1856

My dear Dr. Mann

It is very difficult to recriticize a critique on oneself. I don't quite like your 'word-sculpture' but if you choose let it stand. I don't quite think that the lines *jar*; they rather rush with the impetuosity of passion, jarring perhaps once or twice.[1] However, 'recalls clearly' is wrong, the memory is a phantasmal one, which he cannot trace to its origin although his meeting

---

[1] Henry Venables Lushington (1856–?), son of Thomas Davies Lushington (*Landed Gentry* and memorial tablet, Boxley Church).

[1] *Tennyson's "Maud" Vindicated: An Explanatory Essay* (see above, p. 000). About a third of the essay is reprinted in *Tennyson: The Critical Heritage,* pp. 197–211.

[2] See above, p. 132 n.

[1] For 'word-sculpture' and 'jar' Mann substituted 'word-painting' and 'rush'.

Maud, who greeted him kindly, did strike an old chord of association.[2] Did you get the proofs which my wife sent? Type and style do very well I think. In that note on the Quaker ought you not to say something of the true war being the war of evil in the heart?[3] What *we* call war is but one of the symptoms.*
Believe me,

Ever yours
A. Tennyson

*If I were with you, we could settle it together *viva voce* much better than by letter. I suppose you could not leave Mrs. Mann nor bring her with you now, but how glad I should be to see you![4]

To TICKNOR AND FIELDS

Text. James C. Austin, *Fields of the Atlantic Monthly*, p. 376.

FARRINGFORD, March 18 and April 17, 1856

Gentlemen
From you alone among all American publishers have I ever received any remuneration for my books and I would wish therefore that with you alone should rest the right of publishing them in future.
I have the honour to be Gentlemen

Your obedient Servant
A. Tennyson

i.e. American editors [*for* editions]. Since writing the above I find that Moxon has promised the exclusive sale of the illustrated edition to Messrs. Appleton and Co. of New York. I regret this letter has not been forwarded sooner; it got mislaid and forgotten.[1]

April 17th

To SIR JOHN SIMEON

MS. Yale.

[*c.* 20 March 1856]

Dear Simeon
On Monday I expect Tom Taylor and wife, Richard Doyle and Venables

---

[2] 'Maud', I. vii. Mann's explanation incorporated Tennyson's words 'chord', 'association', and 'phantasmal'.

[3] Mann changed it to: The 'real war', against which 'public opinion should be taught to array itself, is that war of evil in the heart, of which all the battles that were ever fought are but so many external symptoms and demonstrations'. See above, p. 138.

[4] They came (*Journal*, 63–4).

[1] 'I see no objection whatever to your complying with the request of Messrs. Ticknor and Fields as far as regards *American* editions of any of your Poems; but you must be good enough to let them clearly understand that you do not include in your wish *English* editions, especially the one which is now in preparation with illustrations. The exclusive sale of this edition I may mention I have promised to Messrs. Appleton and Co., of New York, who are in a position to do more with it than any other house in America' (Moxon to Tennyson, Thursday [n.d.], TRC).

so that it is more than probable that I cannot be with you to see the hounds throw off, which yet I should well like to see for though no huntsman, I love all country sights and sounds.[1] I hope you will come to us some day when my friends are with me. Do not come on Tuesday i.e. if you do so with the expectation of taking me back. I myself care not much for the books: it was Mrs. Leacock[2] who wanted me to see them. Thanks however for the pains you have taken and I trust your pains may have turned up some prize of woodside for yourself. Seymour is the most uncourteous animal I ever dreamed of, or Estcourt the most lazy (we are now (it being 9 weeks since I first mentioned the matter to Estcourt))[3] obliged to warehouse the furniture in our old Twickenham house—in London. Seymour himself having originally forced us to take the house for three years, or not at all though he had brought us down to Freshwater on the express condition that we should have it to try for one year. Have you seen E? I shall have to give up this place out of pure disgust at the conduct of Seymour I expect.

Ever yours
A. Tennyson

I have done some of my Merlin Idyl which promises well I think. I fear I have been giving you a world of trouble by my questions about woodsides. Forgive me.

To ROBERT JAMES MANN

Text. *Memoir*, i. 405.

[April 1856]

Thanks for your *Vindication*. No one with this essay before him can in future pretend to misunderstand my dramatic poem, 'Maud':[1] your commentary is as true as it is full, and I am really obliged to you for defending me against the egregiously nonsensical imputation of having attacked the Quakers or Mr. Bright: you are not aware, perhaps, that another wiseacre accused me of calling Mr. Layard an 'Assyrian Bull!'[2]

Yours very truly
A. Tennyson

---

[1] For the visit with the Tennysons, see *Journal*, pp. 62–3. See also below, p. 169.
[2] Unidentified.
[3] This is Charles Wyatt Estcourt (1820–66), of Gatscombe House, IW, an attorney, not his brother, Arthur Harbottle Estcourt (1822–98), barrister-at-law, Lincoln's Inn (1850), later Deputy Governor of the Isle of Wight. See below, p. 000. (Foster; *Landed Gentry*; White's *Hampshire*; *Journal*).

[1] Emily Tennyson was less enthusiastic. 'I do most heartily agree with you,' she wrote to Spedding (27 June 1856, TRC), 'that a thing must stand or fall of itself, that in the end the great and good will assert its own rights. At least I think you think this and I am sure I do. So I was utterly against that Defence Vindication [as] it was called however kindly meant.'
[2] 'Maud', I. 233. Austen Henry Layard (1817–94; GCB 1878), an excavator (rather than an archaeologist) who discovered the bas-reliefs (now in the British Museum) from and near Nineveh. After 1851 he 'devoted himself to politics' (*DNB*), and at this date was MP for Aylesbury. In 1869 he married his cousin Enid Guest (see below, p. 469 n.).

To ALAN KER

Text. Materials, ii. 162.

FARRINGFORD, FRESHWATER, I. W., April 6, 1856.

My dear Alan

We are going to buy this house and little estate here, only I rather shake under the fear of being ruined. If we buy it I need not say how glad we should be to see you here some happy day when you return.[1]

Ever yours
A. Tennyson

EMILY SELLWOOD TENNYSON to GEORGE STOVIN VENABLES

MS. National Library of Wales.

FARRINGFORD, April 19 [1856]

Dear Mr. Venables

Will you look down from your great castle upon that little cottage of a Solent and then you will dimly descry Alfred and possibly me and a great party from Swainston and another from Westover and others from Norton, all our neighbours in fact if you could but know them. The Swainston party is to come for dinner or meaty tea here as the hour may be. I wish you could come too on the 23rd. Perhaps you will.[1]

I would you could give a better account of Park House.

Things are not yet settled further than that we are to have the place except the orchard for 6750 to be paid on November 23. We have asked for the sale to be on the 8th if it is to be, but we have not yet heard whether the title is good or not. For the orchard Mr. Seymour asks 150 which as the rent is less than £3 is rather a big sum. I believe we shall not buy it.

Merlin[2] is all written down, quite finished I think, but not much else done. He troubles himself that the Idylls do not form themselves into a whole in his mind and moreover that the subject has not reality enough.

I am afraid you are feeling this cold very much. Baby has a little cold but we are all otherwise pretty well.

We admire the wrong raveneth. It seems as if anything that sounds so grand must be right. It is a pity you cannot recommend the bull-dog practice founded on it as hopeful.[3]

---

[1] From the West Indies (see *Background*, p. 161).

[1] 'A naval review took place [23 April] at Spithead in the presence of Her Majesty, on an unprecedented scale, both as to the amount of the force engaged [25 ships, 1018 guns] and the number of spectators whom it attracted' (*Annual Register*). See *Journal*, pp. 65–7. Swainston (Sir John Simeon) and Westover, seat of the Hon. William Henry Ashe a-Court-Holmes (1809–91), who succeeded in 1860 as 2nd Baron Heytesbury; Norton Lodge was the seat of Admiral Sir Graham Eden Hamond, 2nd Baronet, and Norton Cottage the residence of his son Captain Andrew Snape Hamond, RN, later 3rd Baronet and Vice-Admiral.

[2] Later, 'Merlin and Vivien'.   [3] The meaning is opaque.

Excuse this wretched paper they have given me. I am ashamed to send it you. Alfred's love.

Very sincerely yours
Emily Tennyson

To FRANCIS PITTIS[1]

MS. Tennyson Research Centre.

[May 1856]

Dear Sir
Provided ⟨I be legally bound to buy⟩ the iron handles, all or any of them, be not included among the fixtures in the sale of the Farringford estate I agree to take them at a valuation.

A. Tennyson

—Pittis Esq.

To ELIZABETH RUSSELL

MS. Viscount Boyne.

FARRINGFORD, FRESHWATER, I. W., May 19, 1856

Dearest Aunt
Emily told me that she had written to you when I was out about the terrible fall you had had. We are here in such an out of the way corner, and my family so very seldom write that I was the very last to hear of your accident. I heard however at the same time that you were going on well. I now write to ask whether you *are* going on well; if you have any amanuensis who would let us know it would be to me I need not say how great a gratification to know that you had not suffered in any way which would affect the use of your arm eventually: pray, dearest Aunt, let me know, for though I write seldom I have not the less affection for you, do not the less joy in your joy, and grieve with your grief—, though I may be somewhat undemonstrative. I hope Emma is with you. I do not like the idea of your being left altogether in hired hands: if she is give her my love.

Prince Albert called on me the other day here, and was very kind in his manner shaking hands in quite a friendly way. We were in the midst of a packing bustle, things tumbled about here and there—my landlord being about to sell his furniture: preparatory to my buying the place: he stood by the drawing room window admiring the view which was not looking its best,

---

[1] Francis Pittis, auctioneer, of Church Street, Ventnor, and Newport (White's *Hampshire*), later alderman (Kelly's *Hampshire and the Isle of Wight*, 1870). Farringford had been rented furnished from Seymour. The auction of his furniture took place on 27 May, the Tennysons having moved out, temporarily, to the Red House, Freshwater. See *The Letters of Emily Tennyson*, pp. 98–9.

and on going away said to a Captain Fenwick[1] who was with him 'I shall certainly bring the Queen—it's such a pretty place.' I tell you this little piece of news because I think it will please you a little in your sickness—if such you yet be; I fear you are. Pray let your scribe tell us all about you. Love from Emily.

Ever yours affectionately
A. Tennyson

EMILY SELLWOOD TENNYSON
to GEORGE STOVIN VENABLES

MS. National Library of Wales.

THE NEW HOUSE, May 21, [1856]

Dear Mr. Venables

I would have answered your kind letter sooner and told you of the Prince's visit had we not been ordered to expect the Queen not by herself but only in this way. The Prince said to one of the gentlemen with him Farringford was a pretty place and he should certainly bring her to see it and there have been commands that the ports should be in readiness for her on Saturday, Tuesday and today so that as we have since last Wednesday been in this red house we have had to go to Farringford and spend hours in the garden waiting for her not liking to intrude into the house. Just now it rains so we have come away and I write to make you laugh at our want of etiquette and that I may do it I will begin at the beginning and tell you how every book was taken out of the room to be stowed away ready for the sale, how the chairs and tables were dancing, sofas and chairs stuffed with brown paper and all untidiness, the floor strewed with toys and cards and I know not what besides. Two loud rings at the bell. The housemaid with a face that terrified me coming close whispered in a mysterious voice 'His Royal Highness Prince Albert.' She begged me to go and speak with his gentleman. I came upon him near the stair-case. He said HRH being in the neighbourhood had asked was Mr. Tennyson at home? 'Yes.' Could HRH speak with him! 'Of course.' I said 'I will go and fetch him, will the Prince (but some way I did not say the Prince) walk into the drawing-room, for it seemed to me more really civil to let him come in than wait at the door until Alfred came. I went upstairs and appeared no more but left Alfred to do the honours or receive the honour rather alone. The Prince shook hands and talked very kindly and pleasantly. He was looking out of the window when Alfred came in and there he remained for he never thought of asking him to sit down. He offered him wine. In going away one of his gentlemen brought him a large bunch of

---

[1] Unidentified. *A List of the Officers of the Army and of the Corps of the Royal Marines* (1855) registers three Fenwicks—Percival Fenwick (see Boase), Thomas Fenwick, and Bowes Fenwick —but the Fenwick mentioned here must have been naval rather than military, for on 11 December 1856, Tennyson dined with Captain Richard Crozier, RN, and there met Captain Andrew Snape Hamond, RN, and his wife, and also 'Capt. and Mrs. Fenwick' (*Journal*, 79–80), who must have been (later) Admiral William Henry Fenwick, retired 1873, listed in *Whitaker's Naval and Military Directory* (1900), as 'formerly an Inspector of Prisons under Home Office'.

cowlips which he took into his own hands. Said they were finer than any others he had seen and that they made good tea. We have since heard that when he got on board he put them in water and said he meant to make tea of them for the Queen and himself. It is a pity that the expectation of seeing the Queen is so much spoilt by the uncomfortable state we are in. The Seymours still in the house, the entrance room nearly impassable from packages and the drawing-room stript of pictures and of some of its furniture. Alfred told the Prince there was to be a sale and apologized for the confusion but I suppose being a foreigner HRH did not well understand what was meant or he would not I should think have proposed to bring the Queen. We could not of course spend the whole week at Swainston with the Milneses as we were asked to do but Alfred spent three or four days and to please him and not to seem sulky to the Simeons I also went there on Thursday and returned on Saturday. A very pleasant visit we had. On Friday we left our names at Osborne but of course only saw the pleasant looking old porter and a policeman. Mr. Stephen (Spring Rice) de Vere, Mr. Monsell, Mr. Wegg Prosser were the other guests at Swainston.[1] Our host was expressing himself very enthusiastically about you. It is so pleasant a house I hope you may be tempted there sometimes and so we may have a double chance of seeing you.

Poor Edmund, his worn look shocked me. I think hearing Merlin and other things cheered him somewhat. We have learned today that Tom has arrived safely.[2] I by no means give up the hope of seeing you this year at P. H.

On Monday Alfred signed the agreement and wrote his cheque for the £1000 and gave instructions for his will. He bids me ask whether you will do us the favour to let him put your name as one of the trustees. He has asked Edmund and he means to ask Sir John a similar favour. We have Mr. Sellar and Mr. Palgrave with us. I fear what with waiting for the Queen and the small house their visit is but a dull one. Excuse this blundering note and believe me,

Very sincerely yours
Emily Tennyson

We have each day had our bairns dressed in their rose-coloured dresses and have taken them with us to wait in the garden.

The sale is fixed for the 27th and 28th. Mr. Seymour means to put all those iron rails into the sale which I fear will cost us an additional hundred pounds or two. Edmund is kind enough to say we may have some of the Somersby pictures. I hope they will come very soon to hide the ghastly look of the walls.

---

[1] All three were converts to Roman Catholicism. Stephen Edward de Vere (1824–1904), brother of Aubrey Thomas de Vere, succeeded as 4th Baronet in 1880 (*DNB*). William Monsell (1812–94), liberal politician, was raised to the peerage as Baron Emly in 1874 (*DNB*). Francis Richard Wegg- Prosser (1824–1911), born Haggitt, assumed his uncle's name in 1849 (Foster; *Who Was Who*). He was MP for Hereford from 1847 to 1852, when he resigned and was received into the Roman Catholic church (*Letters and Diaries of John Henry Newman*, ed. Dessain and Kelly, xxi. 568).

[2] Edmund Lushington ('worn' because of his son Eddy) and his brother Thomas Davies.

To ?

MS. Scottish Record Office.

FARRINGFORD, June 13, 1856

Sir

Mrs. Murray[1] has my full permission to publish her music to my words of the Light Brigade. I am, Sir,

Your obedient servant
A. Tennyson

To WILLIAM YOUNG SELLAR

Text. *Materials*, ii. 165–6; draft *Materials*, iv. 93.

FARRINGFORD, June 16, 1856

My dear Sellar

I have received your grateful gift, (this [first] 'gift' I do assure you is not of malice prepense but oozed out of the pen's nibs of its own black will, not having any meaning in it), grateful both for the author's sake and the maker's gift. What does it cost? for I did not tell you to give it to me and I like to pay my debts, so say and postage stamps will pour in upon you. Another thing, don't quote lines you may remember of mine (unpublished of course I mean). F. [P.][1] has been doing so and they have travelled down to Pau and they might as well go to pot, for I have before this seen unpublished lines of mine printed with a little alteration in verse-books of others, not I dare say dishonestly, an author may not know when a verse buzzes in his head whether it is a bee from his own hive or no.

My second poem ('Enid') progresses rapidly but is a little harder to manage than 'Merlin.'

Kindest regards to Mrs. Sellar. I suppose it is not of much use sending love to your bairn, who had scarce come to his memory when I saw him, but I send him a shadowy kiss across the Firth of Forth.[2] This place is splendid now. I wish you were here.

Evermore yours
A. Tennyson

My wife's best remembrances.

To JAMES THOMAS FIELDS

MS. Harvard.

FARRINGFORD, FRESHWATER, ISLE OF WIGHT, June 18, 1856

Dear Sir

I have received the £20 you were kind enough to send me; I have just

---

[1] See above, p. 134.

[1] Palgrave. [2] See above, p. 68.

bought a home and spent a vast deal of money, too, on furniture; so your present was all the more acceptable.

Yours truly
A. Tennyson

I have written the Bugle song[1] out for Mrs. Fields, not very satisfactorily I fear, having made a mistake in it.

To EMILY SELLWOOD TENNYSON

MS. Tennyson Research Centre.

[26 June 1856][1]

Dearest

I called on Mr. Hallam yesterday but neither he nor any of them were in—so I left my name and direction. I called too on Lady Ashburton who asked me if I went to Scotland to their house near Inverness. Lewis Fytche and Anne Belgrave[2] called yesterday and I dined at Parker's and met Helps and Bell who writes the Poets—altogether a pleasant evening.[3] It is frightfully hot here and I begin to wish myself back again. I find Enid[4] stops quite truncated. I cannot write a line for the bustle and the dining and the heat. Edmund wants me to go to Park House and I suppose I must.

Thine ever
A.T.

Don't bother thyself anymore with stitching—Anne wrote off to Tilly—as to *valuing* carpets, that is *de trop*.[5] Palgrave has got for us beautiful prints of the Sistine Chapel which I shall bring down probably.

To CHARLES RICHARD WELD

Text. Agnes Grace Weld, *Glimpses of Tennyson*, pp. 34–5.

[*c.* 1 July 1856][1]

A thousand thanks for your kindness in sending me your 'Brittany'.[2] Very

---

[1] 'The splendour falls on castle walls', *The Princess*, iii. 3.

[1] Postmark.

[2] Unidentified, but probably a Lincolnshire acquaintance. Foster lists a Charles William Belgrave, Venn a Thomas Belgrave, both sons of Thomas Belgrave, of Louth; there were cousins in Stamford (*Landed Gentry*).

[3] John William Parker, Arthur Helps, and Robert Bell (1800–67: *DNB*), journalist, editor, writer, 'chiefly remembered . . . [for] his annotated edition of the English poets, 24 vols., 1854–7'. [4] The Geraint and Enid Idylls.

[5] 'We stop at the barn and look at Merwood's bits of carpet which he thought might do for us. I had sent to beg he would not wait but there he sat in the barn his carpet spread out of doors' (*Journal*, 4 June, p. 72).

[1] It is not certain, or even likely, that the two paragraphs (the second of which also exists in an autograph fragment, TRC) belong to the same letter, since the printed version combines four or five letters.

[2] See above, p. 134.

refreshing to me after the almost daily verse-books that are sent. It must be *pessimi poetoe soecli incommoda*, as Catullus happily calls them. . . .[3]

Pity me; scores of letters to answer, I snatch a moment to say these words to you. I can no more (as people say when they die on the stage).

To COVENTRY PATMORE

MS. Liverpool City Libraries.

July 10, 1856

My dear Patmore

Many thanks for your lanthorn-bug as the Yankees call him:[1] we saw his sidelights but his under-one seems extinct. I am in great fright about him lest he should exhale before he gets back to you. It was very kind in you to send him. Thanks also for the microscope. I have one, but I will keep this as a relic of you. I like what I have read of your espousals as well I think as the 1st part, though it does not *seem* so fresh to me from having read the 1st part.[2] Mine and my wife's kind remembrances to Mrs. Patmore.

Ever yours
A. Tennyson

Let us know whether the beetle arrives safely, poor fellow I am very sorry for him.

JAMES SPEDDING *to* ALFRED TENNYSON

MS. Tennyson Research Centre.

60, LINCOLN'S INN FIELDS, July 15, 1856

My dear Alfred

A parcel has come from Pope and Plante containing a silk elastic thigh hose for you.[1] Shall I send it to you at Farringdon [*sic*]?—I sent off a box of prints the other day by Palgrave's desire. I hope it has arrived safe.

I am still of opinion that Merlin would not have been talked over by that kind of woman; and that the effect of the poem is much injured by the predominance of harlotry. Neither do I agree with A. de V. and Sir J. Simeon that the grosser temptation is the one which was most likely to be successful in such a case. So when I say this hereafter, or agree with numbers of people

---

[3] 'Burdens of the age, worst of poets' (Catullus, Poem 14, l. 23).

[1] A note reads: 'This note of the Poet Laureate accompanied a live specimen of the Pyrophorus noctilucus or West Indian Firefly, which I gave Mr. Patmore to send to him. I am sorry that Alfred Tennyson did not see the full green phosphoric light of the under part, behind insertion of plate to which the hind legs are attached. I fear he did not adopt the suggestion I gave Patmore of throwing the firefly into water first. On the day he arrived, this treatment made all three lights brighten up. Next day he went by post to Newcastle to be dissected by Mr. Albany Hancock, so that poor Pyrophorus has an honoured memory in being posted to a poet, by a poet, posted to and dissected by an anatomist. [signed] 'A White.'

[2] *The Espousals* (1856), following *The Betrothal* (1854).

[1] For varicose veins. Pope and Plante were hosiers, shirt-makers, and surgical elastic stocking manufacturers, 4 Waterloo Place, Pall Mall.

who will say it, I am not to be accused of desertion, or of being the editor of any review.[2]

Yours ever
James Spedding

To ELIZABETH RUSSELL
MS. Viscount Boyne.

[*c*. 16 July 1856][1]

Dearest Aunt
  We are in the hurry of packing as this is our last day before leaving this house for two months, meaning to let it and get a little change of air but I cannot refrain, since I heard this morning from Clara
Palmer that you [   ]
passages in Maud [   ]
and expressing my [   ]
should have foll[   ]
dream. I decl[   ]
that you are utt[   ]
as well say tha[   ]
madman in the [   ]
should be such [   ]
make personal [   ]
upon the Russels. I really could find it in my heart to be offended with such an imputation, for what must you think of me if you think me capable of such gratuitous and unmeaning personality and hostility? I am as sensitive a man as exists and sooner than wound another in such a spiteful fashion would consent never to write a line again. ⟨Assure yourself that you utterly mistake⟩ yea, to have my hand cut off at the wrist. Why, if you had the least suspicion that I had acted in this way did you not inquire of me before? now see, you, the kindliest and tenderest of human beings, how you have wronged me, and nourished in your heart this accusation as baseless, no, more baseless than a dream, for dreams have some little foundation in past things: but pray put it all out of your head and believe me always [   ]

Y[ours affectionately]
[A. Tennyson]

---

[2] The discussion about Merlin continued, and on 18 [?] September Emily Tennyson replied from Builth (see *The Letters of Emily Tennyson*, pp. 102–3).

[1] Docketed by the recipient: 'Alfred from Farringford | recd July 18-56 | respecting Maud'. The excision of the signature on page 2 of course also removed part of page 1. Elizabeth Russell suspected (with some reason) that 'Maud', I. 330–88, alluded to her deceased husband's fortune, inherited from *his* father, a 'self-made coal millionaire'. See i. 2–3 n., with the references to Rader.

I have written in
great haste. I hope I [have]
said nothing to give you p[ain.]
I am sure I do not int[end]
so to do but simply to
defend myself. Emily's l[ove.]

EMILY SELLWOOD TENNYSON' JOURNAL

Text. Materials, ii. 167–71.

July 18th. to the *27th.* The journal says that on the 18th A. and E. T. set off for Wales with the children, and stayed at 'The Hand' at Llangollen. The good old ladies were very sorry that their best rooms were taken, but the harper played the children Welsh airs, and all soon forgot the uncomfortable quarters. My father and mother then took Mrs. Griffith's cottage, the garden full of roses and other bright flowers with the castle Dinas Bran on the conical hills behind. The hillside glowed with foxgloves. The early dawn lay on the hills like streaks of snow. One day they visited Eliseg's pillar on a knoll gay with wild roses standing in a cornfield. Eliseg was father of Brockmael a famous prince of Powis who was slain in the battle of Chester 607 A. D. Another day A. T. was especially charmed with the view, the river running gold between shadowy trees, the town and valley glowing in the sunset with columns of smoke bright against the dark hill side. On this journey A. and E. T. began to learn Welsh and tried to read passages from the Welsh translation of the Psalms, Hanes Cymru, the Mabinogion, Aneurin, and Llywarch Hen with the aid of local schoolmasters and a dictionary.[1]

The journal then continues—July 27th, A. T. has taken long walks in all directions. He finished and read me the passage in 'Enid' when Geraint asked for Enid, and her mother told her. We were on the terrace in the garden.

July 28th. We drove to Bala,[2] and admired the valley beyond Llangollen. The lake a beautiful violet colourwith white breakers. Our landlady Mrs. Lloyd wanted to give him her precious 'Book of the Bards,'[3] but he will not accept it.

Aug. 1st. He has finished the tournament in 'Enid' and read it to me.

Aug. 2nd. To-day he made the stately queen's answer to Geraint. He said

---

[1] Thomas Price, *Hanes Cymru* (1842: Welsh history to 1282), Lady Charlotte Guest's translation of *Mabinogion* [vol. 1], and a 'MS copy probably made *c.* 1856 in the British Museum' of Llywarch Hen, *The Heroic Elegies and Other Pieces*, are all listed in *Tennyson in Lincoln*, i, Nos. 1824, 1408, 1466. See below, p. 000. Aneurin, author of *Gododin*, like Llywarch Hen and Taliessin, is supposed to have lived in the fifth century.

[2] 'As the south-west that blowing Bala lake | Fills all the sacred Dee' ('Geraint and Enid', ll. 928–9).

[3] Perhaps Evan Evans, *Some Specimens of the Poetry of the Antient Welsh Bards*, translated into English, with notes (1764).

that the mountain opposite looked to-day like Parnassus. He and I had long talks about the Infinity of the Universe and about God.

Aug. 4th. Dolgelly. We walked into the field near the Golden Lion [Hotel]. A lovely field it is, encircled by bright streams, mountains beyond, a bridge and church tower in foreground covered with ivy, and Cader Idris towering with its woods over the church and the town.

Aug. 6th. His birthday. We went to the 'Torrent Walk,' a glorious view of Cader Idris over wooded hills at an opening of the road. 'His high rejoicing lines' he said of Cader Idris, he particularly liked the still pools of the torrent. Masses of willow herb and meadowsweet. The Welsh women were very demonstrative, one woman seized on little Lionel and hugged and kissed him as if she were crazy. A. T. bathed in the torrent and delighted in the clearness and in seeing the 'bottom agates'[4] far below.

Aug. 12th. Barmouth (Mrs. Meredith's home). He said that the drive here is beautiful when the tide is in and Cader Idris not veiled in clouds. I admired the place as much as he could wish me to do, I thought I never saw anything more beautiful in its way than the mountain bank with exquisite lights and shadows on crags and dark groves and fields. The sea and the sandhills radiant with sunlight. We had a delightful walk over the cliffs. Heath gorgeous.

Aug. 15th. He walked to Harlech. His old admiration of Harlech continued. (He bathed regularly in the sea.)

Aug. 20th. Mrs. Wynne of Aberam[f]fra[5] sent a beautiful nosegay. Raining all our drive to Harlech, still we could see something of the grand view of Harlech coming into the town. The castle above the marsh backed by dark wild mountains. I admired Harlech more than any other place I have yet seen in Wales.

Aug. 22nd. We set off in a car to Cwm Bychan (giant steps), set down on the banks of a clear stream which rushed past the fields of new mown hay. We sent to the Llyn road on stepping-stones over a bog, plenty of sweet gale. We came to the Llyn[6] in the midst of bare rocks. When he reached the giant steps he was too tired to do more than go up a hundred or so. A pity, for they are so mysterious there up on the mountain placed by the hands of those of whose very race there is no tradition.

Aug. 26th. He walked with Mr. Hughes the shopkeeper to a caldron cut out in the rock in a farm house about two miles from Harlech. On our way to the Tan-y-bwlch Arms, Mr. Hughes turned out to be the druggist of whom A. T. used to buy figs long ago at Barmouth.[7] He talked to A. T. of the bards and of education and of what he deemed its evil effects. Tan-y-bwlch very full. A. T. read me some of Ebenezer Williams's book on the manners of the Celtic nations.[8]

Aug. 30th. Drove through the misty rain to F[f]estiniog. Found the poor blind harper sitting with his head on his hands resting on his harp. He played

---

[4] *The Princess*, ii. 306.

[5] Aberamffra House, on the road from Dolgelly to Barmouth (*Black's Picturesque Guide to Wales*, 1882, p. 190).   [6] Lake, pond, or pool.   [7] In July 1839 (i. 172-3).

[8] *Eliezer* Williams (1754-1820: *DNB*), 'An Historical Essay on the Manners and Customs of the ancient Celtic Tribes', *Works* (1840).

airs to the delight of the children, and afterwards floating Welsh melodies, very sad.

Aug. 31st. A. T. found not only one waterfall but two, one a long silver stream, below were gloomy depths, arches of rocks and still pools. Then to church, voices very beautiful and well trained, the singing among the mountains touching. We looked at the sunset. The gravestones 'smiling in a golden light'[9] make him talk of the Resurrection. He told me that he 'heard the roar of the great cataract at a distance through the noise of the smaller one,'[10] by which he sat. He found the lake of [Llyn-y-Morwynion] very bare and desolate but he saw much to admire.

Sept. 2nd. He set off with Mr. Edwards over the mountains to Mr. Lloyd's[11] and saw the priceless old Welsh MSS., a Druid's egg (round and half purplish half whitish), some Bards' beads, a stone inscribed with the name of Geraint ap Erbin, a spear-head like a Greek spear and three daggers found together—slipt into a hole of rock. We read Stephens's *Cymry* in the evening.[12]

Sept. 4th. He took the children to the falls of Cynfael. The guide, a widow woman, helped to carry them. He said that the pictures and poses of the woman carrying the children in that wild scenery were beautiful.

Sept. 6th. We set off in a double car with two horses for Dolgelly. The vale of Llan-y-Llyd very fine, Cader Idris appearing at the end.

Sept. 8th. He went up Cader Idris. Pouring rain came on. We waited a long time for him. I heard the voice of waters, streams and cataracts, and I never saw anything more awful than that great veil of rain drawn straight over Cader Idris, pale light at the lower edge. It looked as if death were behind it and made me shudder when I thought he was there. A message came from him through the guide that he had gone to Dolgelly. He admired Tal-y-Llyn, and saw some grand effects in going up Cader Idris but the rain spoilt his view.

To Llanidloes. Distant range crimson or rather plum-coloured, then to Builth. We admired the valley of the Wye as it opened fold after fold. The

---

[9] Quote unidentified.

[10] See 'Geraint and Enid', ll. 170–5 and note: 'A memory of what I heard near Festiniog, but the scenery imagined is vaster' (Ricks, p. 1555).

[11] Very likely, Charles Edwards (d. 1889), of Dolserau Hall, about two miles north-east of Dolgelly, in the vale of the Wnion. He succeeded to the Dolserau estate in 1858 and was at one time JP and DL for Merioneth and Cardigan; High Sheriff for Merioneth in 1871; MP for the borough of New Windsor 1865–8. He had a London residence at 57 Great Cumberland Place, Hyde Park (*Black's Picturesque Guide to Wales*, p. 181; Thomas Nicholas, *Annals and Antiquities of the Counties and County Families of Wales* [2 vols., 1872], ii. 660, 702; *Walford's County Families of the United Kingdom*, 1904, p. 317).

He took Tennyson to see John Lloyd (1812–65) of Rhagatt, near Corwen, Merionethshire: 'The mansion contains a number of valuable paintings, many from the hand of the late Mr. Lloyd himself, who was an accomplished artist; and a collection of pre-historic remains—fossil bones, flint and other instruments, not long since discovered in the clefts of the limestone rock on the estate' (Nicholas, ii. 705). See also Foster; *Landed Gentry*.

[12] Thomas Stephens, *The Literature of the Kymry: being a Critical Essay on the History of the Language and Literature of Wales during the Twelfth and Two Succeeding Centuries* (1849), a well-known and prize-winning book (Allibone).

Wye, 'a river of fountains,' with a sweet and gentle voice (that reached far notwithstanding) 'sometimes like a summer shower.'

Sept. 15th. He went to Brecon. Mr. and Mrs. Lister Venables[13] called to ask us to meet Mr. G. S. Venables.

Sept. 16th. A. T. went to Caerleon.[14]

To EMILY SELLWOOD TENNYSON

Text. *Materials,* ii. 171.

CAERLEON, September 16, 1856

The Usk murmurs by the windows and I sit like King Arthur in Caerleon. I came here last night from Newport. This is a most quiet half ruined village of about 1500 inhabitants with little museum of Roman tombstones and other things.

To EMILY SELLWOOD TENNYSON

MS. Tennyson Research Centre.

HANBURY ARMS, [CAERLEON,] September 17, 1856

Dearest

The people here (Mr. Jones the Vicar and Mr. Lee a landed proprietor who lives in a large house near the amphitheatre—the round table of the king) are exceedingly kind.[1] I am going to drive with Mr. Lee today and he has given me his book about Caerleon. I suppose they have found me out though they have never alluded to my status. I think it will be better for you to come over to Brecon some day next week and meet me there, stop a day or two there while I go to Llandovery and then start for the Island. What say you? Let me know.

Thine ever
A. T.

If you can concoct a kind letter to Mary [Ker] I think you had better do it—poor soul she means no ill—then I will add to it.

---

[13] The Revd Richard Lister Venables (1809–94), of Llysdinam Hall (older brother of G. S. Venables), whose wife (m. 1834, d. 1865) was the daughter of 'Gen. Poltaratsky, of Russia' (*Landed Gentry*).

[14] 'Alfred is at Caerleon, or was when he wrote the letter I have today. He left me for it on Monday. Till then we have been wandering about together but our purse had grown so lean it seemed best for me to stay here with the bairns. We hope to be home at the end of the month' (*The Letters of Emily Tennyson,* p. 103).

[1] John Edward Lee (1808–87: *DNB*), antiquary and geologist (FSA, FGS). He was born near Hull, but after travelling in Russia and Scandinavia, moved to Caerleon (the 'large house' is the Priory) and 'took an active part in forming a County Antiquarian Association' (Allibone). He wrote *Delineations of Roman Antiquities Found at Caerleon* (1845) and *Description of a Roman Building and Other Remains Lately Discovered at Caerleon* (1850: see *Tennyson in Lincoln,* i, No. 1378). Lee sent the Tennysons a 'kind note' and a copy of Rees, *Lives of the Cambro British Saints (Tennyson in Lincoln,* i, No. 1864); he is mentioned in Nicholas, *Annals and Antiquities,* ii. 723, 769.

To EMILY SELLWOOD TENNYSON
Text. Materials, ii. 172.

September 18, [1856]

The Lees are going to drive me over to Usk to-day and to Caerphilly on Monday, and from Caerphilly I shall go to Merthyr Tydvil from which place I believe there is a Tuesday coach to Brecon.

To EMILY SELLWOOD TENNYSON
Text. Materials, ii. 172.

September 19, [1856]

I have just returned from Raglan, the ruins of which are magnificent, but I saw not much of them as it was raining though with occasional glorious bursts of sunshine and a rainbow. It is a place to spend a week in but I could not afford more than an hour and a half.
Llandovery must I think wait till another year.

EMILY SELLWOOD TENNYSON's JOURNAL
Text. Materials, ii. 172.

Sept. 23rd. Heavy showers but we got safely to Brecon. Neither he nor I admired this part of the Wye as much as that at Builth. The situation of the Castle Hotel beautiful.
Sept. 24th. We walked in the garden with Mr. Lloyd and saw the bit of ruined Castle adjoining the Hotel. The terraced garden with its bright flowers was a lovely foreground to the Usk, and to the town with its churches and bridge, and the high hills here wooded, there coverd with furze, or with green stubble-fields, Cader Arthur beyond. Horses fording the Usk picturesque. He and I felt the Litany very impressive as we heard it in that desolate looking but fine church. A young lime tree with yellow leaves made a rich picture overshadowing a monumental slab in the wall of the church. This tree was rooted in the wall.

To ROBERT JAMES MANN
Text. Materials, ii. 140, and draft *Materials*, iv. 74.

FARRINGFORD, [*c.* 3 October 1856]

Dear Dr. Mann
Many thanks for your very delightful little astronomical book and the pamphlets, one of which I have seen before.[1] I hope before you settle down at

---

[1] Probably Mann's *Guide to Astronomical Science* (1856: 18mo) but possibly his *Guide to the Knowledge of the Heavens* (1852, also 18mo). The pamphlets were probably his *Lessons in General Knowledge*, Series 1, 2, 1855; 3, 1856 (Allibone).

Bonchurch for the winter that you and Mrs. Mann will come and stop some days with us. That sovereign which you paid for your accommodation at the Villa Doria (as we call the Red House of Mr. Dore)[2] has always stuck in my gizzard like an unswallowed bit of hard apple. Come then once more and let me, by whatever hospitality I can show you, atone for suffering you to pay what I should have done. Moxon was here the other day and told me he sent your essay to all the Reviews and they took no notice, the snobs, I suppose they durst not, have you lost upon it? I fear so. I have heard it praised by men who knew, and should like to learn that you are no sufferer by your chivalrous defence of the heroine. Come if you can, you shall always be welcome.

Yours
A. Tennyson

My wife's kind regards. We have only been back out of Wales for a day or two.

To JOHN WILLIAM PARKER

MS. Doheny Library, St. John's Seminary, Camarillo, California.
FARRINGFORD, FRESHWATER, ISLE OF WIGHT, Sunday, October 5, 1856
My dear Parker
I am here after my tour. Whenever you like to run over I shall be happy to entertain you for as long as you find leisure to stay. So pray come and if [you] can bring Mr. Bell[1] with you so much the better.

Yours very truly
A. Tennyson

To BENJAMIN BAINES

MS. Rosenbach Foundation.
FARRINGFORD, FRESHWATER, ISLE OF WIGHT, October 6, 1856
Dear Sir
I have bought an estate here and am bound under a penalty of £500 to pay the money into Drummond's bank[1] by the 23rd November. I cannot raise the sum without selling out the shares (£1700) in the East Lincolnshire which you bought for me about three years ago at £145 a share. I see now that they range at 139–141. I shall I fear be a loser to some small extent, but I must leave it to you to watch the market and make as good a sale as you can. Let me hear from you in reply. I am, dear Sir,

Yours truly
A. Tennyson

---

[2] John Dore (White's *Hampshire*). See *Journal*, p. 51.
[1] Robert Bell (see above, p. 153).
[1] 49 Charing Cross, SW.

To ARTHUR HUGH CLOUGH[1]

MS. Ruth Mulhauser.

[15 October 1856]

Dear Clough

Where can you be in this frightful storm and fury of wind and rain? I have waited half an hour. Come and dine with me some day. We always dine at 5. I suppose I mustn't ask Mrs. Clough before my wife calls. We did not know that she was with you.

Yours
A. T.

Will you come tomorrow at 2 o'clock. We give a lunch at 2 to a country party.[2]

To WILLIAM ALLINGHAM

Text. Letters to William Allingham, pp. 277–8.

October 21, 1856

My dear Allingham

I daresay you have cursed me in your heart[1] for not sending your book before now.

I have been away travelling for more than two months in Wales and did not receive your book till long after you had sent it.

My opinion of your poem is that Georgy Levison is very good and graphic —the man I mean. The poem seems in parts too fine, in the style of the last century, and some of the worst parts of Wordsworth, a style which he inherited and could not quite shake off.

For instance your Corinthian bush means currants—why not say 'currant bush' at once. Wordsworth has 'the fragrant beverage drawn from China's herb' for tea.[2] This sort of avoidance of plain speaking is the more ungrateful

---

[1] Arthur Hugh Clough (1819–61: *DNB*) had published *The Bothie of Toper-na-Fuosich* (1848; reprinted posthumously as *The Bothie of Tober-na-Vuolich*) and (with Thomas Burbridge) *Ambervalia* (1849), out of which Clough's forty short poems were reissued in 1850. ('Amours de Voyage' appeared serially in the *Atlantic Monthly* in 1858, 'Dipsychus' posthumously in *Letters and Remains*, 1865.) Clough returned to England, after a visit to America in July 1853, and married Blanche Smith in 1854. At this time he was private secretary to Robert Lowe and Vice President of the Privy Council Committee on Education, and was holidaying at Freshwater, 'in a cottage, just above Allum Bay, famous for its coloured sands, red, white, yellow, black, orange . . ., and about a mile from the Needles' (*The Correspondence of Arthur Hugh Clough*, ed. Frederick L. Mulhauser, ii. 520). When and how he met Tennyson (if this is not the first meeting) is not evident, but it must have been through Palgrave (or possibly Jowett), all contemporaries at Oxford. See *Tennyson in Lincoln*, i, No. 765, and below, pp. 276–8.

[2] Fourteen guests (including 'Mdlle Guyangos') are named in *Journal*, p. 76.

[1] Job 1:5.

[2] 'The beverage drawn from China's fragrant herb', *The Excursion*, ix. 530–1. Even Wordsworth, owning that it was 'somewhat too pompous', altered it in 1828 (published 1837). See *The Poetical Works of William Wordsworth*, ed. De Selincourt and Darbishire, v. 304, 474. Tennyson's edition was *Poems*, 5 vols., 1827, now owned by Mark L. Reed, who supplied the information (see *Tennyson in Lincoln*, i, No. 2367).

to me in your poem because other parts of it are quite unadorned and justly simple. Georgy himself as I said is well-drawn and remains, a picture upon the memory, and will remain I hope to do you honour in men's eyes.

The other poems[3] I have had scarce time to look at since my return, but I may tell you that my little boy, four years old, repeats your 'Robin' with great unction.

Yours ever, in all haste, but very truly
A. Tennyson

Mind, I like your Poem and therefore I say about it what I have said. It is *worth* correction. I said I had not read the others; I meant so as to give them their due consideration. 'Mea culpa' I admire much. My wife's kind regards to you.

To BENJAMIN BAINES

MS. Rosenbach Foundation.

FARRINGFORD HOUSE, FRESHWATER, I. W., October 23, 1856

Dear Sir

I have a further grace given me till the 2d of December which is not much. You of course know these matters much better than I do and I must leave it in your hands. If you think it better to sell to the party whom you mention than to wait a little longer, do so. I feel sure that you will not effect the sale without a proper regard to the interest of the vendor. I am

Faithfully yours
A. Tennyson

To WILLIAM RICHARDSON DEMPSTER

MS. Gordon Ray.

FARRINGFORD, FRESHWATER, ISLE OF WIGHT, October 25, 1856

My dear Dempster

I am very glad to hear that you are in England once more—though grieved with your grief which forces you into travelling. Is there any chance of your coming to see me here, as I fear there is not much chance of my visiting London for some time yet. You have not said how long you intend to remain in London or in England. Of course *if* I came to London I would find you out. I religiously preserve the Niagara walking-stick you gave me so long ago, never using it or only on occasions of state which rarely indeed occur.

Pray come here if you can.[1] It is a very pretty place and has a fine air, and

---

[3] In manuscript. 'George Levison; or, The Schoolfellow', 'Robin Redbreast', and 'Mea Culpa' all first appeared in book form in Allingham's *Poems*, published by Ticknor and Fields, Boston, 1861.

[1] Dempster arrived on the 29th, left on the 1st. Tennyson gave him a copy of *Maud, and Other Poems*, A New Edition, 1856 (inscribed 'W. R. Dempster from A. Tennyson', now at Texas Christian University, a hitherto unrecorded state) with the six concluding lines added by hand (with three variants: 'and the war *go* down', 'I have felt *for* my native land', 'doom assign'd').

my wife will be very glad to make your acquaintance and I will introduce you to two pretty boys which have been born to me since I saw you last. Believe me, my dear Dempster,

Yours very truly
A. Tennyson

To WILLIAM RICHARDSON DEMPSTER

MS. Texas Christian University.

[26 October 1856]

My dear Dempster

Pray pardon me: the paper about the boats was left out of my last, by some mischance. I have often so many letters to write, that mine and my wife's (who writes many for me) day are half taken up with it. While other letters were being written, mine to you was laid aside and sent at last without the printed papers.[1]

Yours ever
A. Tennyson

ARTHUR HUGH CLOUGH *to* ALFRED TENNYSON (extract)

Text. P. G. Scott, 'Tennyson's Celtic Reading,' *Tennyson Research Bulletin*, No. 2 (Nov. 1968), p. 5.

November 1, 1856

The best collection of Welsh books is, I am told, to be found in the Library of the Gwynneddifion Society in London. . . . it would be easy to get access to it. The Myvyrian Archaeology is reported 'very scarce'—a copy in the Jesus College Library—I have some hopes of getting a copy of Llywarch Hen for you.[1]

COVENTRY PATMORE *to* ALFRED TENNYSON

Text. P. G. Scott, 'Tennyson's Celtic Reading,' *Tennyson Research Bulletin*, No. 2 (Nov. 1968), p. 5.

November 4, 1856

The Welsh publisher has vanished from Holywell Street, and no other seems to have taken his place. I will, however, make further enquiries. Emily [Patmore] and I are jointly executing a copy of Llywarch Hen, but you must be patient, as it requires more time to copy Welsh accurately than English.

---

[1] The letter is written on the inside of the envelope and flap. Enclosed is 'A printed table of steamboat sailings between Yarmouth and Lymington, Winter Service, 1856'.

[1] See below, p. 167.

The Elegies seem to be strange trash for the most part—at least in the literal translation.[1]

To ELISHA KENT KANE[1]

MS. Indiana University.

FARRINGFORD HOUSE, FRESHWATER, ISLE OF WIGHT, November 4, 1856

Dear Sir

Your book has not yet reached me here in this remote place, but as I learn with much regret that the state of your health obliges you to leave England very soon I will not wait to see it before I write to request you will do me the favour of allowing me an opportunity to thank you in person for what I am told are your kind expressions towards myself in your book, and for the honour you have done me by giving my name to that noble pillar. My wife and I hope that you will feel equal to coming so far out of your way to your ship, as to pay us a visit here and that a little rest will soon restore you to your former health. Believe me, dear Sir,

Yours very truly
A. Tennyson

P. S. If there be a Miss Cross in your house, and if it be the Miss Cross whom I knew in Scotland,[2] will you give her my best regards?

To BENJAMIN BAINES

MS. Rosenbach Foundation.

FARRINGFORD, FRESHWATER, I. W., November 6, 1856

Dear Sir

I have no doubt that you have managed for me as well as possible under the circumstances. It is of course rather annoying to lose so much, but I had

---

[1] See above, p. 156 n., and below, p. 167.

[1] Elisha Kent Kane (1820–57), American Arctic explorer, sailed in 1850 as Senior Medical Officer on the first Grinnell expedition in search of Sir John Franklin. His book *Arctic Explorations: the Second Grinnell Expedition in Search of Sir John Franklin, 1853, '54, '55* (2 vols., 1856) is inscribed 'A. Tennyson Esq., with my warm regard. E. K. Kane, London Nov. 4' (*Tennyson in Lincoln*, i, No. 1286). The 'noble pillar' on the north Greenland coast Kane described (i. 224) as a 'solitary column or minaret tower, as sharply finished as if it had been cast for the Place Vendome. Yet the length of the shaft alone is four hundred and eighty feet, and it rises on a plinth or pedestal itself two hundred and eighty feet high'; 'I remember well the emotions of our party as it first broke upon our view. Cold and sick as I was, I brought back a sketch of it, which may have interest for the reader, though it scarcely suggests the imposing dignity of this magnificent landmark. Those who are happily familiar with the writings of Tennyson, and have communed with his spirit in the solitudes of wilderness, will apprehend the impulse that inscribed the scene with his name.' See also *Memoir*, i. 382–3, *Tennyson in Lincoln*, ii, Nos. 5712–13, and Charles W. Shields, 'The Arctic Monument Named for Tennyson by Dr. Kane', *County Magazine*, lvi (Aug. 1898), 483–91.

[2] See above, p. 69.

made up my mind to lose—it could not be helped. I send you the certificates in a registered letter and am much obliged to you.

Yours truly
A. Tennyson

To ELISHA KENT KANE

Text. Memoir, 1899, p. 322.

[c. 12 November 1856]

Dear Dr. Kane

Only yesterday, and then too late for me to return you thanks by that day's post, arrived your present. The book is really magnificent. I do not think I ever met with one which gives such vivid pictures of Arctic scenery. Nay I am quite sure I never did; and indeed I feel that I owe you more thanks for it, and for your warm-hearted inscription, and your memorial of me in the wilderness than I could well enclose in as many words. So I will say nothing about it, only beg you to accept that volume of my poems containing the line which (as Charles Weld writes)[1] came into your mind when you stood first before the great greenstone minaret. . . . Believe me, dear Dr. Kane,

Yours ever
A. Tennyson

ARTHUR HUGH CLOUGH to FRANCIS JAMES CHILD[1]

Text. The Correspondence of Arthur Hugh Clough, ed. Frederick L. Mulhauser, ii. 520–1 (extract).

November 13, 1856.

Tennyson is going on with fragments, or idylls as I believe he calls them, on the Morte d'Arthur subjects. Two considerable ones are complete and he seems to be working steadily—studying Welsh moreover—I like him personally better than I do his manner in his verses; personally he is the most unmannerly simple big child of a man that you can find.[2]

---

[1] Weld's letter (Yale), 10 November from Somerset House, cites 'As in strange lands a traveller walking slow | [. . .] then thinketh, "I have found a new land, but I die" ' ('The Palace of Art', ll. 277–84). Kane's party, frozen in, had abandoned ship and made their way to Greenland. His health was affected, and he died the following year. For Kane's inscription, see above, p. 165 n.

[1] Francis James Child (1825–96), Professor of English at Harvard, noted especially for his *English and Scottish Popular Ballads* (5 vols., 1883–98).

[2] 'Clough is a very gentle soul. A. likes his poems but not his Hexameters. "The mazy strengths of abstraction" he called a humble[?] end of an Hexameter' (Journal, 16 October 1856, in draft *Materials*, iv. 90).

18 *November* 1856

To THOMAS BUCHANAN READ[1]

MS. Historical Society of Pennsylvania.

PARK HOUSE, MAIDSTONE, November 18, 1856

My dear Sir

I shall be in town at Mr. Charles Weld's of the Royal Society on Thursday evening, and shall be glad to see you if you can find leisure to come—shall also be glad to see you if you can come to Freshwater in the Isle of Wight, where I live. Meanwhile I am,

Truly yours
A. Tennyson

To ROBERT JAMES MANN

Text. *Materials,* ii. 140–1.

[? *c.* 3 December 1856]

Dear Dr. Mann

Tell me did you when here tear out of the Geometry[1] you gave me, in some repentant mood, the inscription you put on the blank leaf and if you did, so be it, if not, who has done it? I find it torn out and suspect the housemaid of lighting fires with my library. Let me know please for I am in some measure troubled about it.

Yours ever
A. Tennyson

Ellis[2] is coming to-morrow, to-day smoke pervades the whole house I am sorry to say.

ARTHUR HUGH CLOUGH *to* ALFRED TENNYSON

Text. P. G. Scott, 'Tennyson's Celtic Reading,' *Tennyson Research Bulletin,* No. 2 (Nov. 1968), p. 6.

[12 December 1856]

I have just received from my uncle . . . both Llywarch Hen and the Gododin—I propose to send them and Palgrave, I believe, is going to pay you a visit before Xmas, but if you are in immediate need of them, I will send them by post.

---

[1] Thomas Buchanan Read (1822–72), American poet and painter. He called on Thursday, 20 November (*Journal,* p. 78). 'Last night, according to arrangement, Tennyson came up to town, and we met at Somerset House, where were several notable people, among the rest Lady Franklin. . . . I was especially convinced that poets are human in my interview with Tennyson last night. He is a noble fellow, but very human, except in his poems, and there he is divine!' (Henry C. Townsend, *A Memoir of T. Buchanan Read* [1889], p. 103).

[1] Possibly one of the *Lessons in General Knowledge* (see above, p. 160 n.).
[2] Charles Ellis, the 'poetic wine dealer' (see above, p. 73 n.).

Llywarch Hen is in Owen's edition, 1792. The Gododin in that of the Revd. John Williams ab Ithel, M. A., Llandovery, 1852.[1]

To GEORGE STOVIN VENABLES

MS. National Library of Wales.

FARRINGFORD, December 18, 1856

My dear Venables

Any book you choose to let me have I shall be grateful for; the Poetae Scenici or another; I merely wanted one as a keepsake.[1] I have not yet written anything to his memory and perhaps never may, so that it will be as well not to mention to any of the L[ushington]s that I ever spoke of such a thing but I do not suppose that you have mentioned it.

Tom's flight and all about the scarlet fever is news to me. I had never heard a whisper of it.[2]

I was sorry to have missed seeing your Father[3] when in Wales. I *did* see the top of his head in the justice room at Rhayader but did not venture to send a message to him. I hope that you left all well at Llysdinam.

I need not say how glad we should be to see you if you could come here before you join the Ashburtons; for my part I shall never take 'my lizard' for an icthyosaur till I have paid for him.

Ever yours
A. Tennyson

My wife's kindest remembrances. Have you read Aurora Leigh?[4] and if [so], how do you like it?

P. S. If I should not see you before you go to Nice, let me beg you now to remember me with all kindness to Lord and Lady Ashburton.[5]

To RICHARD DOYLE

MS. Brook Club, New York, N.Y.

FARRINGFORD, December 19, 1856

My dear Doyle

Simeon brought me the other day your landskip or seaskip for it is both.

---

[1] See above, p. 164; also below, p. 387 and n. for Williams ab Ithel.

[1] Of Henry Lushington whose deathbed will left all his books to Venables (along with his villa on Malta). See *Tennyson in Lincoln*, i, No. 826: Karl Wilhelm Dinsdorf, *Poetae Scenici Graeci* (1830), inscribed (presumably by Venables): 'Henry Lushington August 11, 1855 Alfred Tennyson's gift. 1858'.

[2] They had dined twice with the Tom Lushingtons a month earlier at Park House (*Journal*, p. 78).

[3] The Ven. Richard Venables, DD (d. 1858), Archdeacon of Carmarthen (*Landed Gentry*).

[4] Elizabeth Barrett Browning's poem (dated 1857) was received 27 November, and Emily Tennyson finished reading it by 3 December (*Journal*, p. 79). Venables reviewed it in the *Saturday Review*, 27 December 1856 (M. M. Bevington, *The Saturday Review, 1855–68*, p. 215).

[5] Lady Ashburton died 4 May 1857.

Did I beg it, as your letter seems to imply?[1] It was very shameful in me. Nevertheless I cannot be very repentant seeing that I have got it and that we are both so much pleased with it. I am not sure that I shall not send you an engraving done from it one of these days, that is if you will permit me to have it engraved. There are first however three separate distances of the downs that I shall get you to put in next time you are here and we hope that may be very soon. Easter at the latest if all be well with us. We have some compunction in asking any one not an American to come on so arduous a journey in winter. Meanwhile, my dear Doyle, believe me,

Yours ever
A. Tennyson

To A. PLACKETT[1]

Text. Memoir, i. 416–17; *Materials*, ii. 175; draft *Materials*, iv. 98.

FARRINGFORD, December 31, [1856]

Sir

I have as you desired considered your poem, and though I make it a rule to decline passing any judgment on poems, I cannot in this instance refrain from giving you a word of advice.

Following your calling diligently, for be assured, work, far from being a hardship, is a blessing, and if you are a poet indeed, you will find in it a help not a hindrance. You might, if you chose, offer these lines to some magazine, but you must not be surprised if they are refused, for the poetic gift is so common in these days that hundreds must have to endure this disappointment, and I should not be an honest friend if I did not prepare you for that.

I should by no means recommend you to risk the publication of a volume on your own account. The publication of verse is almost always attended with loss. As an amusement to yourself and your friends, the writing is all very well. Accept my good wishes and believe me,

Your obedient servant
A. Tennyson

---

[1] On 5 December Doyle had written (TRC): 'On the last day of my most agreeable visit to Farringford I began a little sketch of the beautiful view seen from your drawing room windows, and you looked over me, as I sat at work, and said you would like to have it. At the time, with the splendid tints of nature before my eyes, my poor attempt at imitation seemed so worthless that it quite shocked me to think of your possessing it who had the glorious original always in sight. I believe I said nothing, and it must have appeared very rude to you. But I secretly determined in my own mind to take it home, and try to improve it, and then to ask you to accept it. . . .

'It is a long time since Easter but this is the first time that I have fallen in with the "right man" going to the "right place". . . .'

[1] Unidentified.

To WILLIAM RICHARDSON DEMPSTER

MS. New York University Libraries.

[17 February 1857]

My dear Dempster

I am sorry to hear that you are not in such good health and spirits as I would wish you to be. London is but a gloomy place to sojourn in for so long if you have not kindly friends and associates to share the burden of the fog and the hour with you—and you do not say whether you enjoyed your trip to Paris: but I trust that the sight of your little daughter on the other side of the Atlantic will cheer you again. I am ⟨myself⟩ a bad comforter today, having [a] swelled face, [a] cold and a rheumatic arm, all small evils but enough to damp the spirits. Do not make any prophecies about your not returning to England. I trust that I shall yet once more have the pleasure of seeing you under my roof.

Kindest remembrances from my wife and kisses from the babes and believe me,

Yours ever
A. Tennyson

To ROBERT JAMES MANN

Text. Memoir, i. 406; *Materials,* ii. 141.

[early April 1857]

Dear Doctor

I am delighted with Miss Sewell's gift,[1] though yet unseen. I should like as I have told her to learn something of the naming of it: can you tell me anything? Please get it framed, we shall be half a year getting it done here. I think it should not have a great white margin except the artist herself desires it. Perhaps the lake was not called after your humble servant but

---

[1] Ellen Mary Sewell (1813–1905: *DNB*), sister of Elizabeth Missing Sewell (1815–1906), novelist and religious writer, of a prominent Isle of Wight family, whose journal entry for 17 April is helpful: 'I meant to have written on Easter Day, but could not find time. I was called away as I wrote the last words to see Tennyson—*Mr.* Tennyson now, for he has become an acquaintance, almost a friend. Ellen did a drawing for him of the New Zealand Lake, named after him, and he came to thank her the other day with Dr. Mann. Then yesterday we dined at St. Lawrence with him, on the occasion of his brother's marriage with Miss Elwes (a cousin of Lady Charlotte Copley) who has been staying some little time with her sister, Mrs. West, at Lord Yarborough's cottage. This morning he came with Dr. Mann again to see another picture which Ellen has done, a water-colour drawing from an engraving in Dr. Kane's book, of a huge natural pillar found in the Arctic regions and called Tennyson's Pillar. I think I could be fond of him; all his friends are. One sees that he is simple and warm-hearted, and unspoilt by the world. I like the shake of his hand especially. We had a very quiet unpretending party at St. Lawrence, only Mr. Hambrough and two clergymen beside ourselves. Mrs. Tennyson was there, and charms me more than he does. She is tall, and slight, and simple, and sensible, with something of a thoughtful melancholy about her which interests one much; not that it is anything approaching to unhappiness, and he seems quite devoted to her' (*The Autobiography of Elizabeth M. Sewell,* ed. Eleanor L. Sewell, pp. 158–9). *Materials,* ii. 255–6, prints Ellen Sewell's letter to Tennyson quoting extensively from Weld's letter to herself.

another. I enclose you the note to Miss Sewell which please deliver and read if you choose.

A. T.

To ?

MS. Yale.

FARRINGFORD, I. W., [? early April 1857]

Dear Sir

I have received and read with much pleasure your press slip, describing the journey made to the Lake to which Mr. Weld gave my name.[1] I have a painting in water colours done from Mr. Weld's sketch of the Lake by Miss Sewell an amateur artist of Bonchurch in this island.

To REGINALD SOUTHEY[1]

MS. Morgan Library.

FARRINGFORD, I. W., April 25, 1857

Dear Sir

I have this morning received the photographs of my two boys. The eldest is very well likenessed: the other, perhaps, not so well. My best thanks. I wish you had come up here when you were at Freshwater. As it is I look forward to the pleasure of making your acquaintance at some future time.

Yours very truly
A. Tennyson

To EMILY SELLWOOD TENNYSON

Text. *Materials*, ii. 179.

LITTLE HOLLAND HOUSE, April 29, 1857

I called yesterday at the London Library and saw Fitzgerald there looking thinnish and worn. I thought Donne said there need be no hurry in sending

---

[1] Frederick Aloysius Weld (1823–91: *DNB*; GCMG 1855) emigrated to New Zealand in 1844, and did much exploring there in 1851 and 1855. He was Premier in 1864–5, Governor of West Australia, 1869, of Tasmania, 1875, of Straits Settlement, 1880–7. Henry Sewell (1807–79: *DNB*) was New Zealand's first Premier (for six days in May 1856) and was Minister of Justice under Weld in 1864–5. Lake Tennyson is a 'lakelet near the source of the Clarence River. Locality of Amuri County' (*The New Zealand Guide*, compiled by Edward Stewart Dollimore). 'It is nearly half-way between Nelson and Canterbury quite in the interior of the country. I had always intended to give a Tennysonian name to some fitting spot and at the time I saw it first I had some lines of "The Princess" running in my head. The mountain peak tall and stately above the rest with a clear evening sun on its summit, I called "The Princess" and the Lake "Lake Tennyson".' (See 'Come down, O maid', *The Princess*, vii. 176–207, and 'Maud', I. 427—Ricks, pp. 835, 1061.)

[1] Reginald Southey (1835–99), at this time perhaps still an undergraduate (BA Oxford, 1857 [Foster], or 1855 [*Who Was Who*]), on Easter holiday on the Isle of Wight. Later, he became a doctor (MD 1861), and from 1883 to 1898 was Commissioner of Lunacy. See *Journal*, pp. 91–3.

the books about King Arthur.[1] Mrs. Brookfield and the Hallams I saw likewise.

To HALLAM TENNYSON

MS. Tennyson Research Centre.

[? 29 April 1857]

Dear little Hallam
    I have got your nice little letter and am much obliged to you for it. I wish you would learn to write for then you might write to me without troubling Mamma.[1] I did not see you waving the handkerchief for I am short-sighted. Kisses to you and little Lionel and be good biscuity boys.

Your affectionate papa
A. Tennyson

To LIONEL TENNYSON

MS. Tennyson Research Centre.

[? 29 April 1857]

Dear little Lionel I hope that you are a good boy at your lessons and obedient to Mamma. Are all the violets gone?

Your affectionate
Papa

To ANNE ISABELLA THACKERAY

MS. Armstrong Browning Library.

Wednesday [? 29 April 1857]

My dear Annie Thackeray
    I can't come 1st because my good hostess and nurse says that I ought not in my present state 2dly because there is a floating invitation sent out to divers friends of mine and acceptable any day till next Monday.

Yours ever
A. Tennyson

---

[1] See above, p. 78. 'I sent the L[ondon] Library books the same day or rather the next and a note to say I had sent them' (*The Letters of Emily Tennyson*, p. 109).

[1] 'He [Hallam] duly read the printed bit and tried some of the rest and with his usual strong feeling of property took great pleasure in saying that part was his' (Emily to Alfred Tennyson, 30 April, TRC).

To EMILY SELLWOOD TENNYSON

MS. Tennyson Research Centre.

Thursday Morning, [30 April 1857]

Dearest

I got the stocking which seems to have been repaired very swiftly and skilfully—this morning.[1]

Old Thoby Prinsep is a Prince of a man.[2] You would delight in the gallant old fellow. Don't get ill, Madam, don't! So no more at present except
        A KISS FOR HALLAM AND A KISS FOR LIONEL
and another for thee.

                                      Thine
                                      A. T.

I ought to tell you there is a charming house to be had now for asking. Mrs. C[ameron] will write to you about her [*sic*]. Don't leave this lying about.

To ANNE WELD (fragment)[1]

MS. County Record Office, Gloucester.

LITTLE HOLLAND HOUSE, Thursday morning, April 30, [1857]

My dear Anne

I could not call yesterday being laid up with a bad foot. Let me introduce the bearer my hostess, Mrs. Prins[ep].

P. S. Don't tell Emily that I have a bad foot.[2]

---

[1] See above, p. 154 and n.

[2] Henry Thoby Prinsep (1792 [or 1793]–1878), civil servant in India from about 1814 to 1843, when he resigned. In 1835 he married Sarah Monckton Pattle, sister of Julia Margaret Cameron. They returned to England in 1843, leased Little Holland House, Kensington, in 1850, and hunted lions to grace the salon. 'Under Sara and Thoby Prinsep the old house enjoyed a St. Martin's Summer which almost rivalled the palmy days of the great house. Sara was able to experience the pleasures and excitement of lion-hunting to the full, and she became very successful at this social pursuit. . . . The fame of Sara's salon was exceeded by the reputation of her cook. She and Thoby kept open house every Sunday afternoon during the summer months, favoured guests being invited to stay on to dinner, which was a movable feast, for on warm moonlit nights the hostess might have the long table laid in the garden or, if indoors, usher her guests from one room to another during the course of the meal. Earlier, the diners, in company with the less favoured confraternity, had sunned themselves in the pleasant gardens or, taking shelter from the heat in the cool lavender-scented house, strolled from room to room or ensconced themselves on chairs and sofas chatting to whom they pleased. Bowls and croquet were provided as diversions for the most active among the distinguished visitors (all Sara's visitors were distinguished in one way or another) and between games they refreshed themselves at the tea tables set out under the tall branching elms and elegantly presided over by their cheerful hostess.' A 'visitor said of the Prinseps' home that it was a haven from which everything had been rigorously excluded but high living and the pursuit of beauty' (Brian Hill, *Julia Margaret Cameron, A Victorian Family Portrait*, pp. 57–8, 60).

[1] The signature and possibly part of the text have been cut out.

[2] 'I hope Cartwright will make thee comfortable. Do not let anyone play tricks with that toe. I think it very likely from thy cold or from the state of thy general health' (*The Letters of Emily Tennyson*, p. 109).

To HENRY HALLAM

Text. Maggs Bros. Catalogue, No. 269, Summer 1911.

LITTLE HOLLAND HOUSE, KENSINGTON, [*c.* 1 May 1857]

I am laid up with a bad foot and cannot stir out. The nail of the great toe having shot out a spur low down into the flesh causing an inflammation, I have twice had to undergo a rather cruel surgical operation owing to this abnormal fancy of the nail.

To EMILY SELLWOOD TENNYSON

Text. Materials, ii. 179–80.

May 1, [1857]

Hunt and Woolner and Palgrave here. Spedding dines here today. I have little or no news except that all people are exceedingly kind.

May 6, [1857]

I have put the sheets in hand to print and shall bring them back with me.[1]

To JOHN FORSTER

MS. Tennyson Research Centre.

60 [LINCOLN'S INN FIELDS,] [? 8 May 1857]

My dear Forster

I should have been to see you before but I am laid up with a bad foot. I shall be here till 5 o'clock. Can you come over?

Ever yours
A. Tennyson

To EMILY SELLWOOD TENNYSON (incomplete) AND HALLAM TENNYSON

MS. Tennyson Research Centre.

[8 May 1857]

Dearest

Hallam's slake[1] is very good. I am really grieved that Gandy's conduct has been so brutal. I wish I had been at home. I would not have allowed her to go on insulting you. This comes of treating a coarse nature *too* kindly.[2] I did not

---

[1] *Enid and Nimuë: the True and the False* (Ricks, p. 1465). See below, p. 179.

[1] Daub.

[2] Gandy was sent away ('I get up early to see dear Gandy off, obliged to send her away for fear of bad effects on our Hallam from favouritism to Lionel whom she had [favoured] from the first'—*Journal*, p. 94), but rejoined them later (see *Journal*, p. 97).

write yesterday—for I had been out to Hallam's to breakfast which upset me and made me so sleepy all the day that I missed the post. I shall be home some day next week probably about the middle. Shall I bring the new nurse and will you troop the other woman out? I hope she won't get hold of my letters or anything else. Last night I. Morier[3] came and was very genial. He is off again to Vienna. Desired particular remembrances to thee. Millais too came and dined at Little H. House and Doyle has dined twice.

Now here is a letter for Hallam

Dear Hallam
When you get this you must turn to Lionel and give him a nice little kiss and you must give another kiss to dear Mama.
This letter comes from

Papa
×××× Thine

E. L. L. called on me a day or two back.

JOHN FORSTER
to EMILY SELLWOOD TENNYSON (extract)

MS. Yale.

46 MONTAGU SQUARE, W., May 9, 1857

I heard *Enid* last night, and cannot help telling you, at once, how absolutely perfect I think it. . . .

It is a great word to say, that Alfred himself never wrote anything more exquisite than this poem, but it has so *strangely* affected me, that I dare confidently to say as much. I cannot detect a flaw. It goes to the very bottom of the depths of truth. . . .

To EMILY SELLWOOD TENNYSON

MS. Tennyson Research Centre.

[9 May 1857]

Dearest
Thou knowest I told thee that I should miss a letter *occasionally*—so if it occurs again don't fancy anything wrong. We, i.e. Mrs. P[rinsep] and Mrs. C[ameron] and I dined with Forster who was immensely jolly and I read

---

[3] *Materials*, ii. 180, expands 'I.' (or possibly 'J.') to 'Joe', but the reference is unquestionably to Robert Burnet David Morier (see above, p. 48 n.), always known as 'Burnet'. (There never was a 'Joe' Morier; Isaac Morier died in 1817, James Justinian Morier in 1849.) Burnet Morier was at this time attaché in Vienna, and spent twenty-three years in diplomatic service in Germany; later he was minister at Lisbon and Madrid, and ambassador at St. Petersburg. He was also the closest friend Jowett ever had (see Geoffrey Faber's fine book *Jowett, A Portrait with a Background, passim*; on p. 91, Morier is called a 'genial young giant'). See also Morier's *Memoirs and Letters*, ed. Rosslyn Wemyss.

Enid to him and Mrs. F[orster] who is a very nice ladylike woman.[1]

I cannot say on what day I shall be home next week. It all depends upon my dentist and whether a tooth will within a certain time *bear* stopping.

Millais offered to do the cut in the Miller's [daughter] over again with a view of the mill but it was too late.[2] Thine, many kisses to thee and thine and mine.

A. T.

To EMILY SELLWOOD TENNYSON

MS. Tennyson Research Centre.

[? 11 May 1857][1]

Dearest

I had a very pleasant evening at the T. Taylor's yesterday.[2] There was a Frenchman there, a wonderful actor, who played a whole disastrous history on the fiddle, imitating all kinds of things, and blew soap bubbles filled with smoke and set them like fruits upon the rosebushes, blew them double, and sent them up like opals to Heaven—altogether curious if not instructive. I have bought the candlesticks but I fear they will not do—they are about half the size of those we have but the same kind of thing, at any rate they will do for the other chimneypieces. I like the paper with the velvet pattern best, I think.[3] Spedding has given me a little picture, very pretty, and so has Taylor and if I make appeal to Mrs. C[ameron] whom I have not seen no doubt I should get more. I will write to Simeon. I should think that I shall return this week but I can't say.

Thine

I was going to write yesterday—but I was told it would be of no use.

To EMILY SELLWOOD TENNYSON

Text. *Materials*, ii. 182.

May 12 [1857]

Forster of course always praises to the height. Got two photographs taken of myself by the man in Bond Street.[1] The kindness of the people here is marvellous.

---

[1] Forster married Eliza Ann Colburn (née Crosbie), widow of Henry Colburn (d. 1855) the publisher, on 24 May 1856 (*DNB*: Renton, *John Forster and His Friendships*, pp. 94–6).
[2] For the Illustrated Edition.

[1] In *Materials*, ii. 157, dated (impossibly) 1 January 1856.   [2] See below, p. 196.
[3] 'Yesterday I went to the Red House to match papers and paint. My success was not remarkable. They have got roses and clematis for the house' (Emily to Alfred Tennyson, 30 April 1857, TRC).

[1] At Cundall and Howlett, 168 New Bond Street, where the children were also photographed on 17 July (*Journal*, pp. 92, 95). Tennyson was photographed by Cundall and Downes in 1861 (see Richard Ormond, *Early Victorian Portraits* i. 454–5).

12 *May* 1857

To THE DUCHESS OF ARGYLL[1]

MS. Tennyson Research Centre.

LITTLE HOLLAND HOUSE, KENSINGTON, May 12, 1857

There is only one man in all London with whom I breakfast, Mr. Hallam, and he is an old man and bound to me by old and dear ties, and I do not like to refuse him.[2] I remember the Chevalier Bunsen[3] very well: I do not think that I shall be in town on Saturday—but will your Grace admit me tomorrow at 12 o'clock and allow me to explain myself and if not, will you not the less believe me,

Yours very truly
A. Tennyson

To EMILY SELLWOOD TENNYSON

Text. Materials, ii. 182.

May 14, [1857]

Have been all morning with the Duke and Duchess of Argyll, both amazingly kind.

To EMILY SELLWOOD TENNYSON

Text. Materials, ii. 182.

May 16 [1857]

The second day after my arrival much to my disgust seven papers announced my arrival, 'from his seat Farringford, Freshwater, I. W.' *Household Words* is the best book for the 'douls' I think.[1] Have been breakfasting with the Duke of Argyll, have not seen Woolner nor Vernon Lushington[2] lately, Archie Peel here.

---

[1] See Appendix C.   [2] But see below, p. 178.
[3] Christian Karl Josias, Baron von Bunsen (1791–1860), distinguished Prussian diplomat and a learned scholar, with an English wife (see Boase), was minister to England from the King of Prussia, 1851–4. See above, p. 5 n. He was an 'intimate' friend of the Argylls, whose 'introduction to him started with Stanley's life of Thomas Arnold (Argyll's *Autobiography and Memoirs*, i. 332–6), who himself had met Bunsen, then minister at the Papal Court in Rome, in 1827, and regarded him with 'all but idolatry' (A. P. Stanley, *Life and Correspondence of Thomas Arnold*, 2nd American Edn., Appleton: New York and Philadelphia, p. 222).

[1] Glossed as 'servants', but we can find no authority for this. It seems rather to mean 'blues' or 'troubles'. Emily Tennyson had written on 30 April: 'Shouldst thou buy any books think of the servants please. Prescotts would do for them' (Prescott's histories are listed in *Tennyson in Lincoln*, i, Nos. 1817–20).
[2] Vernon Lushington (1823–1912), QC, son of Stephen Lushington (1782–1873), was a barrister at the Inner Temple, and from 1877 to 1900 was judge of the county courts of Surrey and Berkshire (*DNB*; *Who Was Who*; Burke's *Peerage*; Amy Woolner, *Thomas Woolner*; *Tennyson in Lincoln*, i, Nos. 1452–3).

To THE DUCHESS OF ARGYLL

MS. Tennyson Research Centre.

Monday morning, [? May 18, 1857]

My dear Duchess

I am very glad that I was able to give some pleasure to yourself and your party, but if anyone had prophecied to me that I should have gone out to breakfast and read my own poems aloud under a tree to any party whatever I should have set him down as a dreamer: Therefore I must conclude that I was charmed and enchanted into it, and read spell-bound, and remain wondering at myself.[1] Many thanks for your kind invitation which I do not refuse and cannot altogether accept, being under a promise to visit the Camerons when I return to town; but I will write again from Farringford; meantime believe me with my best remembrances to the Duke,

Yours most truly
A. Tennyson

To THE DUCHESS OF ARGYLL

MS. Tennyson Research Centre.

FARRINGFORD, May 21, 1857]

My dear Duchess

Our house is at present full of visitors and will be so for some time: my wife cannot leave home but begs me to express her best thanks for the invitation given her. *I* must come to Town for a day or two presently, and I will then call at Argyll Lodge and if the Duke still wish me to read Maud, and can find a leisure hour, and if possible an after-dinner one, I will read D. V.

I shall value the Testimony of the Rocks[1] as your Grace's gift. I would have acknowledged it earlier, but I had left Little Holland house before the messenger returned and the Book came to me by post. Believe me,

Yours most truly
A. Tennyson

To THE DUCHESS OF ARGYLL

MS. Tennyson Research Centre.

FARRINGFORD, I. W., Saturday, [? 6 or 13 June 1857]

My dear Duchess

Many thanks for your kind note. When I come to town which will I trust be shortly, I will call. The Marshalls of Coniston Water have engaged us for August and whether we can come to Inverary is at present a matter of great uncertainty. I wish if possible to let my house here for the summer before I move; and this is a rather difficult thing to accomplish as I scruple to entrust the business to an agent from fear of being flooded by crowds of

---

[1] See below, p. 179.

[1] Hugh Miller's book (1857). See i. 276 n.

inspective cockneydom. It really is the prettiest place I know on this southern coast and has only to be seen to be appreciated.

The poems which I read on the lawn at Argyll Lodge are printed truly, but not, at least at present, to be published.[1] I have heard of 'a blustering mouth' (I quote from a letter—no name given) a man, a friend it was said, to whom I read or showed the Nimuë; who in lieu of giving his opinion honestly at the moment, apears to have gone brawling about town, saying that such a poem would corrupt the young, that no ladies could buy it or read it etc. etc. Such chatter is as unhandsome, as the criticism is false. Nevertheless why should I expose myself to the folly of fools (* in an age which Byron and Wordsworth made and left undramatic?). I should indeed have thought that the truth and purity of the wife in the first poem might well have served as antidote to the untruth of the woman in the second. Perhaps I shall wait till I get a larger volume together and then bring out these with others. Pardon me all this about myself and my book: it is but an answer to your question.

We should really be delighted to visit Inverary if we could. The uncertainty as to whether we can has kept me from answering the Duke's letter of invitation. Will your Grace make my excuses for me and believe me whether we come or no,

Yours most truly
A. Tennyson

*This is put too strongly but is it not in a measure true?

To ?

MS. Brotherton Collection.

FARRINGFORD, June 8, [? 1857][1]

Sir

I am much obliged for the compliment you intended me in the dedication of your volume to myself.

I am requested by one of the authors[2] of 'Lives of the Laureates' to enclose you this prospectus that you may know such a book is in existence. I think it may influence you as to the publication of your own. I am, Sir,

Your obedient servant
A. Tennyson

---

[1] *Enid and Nimuë: the True and the False* (see above, p. 174).

[1] Watermarked 1856.
[2] Wilfred Stanton Austin, Jr., and John Ralph, *The Lives of the Poets-Laureate with an Introductory Essay on the Title and Office*, 1853 (Ben Jonson to Wordsworth, with Tennyson mentioned only in the Preface).

EMILY SELLWOOD TENNYSON
to GEORGE STOVIN VENABLES

MS. National Library of Wales.

FARRINGFORD, June 12 [1857]

My dear Mr. Venables

Many thanks for your kind letter. Before you reconsider those poems I wish to say a word to you if I can. For it must be confessed that one way or the other I am nearly worn out—what with a rebellious household, drains done in the winter to be done again and other things.[1]

First then those poems are intended for a whole. Two old stories 'The False and the True' (meaning Love, that is why Merlin is called 'Nimue.' Judgements are, I know, divided as to the expediency of choosing the stories but granting them chosen must not knights of the old story be dealt with in the old way—their fights and their lives?

I fear I shall be obliged to come to London for a doctor but do not say anything to people about it. I hope there is nothing seriously amiss. I suppose I want rest. Our love to Frank. I feel altogether too sad about things to write. Glad as I am that he should be with you I cannot but know what it means.[2]

Very sincerely yours
Emily Tennyson

We quite agree with you about Pictures to Poetry and always did.[3] About a week ago 1300 had been sold. A few lines in the beginning of Merlin are all that have been put in, not the scandalous stories.[4] They are just the same. Perhaps it would be better to suppress the poems altogether. I am quite sure that they are poems of a grand moral feeling. Others can judge better than I whether the manner of putting them is what the age will not bear.

To GEORGE STOVIN VENABLES

MS. National Library of Wales.

[? mid-June 1857]

Dear Venables

I have taken E. L. L.'s advice in the matter of the Poems: therefore I beg

---

[1] 'Dr. Mann reports the progress of drains and stoves which he has been so good as to superintend for us' (*Journal*, p. 79).   [2] The meaning is not clear.

[3] 'I am sorry to hear that with few exceptions you would not care to have the illustrations as a gift. All I can say is that neither labour nor expense has been spared in the getting up of the book—the best artists have been employed, and for the designs and engraving alone I have paid upwards of £1500. The price of the book will be either 30/ or 31/6. Mr. Routledge it is true makes the price of his annual volumes a guinea, but your friends should bear in mind that he pays *nothing* for copyright' (Moxon to Emily Tennyson, April 1858, quoted in Hagen, *Tennyson and His Publishers*, p. 105). Moxon printed 10,000 copies of the Illustrated Edition, which appeared in the second half of May (*Publishers' Circular*, June 1857, p. 234).

[4] In l. 5 of 'Merlin and Vivien' the phrase 'wily Vivien' first read 'harlot Nimue', then 'wanton', then 'wileful'. See John Pfordresher, *A Variorum Edition of Tennyson's Idylls of the King*, p. 501.

you to destroy my proofs which my wife sent.[1] I shall wait till I have a bigger book.

Yours ever
A. Tennyson

To WILLIAM MAKEPEACE THACKERAY

MS. Berg Collection.

FARRINGFORD, I. W., [June 1857]

My dear Thackeray

Your American friend and poet-traveller has never arrived.[1] He has I suppose changed his mind. I am sure I should have been very glad to see him for my 'castle' was never yet 'barricaded and entrenched' against good fellows. I write now this line to say that after the 30th I shall not be here.

My best remembrances to your daughters whom I have twice seen once as little girls and again a year or so back.[2]

Yours ever
A. Tennyson

To THE DUCHESS OF ARGYLL

MS. Tennyson Research Centre.

[? mid-June 1857]

My dear Duchess

I will come to dinner at 7.15—trusting that your party is a *very* quiet one.

Yours most truly
A. Tennyson

---

[1] For the extant proofs of *Enid and Nimuë: the True and the False*, see John Pfordresher, *A Variorum Edition of Tennyson's Idylls of the King*, pp. 25–30.

[1] Bayard Taylor (1825–78), traveller and travel-writer, poet, novelist, and (1870–1) translator of *Faust*, who in fact came on 19 June (*Journal*, p. 94; Thackeray's *Letters and Private Papers*, ed. Gordon Ray, iv. 46–8). Taylor's book *Northern Travel: Summer and Winter Pictures of Sweden, Denmark, and Lapland* (see *Tennyson in Lincoln*, i, No. 2167) was published in 1857, and he of course talked of his travels: 'Among other things he told my father that the most beautiful sight in the world was a Norwegian forest in winter, sheathed in ice, the sun rising over it and making the whole landscape one rainbow of flashing diamonds' (*Memoir*, i. 418). The Duke of Argyll, whom Taylor met at Lord Houghton's ten years later, said to him: 'Do you know that *you* were the cause of Tennyson's visit to Norway [in July–August, 1859]? After he read your book he could not rest until he went there himself' (*Life and Letters of Bayard Taylor*, ed. Marie Hansen-Taylor and Horace E. Scudder, ii. 473–4). See also below, p. 207.

Taylor's second visit to Tennyson, in February 1867 (*Journal*, pp. 258–9) got him into hot water: see below, pp. 453–4, 514 n.

[2] See below, p. 333 and n.

To FERDINAND FREILIGRATH [?]

MS. Armstrong Browning Library.

[June or July 1857]

My dear Sir
 My friend Mr. Taylor who says that he met you this year tells me that you take it hardly that I never thanked you for your translation of my poems. I should think it very probable that my letter miscarried, but I have no recollection whether I wrote or not. At any rate I trust you will now accept my best thanks for your able and conscientious translation and believe me
 Yours faithfully
 A. Tennyson

To ROBERT JAMES MANN

Text. Materials, ii. 141–2.

July [9], 1857

Dear Dr. Mann
 I am glad for one thing that you are going to Natal, we shall gain by having a man of science out there; I need not say that I am grieved for another thing, viz. the losing you and Mrs. Mann for I fear a long while. I believe that the climate will be good for her and that is or should be some matter of consolation, a great change indeed from your Eastwind-bitten Norfolk![1] All our good wishes go with you and help like the pilot to steer you into haven! Farewell then, since farewell must needs be said and hearty welcome to Farringford whenever you return till which I am
 Yours most truly
 A. Tennyson

 I wished for you much yesterday. Merwood brought me a lump of snake's eggs and I picked carefully out two little embryo snakes with bolting eyes and beating hearts. I laid them on a piece of white paper. Their hearts or bloodvessels beat for at *least* two hours after extraction. Does that not in some way explain why it is so very difficult to kill a snake? I was so sorry not to have you and your microscope here.

To CHARLES RICHARD WELD

MS. Tennyson Research Centre.

Monday, [13 July 1857]

My dear Weld
 I have received your Irish book and read not all but a good deal of it and

---

[1] Mann, invited to Natal by Bishop Colenso, remained there nine years. 'Two years after his arrival he was appointed to the newly established office of superintendent of education.... The climatic condition of the country, with its severe and frequent thunderstorms, led him to the special study of meteorology, and the careful series of observations which he carried out ... are of considerable value' (*DNB*).

like it as I do all your books.[1] We shall be coming up to town in a day or two. Can you, if wanted, give *me* a bed: I must go either to Spring [Rice] or to the Camerons or you, but I should prefer coming to you. Love to Anne.

Ever yours
A. Tennyson

To THE DUCHESS OF ARGYLL

MS. Tennyson Research Centre.

GRASBY, July 27, 1857[1]

My dear Duchess

I am just going to Manchester and before I go snatch a moment to answer you. I do hope that we shall be able to come to Inverary in October. Doubtless in your Castle some top of a tower, some bottom of a Donjon, some 'coigne of vantage'[2] somewhere may be found where I may smoke my pipe and ruminate as is my wont.

As to 'the idle words' I have learnt who was the Author of them—not without sorrow: an old college friend. He went to my publisher[3] and asked for the loan of the proofsheets, and got them, and then publicly abused them. The cause alleged for this I who like the man will not believe: let it pass.

I am sorry that I did not see Sumner,[4] but some time or other you will tell me his messages from Longfellow—meanwhile believe me

Yours ever
A. Tennyson

THE TENNYSONS AT THE MANCHESTER ART TREASURES EXHIBITION[1]

Text. Nathaniel Hawthorne, *The English Notebooks*, ed. Randall Stewart (Modern Language Association of America and Oxford University Press: New York and London, 1941), pp. 553–4.

[30 July 1857]

... Tennyson is the most picturesque figure, without affectation, that

---

[1] *Vacations in Ireland* (1857).

[1] As the *Journal* shows, they left Farringford on 16 July, spent two nights in London, and on the 18th went to the Charles Tennyson Turners at Grasby.

[2] *Macbeth*, 1. vi. 7.   [3] Probably Milnes (see below, p. 206).

[4] Charles Sumner (1811–74), Senator from Massachusetts 1851–74, was an aggressive abolitionist. He was recovering from a beating, in May 1856, by Representative Preston S. Brooks, nephew of Senator Andrew Pickens Butler, of South Carolina, whom Sumner had attacked in a violent anti-slavery speech. Sumner dined with the Tennysons at Farringford in October 1859 (*Journal*, p. 139), and his letter of thanks to Emily Tennyson is printed in *Materials*, ii. 252–3. See *Tennyson in Lincoln*, i, No. 2129. Sumner first met the Argylls in 1848 or 1849, and they became 'very intimate friends' (Argyll, *Autobiography and Memoir*, i. 411–2).

[1] The Manchester Art Treasures Exhibition, for which a palace was erected at Old Trafford, a suburb, was an immense affair, bringing together works of art from all over Great Britain: paintings by Ancient Masters, Modern Masters, from the British Portrait Gallery, sculpture,

I ever saw; of middle-size, rather slouching, dressed entirely in black, and with nothing white about him except the collar of his shirt, which methought might have been clean the day before. He had on a black wide-awake hat, with round crown and wide-irregular brim, beneath which came down his long black hair, looking terribly tangled; he had a long pointed beard, too, a little browner than the hair, and not so abundant as to incumber any of the expression of his face. His frock coat was buttoned across the breast, though the afternoon was warm. His face was very dark, and not exactly a smooth face, but worn, and expressing great sensitiveness, though not, at that moment, the pain and sorrow which is seen in his bust. His eyes were black; but I know little of them, as they did not rest on me, nor on anything but the pictures. He seemed as if he did not see the crowd nor think of them, but as if he defended himself from them by ignoring them altogether; nor did anybody but myself cast a glance at him. Mr. Woolner was as unlike Tennyson as could well be imagined; a small, smug man, in a blue frock and brown pantaloons. They talked about the pictures, and passed pretty rapidly from one to another, Tennyson looking at them through a pair of spectacles which he held in his hand, and then standing a minute before those that interested him, with his hands folded behind his back. There was an entire absence of stiffness in his figure; no set-up in him at all; no nicety or trimness; and if there had been, it would have spoilt his whole aspect. Gazing at him with all my eyes, I liked him well, and rejoiced more in him than in all the other wonders of the Exhibition.

Knowing how much my wife would delight to see him, I went in search of her, and found her and the rest of us under the music-gallery; and we all . . . went back to the saloon of Old Masters. So rapid was his glance at the pictures, that, in this little interval, Tennyson had got half-way along the other side of the saloon; and, as it happened, an acquaintance had met him, an elderly gentleman and lady,[2] and he was talking to them as we approached. I heard his voice; a bass voice, but not of a resounding depth; a voice rather broken, as it were, and ragged about the edges, but pleasant to the ear. His manner, while conversing with these people, was not in the least that of an awkward man, unaccustomed to society; but he shook hands and parted with them, evidently as soon as he courteously could, and shuffled away quicker than before. He betrayed his shy and secluded habits more in this, than in anything else that I observed; though, indeed, in his whole presence, I was indescribably sensible of a morbid painfulness in him, a something not to be meddled with. Very soon, he left the saloon, shuffling along the floor with

---

ornamental art, water-colour drawings, and historical miniatures. It was opened on 5 May by Prince Albert (the Queen's visit was on 17 June), and closed on 17 October, having attracted 1,335,915 visitors. A good account of it is in the *Annual Register*, but the best is in *The Art-Treasures Examiner: A Pictorial, Critical, and Historical Record of the Art-Treasures Exhibition at Manchester in 1857*, published in Manchester by Alexander Ireland (1810–84: *DNB*), publisher and business manager of the *Manchester Examiner*, who pointed out Tennyson to Hawthorne, and in London by W. H. Smith. Nathaniel Hawthorne (1804–64), Consul at Liverpool 1853–7, saw Tennyson at the Exhibition on Thursday the 30th, and his wife saw the whole family, with nurse, on Friday the 31st.

[2] Probably, the William Fairbairns (see below, p. 187).

short irregular steps, a very queer gait, as if he were walking in slippers too loose for him. I had observed that he seemed to turn his feet slightly inward, after the fashion of Indians. How strange, that in these two or three pages, I cannot get one single touch that may call him up hereafter.

I would most gladly have seen more of this one poet of our day, but forebore to follow him; for I must own that it seemed mean to be dogging him through the saloons, or even to have looked at him, since it was to be done stealthily, if at all. I should be glad to smoke a cigar with him. Mr. Ireland says, that having heard that he was to be at the Exhibition, and not finding him there, he conjectured he must have gone into the contiguous Botanical Gardens to smoke; and sure enough, he found him there. . . . He is exceedingly nervous, and altogether as un-English as possible. . . .

Un-English as he was, sallow, and unhealthy, Tennyson had not, however, an American look. I cannot well describe the difference; but there was something more mellow in him, softer, sweeter, broader, more simple, than we are apt to be. Living apart from men, as he does, would hurt any one of us more than it does him. I may as well leave him here; for I cannot touch the central point.

Text. Journal

[31 July 1857] Our pleasant visit ends.[3] I go with a sad heart. We walk down part of Charley's Walk before going. He takes us to the Station. At Manchester A. and Mr. Woolner meet us and after luncheon we go to the Exhibition. Our servants fortunate to find rooms at the Waterloo Hotel. Meanwhile A. and I see British shields and suits of Metal at the Exhibition and go to the Botanical Gardens and admire the white and yellow water lilies and see the Victoria Regia.[4] I meet a kind Quakeress while he is away a minute who speaks to me. I have tea, he soda water. We dress and go to hear Dickens read his Christmas Carol in the Free Trade Hall.

[3] Tennyson left Grasby on Monday the 27th, as his letter of that date and the *Journal* both evidence, and in Manchester 'pitched his tent in semi-incognito at a quiet old hostelry where his expressed wish to be free from visitors prevented intrusion' (Francis Espinasse, *Literary Recollections and Sketches*, p. 358 n.). Emily Tennyson, despite the evidence of the *Journal* (p. 97), left Grasby not on 1 August but the day before, since she heard 'Dickens read his Christmas Carol in the Free Trade Hall' on 31 July (date in Edgar Johnson, *Charles Dickens*, ii. 876). Tennyson was thus in Manchester not 'for an overnight stop' or for a 'flying visit to the Great Exhibition', as R. B. Martin has it (p. 416), but in fact for six days—time enough indeed to have his photograph taken (see Andrew Wheatcroft, *The Tennyson Album*, pp. 70–1), to spend an evening with Frank Jewsbury (Espinasse, pp. 358–9 n.; Charles Tennyson, p. 306), and to visit the Exhibition at least *five* times—between Tuesday, 28 July and Saturday, 1 August. The first three visits (two with Woolner) are recorded in *The Art-Treasures Examiner*, p. 168.

[4] They traversed the entire length of the building and then went next door to the Botanic Gardens. The 'Victoria Regia', the stupendous water-lily (with flowers up to sixteen inches across, pads up to seven feet, on which a child could sit), was brought from British Guiana in 1850 to Chatsworth (where Joseph Paxton built the Lily House, forerunner of the Crystal Palace, specially for it). A Victoria Regia infant's cot is pictured in Frances Lichten, *Decorative Art of Victoria's Era*, p. 32.

186   31 *July* 1857

Text. Rose Hawthorne Lathrop, *Memories of Hawthorne* (Houghton Mifflin, Boston and New York, 1897, pp. 332–3, with omissions supplied from MS, Berg Collection: Sophia Hawthorne to Elizabeth Peabody, 1 August 1857.[5]

[31 July 1857] [But our day was made illustrious by seeing Tennyson again, and for half an hour or more!] We went up into the gallery of engraving to listen to the music; and suddenly Una exclaimed, 'Mamma! there is Tennyson!' He was sitting by the organ, listening to the orchestra.[6] He had a child with him, a little boy, in whose emotions and impressions he evidently had great interest; and I presumed it was his son. I was soon convinced that I saw also his wife and another little son, [and perhaps his eldest daughter]—and all this proved true. It was charming to watch the group. Mrs. Tennyson had a sweet face, and the very sweetest smile I ever saw; and when she spoke to her husband or listened to him, her face showered a tender, happy rain of light. She was graceful, too, and gentle, but at the same time had a slightly peasant air. [I do not know whether she be a born lady or not.] The children were very pretty and picturesque, and Tennyson seemed to love them immensely. He devoted himself to them, and was absorbed in their interest. In him is a careless ease and a noble air which show him of the gentle blood he is. He is the most romantic-looking person. His complexion is *brun*, and he looks in ill health and has a hollow line in his cheeks [and a nervousness in his manner]. Allingham, another English poet, told Mr. Hawthorne that his wife was an admirable one for him,—wise, tender, and of perfect temper; and she looks all this; and there is a kind of adoration in her expression when she addresses him. If he is moody and ill, I am sure she must be a blessed solace to him. When he moved to go, we also moved, and followed him and his family faithfully. By this means we saw him stop at his own photograph, to show it to his wife and children; and then I heard them exclaim in sweet voices, 'That is papa!' Passing a table where catalogues were sold [, his eldest daughter and] youngest son stopped with the maid to buy one, while Tennyson and his wife went on and downstairs. So then I seized the youngest darling with gold hair, and kissed him to my heart's content; and he smiled and seemed well pleased. And I was well pleased to have had in my arms Tennyson's child. After my raid, I went on and then found Tennyson looking upstairs after the rest of his [family].

Text. Journal

[1 August 1857]. Next morning Mr. Woolner breakfasts with us and we go again to the Exhibition. See Hunt's pictures, Turner's sketches and Mulready all of which please A. more than anything I think and me very much also. Gainsborough's beautiful portrait the Blue Boy and Mrs. Graham.

[5] Hawthorne's wife to her sister.
[6] By the organ, as the floor plan shows, they were strategically situated for coping with childish urgencies—halfway between the lavatories and the first-class refreshment room.

We see also Mr. and Mrs. Garrick. Pope's face in latter[7] almost makes me weep. We set off for Coniston before one. At the Station find Mr. and Mrs. Jewsbury, Mr. Woolner, and a Mr. Smith I think. A gray gentleman who came years ago to see A. at Coniston and found him gone.[8] We arrive at Tent Lodge between seven and eight and find that Mr. and Mrs. Marshall, Mr. Spring Rice and Gandy have been several times to look for us. A goes to dine with the Marshalls. Mr. Allingham comes in the evening.

To WILLIAM FAIRBAIRN[1]

MS. University of Edinburgh.

[early August 1857]

My dear Sir

It was very kind in you to send me Mr. Gaskell's two lectures: they are not uninteresting; though many of the words are not merely Lancashire ones but old friends of mine.[2]

I would have driven my wife down to call upon Mrs. Fairbairn if there had

---

[7] The two words 'in latter' (inserted above the line by Hallam Tennyson) are a desperate guess. 'Pope's face' is certainly Godfrey Kneller's portrait of Alexander Pope (No. 273 in the catalogue), but Jonathan Richardson's 'Alexander Pope, the Poet, and His Dog Bounce' was also exhibited (No. 271). (See *Catalogue of the Art Treasures of the United Kingdom Collected at Manchester in 1857*, priced at 1*s.*, and W. K. Wimsatt, *Pope's Portraits*, pp. 61, 86.) Gainsborough painted David Garrick five times. In the painting referred to here 'the great actor is looking at the spectator with an expression of acute intelligence, a smile hovering about his lips, and a good-humoured roll of the eye'. The portrait of Mrs Garrick, sometimes attributed to Nathaniel Hone, shows her 'leaning on her guitar, her face so wreathed with smiles that it is quite pleasant to look upon'. (See *The Art-Treasures Examiner*, p. 296.)

[8] Frank Jewsbury (1819–78) was the brother of Geraldine Jewsbury (1812–80), novelist and friend of the Carlyles. Her correspondence with Jane Welsh Carlyle was edited by Mrs Alexander Ireland (*DNB*). The 'gray gentleman' may be Henry Smith (see i. 324). 'Frank Jewsbury once came upon Tennyson and Woolner the sculptor looking at pictures in the great Manchester Art Exhibition of 1857, and invited them to spend an evening with the Shandeans [a literary society] at his house. "Tennyson inquired rather gruffly what he was to do when he got there, but on learning that the invitation came from a brother of Miss Jewsbury, whom he had known in London, he accepted it." He talked little during the evening but smoked much and listened, accepting graciously a correction in the punctuation of *Locksley Hall*, which little John Stores Smith was presumptuous enough to suggest to him. He stayed till two or three in the morning, keeping his cabman waiting for hours, and declared upon leaving that he "had never in his life met with such an odd set of fellows"' (Susanne Howe, *Geraldine Jewsbury, Her Life and Errors*, 1935, p. 37—based closely on the account in Francis Espinasse, *Literary Recollections and Sketches*, pp. 358–9 and n.).

[1] William Fairbairn (1789–1874: *DNB*; created baronet 1869), well-known Scottish engineer and wealthy entrepreneur who had settled in Manchester, where his engineering works (at Ancoats) was one of the great factories visited by tourists. Tennyson had met him at Lady Ashburton's in January 1856. Fairbairn's wife, the former Dorothy Mar (d. 1882), was a native of Morpeth, Northumberland. His son, Thomas Fairbairn (1823–91; see below, p. 217 n.), was Chairman of the Executive Committee of the Exhibition. (See *The Life of Sir William Fairbairn, Bart., Partly Written by Himself*, ed. William Pole, 1870; reprinted 1970.)

[2] William Gaskell (1805–84), husband of Elizabeth Gaskell, was a Unitarian minister and Professor of English History and Literature at Manchester New College 1846–53. His 'Two Lectures on the Lancashire Dialect' (1844) were appended to the fifth edition of *Mary Barton* (*DNB*).

been a moment's leisure while we were at Manchester. She had two glimpses of the Exhibition and would willingly have spent a week there. If we return that way I shall be well pleased to see it and yourself once more.[3] My remembrances to Mrs. Fairbairn and believe me

Yours very truly
A. Tennyson

To THE DUCHESS OF ARGYLL

MS. Tennyson Research Centre.

FARRINGFORD, I. W., November 5, 1857

My dear Duchess

We returned last night and found your kind note of inquiry. It is granted that I ought, if I promised, to have written before, but I waited till I could inform you of our safe arrival. I assure you that my recollections of Inverary are as sunny as the sky was cloudy during my week's visit, and I wish that I could have stayed to see Dun—— (how is it spelt)[1] 'like the back of a tortoise-shell cat' as the Duke said. Further south in many places the great elms kept a solid green and had hardly changed a leaf. I wish too that I had not missed C. Sumner. I had heard, or I had hoped, that he would pay me a visit here. On the day when we parted we were also parted from our luggage, which had not arrived at Tarbert when the steamer came to the little pier, so we went on with the children and left the nurse to come after with bag and baggage. Farewell and believe me,

Yours and your Duke's ever
A. Tennyson

ALFRED AND EMILY SELLWOOD TENNYSON to JAMES GARTH MARSHALL[1]

MS. Tennyson Research Centre.

November 10, 1857

My dear J. G. M.
Lo! your 17£ which acknowledge please!

Yours ever
A. T.

Pardon Ally, he has forgotten his 'manners'. I have had the most wicked desire to cram M. A. M. morning, noon and night not with Oxford and Cambridge intellectual dainties but with vulgarest beef, mutton and bread. I know she will starve herself to death yet and in no good cause. May be you

---

[3] No letters written during the three-month holiday in the Lake District and Scotland have turned up, but Emily Tennyson's *Journal*, as published, supplemented by additional Journal passages in *Materials*, ii. 187–91, and with a few details from the manuscript journal (TRC), gives much evidence about their daily activities. See Appendix D.

[1] Dunrobin? Dunstaffanage? Dunaverty? (see below, p. 191).

[1] See i. 96 n. 'M. A. M.' is Marshall's wife, Mary Alice (née Spring Rice).

will say I have forgotten mine too. Joy that the lecture is well over. Love to M. A. M. and all of you. I heard Ally dilating on the glories of the visit more than once in society.

To GEORGE WIGHTWICK[1]

MS. Robert Taylor.

FARRINGFORD, FRESHWATER, I. W., [? November 1857]

My dear Mr. Wightwick

'The circumstance is' *not* 'forgotten by' me, by any means. I remember the whole of my Plymouth visit, to the minutest circumstance, even to the cabman's rowing us for smoking in his cab. I have never been through Plymouth since, or I should have knocked at your hospitable gates again, and solicited admittance. Grieved am I that you give so poor an account of Mrs. Wightwick who seemed to me when I saw her so brimful of sparkling life and gaiety. Pray give her my kindest remembrances. I myself have married since I saw you, nay, have been married for more than seven years, and have two very pretty boys.

Many thanks for your very kind invitation. If ever I am in your neighbourhood[2] I will come and see you, and if you ever be in this island come to me. I live in a house on a hill between the Solent and the Channel and have lovely views of both seas.

I wish I had left a less truncated memorial of my presence under your roof than that inch of clay which you have drawn so carefully. Farewell, dear Mr. Wightwick, and believe me

Yours most truly
A. Tennyson

Your letter has no date: but I answer it as soon as received.

To COVENTRY PATMORE

MS. Tennyson Research Centre.

[? 4 December 1857]

My dear P.

I called on Simeon and he showed me your essay.[1] p. 144 shows me that you are (whatever the merits of the rest of your essay) frightfully out.

---

[1] See i. 292 n. Caroline Wightwick (née Damant), his wife, died in 1867.
[2] Not Plymouth now, but Portishead, Somerset, which also had a charming view.

[1] 'English Metrical Critics', *North British Review*, xxvii (Aug. 1857), 127–61. In *Memoir*, ii. 469–70, and *Materials*, ii. 321, under implied dates of 1860 and 1861. Patmore had said that the 'six-syllable "iambic" is the most solemn of all our English measures', citing as an example the first stanza of his own poem 'Night and Sleep' (from *Tamerton Church-Tower and Other Poems*, 1854). Tennyson's first 'Specimen' duplicates the metre of Patmore's example. Patmore went on to say that the addition of an iambic foot to lines 1–6 and 8 would 'change this verse from the slowest and most mournful, to the most rapid and high-spirited of all English metres'. Tennyson's second 'Specimen' accordingly adds an iambic foot to the verses.

Specimen of the most most mournful English metre

Is this the most solemn

> merry it is
> How glad I am to walk(!)
> With Susan on the shore!
> *do*
> How glad I am to talk!
> o'er and
> I kiss her ten times o'er.
> I clasp her tender waist
> We kiss—we are so fond—
> When she and I are thus embraced
> There's not a joy beyond

Is this rapid and high-spirited

> Specimen of the merriest

> How strange it is, O God, to wake,
> To watch and wake while others sleep,
> Till heart and sight and hearing ache
> For common objects that would keep
> Our awful, inner ghostly sense
> Unroused, lest it by chance should mark
> The life that haunts the emptiness
> And horrors of the formless dark.

CHARLES BEAUMONT PHIPPS *to* ALFRED TENNYSON

MS. Tennyson Research Centre.

WINDSOR CASTLE, December 23, 1857

Sir

It has appeared to Her Majesty the Queen that an additional verse to 'God Save the Queen,' having reference to the occasion, might with very good effect be sung at the State Concert which is to be given at Buckingham Palace upon the Evening of the Wedding of the Princess Royal[1]—and I am commanded to request that you will be good enough to think whether you can frame a Suitable verse for that occasion. I have the Honor to be, Sir,

Your obedient humble Servant
C. B. Phipps

Alfred Tennyson Esqre

---

[1] On 25 January 1858 Victoria Adelaide Mary Louisa (1840–1901), the oldest child, married Crown Prince Frederick William of Prussia (1831–88), later (9 March 1888), on the death of his father, King of Prussia and Emperor of Germany for ninety-nine days (he died 15 June). See the accounts of the wedding in the *Annual Register* or *Illustrated London News*, Supplement, 30 January 1858, pp. 117–28.

27 *December* 1857

To CHARLES BEAUMONT PHIPPS

MS. Tennyson Research Centre.

[27 December 1857]

It appeared to me that Her Majesty would like the expression 'Rose of May' none the less for its being Shakespeare's: but if it seems in any way out of place this reading might be substituted.

> Let both the Peoples say,
> God be thy strength and stay!
> God bless thy marriage day!
> God save the Queen

If this version be adopted, then, to avoid sameness of phrase, the second line of stanza 1st should begin 'Long be' or 'So be.'[1]

To THE DUCHESS OF ARGYLL

MS. Tennyson Research Centre.

[30 December 1857]

My dear Duchess

I write to wish Your Grace what everyone wishes everyone over the deathbed of the Old Year; only I wish my wish to seem a little warmer than everyone's to everyone: I would wish you a Merry Christmas too; but alas the good old fellow is gone, he slumbers with ex-Christmases and is past wishing. Likewise I would say how welcome to me and my wife your last letter was—as yours surely must always be—and how glad we both were to hear that the Duke had regained his health. You ask what I have been doing? Sweeping and rolling lawns, gardnerlike, not having Duna———[1] (I always forget the spelling) to climb; reading Livingston,[2] Bayard Taylor's Summer and Winter pictures (very picturesque they are), Grant's Aristotle and other books; watching our blue little bay and the rosy lights on the cliffs: besides which strenuous employments and enjoyments I have written what for want of a better name may be called a Sea-Idyl,[3] of the modern kind, and ½ of an Ode to Reticence[4] which has ended in Silence, and I know not what else save it be my Opus Magnum, two stanzas added to 'God Save the Queen' at that Queen's command, on the subject of the Princess's marriage. I answered Col. Phipps's letter by return of post and this morning have an answer, that Her Majesty approves of them. I cannot say that my own workmanship pleases me, but the metre is so lumpish and dragging that Phoebus Apollo

---

[1] Tennyson sent *two* stanzas (Ricks, p. 1795), both adopted and both 'sung by all the principal performers and chorus' (*Illustrated London News*, Supplement, p. 123).

[1] Dunaverty, in Argyllshire.

[2] David Livingstone, *Missionary Travels and Researches in South Africa*, 1857 (*Tennyson in Lincoln*, i, No. 1404); for Taylor and Grant, see above, pp. 181 n., 95 n.

[3] 'Sea Dreams' (Ricks, pp. 1095–1105).

[4] 'Reticence' (Ricks, pp. 1796–7; dated *c.* 1869 in *Memoir*, i. 87–8).

would tear his hair over it. Since sending these stanzas I have a sort of horror that in some modern version the line 'Clothe them etc.' must occur. I have only the oldest form in Chappell's Book of Songs.⁵ Can you tell me whether my fears have any foundation.

I send the stanzas but please do not show them, and I send you also Phipp[s]'s letter which to my mind has something cold about it. When I sent my Illustrated Edition the Queen sent through Phipps a letter of thanks. Now, perhaps I am only doing my duty, therefore not thanked—how is it?

Yours ever
A. Tennyson

To LEIGH HUNT

MS. University of Iowa.

January 5, 1858

My dear Leigh Hunt

I was very glad to see your remarkable handwriting once again. Thanks for your letter. You would have given an additional value to the book had you made the marginalia you desired to make.

Your letter arrived some time after date and the book later still.¹ A happy New Year to you, my dear Leigh Hunt, Farewell.

Yours
A. Tennyson

To MARGARET GATTY[1]

Text. Christabel Ward Maxwell, *Mrs. Gatty and Mrs. Ewing*, p. 127. (London: Constable, 1949).

[? early January 1858]

Dear Madam

I have received your kind present and beg you to accept my hearty thanks.

---

⁵ *Tennyson in Lincoln*, i, No. 3309.

¹ Hunt's letter (29 December [1857], TRC), spoke of sending, for his friend Benjamin Moran, of the United States Legation, a copy of the 'new American edition' of Tennyson's works, Moran being 'coy of doing it in his own person'. 'I had wished to be assuming enough to read it through first, pencil in hand, *more meo*, and mark the passages that most pleased me in the hope that it might give more pleasure to yourself.' Another letter from Hunt, on 7 January (TRC), acknowledging Tennyson's, voices his willingness to supply the marginalia if a copy of the poems were sent to him.

¹ Margaret Gatty (1809–73), writer for children, was a far more interesting person than these *Letters* or the *Journal* (or her own letters or journal) suggest. Her mother died when she was two, and her father, Alexander John Scott (who had been Nelson's chaplain in the *Victory*, and of whom, with her husband, she wrote a biography), himself a bibliophile, brought her up in his own image. Her first stories, *The Fairy Godmother and Other Tales* (1851), were followed by the first series (of five) of *Parables from Nature*, illustrated by herself, in 1855, and then by her most famous book, *Aunt Judy's Tales* in 1858. She founded and edited *Aunt Judy's Magazine for Children* in 1866 (*DNB*). The best source of information is Mrs Maxwell's book from which this letter is taken.

? early January 1858 193

When my two little boys are old enough to read I will take care they make friends of your books. May this—1858—come and go happily to you and yours.

Yours very truly
A. Tennyson

To FREDERICK LOCKER[1]

MS. Armstrong Browning Library.

February 1, 1858

Sir

Thanks for your clever little book. I have such reams of verses to acknowledge that I cannot even get through the work of thanking the authors for them.

A furious letter of insult from one, whom I had neglected, has so alarmed me just now that I dared not put off acknowledging your book—any longer. But I *read* your book, otherwise I should not have called it clever. Now there are twenty more to answer. Farewell.

Yours
A. Tennyson

In the eighth year of my persecution

Frederick Locker Esq.

To ROBERT JAMES MANN

Text. Materials, ii. 142–3.

FARRINGFORD, [3 February 1858]

My dear Doctor,

I think your mail goes on the 5th and this is the 3rd and I suppose that you expect me to write you a long letter. You will hardly get that from me who

---

(Mrs Ewing was Margaret Gatty's daughter, Juliana Horatia Ewing, the 'Aunt Judy' of the tales and magazine. Mrs Maxwell is a descendant.)

The 'kind present' of the letter was *Parables from Nature*. A friend had written to Mrs Gatty (1857): 'I have met Tennyson. We have spent two evenings in his society—have you heard him read his *Morte d'Arthur* and *Break, Break*? Do you not envy me? I have a message from him to you. I am to tell you that he admires *The Unknown Land* in your *Allegories from Nature*, as much as anything he has ever read' (*Mrs. Gatty and Mrs. Ewing*, pp. 126–7). See *Journal*, p. 104.

[1] Frederick Locker (1821–95), poet and bibliophile, author of *London Lyrics* (1857), editor of *Lyra Elegantiarum* (1867), an anthology of light verse, and creator of the Rowfant Library. In 1850 he married Lady Charlotte Bruce (d. 1872: see vol. iii, letter to Edmund Lushington, 28 April 1872), daughter of the 7th Earl of Elgin. Their daughter, Eleanor Locker, married Lionel Tennyson in 1878. On 6 July 1874 he married Hannah Jane Lampson, of Rowfant, Sussex, in Westminster Abbey (Tennyson was present), and in 1895 added her name to his. Locker-Lampson was a witty, charming man about town, and a connoisseur. Tennyson said he 'looked like a famished and avaricious Jew'. His posthumous book *My Confidences, an Autobiographical Sketch Addressed to My Descendants* (1896) makes good reading, but, especially with regard to Tennyson, could better be called 'My Reticences'. A note in Locker's hand on p. 1 reads: 'This is the 1st letter I had from Lord Tennyson. We were then perfect strangers to each other.'

hate letter writing, and whose whole morning energies are consumed by writing wretched acknowledgements of wretched little books of verse-work, which is no work and which leaves one sick and sad; and you will, like every sojourner in another land than his own, want news. None have I to give except what you yourself see in the *Times*. How should I living here in solitude?

Our winter has been the mildest I have ever known. I read of ripe pomegranates hanging on a houseside at Bath and I myself counted scores of our wild summer roses on a hedge near, flourishing in December and lasting on into January, though now gone for the temperature has changed. They were perfectly fragrant and I brought home a bouquet of them and put them in water. You ask after the farm? I cannot say that Merwood is going on satisfactorily, very niggard of manure in the fields and ever doing his best to reave me of my rent by working at little odd jobs as a set off, so that at the end of the year, all things deducted I get almost nothing. I am now building a little summerhouse[1] to catch the Southern sun in Maiden's Croft, if you remember what field that is. I shall sit there and bask in the sunbeams and think of you far south. How I should love to roam about that parklike scenery of which you give such a fascinating account.

My two boys are pretty well, but have both had influenza from which my wife and I are still suffering, for we live not in your Natal but in our natal land; what a bad pun! After that you can expect nothing from me, so I leave you to digest it, not however without begging you to present my kind remembrances to Mrs. Mann, so believe me both,

Yours ever
A. Tennyson

I may tell you however that young Swinburne called here the other day with a college friend of his, and we asked him to dinner and I thought him a very modest and intelligent young fellow. Moreover I read him what you vindicated, but what I particularly admired in him was that he did not press upon me any verses of his own.[2] Goodbye. How desolate No. 7 B. T. must feel itself.[3]

---

[1] Pictured in *The Homes of Tennyson Painted by Helen Allingham, Described by Arthur Paterson*, facing p. 44, and in Andrew Wheatcroft, *The Tennyson Album*, p. 105.
[2] On 12 January Algernon Swinburne, of Bonchurch, and his guest, Edwin Hatch, both Oxford undergraduates, 'Called on Tennyson at his house at Farringford: first in morning when we talked not much, he being busy with his poem. Then at dinner with him and Mrs. Tennyson: stayed till long after midnight in his glorious little room, but what he said is to be remembered not here but in my soul for ever.' Next day Hatch continued: 'At Freshwater with Algernon, talking about him whom we had left the night before: called again, but without seeing him' (Hatch's Diary, unpublished: see *The Swinburne Letters*, i, pp. xlvii, 14 n.)
[3] Bonchurch Terrace, IW, where Mann had stayed.

To EDWARD MOXON

MS. Brotherton Collection.

February 8, 1858

My dear Moxon

[*1¾ lines inked out*] We are run dry at the Bank. Could you pay us in fifty pounds towards the housekeeping? I send the workman's letter. It may be worth attending to. I mean publishing May Queen or so, separately at 3*d* or 6*d*.[1] I am sorry to hear your brother is so unwell. We have all been so here.

Yours ever
A. Tennyson

To THE DUCHESS OF ARGYLL

MS. Tennyson Research Centre.

FARRINGFORD, I. W., February 9, 1858

My dear Duchess

I am very glad that the people showed such a spirit of affectionate loyalty on the occasion of the Princess's marriage.

It was very kind to send me that little note. As to my stanzas I do not pique myself upon them: they are neither much better nor worse than the rest of that loyal confection. It might be possible, with some trouble, to accommodate the air with better words than it has at present, though 'send her vic' is loud and stately enough and might be kept.[1]

Would you like to see one of the pretty things which (as I think I told you at Inverary) I now and then receive? here it is. I had it immediately after the marriage. The key to this composition is that I did not acknowledge the receipt of a book of translations from the English poets, sent me by this Chevalier, some French refugee, a total stranger to me. I answered this by acknowledging his book, taking not the slightest notice of his letter—a touch of satire, perhaps too fine for him to feel.[2]

I trust that you and yours have escaped this hideous influenza which has knocked us all down here, children and all, but is now passing away.

Our best remembrances to the Duke and to such of your young ones as recollect us and believe me

Yours ever
A. Tennyson

Both the boys seeing me writing and hearing to whom say 'love and kisses.'

---

[1] This may be the germ of *Moxon's Miniature Poets, A Selection from the Works of Alfred Tennyson* (1865). See below, pp. 196, 199, 382, 383.

[1] See above, pp. 190–2.
[2] *Beautés de la poésie anglaise* (2 vols., 1857). See above, p. 128.

196   1 *March* 1858

To ARTHUR HELPS

MS. W. A. E. Karunaratne.

FARRINGFORD, I. W., March 1, 1858

My dear Helps

Thanks for Oulita[1]—I have not read it but have cut it open which looks as if I meant to read it.

My complaint against the time and my office of Poet Laureate is not so much that I am deluged with verse as that no man ever thinks of sending me a book of prose—hardly ever. I am like a man receiving perpetual parcels of currants and raisins and barley sugar and never a piece of bread.

When you talk of sending 'tribute to a Royal man' see what an unhandsome allusion you make to my position in H. M.'s household!

I remember that Sunday morning at Tom Taylor's very well and what a pleasant bit of talk I had with you.[2] Believe me, my dear Helps,

Ever yours
A. Tennyson

To THE DUKE AND DUCHESS OF ARGYLL

MS. Tennyson Research Centre.

March 5, 1858

My dear Duke and Duchess

Glad am I to hear the good news—doubly glad to us as coming first from little Lady ——'s own mamma, and so proving that all was well with both.[1]

Ever yours
A. Tennyson

To JOHN WILLIAM PARKER

MS. Kenneth Rendell.

FARRINGFORD, April 23, [1858]

Dear Sir

Your letter interests me very much. I am too unskilled in the practical working of these things to venture to give an opinion respecting your suggestions but I will name them to one whose whole aim in life is to meet these great social questions fairly not only in theory but in practice.[1]

It is my wish to do as you desire as to the publication of the more popular of my own poems separately but Mr. Moxon has been very ill and still continues so ill that his doctors forbid any attention to business, in consequence I have had no answer on the subject.[2]

---

[1] *Oulita the Serf*, a tragedy in blank verse (1857), 'in which the evils of serfdom were depicted' (*Correspondence of Sir Arthur Helps*, ed. E. A. Helps, pp. 7, 215–16).

[2] See above, p. 176.

[1] The birth of the fifth daughter, Frances (d. 1931).

[1] James Spedding? John Simeon? [2] See above, p. 195, and below, p. 199.

I am truly sorry to hear that you have been suffering. If I were talking with you I could say many things, but letter-writing is very disagreeable to me. It is not the way in which I naturally express my thoughts and feelings. Yet I will add that I trust we may both live to see the day when every industrious man may be able to earn enough for life both for himself and his wife and children: food, raiment, shelter and leisure for that sound education of the human being which makes mankind know what it is possible for him to understand of God's world and his own work in it. How important a help to this education I deem labour itself to be I cannot tell you but then by labour I do not mean over-work, though even this is perhaps better than no work at all, may certainly be so, if endured with a high heroic Christian spirit as it so very often is. I am, dear Sir,

Yours truly
A. Tennyson

BENJAMIN JOWETT to ALFRED TENNYSON

Text. Materials, ii. 196–8.

April 30, 1858

My dear Tennyson

I have great pleasure in sending some books which I hope you will accept, the best books in the world except the Bible, Homer, and Plato.

I take the opportunity also of enclosing Lempriere's *Dictionary*. The price is 1s. 6d. The bookseller valued it so little that he offered to give me the book. I have added two or three other books which I thought you might like to see, the translation of the Vedas as a specimen of the oldest thing in the world, Hegel's *Philosophy of History* which is just 'the increasing purpose that through the ages runs'[1] buried under a heap of categories. If you care to look at it will you turn to the pages I have marked at the beginning? It is a favourite book of mine. I do not feel certain of the impression it will make on anyone else.

I also send you the latest and best book on Mythology and Bunsen's new *Bibelbuch* [of] which the little I have read seems to be an interesting and valuable introduction to Scripture. What a cartload of heavy literature. Do not trouble yourself to read or to send it back to me: I will carry it away some day myself.[2]

I fear I have no news to tell you, and 'the art of letter-writing' Dr. Johnson says 'consists solely in telling news,' except that Grant hopes to be married in the summer: also that he is likely to be Editor of a new Review which J. W. Parker is starting, this however is not quite settled and therefore not to be mentioned. I love Grant; he always seems to me besides his other virtues to be a 'comfortable thing.'

May I say a word about 'mosquitoes'? Anyone who cares about you is deeply annoyed that you are deterred by them from writing or publishing.

---

[1] 'Locksley Hall', l. 137.
[2] He seems to have taken them away later. For the *Vedas*, see *Tennyson in Lincoln*, i, No. 2268; the Plato (see next letter) may be No. 1790, and the Mythology No. 1301.

The feeling grows and brings in after years the still more painful and deeper feeling that they have prevented you from putting out half your powers. Nothing is so likely to lead to misrepresentation as the indulgence of it. Persons don't understand that sensitiveness is often combined with real manliness as well as great intellectual gifts and they regard it as a sign of fear and weakness.

A certain man on a particular day has his stomach out of order and the stomach 'getteth him up into the brain,' and he calls another man 'morbid.' He is morbid himself and wants soothing words and the whole world is morbid with dissecting and analysing itself and wants to be comforted and put together again. Might not this be the poet's office to utter the 'better voice' while Thackeray is uttering the worse one. I don't mean to blame Thackeray for I desire to take the world as it is in this present age crammed with self-consciousness, and no doubt Thackeray's views are of some value in the direction of anti-humbug.

But there is another note needed afterwards to show the good side of human nature and to condone its frailties which Thackeray will never strike. That note would be most thankfully received by the better part of the world.

Give my love to Hallam and Lionel. Tell Hallam I have put his letter 'where I can always see it,' and that I read every day about 'Louise.'

No more about 'mosquitoes,' I have bored you enough. With most kind regards to Mrs. Tennyson.

Ever yours truly
B. Jowett

To BENJAMIN JOWETT

MS. University of Virginia.

FARRINGFORD, May 4, 1858

My dear Jowett

How very kind to send me that delicious little Plato and the other books! I am unworthy of the Plato knowing so little of him. Shall I try to make myself worthy by reading this? Perhaps. Your Hegel did not arrive with the rest which was of no consequence as I have the book here.[1] Only you can tell me what page the passage marked by you, is in. As to your 'mosquitoes' [?, *words heavily inked out*] you are not altogether right, but in what fashion you are wrong I will not say here—loving you and hating letterwriting—so believe me, dear Jowett with all thankfulness

Yours always
A. Tennyson

---

[1] See *Journal*, p. 114. They were reading Hegel's *Philosophy of History* on 25 February and later (*Journal*, pp. 109, 113–14).

To EMILY SELLWOOD TENNYSON

Text. *Memoir*, i. 376.

May 21, [1858]¹

Grove called and will be ready to show us the Crystal Palace. On Friday I dine with Frederick Locker, on Saturday with Forster.

To EMILY SELLWOOD TENNYSON

Text. *Materials*, ii. 199.

LONDON, May 23, 1858

I am told not to try to see the picture galleries they are so full but indeed I saw yesterday the panorama of Lucknow which is striking and may be, shall see the Delhi one to-day.¹ I dine with Garden on Sunday.

To JOHN WILLIAM PARKER

MS. Yale.

FARRINGFORD, June 3, 1858

Dear Sir

I send the accompanying letter written, as you will perceive, soon after the receipt of your last, as the best proof I can give that you did not offend me. How should you? I receive so many letters that it is not easy to answer all.

Mr. Moxon has been for some time past forbidden by his doctor to attend to business, so that I have not been able to communicate with him about the publication of the more popular of my poems in separate little volumes.

He objected to the publication of a selection in one volume, which I proposed, in consequence of your first letter.¹ I am, dear Sir,

Truly yours
A. Tennyson

To EMILY SELLWOOD TENNYSON

MS. Tennyson Research Centre.

[10 June 1858]¹

I took the key of my garret with me which does not matter. Squire was on board and very civil and told me for I could not see so far that you waved in

---

[1] Dated 1854 in *Memoir*, but Tennyson and Locker met in 1858 (see above, p. 193 n.).

[1] Robert Burford's Panorama, Leicester Square. See the excellent discussion in Richard Altick's *Shows of London*; an illustration on p. 134 shows the rotunda from the Cranbourne Street entrance, with the very titles mentioned in this letter.

[1] See above, p. 196. Moxon died on 2 June.

[1] Postmark.

answer to my hat-waving. I told him about the 6 shillings I had to pay for the wine—and he was astonished and I told Perring and he was indignant.[2] Perring paid it to Yarmouth. Squire told me to let parcels be directed to the care of himself at Yarmouth. The picture-parcel I am told is there now and Squire told me he would send it up. We are cheated every way I don't doubt. I did not suffer much from hay-fever, and arrived a quarter to 11.

Now I want you to take an airing every fine day in Lambert's carriage while I am away. *Don't neglect* this. I am sure it will do you more good than anything and I cannot be easy except you do it—so *pray, pray* do. What *is* a little money to the keeping thee in health?

Thine dearest
A.T.

You had better keep the sheets till I write again.[3] I shall see Forster today I hope. × × × Love to Hallam and Lionel.

To FRANCIS TURNER PALGRAVE

MS. Morgan Library.

Friday, [? 11 June 1858]

My dear Palgrave

I am for some days at Burlington House; if you can, you will come and see me.

Yours ever
A. Tennyson

Come if you can today and dine here at 6, quite quietly—only Mr. and Mrs. Weld.

To EMILY SELLWOOD TENNYSON

MS. Tennyson Research Centre (fragment).

[14 June 1858]

—down at Little Holland House yesterday afternoon and dined there. Half London on the lawn. Too many to be pleasant. Had a long talk with Mrs. Sartoris[1] who enquired kindly after you. Saw Aubrey de Vere also. Woolner told me that [Holman] Hunt has written to say he will come down. I have

---

[2] Perring has not been identified. William Squire, Esq., owner of The Retreat, Easton Farm, was the Mayor of Yarmouth (White's *Hampshire*). William Tooley Lambert was the landlord of Plumbly's Hotel, Freshwater.

[3] Proof-sheets of 'Guinevere'.

[1] Adelaide Sartoris (1814?–79), née Kemble, soprano and author, sister of Fanny and John Mitchell Kemble. Lady Constance Leslie wrote that she remembered 'well the Sunday, June 13, 1858, when we were dining with the Prinseps, Alfred Tennyson, Rossetti, Tom Taylor, Adelaide Sartoris, Edward Burne-Jones, Coutts Lindsay, and Richard Doyle, Adelaide Sartoris sang his own songs to Tennyson' (M. S. Watts, *George Frederic Watts*, i. 160). See above, i. 72 n., and *The Swinburne Letters*, ii. 24–5, vi. 184.

forgotten his direction. Wilt thou write and tell him to come down with me and where I am.² No more today. It is very hot. I suppose I shall be down next week. I soon tire of London.

Thine dearest
A. × × × × × × ×

Papa sends love to Hallam and Lionel. Perhaps you had better send that letter of Moxon's which states that the last 225 is to be paid next month. It *may* be wanted.

To EMILY SELLWOOD TENNYSON (incomplete)

MS. Tennyson Research Centre.

[15 June 1858]

My lowlying tooth and another old stump were pulled out yesterday and two others cut down not without pain but not so much as I expected. I dreamt last night that little Hallam called out help me, help, help, and running out I found the part [?] full of soldiers. We had been talking about the invasion which made my dream. Today I am going to dine with Forster and we are to talk over matters. I have not yet answered poor White. I fear that I shall have to be away two weeks longer for the mould cannot at present be taken. Only if you wish I can come home and come again.

Thine ever × × × × × ×
A. T.

To EMILY SELLWOOD TENNYSON

MS. Tennyson Research Centre; *Materials*, ii. 199.

[? 16 June 1858]

[Called at Argyll Lodge,] the Duke and Duchess at Carlsbad and the Marquis of Lorne. The other children were in the garden and as soon as they saw me ran and made me a pretty bouquet of flowers.¹ Lord Colin² said he remembered Hallam very well.

The Sutherland Duchess³ crost over twice at the Queen's ball to Mrs. Prinsep (I called there after Argyll Lodge) and asked after me, you and the children and said all manner of gracious and kind things, how the Argylls valued us, grand simplicity of character etc. which was the more remarkable says Mrs. Prinsep because the Duchess never notices her in general.

So I add this little bit of news. *Mind you drive out!*

---

² Hunt went to Farringford for several days in late June (*Journal*, p. 117).

¹ See below, p. 208.   ² The Argylls's fifth son (1853–95).
³ The Duchess of Sutherland (Harriet Elizabeth Georgiana Howard, daughter of the 6th Earl of Carlisle), mother of the Duchess of Argyll, was Mistress of the Robes to the Queen. She died 27 October 1868 (see below, p. 510 n.).

To EMILY SELLWOOD TENNYSON

Text. *Materials*, ii. 200.

June 17, [1858]

I saw some fine pictures at the British Institution with Anne Weld yesterday.

To EMILY SELLWOOD TENNYSON

MS. Tennyson Research Centre.

[18 June 1858]

I hope thou hast been enjoying thyself as it appears the children have been enjoying themselves. I have yet got no calls finished. It is so difficult a matter in London except one keeps one's own carriage. It is much cooler here this morning and I am going to Barrett's but I do not know whether he can yet do anything. I am glad the children have got 2 little companions. I spent all yesterday at the South Kensington museum, a very interesting place. At Parker's in the evening I met Pollock and Clark the Editor of poor Brimley's Essays.[1] Love and kisses to little Hallam and Lionel.

Thine dearest
xxxxxx A.

To EMILY SELLWOOD TENNYSON

MS. Tennyson Research Centre.

[19 June 1858]

The teeth cannot be finished for three weeks so that as far as I see at present (I have to go to Barrett again on Tuesday) I shall be at home on Wednesday evening—in that case perhaps it would be less expensive to return by Lymington and Lambert's fly might wait for me across the ferry at Norton. There can be no objection in using our carriage with the donkey, if one has not to pay, but I think you might ask Mr. Lubbe [?] about it in the village. I am sorry to hear thou hast had pain again. I have made no plans about moving with any friend: but I will talk with thee when I return. Kiss the boys for me. Thine dearest

xxxx A.

I don't much fancy Seymour having the house after his ungentlemanly behaviour. Sir F[rancis] P[algrave][1] has sent me his books 'with the author's admiration and respect' which for an old man is very handsome.

---

[1] William George Clark (1821–78), Shakespearean scholar, fellow and then tutor at Trinity College, traveller (in 1856 he toured in Greece with W. H. Thompson, and in 1858 published *Peloponnesus, or Notes of Study and Travel*—see *Tennyson in Lincoln*, i, No. 758). See above, p. 136 n.

[1] See above, p. 27 n. The books were *The History of Normandy and of England* (4 vols., 1851–64), vols. 1, 2, 1851, 1857 (see *Tennyson in Lincoln*, i. No. 1733).

To WILLIAM MOXON[1]

MS. University of Kansas.

[*c.* 25 June 1858]

Dear Mr. Moxon

I am much obliged to you for your kindness in paying the last instalment to my account. I send a stamped receipt as required.

I did not mean by what I wrote to press matters inconveniently—only of course the sooner matters are arranged again the pleasanter, as one necessarily feels unsettled at present. Believe me, dear Mr. Moxon,

Yours truly
A. Tennyson

To CHARLES RICHARD WELD

MS. Tennyson Research Centre.

Monday, June 28, 1858

My dear Weld

I have written today to William Moxon the barrister, urging him to appoint an early meeting with yourself and arrange or rather rearrange my relations with the house of Moxon.

I had a dreadful journey home. Sneezing every moment all the way and both eyes streaming with tears: nothing excites my hay fever so much as the dust of a train. When I got out at Southampton, some one of the officials at the station said 'Sir, you look like a miller: brush the gentleman, Jacob.' So Jacob brushed me.

To MR CHOLMONDELEY[1]

Text. Transcript (by Humphrey House) from Hopkins's Notebook.

FARRINGFORD, July 5, 1858

17 *d.*

With Mr. Alfred Tennyson's Compliments and apologies that the payment of his debt has through a mistake been so long delayed.

Mr. Tennyson is going from home but if Mr. Cholmondeley would like the books during his absence he requests that they may still come to Farringford as usual.

---

[1] William Moxon (b. 1808), younger brother of the publisher. See Hagen, *Tennyson and his Publishers*, p. 107, and below, p. 210 n. See also *Men-at-the-Bar* (1885). The letter is written on mourning paper.

[1] Probably Reginald Cholmondeley (1826–96), of Condover Hall, Salop (*Landed Gentry*), who called at Farringford in July 1857 (*Journal*, p. 94). Nothing in the letter is clear, including the Hopkins connection (though Gerard Manley Hopkins attended Cholmondeley Grammar School, Highgate).

WILLIAM MICHAEL ROSSETTI, *SOME REMINISCENCES*, i. 247-8.

July 1858

In July 1858 Tennyson stayed at Little Holland House with the Prinsep family; he sat to Mr. Watts for a portrait, and was inevitably 'the observed of all observers.' One day my brother and I were there, conversing (like numerous others) with the poet; some of us were asked to stay on to dinner. I noticed that Mrs. Prinsep gave a distinct invitation to my brother for this purpose, I being close by him, but was not quite clear whether she had or had not included myself. Tennyson observed, 'I shall see you again at dinner.' 'Well,' I replied, 'I am not certain that I was asked.' 'Oh yes,' rejoined he, 'I am satisfied you were asked; better stay.' And stay I did. But, on sitting down to table, I perceived with some dismay that Mrs. Cameron, who had been present all the afternoon, and who reappeared in the evening, was not at dinner; and compunctious visitings beset me to the effect that after all I had not been asked, and must be looked upon as *de trop*, and that Mrs. Cameron must good-naturedly have foregone her place at the board so that I might not be put to open shame. What can one do under such circumstances? One thing that can be done is to put a good face on it, and resolve to pass a pleasant evening. I was equal to this emergency, and *did* pass a very pleasant evening.

To EMILY SELLWOOD TENNYSON

Text. *Memoir*, i. 428-9.

[late July 1858]

Started from Hull on July 23rd.[1] Saw E[mily] on board the little New Holland Steamer, and waved my handkerchief as both our boats were moving off: watched the two lights of Spurn Point till they became one star and then faded away. Next day very fine but in the night towards morning storm arose and our topmast was broken off. I stood next morning a long time by the cabin door and watched the green sea looking like a mountainous country, far off waves with foam at the top looking like snowy mountains bounding the scene; one great wave, green-shining, past with all its crests smoking high up beside the vessel.[2] As I stood there came a sudden hurricane and roared drearily in the funnel for twenty seconds and past away.

Christiansand. Went up into the town and saw the wooden houses.

---

[1] The Tennysons left home on 9 July (apparently), to visit his mother and the Jesses in Hampstead, staying at Britannia Cottages, before being rescued by Mrs Prinsep on 16 July and taken to Little Holland House, where Watts painted the portrait of Tennyson now in the National Gallery of Victoria, Melbourne (reproduced in Richard Ormond, *Early Victorian Portraits*, ii, Plate 897). From there they went to Grasby, and then, on 23 July, Tennyson's wife and brother Horatio accompanied him to Hull, whence he sailed to Norway. See *Journal*, pp. 118-19.

[2] See 'Lancelot and Elaine', ll. 480-4 (Ricks, p. 1634).

CHRISTIANA, August 1, [1858]

Magnificent seas on the way here. At Christiansand called on a Mr. Murch, and the Frau Murch gave me a splendid bouquet of flowers: arrived here at 6 this afternoon. I write this at the house of Mr. Crowe, consul, looking over the Sound—very pretty in the evening light. Am not quite certain whether I shall join Barrett and the other.

CHRISTIANA, August 2, [1858]

I let Barrett and Tweedie[3] go by themselves to Bergen. I am starting to-day to see the Riukan Foss with Mr. Woodfall, a very quiet sensible man, and we shall take our time. I have had great kindness from the Crowes. Yesterday a Norwegian introduced himself at the hotel, and began to spout my own verses to me; and I likewise rather to my annoyance found myself set down in the Christiana papers as 'Den beromte engelske Digter.'

I have seen the Riukan Foss. Magnificent power of water; weird blue light behind the fall.

THOMAS WOOLNER *to* LADY TREVELYAN (extract)

MS. Trevelyan Archives, University Library, Newcastle-upon-Tyne (transcript by Raleigh Trevelyan).

29 August 1858

The Tennysons were in town a few days ago; he had been to Norway, and for the short time he was there the country pleased him very much; one waterfall 900 ft. high particularly struck him. He told me one Norwegian Gentleman found out who he was and came straight up to him and commenced quoting Tennyson's poetry in English with a most distracting accent as you may imagine. He stayed all the morning with me in my studio, then we went for me to see Mrs. Tennyson, and afterwards went to Putney and dined with the Camerons. The next day we all went to the Crystal Palace, and I made them carefully inspect the 'Bartolemes Colleone',[1] which after a sound inspection they all pronounced wonderful. Neither of them had seen it

---

[3] Henry John Barrett, his dental surgeon, and possibly Alexander Tweedie (1794–1884), FRS, at this time Physician to the London Fever Hospital; he was a voluminous writer on medical matters, and was still practicing at the time of his death (*DNB*). For Woodfall, see below, p. 409 and n. Crowe could be Fritz Hauch Eden Crowe, RN, CB 1902, retired with the rank of Captain in 1896, having served in Peru and Sudan, and also as British Consul-General, Lourenço Marques. He died 11 August 1904 (*Who Was Who*; *Whitaker's Naval and Military Directory and Indian Army List*, 1900). The Mr Crowe who went to Farringford in March 1860 (*Journal*, p. 146) was probably Eyre Evans Crowe (1799–1868: *DNB*), historian and novelist, whose son Joseph Archer Crowe (1825–96: *DNB*), though himself a consul-general, was already much too distinguished a journalist and (with Cavalcaselle) art critic, to be a mere consul in Norway. Joseph Archer Crowe married in 1861; Tennyson knew the Crowes through Thackeray. (See Sir Joseph Crowe, *Reminiscences of Thirty-five Years of my Life*, 1895, pp. 81, 430; *The Thackeray Letters*.)

[1] Verrochio's famous equestrian statue in Venice of the Italian general Bartolomeo Colleone (1400–75), specially cast for the Crystal Palace.

before, so that it was a great pleasure to show it them. Tennyson went in the evening with Mrs. Cameron to dine with the Prinseps; I could not go as I had to dine with Holman Hunt to meet Lear, who is just returned from Jerusalem with I should think one of the noblest portfolios of sketches ever carried by man or woman, they are chiefly of Jerusalem and its adjacent country; there are a few of Petra, where poor Lear was robbed, stripped, pinched and beaten in the most shameless way unprovokedly by the Arab Vermin that infest that part of this earth. . . .

You will be charmed to hear that royal Alfred has done another of his Arthur Poems, which is so grand and perfect, taking the perfection with the vastness, I think you will say there is nothing in our language to surpass it. The subject is where Guenevere is in the Abbey after her crime has been declared; she is first talked to and unconsciously tortured by a garrulous little novice; after a while the King himself comes and talks his view of things to her: in all his speech there is such a height of dignity of piercing tenderness it quite melts the soul on reading it; he says what he wants to say and leaves the Queen aghast; then the description of Arthur, as watched by his wife, when departing to his last battle, is appalling from its simplicity and colossal greatness, it feels as if he were beholding the ends of things. He is now engaged upon a fourth, which is to be the Fair Maid of Astolat's love for Sir Launcelot; which will make all the others complete. Besides these he has written a pastoral kind of poem, which is fine in a simple way; then there is one of a man who has lost his money by speculations which also is very fine in many respects and on the whole I may say it is quite worthy of him. So you see there is a great treat in store for you some day. Pray tell no one of Tennyson's subjects, for he makes a loud to-do if he thinks his poems get commented on before they are published: and as he reads them to very few persons he can generally tell where the report sprang from when he hears anything of them. He is in a state of wrath against Monckton Milnes for giving vent to public criticisms concerning his unpublished poems. . . .

I have not got rid of Tennyson's bust yet, although there has been a subscription going on for 5 months; the object is to place it in Trinity Library, Cam., Vernon Lushington is the person who is managing it, and I am sorry to say he has placed so many restrictions in the way of subscribing that I think it can never succeed; if he had made no restrictions the list need scarcely have been open more days than it has been months: and most unfortunate for me, although this has been represented to him repeatedly by mutual friends and he knows how seriously I am in want of the money, yet singular to say he will not give up the least of his crotchets, and he is so kind and gentle in his manner that I cannot press the matter very strongly through fear of wounding him. He is doing my reputation a mischief, keeping me out of my money—for Fairbairn told me the other day he meant to persuade Lord Ashburton to buy it, but of course this affair stopped him— and making Tennyson himself anything but pleased, for he says it is 'disgracing' him, that a subscription should be so long on hand for placing a bust of him in his own College. More than a year ago I lost the sale of the bust through Vernon's scheme getting talked of, although it was not begun;

Fairbairn himself wanted to buy it and was vexed when he was told I had promised it to Cambridge, so altogether it certainly is hard upon me that Vernon will not allow those persons to subscribe who are really anxious to do so and feel themselves aggrieved that they are unable. . . .

WILLIAM MICHAEL ROSSETTI *to* FRANCES ROSSETTI

Text. Ruskin: Rossetti: Preraphaelitism, p. 208.

FRESHWATER GATE, September 1, 1858

. . . Tennyson has been back since Friday, and took the trouble of looking me up on Saturday; but bent his steps through some mistake to Alum Bay—some six times too far off—where of course he could learn nothing of me. I spent Monday very pleasantly at his very commodious house (not half a mile from here), and shall return as often as I can spare myself from here. He found the Norway travelling very laborious. He and his wife (a most lovely human creature) like Gabriel's *Arthur Watched by Weeping Queens* as well as or better than, any other illustration in the edition. . . .

ALFRED AND EMILY SELLWOOD TENNYSON *to* THE DUCHESS OF ARGYLL

MS. Tennyson Research Centre.

FARRINGFORD, FRESHWATER, I. W., September 2, 1858

My dear Duchess

I was very glad to see your handwriting once more and to learn that you had all returned safe and well and that the Duke had benefited by his journey.[1] We were very nearly going to the Styrian Alps ourselves, but the scheme was given up and instead of that I went alone to 'Norroway out o'er the saut-sea faem'[2] in the Scandinavia: we had something of a storm by the way (the same I believe which blew down trees and did other damage in London) it broke the top of our mast—that is very unnautical and untechnical but forgive it—and blew some of our sails loose; but I who had never seen so grand a sea at sea felt as it were in my element.[3] In Norway I saw what I went chiefly to see, the Riukan Foss, which being interpreted is Reeking Force and which Bayard Taylor, the American traveller, calls the loveliest waterfall in the world.[4] I shall not describe, only say that I who had always been disappointed in waterfalls was not so in this: other Fosses I saw with a wealth of water in them; for mine was a Foss-tour and I did not 'do' much Norway, but kept mostly to the lower lands, scared it may be by the accounts of the beds or no-beds up in the mountains—but I will answer the questions asked.

---

[1] See above, p. 201.
[2] Tennyson's recollection of Walter Scott's addition to 'Sir Patrick Spens' (Child 58; see *English and Scottish Popular Ballads*, ed. Sargent and Kittredge, p. 648).
[3] See above, p. 204. [4] See above, p. 181 n.

The boys are pretty well—many thanks—my wife not so well. 'When is Queen Guinevere to come out'? I don't know. 'Is she to come out with the other two'? Yes, and with yet another if I can get it finished. I am sorry that you 'have heard *that* of the Queen which makes you long for her very much' for like enough you will be disappointed. Our universal chatter does this harm to nature, books and men too often.

I think now the questions are answered. Here are two of mine. How does Inverary look? as beautiful as ever, or lessened and darkened by being regarded through Styrian spectacles? Is Argyll Lodge to be henceforth unduchessed? I heard a rumour to that effect in town and that you were going to reside chiefly in the North. I hope not so. Tell little Edith that if she was happy in playing little hostess to me, I, old fellow as I am, was not ungrateful for the pretty bouquet which she gave me.[5] My wife's love.

Yours and the duke's
A. Tennyson

Watts has done a portrait of him which I should like you to see.[6]

E. T.

ALFRED AND EMILY SELLWOOD TENNYSON *to* LEWIS FYTCHE

MS. Tennyson Research Centre.

October 4, 1858

My dear Lewis

All good wishes and congratulations from us both to you both![1]

Your affectionate cousin
A. Tennyson

It is very kind of you to want us with you on your day of days and we should have liked much to have been with you but it cannot be. We hope you will take us on your wedding tour. Love to all,

Your affectionate
E. T.

To ANNE HODGSON [?][1]

MS. Tennyson Research Centre.

FARRINGFORD, FRESHWATER, I. W., October 25, 1858

My dear Mrs. Hodgson

I am no letter-writer as all my friends either know or should know: but

---

[5] See above, p. 201.   [6] See above, p. 204 n.

[1] He married Susan Skipworth on 28 October (see above i. 170 n.; *Landed Gentry*, 1871).

[1] Probably the daughter of John Palmer Hollway, of Boston. She married Shadworth Hodgson, of Boston, and their son, Shadworth Hollway Hodgson (1832–1912: *DNB, Who Was Who*, Allibone), became a philosopher of considerable distinction (his wife and only child died in 1858). She is not the 'Miss Hollway' of i. 286, whom Charles Tennyson Turner met in July 1866:

since you refuse to accept my wife for secretary and appear to make it a matter of courtesy that I should write to you in my own hand—why of course I must answer yours—at least so far as to tell you where the better correspondents of the family are to be found.

My mother and my sister Matilda have made their home with the Jesses at Rose Mount, Hampstead, and no doubt Mary and her husband who are now in England and I believe at Manchester will settle somewhere near them for the winter. Horatio is married and will probably be this winter in London, for he has a house in Gloucester St., Belgravia, No. 42. As for ourselves we live all the year round here except about a couple of months in the summer. I am glad to hear so good an account of yourself and your family and in the hope that you will soon be permanently stronger remain

Yours truly
A. Tennyson

To BRADBURY AND EVANS[1]

Text. Tennyson Research Centre (transcript by Emily Sellwood Tennyson).

October 29, 1858

Dear Sirs

I send the enclosed for your perusal.

After very weary waiting for months and rejecting splendid offers from first rate publishers because I chose to stick by the house of Moxon, I am treated at last discourteously and untruthfully by William Moxon. I decline entering into any business till all this is explained and apologized for.

I am coming to town on Monday.

Yours truly
A. Tennyson

EMILY SELLWOOD TENNYSON to JOHN FORSTER

MS. Tennyson Research Centre.

October 31, 1858

My dear Mr. Forster

Sunday the post goes early. I must write a line of hearty thanks for your letter. I copy the passage concerning you from Mr. Evans' letter telling you at the same time that I have copied the whole letter for Charles Weld.

'Before Mr. Forster went out of town we consulted him as to the propriety

---

'very fine night on our return from the Charles Barnards. Miss Hollway there; she knew Alfred when she was a little girl' (Memorandum Book for 1866, TRC; transcribed by Roger Evans).

[1] William Bradbury (d. 1869) and Frederick Mullett Evans (1803?–69), partners, were the owners of *Punch*, publishers (notably of Dickens, for a while), and printers (Moxon's, and therefore Tennyson's). After Moxon's death they managed the business until 1864, when J. Bertrand Payne took over (Merriam, *Edward Moxon*, p. 194). They appear frequently in the letters of Dickens, Thackeray, and Meredith. See also below, p. 230.

of getting forward with the Illustrated Edition of the Princess; and by this post we send the first two sheets etc.'

Upon which Alfred commented last night almost in the words of your letter. He felt sure you could have given no advice. We will not interfere personally in anything concerning this matter. All shall go through yourself and Charles Weld since you with such exceeding kindness consent that so it shall be. It seemed necessary to send some sort of answer to B. and E. Now Alfred desires that there should be a stop put to this Illustrated Edition of the Princess until something concerning it be decided.

I enclose a statement of facts respecting the Illustrated Edition. They must be taken as *mine* in which he as far as he remembers concurs. You will see that there has been no arrangement whatever respecting the Princess. On the contrary we were utterly astonished when we heard that Maclise was in Italy or had been there making drawings for it.[1]

Alfred of course will not come to town since you and C. Weld advise that he should not.

Ever gratefully yours
Emily Tennyson

A STATEMENT OF FACTS RESPECTING THE ILLUSTRATED EDITION OF MY POEMS[1]

MS. Tennyson Research Centre.

[31 October 1858]

The Illustration of the Poems was entirely the late Mr. Moxon's proposal on occasion of the encouragement given him to such a publication by different booksellers with whom he had transactions respecting the Illustrated edition of Keats. (They would take so and so but if they had been Tennyson they would have taken many more.) That I objected at first is implied by the promise of [£]2000 which is referred to in the letters and which he engaged to make for me by the Illustrated Edition within a short time, I think three years.

When I had once consented to the thing being done I on many accounts urged its speedly completion and for Moxon's sake I am heartily sorry if the speculation proved a failure.

---

[1] *The Princess*, with twenty-six illustrations engraved from drawings by Daniel Maclise, was published in 1860.

[1] In Emily Tennyson's hand. An incomplete draft (TRC) of this statement, in the same hand, concluding with a message to Forster, reads: 'My banking book proves that I accepted the 2000 for the Illustrated Edition according to the arrangement in Edward Moxon's letter. | The absence of any notice of the edition in my Christmas bill confirms this. William Moxon paid the last instalment of the 2000 himself. I gave him a stampt receipt. | Alfred is certain he never agreed to The Princess unless it were by ⟨grumbling acquiescence in something said [?]. But even[?] this he does not at all remember⟩ silence. I will of course copy anything answer anything do anything I can to lessen your trouble dear Mr. Forster. Between ourselves I will even come up to Burlington House alone if it would be desirable to question me personally.'

That I accepted the 2000 in lieu of the much larger sum I had reason to expect proves that I was not greedy of gain.

As to the Princess, I was one day astonished by hearing that Maclise was in Italy or had been in Italy (I forget which) making drawings for an Illustrated edition having to the best of my belief never had a word with Moxon on the subject except that he once said in a casual manner, 'We must get Maclise to illustrate the Princess' to which I as casually answered 'Oh ho' and thought no more about it until the news of Maclise came. Neither did Mr. Forster communicate with me on the subject.

Not long before Moxon's death I through my wife remonstrated and suggested that the Illustrations might be published separately. This is the first I have seen of the Illustrations.

To EMILY SELLWOOD TENNYSON

MS. Tennyson Research Centre.

Wednesday, [17 November 1858]

I do not see how I can possibly be home till Friday morning perhaps not till Saturday. Business is not yet concluded. And I must not let Maclise's designs be published this Christmas if possible—they are too wide of the text.

If Mrs. Gatty were to come on Thursday though I were away she would satisfy what she called the wish of her heart, to be under my roof.[1]

My cold continues not bad but bothering. Love to the bairns.

thine ever
A.T. × × × ×

To DR AND MRS ROBERT JAMES MANN

Text. draft *Materials*, iv. 74.

[December 1858]

Dear Doctor and Mrs. Mann

You know that any day I would as soon kill a pig as write a letter—'heaven first sent letters for some wretched aid!' so I think Eloisa says to Abelard in Pope.[1] For 'aid' read 'curse.' Yet I feel that to friends over the sea a word is due—if it be only to say how well we remember you and how often we wish

---

[1] Five letters dated this month from Emily Tennyson to Mrs Gatty are in the Boston Public Library: 'I dare not ask you to run the risk of crossing the Solent on the slight chance of finding my husband at home this week as we are bid hold ourselves ready to go to Town this week on important business' (8 Nov.); 'My husband is not able to say when he can be home before to-day and perhaps not then but if it would be more agreeable to you to wait for him here than where you are, I hope you will come to-morrow to me' (17 Nov.); 'I pray you do not distress yourself. ... He has more than once expressed his fear that you may be inconvenienced by his detention in Town. I am very sorry to tell you that matters were not after all settled yesterday and this morning he tells me that it is impossible that he should come to-day and that it may be Saturday' (18 Nov.). See *Journal*, p. 127.

[1] Line 51 (mistranscribed or misremembered): 'sent' for 'taught'; 'wretched' for 'wretch's').

you back again. Are you coming back? soon? it is well for Mrs. Mann that she is not here now. Cough and cold rage. November gave us such an unusually sharp stroke of iron frost as generally does not fall till January. I have (according to my wife's prescription) honey plastered my chest every night for a week till it is a mass of weals but my cough still continues. I should like much to know whether you have made out any new nebulae or discovered anything new in the old; what you have been about scientifically? I don't I know deserve to be answered, but shall be grateful if answered, at your convenience: you know *you* have not to cast about, *you* have something to tell—we living in the old place and looking on the old views and running in the old ruts, little or nothing but what you know already; and your last, though to my shame left so long unacknowledged was very interesting. I have been in a heap of troubles touching publishing matters, which are not quite over yet. —Good-bye, good friends. May you be happy till we meet again as surely some time we shall.

Yours ever
A. Tennyson

To TICKNOR AND FIELDS

MS. Yale.

FARRINGFORD, December 11, 1858

Dear Sirs

I have received your kind present of £20 and thank you. I will take care that you have the proofs of my new volume[1] in time enough to get the start of other American publishers—but I cannot tell you when it will be ready and I wish that you would disabuse your own minds and those of others, as far as you can, of the fancy that I am about an Epic of King Arthur.

I should be crazed to attempt such a thing in the heart of the 19th Century. Believe me

Yours very truly
A. Tennyson

To SIR FRANCIS PALGRAVE

MS. Brown University.

FARRINGFORD, FRESHWATER, ISLE OF WIGHT, December 27, 1858

My dear Sir

A thousand thanks for your kindness in sending me a book which I have long wished to have—but never had courage enough to purchase—Milman's Latin Christianity.[1]

I am very glad to hear from your son that your History is progressing,[2] and

---

[1] *Idylls of the King*, published July 1859.

[1] Henry Hart Milman, *History of Latin Christianity* (6 vols., 1854–5: see *Tennyson in Lincoln*, i, No. 1590)—bought by F. T. Palgrave (*Journal*, p. 128).

[2] *History of Normandy and of England* (see above, p. 202).

has now arrived at the portion which will most interest Englishmen. Believe me

Yours very truly
A. Tennyson

Sir F. Palgrave, etc. etc.

EMILY SELLWOOD TENNYSON
to GEORGE STOVIN VENABLES

MS. National Library of Wales.

FARRINGFORD, January 29, 1859

My dear Mr. Venables

They are very good in writing to me as they are in all other things and you are very good too to write. I did not know until the other day that you could be with them even so long as this. I dread the idea of your leaving them and I trust you will not have to do it. I fear indeed those sufferings must be terrible. The continual cry of one's heart is enough, enough: Stay thy hand. It is so hard to raise oneself to such a height of faith as to accept such continual sorrow and suffering for them even though it does prove them to be among the best the world has ever seen and beloved of God accordingly.[1]

Alfred has not been well lately. I always felt the ground hollow beneath one and now this succession of open graves at Park House makes one feel it more than ever, makes one live almost as much in expectation of death as of life. An awful world truly. How is it that the world for the most part so well contrives to forget it. I am not grown into a doleful heart for all I say. I think the boys find me not at all a bad playmate. I am only rather more nervous about illness than usual.

Have you heard anything of the Marshalls lately! I think with the greatest admiration of Kate Morgan. There is something very touching in Miss Heathcote's consciousness that she is unfit for the sick-room but I do wish that they had another with them who is fit.

Believe me, my dear Mr. Venables, with many thanks for your goodness in writing and telling me how she liked those poems of long ago.

Ever yours most truly
Emily Tennyson

---

[1] Lushington deaths had been frequent: Louisa in 1854, Henry in 1855, Edmund Henry, son of Edmund Law and Cecilia, in 1856, Mrs Stephen Rumbold Lushington, of another branch, also in 1856, Thomas Davies on 17 June 1858, and Edmund Ansell, son of James Law Lushington (1822–1905), who was born and also died in 1859. This letter was occasioned by the severe illness of Maria Catherine Lushington, who recovered and survived until 1891.

31 *January* 1859

To WILLIAM COX BENNETT

MS. University of Virginia.

FARRINGFORD, I. OF WIGHT, January 31, 1859

Dear Sir

Many thanks for your book of songs:[1] two of them I had read with pleasure long ago—'the gentle summer rain' and 'the lanterns.' I wish you all success and am

Yours very truly
A. Tennyson

To JOHN W. KING[1]

MS. Tennyson Research Centre.

FARRINGFORD, February 4, 1859

Mr. Alfred Tennyson presents his compliments to *Mr. Whing* and begs to thank him for his 'Earnest *Pilgrim*' and for his kind words which accompany it.

Mr. Tennyson hopes Mr. Burnard Neville[2] is well and prosperous.

JOHN W. KING *to* EMILY SELLWOOD TENNYSON

MS. Tennyson Research Centre.

February 6, 1859

Madam

The name on the Title-page of my book is

J: W: King

The title of the book

'Ernest *the* Pilgrim'

and the gentleman named in my note

Neville Burnard

---

[1] *Songs by a Song-writer. First Hundred* (1859). The poems are Nos. 33 and 51: 'A Summer Invocation' and 'The Cry of the Awful Lanterns'.

[1] John W. King (*fl.* 1850s) was a writer of whom little seems to be known other than the titles of his works. Besides *Ernest the Pilgrim, A Dramatic Poem* (1859: *Tennyson in Lincoln*, i, No. 1319), he wrote *The Patriot, A Poem* (1853); *Ebenezer Elliott: A Sketch* (Sheffield, 1854); *Characters and Incidents, or Journeyings through England and Wales* (1856); *James Montgomery, A Memoir, Political and Poetical* (1858); and *Continental Europe from 1792 to 1859* (1859). We find no evidence that he was a clergyman, and, regrettably, though not without colour of his own, he was certainly *not* the Lincolnshire Anglican parson, hunter, gambler, turf devotee noticed in Boase, Francis Hill (*Victorian Lincoln*, p. 173), or R. B. Martin (p. 419). Indeed, since he wrote on Elliott and Montgomery, it is reasonable to assume that he was himself from Sheffield.

[2] Neville Northey Burnard (1818–78) was a sculptor, especially of portrait busts. See the next two letters, and i. 291 n. (*DNB*; Richard Ormond, *Early Victorian Portraits*).

not Burnard Neville.

I am, Madam,

Yours very sincerely
John: W: King

EMILY SELLWOOD TENNYSON *to* THOMAS WOOLNER

MS. Tennyson Research Centre.

FARRINGFORD, February 6, 1859

My dear Mr. Woolner

It is a great pleasure to hear of your being so busy and soon I hope to hear that a dozen men in your studio are also busy under your orders. Pity me! Behold my poor little note meant to be so courteous returned to me by some clown or the other named King who had joined the W and K together WK so that being involved with the letters above I took the name for Whing. I hope I do not often make mistakes in my letters to these strangers. At all events I have never been accused of any before. I do plead guilty to having looked at no more than the end of the letter at the time of answering it. You can understand this knowing how hard the labour of answering all the letters we receive. The name of the book I wrote from memory. Mr. Neville Burnard has dined with us and I sit opposite a bust of his, his gift, very often at dinner but some way having once been intimate with one of the surname of Neville[1] and having had family connections of the Christian name of Bernard I do naturally reverse the order of his names. I am sure he is not nice[?] to insult me for it himself.

Alfred is so disgusted at this man King for having returned my letter that he will not let me write in his name and of course I will not sanction the man's impertinence by addressing him in my own. So if you ever meet Mr. Neville Burnard tell him if you think of it I regret the mistake made in my hurry.

Alfred is better. Poor Mrs. Cameron has had a fire in the house of which I have not heard the particulars. Both our kindest thanks for your letter,

Very sincerely yours
Emily Tennyson

To THE DUCHESS OF ARGYLL

MS. Tennyson Research Centre.

FARRINGFORD, I. W., March 8, 1859

My dear Duchess

I really do not know when 'King Arthur' is to come out.[1] I so thoroughly nauseate publishing that I could be well content to be silent for ever; however the Poems—there are four of them (Your Grace heard two) are finished and,

---
[1] See i. 152 n.
[1] *Idylls of the King,* July 1859.

for want of a better name, to be called 'the King's Idylls.' I expect to be in London very shortly: had I known of this early expedition into Scotland I should surely have made an effort to have come up earlier. We are very sorry to hear that there has been so much illness amongst you. As to ourselves I have not been well for some weeks and my wife is now suffering from a very severe cold and cough. The 'bairnies' prosper. I hope the Edinburgh school is a success. Present our best remembrances to the Duke and believe me

Yours ever
A. Tennyson

To EMILY SELLWOOD TENNYSON
MS. Tennyson Research Centre.

Wednesday, March 23, 1859

Dearest

I had Mr. Squire[1] and his family with me as far as Bishopstoke and Charles Simeon[2] from Basingstoke, from whence to town we fumigated a coupe. Poor Sir John is lying unwell at Crawly's Hotel and I am going to call upon him. We dined yesternight at the Oxford and Cambridge Club. Forster not there but Garden, Monteith, Robertson,[3] Clough, William Lushington[4] an elder brother of Vernon's etc. I have done nothing yet—I think of getting the two MS. printed. That's all at present. I suppose Rosa Chawner's book had better be subscribed for.[5] You must tell her that I am in town and that you are in the habit of answering my letters even to particular friends—my best regards to the Fraulein and love to the little ones.

Thine ever
A. T.

To EMILY SELLWOOD TENNYSON
MS. Tennyson Research Centre.

March 24, [1859]

I have been sitting with Simeon and reading Nimuë to Walter White all this

---

[1] See above, p. 200 and n.
[2] Charles Simeon (1816–67), brother of Sir John and captain in the 75th Regiment (*Peerage*).
[3] James Craigie Robertson (1813–82), Canon of Canterbury, and author of *History of the Christian Church from the Apostolic Age to the Reformation* (4 vols., 1852–73; revised, 8 vols., 1874–5) and *Becket, Archbishop of Canterbury* (1859: *Tennyson in Lincoln*, i, No. 3078). He was a Trinity man (BA 1834), and was 'well and long acquainted with Tennyson' (*DNB*).
[4] William Bryan Lushington (1824–88), barrister-at-law (*Peerage*).
[5] See above, p. 92 and n., and i. 296 n.

morning and have done nothing as yet.[1] Froude is coming here tonight, Palgrave and others—I have no news. I shall get a carriage tomorrow and make all calls. I have got thine. I am averse to being exhibited,[2] but not so to having my name appended to the Rajah Brooke paper.[3] Perhaps you won't get a letter tomorrow as I may be out all day calling. I am not less as thou knowest

Thine
A. T.

To HALLAM TENNYSON

MS. Tennyson Research Centre.

March 24, [1859]

My dear little Hallam

I got your nice letter and thank you for it. I hope you will soon know Latin and write to me in Latin.

I suppose if you have pulled a tooth out that there is another coming.

Are the almond blossoms all gone yet? Kiss Lionel for me and do you both be good and obedient and not vex Mamma while Papa is away.

Your affectionate Papa
A. Tennyson

Don't cry if you hurt yourself while I am away but bear pain like a man.

---

[1] 'Tennyson in town. He read to me one of the chapters of his Legends of Arthur . . . a grand musical intonation in his deep sonorous voice. We stood by the mantelpiece in my office, and he read on one hundred and forty pages, till the story was finished. 'Tis admirably told, the contrast between Merlin's and the harlot's nature well sustained, and the way in which he yields at last is most skilfully conceived. There is however that in it which will shock the "unco guid" folks. Spoke my mind freely and advised him to publish. Dined with him at Weld's, Barrett and P[algrave] of the party. The latter an incessant babbler' (*The Journals of Walter White*, p. 150).

[2] Woolner had urged Watts to send the new Tennyson portrait to the Royal Academy Exhibition, but Watts feared that Tennyson would object. Woolner therefore appealed to Emily Tennyson: 'for I think it a pity that it should not be seen by the world, in order to help correct the base and false impression give by Brodie's bust and Mayall's photographs: for altho' the view of the character chosen is not what altogether satisfies either you or me, still it is a high and noble work of art and would do a great deal of good in assisting public taste, and unless there were any real objection it would be a pity not to let it be publicly seen' (Amy Woolner, *Thomas Woolner*, p. 1675). Emily Tennyson replied: 'I have told Alfred that if you do not hear to the contrary before Sunday, you may conclude that the portrait may be exhibited' (*The Letters of Emily Tennyson*, p. 132). It was first exhibited, in fact, by Colnaghi in 1860 (Richard Ormond, *Early Victorian Portraits*, i. 447).

[3] James Brooke (1803–68: *DNB*), Rajah of Sarawak. Thomas Fairbairn (who named his fourth son 'James Brooke' and commissioned Woolner's bust of Brooke) and his (and Brooke's) friend A. H. Novelli had instituted 'an appeal to the nation on behalf of Sir James as the Government has refused to do anything for him' (*Thomas Woolner*, p. 166; see also pp. 152–3). Woolner introduced Tennyson to Novelli (not Vincent Novello) in April (*Journal*, p. 133). See below, p. 256.

To EMILY SELLWOOD TENNYSON

Text. Materials, ii. 214.

March 25, [1859]

I have been carried off to Little Holland House. I shall go up to Hampstead ('mother's') on Monday. On Sunday I go to dine with Owen.

I am much touched by Lord Lansdowne[1] at his age coming to call on me. Had a talk with the Duc D'Aumale[2] about France.

Saw Tom Hughes[3] to whom I take much.[4]

To EMILY SELLWOOD TENNYSON

MS. Tennyson Research Centre.

LITTLE HOLLAND HOUSE, KENSINGTON, Saturday, [26 March 1859]

Dearest

No news except that the Duke and Duchess have just called and I told them (as they wanted to hear me read the M[aid] of A[stolat][1] and I had promised Woolner to read it to him here tonight) to come here at 10 o'clock and they are coming accordingly. The Duke looks unwell, the Duchess very well—enquired very kindly after you and the boys. Give them my love and believe me

Ever thine with crosses
A. T.

Written in great haste the fly waiting.

---

[1] Henry Petty-Fitzmaurice (1780–1864), 3rd Marquis of Lansdowne. With an Edinburgh education and a Cambridge (Trinity) degree, he had the best of two worlds. A prominent Whig and a fixture of the original Holland House (and a cousin of Lord Holland), he was in the cabinet as Lord President of the Council under Grey and Melbourne (1830–4, 1835) and Russell (1846–52), but, though a Whig, he was, like Wellington (whom he succeeded as 'informal adviser to the crown') politically more of a gyroscope than a strict party man (*DNB*).

[2] Henri Eugène, Louis Philippe d'Orléans (1822–97), fifth son of Louis Philippe. He lived in England after the 1848 revolution until 1871, when he returned to France as Deputy in the National Assembly. He bequeathed to the Institute of France the splendid chateau of Chantilly and the Musée Condé.

[3] Thomas Hughes (1822–96), author of *Tom Brown's School Days* (1857), *Tom Brown at Oxford* (1861), and *The Scouring of the White Horse* (1859), illustrated by Richard Doyle (1859: see *Tennyson in Lincoln*, i, No. 1206).

[4] Added here in *Materials*, ii. 215: 'A. T. saw Hunt's picture[s?] which he described as "still growing in power and beauty.") In the way of sights he contented himself with some pictures on sale at Christie's where unfortunately someone asked in a loud tone whether that was not Alfred Tennyson, which spoilt his picture-seeing; and on other days he went to the Zoological gardens, and the British Museum where he saw some exquisite old illuminations with which he was enchanted.'

---

[1] 'Lancelot and Elaine'.

EMILY SELLWOOD TENNYSON to ALFRED TENNYSON

MS. Tennyson Research Centre.

FARRINGFORD, March 26, 1859

Own dearest

So thou art in the Enchanted Palace[1] once more. I do not doubt that thou art happy and I hope it will do thee good. I saw by the papers that the Argylls are in London, whether at their Lodge did not appear, but of course thou wilt see them. It was very good in thee to send me thy dear letter in spite of moving quarters. Take care of thyself. I think thou wilt consent to the portrait being exhibited because after all the horrible slanders of thy face I want people to see something truer to thee.[2]

I enclose this Literary Fund paper which is interesting and deserves attention, does it not?[3]

To Mr. Kingsley's letter I will reply saying that thou wilt answer on thy return.[4]

There is a letter from Mr. Edmund announcing the probable appearance of Mr. Henry Glas[s]ford Bell (Sherrif Bell)—a friend of Edmund's with an introduction from himself and his (Mr. Bell's) friend Lord Mackenzie a Scotch judge.[5] He or they are to come some day early next week.

I should not think of settling anything about Mathilde without thee.[6] She seems to feel that it is scarcely worth while to come back to England for so short a time, but that it would have been better if she could have stayed on indefinitely now. I told her thou hadst expressed a wish that she could have stayed now seeing that it would so soon be time to put Hallam under care of a tutor.

I have asked her to make inquiry for a German tutor and I have told her that perhaps we should arrange for him to lodge in the village but that this would depend partly on the person and would be matter for after arrangement. But when thou art at home again we can talk of this. It is not fair to trouble thee with plans while thou art away. Mathilde stays till next Saturday.

There have been divine lights on land and sea. 'Glorious lights' as little Lionel has more than once exclaimed. Love to the Principessa. My pain is better—Hallam's cold nearly gone. God bless thee dearest.

Thy own loving wife
E. T. x x x x x x x x x

I have written to Mr. Kingsley saying that thou art on the move and that I fear he will have no answer from thyself for some days.

---

[1] Little Holland House.   [2] See above, p. 217 and n.   [3] Unidentified.

[4] Kingsley's letter (*Memoir*, i. 443) had asked permission to reprint his review of *In Memoriam* (see i. 322–3 n.).

[5] Edmund Lushington introducing Henry Glassford Bell (1803–74), advocate and then sheriff [i.e. county judge] and sheriff principal, Glasgow: 'He has been called "the last of the literary sheriffs"' (*DNB*). See below, p. 430. Thomas Mackenzie (1807–69), who had himself been sheriff, 'was raised to the bench' in 1854 'with the title of Lord Mackenzie' (*DNB*).

[6] Mathilde was apparently the boys' nurse (see below, p. 224).

Poor Charles.[7] Perhaps we shall be able to do something towards convincing Louy but I fear not because she is fully aware of what has been so often said by others that abstinence is easier than moderation.

If you could bring back some very good quill pens I should be very much obliged to thee. I cannot get anything decent by way of a pen either here or at Yarmouth or Newport. I suppose everyone uses metal pens now.

To SARAH MONCKTON PRINSEP (incomplete)
MS. Tennyson Research Centre.

[late March or early April 1859]

O Principessa

Will some of the adoring sisterhood hint to the Goddess of Eastnor Castle and Little Holland House that she must really burn or hermetically seal up that copy of Guinevere taken surreptitiously under cloud of night?[1] for I know not when—in such relations I stand to the honourable firm I have to do with—it can be made public. Why should it, as I think and fear it may do, in these many tongued days, come out parcel-wise in misquoted quotation, or altogether basely distilled through some imperfect alembic in consequence of the Goddess's overgenerosity and want of caution. The Goddess spake of two or three—but two or three = the world O Principessa and therefore I petition the Goddess to burn—burn—burn— And, O princess, with respect to the Heavens and the Earth, have regard to me, a silverheaded many wrinkled man, if you that are everblooming, always believed to be your own daughter, and know no touch of time, can sympathize with decadence and infirmity

To EMILY SELLWOOD TENNYSON
MS. Yale.

Friday, [April 1, 1859]

Allow me till Monday—I stay with regret—but among other reasons poor Watts[1] is in the midst of a very fine portrait of myself much superior (people

---

[7] A relapse into his opium addiction.

[1] At Little Holland House, Tennyson had read 'Guinevere' and, apparently, distributed a few copies. Lady Somers (see Appendix A), the 'Goddess of Eastnor Castle', made two or three copies on the sly, and Tennyson, learning the news, reacted predictably—except for casting himself wittily as Tithonus importuning Aurora, Goddess of the Dawn.

[1] George Frederick Watts (1817–1904: *DNB*), the celebrated painter and sculptor (see above, p. 204 n.), familiarly known as 'Signor'. In 1864 Ellen Terry (1847–1928: *DNB*; Dame, 1925), the actress, became his child-wife—for some months: they separated in 1865, divorced in 1877. She acted with Irving in Tennyson's dramas *The Cup* (1881) and *Becket* (1893). See Tennyson's letters to her in vol. iii, 5 January and 26 February 1881.

say) to the last.[2] Poor Watts is so rapt in this—calling it his great work and thinking he may not live—that I stay though unwillingly and longing for [home].

To EMILY SELLWOOD TENNYSON

MS. Tennyson Research Centre.

[? 2 April 1859][1]

I hope thou wast not too much disappointed at my non-appearance today. Expect me on Monday. I have just seen Ruskin. His note to Mrs. Prinsep may amuse thee.

He says the Signor's portrait of me is the grandest thing he has seen in that line—but so he said of the bust—I trust thy pain is better.

Thine
A.

I suspect the Post Office and so got my letters directed in another hand.

To THE DUCHESS OF ARGYLL

MS. Tennyson Research Centre.

LITTLE HOLLAND HOUSE, [? 2 April, 1859]

My dear Duchess

I wish I could, but I can't, as tomorrow is my last day in town and almost every minute of it engaged.

Yours ever
A. Tennyson

To THOMAS HARDWICKE RAWNSLEY

MS. Harvard.

FARRINGFORD, ISLE OF WIGHT, April 25, 1859

My dear Rawnsley

I have been so unwell for the last few days with head-ache and face-ache—owing to having caught cold while working in my grounds, while a bitter Easter was blowing and a hot sun shining—that I could scarce settle to anything—not even to answering a letter.

---

[2] This picture, the 'great moonlight portrait' (now at Eastnor Castle), is reproduced in *Memoir*, i, facing page 428. 'While this . . . portrait was being painted, the Laureate, who was then writing the idyll, "Elaine, the Fair", asked Signor [i.e. Watts] what was in his mind when he set to work upon a portrait, and the words of his reply, having passed through the mind of the poet, lie embedded in the poem' (M. S. Watts, *George Frederic Watts*, i. 170). See 'Lancelot and Elaine', ll. 329–35.

[1] Dated November [1858] in *Memoir*, i. 431.

When you write to Mr. Edward Trollope[1] will you be so good as to thank him in my name for his kind invitation to the meeting of the Lincoln and Nottingham Archaeological Society at Grimsby—and tell him that as I expect guests in May I cannot well present myself there on that occasion. As to belonging to their Society if they only want me as an Honorary member, I am sure my name is quite at their service.

My wife and I beg our united kind remembrances to Mrs. Rawnsley and yourself and hope that you will soon come to us when you are upon our island for we have more than once heard of your being here. We very seldom go into Lincolnshire and have never visited, being there, except at Grasby, which is as you know several hours' journey from Halton, but after your invitation, we *will* try if all be well to get to you.

Thanks for your inquiries after my boys: they are well and merry. Anne Weld is with us and sends her best regards. Believe me, my dear Rawnsley,
Yours very truly
A. Tennyson

To THE DUKE OF ARGYLL

Text. Tennyson Research Centre (transcript).

FARRINGFORD, I. W., April 26, 1859

My dear Duke

I ought to have sent my thanks ere this for the Geological Essay;[1] but as I have not, accept them now. It interested me a good deal.

Are you coming Freshwaterward and seawaterward this May? I hope so
Yours always
A. Tennyson

To THE DUKE OF ARGYLL

Text. Tennyson Research Centre (transcript).

FARRINGFORD, I. W., April 29, 1859

My dear Duke

As far as I can see and except those French and Russian Rogues land in Freshwater Bay, we shall be here in May—16th to 20th—and 'the Queen' also.[1]

---

[1] Edward Trollope (1817–93) was at this time Rector of Leasingham, Lincs., and was in overdue time (1877) Bishop Suffragan of Nottingham, but it was as an antiquary that he 'was most widely known' (*DNB*).

[1] 'Geology: its Past and Present. Being a lecture delivered to the members of the Glasgow Athenaeum, January 13, 1859' (Argyll's *Autobiography and Memoirs*, ii. 596).

[1] The Argylls dined with the Tennysons on 23 and 24 May (*Journal*, pp. 134–5). 'The Queen' refers to 'Guinevere' (see below, p. 228).

My wife is I hope getting better as the weather gets warmer. We hope that your project will not fall to the ground.

Yours ever
A. Tennyson

To JULIA (HALLAM) CATOR

MS. Yale.

[late April 1859]

>   Here with his wife and children
>   rests
>   Henry Hallam
>   The Historian
>   only son of the late John Hallam, D. D., dean of
> Bristol
>   ⟨and Eleanor Robert his wife⟩
>   Born 9th July 1777: died 21 January 1859 ⟨in his 83
> year⟩
>   Blessed are the dead

My dear Julia

The simpler the epitaph on so great a man as your father, the better. Such an epitaph as I have here suggested, besides meeting his own wish on the subject, contrasts favourably with the rather-too-full ones (touching and beautiful as they are) which are already in the church. If he were *my* father I would even omit the parentage, but you will let me hear again on this point. My wife's best love. She has been very unwell, but is better. I myself am suffering from face-ache and must conclude.

Ever yours affectionately
A. Tennyson

ALFRED AND EMILY SELLWOOD TENNYSON to CHARLES RICHARD WELD

MS. Berg Collection.

[early May 1859]

My dear Weld

I send you the song in *its last form*. I don't think the Times will put it in—but you can try if you like—another paper will—to be signed T.[1]

---

[1] 'Riflemen Form!' (Ricks, pp. 1110–11), a reworking of 'Rifle-Clubs!!!' (see above, p. 20, and Ricks's notes pp. 1110, 1778–9). Added in red ink by Weld: 'The lines appeared in the "Times" Monday May 9, 1859—and on Thursday May 12 the Government sanctioned the formation of the Volunteer Rifle Corps. The "Lines" were copied into a great number of papers.' Weld's note is misleading and perhaps disingenuous, for the War Office circular authorizing the Volunteer Rifle Corps was the direct result of a public meeting in St. Martin's Hall, Long Acre, on 16 April, organized by Alfred Bate Richards (see below, p. 522 n.).

Will you copy this out: I haven't time today to send it to Mr. Gatty. I sent him a faulty version and told him to put it into a country paper. [A. T.] I will copy it for Mr. Gatty. So do not trouble yourself dear Charles.

Yours very affectionately
E. T.

To GEORGE STOVIN VENABLES

MS. National Library of Wales.

May 16, 1859

My dear Venables

I have nothing by me of the kind that you require.[1] I know I did once intend to write a stanza or two at your request, but I never got it done or if I did it has past away from memory—I am at present correcting proofs which are a vile nuisance to me, excited as I am about national matters.

Ever yours
A. Tennyson

EMILY SELLWOOD TENNYSON to GEORGE STOVIN VENABLES

MS. National Library of Wales.

[16 May 1859]

My dear Mr. Venables

I very much regret that it is so but I fear the thing could not be done now. I think it must be done when some occasion which naturally suggests it arises. He is a good deal fretted by proof sheets at present.

I hope you leave all well at your home. I am better than I have been but not very well. The boys' nurse who was married has had to return to her husband[1] so they are rather disorderly now for the new nurse has not been much used to children.

Is there any chance of seeing you here before long? If certain things would arrange themselves we might ask if you could come on a certain day which always seems the most satisfactory sort of invitation. I trust this *will* be before long.

Ever most sincerely yours
Emily Tennyson

---

[1] A memorial verse to Venables's edition of Henry Lushington's *The Italian War, 1848–49, and The Last Italian Poet: Three Essays*, with a Biographical Preface by George Stovin Venables (1859). See *Tennyson in Lincoln*, i, No. 3353.

[1] Mathilde (see above, p. 219, and *Journal*, p. 132).

To SAMUEL AUSTIN ALLIBONE[1]

MS. Huntington Library.

FARRINGFORD, I. OF WIGHT, May 24, 1859

Sir

I have only just received the first volume of your work. It has been lying all this time at 44 Dover St., Piccadilly, and I was not aware that there was so sumptuous a book waiting for me. Many thanks. The very few names I have looked at seem to be treated carefully and satisfactorily. I am, Sir,

Your obliged servant
A. Tennyson

To ?

MS. Morgan Library.

FARRINGFORD, I. W., May 25, 1859

Sir

I have only just received your Constitutional press[1] for which accept my thanks. It was [or lay?] at 44 Dover St. for some time and was then forwarded to me along with books and parcels. It is so contrary to the wont of my whole life to write in Magazines that I cannot accept your proposal, but I will become your subscriber—at least for a year. I am, Sir,

Your obedient servant
A. Tennyson

EMILY SELLWOOD TENNYSON *to* MARGARET GATTY

MS. Boston Public Library.

FARRINGFORD, June 3, 1859

My dear Mrs. Gatty

I ought to have answered your kind letters before but I have had a great deal to do in many ways and have not yet grown very strong so I hope you will excuse me and now that I write I have not very good news to tell for poor Ally has, for this week past, been far from well having suffered both from swelled face and hay-fever. He was to have taken his proofs[1] up last Saturday but was not able. If he be well enough perhaps he will go on Monday. He has been also vexed at hearing that the American edition of his books is sold at Paris for three francs. Certainly our descendants in the far West cannot boast of honesty as one of their good qualities.

---

[1] Samuel Austin Allibone (1816–89), compiler of the great *Critical Dictionary of English Literature and British and American Authors* (3 vols.; Philadelphia: Lippincott, 1858–71).

[1] This obscure publication began in 1858, and lasted until March 1860 (Michael Woolf, *Waterloo Directory of Victorian Periodicals*). Emily Tennyson wrote to the Gattys 24 December 1859 (Boston Public Library): 'Someday I must send you the answer from the Constitutional Press. A "present compliments" answer to the expansive sorrowing of Alfred's letter closed by the offer of a Poem.'

[1] *Idylls of the King*, published in July.

We have had a good many guests lately, Mrs. Norton and her son Brinsley with his Capriote wife and Mr. and Mrs. Theodore Martin are the last.[2] Mrs. Martin gave an interesting account of Mr. Craig's astonishment and delight when some fellow-workmen wherever she works called at her little lodging and told her she had the prize.[3] She and her husband dine with us today. They were both strangers to me before yesterday.

I wish we could lend you some of our company since you say you sometimes feel the want of a little more.

The boys are pretty well though the changeable weather is rather trying for them. I hope you are all well in spite of it. Did I tell you of our making Bay-windows in three of the attics and raising two at least of the ceilings? Also of the platform Ally has devised at the top of the house to look at once on the two seas. With our kindest regards to you both believe me

Very truly yours
Emily Tennyson

To EMILY SELLWOOD TENNYSON

MS. Tennyson Research Centre

Saturday, [11 June 1859][1]

Dearest

I came up without one sneeze. I am at Mr. Byrne's chambers, No. 1, Tanfield Court, Temple.[2] No time for more today.

Thine
A. T.

I saw Frank who said he had despatched a coronetted letter to me at Farringford. I suppose the Duke's.

---

[2] See i. 233 n. Brinsley Norton (1831–77) 'married an Italian peasant girl of Capri, "who turned out the best of wives and mothers", and in 1875 succeeded his uncle as fourth Lord Grantley' (*DNB*). Theodore Martin (1816–1909: *DNB*), knighted in 1880, was by profession, on one hand, a parliamentary agent (a solicitor) and, on the other, a versatile man of letters— poet (Bon Gaultier *Book of Ballads*, with Aytoun), translator, biographer (of Aytoun, the Prince Consort, and others). In 1851 he married Helen Faucit (1817–98: *DNB*) the actress, and spent the rest of his life adoring her.

[3] Mr Craig is not identified, and the allusions are not explained in Martin's *Helena Faucit (Lady Martin)*, 1902. Helena Faucit was acting in Glasgow in March, and she and her husband went to Paris for the Whitsun holidays soon after the date of this letter.

---

[1] Postmark.

[2] George Grey Byrne (*c.* 1827–62), BA Oxford, 1850; barrister-at-law, Inner Temple, from 1850 (Foster). His connection with Tennyson may have been through Franklin Lushington.

To THE DUCHESS OF ARGYLL

MS. Tennyson Research Centre.

—AT G. G. BYRNE'S I TANFIELD COURT, TEMPLE, [13 June 1859]

Dear Duchess

Your letter dated Tuesday only reached me this morning. I am engaged on Tuesday, Wednesday and Thursday.

Yours ever
A. Tennyson

To EMILY SELLWOOD TENNYSON

Text. Materials, ii. 219.

LONDON, June 13, [1859]

Val. Prinsep and Mrs. Dalrymple found me out yesterday and drew me to dine at Little Holland House. Mrs. Sartoris was at the Prinseps' and sang some of my things with the most splendid voice, and some Scotch Ballads.[1]

EMILY SELLWOOD TENNYSON to JAMES THOMAS FIELDS

MS. Huntington Library.

FARRINGFORD, June 14, 1859

Mrs. Alfred Tennyson presents her compliments to Mr. Fields and begs to say that she much regrets Mr. Tennyson is not at home. How long his affairs may detain him in Town is uncertain but if Mr. Fields would take the trouble of calling at Mr. Byrnes, 1 Tanfield Court, Temple, he might perhaps ascertain when there is a chance that both Mr. and Mrs. Tennyson may have the opportunity of welcoming Mr. and Mrs. Fields to Farringford.

About ½ past 11 is the most likely time to find Mr. Tennyson at the Temple.

James T. Fields Esqre
Care of Messrs. Trubner and Co.
Paternoster Row
London, EC

---

[1] Valentine Cameron Prinsep (1838–1904: *DNB*), the painter, was the son of Henry Thoby and Sarah (Pattle) Prinsep. For Mrs Dalrymple and Mrs Sartoris, see Appendix A and above, p. 200 n.

To EMILY SELLWOOD TENNYSON

MS. Tennyson Research Centre.

Tuesday, [14 June 1859][1]

Dearest

Thou thinkest so much of the day that I must begin to think of it too—thanks for the Syringa (I don't know how to spell it) which I suppose stands for orange blossom though why orange blossom should symbol marriage I don't know. I have seen nothing yet, hating to go to public exhibitions. The Duchess sent me another note last night to ask me to go to Stafford House[2] on Saturday at noon or Friday afternoon. I shall choose the latter I think—to read The Queen Guinevere to her mother. I can't go to Park House at present but I think when we move we might all go there for a few days. Arnold you know said I was not to pay him at all if he did not get finished before my return—which he understood then would be in a week. Thine, dearest, marriage days and all with no crosses but many × × × × × × ×

A. T.

I hope I shall be able (as I see Barrett today) to tell thee when I can come back.

To HALLAM TENNYSON

MS. Tennyson Research Centre.

[14 June 1859]

Dear Hallam

Thanks for your roses and myrtles and oranges and good wishes: and do not be lazy at your lesson while Papa is far away: but let him hear a good account of you when he returns. And do you and Lionel be good boys now and so you will I hope grow up to be good men. Kisses to both of you,

Your affectionate
Papa

To EMILY SELLWOOD TENNYSON

Text. Materials, ii. 199.

[mid-] June [1859]

Many people here are getting very much alarmed about the French, others are not at all so.[1]

---

[1] Postmark.
[2] Stafford (now Lancaster) House, residence of the Duke and Duchess of Sutherland, and by common consent the finest private residence in London. Tennyson went on Friday (see below, p. 229).

---

[1] See below, p. 232 n.

EMILY SELLWOOD TENNYSON
to JAMES THOMAS FIELDS

MS. Huntington Library.

FARRINGFORD, June 16, 1859

Dear Sir

I regret to say that my Husband will be detained still 8 or 9 days longer in Town. After that we shall if all be well have much pleasure in seeing yourself and Mrs. Fields at Farringford.

Truly yours
Emily Tennyson

James Fields Esqre
Messrs. Trubner and Co.
Paternoster Row
London

To EMILY SELLWOOD TENNYSON

MS. Tennyson Research Centre.

[18 June 1859][1]

Dearest

I read to the Duchess yesterday Guinevere. They asked very kindly after you. There was Gladstone and Mrs. Gladstone and the Duke of Argyll and Mr. Howard:[2] and I suppose my reading was effective though I was conscious that I did not read my best. You see the Duke is in again and also the Duchess of Sutherland as Mistress of the Robes.[3] Love to the boys. I write in great haste, Frank waiting to go to the British Museum with me. Love to the boys. I shall be back next week I hope. Get carriages and drive out.

Thine
A. x x x x x x

---

[1] Postmark.

[2] Probably William George Howard (1808–69), Rector of Londesborough, Yorks., who succeeded his brother as 8th Earl of Carlisle in 1864. He and two younger brothers, Charles Wentworth George Howard (1814–79) and Captain (later Admiral) Edward Granville George Howard (1808–79), later Lord Lancaster, uncles of the Duchess, were at Argyll Castle during the Tennysons' visit in October 1857 (see Appendix D). The six sons of the 6th Earl of Carlisle were all named George, the six daughters Georgiana, and the 7th and 8th earls were uncles of the Duchess of Argyll.

[3] The Earl of Derby's cabinet resigned officially on 17 June. 'The new Ministry, formed by Lord Palmerston in June, 1859, was a very strong one, representing as it did all sections of the Liberal party. The Duke had accepted the office of Privy Seal' (Argyll's *Autobiography and Memoirs*, ii. 137).

To WILLIAM EWART GLADSTONE

MS. British Library.

June 21, 1859

My dear Mr. Gladstone

I am glad that you were not disappointed with Guinevere, and I would come and breakfast with you if I ever went out to breakfast. I used occasionally to breakfast with Mr. Rogers and Mr. Hallam, but they were men of so great an age that it would have been irreverent to refuse their invitation.

Yours very truly
A. Tennyson

To EMILY SELLWOOD TENNYSON

MS. Tennyson Research Centre.

[21 June 1859][1]

Dearest

I went to the Handel celebration.[2] It was magnificent both sight and sound and I only wished for thee there.

I stick to coming down on Saturday if I *can*: it is just possible it may be Monday.

I shall certainly treat with Edmund Venables as Lady Lyndhurst has vouchsafed his answer.[3]

Thine
A. T. × × × × × ×

Evans has offered me £100 for the old woman to put in his new paper. I think I *ought* to take it.[4]

To FRANCIS TURNER PALGRAVE [?]

MS. British Library.

Wednesday, [22 June 1859]

My dear P

I am vext that I was out. I am today going down to Little Holland House

---

[1] Postmark.

[2] A centenary commemoration of Handel's death, in the Crystal Palace, 20, 22, and 24 June. A chorus of 2,765, with a band of 393, sang the *Messiah* on the opening day, *The Israelites in Egypt* on the closing day (*Annual Register*).

[3] Edmund Venables (1819–95), antiquary and divine, was curate at Bonchurch, IW, 1853–5, 'and for some years after 1855 he remained there taking pupils' (*DNB*). Lady Lyndhurst (née Goldsmith, d. 1901) was the second wife of John Singleton Copley (1772–1863), Baron Lyndhurst, son of the portrait painter, statesman, and Lord Chancellor, 1827–30. Farringford was to be let during August–September.

[4] '"The Old Woman" ['the Grandmother'] is to come out in "Once a Week". Alfred could not very well refuse his own printer' (Emily Tennyson to Alfred Gatty, 9 July, Boston Public Library). See also *The Letters of Emily Lady Tennyson*, pp. 138–9. 'The Grandmother' (Ricks, pp. 1106–10) was published in the third number of *Once a Week* as 'The Grandmother's Apology'. For Evans, see above, p. 209 n.

to have my portrait finished by Watts. Could you not manage to come down. You will see Watts's Gallery[?], worth seeing. Why *does* Lady Lyndhurst not return an answer? I have other applications—and shall close with them if I do not hear from her quite immediately. Indeed I do not know whether my wife has not already let the house but I think not.

I stop till Saturday at Little Holland House, then go Farringfordward.

Ever yours
A. Tennyson

To EMILY SELLWOOD TENNYSON

MS. Tennyson Research Centre.

Saturday, [25 June 1859][1]

Dearest

I am going to give my proofs for publication today. The bother they have been to me has not been small: then follows the abuse: but I am fixt not to read it. The Grandmother is only for that copy of 'Once a week' and is my property not Evans's, so make thyself easy. I wish thou would'st have gone out in carriages as I requested thee. Haven't I made £200 in this very journey to town and can't I afford to hire a carriage? I rather fear that two in the house may inconvenience thee, if Margaret[2] has gone: but we must manage as well as we may. I go to Putney today to meet the Grants and Simeon and Lord Monteagle, and the Brookfields. I ceded to this but I would much rather have come back to thee. We shall start by the 11 o'clock express from Waterloo. Let a fly therefore wait by the ferry. I am all the better for coming here.

The children's b[ab]y-talk[?] is touching and curious—love to them. I hope Barrett will send the brushes in time. I wrote to him so to do. My new teeth serve me much better than the old and he says are almost indestructible. Mrs. Prinsep is sending a pretty present of ⟨horns⟩ bugles to the bairns: but better not tell them they will sound well on the downs. Now goodbye, dearest, in hopes to see thee on Monday.

thine
A. x x x x x x

Papa coming home on Monday afternoon! with Mr Cameron and Uncle Fred!

---

[1] Postmark.   [2] Aut ancilla aut ignota.

To EMILY SELLWOOD TENNYSON

MS. Tennyson Research Centre.

[25 June 1859]

The very last news! just got it in the Strand—rather awful!

A. T.

evening papers not yet out.[1]

EMILY SELLWOOD TENNYSON
to JAMES THOMAS FIELDS

MS. Massachusetts Historical Society.

FARRINGFORD, June 30, 1859

My dear Sir

I have pleasure in copying the title page for you as it is to stand.[1] We think we shall be here until the middle of next month and if we knew when you are likely to be here we would reserve rooms for Mrs. Fields and yourself. Believe me, my dear sir,

Truly yours
Emily Tennyson

Idyls of the King
By Alfred Tennyson D. C. L.
Poet Laureate
⟨'God has not made since Adam was,
The man more perfect than Arthur.'
Brut ab Arthur.⟩
'Flos regum Arthurus,
Joseph of Exeter
London

---

[1] The note is scribbled on the inside of the envelope flap. Enclosed is a press release on the battle of Solferino: 'SECOND EDITION | Daily Telegraph office, | Saturday Morning, 10 A.M. | The following most important telegram was received at Mr. Reuter's office, Saturday, June 25th, at 8 30 a.m.:—Paris, Saturday, 7.45 a.m. | THE EMPEROR TO THE EMPRESS. | Cavriana, Friday evening. | Great battle, great victory. The whole Austrian army formed the line of battle, which extended 5 leagues in length. We have taken all their positions, and captured many can[n]on, flags, and prisoners. The battle lasted from four o'clock in the morning till eight o'clock in the evening.'

[1] Not quite. The English edition read 'Idylls', and both English and American editions deleted the first quotation (lined through in this letter and hence given in angle brackets). See below, p. 235.

EMILY SELLWOOD TENNYSON
to JAMES THOMAS FIELDS

MS. Huntington Library.

FARRINGFORD, July 6, 1859

My dear Sir
There are two hotels near us and we hope to see as much of you as convenient to you while you are here. Plumbley's is that to which we went on first coming here. Murrow's is on the sea-shore.[1] Plumbley's higher up but overlooking the sea. Believe me

Truly yours
Emily Tennyson

Mr. Tennyson may have to go to Jersey.

James T. Fields Esqre
23 Northumberland Street
Strand, W.C.

THE DUKE OF ARGYLL *to* ALFRED TENNYSON

MS. Tennyson Research Centre.

LONDON, July 14, 1859

My dear Mr. Tennyson
I think my prediction is coming true—that your 'Idylls of the King' will be understood and admired by many who are incapable of understanding or appreciating many of your other works.

Macaulay is certainly not a man incapable of *understanding* anything; but I knew that his tastes in Poetry were so formed in another line, that I considered him a good test—and three days ago, I gave him 'Guinevere.'

The result has been, as I expected, that he has been *delighted with it*. He told me that he had been greatly moved by it, and admired it exceedingly. Although by practice and disposition he is eminently a Critic, he did not find one single fault. Yesterday I gave him the 'Maid of Astolat,' with which he was delighted also.[1]

I hear the article in the 'Edinburgh Review' is not to contain much criticism—consists to a great extent of long extracts. But I have not seen it myself—nor am I sure who wrote it.[2]

How are you standing this tropical heat—and Mrs. Tennyson? Let us have a good account of yourselves.

This Peace is abominable: and you should be perpetually telescope in hand,—watching for the 'Liberator of Italy'—who has proclaimed to his

---

[1] Thomas Murrow's Royal Albion Hotel (White's *Hampshire*). For the visit, see below, p. 235.

[1] Macaulay lived in 'a charming villa next door to us on Campden Hill' (Argyll, *Autobiography and Memoirs*, ii. 71). See below, p. 236.

[2] Coventry Patmore, 'Tennyson's "Idylls of the King"', *Edinburgh Review*, cx (July 1859), 247–63.

soldiers that he stops because the contest is no longer in the *interests of France!*³

Yours most sincerely
Argyll

ALFRED AND EMILY SELLWOOD TENNYSON
to SIR ALEXANDER GRANT

MS. Yale.

[mid-July 1859]

My dear Grant

A thousand thanks: I shall have another memorial of you though I want no memorials whereby to remember you.¹ I find my name written by you in Oersted Oct. 1854.² So long have we known each other.

I felt and still feel the loss of you for there is no man living from whom I part more unwillingly.

My love to your wife and mother and Heaven speed you on your voyage!

Ever yours
A. Tennyson

My love and God bless you all ever.

E. T.

JAMES THOMAS FIELDS
to HENRY WADSWORTH LONGFELLOW

Text. James C. Austin, *Fields of the Atlantic Monthly,* pp. 396–7.

BONCHURCH, ISLE OF WIGHT, July 18 [for 17], 1859

My dear Longfellow

It is Sunday morning in England, and we have just arrived here, in one of the most charming English rural spots, direct from Tennyson's house at Farringford where we staid two days. Mrs. Tennyson sent to us in London saying we must come to her place when we arrived in the Island, but we drove to a hotel from which both the bard and his wife insisted upon bringing

---

³ On 7 July the emperors of Austria and France agreed upon an armistice, and on the 11th a treaty of peace was signed. Napoleon III's face-saving proclamation said that his troops had 'liberated Piedmont and Lombardy', and had 'only stopped because the conflict was assuming a magnitude no longer in proportion to the interests that France had in this formidable war' (*Annual Register,* p. 252)—diplomatese meaning that the battle of Solferino on 24 June was too costly, and the opposition of the clerical party in France too powerful.

¹ Grant was leaving for India, and the 'memorial' must have been either 'The Ancient Stoics', in *Oxford Essays,* vol. 4 (1858), or his edition of Aristotle's *Ethics* (see above, p. 95 n.).

² Hans Christian Oersted, *The Soul in Nature,* inscribed by Grant: 'Alfred Tennyson. Freshwater, Oct. 1854' (*Tennyson in Lincoln,* i, No. 1706).

us.[1] A most hearty welcome greeted us, and we found we were several days behind the time they had looked for us. I had already met Alfred the Great in London where he had gone to read the proofs of his new volume. We sat down together over the sheets one day in the Temple and talked over certain passages about which he seemed doubtful. The title then was 'The True and The False' which he afterwards altered as it now stands. As you have never seen him I will try to make him out on paper for your inspection. A tall stooping figure clad in sober grey, beard full and flowing, moustache, long stringy hair, and spectacles. His voice is shaggy-rough, and his gait moves with his voice. His 'rear [near?] sight' does not improve his general appearance, as you may imagine. In his own house and grounds (he owns some hundred and fifty acres) he stumbles about in a kind of Tennyson fix which he does not seem to be trying to move away from. One morning he read to us the whole of 'Maud' in a style I cannot soon forget and on another occasion he read 'Guinevere' from the new volume. 'Come into the garden Maud' he gave in a kind of chaunt, most impressive. I shall have much to say to you of him when we meet which I cannot write, but I will note down here that he strikes me constantly as the greatest man I have ever met in England. His Knowledge is most wonderful, and when he talks he says things that are apt to send a thrill with the words. His usual tone is a low unmelodious thunder-growl, but when he chooses he can melt as well as rasp with his Lincolnshire tongue. When he appears at the table in the morning with his old slouched sombrero hat, reading his letters while he takes his breakfast, he is apt to stick dagger-words up and down the present Emperor of France whom he variously designates as a beggar and a scoundrel. But I will not *write* of him any more. He has treated us both with marked kindness, and his lovely wife has made us feel the warmest friendship for the whole household. His two boys, Lionel and Hallam, are dream-picture-children, fair like their mother and as gentle too.

We have enjoyed every day of our sojourn here in dear Old England. All tongues ask for you, and every body loves you. 'Give my *love* to Longfellow' said Tennyson when we parted last night. The 'Golden Legend' is his favorite I think. My wife thanks you again for the flowers you brought her that morning she sailed away from home.

Ever yours
J. T. F.

[1] On Wednesday, 13 July, they 'Passed a miserable night at the Fountain [Hotel, High Street, West] Cowes', and next day took a fly to Plumbly's Hotel, whence, after resting and repacking, they moved to Farringford'. See the account of the visit in M. A. Dewolfe Howe's article 'The Tennysons at Farringford: A Victorian Vista. Drawn from the Unpublished Papers of Mrs. James T. Fields', *Cornhill Magazine*, lxiii (Oct. 1927), 447–57. See also Annie Fields, *Authors and Friends*, pp. 337–55.

To THE DUKE OF ARGYLL

Text. Tennyson Research Centre (transcript).

FARRINGFORD, Monday, July 18, 1859

My dear Duke

Doubtless Macaulay's good opinion is worth having and I am grateful to you for letting me know it—but this time I intend to be thickskinned—nay, I scarcely believe that I should ever feel very deeply the pen-punctures of those parasitic animalcules of the press, if they kept themselves to what I write, and did not glance spitefully and personally at myself. I hate spite.

The heat is very much abated—my wife is all the better for the heat but still far from well. We expect to be in town presently. Will no one put that second sight-seen bullet into Louis Napoleon's forehead *before* he gets to London?[1] When was Europe so insulted?

Yours ever
A. Tennyson

Best remembrances to the Duchess.

To THE DUKE OF ARGYLL

Text. Tennyson Research Centre (transcript)

E. L. LUSHINGTON'S, PARK HOUSE, MAIDSTONE, July 29, 1859

My dear Duke

Your last note was very welcome to me, and if I did not answer it earlier, why—I was all the more to blame—answered partly it was by my wife's copy of the song requested, which I hope arrived safely.[1] She has set it to music far more to the purpose than most of Master Balfe's.

'Red-cap' is, or was when I was a lad, provincial for 'Gold-finch.' Had I known it was purely provincial I should probably not have used it.[2] Now the passage has stood so long that I am loth to alter it.

I suppose the 'well known Author, himself a Poet' who is not to be named is L——n or possibly A——n.[3]

Ever yours
A. Tennyson

---

[1] 'Napoleon haunts his thoughts. He believes him about to attack England. Will America help us? he cries— we are but 50,000 against 600,000' (Mrs James T. Fields's travel diary, 14 July, quoted by Howe—see above, p. 235 n.).

[1] Not 'Riflemen, Form' (see *Memoir*, i. 451 n.) but 'Hands All Round' (Ricks, pp. 1002–4, 1310–1), printed with the music in *Tennyson and His Friends*, pp. 481–4. Argyll had asked for 'The Great Name of England round and round' (*Memoir*, i. 451). 'Mr. Paul takes a stanza of 'Up, Jack Tar' for Balfe to set' (14 May 1859, *Journal*, p. 134). Balfe set to music a dozen Tennyson songs (of which the most famous by far is 'Come into the Garden, Maud') but not apparently 'Jack Tar' (see Gooch and Thatcher, pp. 509–629).

[2] 'The Gardener's Daughter', l. 94.

[3] Tennyson is quoting Argyll, and if the letters are accurate, the names may be Lytton and Aytoun, but Argyll's reference is probably to Patmore's review of the *Idylls of the King* (see above, p. 233 n.).

early August 1859   237

To ROBERT STEPHEN HAWKER

Text. C. E. Byles, *The Life and Letters of R. S. Hawker,* facsimile facing p. 196.
PARK HOUSE, MAIDSTONE, [early August, 1859]

My dear Mr. Hawker

I have just received your kind present. Many thanks. I sent you my book, that is, I told my Publisher to send it you: had it past through my hands I would have written in it.

I did not know that Bos was only one -s'd.[1]

Yours ever
A. Tennyson

P. S. The verses are too complimentary for me to put faith in.[2]

EMILY SELLWOOD TENNYSON
to MRS JAMES T. FIELDS

MS. Huntington Library.
ASHBURTON COTTAGE, PUTNEY HEATH, August 6, 1859[1]

My dear Mrs. Fields

Your kind letter ought to have been answered before this. You must forgive the delay. I was so completely overworked before I left home and then at Park House so many had so much to say to me I could scarcely find a few minutes for anything but talk. Now I am alone in my room for a little while and I will not let the opportunity slip of thanking you for all the kind things you say and assuring you that we too have pleasant recollections of your visit and moreover a hope that it will not be the last to us at Farringford.

Since we received your letter Alfred has had a very nice letter from Messrs. Smith and Elder. This was sent after us and has also remained unanswered till to-day. I do not know if any arrangement with them about a selection would be practicable consistent with Alfred's wish to support the House of Moxon all he can. I hope however he will have an interview with one of the Firm. As Mr. Fields' name is mentioned by them I conclude I am not betraying any confidence in mentioning the subject. Will you thank him for his kind offer to help us in the matter.

I trust you will like the Portrait as well as I do.[2] I have already mentioned your desire to see it to Mrs. Cameron, a sister of Mrs. Prinsep, the Lady of

---

[1] 'Guinevere', l. 289. 'Boss' became 'Bos' in the second edition (1859).
[2] 'When the "Idylls" appeared in 1859, Tennyson sent a copy to Hawker, who acknowledged the gift in a set of verses, (Byles, p. 195): 'To Alfred Tennyson, Laureate, D.C.L., On his "Idylls of the King"', four quatrains dated August 1859, printed in Hawker's *Poetical Works,* ed. J. G. Godwin (1879), p. 207. He refers to Tennyson as 'A Bard ... the mightiest of his race', and concludes: 'He!—would great Arthur's deeds rehearse, | On grey Dundagel's shore; | And so, the King! in laurelled verse, | Shall live, and die no more!' See *The Letters of Emily Lady Tennyson,* p. 144.

[1] 'We go to Park House and then to the Camerons at Ashburton Cottage' (*Journal,* p. 138).
[2] See above, p. 220. 'I want you to see Watts' picture of me in London,' Tennyson had said to Annie Fields (Howe, p. 452).

Little Holland House, but perhaps it would be pleasanter to have a line to herself so I will ask Alfred to write it for you. With all good wishes from us both for you both and very kind remembrances. Believe me, my dear Mrs. Fields,

Most truly yours
Emily Tennyson

EMILY SELLWOOD TENNYSON
to FREDERICK JAMES FURNIVALL

MS. Huntington Library.

ASHBURTON COTTAGE, PUTNEY HEATH, August 11, 1859

Dear Sir

My husband is just going abroad and has so much to do that I feel sure you will excuse him when he deputes me to thank you for your great kindness in thinking of him when you received the St. Graal.[1] He must now hope to see it in May. Believe me with thanks, dear Sir,

Truly yours
Emily Tennyson

To EMILY SELLWOOD TENNYSON

Text. Materials, ii. 221.

RADLEY'S HOTEL, SOUTHAMPTON, August 16, [1859]

Had my warm bath, and boiled fowl for dinner and have been over the Vectis, the name of the vessel, not Tagus, Tagus being repaired, or running alternately with the Vectis, the vessel very prettily got up and painted, and apparently scrupulously clean. Brookfield keeps up my spirits by wonderful tales, puns, etc.[1] I find that neither Palgrave nor Grove[2] wants to move except as I will and they are quite content to remain at Cintra.[3]

---

[1] *Seynt Graal*, or *The Sank Ryal*. The History of the Holy Graal, partly in English verse, by Henry Louelich, Skynner . . . ; and wholly in French prose by Sires Robier Sorron. . . . Ed. from MSS in the library of Corpus Christi College, Cambridge, and the British Museum (2 vols., 1861–3). Furnivall's 'earliest editorial labour was spent upon an edition of the *Seynt Graal* for the Roxburghe Club'—John Munro, in *Frederick James Furnivall, A Volume of Personal Record*, p. xlvi. See below, p. 268.

[1] Brookfield's Diary, 16 August: 'Left London by three o'clock with Alfred Tennyson and Palgrave. Found Jane and the children at Bullar's, where I joined them at dinner. At nine thirty to Tennyson and Palgrave at Radley's for a couple of hours when they were joined by Grove, who was going with them to Lisbon. *Alfred had entered his name E. Tennyson, Esq*' (*Mrs. Brookfield and Her Circle*, ii. 482–3).

[2] Florence Craufurd Grove (1838–?), an 'old friend' of Palgrave's, 'well-known as a strenuous climber in Alps and Caucasus' (*Materials*, ii. 224). Apparently a student at Lincoln's Inn at this time, he was called to the bar in 1862. In 1864 he published a book *The Frosty Caucasus* (*Men-at-the-Bar*; Allibone).

[3] This sentence must be from a later letter (see p. 239).

To EMILY SELLWOOD TENNYSON

Text. Memoir, i. 438.

August 17, [1859]

Have passed a night somewhat broken by railway whistles.

To EMILY SELLWOOD TENNYSON

Text. Memoir, i. 439; Materials, ii. 222; draft Materials, iv. 124.

BRAGANZA HOTEL, LISBON, August 21, [1859][1]

Just arrived at Lisbon and settled at the Braganza Hotel after a very prosperous voyage though with a good deal of rolling. We merely touched at Vigo which looked fruitful, rolled up in a hot mist, and saw Oporto from the sea, looking very white in a fat port-wine country. It is here just as hot as one would wish it to be but not at all too hot. There was a vast deal of mist and fog all along the coast as we came. Lisbon I have not yet seen except from the sea, and it does not equal expectation as far as seen.* Palgrave and Grove have been helpful and pleasant companions, and so far all has gone well. We [are going to see a bull-fight this evening but not a bloody one and] shall go to Cintra either to-morrow or next day.[2] It is said to be Lisbon's Richmond and rather cockney though high and cool. The man who is landlord here is English and an Englishman keeps the hotel at Cintra. I hope with good hope that I shall not be pestered with the plagues of Egypt. I cannot say whether we shall stick at Cintra or go further on. Brookfield gave a good account of the cleanliness of Seville at the Reyna.[3]

*Except the convent chapel at Belem.

To EMILY SELLWOOD TENNYSON

MS. Tennyson Research Centre.

CINTRA, August 23, [1859]

Dearest

We drove over Lisbon yesterday in a blazing heat and saw the church of St. Vincent, and the Botanic Gardens where palms and prickly pears and enormous cactuses were growing, and enormous oleanders covered all over with the richest red blossom and I thought of our poor one at Farringford that won't blossom. There were two strange barbaric statues at the gate of the garden, which were dug up on the top of a hill in Portugal, some call them Ph[o]enician but no one knows much about them. I tried to see the

---

[1] The best accounts of this trip (unmentioned in R. B. Martin's *Tennyson*) are in Gwenllian F. Palgrave, *Francis Turner Palgrave*, pp. 58–62, and D. G. B. Wicks, 'Tennyson in Portugal', *Tennyson Research Bulletin*, No. 2 (Nov. 1968), based partly on Palgrave's manuscript account of the journey.

[2] 'We are going to see a bull fight this evening but not a bloody one, and shall go to Cintra tomorrow or next day' (Wicks, p. [9], from Palgrave).

[3] The Brookfields were in Seville in 1852 (*Mrs. Brookfield and Her Circle*, ii. 376–7).

grave of Fielding the novelist who is buried in the Protestant cemetery but could find no one to let me in. He lies among the cypresses. In the evening we came on here: the drive was a very cold one and the country dry, tawny and wholly uninteresting. Cintra disappointed me at first sight, and perhaps will continue to disappoint though to Southern eyes from its evergreen groves in contrast with the parched barren look of the landscape it must look very lovely: but as yet I have not seen much of it. I climbed with Grove to the Pena, a Moorish-looking castle on the top of the hill, which is being repaired and which has gateways fronted with tiles in patterns, these gates look very much like those in the illustrated Arabian nights of Lane. It is not yet decided whether we shall stay here or go on to Seville and Gibraltar. You might write to the Post Office, Gibraltar on a chance, but I do not know whether I shall receive it. Thou wilt hear from me occasionally but must not be disappointed if it be only at rare intervals: whether I can hear from thee is very uncertain: but I hope thy letter at Lisbon will say when thou goest to Grasby that mine may not be delayed in England. I continue pretty well and have not been bitten. Kiss the boys for me and believe me

Thine ever x x x x x x x
A. T.

To EMILY SELLWOOD TENNYSON

Text. Memoir, i. 440.

August 26, [1859]

It is, I think, now decided that we are to go on to Cadiz and Seville on the 2nd, and then to Gibraltar and possibly to Tangiers, possibly to Malaga and Granada. The King's Chamberlain has found me out by my name:[1] his name is the Marquis of Figueros or some such sound; and yesterday even the Duke of Saldanha came into the *salle à manger*, described himself as 'having fought under the great Duke, and having been in two and forty combats and successful in all, as having married two English wives, both perfect women,' etc., and ended with seizing my hand and crying out 'Who does not know England's Poet Laureate? I am the Duke of Saldanha.'[2] I continue pretty well except for toothache; I like the place much better as I know it better. A visit to Santarem (the city of convents) was greatly enjoyed.[3]

[1] Tennyson had registered as 'E. Tennyson', but at 'Lisbon a newspaper correspondent whom he had visited had advertised his arrival in a local newspaper' (Wicks, p. [10]). The journalist was a Mr Lewtes: 'Daily News correspondent—he was very civil to me during my short stay in that city' (Tennyson letter, 9 July 1860, quoted in Sotheby Catalogue, 20 May 1975, Lot 395).

[2] Oliviera e Daun, João Carlos, Duke of Saldanha (1780–1876), statesman, was from 1871 the Portuguese minister in London. Larger than life, both physically and temperamentally, as *Vanity Fair* (2 September 1871) emphatically demonstrates in caricature and letterpress, he had been in and out of governments, at home and abroad, before 1859, and had 'acted the part of Cromwell with the effete and worthless Government' of Portugal.

[3] The last sentence (not in *Materials*, ii. 223) is probably Hallam Tennyson's addition. The visit to Santarem took place on 5 September (Wicks, p. [12]).

To EMILY SELLWOOD TENNYSON

Text. Memoir, i. 441.

LISBON, September 2, [1859]

The heat and the flies and the fleas and one thing or another have decided us to return by the boat to Southampton which starts from this place on the 7th. We propose on arriving at Southampton to pass on to Lyndhurst to spend two or three days in the Forest.[1]

To EMILY SELLWOOD TENNYSON

Text. Memoir, i. 442.

SOUTHAMPTON, September 13, [1859]

Arrived, and going on to-morrow to Lyndhurst, where I shall stop two or three days, then I am going on to Cambridge with Palgrave from a longing desire that I have to be there once more.

CROWN HOTEL, LYNDHURST, [*c.* 15 September 1859]

Palgrave has been as kind to me as a brother, and far more useful than a valet or courier, doing everything. His father is away at Spa, he (Palgrave) is horrified at being alone. I gave him hopes of his being with me till his father returned and I do not therefore like to leave him.

CAMBRIDGE, September 20, [1859]

I have been spending the evening with my old tobacconist in whose house I used to lodge,[1] and to-morrow I am to dine with Macmillan. I admire Jesus Chapel which is more like a Church than a Chapel.

---

[1] 'He enjoyed tolerably his trip to Lisbon, but was exceedingly ill for some days, brought on by the wine and vile food of the country: Palgrave, who was with him, was in a fright about him for some while: his and Tennyson's fear was lest the fact should get into the papers and frighten Mrs. Tennyson at home: she was staying at Maidstone with the Lushingtons while he was away. A few days after their arrival at Lisbon, all the grandees, who had discovered Tennyson's identity, came flocking to pay their compliments and offer him their services. The same thing occurred at Copenhagen last year——the result, you see, of becoming famous: perhaps it would have been ditto for M. F. Tupper, who is, I hear, the especial pet poet of H.M.G.M. the Queen. If so, all that the reflective mind can remark is that she is true to her race; for an ancestor once denied access to some of Hogarth's works after this fashion "Dak'em away; O dak'em away; I hates boetry and baintin"' (Woolner to Lady Trevelyan, 18 October 1859, Trevelyan Archive, University Library, Newcastle-upon-Tyne, transcript by Raleigh Trevelyan).

[1] 'The apprentice at the tobacconist's where A. lodged recognizes him and puts a paper in his hand' (*Journal,* p. 138.)

Text. Materials, ii. 223.

September 23, [1859]

Going to Park House on Friday.

ALEXANDER MACMILLAN[1]
to EMILY SELLWOOD TENNYSON

MS. Tennyson Research Centre.

CAMBRIDGE, September 29, 1859

Dear Madam

I am afraid you will think that I am making a somewhat too rapid response to the kind invitation which you and Mr. Tennyson gave me. But you will not hesitate to say if you would rather not see me down at the Isle of Wight at present. The occasion of my proposing to come so speedily is that Professor Masson[2] and myself had arranged to take a two or three days run together somewhere before our winter's work fairly begins, and on talking over the question of place today, it occurred to us that we could not do better than come to the Isle of Wight, especially if we had a chance of an hour or two with Mr. Tennyson and yourself. If you would kindly let me know if you are at home, and whether you could conveniently see us, we propose coming on Friday and being about the I[s]land up till Monday. Any time within these bounds we could call on you. I cannot help telling you what deep joy Mr. Tennyson's visit gave and has left in our household. If you will pardon my intruding my private matters on you, I would like to tell you how Mr. Tennyson is linked in the minds of myself, my wife and sister-in-law who lives with us by bands deeper than as a writer of noble poetry, though as such he is indeed dear to us as to thousands of English speaking people. The two men who were nearest to me in relationship, were, happily for me, also nearest to me in love and intellectual intercourse. My brother Daniel, who was my partner in all ways, for eighteen years of most blessed intercourse—(we had been separated by circumstances in earlier life)—was the first who introduced me to Mr. Tennyson's poetry. Ever since 1842, when the first 2 volume edition was published, there has been no book, but one, so often in our hands, or whose words have been so often on our lips. Each successive publication was hailed with a fresh joy and conned and discussed and read and re-read together till every sentence was familiar to us. Our most earnest aspirations after any nobleness in life or thought got its best expression oftenest I believe in the words of these books. For the last few years of his life, he was a hopeless invalid. His disease—pulmonary—was one, we knew, that could not but take him from us very soon and he and we were both conscious

---

[1] Alexander Macmillan (1818–96) and his brother, Daniel Macmillan (1813–57: *DNB*), booksellers and publishers. See i. 322–3 n. Macmillan became Tennyson's publisher in 1884.

[2] David Masson (1822–1907), Professor of English (University College, London, 1853–65; Edinburgh, 1865–95), biographer of Milton, edited *Macmillan's Magazine* from the first number in November 1859 until December 1867.

for at least two years before he went, that any day almost might be the last of our intercourse. You may perhaps judge how [and] in what spirit we read 'In Memoriam' together. It and Mr. Maurice's books were the constant companions of our fireside, or of any pleasure outing we had. Then besides my brother, my wife's brother George Brimley had been for some years before my marriage about my most intimate my[?] friend next to my brother.[3]

I need hardly tell you how he admired and, intelligently, Mr. Tennyson['s] poetry. The Essay which he published in the Cambridge Essays was written at a time when we were constantly together, and many of the points were discussed long and earnestly between us. He was naturally a man of keen critical faculty. I was by temperament more enthusiastic and the results arrived at in the Essay were not always what I sympathised with. But deeper and more important by far than any mere criticism, was the hold which Mr. Tennyson's poetry took on my dear friend and brother's feelings. He, like my brother Daniel, was under the influence of a fatal and most painful disease. His naturally critical and sceptical mind had led to a considerable extent to loss of any distinct hold on things unseen. Mr. Tennyson's 'In Memoriam,' I have reason to believe, came home to him with great power and had a blessed influence on his whole life after. In a most beautiful article which he wrote in the Spectator,[4] under the title of Christmas Thoughts for 1857, he manifested this influence strongly and I think every Christmas eve afterwards at our family gatherings that noble hymn 'Ring out Wild Bells' was read. In May 1857 dear George was taken from us, and in a month after Daniel took his last farewell of us too. Two nobler or braver or more living men I cannot ever hope to know again in this world. Their memory is wound up in every act and work of my daily life; and so it is with my dear wife and sister. 'In Memoriam' is still often read at our fireside and every line is linked with the memory of those two blessed brothers.

You will understand how when the man to whom we owe so much, that is thus deeply woven up with so precious memories, came among us, he came not alone, but seemed almost to give us back what we had lost. And when we found him so kind and genial, I hope he would forgive us if we seemed to treat him as [an] old and most familiar friend.

You will forgive me if I have written thus to you in a strain that is usually only permitted to intimate and long continued friends. But I could not refrain from expressing to you thus some of the deep debt of gratitude and love I and my household feel to your husband and entering thus freely on the grounds of it.

Do not, I beg of you, hesitate to say if our coming to see you at this time would at all inconvenience you and I will willingly defer the pleasure I promise myself till some future and more convenient opportunity. Believe me, dear Madam,

Most respectfully and gratefully yours
Alexander Macmillan

---

[3] See above, p. 136 n.   [4] *Spectator*, xxx (26 Dec. 1857), 1350–1.

3 October 1859

To THE DUKE OF ARGYLL

Text. Tennyson Research Centre (transcript).

FARRINGFORD, October 3, 1859

My dear Duke

We are delighted to hear that your Duchess has added another scion to your race, and that Mother and child are both prospering. I had fancied that the event would have come off while I was in Portugal (for in Portugal I have been) and made enquiries 'thereanent' of Mr. Henry Howard but he could tell me nothing.[1]

If I came back with 'bullion' in the Tagus, it was nowhere in my packages and the Captain and crew kept their treasure a profound secret.[2] I went to see that Cintra which Byron and Beckford[3] have made so famous: but the orange trees were all dead of disease, and the crystal streams (with the exception of a few sprinkling springlets by the wayside) either dried up, or diverted through unseen tunnels into the great aqueduct of Lisbon. Moreover the place is cockney and when I was there, was crammed with Lisbon fashionables and Portuguese nobility; yet Cintra is not without its beauties, being a mountain of green pines rising out of an everywhere arid and tawny country, with a fantastic Moorish-looking castle on the peak, which commands a great sweep of the Atlantic and the mouth of the Tagus: here on the topmost tower sat the King (they say) day by day in the old times of Vasco da Gama watching for his return, till he saw him enter the river: there perhaps was a moment worth having been waited for. I made some pleasant acquaintances, but I could not escape autograph-hunters—a certain Don Pedro Something even telegraphed for one after I had returned to Lisbon.

As to Macaulay's suggestion of the Sangraal I doubt whether such a subject could be handled in these days, without incurring a charge of irreverence. It would be too much like playing with sacred things. The old writers *believed* in the Sangraal. Many years ago I did write Lancelot's Quest of the Grail in as good verses as I ever wrote—no, I did not write—I made it in my head, and it has now altogether slipt out of memory. My wife, I am

---

[1] The Duke had written on 23 September (TRC) that the Duchess had 'just been happily confined of a daughter'—Mary Emma (1859–1947), their sixth. Henry George Howard (1818–79), youngest son of the 6th Earl of Carlisle (see above, p. 229 n.), after Trinity College, had been attaché to the embassy or secretary of legation in Paris, The Hague, Lisbon (June 1848–February 1851), Vienna, Paris (December 1853 to March 1858), and was then appointed envoy to Tuscany (and resigned) in 1858. (See Dod, *Peerage, Baronetage, and Knightage*, 1855, p. 628; obituary, *The Times*, 14 August 1879, p. 10). He was not 'English minister at Lisbon in 1859'—*Memoir*, i. 456 n., confuses him with Henry Francis Howard (1809–98; GCB 1863), son of Henry Howard of Corby Castle (*Landed Gentry*).

[2] Argyll professed to be mystified when 'an inscrutable paragraph appeared in the Papers to the effect that a Lisbon steamer had brought a lot of Bullion, "*and* the Poet Laureate". As we had not heard you speak of any intention of going either to Portugal or elsewhere abroad . . . we are greatly puzzled by the above; and I am charged by Her grace to ask you what you have been doing and seeing' (TRC).

[3] Beckford lived there for a while in 1794–5, and Byron wrote about Cintra (and Beckford) in *Childe Harold*, i. 236–314.

sorry to say, has been very unwell and is at this moment in bed with a severe cold—but desires her best remembrances.

Yours ever
A. Tennyson

To WILLIAM MAKEPEACE THACKERAY
Text. Memoir, i. 446–7.

FARRINGFORD, [6 November 1859]

My dear Thackeray

Should I not have answered you ere this 6th of November?[1] surely: what excuse? none that I know of: except indeed, that perhaps your very generosity and boundlessness of approval made me in a measure shamefaced. I could scarcely accept it, being, I fancy, a modest man, and always more or less doubtful of my own efforts in any line. But I may tell you that your little note gave me more pleasure than all the journals and monthlies and quarterlies which have come across me: not so much from your being the Great Novelist I hope as from your being my good old friend, or perhaps from your being both of these in one. Well, let it be. I have been ransacking all sorts of old albums and scrap books but cannot find anything worthy sending you. Unfortunately before your letter arrived I had agreed to give Macmillan the only available poem I had by me ('Sea Dreams'). I don't think he would have got it (for I dislike publishing in magazines) except that he had come to visit me in my Island, and was sitting and blowing his weed vis-à-vis. I am sorry that you have engaged for any quantity of money to let your brains be sucked periodically by Smith, Elder and Co.: not that I don't like Smith[2] who seems from the very little I have seen of him liberal and kindly, but that so great an artist as you are should go to work after this fashion. Whenever you feel your brains as the 'remainder biscuit'[3] or indeed whenever you will, come over to me and take a blow on these downs where the air as Keats said is 'worth sixpence a pint.'[4] and bring your girls too.[5]

Yours always
A. Tennyson

---

[1] Thackeray's marvellous letter (Memoir, i. 445–6; MS, Yale), written in two parts, early September and 16 October, praised *Idylls of the King* and (later) expressed regret that Tennyson had refused Smith, Elder a poem for the first number (January 1860) of the *Cornhill Magazine*, of which Thackeray was the editor. In the event, Tennyson sent 'Tithonus' (see below, pp. 248, 252).

[2] George Smith (1824–1901) earned immortality by founding (1882) and publishing *DNB*, and also designing the *Concise DNB*. He became head of the firm of Smith, Elder (founded in 1834 by his father and Alexander Elder) in 1848. See below, p. 248.

[3] *As You Like It*, II. vii. 36.

[4] See above, p. 92.

[5] Thackeray: 'You don't know how pleased the girls were at Kensington [Little Holland House] t'other day to hear you quote their father's little verses, and he too I dare say was not disturbed' (*Memoir*, i. 446).

To ALEXANDER MACMILLAN

MS. Yale.

FARRINGFORD, ISLE OF WIGHT, November 18, 1859

My dear Macmillan

Many thanks for your enclosure—I enclose the receipt signed. I think I see why you want the second title—but 'a modern Idyll' is too much: 'an Idyll' will be sufficient.[1]

I trust that your Magazine will prosper. I have not seen the Saturday Review,[2] nor know what it says: but, O my friends, look to your Round Table and make it lighter, or it will drag all of you down.

Yours ever
A. Tennyson

P. S. You will—of course—send me proofs: my wife, thanks, is somewhat better.

To CHRISTIAN BERNHARD TAUCHNITZ[1]

Text. [Curt Otto,] *Der Verlag Bernhard Tauchnitz 1837-1912*, pp. 120-1 (Leipzig: privately printed, 1912).

FARRINGFORD, ISLE OF WIGHT, November 18, 1859

I have no recollection of having received any communication from you through Messrs. Williams and Norgate,[2] and I should scarcely have forgotten it if I had: Mr. Max Müller[3] spoke to me on the subject more than a year ago, and I replied that as I was about to publish a new volume, I thought it would be better to wait until it was published. When it was published this summer I desired Messrs. Moxon to forward you a copy, which I trust that you received. Now I must request you to be so kind as to communicate with

---

[1] 'Sea Dreams, An Idyll', published in *Macmillan's Magazine*, January 1860 (see above, p. 191).

[2] An anonymous review, favourable and respectful, of *Idylls of the King*, *Saturday Review*, viii (16 July 1859), 75-6.

[1] Christian Bernhard Tauchnitz (1816-95), German printer and publisher, whose Library of British and American Authors, cheap paper reprints (begun in 1841), were for many years the staple reading fare of English-speaking travellers on the continent. Exceptional in many ways, Tauchnitz was apparently unique in paying fees to foreign authors before international copyright treaties existed. 'Had Baron Tauchnitz never paid English authors a penny, their gain would all the same have been immense. He obtained for them a vast, an unimaginably vast, public' (Matilda Betham-Edwards, 'A Visit to Baron Tauchnitz', in *Mid-Victorian Memories*, 1919, pp. 84-91). Even so, the cheap editions, smuggled into England, created problems: see below, pp. 487-8, 496. Tauchnitz was raised to the rank of baron in 1860 (*Men of the Time*, 1884; Simon Nowell-Smith, 'Firma Tauchnitz, 1837-1900', *The Book Collector*, xv [Winter 1966], 423-36).

[2] Tauchnitz's London agent was Sydney Williams of the publishing firm Williams and Norgate (Nowell-Smith, p. 431).

[3] Friedrich Max Müller (1823-1900: *DNB*), orientalist and philologist, had settled at Oxford in 1848, was Taylorian Professor 1854-68, and a fellow of All Souls, where Tennyson breakfasted and dined with him in August 1860 (see below, p. 262). See also *Journal*, p. 47.

Messrs. Bradbury and Evans on the subject, as I leave all business matters in their hands.[4]

Allow me to add that I have long known and admired your books. They are beautifully done.

To CHRISTIAN BERNHARD TAUCHNITZ

Text. Der Verlag Bernhard Tauchnitz, p. 121.

FARRINGFORD, ISLE OF WIGHT, December 12, 1859

I did not know that you were in England and am sorry to have missed seeing you. I shall be very glad to see you at my house here when you make another visit to our shores.

You can publish my poems in any order you choose, so that you give the dates. I am sorry that I know of no engraving. There is a likeness of me (said to be a very good one) by Mr. Watts at Little Holland House, Kensington, but no engraving has been made from it: there is also a photograph—when there is a good engraving from Watts' picture made, I will send it—I send you here a photograph from the very successful bust by Woolner; but whether it will be of any use to your book, you must yourself be the judge.

To WILLIAM ALLPORT LEIGHTON [?][1]

MS. Yale.

FARRINGFORD, ISLE OF WIGHT, December 24, 1859

My dear Leighton

I am very glad to hear of you again, and to be reminded of our far-off Cambridge days and should like much to see you, though perhaps you would be shocked to see my calvitude[2] and the furrows which time has drawn since those old days. I am sorry that I cannot find any copies of the Book you ask for. The few which I had I have either given away or lent and to unreturning knaves. I am grieved for my own sake that this is the case as well as for yours.

10 a line to what I *did* receive is as a crocodile to an eft. I wish the liars *had* told the truth—in more senses than one.

I have got into a horror of writing letters so that you are to be all the more obliged to me for this—I and my wife will always be glad to see you here.

---

[4] Emily Tennyson wrote to Bradbury and Evans on 21 November (MS *Punch* office): 'I enclose a letter from Herr Tauchnitz and Mr. Tennyson bids me request that you will be so kind as to arrange for the publication of his Poems either by him or Messrs. Trubner from whom Mr. Tennyson has also heard on the subject and who through Mr. Nutt offered 50£ which does not seem to us very liberal nor to Mr. Weld neither. You will probably hear from Herr Tauchnitz as he has been requested to communicate with you on the subject. I think Mr. Tennyson would give him the preference.'

---

[1] See i. 72 n.   [2] Baldness (not in *OED*).

A happy Christmas to you and yours and a new year as happy as the Christmas.

> Ever yours
> A. Tennyson

To MRS RICHARD MONCKTON MILNES

MS. Trinity College.

FARRINGFORD, I. W., December 24, 1859

My dear Mrs. Milnes

I remember Cookesley[1] very well—he acted in Bombastes with your husband at King's, how long ago I daren't say: I am obliged to you for your little maid's Christmas box. My classics are I fear rather stale and never were very accurate but the translation seems to me generally very good,—here and there, or rather once or twice, not so good.

My wife's best remembrances to yourself and Richard

> Ever yours
> A. Tennyson

To GEORGE SMITH

MS. Yale.

December 26, 1859

My dear Sir

I send you my Poem—Tithonus[1]—it is between 70 and 80 lines long. When published I should like this sort of announcement to precede it.

> My dear Mr. Ed.
> or
> My dear Thackeray
> or
> whatever you think best

You ask me for a poem. Will you accept one which was written about a quarter of a century ago? It is a pendant to my 'Ulysses'?

Macmillan has my Idyl for a year and I suppose that you will want this for an equal time.

> Yours very truly
> A. Tennyson

---

[1] William Gifford Cookesley (1802–80: *DNB*), classical scholar, had been at King's College, Cambridge (BA 1825 or 1826, MA 1827; elected Apostle, 1828), was assistant master at Eton and (in 1857) Vicar of Hayton, Yorks., thirty miles or so from Fryston. The translation referred to must have been Cookesley's edition of *Eton Selections from Ovid and Tibullus, Electa ex Ovidio et Tibullo . . . Notas quasdam Anglice scriptas adjecit* (Eton, 1859). 'Bombastes' is William Barnes Rhodes's burlesque *Bombastes Furioso* (1810). See below, p. 254.

[1] Ricks, p. 112 (see below, p. 252).

I am very glad to hear that your magazine is so prosperous. My thanks and my wife's for your good wishes. I should like to see the illustration before published, and of course the proof of the Poem.[2]

EMILY SELLWOOD TENNYSON
to ALEXANDER MACMILLAN

MS. Berg Collection.

FARRINGFORD, January 25, 1860

My dear Mr. Macmillan

I ought to have answered you before but I have had a great deal of writing these two days so I hope you will pardon me for not having done it. And may I also be pardoned for saying that the song is in four time not in three according to my notion.

[*two bars of music*] this or this as you will

What does little Birdie say[1]

I presume that I am to return the music as it is in manuscript. Many thanks. Alfred is suffering from his face. I am better when perfectly quiet and the boys are pretty well in spite of all our storms.

May I venture to express hope that the Magazine succeeds.[2] With our united kind regards believe me

Very truly yours
Emily Tennyson

---

[2] Tennyson never published with Smith, Elder, but he could have. 'While Henry King was still a partner in Smith, Elder Co., and the *Cornhill Magazine* was being planned, the senior partner, George Smith, had an amusing experience in this connection. The "Idylls of the King" had recently appeared, and the publisher had in mind a further series for his new magazine. In the interview at which this suggestion was discussed he offered Tennyson five thousand guineas for as many lines as were contained in the "Idylls" already issued, on the understanding that he should have the right to publish them for three years after their first appearance in the *Cornhill*. It was a record offer for English poetry up to that time, and as the publisher afterwards wrote in his reminiscences, quoted in Dr. Leonard Huxley's history of "The House of Smith, Elder", might fairly be described as extravagant. Tennyson, however, listened to the proposal quite unmoved, asking Smith to smoke with him and chatting pleasantly, but giving no idea as to whether the proposal was acceptable. Shortly afterwards Mrs. Tennyson came into the room, and Tennyson, addressing her, said: "My dear! We are much richer than we thought we were. Mr. Smith has just offered me five thousand guineas for a book the size of the 'Idylls', and", he continued, "if Mr. Smith offers five thousand, of course the book is worth ten!" A remark at which they all laughed. Nothing came of the proposal' (F. A. Mumby, *The House of Routledge, 1834–1934*, pp. 186–7).

[1] 'My friend Mr. Amps has set the "baby song" to music. I do not know enough of music to judge whether it is good and suitable. If it were I should like it published if Mr. Tennyson has no objection. Remembering your feelings on the subject, I should like very much to have your opinion—if you do not feel it a trouble to give it' (Macmillan to Emily Tennyson, 18 January, BL). Gooch and Thatcher list forty-two settings of this lyric, but none by William Amps (1824–1910), organist and composer (Venn). See below, p. 253, and also I. A. Copley, 'Lady Tennyson, Composer', *Tennyson Research Bulletin*, No. 2 (Nov. 1976), 209–10.

[2] *Macmillan's Magazine* (see above, p. 242 n.).

EMILY SELLWOOD TENNYSON
to FREDERICK GODDARD TUCKERMAN

MS. Harvard.

FARRINGFORD, January 25, 1860

My dear Sir

It seems to grow more and more impossible to my husband to write letters so lest you should have any cause to think your welcome letter less welcome than it really was I must be allowed for the present to thank you in his name though he has the intention of thanking you himself which I hope will some day be fulfilled.

I am glad you like the Idylls. I think Guinevere is my favourite but each differs so much from the other that it is difficult to compare them.

Many thanks for what you say about 'grigs.'[1] One gets some of those out of the way words one knows not how. In England they come chiefly as provincial words and I think in this case have generally a meaning true to their origin.

Our beautiful views will, I fear, be spoilt before long. People are seized with a building mania. Already a bit of our sea is built out from us and we are obliged to buy land at the rate of a thousand pounds an acre nearly to prevent more of the bay being hidden by ugly brick houses. The son of Sir Charles Barry,[2] one of our great architects, has been sent down to look for building sites in different directions and we begin to say perhaps we shall be driven from our home by [the] press of people. If our down were no longer lovely we could not stay. We could only be here in the winter when it is too stormy for visitors.

It is extremely kind in you to think of Hallam. Both he and Lionel take great delight in History. The quasi historical 'Heroes of Greece' by Kingsley also took their fancy very much. I think it must be something like 'Tanglewood Tales.'[3] We had Mr. and Mrs. Kingsley staying with us in the autumn which was very pleasant.[4] Is there any chance of our seeing you soon in England again? I have often thought of writing to you but I have been much out of health ever since two autumns, one in Wales and the next at the Lakes. Last summer I was forbidden to write having been taken very ill when Alfred was away in Lisbon and Cintra three or four weeks.[5] The year before he went to Norway for three weeks and was out in a great storm going. He liked his Northern trip very much the best though he only went to see some waterfalls, the Reichenfalls and others.

We have had the pleasure of making the acquaintance of Mr. and Mrs. Fields, also of Mr. Charles Sumner, this year and you know that this must have been a pleasure.[6]

[1] 'The Brook', l. 54, glossed by Tennyson as 'crickets' (Ricks, p. 1027 n.).
[2] Sir Charles Barry (1795–1860) and Edward Middleton Barry (1830–80), who worked with his father and carried to completion the Houses of Parliament after the elder Barry's death on 12 May (*DNB*).
[3] Charles Kingsley, *The Heroes, or Greek Fairy Tales for My Children* (1856), and Hawthorne's *Tanglewood Tales* (1853). [4] *Journal*, pp. 149–50.
[5] See above, pp. 156–60 (Wales), Appendix D (Lake District), 238–41 (Portugal), 204–5 (Norway).
[6] See above, pp. 232–3, 183, and below, pp. 317, 318.

25 *January* 1860

I think that you who have so kindly and generously interested yourselves in the fate of my Uncle and his companions will rejoice in the success of McClintock's expedition however short this falls of whatever one could desire.[7]

My letter was broken off. I feel as if there were more I wanted to say but here I think I must end begging you to accept our united very kind remembrances and to believe me

Very truly yours
Emily Tennyson

To ?[1]

MS. University of Kansas.

FARRINGFORD, FRESHWATER, I. W., January 27, 1860

My dear Sir

It is so many years since I had the pleasure of seeing you that I feel perhaps some reluctance in intruding upon your time to ask a favour. However hearing that to you belongs the choice of a sculptor for the Franklin monument allow me to introduce to you my friend Mr. Woolner—at least in writing. Doubtless you know his name as one generally reckoned among the first of our sculptors: I have no doubt myself he is the first for this kind of work: himself I am sure you would esteem as a man of thoroughly upright and kindly heart, clear and vigorous intellect and high imagination. Though very much engaged he would like well to have this commission.

My wife begs to be kindly remembered to you and I am, my dear Sir,

Very truly yours
A. Tennyson

---

[7] Lady Franklin, the widow, had financed the expedition of the *Fox*, under Captain (later, Admiral Sir) Francis Leopold McClintock, to search for the lost *Erebus* and *Terror*. McClintock's account of the celebrated discovery, *The Voyage of the "Fox" in the Arctic Seas: A Narrative of the Discovery of Sir John Franklin and His Companions* was inscribed by Lady Franklin to Emily Tennyson (*Tennyson in Lincoln*, i, No. 3355). See *DNB* and *Journal*, pp. 141–2 ('MacKintosh', p. 142, is a mistranscription of 'McClintock').

[1] Unidentified, but probably a Lincolnshire acquaintance, and, if so, probably Sir John Richardson (1787–1865: *DNB*), Arctic explorer and naturalist, who had accompanied Franklin on the first two expeditions (1819, 1825) and conducted the first of the searches (1848). He was himself a Scot, but his second wife was Mary Booth (d. 1845, daughter of John Booth of Stickney, Lincs., and niece of John Franklin: see i. 311 n.), and his third wife was Mary Fletcher, daughter of Eliza Fletcher (see i. 338 n.). The monument is the bronze statue of Franklin by Charles Bacon (1821–85), unveiled by Richardson in Spilsby, Franklin's native village, in 1861 (reproduced in *Illustrated London News*, xxxix [1861], 338, and in *The Life, Diaries and Correspondence of Jane, Lady Franklin*, ed. Willingham Franklin Rawnsley, facing p. 156; see also Richard Ormond, *Early Victorian Portraits*, i. 181).

27 *January* 1860

To THE DUKE OF ARGYLL

Text. *Memoir,* i. 458–9.

[27 January 1860][1]

My dear Duke

I sympathised with you when I read of Macaulay's death in the *Times*.[2] He was, was he not, your next-door neighbour? I can easily conceive what a loss you must have had in the want of his brilliant conversation. I hardly knew him: met him once, I remember, when Hallam and Guizot[3] were in his company: Hallam was showing Guizot the Houses of Parliament then building, and Macaulay went on like a cataract for an hour or so to those two great men, and, when they had gone, turned to me and said, 'Good morning. I am happy to have had the pleasure of making your acquaintance', and strode away. Had I been a piquable man I should have been piqued, but I don't think I was, for the movement after all was amicable.[4] Of the two books I should, I think, have chosen the Crabbe, though Macaulay's criticisms on poetry would be less valuable probably than his historical ones.[5] Peace be with him!

As to the *Sangreal*, as I gave up the subject so many long years ago I do not think that I shall resume it.[6] You will see a little poem of mine in the *Cornhill Magazine*. My friend Thackeray and his publishers had been so urgent with me to send them something, that I ferreted among my old books and found this 'Tithonus,' written upwards of a quarter of a century ago, and now queerly enough at the tail of a flashy modern novel.[7] It was originally a pendent to the 'Ulysses' in my former volumes, and I wanted Smith to insert a letter, not of mine, to the editor stating this, and how long ago it had been written, but he thought it would lower the value of the contribution in the public eye. Read in Browning's *Men and Women* 'Evelyn Hope' for its beauty, and 'Bishop Blougram's Apology' for its exceeding cleverness, and I think that you will not deny him his own.[8] The *Cornhill Magazine* gives a very pleasant account of Macaulay.[9]

Yours ever
A. Tennyson

---

[1] Tennyson replies to Argyll's letter of 20 January (TRC; *Autobiography and Memoirs*, ii. 572); and Argyll replied to this one on 28 January (TRC), the day he received Tennyson's.

[2] Macaulay's death, on 28 December, was announced in *The Times* on 31 December, p. 6 ('the greatest of English writers whom the nineteenth century has produced. Orator, Essayist, Poet, and Historian—in all these fields of literary activity *Macaulay* has won for himself the first place'); a long obituary was in the same issue (p. 7).

[3] François Pierre Guillaume Guizot (1787–1874), French historian and statesman ('Tupper and Tennyson, Daniel Defoe, Anthony Trollope and Mister Guizot'—*Patience*).

[4] But it must have rankled, for he recounted the same story ten years later; see *Tennyson at Aldworth: The Diary of James Henry Mangles*, ed. Earl A. Knies, p. 51.

[5] Argyll had chosen Pietro Sarpi's *History of the Council of Trent* over Crabbe's *Tales of the Hall*, both with Macaulay's pencilled notes.   [6] See above, p. 244.

[7] See above, pp. 245, 248. The 'flashy modern novel' was Trollope's *Framley Parsonage*.

[8] Argyll to Tennyson, 20 January (TRC): 'You once told me you admired some of Browning's Poetry. I wish you could tell me now, *what*? for all I have read seems to me raving nonsense.'

[9] 'Nil Nisi Bonum', *Cornhill Magazine*, i (Feb. 1860), 129–34; anonymous, but in fact by Thackeray (*Wellesley Index*).

EMILY SELLWOOD TENNYSON
to ALEXANDER MACMILLAN

MS. Berg Collection.

FARRINGFORD, February 1, 1860

Dear Mr. Macmillan

I am extremely sorry that the music has not arrived. I sent it at the same time that I sent my last note to you.[1] You are quite at liberty to use your own discretion about giving leave to publish music with those words. I do not doubt that you will use more than we do in such matters.[2]

You must allow Alfred to subscribe to your Magazine. I have not yet had time to look at it.[3] Many thanks for sending it. With our kind regards,

Very truly yours
Emily Tennyson

Will you let Alfred know what he is in your debt for corrections if you please.[4]

ALFRED AND EMILY SELLWOOD TENNYSON
to CHARLES KINGSLEY

MS. Robert Taylor.

FARRINGFORD, February 1, 1860

My dear Kingsley

Of course my name is at your service.[1]

Yours ever
A. Tennyson

I hope Mrs. Kingsley is well and you much better, dear Mr. Kingsley.

E. T.

---

[1] See above, p. 249.

[2] 'I will take it for granted that you leave me to give permission as to the publication of the words to Music as I see fit. I fancy that it is rather to the benefit of the general popularity of an author that his songs should be about in people's drawing rooms and it is surely a benefit to the public that they should have a better article in this line than they have been used to' (Macmillan to Emily Tennyson, 30 January, BL).

[3] 'I am glad to say', Macmillan continued, 'that the Magazine is selling better now than it did at first. Our big contemporary the Cornhill does us no harm so far as we can see. Those learned in periodical sale told us that we would fall off one third from the first start. We have instead risen nearly that. Mr. Tennyson's poem has no doubt been of service to us in a permanent sense, though perhaps the sale of the individual number was not so much larger as we might have looked for.'

[4] In 'Sea Dreams'.

[1] Probably in connection with the Regius professorship at Cambridge, officially offered and accepted in May.

254   *2 February* 1860

To RICHARD MONCKTON MILNES

MS. Trinity College.

FARRINGFORD, I. W., February 2, 1860

My dear Milnes

Will you do me the kindness to read the enclosed from my brother-in-law Captain Jesse on behalf of his son Arthur Henry Hallam?[1] I would fain help him if I could but my *political* influence = nil. Can you do anything for him? Speak of him to the Speaker as a candidate for this clerkship? or advise me what to do? And so with mine and my wife's remembrances to Mrs. Milnes (tell her, please, that I have discovered on rereading more than one mistake in C[o]okesley's translation and therefore must have overpraised it)[2] I am

Yours ever
A. Tennyson

To CHRISTIAN BERNHARD TAUCHNITZ

Text. *Der Verlage Bernhard Tauchnitz*, p. 121.

FARRINGFORD, February 6, 1860

I am much obliged by your kind offer to send me copies of your edition of my Poems.[1] I should like to possess a copy or two. I have no objection to your arrangement of the Poems. I do not think there is any need to change the title or add to it in any way if you retain the dates of publication as I should wish.

I was not aware that Messrs. Smith and Elder had the copyright of my portrait by Lawrence. The lips are considered too thick in this portrait.[2]

---

[1] Arthur Henry Hallam Jesse, 'of the Exchequer and Audit', was born at Boxley, Kent, 18 Janaury 1843, was 'living unmarried' in 1902, and died 10 August 1903 (Jesse family tree, TRC; see also *The Letters of Arthur Henry Hallam*, pp. 800–1.) Milnes replied on 15 February (TRC): 'I spoke to the Speaker [John Evelyn Denison, 1800–73, later Viscount Ossington] about your nephew and he spoke to me—to the effect that he had not a single appointment about the House of Commons—all of them being in the hands of Sir Denis Le Marchant [1839–1915, 2nd baronet], Chief Clerk. I don't agree with you that you have no political influence. I venture to say that before Walter Scott had got your fame he had provided for a dozen cousins. You may be quite sure that any application of yours to the head of any department—to Gladstone, the Duke of Newcastle, Sidney Herbert or in fact any one—would be courteously received. All I can do is to be on the look out if I can serve your nephew which I would fain do for your sake and "in memoriam"'. See the next letter.

[2] See above, p. 248.

[1] Vols. 1–4 (bound as two) of Tauchnitz's twelve Tennyson volumes (no portrait included). See *Tennyson in Lincoln*, ii, No. 3608.

[2] See i. 235–6 n., and below, p. 340. Tennyson called it 'blubber-lipt' (*The Letters of Edward FitzGerald*, iv. 434).

17 *February* 1860

To WILLIAM EWART GLADSTONE

MS. British Library.

FARRINGFORD, I. W., February 17, 1860

My dear Mr. Gladstone

Will you grant me one moment's audience in the midst of your great patriotic labour?[1] I will not detain you longer. 'In medias res.' Hallam's Godson, my nephew, Arthur Henry Hallam Jesse, is anxious to obtain a junior clerkship in the House of Commons. I am told that one will become vacant this year: and his parents have urged me to ask you to say a word for him which I am sure you will do for the sake of old memories. Had I known Sir Denis le Marchant who gives these things away I would not have invaded your time, which is, at this hour especially, so invaluable to your country. Believe me,

Yours respectfully
A. Tennyson

EMILY SELLWOOD TENNYSON *to* ALFRED GATTY[1]

MS. Boston Public Library.

FARRINGFORD, March 12, 1860

My dear Mr. Gatty

I hope you will forgive me for not having acknowledged at once Mrs. Gatty's kind gift of your lecture. I have been and am so unwell from a bad cough. In its pauses I have, however, contrived to read the lecture. I need not say I have read it with much interest but I am too stupid and too coughy to write more about it.

When I am better I mean to write to Mrs. Gatty and ask her if she will give us the pleasure of seeing her here with Dr. Wolff. I suppose she is now with him and is I hope the better for the change.[2]

With our united kind regards and best thanks believe me

Very truly yours
Emily Tennyson

---

[1] Gladstone, as Chancellor of the Exchequer, had brought forward the 'Great Budget' and the Commercial Treaty with France on 10 February (see Morley's *Life of Gladstone*, ii. 18–41, and *Annual Register*, pp. 25–97).

[1] Alfred Gatty (1813–1903: *DNB*), clergyman and devotee of Tennyson's poetry, was the husband of Margaret Gatty (see above, p. 192) and Vicar of Ecclesfield, Yorks., from 1839 until his death (Foster). His lecture before the Literary and Philosophical Society of Sheffield, 6 December 1859, was published in 1860 as *The Poetical Character: Illustrated from the Works of Alfred Tennyson*. He was also the author of *A Key to Tennyson's In Memoriam* (1881).

[2] A note by Gatty at the head of this letter reads: 'I think you had best anticipate the invitation by stating the *utter impossibility* of your accepting it. If the Dervish were to know it would unsettle him. So prevent its coming'. Dr. Joseph Wolff (1799–1862), a continental Jew who converted to Christianity and became a noted Anglican missionary to the Middle East and India, was Vicar of Ile-Brewers, Somerset. Author of *A Mission to Bokhara* (1845), he was a close friend of Mrs Gatty, who advised him with the preparation of his autobiography, *Travels and Adventures* (1860). Wolff visited Farringford in June, preached in the parish church, read prayers

To THE DUKE OF ARGYLL

Text. Tennyson Research Centre (transcript).

FARRINGFORD, April 5, 1860

My dear Duke

My fear is that if you 'invade' us the whooping cough will invade you and yours. Half our parish whoops. My wife has kept her room for six weeks, having caught it a second time and been terribly shattered by it. My two little boys also have it and their nurse is laid up and two other of the servants cough suspiciously. Under these circumstances I can scarcely advise yourself and your Duchess to come, sorry as I shall be to miss your society.[1] I should have been in town some weeks ago if it had not been for this. As the worst appears to be over I shall I think go to town in about three or four days time but if you have courage to come, let me know and I will wait.[2]

Our best regards to the Duchess of whom we grieve to hear so indifferent an account.

Yours always
A. Tennyson

To AUGUSTUS HENRY NOVELLI[1]

MS. Kenneth Rendell.

April 30, 1860

My dear Novelli
    Arrived—many thanks—from

Yours ever
A. Tennyson

P. S. My regards to your wife: mine I am glad to say is somewhat better.

---

in the afternoon, and gave a lecture in Freshwater. See *The Letters of Emily Tennyson*, p. 149; *Journal*, pp. 146–7; and *Memoir*, i. 460. He was called the 'Dervish'—no doubt because of his 'extraordinary vitality and nervous energy' (*DNB*). 'Dr. Wolff arrived last night. His talk has an inspiration that cannot be withstood and he is so gentle and kind withal that one must like him as much as one wonders at him. I am a good deal exhausted with the excitement for I have not yet recovered my usual portion of strength.' 'Pray tell Mrs. Gatty that we find Dr. Wolff has an eastern dignity and courtesy in addition to the Dervish inspiration' (Emily Tennyson to Gatty, 7 and 11 June 1860, Boston Public Library).

[1] Argyll wrote the next day (TRC) that they had no fear of whooping cough, all having had it, and would come on to Freshwater the next week—as they did, staying 'at the Hotel' and spending three evenings with the Tennysons (*Memoir*, i. 459; *Journal*, p. 144).

[2] He went to London to the dentist on 16 April and on the 19th, at Macmillan's, wrote 'his name in capitals on the rim of the big round table'. He also recited 'Boadicea' and 'stayed till half-past one in the morning' (Derek Hudson, *Munby, Man of Two Worlds*, p. 59; Charles Morgan, *The House of Macmillan, 1843–1943*, p. 53).

[1] Augustus Henry Novelli (born in Manchester, *c.* 1820, son of Philip Novelli), BA Glasgow 1836, admitted to Trinity 1836, migrated to Pembroke 1839, readmitted to Trinity 1840 (Venn). Formerly from Northaw, Herts., he apparently settled in Aberystwyth, where Woolner visited him. 'While I was with the Rajah [James Brooke] his friend Novelli, who is also Fairbairn's *most* intimate friend, asked me to come to Aberystwyth and spend a few days with him.... He is one

PRINCE ALBERT to ALFRED TENNYSON

Text. *Memoir*, i. 455.

BUCKINGHAM PALACE, May 17, 1860

My dear Mr. Tennyson

Will you forgive me if I intrude upon your leisure with a request which I have thought some little time of making, viz. that you would be good enough to write your name in the accompanying volume of your 'Idylls of the King'?[1] You would thus add a peculiar value to the book, containing those beautiful songs, from the perusal of which I derived the greatest enjoyment. They quite rekindle the feelings with which the legends of King Arthur must have inspired the chivalry of old, whilst the graceful form in which they are presented blends those feelings with the softer tone of our present age. Believe me,

Always yours truly
Albert

TWO VIEWS OF TENNYSON

(i) . . . The *looking* at him would be the most capital offence of all if he were Ruler of the Universe—and yet he is so worth looking at—so grand in form and character and even in his shrinking [from others] there is a sad and serious helplessness. . . .

. . . Alfred's wood may satisfy any forester. His place is a perfect beauty but it does not satisfy him. His prairies are all enamelled with the purple orchis and golden cowslip—the orchis being of that rich Violet which is the robe of Kings and the golden Cowslip and burnished buttercup bordering this purple with a golden band.

He sees the beauty but he *feels* it not—his spirits are low—and his countenance serious and solemn. Every trifle of life disturbs him—the buildings

---

of the most fascinating men I ever met. He has the soul of a poet with the profoundest comprehension of business in its minutest details: the Rajah calls him Prince of British Merchants; and altho' this Prince has one of the most enormous businesses in the World, he wields it all as lightly as a lady plays with a feather; he perfectly astounds by his cleverness, for his accomplishments never seem to end; he plays the piano exquisitely and his own compositions make one think he has devoted his whole life to the art of music; to see him play billiards one would think he must have been a billiard marker, for he beats any gentleman player and gives long odds. I shall tell you plenty about him when I see you. Fairbairn always promised me as the highest compliment he could pay me, that he would introduce me to his friend Novelli, and altho' I believed he was a nice fellow from his report, yet I never imagined him to approach what I really found him. To make his happiness complete he has a most charming wife and two children' (Amy Woolner, *Thomas Woolner*, pp. 152–3). Woolner introduced Novelli to Tennyson at Little Holland House early in April 1859 ('Very pleasant that he should get to know these great practical men'), and Novelli visited Farringford in December (*Journal*, pp. 133, 141). 'Novelli and Company, merchants' had offices in London in 1860 at 2 Crosby Square, Bishopsgate Street Within (*P.O. London Directory*), and later at Billiter House, Billiter Street (*City of London Directory*, 1844). See above, p. 217 n.

[1] The autographed copy is now in the Royal Library, Windsor. The 'Dedication' (Ricks, p. 1467) to *The Idylls of the King* begins: 'These to His Memory—since he held them dear'.

getting up are a nightmare to him—the workmen *not* getting on are a daily vexation to him—his furniture has not come[1]—the sculptures for his hall have miscarried or been delayed—the tradesmen cheat him—the visitors look at him—Tourists seek him—Americans visit him—Ladies pester and pursue him —Enthusiasts dun him for a bit of stone off his gate—These things make life a burden and his great soul suffers from these insect stings. . . .

A little thing pleases him for a little while. The Prince Consort writes him a very *friendly* letter sends the Queen's or his own Copy of the Idylls asks for an Autograph! and Alfred meditates seriously and pleasantly on it all—declares he does not know what form of answer to write—and then fashions and frames a *perfect* answer. . . . All that he has is so great and grand—if he would only live in his own *divine* powers and not suffer the merest terrestrial trifles to magnify themselves into misfortunes heaped on him (Julia Margaret Cameron to her husband, 25 May 1860, Sotheby's Catalogue, 14 Mar. 1979, Lot 266).[2]

(ii) Alfred Tennyson came in the morning in an agreeable mood, though it *was* in the morning. His agreeable moods are generally in the evening. After I was in bed, Mrs. Cameron wrapped a shawl round her head and went down to the beach, and finding a most magnificent state of things there, she sent for Alfred, who joined her, and whom she left to make the most of it. He seems to be independent of weather. Mrs. Cameron says that in one of the great storms of this year he walked all along the coast to the Needles, which is six miles off. With all his shattered nerves and uneasy gloom, he seems to have some sorts of strength and hardihood. There is a great deal in him that is like ——. But his tenderness is more genuine, as well as his simplicity; and he has no hostilities and is never active as against people. He only grumbles. . . . He wants a story to treat, being full of poetry, with nothing to put it in (Henry Taylor to his wife, 2 or 3 June 1860, *Autobiography*, ii. 192).

---

[1] 'We have been very unfortunate about our furniture agent. After having spent 500 £ and more including agency the furniture is by no means what I ordered and what we should have had for a 150 less nor is it yet finished though begun three months ago' (Emily Tennyson to Mrs Gatty, 25 July, Boston Public Library).

[2] The description of the letter continues: 'Young Hardinge [Cameron (1846–1911)], on arriving to have Greek lessons from Tennyson, found the poet mowing his lawn with [a] two-handle scythe and carefully removing every dandelion (". . . He gave the remaining *one* to Har and says Hold it tight in your hand for if you don't the seed will blow away and sow itself—But I must let it go *somewhere* says Har—Oh yes anywhere you like—but not in my fields—In any one's field but your's said Har Sotto Voce . . ."); further relating how Tennyson had forbad them to pick hyacinths from his woods (". . . they were for a bride herself a hyacinth tall and stately—tranquil and tender . . .") but how Mrs. Tennyson, repenting of this hardheartedness, sent round six dozen the next day; she then compares Tennyson rather unfavourably with her other idol, Sir Henry Taylor, giving an amusing example of the former's timorousness . . ." He [Taylor] delights in his fellow creatures whilst A T fears them all. He Alfred begs me to conduct him to his gate 'for there is someone coming—!' 'Oh a poor old Woman hobbling along', I tell him—'Oh is it'—T thought it was some fashionably dressed Lady in his answer—No Lady or Woman in any form would H. T. turn from. . . .'

To THE DUCHESS OF ARGYLL

MS. Tennyson Research Centre.

FARRINGFORD, I. W., July 12, 1860

O Duchess

Why should you reproach me? Dumb to all the world, have I ever refused to answer you? Have I not made your Grace that striking example which proves the rule?

No—I never wrote anything on Macaulay's death: this is one of those hoaxes in which the Transatlantic soil is so fertile. The stanzas were sent to me in an American paper some weeks ago. Very glad am I to learn that your healths are so far reestablished—myself am hay-feverous with inflaming and ever reinflaming and weeping eyes. My wife and the boys cough still but the whoop has returned to owl-land. I suppose that we shall move in about a fortnight when I hope that we may find you and the Duke still at Argyll Lodge. Meanwhile, believe me,

Yours ever
A. Tennyson

To JOHN AULDJO[1]

MS. Rosenbach Foundation.

July 13, [1860]

Mr. Alfred Tennyson presents his compliments to Mr. Auldjo and will be much obliged to him if he will say whether 'L'Histoire Générale des Hommes du XIXe Siècle' is a bonâ-fide publication:[2] and whether one would be right in enclosing a cheque to Le Secrétaire de la Direction de l'Histoire Générale, 27 Terrassière, à Genève.

Mr. Tennyson begs Mr. Auldjo to excuse the trouble he is giving him: but he has failed to obtain information through other channels in England.

---

[1] John Auldjo (1805–86), amateur scientist, fellow of the Royal Society, the Royal Geographical Society, the Geological Society, and the Statistical Society, author of three books—on his ascent of Mont Blanc in 1827 (published 1828), Vesuvius and its eruptions (1832), and a trip to Constantinople and some of the Greek islands (1833)—and a longtime friend and correspondent of Bulwer-Lytton, suffered financial reverses in 1859, and thereafter resided on the Continent. He married Caroline H. Hammet in Paris early in 1860, and in the summer they went to Geneva, where they settled, and where Auldjo was acting British Consul 1870–1, and then Consul 1872–86. (Boase; J. M. Bulloch, 'John Auldjo, F.R.S.', *Notes and Queries*, clxvi [12 May 1934], 327–32). A Mrs Auldjo, aged eighty-five, 'of Bryanston-square, relict of John Auldjo, esq., of Mottingham House, Kent' died 18 February 1861 at the Lodge, East Cowes, IW (*Annual Register*, p. 397), where she resided with Henry Auldjo, Esq. (White's *Hampshire*, p. 624); one of them, perhaps indirectly, must have given Tennyson John Auldjo's name and address.

[2] *L'Histoire Générale des hommes vivants, et des hommes morts dans le XIXe siècle. Recueil de mémoires etc. Par des écrivains de diverses nations* (7 vols., Geneva, 1860–82 ('imperfect; wanting the rest') is in the British Library.

To MRS. JERROLD[1]

MS. Tennyson Research Centre.

FARRINGFORD, July 18, 1860

Mr. Alfred Tennyson presents his compliments to Mrs. Jerrold and has the honour to grant the permission which Mrs. Jerrold requests to publish her music to his poem of The Rivulet and to dedicate it to himself.

To THE DUCHESS OF ARGYLL

MS. Tennyson Research Centre.

July 27, 1860

My dear Duchess

I had hoped to have been in London ere this, and to have thanked you viva voce for the Duke's shadow[1] which is, however, by no means so satisfactory as the Duke's substance—but we have had many troubles and bothers which have delayed us. I hope that we shall move in about 10 days and that we shall find you among the roses and larkspurs of Argyll Lodge.[2]

Ever yours
A. Tennyson

in haste and in the midst of letterwriting (strange to say) paying off old long-due debts—of correspondence, I mean.

To JAMES THOMAS FIELDS

MS. Harvard (transcript).

July 30, 1860

My dear Sir

You have behaved as crazily or as generously as Glaucus in Homer who exchanged his golden armour for Diomed's brass:[1] in return for an old brambleroot choked with the accumulated oils of three-dozen fumigations you have sent me a maiden Brier of I know not what value. Many thanks. I am glad that your walk did not disappoint you. Farewell and all prosperity!

Yours ever
[A.] Tennyson

---

[1] Unidentified, but possibly the wife of William Blanchard Jerrold (1826–84: *DNB*), journalist and author, whose father, Douglas William Jerrold (1803–57: *DNB*), author, editor, playwright, and wit, Tennyson knew. No music by Mrs Jerrold is listed in Gooch and Thatcher. 'The Rivulet' is probably the lyric from 'Maud', I. xxi: 'Rivulet crossing my ground' (Ricks, pp. 1074–5). The letter is in Emily Tennyson's hand.

[1] A photograph ('pretty good') enclosed in an undated letter (TRC).
[2] 'We are in great beauty—with roses and quantities of the dark blue Larkspurs', the Duchess had written (TRC).

[1] *Iliad*, vi. 236.

Mine and my wife's best thanks to Mrs. Fields for her kind message. We should have been so glad to have seen her likewise!

To ?[1]

MS. Huntington Library.

FARRINGFORD, I. W., August 1, 1860

Dear Sir

I fancied that you were about to follow your letter in person to these parts at once—and therefore did not answer. On referring to it I see that the date of your arrival is uncertain. Lest you should come and find us out I send this note to tell you that for two months about from this time, more or less, I and mine move from home. After my return I need not say that I shall delight in welcoming you under my roof: believe me (with many thanks for your 'book').

Yours very truly
A. Tennyson

THE JOURNALS OF WALTER WHITE, pp. 151–2.

August 10, 1860. Dined with Mr. and Mrs. Tennyson at Burlington House. Palgrave and Woolner of the party; Spedding came in at tea-time. The Laureate talked of going to the Levant,[1] to West Indies, Cornwall or Brittany.

August 14. Talk with Tennyson concerning Dartmoor, Cornwall, and the Scilly Isles. He thinks of writing something more about King Arthur, urged thereto by Mr. Gladstone and others. If he does there will be a chasing and marching of Arthur and Sir Modred from Tintagel down to Lyonesse, the now submerged region beyond Land's End. He commonly composes while smoking, and keeps the lines long in his head before writing them down; dislikes the labour of writing and so loses many thoughts by delay. He once had three hundred lines in mind concerning his Lancelot and his quest for the Sangrail, and lost them all through leaving them too long unwritten. Does not remember if he has written more in one place than another; writes wherever he may happen to be. 'Locksley Hall' was written at High Beach [*sic*] in an old house which has since been pulled down.[2] He admires the Vale of Thames between Maidenhead and Streatley, and now departs for Oxford preparatory to journeyings in Devon and Cornwall.

---

[1] Perhaps Martin Tupper, whose volume ('book'?) *Three Hundred Sonnets* was published in April.

[1] Tennyson 'thinks of going with Palgrave to Constantinople for a few weeks; but he never definitely makes up his mind what he will do until the last' (Woolner to Lady Trevelyan, 5 August, Trevelyan Archive, University Library, Newcastle upon Tyne, transcript by Raleigh Trevelyan).

[2] See below, p. 286.

To EMILY SELLWOOD TENNYSON

MS. Tennyson Research Centre.

ALL SOULS READINGROOM, OXFORD, Saturday, [18 August 1860]

Dearest

I hope thy journey was accomplished safely and speedily and that you found a train from Retford.[1] This day here is very vile and must I fear be very cold and damp at Grasby. [Before my] departure called [on?] Palgrave with his Syrian brother,[2] a very interesting man in an Eastern dress with a kind of turban, having just escaped from his convent in the Syrian deserts, where several of his fellow monks were massacred—but Frank P. kept up such a shouting with Woolner that I could not very well hear what the brother said. However F. P. was obliged to stop for a week at Hampstead till the brother goes to Paris where he will have an interview with the Emperor on the affairs of the east: I started off alone and I believe that in a week's time H. Hunt, V. Prinsep and F. P.[3] will join me at Penzance. Woolner (like a good fellow) followed me here yesterday that I might not feel lonely and this morning we breakfasted with Max Müller and are going to dine with him at 7.

Kisses to the boys. I cannot well say whither thou art to direct but at Penzance Post Office in a week's time I shall hope to find a letter.

Thine ever × × × × ×
A. T.

Love to your father! Max Müller will like (he says) to take my sea-villa if not tenanted for September. Wilt thou write and ask and send me the answer to Penzance. Woolner dispatched the watch yesterday.

To EMILY SELLWOOD TENNYSON

BIDEFORD, August 21, [1860]

We came here last night at 7 o'clock. I and Woolner are going down the coast to Tintagel where we shall stop till the others join us [*Memoir*, i. 460].[1]

---

[1] 'We having been misinformed as to the trains, the boys and myself end our railway journey by coal train, much to their delight' (Journal).

[2] William Gifford Palgrave (1826–88), F. T. Palgrave's younger brother, had been a Jesuit missionary in India and Syria, and in 1862–3, 'passing as a Syrian christian doctor and merchant', he undertook the dangerous assignment described in his most famous book *Narrative of a Year's Journey through Central and Eastern Arabia* [1865] (*DNB*). See *Tennyson in Lincoln*, i, No. 1743, and Gwenllian Palgrave, *F. T. Palgrave*, p. 82, and below, p. 502. Mrs Cameron's glamorous photograph of him is in *Victorian Photographs of Famous Men and Fair Women*, Plate 25, and in Andrew Wheatcroft's *Tennyson Album*, p. 32. Another, equally glamorous, is in Benjamin Braude's article 'William Gifford Palgrave, Mysterious Arabist', *Harvard Magazine*, xxxxvii, No. 3 (Jan.–Feb. 1985), 40–1. He died in Montevideo 30 September 1888. Tennyson's wonderful tribute 'To Ulysses' (Ricks, p. 1396), written early in 1888, merges Palgrave ('Ulysses, much experienced man') with his book *Ulysses*, published in November 1887.

[3] Holman Hunt, Val Prinsep, and F. T. Palgrave.

[1] Palgrave's account of the Cornwall tour is much fuller in *Materials*, ii. 309–17, than in *Memoir*, i. 461–5.

BUDE, August 23, [1860]

Fine sea here, smart rain alternating with weak sunshine. Woolner is with me and very kindly. We go off to-day to Boscastle which is three miles from Tintagel [*Materials*, ii. 304].

August 23, [1860]

Arrived at Tintagel, grand coast, furious rain. Mr. Poelaur would be a good name to direct to me by [*Memoir*, i. 461].

TINTAGEL, August 25, [1860]

Black cliffs and caves and storm and wind, but I weather it out and take my ten miles a day walks in my weather-proofs. Palgrave arrived to-day [*Memoir*, i. 461].

To HALLAM TENNYSON

MS. Yale.

TINTAGEL, August 25, 1860

My dear Hallam

I was very glad to receive your little letter. Mind that you and Lionel do not quarrel and vex poor mamma who has lots of work to do: and learn your lessons regularly: for gentlemen and ladies will not take you for a gentleman when you grow up if you are ignorant. Here are great black cliffs of slate-rock and deep black caves and the ruined castle of King Arthur and I wish that you and Lionel and mamma were here to see them.

Give my love to Grandpapa and to Lionel—and work well at your lessons —I shall be glad to find you know more and more every day.

Your loving papa
A. Tennyson

To EMILY SELLWOOD TENNYSON

TINTAGEL, August 28, [1860]

We believe that we are going to-morrow to Penzance or in that direction. We have had two fine days and some exceedingly grand coast views. Here is an artist, a friend of Woolner's (Inchbold),[1] sketching now in this very room. I am very tired of walking against wind and rain [*Memoir*, i. 461].

UNION HOTEL, PENZANCE, August 31, [1860]

I am so very much grieved for poor Simeon's loss of his wife;[2] it casts quite a gloom on my little tour, what will he do without her and with all those children? I have now walked ten miles a day for ten days, equal 100, and

---

[1] John William Inchbold (1830–88: *DNB*), landscape painter with Pre-Raphaelite affinities, much admired by Ruskin. His *Tintagel* (1862) was probably begun at this time.
[2] She died on 24 August, survived by six children.

I want to go on doing that for some time longer. I am going to-morrow to Land's End and then I must return here, and then I go to the Scilly Isles and then again return here. Mary must not run away with the Prince Consort's letter to the West Indies.[3] [*Materials*, ii. 305–6].

LAND'S END INN, September 5, [for 1, 1860]

I will write to Simeon to-day, though I rather shun writing to him on such a subject, for what can one say, what comfort can one give? We are here at this racketty, rather dirty inn, but we have had four glorious days and *magnificently coloured seas*. To-day the Scilly Isles look so dark and clear on the horizon that one expects rain. [*Memoir*, i. 462].

To SIR JOHN SIMEON

MS. Syracuse University.

LAND'S END INN, [1 September 1860]

My dear Simeon
It was only late last night that I heard from my wife that dear Lady Simeon had past away. There is nothing consolatory that I or anyone else can say which would not seem flat and stale to you under so sudden and so great a sorrow. I dare only speak for myself and tell you that my heart aches for and with you in your lonely house. Certainly to be separated, for what remains of life, from one so surpassingly sweet and true and gentle is a doom most terrible—but you will bear up, will you not? for you are brave, and you have children, and you have faith—and she lives, you know. She is not really gone.

Yours most affectionately
A. Tennyson

To EMILY SELLWOOD TENNYSON

PENZANCE, September 6, [1860]

I start in an hour by the boat for the Scilly Isles. The weather is splendid and the sea as calm as any lake shut in on all sides by hills. Woolner goes back to London and Palgrave continues with me. [*Memoir*, i. 463]

ST. MARY'S, SCILLY ISLES, September 9, [1860]

Captain Tregarthen, who has the packet and the hotel here,[1] has brought me my letters: the packet only goes three times a week. I shall stop here till

---

[3] Mary Ker, his sister.

[1] 'Between us we nearly ate the rough but hospitable "Tregarthen's Inn" empty.... Many a little voyage, by sail or oar, did we make in that miniature Archipelago.... One was to the smallest of the main islands that formed the bay, where we rambled over great stones and heather, Tennyson all the while carrying a volume of Homer, looking into it when we rested, and leaving it on the rock' (Palgrave, in *Materials*, ii. 313).

Wednesday; there are West Indian aloes here thirty feet high, in blossom, and out all winter, yet the peaches won't ripen; vast hedges of splendid geraniums, a delight to the eye, yet the mulberry won't ripen. These Islands are very peculiar and in some respects very fine. I never saw anything quite like them. [*Memoir*, i. 463]

THREE TUNS, LIZARD, September 11, [1860]

At the Lizard; and intend coming on to Falmouth. Hope to be at Brockenhurst next Saturday, but if not there, I shall have turned aside to see Avebury and Silbury Hill. [*Memoir*, i. 463]

FALMOUTH, September 20, [1860]

Have not found it easy to write every day in the bustle and bother of travellers' inns. I am now writing on my knees in my bedroom at a fishmonger's, there being no room at the Hotel and the whole town mad with a bazaar for riflemen, who get drunk every night and squabble and fight and disgrace themselves and their corps.[2] We left Hunt and Val Prinsep hard at work at the Lizard, sketching on a promontory. One farmer was astonished at Val's legs and wished to feel them to find out whether they were real or false.[3] [*Materials*, ii. 307]

RED LION INN, TRURO, September 22, [1860]

Found out at Falmouth in the Polytechnic Hall where there was a show of pictures and other things, likewise a painting of my 'Guinevere' from the hand of the Secretary of the Society,[4] not badly done. Now we are going to Perran Sands about nine miles from here to stop the Sunday. [*Materials*, ii. 307]

---

[2] 'But at the foot of the stairs, when we entered the inn, stood certain small damsels who put their pretty hands in ours and insisted on leading us to a bazaar—doubtless for some holy purpose—going on within the ball-room above. Like all good men and poets alive to the spell of a little child, especially if a girl, Tennyson yielded at once. But the room was crowded, and although we knew no one, yet there were several in the throng who recognized a face and figure which it was not easy to forget. People behaved with perfect good manners . . . ; yet interested looks were aimed, strange passages opened before us in the assemblage; in short, the poet was detected (unperceived as yet to his shortness of sight), and I took the liberty of warning him off the premises: remaining, at his wish, to save the look of unsociability; and hence to receive many enquiries about so distinguished a companion' (Palgrave, in *Materials*, ii. 315).

[3] Prinsep (see above, p. 227) was a young giant, as the Spy cartoon in *Vanity Fair* (13 January 1877) attests.

[4] J. Sydney Willis Hodges (1829–1900), who painted portraits of many notables, exhibited thirty-five pictures at the Royal Academy, eight at the British Institution, 1854–93, and also wrote poems and several novels (*Bryan's Dictionary of Painters and Engravers*). See below, p. 266.

CHAUNTECLEER AND THE COLFOX[1]

Text. Caroline Fox, *Memories of Old Friends* (2nd edn., Philadelphia: Lippincott, 1884, pp. 349–51.

FALMOUTH, September 22, 1860

Alfred Tennyson and his friend Francis Palgrave at Falmouth, and made enquiries about the Grove Hill Leonardo, so of course we asked them to come and see it; and thus we had a visit of two glorious hours both here and in the other garden.[2] As Tennyson has a perfect horror of being lionized, we left him very much to himself for a while, till he took the initiative and came forth. *Apropos* of the Leonardo, he said that the head of Christ in the Raising of Lazarus was to his mind the worthiest representation of the subject which he had ever seen. His bright, thoughtful friend, Francis Palgrave, was the more fond of pictures of the two: they both delighted in the little Cuyp and the great Correggio; thought the Guido a pleasant thing to have, though feeble enough; believed in the Leonardo, and Palgrave gloated over the big vase. On the leads we were all very happy and talked apace. 'The great T.' groaned a little over the lionizing to which he is subject, and wondered how it came out at Falmouth that he was here; this was *apropos* of my speaking of Henry Hallam's story of a miner hiding behind a wall to look at him, which he did not remember; but when he heard the name of Hallam, how his great gray eyes opened, and gave one a moment's glimpse into the depths in which 'In Memoriam' learned its infinite wail. He talked a good deal of his former visit to Cornwall, and his accident at Bude, all owing to a stupid servant-maid.[3] In the garden he was greatly interested, for he too is trying to acclimatize plants, but finds us far ahead, because he is at the western extremity of the Isle of Wight, where the keen winds cut up their trees and scare away the nightingales in consequence. But he is proud and happy in a great magnolia in his garden. He talked of the Cornish, and rather liked the conceit of their countryism; was amused to hear of the refractory Truro clergyman being buried by the Cornish miners, whom he forbade to sing at their own funeral; but he thought it rather an unfortunate instance of the civilizing power of Wesley. By degrees we got to Guinevere, and he spoke kindly of S. Hodges's picture of her at the Polytechnic, though he doubted if

---

[1] Caroline Fox (1819–71: *DNB*), diarist and tuft-hunter: she rarely left her home, Penjerrick, in Falmouth, and she knew everyone. She was the daughter of Robert Were Fox (1789–1877: *DNB*), the scientific writer.

[2] 'One [invitation] came from a gracious and lively minded lady, whose narrative (not wholly accurate) was published a few years since. She said that her father's garden was much admired, and hoped Mr. Tennyson might be interested by the sight of it. The lady and her family were entire strangers to us both: but the visit, we thought, need not be long, and would leave us leisure for some expeditions. However, between talk and garden and the house with its collections, so long a time went by that it was decided to fly to regions of lesser culture and leave Falmouth unexplored; and I felt again that Tennyson's anxiety not to be recognized was no assumed or morbid shyness' (Palgrave, in *Materials*, ii. 316). Grove Hill was the seat of Caroline Fox's brother, Robert Barclay Fox (1817–55), succeeded by his son Robert Fox (1845–1915). See *Landed Gentry*.

[3] See i. 288–90.

it told the story very distinctly. This led to real talk of Arthur and the 'Idylls,' and his firm belief in him as an historical personage, though old Speed's narrative has much that can be only traditional. He found great difficulty in reconstructing the character, in connecting modern with ancient feeling in representing the ideal king. I asked whether Vivien might not be the old Brittany fairy who wiled Merlin into her net, and not an actual woman. 'But no,' he said; 'it is full of distinct personality, though I never expect women to like it.' The river Camel he well believes in, particularly as he slipped his foot and fell in the other day, but found no Excalibur. Camel means simply winding, crooked like the Cam at Cambridge. The Welsh claim Arthur as their own, but Tennyson gives all his votes to us. Some have urged him to continue the 'Idylls,' but he does not feel it expedient to take people's advice as an absolute law, but to wait for the vision. He reads the reviews of his poem, and is amused to find how often he is misunderstood. Poets often misinterpret poets, and he has never seen an artist truly illustrate a poet. Talked of Garibaldi, whose life was like one out of Plutarch, he said, so grand and simple; and of Ruskin, as one who has said many foolish things; and of John Sterling, whom he met twice, and whose conversational powers he well remembers.

Tennyson is a grand specimen of a man, with a magnificent head set on his shoulders like the capital of a mighty pillar. His hair is long and wavy and covers a massy head. He wears a beard and a moustache, which one begrudges as hiding so much of that firm, powerful, but finely-chiselled mouth. His eyes are large and gray, and open wide when a subject interests him; they are well shaded by the noble brow, with its strong lines of thought and suffering. I can quite understand Samuel Laurence calling it the best balance of head he had ever seen. He is very brown after all the pedestrianizing along our south coast.

Mr. Palgrave is charmingly enthusiastic about his friend; if he had never written a line of poetry, he should have felt him none the less a poet; he had an ambition to make him and Anna Gurney[4] known to each other as kindred spirits and of similar calibre. We grieved not to take them to Penjerrick, but they were engaged to the Truro river; so, with a farewell grasp of the great brown hand, they left us.

To EMILY SELLWOOD TENNYSON

Text. Materials, ii. 307.

CLARENCE HOTEL, EXETER, September 26, [1860]

Propose to be home on Thursday through Salisbury.[1]

---

[4] Anna Gurney (1795–1857: *DNB*), Anglo-Saxon scholar (probably a cousin). See Gwenllian Palgrave, *F. T. Palgrave*, pp. 22–3.

[1] On the same day Woolner wrote to Lady Trevelyan from London: 'I am sorry the Tennysons are not going to you this year; I know Mrs. Tennyson would have liked [to] for I have heard her say how much she would like Alfred to know you and Sir Walter. When I was

23 *October* 1860

To FREDERICK JAMES FURNIVALL

MS. Huntington Library.

FARRINGFORD, October 23, 1860

My dear Sir

Mr. Shorter[1] has my permission to insert the poems you mention. I am going to make it a rule not to grant any more of these applications, for so my printer[2] advises me, but as the rule is not yet made Mr. Shorter is very welcome to the May Queen and the other two.

Many thanks for the Proofs of the St. Graal[3] which you were kind enough to send me some time ago and believe me,

Yours very truly
A. Tennyson

F. J. Furnivall Esqre
Old Square
London, W. C.

To THE EDITOR OF THE *CALBOURNE MAGAZINE*[1]

MS. University of Indiana.

FARRINGFORD, November 21, 1860

Mr. Alfred Tennyson presents his compliments to the Editor of the Calbourne Magazine and requests him to put his name down as a subscriber for 2 copies of his Magazine.

EMILY SELLWOOD TENNYSON *to* FREDERICK JAMES FURNIVALL

MS. Huntington Library.

FARRINGFORD, November 26, 1860

My dear Sir

Mr. Tennyson was going to write you but he has such a bad tooth ache

---

with A. T. at the Scilly Isles he was grumbling that he had to go home to entertain guests; he was always asking me questions about Sir Walter, and seemed to take a great interest in him; I think that wild Trevelyan legend of the White Horse fascinates rather and makes him wish to see the descendent of such a favored man. I saw Palgrave this afternoon who had just returned from his tour, having left Tennyson at Salisbury. Hunt and Val Prinsep they left somewhere near Falmouth making sketches' (Trevelyan Archives, University Library, Newcastle-upon-Tyne, transcript by Raleigh Trevelyan).

[1] *A Book of English Poetry: for the School, the Fireside, and the Country Ramble* (1861), ed. Thomas Shorter (d. 1899), anthologist, author, and first Secretary of the Working Men's College (see Allibone and J. F. C. Harrison, *A History of the Working Men's College, 1854–1954* [1954], pp. 50–1). Besides 'The May Queen', Shorter printed an extract from 'The Ode on the Death of the Duke of Wellington' and 'You ask me why' (entitled 'Britain').

[2] Bradbury and Evans.   [3] See above, p. 238 and below, p. 269.

[1] No copy of the magazine has been traced. Calbourne is a village on the Freshwater road, five miles south-west of Newport, a mile and a half from Swainston, home of Sir John Simeon.

that he told me to say for him how much he thanks you for your kindness in sending the San Graal.¹ He is indeed very grateful for the interest you show in his pursuits.

Very truly yours
Emily Tennyson

F. Furnivall Esqre
3 Old Square, Lincoln's Inn
London W. C.

To THE DUCHESS OF ARGYLL

MS. Tennyson Research Centre.

FARRINGFORD, I. W., December 3, 1860

My dear Duchess

Should I not have answered before this? I think I should. Is there any use in making my apology? Something of an apologetic nature is somewhere in the depths of my heart, but refuses to dress itself in words and come forth. So let it be where it is. As to my Cornish tour, after which you are kind enough to enquire, I send for answer a paragraph from a Cornish paper which was transmitted to me after I had reached home. It is not quite right, not extravagantly wrong. I was comfortable enough while I could preserve my incognito but I was found out at a bazaar in aid of the Rifle-fund at Falmouth¹—and fled to Truro, where I did *not* stop at the Red Lion because it was the natal home of Sam. Foote.² I am sorry for the occasion of the Buxton visit and hope that it has proved beneficial, but I scarce had dreamed that Rheumatism would have attacked so tender a blossom as Lady Edith. I that love all wild and desolate places envy you your imprisonment in that 'ultima Thule' Tyree.³ I have seen it afar off and longed to be in it. Glad am I that dear good Bunsen's latter hours were cheered by the gleam of light from Italy.⁴ I hope it is more than a gleam but Garibaldi the brave and guileless is at any rate, a light for ever. We shall hear of him again.

¹ See above, p. 268.

---

¹ See above, p. 265.

² Samuel Foote (1720–77), actor, dramatist, wit, buffoon, 'was born at a home in Truro long known as Johnson Vivian's'' (*DNB*).

³ An island of the Inner Hebrides, Argyllshire. On 22 September 1863 Argyll wrote to Tennyson (TRC): 'Tyree is a curious Island—three low Hills, all the rest nearly quite flat—but clovery, and fertile—with a population of 3000 creatures who live in strange Beehive like huts very well built—and very neatly thatched. But consecutive bad seasons have reduced a great number to poverty and I have to pay them instead of them paying me, which is an unpleasant turning of the table. On looking out one sees only the Ocean—over rocky knolls—or over Sandy dunes—and on the sky line the great Light-House of the "Skerryvore"—a column of granite rising out of the Sea to the height of 160 feet having its feet always in the waves—a noble monument of human skill and knowledge.'

⁴ Bunsen (see above, p. 177) died on 28 November. The 'gleam of light' was the possibility of Italian unification under Victor Emmanuel II. Garibaldi, refusing to accept the King's proffered 'honours and emoluments', 'quitted Naples for the Island of Caprera on the 9th of November, two days after Victor Emmanuel entered it' (*Annual Register*, p. 244).

My wife desires her love. She has many nights of sleeplessness and pain: I too suffer from face-ache.

I expect to be in London before Christmas and will if possible call at Argyll Lodge. Believe me always

Yours and the Duke's
A. Tennyson

How are the Duchess of Sutherland's eyes?[5]

To ROBERT GORDON LATHAM[1]

Text. J. Holt Schooling, 'The Handwriting of Alfred Lord Tennyson', *Strand Magazine*, viii (1894), 603 (facsimile).

[December 1860][2]

My dear Latham

You never did send me the book—even of the single sheet of MSS which you sent I shall be most perplext to find the whereabouts.

If you want that, and if I ever should find it, why then you shall have it.

Yours ever truly
A. Tennyson

TWO VIEWS OF TENNYSON, JANUARY 1861

January 23, 1861

We found the glorious old god as godlike as ever.[1] . . . Nothing could be kinder than both Mr. and Mrs. Tennyson—he in his great blind superhuman manner, like a colossal child—and his often repeated disappointment that we could not stay longer near them was evidently as unfeigned and straight-spoken as everything, large and little, that comes out of that mouth, with which he rather seems to think aloud than, in the ordinary acceptation, to

---

[5] Mother of the Duchess of Argyll.

[1] Robert Gordon Latham (1812–88: *DNB*), MD, ethnologist, and philologist, born at Billingborough, Lincs. Tennyson had met him in the train at Peterborough in November 1849 (see Appendix, vol. iii).

[2] The facsimile notes: 'Written in December, 1860'. Woolner wrote to Lady Trevelyan on 1 January 1861: 'Palgrave has just returned from Farringford where he left the Tennysons very well save a cough which troubles the lady of that house. I think I told you of a collection of English lyrics that Palgrave has been making [*The Golden Treasury*, 1861]: he took his batch of poems for the Poet to give his opinions on, and says that well as he knew Tennyson's powers of insight into poetry he was nevertheless astonished at the precision and profundity of his judgments in each poem, in giving its characteristics without any hesitation, and compares his judgment to the fine touch of Durer or Leonardo' (Trevelyan Archives, University Library, Newcastle-upon-Tyne, transcript by Raleigh Trevelyan).

[1] See *Journal*, p. 153. The Dobells wintered at Niton, IW, for several years.

speak. When E[mily][2] told him, in the morning, that we were going to bring an authoress, his horror at 'writing women' was grotesque to behold. . . . (Sydney Dobell to his father [John Dobell]: *The Life and Letters of Sydney Dobell*, ed. E[mily] J[olly], ii. 178).

[late January 1861]

I paid my annual visit to Tennyson last week.[3] Shall I tell you about him? This year he has written nothing but a short piece called 'Boadicea,' in a very wild peculiar metre, with long lines and innumerable short syllables. It is very fine, but too strange to be popular. He has been ill, and greatly suffering and depressed I fear. The more I see of him the more I respect his character, notwithstanding a superficial irritability and uneasiness about all things. I have a pleasure in repeating this about him, because I find he is so greatly mistaken by those who don't know him or only know him a little. No one is more honest, truthful, manly, or a warmer friend; but he is as open as the day, and, like a child, tells any chance comer what is passing in his mind. He sometimes talks of going on with 'King Arthur.' For my own part I hope he won't; he has made as much of it as the subject admits. Twenty years ago he formed a scheme for an epic poem on 'King Arthur' in ten books; it is perhaps fortunate for himself that circumstances have prevented the completion of it. He dislikes Byron, but speaks very generously and warmly of Wordsworth. The subject on which I think he is most ready to converse—sometimes over a pipe—is (what do you think?) a future state, of which he always talks with a passionate conviction. He is the shyest person I ever knew, feeling sympathy and needing it to a degree quite painful. Please not to repeat this to the vulgar, who can never be made to understand that great mental troubles necessarily accompany such powers as he possesses. I should not tell it you if I did not think *you* would comprehend it (Benjamin Jowett to Margaret Elliott, *Letters of Benjamin Jowett*, ed. Abbott and Campbell, pp. 171–2).

To WILLIAM BARNES[1]

MS. Dorset Natural History and Archaeological Society.

FARRINGFORD, February 28, 1861

Sir

I was from home when your kind gift came. I have for many years known

---

[2] Mrs Dobell (née Fordham). The 'authoress' was Emily Jolly, author of a dozen or so anonymous novels (Allibone). 'She also wrote under the initials "E. J." and "Lady who prefers to be anonymous." Her contributions to . . . [*Household Words* and *All the Year Round*] were reprinted in 1875 under the title *A Wife's Story and Other Tales*' (Albert Johannsen, *The House of Beadle and Adams and Its Dime and Nickel Novels, The Story of a Vanished Literature*, ii. 166).

[3] Jowett arrived at Farringford on 15 January (*Journal*, p. 153).

[1] William Barnes (1801–86: *DNB*), the 'Dorsetshire Burns'. The 'kind gift' was his *Poems of Rural Life in the Dorset Dialect* (2nd edn., 1847), inscribed: 'With the author's kind respects' (*Tennyson in Lincoln*, i. No. 3494). For Barnes's visit to Farringford, with Allingham, in November 1865, see *Memoir*, i. 513 (fuller than Allingham's *Diary*, pp. 126–8). He was also a philologist, whom Swinburne thought 'much better as a lexicographer . . . than as a poet' (*The Swinburne Letters*, vi. 211).

and admired this volume of your Poems but I need not say that I value this copy with an especial value as coming from yourself. I have the honour to be, Sir,

Your obedient and obliged servant
A. Tennyson

To ?

MS. University of Kansas.

FARRINGFORD, March 4, 1861

Sir

As it might be a work of some days to get bank notes here I send a cheque for £15 requesting an acknowledgement. With good wishes, I have the honour to be, Sir,

Your obedient servant
A. Tennyson

I should certainly again recommend you to apply to the literary fund where perfect secrecy is observed.

To THE DUCHESS OF ARGYLL

MS. Tennyson Research Centre.

[FARRINGFORD,] [12 March 1861]

My dear friend

I do not know the measure of your sorrow but know that you must be sorrowing, and sorrow for the loss of one so near is so sacred that I hesitate to approach you even with a kind word and wish lest I should disturb the silence.[1]—My one word and wish is only God bless you—in which I need not say that my wife cordially joins—

Perhaps the Duke will let us know how you are and how the Duchess of Sutherland bears her great loss.

Ever yours
A. Tennyson

To ANNA MARIA HALL[1]

MS. Historical Society of Pennsylvania.

FARRINGFORD, March 20, 1861

Madam

I regret that I cannot have the pleasure of sending you a Poem for your

---

[1] Her father, the Duke of Sutherland, died 22 February. Argyll (answering this letter) wrote on 13 March (TRC): 'a nobler and gentler spirit never breathed and I don't think I ever saw such a general mourning among all—even slight acquaintances.... The attachment of all His children to the Duke was something beyond the ordinary measure of that relationship.'

[1] See i. 223–4. Mrs Hall was the founding editor of the *St. James's Magazine*, which began publication in April 1861.

Magazine as I have refused and been obliged to refuse similar requests even from personal friends, such requests having become too numerous to grant. I have the honour to be, Madam,

Your obedient servant
A. Tennyson

EMILY SELLWOOD TENNYSON to EDWARD LEAR

MS. Tennyson Research Centre.

FARRINGFORD, April 2, 1861

My dear Mr. Lear

I wrote to you on Sunday but you were gone and since that time I was in my room for nearly a week with three brief exceptions in evenings when I was brought down. I have been very ill but I have been daily gaining strength now.

Nothing settled about C. R. W. Not a word more about cause from them. From Grasby rather vague words. I will let you know when anything is settled.[1]

Frank came on Monday and none could be more welcome as you know.[2] He is as ever I think when one is in love. With him though his manner is different in society. He looks well and is cheerful.

I cannot say more today. I hope you are somewhat better. Our love

Ever yours
E.T.

I need not wish you to say nothing about C. R. W. more than you can help.

To ?

MS. University of California at Los Angeles.

FARRINGFORD, April 22, 1861

Sir

I regret that I cannot help your protégé my vote being already promised. I have the honour to be, Sir,

Your obedient servant
A. Tennyson

---

[1] Charles Weld had been forced to give up his position at the British Institution, in Burlington House. 'The offence is of the nature we believed it to be but we have had no particulars. Continual threats of self-destruction come to one[,] and all at present in that quarter is dreary and dark. The only hope of improvement is in occupation and that under the circumstances is not easy to find.' 'Poor C. R. W. is so ill owing to want of sleep through his trouble, that his doctor orders him immediately to leave Town. He is to come here tomorrow. I think I forgot to tell you, that the reasons assigned to the Council after giving up the office are simply "family reasons"' (Emily Tennyson to Edward Lear, 15 April [*The Letters of Emily Tennyson*, p. 156], and 22 April [TRC]).

[2] Frank Lushington (see below, p. 281).

To EMILY SELLWOOD TENNYSON

Text. Materials, ii. 328.

LONDON, [early May 1861]

I was going to start by the 5 [o'clock] train tonight and stop at Southampton and see Rogers' gardens[1] the next morning before starting, but Simeon coming in would have me dine with him at the Garrick.

To EMILY SELLWOOD TENNYSON

MS. Tennyson Research Centre.

[WINCHESTER,] [22 May 1861]

Dearest

I have had a long walk—country a good deal better than that about B. Walked to Chilcourt. Little church yellow-lichened in a million-buttercupped churchyard. Three tombstones in a row:

Sacred to the Memory of

Harriet so and so, 42 years servant of the Revd. H. S. (I forget the name)
To the Memory of John *35 years servant of the Revd. H. S. (the same name)*
To the Memory of *32 years servant of the Revd. H. S.*

All three tombstones in a row erected by the Revd. Master. Thought it was creditable.

I found no bed at the George, the Hampshire militia being here in great force but this inn on a back street (the Royal) is quiet, clean and almost cheering[?] with a green garden. I got up to the top of the hill which I told Hallam was called King Arthur's Table—with the fir-clump on it.

I trust you got home all right. If fine tomorrow here, I complete my week of walking—if not, possibly I go townward.

Warburton[1] out of the town. Mrs. W., the cocky page assured me, wouldn't see me (I did not give my name) because she was just sat down to lunch. British, that!

---

[1] William Henry Rogers, 'nurseryman and seedsman, and landscape gardener, 13 High Street, and *Red Lion Nursery*', Southampton (White's *Hampshire*), p. 188). See *Journal*, p. 156.

[1] William Parsons Warburton (1826–1919), from Ahaseragh, Ireland, matriculated at Oxford from Balliol in March 1845 (BA 1849, first class Lit. Hum.); he was ordained in 1851, and was a fellow of All Souls 1849–53. From 1851 to 1881 he was (like Matthew Arnold, with whom he corresponded) Inspector of Schools, and in 1881–5 of training colleges. He was Honorary Canon of Winchester 1881–7, Canon from 1885, and he lived at Winchester in the Close even in the fifties (Foster, Allibone, White's *Hampshire*, *Journal*, *Memoir*, *George Eliot Letters*, ed. Haight, v. 420).

To EMILY SELLWOOD TENNYSON

MS. Tennyson Research Centre.

CAMELOT, May 23, 1861

Another long walk today—broke my back as it were—but feel very well—going tomorrow by 12 [o'clock] train to London—shan't get my walk I'm afraid.

Thine ever
A. T.

Love to the boys: tell Lionel he's a

CHATTERBOX!!!

and must learn to keep the peace, meantime to observe the direction.

I shall try at the Old Hummums[1] but don't expect a bed—write again tomorrow.

May 25, [1861]

I have asked the Welds down. I am going to-night to Lyndhurst I think but [am] not certain. [*Materials*, ii. 329].

To THE DUCHESS OF ARGYLL

MS. Tennyson Research Centre.

FARRINGFORD, May 29, 1861

My dear Duchess

I have just returned and am just going to set out again to the New Forest. I shall put up at the Crown Hotel, Lyndhurst, which is about 2 hours from Farringford—the moment I hear of your arrival at Freshwater I will come home again.

Yours always with best remembrances to the Duke. I am glad that your mother is well.

A. T.

To EMILY SELLWOOD TENNYSON

Text. *Materials*, ii. 329.

CROWN HOTEL, LYNDHURST, June 1, [1861]

Arrived safe enough, there was no omnibus to meet the train, so I walked. I found some very pretty new lawns[1] in the Forest after arriving.

---

[1] See i. 227 n.

[1] Draft *Materials*, v. 22, reads 'plants'.

LYNDHURST, June 3, [1861]

I wish Edmund Lushington would have come to-day,[2] I want to be off. It is only 13 miles from this place, minus boat to Farringford so I intend to walk.

LYNDHURST, June 4, [1861]

I shall be home to-morrow. The postmistress here has written wanting to take my portrait.[3]

THE TENNYSONS IN FRANCE, JULY–SEPTEMBER, 1861: ARTHUR HUGH CLOUGH *to* BLANCHE CLOUGH (extracts)

Text. *The Correspondence of Arthur Hugh Clough*, ed. Frederick L. Mulhauser.

MONT DORE, Sunday, July 21, [1861]

This morning about 8 ½ going across the *place* to the café, whom should I see but Tennyson? he and she and Dakins and the 2 boys and a maid are all here—he and Dakins had been here two days. They go to the Pyrenees and I am to follow them. . . . They go tomorrow.[1] . . .

Today I rode with him and Dakins walking and put'em into the road up to Pic de Sancy which I hope they reached—'tis a beautiful day for it and then I came back and took Hallam, ride and tie, to la cascade de Quereult. They were at Royat last Sunday when I went there from Clermont for my walk. They haven't flourished very much, by Mrs. Tennyson's account, as yet—inns have been inconvenient etc., etc. However I hope today has pleased him. . . .

I write at ½ past 7. Tennyson and Dakin[s] have returned in safety after a long day in the hills. [ii. 591]

---

[2] He joined Tennyson in the New Forest the next day (*Journal*, p. 157).

[3] A letter (Maggs Bros. Catalogue 295, Sept.–Oct. 1912, Lot 3658) to H[erbert] Watkins, photographer, 3 June 1861, 'in answer to a request to take portrait: "I regret that it is not in my power to grant your request"' was endorsed by [?] Watkins: 'He did sit later on.' This perhaps refers to the problematical photograph attributed (by Andrew Wheatcroft, *The Tennyson Album*, pp. 66–7, and by Helmut Gernsheim) to Lewis Carroll, but alternatively (by W. D. Paden) to Cundall and Downes (see Richard Ormond, *Early Victorian Portraits*, i. 453; ii, Plate 901). Yet Herbert Watkins, the well-known photographer of the period, at 215 Regent Street and later 28 St. George Street, Hanover Square, was probably not postmistress at Lyndhurst.

[1] The trip is recounted in *Memoir*, i. 472–6 (negligible variants in *Materials*, ii. 329), and *Journal*, pp. 158–63. Henry Graham Dakyns (1838–1911), Rugby and then Trinity (BA 1860, MA 1864) was the first resident tutor for Hallam and Lionel, 1860–1; Housemaster and Assistant Master at Clifton College, 1862–89, where he came to know John Addington Symonds (see Venn, and especially the informative note in *The Letters of John Addington Symonds*, ed. Herbert M. Schueller and Robert L. Peters, i. 388). See also P. G. Scott, 'Tennyson and Clough', *Tennyson Research Bulletin*, i, No. 3 (Nov. 1869), 64–70. A photograph of Dakyns with Hallam and Lionel, 1861 [for 31 July 1862?—see *Journal*, p. 174], is in Wheatcroft's *Tennyson Album*, p. 76.

LUZ, Monday, August 12, [1861]

Tennyson was a little poorly again, when I saw them, and Lionel had also been ailing. They reached Luchon about 8 p m on Friday—and were pretty well settled for the night when I bade them good-bye at ½ past 9. I don't think he'd like Luchon, but I believe they would very likely stay a week there. It is a very Parisian place—people flaunt about and wear strange Parisian-mountain-costumes—'tours de têtes' of all kinds. I bought a tour de tête myself there, viz. a brown or grey wide-awake, having worn the old black one till then. [ii. 598]

LUCHON, Monday, August 26, [1861]

Yesterday at ½ p. 6 a.m. left Arreau and came up a long valley to the top of another Col and so down to Luchon before ½ p. 11. There I soon found out the Tennysons, who are very comfortably established in pleasant lodgings out of the town, in maize fields, not far from the river—the boys however not altogether well and Mrs. T[ennyso]n and they pretty much confined to the house and the roads just by. He and Dakyns have walked about a good deal, and the stay here has been in that respect successful enough, I suppose. On Thursday they will start and come Luz-wards, and be there on Saturday. I shall go back a cheval tomorrow, by the way I came, which is agreeable enough to be worth doing twice. . . .

The Tennysons won't return I think before the latter end of September— I dare say they'll be 3 weeks more Pyreneeing about; and will perhaps return by Brittany. [ii. 600–1]

[LUZ], Monday, September 2, [1861]

Plans still undetermined! Tennyson was here with Arthur Hallam 31 years ago and really finds great pleasure in the place. They staid here and at Cauterets—Oenone, he said, was written on the inspiration of the Pyrenees —which stood for Ida. Well, I shall go to Pau, I think, on Thursday, but if there's anything special write *also* to Cauterets, for perhaps it may be a convenience to them if I take Mrs. Tennyson and the boys there—and at worst they will get your letter for me. . . .

The weather continues very hot—and the Tennyson boys not very well. Today he and Dakyns go to Gavarnie and sleep, which I shan't. I suppose they'll stay at least a fortnight more in these parts, and he wants to go to Chartres, and Rennes (to see some Breton remains) on their way home. [ii. 602]

LUZ, Friday, September 6, [1861]

We went up the Pic [du Midi], which proved fully equal to all expectations though there was haze over the plain and over the remoter ends of the chain—left at 8 ½ got to the top at 1 ¼, having refreshed hastily at a sort of inn an hour from the top. Staid on top till 3 ¼ and got home at 6 ½. Tennyson rode up and walked back. It is a very complete view of the chain, as we saw it, only from the Maladetta to the Pic du Midi d'Ossau—our Pic du Midi lying detached or only tacked-to by the thin Col du Tourmalet some way to the North—Today we *all* go to Cauterets, having got money, which was the difficulty. I hope I may get a *line* from you there—They'll probably stay a week in lodgings. . . .

Tennyson and Dakyns have walked on to Cauterets and I and the family follow in a calèche at 2. [ii. 602][2]

CAUTERETS, September 7, [1861]

The Tennysons are disposed to stay here a week. I must depend on your letters, for which I have written to Pau, but it is possible I may stay on with them. I came with Mrs. T[ennyso]n and the nurse and children yesterday—he and Dakyns having walked on, as I told you. Today is heavy brouillard down to the feet or at any rate ancles of the hills—and little to be done—

It's pretty quick travelling from these places to Paris—1 day to Pau, 1 to Bordeaux, 1 to Paris,—so if you really get an escort and start I shan't be long. But I confess I am rather for the 2d October, as before, for various reasons.—It would be among other things a charity to these Tennysons; for Dakyns is to go away for a month most likely, perhaps this next week, and A. T. is but helpless by himself and thinks himself even more so than he is. I hope the boys will get better here, for it is *some weeks* now that they've been out of order—Lionel particularly.

6 ½ p m —I've been out with A. T. for a walk—to a sort of island between two waterfalls with pines on it, of which he retained a recollection from his visit of 31 years ago—and which, moreover, furnished a simile to the Princess[3] —The weather however continues to be *brouillard* not *sec*. He is very fond of this place evidently—and it is more in the mountains than any other and so far, superior—Today it is even cold, but what it is in hot weather, is another thing—for it is much in a hole. [ii. 603]

BARON DUFFERIN AND CLANDEBOYE[1]
to ALFRED TENNYSON

MS. Tennyson Research Centre.

CLANDEBOYE, BELFAST, September 24, 1861

My dear Mr. Tennyson

I wonder if you will think me very presumptuous for doing what at last,—after many months' hesitation,—I have determined to do?

You must know that here in my park in Ireland there rises a high hill, from the top of which I look down not only on an extensive tract of Irish land, but

---

[2] 'There was a fairly large party of us, the Tennysons, Clough, and myself, some walking, and some driving. Tennyson walked, and I being the young man of the company, was the great man's walking-stick. When we came to the valley—I knew it was a sacred place—I dropped behind to let him go through it alone. Clough told me afterwards I had done well. He had noticed it, and the Poet said—and it was quite enough—"Dakyns isn't a fool!"' It was that evening that Tennyson wrote 'All along the valley' (Henry Graham Dakyns, 'Tennyson, Clough, and the Classics', in *Tennyson and His Friends*, p. 205).

[3] *The Princess*, v. 336–7 (see *Memoir*, i. 475).

[1] See Appendix E.

24 September 1861

also on St. George's Channel, a long blue line of Scotch coast, and the mountains of the Isle of Man. On the summit of this hill I have built an old-world tower, which I have called after my mother, 'Helen's Tower'. In it I have placed on a golden tablet the enclosed verses, which my mother wrote to me on the day I came of age, and I have spared no pains in beautifying it with all imaginable devices. In fact, my tower is a little 'Palace of Art'. Beneath is a rough outline of its form and situation.

[*sketch*]

Now there is only one thing missing to make it a perfect little gem of architecture and decoration, and that is '*A Voice*'. It is now ten years since it was built, and all that time it has stood silent. Yet, if he chose, there is one person in the world able to endow it with this priceless gift, and by sending me some little short distich for it, to crown it for ever with a glory, it can not otherwise obtain, and render it a memorial of the personal friendship which its builder felt for the great Poet of our Age.[2]

I do not know whether I have rightly expressed myself when I say 'distich', but I mean something of the kind that was carved long ago on a tower in Scotland.

> Earth builds upon Earth,—Castles and Towers,
> Earth saith unto Earth,—'all shall be ours'
> Earth walks upon Earth—glistening in Gold
> Earth goeth unto Earth,—sooner than it wold.[3]

At one time I thought of carving on it these words,

> I stand four-square to every wind that blows,[4]

but on reflection I felt I had no right to deface one of the noblest lines that was ever written in any language.

Will then Mr. Tennyson reward my reverence with some little gem from the same mine from whence that was dug? and send it me with the additional grace of its having been expressly designed for 'Helen's Tower'![5]

Whether he does or not, his petitioner will always remain

His devoted admirer and servant
Dufferin

---

[2] The close and signature at this point in *Memoir*, i. 477–8, were added by Hallam Tennyson.
[3] See *The Middle English Poem Erthe upon Erthe Printed from Twenty-four Manuscripts*, ed. Hilda M. R. Murray (EETS, 1911).
[4] 'O fallen at length that tower of strength | which stood four-square to all the winds that blew', from 'Ode on . . . Wellington', ll. 38–9.
[5] The studied charm of the Baron, the potent glamour of the verses, the seductive susurrations of the poet's 'passion of the past' all fused with the spell of his renewed love of home into 'Helen's Tower' (Ricks, p. 1126), forthwith. See below, pp. 313, 317, and Appendix F.

30 *September* 1861
ROBERT BROWNING *to* GEORGE BARRETT (extract)
Text. Letters of the Brownings to George Barrett, ed. Paul Landis, with Ronald E. Freeman, p. 275.

[30 September 1861]

Strange to add, while on the train [from Paris to Boulogne], I was thinking of the meeting we had with Tennyson ten years ago on our first return to England—catching a glimpse of him at Paris, and looking out of the window, there *was* Tennyson again entering the carriage! I could not believe my eyes: at Boulogne, I went with Pen to the quay—the Folkestone boat was about to leave. I said, 'I will show you Tennyson': We went close—he was there with his wife and two children. I would not be recognized, but stood looking for a quarter of an hour till they left. He, too, therefore escaped the same danger.

To BARON DUFFERIN AND CLANDEBOYE
Text. Tennyson Research Centre (transcript by Dufferin).

[? early October 1861]

Dear Lord Dufferin

This my wife likes best: she is most likely right: but read the scratches.[1]

Yours ever
A. Tennyson

'To and thorough doomsday fire' has its merits for 'an old-world Tower' [I] do like this best. E. T.

To EMILY SELLWOOD TENNYSON
MS. Yale.

2 MITRE COURT BUILDINGS, TEMPLE [29 October 1861]

The Boat was late for in starting it got entangled with the cattle boat behind it and the wind was so high that it was some time before we righted ourselves. So I had five weary hours at Lymington and ¾ of an hour at Brockenhurst and did not reach this till near half past 10 o'clock and had to send a boy from the Mitre Tavern to get the key from the laundress. This morning I went to Dr. Jackson[1] who was exceedingly kind, and took no fee, and recommended me to take a chlorine bath and walked with me to the Establishment half a mile off and gave directions there. He says that I am in an anoemitous, i.e. bloodless and bileness, condition and must take nitric acid or something of that kind, and several of these baths, and a mustard

---

[1] See Appendix F.

[1] Dr John Jackson, husband of Mrs Cameron's sister Maria (see below, p. 284 n.). The ailments were some form of neural dermatitis (probably eczema) and a 'torpid liver' (see below, p. 283).

plaster for three nights ten minutes a time—he gave me a long consultation. Barrett I shall go to tomorrow. Love to boys.

Thine ever
A.

To EMILY SELLWOOD TENNYSON (fragment)

MS. Yale.

[2 MITRE COURT BUILDINGS] [2 November 1861][1]

I must contrive to see Sandford and give up the inauguration ode—I can't accomplish it satisfactorily to myself.[2]

Frank has just told me of his engagement. I wish the lady had more money.[3]

I saw Lear too this morning. His paintings of the Dead Sea and an Egyptian sunset are very fine.

To EMILY SELLWOOD TENNYSON

Text. Materials, ii. 339.

November 4, [1861]

I saw mother yesterday, wonderfully well and hearty, far better indeed than when I saw her last, but the shawl (for her) I quite forgot. I must take it next time. Frederick and Giulio[1] were at mother's. The latter goes in for his examination to-day, he is very confident. F. has got wonderful stories of his elbow being forked by the d——l, as he wrote, and strange things coming out on the paper in a strange hand.

November 5, [1861]

Dr. Jackson's kindness is in this hard worky-day world amazing.

---

[1] *Materials*, ii. 339.
[2] 'Ode Sung at the Opening of the International Exhibition' (Ricks, p. 1127), written at the request of Francis Richard Sandford (1824–93; created 1st Baron Sandford 1891), who, as organizing secretary of the exhibition, made his request in a letter (*Materials*, ii. 338–9), saying that William Sterndale Bennett (1816–75: *DNB*), the composer, would arrange the music for the 'unaccompanied chorale' for 'a mass of voices'. See *Memoir*, i. 480; *Journal*, pp. 163–4, 171; and below, pp. 292, 307.
[3] He married Kate Maria Morgan (d. 1928) on 20 January 1862 (*Landed Gentry*). See above, p. 273.

[1] Frederick Tennyson and his eldest son.

November 6, [1861]

I have seen Profesor Sterndale Bennett and given him my Ode.[2]

November 9, [1861]

Tell Hallam I have just come in from seeing the Lord Mayor's show, and very grand the gilt coach of the Mayor was.[3] The chrysanthemums at the Temple are wonderful, a splendour like that of midsummer.

To THE DUKE OF ARGYLL

Text. Tennyson Research Centre (transcript).

AT G. S. VENABLES, 2 MITRE COURT BUILDINGS, TEMPLE, November 10, 1861

My dear Duke

I had intended to write yesterday so that my answer might have reached Cliveden on the 10th,[1] and I scarcely know why I did not: perhaps because in these chambers, I had lighted on an old and not unclever novel 'Zohrab the hostage,'[2] partly perhaps because I had fallen into a muse about human vanities, and 'the glories of our blood and state' (do you know those grand old lines of Shirley's?).[3] This must have been suggested by the progress of His Majesty the Mayor down the Strand where I was entangled for half an hour in a roaring crowd and hardly escaped unbruised—however what with

---

[2] 'In November, 1861, Tennyson sent him [Bennett] a message to the effect that he had written something, that he felt nervous about it, and would like to talk it over with him. Thereupon Bennett went to the chambers in the Temple where Tennyson was stopping with a friend. He was fascinated by the quaint occupation in which he discovered the poet completely absorbed, viz. that of drying tobacco on the hobs of the grate; he thought, as a listener, that the reading of the poem was curiously monotonous; but when, before leaving, he ventured to confide his own anxiety and spoke of public criticism as sitting at his elbow when he tried to compose, the words of sympathy which followed, and Tennyson's assurance that he himself knew that feeling only too well, went to his heart.

'When Bennett made a study of the words, he thought them too elaborate to be set to a simple Chorale and to be sung entirely by unaccompanied voices, according to the original wish of the Commissioners. Indeed, with regard to one section of the Ode, he felt doubtful how it would yield to his musical treatment at all. When, in the course of composition, he found it manageable, then he was relieved, and would afterwards playfully say that he had set "The Exhibition Catalogue" to music; for the nineteen lines in question contained the poet's enumeration of the "marvels" gathered within "the long laborious miles of Palace". To illustrate such a poem Bennett desired an orchestral accompaniment. An orchestra was to be used by the other composers, so he asked and was granted permission to employ it' (J. R. Sterndale Bennett, *The Life of William Sterndale Bennett*, pp. 304–5). The 'other composers' invited were Meyerbeer to represent Germany, Auber for France, Verdi for Italy.

[3] The Lord Mayor's Day Procession; see the next letter.

[1] Cliveden, Taplow, Bucks., the 'beautiful villa' bought by the Duke of Sutherland in 1852 (Argyll, *Autobiography and Memoirs*, i. 419), and later bought by the even richer Astors, where, in a letter of 28 October (TRC), Argyll had written that he and his Duchess would arrive on 10 November.

[2] By James Justinian Morier (1832).

[3] 'The glories of our blood and state | Are shadows, not substantial things', James Shirley, *Contention of Ajax and Achilles*, iii. 1. See above, p. 113.

the novel and what with the musing-fit I let the post slip: but this morning let me say that I am grateful for the enquiring after myself and mine: of myself indeed I have no good account to render, being very far from well, living at a friend's rooms here in the Temple and dancing attendance on a doctor. France, I believe, overset me, and more especially the foul ways and unhappy diet of that charming Auvergne: no amount of 'granite craters, or chestnut-woods, or lava-streams'[4]—not the Puy de Dome which I climbed, not the Glen of Royat, where I lived, nor the plain of Clermont seen from the bridge there, nor the still more magnificent view of the dead volcanoes from the ascent to Montdore could make amends for these drawbacks: so we all fell sick by turns: my wife is better since our return and the boys are well enough though they suffered too at the time; but I remain with a torpid liver,[5] not having much pleasure in anything—yet I can still grieve with my friends' griefs and am therefore sorry for the occasion which exiles your good and kind Duchess though it be but for this December:[6] I am sure the Duchess will sympathize with my disgust at having my Freshwater (where I had pitched my tent, taken with its solitariness) so polluted and defiled with brick and mortar, as is threatened. They talk of laying out streets and crescents, and I oscillate between my desire of purchasing land at a ruinous price in order to keep my views open, and my wish to fly the place altogether. Is there no millionaire who will take pity on the wholesome hillside and buy it all up?

'Boadicea'—no, I cannot publish her yet—perhaps never, for who can read her except myself?[7] I have half consented to write a little ode on the opening of the International Exhibition. The commissioners prest me: I should never have volunteered; for I hate a subject given me, and still more if that subject be a public one.

Present my best remembrances to your Duchess and to the Duchess of Sutherland. I am half afraid to inquire after Her Grace's eyesight lest I should hear ill news.

Yours, my dear Duke, always
A. Tennyson

To EMILY SELLWOOD TENNYSON

Text. Materials, ii. 340; draft *Materials*, v. 28.

November 12, [1861]

I am grieved to hear about the pines falling. I had always expected that

---

[4] Argyll to Tennyson, 28 October (TRC): 'And have you seen *Auvergne*? I always wish to go there. It must be beautiful—granite Craters—and chestnut woods or Lava streams.' For the French trip, see above, pp. 276-8.

[5] See above, p. 280. 'Bagnères de Luchon and the glorious excursions round were new to my husband and are still almost unknown to me as I stayed at home to amuse my sick boys and to watch over them for in such young creatures perpetual diarrhoea even when not bad makes one very anxious' (Emily Tennyson to Mrs Gatty, 10 October 1861, Boston Public Library).

[6] The Duchess had been so ill the previous winter that they intended 'to pass December on the shores of the Mediterranean this year' (TRC).

[7] See above, p. 271.

great ivied one to go, but I am not the less sorry. I am glad Keeping believes in the water power of the Bagshot sand.[1]

November 13, [1861]

The Duchess of Sutherland has sent me an invitation which I shall not accept. The Duke of Argyll advises me strongly against buying land at building prices. He has been, and I told him Woolner's fisherman's story[2] which broke him down a little, and then he would hear my 'International Ode' which he said was very fine.[3]

November 14, [1861]

A very shrill-sounding storm here. I am afraid more of my pines are gone.

To MARIA (PATTLE) JACKSON[1]

MS. University of Texas.

November 14, 1861

My dear Mrs. Jackson

On reconsidering matters I wish to change my [mind] and to accept your

---

[1] Henry Keeping, 'our local geologist', was proprietor of a lodging house at Colwell Bay in Freshwater parish (White's *Hampshire*, p. 630) and curator of the Woodwardian (Geological) Museum, Cambridge (see below, p. 328; *Memoir*, i. 366; *Journal*, pp. 171, 178, 182; and Pollock, *Personal Remembrances*, ii. 116). The Bagshot Beds of Alum Bay, near Farringford, familiar to geologists, are 'a series of sands and clays of shallow-water origin, some being fresh water, some marine.... In the Isle of Wight the lower division is well exposed at Alum Bay...; here it consists of unfossiliferous sands... and clays.... The leaf-bearing clays of Alum Bay and Bournemouth are well known, and have yielded a large and interesting series of plant remains ... (*Encyclopaedia Britannica*, 11th edn., iii. 207). 'The shore at Alum Bay is a flat belt of minutely pulverised sand, of various colours, overhung by perpendicular, shelving, and projecting cliffs, several hundred feet high. These cliffs are deeply perforated and torn by chasms and caverns, and streaked by spouting streams and playful cascades. They display strata of white, red, and blue chalk; disposed horizontally, like stripes in an artificial fabric; and much of their under strata being gravelly or otherwise friable, and fully exposed to the erosion of sea or weather, they have extensively come down in tremendous *landslips*, and strewn their huge fragments on the beach' (White's *Hampshire*, p. 593).

[2] For the prose draft, the source of 'Enoch Arden', which Woolner gave Tennyson on 11 November, see Amy Woolner, *Thomas Woolner*, pp. 208-12. See also P. G. Scott, 'The Sources of "Enoch Arden" and "Aylmer's Field"', *Tennyson Research Bulletin*, No. 2 (Nov. 1968), 30-1.

[3] Both the Duke and Duchess wrote on 17 November praising the 'Ode', and of lines 29-31 the former said: 'The 3 lines you speak doubtfully of are beautiful—but in some respects "Hope" would be better than "dream"; which implies that the "goal" besides being "far away" is altogether visionary. Still, I do so heartily agree with the disbelief in *mere* Commerce being—ever —the Healer of the Nations, that I can't find fault with this vision being treated as a Dream.' Tennyson (preferring his gold to Argyll's brass) let 'dream' stand.

[1] Julia Margaret Cameron's sister. Her husband, Dr John Jackson (1804-87), a native of Lincolnshire (and fellow pupil of Tennyson at Louth), had been Professor of Medicine at Calcutta Medical College. He retired in 1855, practised for a while in London, and then 'set up his plate at Saxonbury, near Frant, in Sussex. The Jacksons chose that rural neighbourhood so that they could have the pleasure of being near their friend, the poet [Coventry Patmore]' (Brian Hill, *Julia Margaret Cameron*, pp. 158-9; see also Champneys, *Coventry Patmore*, especially ii. 189-218, and Colin Ford, *The Cameron Collection*, p. 121.

very kind offer of a bed at Hendon and of the carriage. I will be ready for it here at the time appointed tomorrow evening. Would you tell your coachman to drive to the top of King's-bench-walk, and stop at the archway to Mitre Court Buildings? I shall be at Mr. Lushington's rooms, 2 Mitre Court Buildings. He himself, I am sorry to say, goes home to-day. Believe me
Always yours
A. Tennyson

To EMILY SELLWOOD TENNYSON

Text. Materials, ii. 340.

November 15, [1861]

I am going to buy a vapour-bath which can be set a-going immediately and doesn't make the least mess. The seal of my letter is Julius Caesar, supposed to have been cut about the time of that mighty man, and given by Palgrave last night.

EMILY SELLWOOD TENNYSON
to MARGARET AND ALFRED GATTY (extract)

MS. Boston Public Library.

FARRINGFORD, November 15, 1861

My dear Mr. and Mrs. Gatty

I am grieved to tell you that my husband has been nearly three weeks in Town under a doctor taking chlorine baths etc.[1] He has not yet returned neither is it certain when he will be allowed to return and when he does the doctor says he will for some time require great care so I fear I cannot fix any time when he will be able to see guests. Otherwise I should gladly have fixed a time for welcoming your friend. . . .

---

[1] See above, p. 280. On 16 November Tennyson was also dreaming of '*mere* Commerce': 'Chapman junior came to me in the office to say that Tennyson was in their counting-house and wished to see me. I went across and found him in conference with the two partners [Edward and Frederic Chapman, the publishers], having told them that his engagement with Moxon's was not likely to be broken. He left presently, took my arm, and we walked down Piccadilly together. He said he could not yet muster courage to come to Burlington House after what had taken place [see above, p. 273 and n.], that he will most likely when next he comes to town. Told me of his visit to France, his disgust at the bad food and stinks of the hotels and boarding-houses. Asked where I had spent my holiday, and promised to give me a little information as to where the poems were written' (*The Journals of Walter White*, p. 153).

To ?

Text. *Materials*, ii. 340; draft *Materials*, v. 28.

November 19, 1861

We have lost poor Clough:[1] he died at Florence of a relapse of malaria-fever on Saturday. It gave me a great shock as it will do my wife.

To EMILY SELLWOOD TENNYSON

Text. *Materials*, ii. 340.

November 20, [1861]

I see that poor Godley[1] too has gone, so we fall one by one. Poor Browning I saw yesterday, very pale (since his wife's death) with a silver beard.[2] He is coming to see me to-night.

MS. Yale.

Thursday, November 21, 1861

I shall be back on Saturday by 3 o'clock boat—God willing.

A.

To WALTER WHITE

MS. Princeton.

[? late November 1861]

My dear Sir

The House used to be called Beech Hill. This was pulled down and Richard Arabin, son of the Serjeant, built another on the site.[1] I told you, I believe, that 2 Mitre Court Buildings, Temple, at the top of the stairs had seen or heard, as far as I recollected, as much of the composition of the Poem in question, as that old house. Since you ask me, I cannot but say that this kind of literary gossip is not interesting to me, when related of others, nor particularly grateful to me when printed about myself.

Yours very truly
A. Tennyson

---

[1] Clough died on 13 November, and was buried in the Protestant cemetery in Florence.

[1] John Robert Godley (1814–61: *DNB*), politician and founder of Canterbury, New Zealand. Woolner was commissioned to make a large statue of him in bronze (Amy Woolner, *Thomas Woolner*, p. 230).

[2] Elizabeth Barrett Browning died in Florence on 29 June, and, like Clough, was buried in the Protestant cemetery.

[1] See i. 152, and above, pp. 261, 285 n.

EMILY SELLWOOD TENNYSON *to* LEWIS FYTCHE

MS. Tennyson Research Centre.

FARRINGFORD, December 9, 1861

Dear Cousin

Will you accept through me Alfred's thanks for your kind note since he has, I grieve to say, been very unwell for some time past. The immediate cause of his present illness seemed to be a chill at Cauterets from which he has never recovered entirely though after nearly a month under a doctor in town he is better than he was.

We were three months in France, the boys and their tutor with us. First, we went to Auvergne and then the Pyrenees but the bad drainage of the houses and the stagnant air of mountain hollows did not suit us though in spite of them we have, I hope, all stored pleasant memories.

Do you know we have turned farmers, that is we were bold enough to undertake our own land this autumn having had the good fortune to find a very clever bailiff in a gardener we value much. We have a great deal to do at present to put things in order after a very slovenly tenant, but I hope when this is done we shall find it answer very well.[1]

The boys ride about on a white pony and if they can coax the men to pull them on cart horses they like it all the better.

Thank you for your kind invitation and thank Mrs. Ffytche too, and will you tell your sister[-in-law] Miss Skipworth that her kind note was answered though the answer never reached her for I am sorry to say it never left Farringford but lay about for months until sending it seemed too late.

Albert is so kind as to send us the Reports of his Province.[2] It is very pleasant to be remembered by him so far away. I trust he is happy in his new position. We return your Christmas and New Year's greetings by a Merry Christmas and a happy New Year to you both. I hope baby Mary thrives to your heart's content. With love from us all, believe me,

Ever yours
Emily Tennyson

We hope you like your new home.[3] We hear it is a very nice place. You know you have half promised to come and see us.

[1] Charles Heard, their gardener since 13 February 1860 (*Journal*, p. 143), became bailiff on 11 October 1861 (succeeding the 'slovenly' Merwood), and tenant on 16 November 1869: 'The Farm is not the source of out of doors interest to A. which I had hoped it might have been when we no longer had that of making new lawns and glades and otherwise altering the grounds at Farringford and the accounts proved too hard work for me with our many letters. But he did like to hear that only the Duke of Richmond's sheep could rival his and I can record as my experience that we did not lose by a home farm though we did not gain except by way of having everything of the best in Farm produce' (*Journal*, pp. 298–9). (Heard's first name, as far as we know, occurs only on a cheque for £30 on 10 February 1863 in John Wilson's Catalogue, April 1981.)

[2] Albert Fytche, Lewis's younger brother (see i. 165 n.). Promoted from Deputy Commissioner of the province of Bassein, he was at the time Commissioner of the Tenasserim and Metaban provinces, 'which formed the northern division of British Burma' (*Burma Past and Present*, i. 127, 164).

[3] Thorpe Hall, Lincs., to which he succeeded on his father's death in 1855 (White's *Lincolnshire*, pp. 228, 253). See i. 21 n., and below, p. 399.

To JAMES THOMAS KNOWLES[1]

MS. Tennyson Research Centre.

FARRINGFORD, December 10, 1861

Sir

I was from home and ill when your double gift arrived.[2] Accept my thanks now. Your task seems to me admirably done. My boys of 9 and 7 could think of little else but King Arthur and his Knights while reading your book and I doubt not it will be hailed with delight by numbers [of] men no less than boys. My wife sends a petition for a Layamon's Brut from you now,[3] that the old Legends of our Country may all be made familiar among us. I have the honour to be, Sir,

Your obedient servant
A. Tennyson

EMILY SELLWOOD TENNYSON *to* MARGARET GATTY

MS. Boston Public Library.

FARRINGFORD, December 17, 1861

My dear Mrs. Gatty

I do not know to what you allude but I cannot allow the poor Queen to have any blame cast on her without saying that she never in any way deserved any at all events as far as we are concerned. We have had nothing

---

[1] James Thomas Knowles (1831–1908; knighted, 1903: *DNB*), editor of the *Contemporary Review* (1870–7), and founding editor of the *Nineteenth Century and After* (1877–1908), was also the organizer of the Metaphysical Society (see below, p. 517 and n.) and the architect of Tennyson's summer residence, Aldworth. For an excellent account of Knowles and his dual career, see Priscilla Metcalf, *James Knowles, Victorian Editor and Architect* (Clarendon Press, Oxford, 1980). Knowles began ingratiating himself with Tennyson in a letter of 13 August 1861 asking permission to dedicate to the poet a modernized Malory, 'as a book for boys', *The Story of King Arthur and His Knights of the Round Table* (1862).

[2] Two copies of *The Story of King Arthur*: one regular issue, with (Knowles regretted) 'childish prints', and one specially bound without them for Tennyson. He wrote to Tennyson on 7 December 1861 that he 'aimed at compiling a book which grown readers might consult as a fair abridgement of the Legends—while children yet might read it for the mild stories' and expressed himself 'anxious to know your own judgment on it—if you think it at all worth your criticism' (Metcalf, *Knowles*, p. 164). Tennyson's response led in 1867 to a friendship of a quarter of a century. Emily Tennyson wrote on 28 October that she amused the boys in Tennyson's absence by reading them 'Mr. Knowles' King Arthur Stories in the evening' (*Journal*, p. 164)—from the proof-sheets that Knowles had sent on 13 August.

[3] And she wrote to Margaret Gatty about Tennyson's absence on this date (Boston Public Library): 'I am sorry that I cannot give you as good an account of Alfred as I could wish. He is certainly better but by no means well in spite of his nearly four weeks doctoring in Town. He does not like to have his few lines called an Ode. An ode must be a free song and not written because asked for and as asked for and besides the fact of his having written the lines was not to be mentioned. There is as yet nothing finished or final as the lines and music must be one if they are to be at all. . . .'

but kindness from her. She never asked for An Ode and certainly we cannot think she could have done it in a wrong way if she had.[1]

I was only speaking in Irish fashion when I spoke of the nest of traitors.[2] I doubt not there are multitudes of loyal hearts in Ireland but the disloyal brawl so loud that their modest voices are scarcely heard above the din and I had just been made very wrathful by Smith O'Brien[3] and by Aubrey de Vere. It is so wicked in those who call themselves Christian gentlemen to keep up old grudges when they know very well that for years England has done all she can for those who are too little inclined to do anything for themselves. Let the gentlemen look to themselves and ask if they at least have not loved England too well. It is just as rational for the Saxon to cry out against the Norman in England as for the Celt to cry out against the Norman in Ireland Scotland or Wales. We are a misled [?] people by events over which we at least have had no countroul [sic]. We should fare poorly apart so let us e'er make the best of it together. I too am partly a Celt I believe and so you will believe from my indignations.

I write this to beg you to unsay anything unkind about the Queen that may have been said. At all times it would be hateful to us to hear most especially now.

Thank you for all your good wishes. We heartily send you the like.

Very truly yours
Emily Tennyson

To PRINCESS ALICE[1] (draft)

MS. Tennyson Research Centre.

[*c.* 23 December 1861]

Hearing of your Royal Highness's strong desire that I should write something on the memory of the Prince Consort, I answer that at present I am unwell and the subject which I have tried is too exciting to me, but that in my own way and at my own time I trust I may be enabled to do honour to

---

[1] See above, p. 281. In a subsequent letter, of 21 December, Emily Tennyson wrote to Mrs Gatty: 'We are in our turn most innocent of ever suspecting that it was you. You spoke of the Papers or a paper saying "that the Ode was pretty freely handed about" and we thought from your letter that they or it had also said something about the Queen. It was the Committee who asked and they meant no harm only they do not understand that it is not easy to write "about 30 lines" on a given subject. Ally could not well refuse to write on so National a subject it was urged. I am very sorry that you should for a moment have thought I was accusing you of anything (I can't make out what) seeing I never meant to accuse anyone of anything only the Irish for unpatriotic talk.... [P.S.] (The lines were given under promises of strict secrecy Ally not having made up his mind whether they were finally to be given.)' (Boston Public Library).

[2] 'But do you know I love not the Irish. I think them a nest of traitors with some honourable exceptions' (letter to Mrs Gatty, 10 December, *The Letters of Emily Tennyson*, p. 162).

[3] William Smith O'Brien (1803–64: *DNB*), Irish nationalist.

[1] Princess Alice (1843–78), Queen Victoria's second daughter, who married Prince Louis (1837–92), Grand Duke of Hesse in July 1862, was with her mother at her father's death in Windsor Castle. The Queen arrived at Osborne, IW, on 19 December (*Journal*, p. 165).

the memory of as gracious, noble and gentle a being as God has sent among us to be a messenger of good to his fellow-creatures. We all honour him—we all love him—more and more since we lost him: there is scarce an instance in History of a person so pure and blameless—is not that some comfort to Her Majesty and Her children, some little comfort in the midst of so great a sorrow?[2]

But I wished to say to your R. H. that when I was some three or four years older than yourself I suffered what seemed to me to shatter all my life so that I desired to die rather than to live. And the record of my grief I put into a book;[3] and ⟨of this book⟩ I continually receive letters from those who suffer telling me how great a solace this book has been to them. Possibly if by and by Your R.H. would ⟨look into this book⟩ consider this record it might give you some comfort. I do not know. I only know that I write in pure sympathy with your affliction and that of your R. mother—

1) and if I sin against precedent in so doing
2) and if I have seemed in any way to have violated the sanctity of your sorrow
3) and if I ⟨trouble you⟩ have troubled you in vain forgive me as your Father would have forgiven me.

A. Tennyson

To SIR CHARLES BEAUMONT PHIPPS

Text. Dear and Honoured Lady, ed. Hope Dyson and Charles Tennyson, pp. 61–2.

FARRINGFORD, December 24, 1861

My dear Sir

The Queen has my full devotion, the Princess Alice my entire sympathy, and with all sincerity I mourn their unspeakable loss.

From your own kind words—if indeed I understand them rightly—I conclude that the thing which I had intended before they reached me—will happily be that most pleasing to Her Majesty and the Princess.[1] I had thought of consecrating an Idyll to the memory of him whom we have lost. I have tried the subject more than once, but I find it too exciting for me to accomplish anything worth preserving at present, for I have been for some

---

[2] Charles Beaumont Phipps (see i. 342 n.) had written to Tennyson on 21 December 1861 (TRC): 'Princess Alice has expressed a strong desire that you should write something upon the late sad, sad event. My beloved master admired your Idylls so much, and dwelt so often upon the beauty of the feelings and thoughts embodied in them, that the Princess thinks that you could, better than anybody else living, idealize this sacred subject . . .'. Charles Tennyson and Hope Dyson believed that the letter drafted here was never sent (*Dear and Honoured Lady*, p. 61), but the letter to Princess Alice, 13 January 1862, draws substantially on this draft.

[3] *In Memoriam*. Tennyson was twenty-four when Arthur Henry Hallam died; Princess Alice was eighteen at Prince Albert's death.

[1] 'A dedication to the Prince's memory of a new edition of the *Idylls of the King* of 1859, which was already with the printers' (*Dear and Honoured Lady*, p. 61).

months unwell and under medical care, and to say the truth poetry is as inexorable as death itself.

At any rate I do trust that somehow at some time I may be enabled to speak of Him as He Himself would have wished to be spoken of—surely as gracious, noble, and gentle a being as God ever sent among us to be a messenger of good to his creatures. I am

Yours very truly
A. Tennyson

To THE DUCHESS OF ARGYLL

MS. Tennyson Research Centre.

FARRINGFORD, January 4, 1862

My dear Duchess

Your letter moved us deeply: I am going to send you in a day or two what I have written on the Prince,[1] and to write again. You make no mention of the Duke or your own health.

Ever yours
A. Tennyson

To PRINCESS ALICE

MS. Tennyson Research Centre (transcript).

[13 January 1862]

Madam

Having heard some time ago from Sir C. B. Phipps that your Royal Highness had expressed a strong desire that I should in some way 'idealize' our lamented Prince, and being at that time very unwell, I was unwilling to attempt the subject, because I feared that I might scarce be able to do it justice; nor did I well see how I should idealize a life which was in itself an ideal.

At last it seemed to me that I could do no better than dedicate to His memory a book which He Himself had told me was valued by him. I am the more emboldened to send these lines to your Royal Highness, because having asked the opinion of a lady who knew and truly loved and honoured Him, she

---

[1] 'Dedication' to the *Idylls of the King* (Ricks, p. 1467), sent on 7 January to the Duchess for her opinion and that of her mother, the Duchess Dowager of Sutherland, Mistress of the Robes to the Queen (*Journal*, p. 166). Next day the Duke and Duchess of Argyll both wrote admiringly of it, though the Duke suggested that 'worthy the sacred name of Gentleman' (which followed l. 40 in place of present ll. 41–2) conclude the poem. His wife was inclined to drop 'Before a thousand peering littlenesses' (l. 25), and they preferred 'clave' to 'cleaved' in l. 10. (These readings exist in Marian Bradley's 'Diaries'.) Tennyson dropped l. 41 for 'Beyond all titles and a household name, | Hereafter, through all times, Albert the Good' (ll. 41–2); he retained l. 25, despite the Duchess's reiterated demurrer (12 January, TRC); and he adopted 'clave'. On January 8, also, the Argylls sent the 'Dedication' on to her mother. By 12 January Tennyson had sent revisions; and in a postscript to the Duchess's letter of that date, Argyll assured him, 'You may well be satisfied—we think' (TRC). See the next letter.

gave me to understand by her reply that they were true and worthy of Him:[1] whether they be so or not, I hardly know, but if they do not appear to be so to Your Royal Highness, forgive me as your Father would have forgiven me.[2]

Though these lines conclude with an address to our beloved Queen[3] I feel that I cannot do better than leave the occasion of presenting them to the discretion of your Royal Highness. Believe me, as altogether sympathizing with your sorrow,

Your Royal Highness' faithful and obedient servant
A. Tennyson

To WILLIAM STERNDALE BENNETT

Text. J. R. Sterndale Bennett, *The Life of William Sterndale Bennett*, pp. 305–6.

FARRINGFORD, FRESHWATER, ISLE OF WIGHT, January 13, 1862

My dear Sir

I wish you would come down and see me, you know you promised to come, pray do.

As to the inauguration poem[1]—when our good Prince left us, I thought it was absolutely necessary to notice his loss and therefore inserted four lines. Afterwards I heard that the Queen did not wish any allusion made to Her loss—so I would not trouble you with the lines. Now I hear (none of my instigating) that Lord Granville showed them to H. M. and she wished them to be included.[2]

Pray come if you can, you start by 11 o'clock train from Waterloo and take your ticket for Lymington—then in half-an-hour the boat crosses.

Yours always
A. Tennyson

---

[1] See the preceding letter. On 11 January the Duchess of Sutherland had written to Tennyson commending his 'beautiful verses': 'I am sure they are this, worthy of yourself, and worthy of the great and tragic subject.... It was a truth that the character was ideal.... How beautiful your termination is! how beautiful the beginning! how beautiful all! (*Materials*, ii. 344). On 13 January Tennyson sent this letter to Princess Alice with the 'Dedication' (*Journal*, p. 166). Marian Bradley, who arrived just as the Tennysons were about to seal the letter, records: 'he gave it me to read. It is a beautiful mixture of a kind of heroic grandeur and simple dignity and tender sympathy in thought and expression—he laughed and said "I hardly know myself in writing anything so unexceptionally correct ..." ('Diaries').

[2] Echoing Matthew 6:14?

[3] Lines 43–53 (beginning 'Break not, O woman's heart, but still endure').

[1] See above, p. 281 n.

[2] See *Journal*, p. 166. Granville George Leveson-Gower (1815–91: *DNB*), 2nd Earl Granville, leader of the Liberal Party in the House of Lords since 1855, and holder of many offices, was President of the Council, 1855–8, 1859–66.

To MARIA (PATTLE) JACKSON

MS. Berg Collection.

FARRINGFORD, I. W., January 14, 1862

My dear Mrs. Jackson

How very kind you are! Count upon me as evermore and especially grateful to yourself and Dr. Jackson; but at present I do not think, except I deteriorate very rapidly, of leaving Farringford.[1]

My best remembrances to the Doctor and your two daughters.

Ever yours
A. Tennyson

PRINCESS ALICE to ALFRED TENNYSON[1]

Text. Memoir, i. 480.

[15 January 1862]

If words could express *thanks* and *real* appreciation of lines so beautiful, so truly worthy of the great pure spirit which inspired the author, Princess Alice would attempt to do it;—but these failing, she begs Mr. Tennyson to believe how much she admires them, and that this just tribute to the memory of her beloved father touched her deeply. Mr. Tennyson could not have chosen a more beautiful or true testimonial to the memory of him who was so really good and noble, than the dedication of the 'Idylls of the King' which he so valued and admired. Princess Alice transmitted the lines to the Queen, who desired her to tell Mr. Tennyson, with her sincerest thanks, how much moved she was on reading them, and that they had soothed her aching, bleeding heart. She knows also how *he* would have admired them.[2]

To PRINCESS ALICE

Text. Yale (transcript).

[c. 16 January 1862]

That any words of mine should be any comfort to those sorrowing as you must sorrow for one so beloved and so worthy of love, is indeed a source of great thankfulness to me, though I know well, it is God alone Who can give real and lasting comfort to such mourners as those are who have lost all you have lost in him. Therefore I will not trouble you with more words, though I might say much of how even the stranger warms to the memory of so good

---

[1] See above, p. 284.

[1] Marian Bradley ('Diaries') noted of this letter: 'Curiously enough it was directed to *Mr.* A. Tennyson—it had no beginning.'

[2] See *Journal*, p. 166. Phipps also wrote on the 15th (TRC): 'Only this moment have I had the privilege of reading your beautiful, too beautiful, because too touching dedication. And I must write, whilst my heart is overflowing, to thank you ... for the beautiful garb in which you have clothed the truth. ...'

and brave a Christian, feeling himself no longer strange, but akin, however distantly and full of yearning for the perfect brotherhood of like deeds, in the same spirit. Believe me, dear Madam,

Yours gratefully
A. Tennyson

To THE DUCHESS OF ARGYLL

MS. Tennyson Research Centre.

FARRINGFORD, January 23, 1862

My dear Duchess

Of course Lord Dufferin is at full liberty to quote the Dedication, as much of it or as little as he may think fit.[1] I have been about to write to him for I know not how long, and ask him how he had decided as to the Helen's-tower inscription. I hope he has not made a medley of the three separate forms which I sent him but has adopted the third.[2]

I am altogether, I assure you, out of love with my Dedication—but I suppose as the Queen has approved of it it must stand as it is: at any rate I am glad that I have soothed her sorrow—

I added a line in the copy which I sent to Her—this—at the conclusion—

May all love
His love, unseen but felt, o'ershadow Thee,
The love of etc.

I am much obliged to the Duke for the interest he took in the poem, and I have adopted his omissions, though, I must confess, that in my inner heart I stick to my old readings—at times.[3]

As far as I can see I shall remain here for several weeks.

I ought to mention perhaps that I missed out the word 'bounteous' in the lines I sent to the Queen and inserted 'kindly' simply because I thought the

---

[1] When Parliament assembled on 6 February, Lord Dufferin, eulogizing the Prince Consort, quoted the concluding lines of the 'Dedication' to the *Idylls* in his remarks moving the Royal Address, which the Lord Chancellor, Lord Westbury, had delivered on behalf of the Queen. See *Journal*, p. 167.

[2] See above, p. 280 and Appendix F.

[3] The Duchess (12 January) had raised a doubt about 'those narrow jealousies' of the Prince 'now silenced' (ll. 15–16); and the Duke (14 January) had been moved to send 'a word—not of literary, but of *Political* criticism'—that 'Those narrow jealousies | Are silenced' should be omitted. Granting that there were such jealousies once, which caused a public outcry and Parliamentary explanation, he believed that they 'had ceased to exist', and feared 'lest the nation may now almost regard as an undeserved imputation on itself a reference which may lead to the supposition in after times that "Albert the Good" had been pursued by "narrow jealousies" so long as he lived' (TRC). On January 18 Argyll was gratified by the alteration to 'all narrow jealousies' ('Because this makes the allusion more general—less specific'); (and perhaps also suspecting a Latinate *double entendre*), he accordingly, advised against the insertion between lines 15 and 16 of 'The sudden fume and petulance of an hour', because 'it is specific and has direct reference to that shameful moment—of which I spoke in my last. Let it be forgotten, if possible' (TRC). Tennyson acceded.

line sounded better—some unhappy critic, possibly, would say that I struck out the word because the Prince had been called *near*.[4] Pereat![5]

Is there any hope* of your crossing the water to us?

Ever yours, my dear Duchess,
A. Tennyson

*Small hope, I fear, as our boats are going to be given up on the 1st of February—so at least I hear.

To THE DUKE OF ARGYLL

Text. Tennyson Research Centre (transcript).

FARRINGFORD, 25 January 1862

My dear Duke

As you have taken so much interest in this Dedication I send you the proof—two of them. I don't know where Lord Dufferin is. Would you have the kindness to forward one of those to him—it is slightly different from the M.S. which you have: but it is the copy which I sent to Princess Alice with only the alteration of 'all' for 'thou'—

My best remembrances to Lord Ashburton. I had once a very pleasant week at his house.

Yours ever
A.

There is a counter-rumour about the boats today and I cannot arrive at the truth.[1]

To SIR CHARLES BEAUMONT PHIPPS

MS. Tennyson Research Centre.

FARRINGFORD, I. W., February 11, 1862

My dear Sir

As there is a new Edition of the Idylls of the King published with the Dedication,[1] I have thought that a copy might perhaps not be unacceptable to Her Majesty.

---

[4] Line 17: 'How modest, kindly, all-accomplished, wise.'
[5] 'Fac pereat vitreo miles ab hoste tuus' Ovid, *Ars Amatoria*, ii. 208 ('In chess, let your knight be taken by a pawn').

[1] See above.

[1] Incorrectly dated by T. J. Wise (*Bibliography*, i. 156) July 1862 (listed in 'New Books' in the *Athenaeum*, 1 February, p. 152, and 'Dedication' printed there on 8 February, p. 191). Phipps replied from Osborne on 18 February: 'The Queen commands me to return to you her best thanks for the new Edition of your "Idylls", with the beautiful dedication.' He also asked Tennyson to direct the publisher to send the Queen several copies of the 'Dedication' printed separately (*Materials*, ii. 344).

If you think so too, will you have the kindness to present this, with every expression of my loyal devotion and believe me,

Yours truly
A. Tennyson

Hon. Sir C. B. Phipps

To WILLIAM HEPWORTH THOMPSON
MS. Trinity College.

FARRINGFORD, February 19, 1862

My dear Thompson

Is there to be a statue of the Prince Consort at Cambridge?[1] If so, don't let the doing of it fall into the hands of Marochetti,[2] if you can help it. He has neither the gifts nor the industry of Foley[3] or Woolner. I really believe Woolner to be a first rate artist: not known indeed as he ought to be and as he would be, if he got this statue to execute. Wherefore I pray you, if your influence be not promised to another use it for him. He has asked me to write to you on this matter but I should have written unasked, for I have not only a great liking for the man, but an admiration of his works.[4]

Yours ever, in haste, my dear Thompson,
A. Tennyson

My wife's best remembrances.

---

[1] So announced in the *Athenaeum* on 22 February, p. 265. Committees had been appointed 'both in Cambridge and in London for the purpose of carrying out the plan'. Thirteen months later, 'notwithstanding an earnest speech by the Master of Trinity in favour of bronze', marble was specified (*Athenaeum*, 14 March 1863, p. 366).

[2] Carlo Marochetti (1805–67: *DNB*), sculptor, ARA 1861, RA 1866, Italian by birth, French by naturalization, moved to England in 1848, and soon found favour with the court and the nobility, though throughout his career in England his work was controversial. In 1857 he had exhibited a bust of the Prince Consort at the Royal Academy.

[3] John Henry Foley (1818–74: *DNB*), ARA 1849, RA 1858, who was born in Dublin and came to London in 1834, became a prolific and imaginative sculptor. In the Albert Memorial the allegorical group *Asia* and the figure of the Prince Consort are his.

[4] On 6 June 1863 the *Athenaeum* reported: 'Mr. Foley has been commissioned to execute the Cambridge Memorial to the Prince Consort,—a marble statue' (p. 751). Woolner got the commission for the statue for the New Museum in Oxford, and was busy with it as early as December 1862 (*Athenaeum*, 6 December 1862, p. 738), though he grumbled in a letter to Emily Tennyson that it was not to be in marble. Executed in Caen stone, the statue was first exhibited in 1864 (Amy Woolner, *Thomas Woolner*, pp. 215, 238).

To THE DUKE OF ARGYLL

Text. Tennyson Research Centre (transcript).

February [25], 1862[1]

My dear Duke

Many thanks for your very interesting letter.[2] Very touching is what you tell me about the Queen. I am of course exceedingly gratified that anything which I have written should have the power to console one whom we all love—strange that a book which when it first appeared was pronounced by more than one clergyman as Pantheistic if not as (I think) one wiseacre commented on it, Atheistic, should have such a power—but after all it is very little that words can do. Time—time—

I have written out for the Princess Royal a morsel from Guinevere.[3] I do so hate rewriting my own things that my pen refuses to trace the Dedication. Her critique on the Idylls is enthusiastic and mingled up with the affection of Her Father as I would wish it to be. As to joining these with the Morte d'Arthur, there are two objections—one that I could scarcely light upon a finer close than that ghostlike passing away of the King and the other that the Morte is older in style and suggestive of a less modern social state—I don't think they would fit together. As it is, I have thought about it for two years and arranged all the intervening Idylls but I dare not set to work for fear of a failure, and time lost.[4] I am now about my Fisherman which is heroic too in its way,.[5]

Yours ever
A. Tennyson

If you call me Mr. Tennyson any longer, I think I must Your Grace you till the end of the chapter.[6]

---

[1] *Journal*, 25 February (p. 168): 'A. writes to the Princess and copies for her "The Passing of Arthur"' [for 'a morsel from "Guinevere"'], in lieu of the 'Dedication' suggested by Argyll.

[2] 'No words can express the love—admiration which the Queen's whole bearing and character inspires one with—when one sees Her under Her great Sorrow—Her gentleness—Her splendid transparency and truthfulness—and Her simplicity. But I want to tell you that she is finding much on which she loves to dwell in your "In Memoriam". She specially desired me to tell you this last night: and she gave me the copy to show "how well it was read"—and how many were the passages she had marked' (Argyll to Tennyson, 23 February, TRC).

[3] Argyll enclosed a letter to Tennyson 'in the Princess's handwriting and at her request' (printed in *Dear and Honoured Lady*, p. 66): 'The first time I heard them [*Idylls*] was last year, when I found both the Queen and Prince quite in raptures about them. The first bit I ever heard was the end of "Guinevere". the last ten pages, the Prince read them to me, and I shall never forget the impression it made upon me hearing those grand and simple words in his voice! He did so admire them, and I cannot separate the idea of King Arthur from the image of him whom I most revered on Earth!'

[4] The Princess Royal (said Argyll) was 'very anxious' that Tennyson should 'make the "Morte d'Arthur" the ending of the Idylls, adding only something to connect it with the ending of Guinevere. Is there any objection to this? None that I recollect. In the end of Guinevere the King is spoken as departing to the Great Battle—and in the "Morte", we should have the worthy close.'

[5] 'Enoch Arden'.

[6] Argyll began his next letter, 27 February: 'My dear — Tennyson', dropping 'Mr.', which he always felt 'abominably incongruous' (TRC).

To THE DUKE OF ARGYLL

Text. Memoir, i. 483–4.

Monday, March 3, 1862

My dear Duke

I have been out on a visit (a very unusual proceeding on my part), and on returning found your letter, which a little dismayed me, for, as you in the prior one had bound me by no promise of secrecy, I, in talking of Her Majesty and her sorrow, did say to two friends, whom I bound by such a promise, that she had found comfort in reading 'In Memoriam,' and had made the private markings therein.

I don't suppose much harm would result even if these broke their promise, for that is all that could be reported; still I am vexed, because if the Queen heard of the report she might fancy that her private comments were public prey. As to those very interesting ones communicated in your last, whether you had bound me to secrecy or not, I should not have dreamt of repeating them: they are far too sacred; and possibly your caution of silence only refers to these.[1]

I hope so. I think it *must* be so. I wrote off the very day I returned to both my friends, urging them to abide by their promise, for in these days of half-unconscious social treachery and multitudinous babble I felt that I ought to make assurance doubly sure. You can scarce tell how annoyed I have been. I hope the Princess Royal got my note and inclosure, but she has not acknowledged it. My letters, I believe, have ere this been opened and stopt at our little Yarmouth P. O. but not in the present Postmaster's time.

My best remembrances to the Duchess.

Yours ever
A. Tennyson

To THE DUKE OF ARGYLL

Text. Tennyson Research Centre (transcript).

FARRINGFORD, March 5, 1862

My dear Duke

Thanks; you have set me at ease, though indeed I thought it must have been, as you now tell me it is:[1] both my friends have written declaring that they have abided by their promise, so that there is not harm done anywhere.

---

[1] As Argyll reported on 27 February (TRC; printed in *Dear and Honoured Lady*, pp. 67–8): 'Indeed some of them seemed so sacred that except to you I should never speak of them. . . . I need not say that I wish to tell these things to you and Mrs. Tennyson *only*. She wished me to see them that I might tell you, but you alone.'

[1] Argyll to Tennyson, 4 March: 'It was only the individual passages in "In Mem:" that I wished you to keep to yourself. That the Queen likes and appreciates "In Memoriam" I have mentioned to several (*worthy*) persons—though even this I would not cast before some S——ne' (TRC).

I need not say that we shall be charmed to see you and the Duchess on the 13th. Shall I send a fly over for you to Yarmouth to Lambert's Hotel?[2]

Ever yours
A. Tennyson

To ?

MS. University of Toronto.

March 18, 1862

My dear Sir

The Artist whom you write about was answered and thanked the next morning after the arrival of his book of Illustrations. I am buried most mornings under a monticule of letters; I and my wife do our best to get them answered. We do our best but cannot get through them all.

Yours very truly
A. Tennyson

To MRS EDWARD EARNEST VILLIERS

MS. Corpus Christi College, Cambridge.

FARRINGFORD, March 20, 1862

My dear Mrs. Villiers

I do not know if you know Woolner's works and I do not know if Lord Clarendon does.[1] If you know them there is I am sure no need of a word from me. If you do not may I say, will you go to his studio, 29 Welbeck Street, for then I am certain that one of the foremost if not in some ways the foremost sculptor of our day will not be without an opportunity of employing his genius on this great National Monument about which we are all on many accounts so anxious.[2]

We hear of you and your daughters at rare intervals, but we hope that you are all well. Believe me,

Yours always
A. Tennyson

To ?

MS. Huntington Library.

FARRINGFORD, March 22, 1862

Sir

It was my intention to return the cutting from the Cambridge Paper when I had the honour of answering your last letter and in looking through the packets of letters lately received for yours I find the letter without the cutting.

---

[2] See *Journal*, p. 169.

[1] See i. 283 n.

[2] The Albert Memorial, designed by G. Gilbert Scott (1811–78: *DNB*), knighted, 1872, when the monument was unveiled.

I have no doubt that I did send it as I intended. I am sorry that it should have missed you. I am, Sir,

Your obedient servant
A. Tennyson

To LOUIS TENNYSON D'EYNCOURT

MS. New York University Libraries.

FARRINGFORD, March 24, 1862

My dear Louis

Many thanks from myself and my wife to you and yours for your kind invitation; but really I scarcely ever go out, and am grown an old fellow, crystallized in my ways, and sticking all the year round to my own hearthstone except when I make one great move to escape the summer or rather Autumn cockneyism of this place: I do not know whether I shall be at the opening of the International Exhibition,[1] but if I am I am bound by more than one promise to spend some days with the Duchess of Sutherland[2]—but I rather think, if I go, that I shall just run up to town and back again; except indeed I be much better in health than I feel myself at present; most likely I shall content myself with reading all about it in the Times.

It is quite true that Princess Alice wrote to me, and the Princess Royal some weeks after;[3] both very kindly and flatteringly, but as I never mentioned the circumstance to anybody I am at a loss to know how it got into the papers—nay, when the Daily Telegraph reported it I took the trouble to write to the Times to beg that the Princess' letter might not be mentioned—and the Editor apparently was courteous enough to attend to my request[4]—not that the Princess cared about it, but that I do.

Thanks again: and with best remembrances to your wife and love to my Godchild. Believe me

Your affectionate cousin
A. Tennyson

I shall be very happy to see you here if ever you pass my way. I ought to have answered before, but there are such myriads of letters to attend to.

---

[1] On 1 May.
[2] See below, p. 308.
[3] See above, pp. 293, 297 n.
[4] 'We are inexpressibly vexed to see a paragraph in the *Daily Telegraph* speaking of the letter from Princess Alice and cannot think who has been so ill judged as to put it in. A. writes to Mr. Dasent [George Webbe Dasent, Assistant Editor of *The Times* 1845–70] to prevent it from slipping into the *Times*' (Journal, 7 February). Despite an exhaustive search of the *Daily Telegraph* for 7 February and adjacent dates, this paragraph has eluded us.

To THE DUKE OF ARGYLL

Text. *Memoir*, i. 484.

March 26, 1862

My dear Duke

I am a shy beast and like to keep in my burrow.[1] Two questions, what sort of salutation to make on entering Her private room? and whether to retreat backward? or sidle out as I may?[2]

I am sorry to hear you were the worse for your journey.[3] I myself am raven-hoarse[4] with cold.

Yours ever
A. Tennyson

WILLIAM STERNDALE BENNETT *to* EMILY TENNYSON (extract)

MS. Tennyson Research Centre.

29 March 1862

I should like to ask Mr. Tennyson if he could give me another line in the last piece. I will endeavour to describe what I want and sketch you my little plan.

         Chorale
1st six lines—
      The same repeated with Instruments
A movement in minor devoted to the lines on the Prince Consort.
'The world compelling plan was thine' (this line recited by itself, voices in unison)

---

[1] Tennyson had received a letter from Argyll (24 March, TRC) with these 'Royal words': 'The Queen wishes the Duke of Argyll to tell Mr. Tennyson to call at Osborne during her next stay there: and to send up his name to Col Biddulph or Lady Augusta Bruce so that the Queen might have an opportunity of seeing Him which She wishes to do very much.' Argyll advised him how to address the Queen and reassured him: '*Don't be afraid of saying anything to Her*—I mean in any direction to which Her own conversation naturally leads you. . . . in these interviews one sees Her in Her own room without any sort of form or ceremony (unless standing can be said to be so)—and what She likes is to be able to *speak* Her sorrow and Her love to those of whom She thinks that they can feel for or with her.'
Thomas Myddleton Biddulph (1809–78; knighted, 1863: *DNB*), was Master of the Queen's household and an equerry. For Lady Augusta Bruce, a lady-in-waiting, see below, p. 303 n.

[2] Argyll's reply, 27 March (*Dear and Honoured Lady*, pp. 68–9), said that upon entering no other salutation than 'a respectful bow' was expected and that the Queen would retire when she wished to conclude the interview, so that the poet would have 'no bother' about how to retreat. He further urged Tennyson to do what seemed natural: 'Don't let yourself be a "shy beast"— and "come out of your burrow—Talk to Her as you would to a poor Woman in affliction—that is what she likes best.'

[3] From the Isle of Wight to London after the visit on 13–15 March (see *Journal*, p. 169): 'I was very ill for a couple of days after we left you. But I am nearly all right again' (Argyll to Tennyson, 24 March, TRC).

[4] *Macbeth*, I. v. 39.

>   Quicker movement
> And lo! etc.
>   Return of the Chorale
>   O ye the wise who think, the wise who reign
>   From growing commerce loose her latest chain
>   (più arioso)
>   And let the fair white-wing'd peacemaker fly
>   To happy havens under all the sky
>   And mix the seasons and the golden hours
>   . . . .
>   Till each man find, etc. etc.

I hope Mr. Tennyson does not mind my request, and if he does not like it, I can manage as it stands.

To MESSRS SUCKLING AND CO. [?][1]

MS. Rowland Collins.

FARRINGFORD, April 5, 1862

Gentlemen

The proof prints arrived quite safely and extremely fine specimens of the art they seem to me. Accept my best thanks for your kind gifts and believe me, Gentlemen,

>   Your very obedient servant
>   A. Tennyson

To THE DUCHESS OF ARGYLL

MS. University of Virginia.

FARRINGFORD, I. W., April 11, 1862

My dear Duchess[1]

Almost ever since the Duke of Argyll left me, I have been laid up with a prostrating cold and a furious cough; and as soon as I began to recover I wrote to Col. Biddulph saying that I would call at Osborne on whatever day and at whatever hour The Queen might appoint: and this morning along with Your Grace's letter comes one from the Colonel, fixing 3 o'clock on Monday next. I am grieved that Her Majesty's second message seems to imply that I ought to have written before.

I am rather afraid of my interview with Her Majesty—if anything be

---

[1] A mere guess—but the prints were perhaps photographs: see *Tennyson in Lincoln*, i, Nos. 5695-7 (or 5980-5?).

[1] In reply to a letter [10 April] (TRC) with a message from the Duchess of Sutherland conveying the Queen's desire that Tennyson come to Osborne. The Queen's direction was for Tennyson to call for Lady Augusta Bruce upon arrival; the Duchess of Argyll's direction was not to delay—'the sooner you go the better'. Tennyson went on 14 April.

expected from me—feeling altogether powerless to give any real consolation to such sorrow as Hers.

Many thanks for your kind letter.

Ever yours
A. Tennyson

To THE DUCHESS OF ARGYLL

MS. Tennyson Research Centre.

FARRINGFORD, April 16, 1862

My dear Duchess

I have had my interview.[1] I requested Lady Augusta Bruce,[2] whom I took to at first sight, to report to me whether (for I was conscious of having spoken with much emotion) I might not have touched upon something which jarred Her Majesty's feelings. I think I cannot do better than send you Lady Augusta's letter[3] which arrived this morning. I see as you know very dimly, yet I saw enough to assure me that Mayall's photographs—those at least which he sent me—do Her grievous injustice. Great sweetness of expression she has, and a kind of stately innocence in her bearing, such as I do not remember to have seen in any other woman.

I do not remember much of what she said; what I do I will tell you when we meet. Afterwards came in Princess Alice and the little Beatrice,[4] the first true-natured and true-manner'd; the little one remarkable for her Pre[-]Raphaelite hair. Tell the Duke that I found 'Your Majesty' easy enough but 'Mam,' which I dislike, met occasionally in a neutral ground with 'Madam' where 'each was either.'

Yours ever
A. Tennyson

I should like the letter back again, please. I had a very kind note from the Duchess of Sutherland this morning. I do so hope the eyes are better since the writing is so much clearer.[5]

---

[1] The Queen noted in her Diary on 14 April: 'I went down to see Tennyson who is a very peculiar looking, tall, dark, with a fine head, long black flowing hair and a beard—oddly dressed, but there is no affectation about him. I told him how much I admired his glorious lines to my precious Albert and how much comfort I found in his "In Memoriam". He was full of unbounded appreciation of beloved Albert. When he spoke of my own loss, of that of the Nation, his eyes quite filled with tears' (*Dear and Honoured Lady*, p. 69). See also *Journal*, p. 170, and Edmund Venables's account in his letter to *The Times*, 20 October 1892, p. 4.

[2] Lady Augusta Bruce (1822–76), daughter of the 7th Earl of Elgin (of the Elgin Marbles) and sister of Lady Charlotte Locker. On 23 December 1863 she married Arthur Penrhyn Stanley (1815–81: *DNB*), who became Dean of Westminster on 9 January 1864.

[3] See *Dear and Honoured Lady*, p. 72.

[4] Princess Beatrice, youngest of the nine children, was barely five years old.

[5] *Dear and Honoured Lady*, p. 72. She had gone to Paris 'to see the greatest of oculists Mon. Grafe—and he has been I think cheering to her about the good eye. The other is an undoubted case of cataract' (Duchess of Argyll to Tennyson, 18 April, TRC).

To LADY AUGUSTA BRUCE

Text. Memoir, i. 485–6.

FARRINGFORD, April 17, 1862

My dear Lady Augusta

Accept my very best thanks for your kind letter.[1] I perceive that it was written on the evening of that day when I called at Osborne, but I received it only yesterday; then I thought that I would wait till the prints arrived, but as they have not I will not delay my answer.

I was conscious of having spoken with considerable emotion to the Queen, but I have a very imperfect recollection of what I did say. Nor indeed—which perhaps you may think less excusable—do I very well recollect what Her Majesty said to me: but I loved the voice that spoke, for being blind I am much led the the voice, and blind as I am and as I told Her I was, I yet could dimly perceive so great an expression of sweetness in Her countenance as made me wroth with those imperfect cartes de visites of H. M. which Mayall once sent me. Will you say, as you best know how to say it, how deeply grateful I am to Her Majesty for the prints of Herself and of Him which She proposes to send me, and how much I shall value Her Gift? I was charmed with Princess Alice. She seemed to me what Goethe calls *eine Natur*.[2] Did he not say that was the highest compliment that could be paid to a woman? and the little Beatrice with her long tresses was very captivating. Thank you also for what you tell me of your own family. True, as you write, I often receive similar communications, but the value of these depends on the value of those from whom they come. I often scarce believe that I have done anything, especially when I meet with too flowery compliments: but when I know that I am spoken to sincerely, as by your Ladyship, I lift my head a little, and rejoice that I am not altogether useless. Believe me,

Yours very truly
A. Tennyson

To THE DUKE OF ARGYLL

Text. Memoir, i. 484.

April 21, 1862

My dear Duke

As you were kind enough to say that you would mention Woolner's name to the Queen, I send a photograph of a work of his, which Gladstone, who saw it the other day, pronounced the first [finest?] thing he had seen after the

---

[1] Printed in *Materials*, ii. 345–7 (long extract in *Dear and Honoured Lady*, p. 72): 'You will receive prints of the Queen and Prince which are forwarded by Her Majesty's command.'
[2] Untraced.

antique. The children are Thomas Fairbairn's, deaf and dumb, not pretty certainly, but infinitely pathetic.[1]

I do not say, show this to her Majesty, you know best, but admit that myself and Gladstone are justified in our admiration.[2]

Yours ever
A. Tennyson

To THE EDITOR OF THE TIMES[1]

Text. The Times, 28 April 1862, p. 8.

April 25, [1862]

Sir

There are two errors in my Ode as it appears in your columns of the 24th.[2]

In the second line 'invention' should be read, not 'intentions'; and, further on [l. 22], 'Art divine,' not 'Part divine.' Be kind enough to insert this letter.

A. Tennyson

To EMILY SELLWOOD TENNYSON

MS. Tennyson Research Centre.

29 WELBECK STREET,[1] Saturday, April 26, 1862

Dearest

I arrived all right and I hope thou art better today. Here it is quite uncomfortably hot. I have seen Paddison[2] who heard my petition that he would let himself be associated with Estcourt in the management of my affairs—said it was an unusual thing, though not unprecedented, and that he would be proud to do anything for me, and has undertaken to write the letter for me to Estcourt. I have left all the papers with him.

I really hope thou art much better today. It seems so very warm here. Spedding is coming to hear me read the Fisherman.[3] Love to all × × × × × ×.

A. T.

---

[1] Thomas Fairbairn (1823–91), 2nd Baronet (see above, p. 187 n.). He was a patron of the arts not only in Manchester, but also as Royal Commissioner for the Great Exhibition of 1851, and the International Exhibition of 1862 (Boase). The life-size statue of the Fairbairn children, 'Brother and Sister; or Deaf and Dumb', was exhibited at the International Exhibition. The photograph, by William Jeffrey (see below, p. 533 n.), is reproduced in Amy Woolner, *Thomas Woolner*, p. 95 (see also p. 216).

[2] Argyll replied on 23 April: 'I shall probably be able to show the Photograph you sent, to the Queen, when I am at Balmoral. It is, as you say, very pathetic but rather ugly. Why could He not idealise a little more the clumsy lines of the Boy! But I suppose it is meant as a Portrait' (TRC).

[1] John Thaddeus Delane (1817–79), editor of *The Times*, 1847–77.

[2] 'Ode Sung at the Opening of the International Exhibition' was published with Bennett's music on 12 April. *The Times* had printed it erroneously from the sheet music. See below, p. 306.

[1] *Chez* Woolner.

[2] Richard Paddison and Son [Howard], solicitors, 37 Essex Street, Strand, WC (*P.O. London Directory*), of a Lincolnshire background (see below, p. 355).

[3] 'Enoch Arden'.

To EMILY SELLWOOD TENNYSON

Text. *Materials*, ii. 51.

April 27, [1862]

I have writen to the Duchess of Sutherland saying I will go on Friday.[1]

To EMILY SELLWOOD TENNYSON

MS. Tennyson Research Centre.

Tuesday [29 April 1862]

Dearest

I am sorry that in thy invalid state thou hast asked so large a party—moreover doesn't it seem by asking the Mildmays[1] when I am not at home, as if *I* wouldn't see them?

Paddison on second thoughts refuses to act along with Estcourt. I saw Chapman who will look over all titles *gratis* and strongly advises me to take both the Woodford and Squire[2] business out of Estcourt's hands, as the business of one is involved with that of the other—he says that Squire cannot sell at all, his son being a minor, except by a direct petition to Chancery.

It is quite impossible for me to call at F. Lushington's. The utmost I can do will be to get to Hampstead.[3] It is fine here but colder than yesterday. Take drives.

Thine × × × × × ×
A. T.

Horrid pen! Gladstone is coming to dine here on Wednesday. On the morning of that day I go to hear the rehearsal of my ode at the Exhibition. I saw Sterndale Bennett yesterday. Didst thou see my letter in The Times?[4] 'Part divine' came funnily enough from the thieves having stolen the ode from a piece of music and taking the p. for piano as part of the text.

Weld dines here today and Fairbairn comes in the evening.

To EMILY SELLWOOD TENNYSON

Text. *Materials*, ii. 351.

April 30, [1862]

I have no tickets for the Exhibition. I refused them altogether. I saw mother yesterday very well and hearty though almost bent double.

---

[1] To Cliveden (see below, p. 308).

[1] The Ven. Carey Anthony St. John-Mildmay (1800–78), Archdeacon of Essex, Rector Sinecure of Shorwell, Isle of Wight, and of Chelmsford, Essex; his wife was Caroline Waldegrave (d. 1878), daughter of 1st Baron Radstock (Foster, *Peerage*, White's *Hampshire*, p. 632).

[2] Woodford was a common name in the vicinity. This one could be John Woodford, farmer, of Easton, Freshwater Parish, or John Lord Woodford, farmer, of Brixton. For Squire, see above, p. 000 n.

[3] To see his mother.   [4] See above, p. 305.

To RICHARD MONCKTON MILNES

MS. Trinity College.

29, WELBECK STREET, [*c*. 30 April 1862]

My dear Milnes

Many thanks: but I don't dine out. I refused Fairbairn on Sunday. Moreover I do not think I shall be in town on Tuesday.

Yours ever
A. Tennyson

To EMILY SELLWOOD TENNYSON

MS. Tennyson Research Centre.

Friday [for Thursday], [1 May 1862]

Dearest

I sent the cheque yesterday which must be signed at the back. I heard the rehearsal[1] yesterday but did not very much approve of it—however the people seemed to like it. Gladstone dined with us last night—a very agreeable and intellectual and most gentlemanly man. I read the Fisherman with which he seemed greatly struck.

I wrote yesterday to Estcourt taking the Woodford and Squire business out of his hands. I hope he will take it kindly. I am grieved thy cough continues.

Thine × × ×
A. T.

I am not at the opening. On Friday evening I go to Cliveden to stop till Monday.

To EMILY SELLWOOD TENNYSON

Text. Materials, ii. 352.

May 2, [1862]

I was not at the opening of the Exhibition but I hear from Simeon and others that the ode went very well![1] One paper reported 'the poet laureate being there in green baize,' probably meant for bays.

---

[1] Of the 'Ode Sung at the Opening of the International Exhibition'.

[1] In appreciation of the 'Ode' the Commissioners of the International Exhibition later gave Tennyson a silver urn and salver inscribed: 'Her Majesty's Commissioners of the International Exhibition of 1862 present this urn to Alfred Tennyson in grateful remembrance for his gift of pure and noble song, 1st May, 1862' (*Athenaeum*, 25 April 1863, p. 557, and 2 May, p. 587). See *Journal*, p. 183.

To EMILY SELLWOOD TENNYSON

MS. Tennyson Research Centre.

[3 May 1862]

Dearest

I came with the Duchess and Gladstone and Charles Howard here last night.[1] We took [the] train to Slough and drove afterwards 7 or 8 miles. They are all very pleasant, and the Duchess specially kind—but the ways of living don't exactly chime with my ways. The place is beautifully fresh and green with a long view of the reaches of the Thames, and vast foreground of lawn starred with all flowers. This is a bad morning for thy cold. I have not a letter from thee this morning but am told to expect one at two o'clock. There is a brother of the Duke of Newcastle, a great invalid, but who is very gentle and amiable.[2] I shall be back on Wednesday I should think. Love to all.

Thine ever × × ×
A. T.

To EMILY SELLWOOD TENNYSON

MS. Tennyson Research Centre.

Sunday, May 4, 1862

Dearest

Yesterday was so bitter that I am afraid thy cold and cough would not be bettered by it. The Duchess drove me out through Lord Grenville's place, remarkable for strange trees and rhododendrons about a sort of wilderness.[1] Lord Dufferin is here this morning as pleasant as ever, and Lady Constance Grosvenor and Lady Taunton, the Duchess's sister,[2] also Gladstone. I read the Fisherman yesterday to the Duchess and the Duke of Newcastle's brother. They were very much pleased with it. I still think of returning on Wednesday —but am not as yet quite sure. Today is warmer here but misty.

Thine × × × × ×
A. T.

I got thine yesterday.

---

[1] To Cliveden, Taplow, Bucks. Charles Wentworth George Howard (1814–79), fifth son of the 6th Earl of Carlisle, brother of the Duchess of Sutherland, and uncle of the Duchess of Argyll, was MP for East Cumberland, 1840–79. The Tennysons had met him in October 1857 at Inverary Castle, when visiting the Argylls (*Journal*, p. 102).

[2] Probably Robert Renebald Pelham-Clinton (1820–67), youngest brother of the 5th Duke of Newcastle, MP for North Notts. Palgrave was also present (*Memoir*, ii. 490).

[1] Dropmore House—built in 1792 by William Wyndham Grenville (1759–1834: *DNB*), 1st Baron Grenville, and occupied by his widow until her death in 1864. (*Materials*, ii. 352, reads 'Lord Granville'.)

[2] Lady Constance Grosvenor (Constance Gertrude Leveson-Gower), daughter of the Sutherlands and sister of the Duchess of Argyll, was the wife of Hugh Lupus Grosvenor, liberal MP for Chester, 1847–69, who succeeded as 3rd Marquis of Westminster in 1870, and was created 1st Duke of Westminster in 1871. Lady Taunton (Mary Matilda Georgiana Howard), youngest daughter of the 6th Earl of Carlisle, sister of the Duchess of Sutherland, and aunt of the Duchess of Argyll, was the second wife of Henry Labouchere, 1st Baron Taunton (1798–1869), who held office in various Whig ministries.

To EMILY SELLWOOD TENNYSON

Text. Materials, ii. 352.

CLIVEDEN, May 5, [1862]

I leave here today at 4 o'clock.[1] We went yesterday to the Chapel Royal and into the Queen's seat and looking down I saw the wreaths of immortelles on the floor.

To THE DUCHESS DOWAGER OF SUTHERLAND

MS. Sotheby's Catalogue, 6 Nov. 1984, Lot 1193.

29 WELBECK STREET, Tuesday, [6 May 1862]

My dear Duchess—I have half a mind to address you as our good Queen does, in the superlative—I want, before I return to my island tomorrow morning, to thank you for your great kindness to me, and letting me have my own way at Cliveden—and to assure you, better than I could do at a railway terminus, how fully and without any, the least, drawback, I believe in you.[1] Believe in me also when I subscribe myself

Affectionately yours
A. Tennyson

To THE DUKE OF ARGYLL

Text. Memoir, i. 493.

FARRINGFORD, May 28, 1862[1]

My dear Duke

I have delayed so long granting the 'absolution,' that like enough by this time you may have forgotten that you desired it.

However it is granted.

---

[1] For London and thence, 7 May, home (*Journal*, p. 171). In London, on 6 May, wrote Walter White: 'Tennyson and Woolner called on me while I was at lunch and partook of ale and bread-and-butter. We told a few stories and had some talk. The poet has written a poem embodying a description of a tropical island, and wishes to see a good view of an Isle to verify his description. The publication of his ode in "The Times" was surreptitious, some one at the Exhibition having copied it from the music, and seeing *p.* for *piano* before 'art', wrote 'part divine', which had to be corrected by the author in a letter to the paper. He complains of the view of the sea being built out from him at Farringford, and says he will depart for a time at the end of this month to get out of the way of Cockneys' (*Journals of Walter White*, p. 154).

[1] The euphoria of the letter *may* be partly attributable to something reported (presumably from Tennyson himself) in 1868 by Walter White: 'Through the Duchess of Sutherland the Queen offered him a baronetcy. He declined. "Can the Queen do nothing for you?" "Yes, if she could shake my two boys by the hand it would help to keep them loyal"' (*The Journals of Walter White*, p. 164).

[1] Dated 1863 in *Memoir*, though clearly a reply to Argyll's letter from Balmoral of 22 May 1862, confessing his sin of having without permission repeated 'In the Valley of Cauteretz' to the Queen ('who was delighted with it'), and asking for 'absolution' (*Materials*, ii. 353). See also below, p. 327.

Only do not, after absolution, begin sinning the sin again with a greater gusto.²

Of course I am glad to have given a moment's satisfaction to our poor Queen, glad too that you give a somewhat better account of her.

I had a very pleasant two days' visit to Cliveden. I sat in your favourite seat which looks over the reach of the river, and regretted that you were not at my side. Gladstone was at C. with me. I had met him before, but had never seen him so nearly. Very pleasant, and very interesting he was, even when he discoursed on Homer, where most people think him a little hobbyhorsical: let him be. His hobby-horse is of the intellect and with a grace.

Yours ever
A. Tennyson

To LADY AUGUSTA BRUCE[1]

MS. University of Virginia.

FARRINGFORD, June 3, 1862

Dear Lady Augusta

You will think me crazy.² I wrote in such haste yesterday to save the post that I quite forgot the main purpose of my letter—at least as far as I can recollect. I fear that though my thanks to the Queen were of course implied in what I wrote I did not expressly request you to present them to Her Majesty. Will you have the kindness to do so—thanks most dutiful and heartfelt for the volumes whether they be a gift or a loan; for on referring to your letter, which merely states that your Ladyship was commanded by the Queen to 'forward' the books that I might read and admire what H. M. had heard and admired, I am horror-stricken lest I may have assumed as a gift what may have been meant as a loan; still I feel that you are so kind and considerate you would have said something about the returning the books had they been to be returned. May I ask for a single line to tell me how this is, and to assure me of your forgiveness of my haste, my stupidity and my troubling you.³

Yours very truly
A. Tennyson

---

² Echoing 'Guinevere', ll. 541–2?

[1] An earlier version of this letter, with the same date but many variants, is in TRC.

[2] On 31 May 1862 Tennyson had received a 'letter from Lady Augusta Bruce saying that she was commanded by the Queen to send . . . [him] two volumes of poems by Zeller and another in which HM has found comfort. They are marked by herself. A precious gift' (*Journal*, p. 172). The 'poems' were those of Caecilie Zeller (1800–76), *Aus den Papieren einer Verborgenen* (2 vols., 1847–8) and perhaps *Lieder einer Verborgenen* (1858). See *Allgemeine Deutsche Biographie* (1900), vol. 45.

[3] She replied on 6 June (*Materials*, ii. 354–5), grieved at her vagueness and assuring Tennyson that his 'first letter was felt to contain a most warm acknowledgement', and that 'Her Majesty was soothed' by his words. The books were a gift: 'The Queen was shocked at my want of distinctness, and bids me say that the vols. not being obtainable here H. M. sent to Germany for them and had them specially bound for you, and I am again to add that "In Memoriam" is still

HENRY TAYLOR to THEODOSIA ALICE TAYLOR

Text. *Autobiography of Henry Taylor*, i. 196.

June 15, 1862

We dined at the Tennysons' yesterday, and in the evening he read us his new poem[1] ['Enoch Arden']–a story (said to be true) which Woolner had read in the diary of a lady who was his fellow-passenger in a voyage to Australia. It is a very powerful poem, of the genus 'Michael.' The fault of the subject, if not of the treatment, was illustrated by its effect upon one of the audience, Mrs. J[ackson]. After an hour and a half, and when the end was near, she went into hysterics.[2] The poem is too purely painful, the pain not being the rich and pleasing pain which poetry ought to produce. It is not so coloured and glorified by imaginative power as to exalt the reader above his terrestrial distress. It is, however, one more variety of the manifestation of Tennyson's genius, and it may be well that he should have so written upon such a theme: and I think that, if he were to regard the poem as I regard it, he might do much to enrich and soften the effect. Mrs. Tennyson must be much stronger than she was when you were here. She was looking less fragile than I recollect to have seen her look before, and very pretty and tender and interesting.

To J. C. RATCLIFF

Text. *Materials*, ii. 355–6.

FARRINGFORD, June 18, 1862

Sir
   I beg to offer you my best thanks for your kind gift and the kind manner of it.[1] The case is magnificent and I shall have it put into a glass box to preserve it. I sincerely hope that your efforts to raise the character, and improve the taste of your manufactures may succeed to your heart's content, and bring comfort and prosperity to your ancient Town after the long days of poverty and suffering. I have the honour to be, Sir,

Your very obedient servant
A. Tennyson

---

the only book besides religious books, to which H.M. turns for comfort. Some of the earlier poems, the sadder ones especially which the Queen knew less, H.M. has found solace in reading.'

[1] 'Enoch Arden'.   [2] See *Journal*, p. 172.

[1] 'A magnificent Blotting book from the manufacturers at Coventry with The Lady Godiva woven in silk' (*Journal*, p. 172).

To ANDREW JAMES SYMINGTON[1]

Text. Materials, ii. 356.

June 23, 1862

Dear Sir

I beg to thank you for your kind gift of *Faroe and Iceland*, and for the kind expressions toward myself which accompany it. Northern subjects have as you say a great interest for me. Believe me, dear Sir,

Truly yours
A. Tennyson

To ?

MS. Yale.

FARRINGFORD, June 27, 1862

Sir

You are most welcome to perform my Inauguration Ode at your benefit concert on Monday night. I have the honour to be, Sir,

Your very obedient servant
A. Tennyson

To THOMAS WOOLNER [?] (fragment)

MS. John Rylands Library.

[? c. 8 July 1862][1]

I hope Coventry has *not* gone to Brighton.

A. Tennyson

My wife has written to him at the B. M.

COVENTRY PATMORE to OCTAVIAN BLEWITT[1]

Text. Basil Champneys, *Memoirs and Correspondence of Coventry Patmore*, i. 185–6.

ELM COTTAGE, NORTH ROAD, HAMPSTEAD, July 9, 1862

Sir

I have just heard that an application has been made for me to the Royal

---

[1] Andrew James Symington (1825–?), Scottish poet, author of miscellaneous books—on Carlyle (whom he knew), Tom Moore, and Wordsworth, and on *The Reasonableness of Faith* and *The Beautiful in Nature, Art, and Life*, as well as *Pen and Pencil Sketches of Faroe and Iceland* (Allibone). See *Tennyson in Lincoln*, i, Nos. 2148–50, and also 3381–2, inscribed (in 1880) to Emily Tennyson 'with kind regards from her 'late brother and sister's friend'—Charles Tennyson Turner (on whom he wrote a short essay).

[1] The date is a (convenient) guess. Emily Patmore died of tuberculosis on 5 July, and a rupture of the poets' friendship was the inadvertent result. See the next two letters; Champneys, *Memoirs and Correspondence of Coventry Patmore*, i. 181–91; and the curt notes to Patmore, 11 June and 28 July 1881 in vol. iii.

[1] Octavian Blewitt (1810–84: *DNB*), Secretary of the Royal Literary Fund.

Literary Fund by Mr. and Mrs. Tennyson. Though done with the kindest intentions, this has been with an entire misapprehension of my circumstances and wishes, and I beg you to favour me by at once stopping any proceedings which may have been commenced in consequence of that application, and by further communicating the substance of this letter to any persons who may have been acquainted with that application. I am, Sir,

Your obedient servant
Coventry Patmore

COVENTRY PATMORE
to EMILY SELLWOOD TENNYSON

Text. Basil Champneys, *Memoirs and Correspondence of Coventry Patmore*, i. 185.

[c. 10 July 1862]

Dear Mrs. Tennyson

I could not feel that the course which your kind anxiety for me induced you to take was one of which I was justified by my circumstances in reaping the fruits. I therefore wrote to Mr. Blewitt to say so, and to stop further proceedings before the business of the monthly meeting commenced. Whatever pressure may be upon me at present is I trust nothing more than I shall now be able to recover from, with the discharge of every obligation, in a moderate period of industry and economy.

With sincere thanks for your kind wishes and endeavours and expressions of sympathy, I am, dear Mrs. Tennyson,

Yours most truly
Coventry Patmore

To BARON DUFFERIN AND CLANDEBOYE

MS. Indiana University.

Tuesday, August 12, 1862

Dear Lord Dufferin

You mistook me. I never said that the two lines were to be inserted without some alteration of the following ones. I send you the inscription thus altered.

I have yielded to Lady Dufferin, but I still infinitely prefer it, without the two lines[1] and as you had it *first* printed.

I send you an autographed 'Idylls' and am

Yours always
A. Tennyson

---

[1] Lines 5–6: 'Love is in and out of time, | I am mortal stone and lime.'

F. T. PALGRAVE: TOUR IN DERBYSHIRE AND YORKSHIRE WITH A. T.

Text. *Materials*, ii. 366–70.

August–September, 1862

It was Tennyson, I think, who always framed the main scheme and locality of our journeys, although the details were left to the pleasure of the moment. This time the country chosen I believe was new to him. . . .

We started from London together: and Leicester must have been the first resting-place. That city did not offer much of the alluring, and we went a few miles off for a ramble in the fine wild grounds of Broadgate, Bradgate. . . .

Derbyshire however was our 'objective point': and through the capital, (which the railway porters shouted forth as *Dirby* . . .), we moved on quickly to Matlock (18 Aug.). After traversing that romantic little valley with its wall of spire-like rocks, we climbed the cliff and walked I forget whither over the rough pleateau above; until, (but by rail, it must have been), Rowsley was reached. Thence we wandered through the desolate rooms and passages of Haddon Hall. Omitting Hardwicke with regret, from Edensor we walked to Chatsworth; the gilded window frames of the great house blazing burnished in the afternoon sun redeemed its somewhat monotonous elevation. By the leave of that dear and deeply-honoured friend whose cruel death eighteen years after,[1] has cast a gloom over Edensor churchyard, we went through the whole house and its meany treasures of art: declining however the great fountain, which we had seen to more advantage when rising among the trees like a silver geyser as we were nearing Chatsworth.

The great conservatory,—Archetype, as is well known, of the Exhibition Building of 1851, and so of all its weary successors in vanity, I think was Tennyson's greatest enjoyment. Filled, not like those in public Botanical Gardens, but at the personal pleasure of that noble-hearted and accomplished man who owned it, this acre of the Tropics enshrined under glass was planted so closely with palm and fern, that Tennyson found in it some faint but attractive image of those gorgeous southern forests which he drew with masterly hand in 'Enoch Arden.'

After Buxton, where we met Tennyson's Trinity comrade of the old days, often amusingly paradoxical and always bright and genial, R. M. Milnes,[2] Castleton and the Peak were the remaining Derbyshire wonders. The vast cavern impressed Tennyson much, where, after passing through a crowd of women who carried on under its shelter their rope-twisting manufacture, we

---

[1] Lord Frederick Charles Cavendish (1836–82: *DNB*), murdered in Phoenix Park, Dublin, was the second son of William Cavendish (1808–91: *DNB*), 7th Duke of Devonshire, the 'noble-hearted and accomplished' owner of Chatsworth.

[2] 'I left Alfred Tennyson in our rooms at the hotel; he is strictly *incognito*, and known by everybody except T[hornhill ?], who asked him if he was a Southerner, assuming that he was an American (Milnes to his sister, 21 August). 'Mr. Palgrave has been here for a third time with Mr. Tennyson, who did not like to be known, as people stared at him so much, which was no wonder, as he wore an immense broad hat and a beard' (Milnes to his elder daughter, 27 August, in T. Wemyss Reid, *Life of Lord Houghton*, ii. 81–2).

were alone in the gloomy recesses, resounding with strange rushings of subterraneous streams, and ferried over a Lethe, smooth as a surface of black marble, in a kind of Charon's boat. The guide had asked before entering on what scale of expence we should like to see the great Hall illuminated. The most complete had been chosen some time before by the Emperor of Russia. 'We will be as grand as Emperors for once,' Tennyson had decreed: and certainly the display, especially of the costly crimson fire, was of a brief magnificence.

From Castleton was a lovely road through the Vale of Hope, contrasted in its sweet greenery with the chilling gray, like that of the Riviera about Mentone, which marks the rocks of the Peak country. This led to Hathersage, where in the churchyard Tennyson examined, (with an interest, I suppose, wholly unconscious of the future), the reputed grave of Robin Hood. Thence by Sheffield and Leeds (a city at that time almost sinfully dirty), to Ripon; where, after the sight of fountains, with the gleaming lakelets of the park, and monastic ruins unequalled in Britain for mass and variety of style, began a delightful trip of near 200 miles altogether in dog-carts, hired from place to place. . . . Visiting by the way the richly picturesque valley of Hackfall, we reached Leyburn on its striking Terrace. Here, two castles were accessible: Middleham, built or inhabited successively by the three Richards, a noble confusion of tower over tower, and huge fallen fragments like rocks, overgrown with foliage, which greatly impressed Tennyson; and Bolton. . . . The road now lay through Wensleydale. . . . At Aysgarth we diverged to the beautiful little waterfalls: turning south at Hawes round the lofty mass of the central moors, and so on till we reached the railway at Clapham.

Somewhere on this journey, I think, it was that, seeing a single farm in a wild lonely region, all by itself, with its own landscape, 'almost its own sky,' here, I said, a man might well choose to take up his abode, the world forgetting etc.[3] Intensely as Tennyson always loved the country, with his ever-wakeful hatred of exaggeration, he corrected my false asceticism; 'if, as in the fairy stories, my choice were no London, or, all London,—all London I should have to decide for.' . . .

At Bolton, our next and last halting-place, the hospitality of the owner's family, and the company of Judge Lushington,[4] bright and active, . . . brought us into the presence of the world. The Priory ruins, rendered sacred to the lovers of poetry by Wordsworth's almost too ideal treatment;[5] the fine Gate House; that valley of unique beauty; the famous leaping place where Wharfe boils and struggles through a rock-strangled chasm, (tempting us much, but terrifying more), the wild climb to Barden Tower; all this we saw. . . .

There, or at Skipton, on Sept. 9, we parted.

---

[3] Pope, 'Eloisa to Abelard', l. 208.
[4] The Duke of Devonshire, with Stephen Lushington (see above, p. 177 n.) reformer and jurist; as counsel to Lady Byron, he was one of those who 'tried to prove her loving lord was mad' (*Don Juan*, i. 210). See below, p. 316.   [5] 'The White Doe of Rylstone'.

To WILLIAM EWART GLADSTONE

MS. British Library.

CASTLE INN, CASTLETON, DERBYSHIRE, August 26 [or 20?], 1862

My dear Mr. Gladstone

Many thanks for your kind invitation which however at present I am not able to say whether I can accept. If I can I will let you know. I trust you are recruiting yourself after the toils of statesmanship and gathering health and strength for another season.

Milnes is much better and in almost his usual spirits. I gave your message to him and he seemed grateful for your remembrance of him. Believe me with best remembrances to Mrs. Gladstone,

Very truly yours
A. Tennyson

To EMILY SELLWOOD TENNYSON

MS. Tennyson Research Centre.

BOLTON A[BBEY] HOTEL, September 6, 1862

Dearest

I have thine of the fifth this morning. I do not know why thou should'st have fancied that I might have come on the 5th. I cannot be back before Tuesday or Wednesday. I have just had a long talk with old Dr. Lushington —he is very full of anecdotes and specially amusing.

I start from here I suppose on Monday, sleep at Leeds and come on next day. I will write once more.

Thine × × × × × ×
A. T.

To THE DUCHESS OF ARGYLL

MS. Tennyson Research Centre.

FARRINGFORD, October 28, 1862

My dear Duchess

Where have I been? I have been—as it were—nowhere: for as there are some people whom society considers nobodies, so there are some tours which in our days are no tours at all—such was mine—to the Peak in Derbyshire— the localities of which are so totally slighted in Scott's Peveril that I cannot believe he ever was there,[1] though the Castleton folk assured me that he had been, even pointing out the house where he stayed—then I passed through Wensleydale in Yorkshire, and ended by renewing my recollections of the lovely Wharfe Valley and Bolton Abbey—not to be called a tour. Yet for the most part we followed horses not steam engines, heard real country talk and saw the humours of landlords. Altogether I have rather enjoyed myself than not.

---

[1] Walter Scott, *Peveril of the Peak* (1822); below, Victor Hugo's *Les Misérables* (1862).

I have not read the 'Misérables.' I have not seen the Duke's article in the Edinburgh,² though I ordered it as soon as published of our Mudie-Man at Yarmouth who in his small way caters for the literary appetites of our narrow neighbourhood—the narrower the better—though I hear, even as I write, the tinkle of the horrible trowels, which tells me it is increasing, nor have I read Charles Sumner's speech at Boston, nor though I like him personally have I your admiration of his politics.³

Very sorry was I to have missed you at Buxton. I was there on a threedays visit to Monckton Milnes⁴—(who was just recovering from a fit of gout) not very long after you had left, and heard of you from Lady Trevelyan, Macaulay's sister,⁵ and like him, they say, but I have no eyes. It is pleasant to hear that your little girl⁶ was benefited by her sojourn there.

So I see by the Times of yesterday that pleasant young gentleman Lord Dufferin is married: for this I was prepared by a very kindly letter he sent me some time ago; but scarcely so for the marriage of Lady Dufferin. How is it? Has Helen's tower spoken too loudly?⁷ I hope not.

My wife, thank you, is not very well but suffering from cold and ear-ache but the boys prosper and all send love.

Remember me to your Duke. When I read of his journey southward all in vain (as it seemed) I thanked Heaven that I was rather P[oet] L[aureate] than Privy Seal.⁸

Always yours
A. Tennyson

To WILLIAM EWART GLADSTONE

MS. British Library.

FARRINGFORD, I. W., October 30, 1862

My dear Mr. Gladstone

To you, as our great financier,¹ I send the enclosed. You are not requested to answer, only to read it (there is not much to read) and see if there be anything in it.

They are my wife's notions, and she, though much afraid of seeming

---

² 'The Supernatural', *Edinburgh Review*, cxvi (Oct. 1862), 378–97. The 'Mudie-man' was probably George Boggs, bookseller (White's *Hampshire*).

³ On 6 October Charles Sumner had extolled Lincoln's preliminary Emancipation Proclamation freeing slaves on 1 January 1863 in a lengthy and fiery address ('lasting about two hours') reported in *The Times*, 20 October, p. 8. See below, p. 318.

⁴ See above, p. 314.

⁵ Hannah More Macaulay (1810–73), who in 1834 married Charles Edward Trevelyan (1804–86: *DNB*), KCB 1848, created baronet 1874.

⁶ Mary Emma, their sixth daughter (see above, p. 244 n.).   ⁷ See above, p. 279.

⁸ Argyll was Lord Privy Seal in Palmerston's second cabinet, 1859–66. He had come to London from Scotland for a cabinet meeting that was apparently called off (*The Times*, 13, 24, 25 October, pp. 7, 6, 7).

¹ Chancellor of the Exchequer.

presumptuous, is yet so anxious on these matters that I told her I would transmit them to you in *confidence*. How does Homer go on?[2] Believe me,

Always yours
A. Tennyson

To ?

MS. Indiana University.

FARRINGFORD, November 5, 1862

Dear Sir

You are quite welcome to my May Queen and Lady Clara Vere de Vere and I am delighted that they should have served so good a purpose. Thank you. I am not often in Bath nor near. Believe me, dear Sir,

Truly yours
A. Tennyson

To THE DUCHESS OF ARGYLL

MS. Tennyson Research Centre.

November 11, 1862

My dear Duchess

Sumner's speech seems to have been very eloquent and enthusiastic and because you believe him to be a true man, and I have faith in a true woman's instincts, I would willingly believe him true also.[1] Yet how is it that an able and honourable man can blind himself to the selfishness of that proclamation? Had it given liberty to the Slaves of those States which remain faithful to the union with promise of compensation to the Slave-owners the case would [have] looked different. But the loosing of all the Demonism in the other states whatever their Treason or their imagined Treason I cannot for a moment tolerate.[2]

And after all is there treason indeed? If I read rightly what has been truly written of the Constitution of those Southern States—No. Slavery there was recognized when each state was received—a sovereign state abdicating part of its sovereignty and laying it before the throne of the Union with a right to resume it at will. I love not Slavery more than Charles Sumner does; but here a cool spectator—not an actor all on fire among these fiery scenes—small praise to me if I love justice more than he. Altogether I am disappointed nay

---

[2] Gladstone had published *Studies on Homer and the Homeric Age* (3 vols., 1868), and his *Homeric Synchronism: An Enquire into the Time and Place of Homer* would appear in 1876. His and Tennyson's divergent views on Homeric versification and the translating of Homer into English led to some touchiness between them. See above, p. 310, and below, p. 417 ff.

[1] See above, p. 317 and n.

[2] 'He had always looked forward anxiously to the total abolition of slavery: but he had hoped that it might be accomplished gradually and peacefully. . . . He would sing with enthusiasm the great chorus of the "Battle-hymn of the Republic": "Singing Glory, Glory Hallelujah! | His soul goes marching on"' (*Memoir*, i. 490 and n.).

disgusted with the Northerners ever yelling and mouthing against their old European mother—who is now at least—the most unaggressive power in the Universe. I suppose it is the overproportion of Celtic blood among them. Look at the three-year-old and four-year-old factions in Tipperary and see whether they don't exemplify my friend Aubrey de Vere's saying 'Give an Irishman an egg every morning to breakfast and the whole world won't contain him.' What are we to do if all the best and highest leave us? and yet with these Articles attempting to define so much that is indefinable and imposing their own definitions as necessities of faith truly one cannot much wonder if men sometimes feel the chains too heavy to be borne.[3]

Yours, my dear Duchess,
A. Tennyson

JULIA MARGARET CAMERON to SIR HENRY TAYLOR

Text. Autobiography of Henry Taylor, ii. 193–4.

[c. 29 November 1862]

Alfred talked very pleasantly that evening to Annie Thackeray and L[ouisa] S[imeon?]. He spoke of Jane Austen, as James Spedding does, as next to Shakespeare! . . . Alfred has grown, he says, much fonder of you since your last two visits here. He says he feels now he is beginning to know you and not to feel afraid of you, and that he is beginning to get over your extreme insolence to him when he was young and you were in your meridian splendour and glory. So one reads your simplicity. He was very violent with the girls on the subject of the rage for autographs. He said he believed every crime and every vice in the world were connected with the passion for autographs and anecdotes and records,—that the desiring anecdotes and the acquaintance with the lives of great men was treating them like pigs to be ripped open for the public; that he knew himself should be ripped open like a pig; that he thanked God Almighty with his whole heart and soul that he knew nothing, and that the world knew nothing, of Shakespeare but his writings; and that he thanked God Almighty that he knew nothing of Jane Austen, and that there were no letters preserved either of Shakespeare's or Jane Austen's, that they had not been ripped open like pigs. Then he said that the post for two days had brought *him* no letters, and that he thought there was a sort of syncope in the world as to him and to his fame. I told him of the mad worship

---

[3] The Duchess replied, on 14 November (TRC): 'War once begun, I fear one must make up one's mind to all possible material injury to the Adversary being fair policy. I doubt whether in Civil war a Government has ever been so fearful of putting into effect its powers as Abraham Lincoln has been. Charles Sumner has great confidence in the humanity of the Negro race, and thinks that the chief effect of the Proclamation upon them will be, in the inducement to strike work. God grant he may be right;—but when the South *began* this war (the South began it) it ought to have known that it might be—surely *would* be—servile as well as civil war. . . . But I wish you would read Mill's short-article in the last Westminster Review "The Slave power"— we agree in every word of it.'

of Swinburne, of —— the Pre-Raphaelite saying that Swinburne was greater than Shelley or Tennyson or Wordsworth.[1]

To SIR REDMOND BARRY[1]

MS. State Library of Victoria.

FARRINGFORD, December 1, 1862

Mr. Alfred Tennyson presents his compliments to Sir Redmond Barry and begs to thank him most sincerely for his kind gift of the Catalogues and acacia seeds and the magnificent samples of corn. The maize is the finest both as to size and colour which Mr. Tennyson has ever seen, the wheat looks fed on sunshine and the oats are if possible more beautiful than the wheat itself. The wheat is being sown here to-day.[2] Mr. Tennyson has great pleasure in requesting Sir Redmond's acceptance of samples of the produce of his own fields and only waits to know whither they are to be sent.

Sir Redmond Barry etc. etc.

To ROBERT HARRISON[1]

MS. University of Chicago.

FARRINGFORD, FRESHWATER, ISLE OF WIGHT, December 2, 1862

Sir

I am told that I may hope the Committee of the London Library will be kind enough to admit me again as a subscriber on payment of my subscription of £2 a year. I should be very glad to enroll myself again amongst your members if it be so; as now, the communication between this and London is so much easier than when I was formerly a member that the box which used sometimes to be a fortnight in arriving need not now be more than a day or two. I have the honour to be, Sir,

Your obedient servant
A. Tennyson

---

[1] See Tennyson to Taylor, 23 [for 24] March 1885, vol. iii.

[1] Sir Redmond Barry (1830–80: *DNB*; knighted, 1862), born in Co. Cork, educated at Trinity College, Dublin, called to the bar in 1838, emigrated to Australia in 1839, and became the first Solicitor-General of Victoria in 1850. In 1851 he was appointed a judge, and in 1855 chosen to be the first Chancellor of the University of Melbourne. He visited England in 1862, and was Commissioner from Victoria to the International Exhibition.

[2] 'A. writes to Sir Redmond Barry to thank him for the Exhibition Catalogue and the seeds of Wattle and the magnificent maize and the Victorian wheat and oats beautiful to behold. A. says that the oats look like stately virgins the colour and the shape are so beautiful. We go to see the wheat sown' (Journal, 1 December). 'Our wheat won a prize at the Exhibition. A. says that the Victorian oats look like stately virgins. The colour and the shape are beautiful' (Journal, 1 January 1863, in Hallam's hand).

[1] Robert Harrison, dates unknown, Librarian of the London Library, 1857–93, author, traveller, translator (Allibone).

To EDMUND LUSHINGTON

Text. Materials, ii. 86 n.

[? mid-December 1862]

Tell Sellar I am glad to hear that he is a candidate for the Edinburgh Latin professorship,[1] since he is not only one of the best Latin scholars living but one of the finest. I mean one of the most keenly and critically sensitive to the individual beauties of each author, as I have found both by conversing with him and by reading some of his essays.[2] Moreover he is such a thoroughly good fellow that I wish him to succeed in whatever he sets his heart upon, and if I say this rather to you than to him, it is only because I cannot so well praise a man to his face.

Yours affectionately
A. Tennyson

To STEPHEN SPRING RICE

Text. Catalogue 78 (Sept. 1972), Lot 151, Kenneth W. Rendell, Inc.; and MS TI/6485B (fragment) Public Record Office, London.

December 20, 1862

[Dear Stephen]

It is long since I heard from or saw you which makes [me] doubly glad to look upon your handwriting again. I am relieved to hear from you that your health has so much improved of late. I had heard it from others, but it is satisfactory that you confirm the report. . . . I am grieved to hear your recount of Lord Monteagle. But how are all the rest of you? Your wife and your innumerable progeny? And am I never to see you again or is the remainder of your days to be wasted on the far west of Mount Trenchard. I subjoin on the opposite page a favourable word for Allingham. You can tear it off and send it to Lord Carlisle. If you don't approve of it let me know and I will see if I can mend it. But I think it will serve the purpose.

[MS] As to Allingham he is a very poor man and has worked hard at his duties for seventeen years or thereabouts, and has moreover a fine poetical talent which should not be let starve.[1]

I will willingly sign my name in his commendation to Lord Palmerston. My wife desires her best regards to you and yours.

Ever yours affectionately
A. Tennyson

---

[1] W. Y. Sellar, Professor of Greek at St. Andrews, was the successful candidate for the professorship at Edinburgh (1863–90). See above, p. 67 and n.

[2] Sellar had published in *Oxford Essays Contributed by Members of the University* (4 vols., 1855–8) 'Lucretius and the Poetic Characteristics of His "Age"' (1855) and 'Characteristics of Thucydides' (1857).

[1] He obtained a Civil List pension in 1864 (see below, p. 367 and n.).

2 January 1863
ALFRED AND EMILY SELLWOOD TENNYSON
to THE DUCHESS OF ARGYLL

MS. Tennyson Research Centre.

FARRINGFORD, I. W., 2d of [January, 18]63

Nothing, dear Duchess, but newspaper nonsense! I am quite as well as usual.[1] My love to the Duke.

Yours affectionately
A. Tennyson

Best New Year wishes from us all to you all. I am thankful to say he is far better now than he was this time last year.

E. T.

To JOHN CHIPPENDALE MONTESQUIEU BELLEW[1]

MS. Rosenbach Foundation.

FARRINGFORD, March 7, 1863

Dear Sir

Since you wrote to me I have written a song of welcome—not an ode.[2] I have ordered Mr. Evans[3] to send a special messenger to Mr. Fechter with a copy as soon as printed. Mr. Fechter is of course not at all bound to have it recited if he does not think it suitable. I am, Dear Sir,

Yours truly
A. Tennyson

---

[1] 'Alfred is as usual and has been far better this autumn and winter than last. I have had many inquiries but I do not know whence the report has arisen' (Emily Tennyson to Mrs Gatty, 4 February, Boston Public Library).

[1] Handwriting unidentified; only the signature is Tennyson's. 'J. W. Bellew', written on the verso, is clearly a mistake for J. C. M. Bellew (1823–74: *DNB*), associated with Charles Albert Fechter (1824–79: *DNB*), actor and theatre manager, whose famous interpretation of Hamlet at the Princess's theatre (1861) was in part due to Bellew. From 1855 to 1867 he was 'one of the most popular of the London preachers' (in 1868 he converted to Roman Catholicism), and as a public reader of literature, he rivalled Dickens and Fanny Kemble (*DNB*).

[2] 'A Welcome to Alexandra' (Ricks, p. 1152), written in honour of the Princess Alexandra (1844–1925), eldest daughter of Prince Christian (later King Christian IX) of Denmark, whom the Prince of Wales married on 10 March in the Chapel Royal, Windsor. On 6 March Tennyson had sent to Windsor a final copy of the poem, which arrived on the evening of the next day, just after Alexandra reached the castle, following a triumphal procession through London. On 8 March, by means of a letter from Lady Augusta Bruce (*Memoir*, i. 489–90), the Queen acknowledged 'with how much pleasure she had read the lines and how much she rejoices that the sweet and charming Princess should be greeted thus'. 'A Welcome' was printed in *The Times* (p. 10) on the day of the wedding. See *Dear and Honoured Lady*, pp. 73–4; *Journal*, p. 182; *Annual Register*, pp. 36–50.

[3] Frederick M. Evans, of Bradbury and Evans.

To THE LORD CHAMBERLAIN[1]

MS. Knox College.

FARRINGFORD, FRESHWATER, ISLE OF WIGHT, March 11, 1863

My Lord

I regret that, owing to my not having been in town, and the intervention of Sunday, I did not receive your Lordship's card of entrance till ten o'clock on the marriage morning. I have the honour to be

Your Lordship's obedient servant
A. Tennyson

The Lord Chamberlain

ALFRED AND EMILY SELLWOOD TENNYSON to LEWIS FYTCHE[1]

MS. Tennyson Research Centre.

[11 March 1863]

With kindest love.

A. [and] E. T.

All went off well here yesterday.[2]

ALFRED AND EMILY SELLWOOD TENNYSON to THE DUCHESS OF ARGYLL

MS. Tennyson Research Centre.

March 11, 1863

Dear Duchess

I did not see the show—perhaps I wish that I had. This is a little lyrical flash, an impromptu which I sent to the Queen and for which she returned me the warmest thanks. Sterndale Bennett wishes to set it.[1] Will you accept it and believe me

Always yours
A. Tennyson

---

[1] John Robert Townshend (1805–90: *DNB*), 3rd Viscount Sydney; created Earl Sydney of Scadbury, 1874; Lord Chamberlain, 1859–66, 1868–74 (*Peerage*, 1877 edn.). See *Journal*, p. 182.

[1] Addressed: 'Mr. Fytche | Eastgate, Lincoln', enclosing 'A Welcome' (Moxon, 1863); the message is written inside the envelope and flap.

[2] The celebration at Farringford in honour of the royal wedding—decorations of flowers and of Danish and English flags, a special cake, a torchlight procession, and a 'very grand' bonfire on the Down (*Journal*, p. 182).

[1] 'A Welcome' (Moxon, 1863). 'Bennett asked and obtained the poet's permission to set the Ode to music. Unfortunately, however, another composer, without waiting to obtain the same permission, hastily set the words in the form of a popular song, and this upset Bennett's project' (*Life of William Sterndale Bennett*, p. 307). Gooch and Thatcher (p. 622) record only a setting by H. Glover (1863).

I had an invitation to the marriage but it arrived too late.[2] My love,

E. T.

To ?

MS. Berg Collection.

FARRINGFORD, March 30, 1863

Sir

I have the pleasure of granting the leave you ask to publish the words from the 'Idylls of the King' with your music. I have the honour to be, Sir,[1]

Your obedient servant
A. Tennyson

HALLAM TENNYSON
to THE EDITOR OF *THE SUNDAY AT HOME*

MS. McGill.

FARRINGFORD, March 31, 1863

Sir

In the last page of your March number for 1863[1] I find mention made of a Frenchman who visited the Tower of Constance in Languedoc 95 years ago. Could you tell me the name of the Frenchman, and where this account is to be found please as Papa has been reading your magazine and wishes to know.

Hallam Tennyson

---

[2] The Duchess replied the next day (TRC): 'I think the Princess of Wales seems to be all that Poet's dream could make her—likely, thank God, to be a great blessing to the Land, and to our loved Queen. She talks of her to my Mother with unbounded satisfaction. The sight in St. George's was one of great beauty and I wish you had been there. I shall never forget the Princess Royal's look up to her Mother, as she paused in the procession and bowed low. It had something of the old reverential times not of our days when English sons are not sure about saying *Father*, and like Governor better.'

[1] Perhaps E. Levien's 'The Song of Love and Death', 1863 (Gooch and Thatcher, p. 534).

[1] 'Religious Intelligence', in *The Sunday at Home: A Family Magazine for Sabbath Reading*, x (28 Mar. 1863), 207–8, an affecting account by the Chevalier de Boufflers (1738–1815) of entering the Tower of Constance at Aigues-Mortes, where fourteen women, guilty of attending Protestant services or of being married to Protestant ministers, were imprisoned under appalling conditions, some from childhood and one for forty-one years. (His account is quoted in Daniel Benoit, *Marie Durand: Prisonnière à la Tour de Constance (1730–1768)*, [1894], pp. 306–9.) On this inspection of the Tower, 11 January 1767, Boufflers accompanied his uncle, Prince Charles-Juste de Beauvau, who, moved with compassion, released some of the prisoners at once on his own authority, and succeeded in gaining royal assent to free all the others, the last being liberated in December 1768. See also Raoul Stéphan, *Histoire de Protestantisme Français* (1961), pp. 195–6, and Samuel Mours and Daniel Robert, *Le Protestantisme en France du XVIIIème Siècle à Nos Jours (1685–1970)* (1972), pp. 149–51.

To EDWARD SILAS

MS. National Library of Wales.

FARRINGFORD, April 16, 1863

Mr. Alfred Tennyson presents his compliments to Mr. Silas and has the pleasure of giving him the permission he asks to publish 'The Owl' with his music.[1]

To JOHN COLAM[1]

MS. Brotherton Collection.

FARRINGFORD, April 17, 1863

Mr. Alfred Tennyson presents his compliments to Mr. Colam and begs to thank him for the ticket of admission to St. James's Hall on the 28th of May.

Mr. Tennyson regrets that being obliged to decline all public meetings he cannot prove the interest he feels in the cause by being present on the 28th.

HALLAM TENNYSON'S DESCRIPTION OF THE VISIT TO THE QUEEN

Text. Dear and Honoured Lady, pp. 76–8.

OSBORNE, May 9, 1863

We all went to Osborne on 9th May 1863. We had our dinner there with Lady Augusta Bruce and then went out driving in one of the Queen's carriages. We saw a beautiful Pinus Insignis that the Prince consort had planted in 1847 and there was a beautiful puzzle monkey at the Queen's dairy, once called and was the old Abbey of Barton. We saw the Queen's dairy. We had pretty glimpses of the sea now and then. We saw the young Princes' and Princess's gardens. There were potatoes and artichokes. There were a great many mares tail about Osborne, asparagus and radishes. We went into a Swiss cottage that the Queen had given to them as a Christmas present.

We saw fossils and birds stuffed and a wolf, very big, and a gentleman brought a fish home and a naughty little puppy tore it to pieces. We saw another Swiss cottage with an old dame of 81 in it. There the Princesses cook and all was beautifully arranged. There was another little room and in there a little shop belonging to the Princess Beatrice about a foot square and at the top [of the shop] was put Grocer Spratt to Her Majesty and Princess. Princess Royal was very fond of cooking biscuits.

---

[1] Gooch and Thatcher, p. 616. Silas is unidentified.

[1] John Colam, Esq., of Croydon, Surrey, Secretary to Royal Society for the Prevention of Cruelty to Animals (Men-at-the-Bar, p. 92).

9 May 1863

Beatrice assured Lady Augusta that she served a large quantity of tea out to Her Majesty and there were really little tea caddies and tea and sugar and all sorts of good things. There was a little fort that Prince Arthur made all by himself with a very little help. It was called Victoria fort and Albert Barracks: there was a little drawbridge. There was the British flag floating gently at the top of a little flag staff and a powder recess and four or five little cannons: there was a moat round the fort. Prince Arthur is destained for an engineer. We saw the pet donkey which used to draw the gun carriage. We drove back to Osborne. We went into one of the drawing-rooms. The Queen came and made a very low bow. Her Majesty shook hands with Mamma and Mamma very courteously went down on one knee and kissed the Queen's hand and the Queen shook hands with Lionel and myself and we shook hands with all the Princes and Princesses except Princess Louise: she only shook hands with Mamma. I had a chat with Prince Leopold about the South of France and Paris, he said he did not like Boulogne. The Princess Louisa asked me whether I could draw, I told her I could not. She can draw beautifully and Prince Leopold can a little: he talked about his fine ships, how he made them as follows (he makes them with paper, he put a match into one of them and it burnt beautifully, it was very windy that day: he put a match into another and it would not burn so he tied two together and they burnt beautifully. There is a little bit of the sea where it is quiet and *that* is where he sails his boats: he talks about building castles in this quiet part of the sea where he sails his boats).

The Queen wears a locket round her neck with thin black velvet. The Queen is not stout. Her Majesty has a large mind and a small body to contain it therein. We went into Lady Augusta's room and had tea. We saw Sir Charles Phipps the Secretary of the Queen, he was a very nice gentleman. (I forgot that after we came from driving we saw Prince Alfred, he looked just like a Norwegian. He shook hands with Papa and was very reverential to him and called him Sir. We saw Prince Louis of Hesse.)

There was a big balustrade outside. We saw the Queen out driving. Her Majesty bowed as she passed by us on the balustrade. Her Majesty drove out with Prince Leopold, Princess Alice, Louis of Hesse and Lady Augusta Bruce. We go home and the porter at the gate smiled when we said how beautiful the Queen was. Her Majesty has a beautiful little nose and soft blue eyes. The Princesses wore dresses, light blue with black spots except Princess Beatrice who was dressed in a sort of checked light blue with a piece of black velvet to tie up her long golden hair. Papa and I saw (as we thought) Princess Beatrice's shetland pony. Princess Beatrice's cat died at seven o'clock that night.

List of Princes and Princesses whom we saw at Osborne exactly in the order we saw them—

Prince Alfred [b. 1844]	Princess Helena [b. 1846]
Prince Louis of Hesse [b. 1837]	Princess Beatrice [b. 1857]
Princess Alice [b. 1843]	Princess Louisa [b. 1848]
[Prince Arthur (b. 1850)]	Prince Leopold [b. 1853]

Princess Beatrice said to Lady Augusta Bruce (not in our presence) (Guste short for Augusta) Guste why do you always call Ma 'Mam'?

Observations:—You must always say 'Mam' when in her Majesty's presence. You must stand until the Queen asks you to sit down. Her Majesty does not *often* tell you to sit down.

Finis

To LADY AUGUSTA BRUCE

MS. Rowland Collins.

May 12, 1863

Dear Lady Augusta

I had no time yesterday to overlook the volume which Her Majesty sent me. I did but see the inscription in the beginning by the Duchess of Kent and Goethe's 'Edel sey der Mensch' in the Prince's handwriting—a poem which has always appeared to me one of the grandest things which Goethe or any other man has written. Perhaps some time or other the Queen will allow me to look at the book again.[1]

The little song which I inserted in it was repeated to H. M. last year by the Duke of Argyll who told me that she approved of it, and I thought it more graceful to give an unpublished than an already printed one.[2] Cauteretz, which I had visited with my friend before I was twenty, had always lived in my recollections as a sort of Paradise. When I saw it once more, it had become a rather odious watering place, but the hills wore their old green, and the roaring stream had the same echoes as of old. Altogether I like the little piece as well as anything I have written: I hope I wrote it out correctly—for I was very much hurried—and I feel sure that in my note to yourself I somewhere or other made pure nonsense of a sentence by putting an 'of' for an 'a' or 'and'.

I have read Guizot's preface, which is just what it ought to be—compact, careful, reverential: I have also dipt slightly into the Meditations, and what I

---

[1] On 11 May a messenger from the Queen brought an Album, in which Tennyson was to 'write something', and two books, *Le Prince Albert, Son Caractère, Ses Discours, Traduit de l'Anglais per Madame de W . . . et Précedé d'une Préface par Mr. Guizot* (Paris, 1863) and *The Meditations* (*Journal*, p. 186). The latter is identified as Karl Sudhoff's in the next letter, and in *Memoir*, i. 491, as Sudhoff's *In der Stille*. Both Tennyson and his wife (*Journal*, p. 186) use the English title *Meditations*, but the same Journal entry in *Materials*, ii. 376, reads '*Meditations from the German*'. Lady Augusta's reply, 19 May (*Materials*, ii. 377) says 'the Meditations', and shows that the Queen had a translation in MS: 'I am to say that the Queen feels as you do that the German is distinctly discernible through the English of "In Memoriam" [*sic*] and felt it when it was submitted to her in MS, but it seemed almost impossible to remove that blemish without obliterating something that it was most desirable to retain.' The 'Specially bound' copy of *In der Stille* presented by the Queen (*Tennyson in Lincoln*, i, 2127) does not include a translation.

The Duchess of Kent, mother of the Queen, died on 16 March 1861, aged seventy-four. Of 'Edel sei der Mensch' from Goethe's 'Das Gottliche', Lady Augusta commented: 'Your enthusiastic appreciation of those lines of Goethe's, which were constantly on the beloved Prince's lips (his especial favourites) is very welcome to the Queen.'

[2] 'In the Valley of Cauteretz' (see above, p. 309 and n.).

have read of them I can quite approve of: their one defect to me being that I discern the German through the translation. Passages here and there which would look quite natural in the original read a little too quaintly in our English: yet I find my appreciation of these essays scarce lessened by feeling that they are a translation. They are true hearted, tender, and solacing, and contrasting advantageously with our disquisitions on these subjects. Does H. M. know the sermons of Robertson of Brighton?[3] he died young, not very long ago. These have always appeared to me the most spiritual utterances of any minister of the church in our times.

I am glad that the Queen remembers my visit with pleasure, and refers to the conversation she held with us, not without interest.

It was very good of you to think of bringing the book: we were sorry, it could not be. Believe me, dear Lady Augusta,

Yours very truly
A. Tennyson

ALFRED AND EMILY SELLWOOD TENNYSON to THE DUCHESS OF ARGYLL

MS. Tennyson Research Centre.

FARRINGFORD, I. W., May 13, 1863

Dear Duchess

Are you well? Is your Duke well? Are your children well? particularly that one which was ailing some time ago. It really pains me to think how long it is since I have seen yourself or Him. Month by month have I been intending to come up to town and look in upon you and yours: but I linger on here: friends visiting, or friends making appointments to visit me, have ever kept me tied and bound to the present or future guest: and so it will be till Whitsuntide.

I have a wish, dear Duchess; but I fear it will be uttered too late for its accomplishment. The Duke in one of his letters told me that he hoped to revisit Farringford. I have a very grateful remembrance of the days when you were with us[1] and shouldn't I and my wife be charmed if you could come again to us this Whitsuntide as quietly and pleasantly as before. He has never seen our Hampstead beds which are very interesting,[2] and I would get our local geologist, Mr. Keeping, to go with us and show him what I think would delight him even more than it did me, inasmuch as he [is] thrice as

---

[3] Frederick William Robertson (1816–53: *DNB*) was the incumbent of Trinity Chapel, Brighton, 1847–53, and during that time won fame for the force and influence of his sermons, creatively edited by H. S. King, then at Smith, Elder, and published posthumously in five series 1855–90. See i. 246 n. and Hagen, *Tennyson and His Publishers*, p. 132. His *Analysis of Mr. Tennyson's 'In Memoriam'*, first published in 1862, was dedicated to Tennyson.

[1] See above, p. 299, and *Journal*, p. 169.

[2] Geological beds at Hempstead (Hampstead, Hemstead, Hamstead) on the north-west side of the Isle of Wight, some three miles east of Yarmouth, rich with fossils. 'The geology at Freshwater is very interesting, and the natural arrangements are like a museum on a large scale, as there is so much to be seen within a small compass, and it is all so accessible. There are places where you can get fossils out of the ground as easily as you take them from the drawers of a cabinet' (Pollock, *Personal Remembrances*, ii. 115).

scientific in these matters. Could you come? Could it be done? If it could, I should strike the stars with my sublime head, as Horace says.[3]

I am sure you will be glad to hear that the Queen admitted myself and wife and two little boys to Her presence on Saturday afternoon. It was a very different interview from that which I had with Her the year before. She had a long talk with us, and we both admired Her, my wife saying afterwards that she had never looked upon a sweeter face and sweet it is, however, the photographer may misuse it. She struck both of us as having great breadth and freedom of intellect, and to be in every way worthy of England's love and honour. Not without humour either; laughing easily at two or three little tales we told Her. So I trust we did not bore Her, for Lady Augusta Bruce said she took her drive later than usual—indeed I feel sure we did not, for the Lady aforesaid wrote to me on Monday that H. M. had exprest great pleasure at our visit and recurred to it with much interest. On Monday too the Queen sent me by the Prince Consort's groom Sudhoff's Meditations, and Guizot's translations of His speeches—wishing me to read the Preface.— also that Album given H. M. by the Duchess of Kent.[4] Lady A[ugusta] said the Queen wished me to write in it anything I liked. I thought I could do no better than inscribe the little song 'All along the valley,' which your Duke repeated to Her last year, and reported that She approved. Do you like to hear these little facts? or do you think I am chattering like old Pepys? only not so amusingly.

I am sure you will come if you can—but perhaps the Queen's going to Balmoral will draw you or at least the Duke after Her by some court-necessity—I am not versed in these matters—though.

Yours always
A. Tennyson

Dear Duchess

My love to you. I am to add from us both, if the Duke have to go to Balmoral would it be possible and would it be pleasant to you both to return with Alfred when he returns from Town whither he hopes to go after Whitsuntide.

Ever yours
E. T.

To ?

Text. *Materials*, ii. 376.

[? *c*. 1 June 1863]

The coins to which you refer are of the time of Gallienus, all except some of his successor Claudius Gothicus. They are copper coins chiefly, some copper washed with silver. There are several of Gallienus, several of Tetricus, father

---

[3] *Odes*, I. i. 36.
[4] See the preceding letter.

and son, one of Salonina, one Postumus, several Victorinus.[1] They are still in my own possession.

To MESSRS CHAPMAN AND HALL [?]

MS. Berg Collection.

FARRINGFORD, I. W., June 5, 1863

Dear Sirs

Accept my best thanks for these two volumes of that true and rare genius, my friend, Robert Browning[1]—I don't know where he is. He would make me very happy if he would come and spend a few days with me here. If you will tell him as much when you see him or write to him, you will increase my obligation to you.

Yours gratefully
A. Tennyson

To ROBERT SEYMOUR BRIDGES[1]

MS. Tennyson Research Centre.

FARRINGFORD, June 11, 1863

Dear Sir

I hope you will not think it unkind that I disclaim the gift attributed to me. I do not doubt that you will at once feel that it would have been a vain thing in me to have sent my portrait to a stranger. I have sent your thanks to the friend to whom I have by chance learnt that they are due and for yourself accept the assurance that since you like to have my portrait I like that you should have it.

Believe me with all good wishes

Truly yours
[A. Tennyson]

---

[1] All from the second half of the third century AD. 'We dug up an urn full of coins here with horses' bones buried round it.' Tennyson 'rubbed and scrubbed the coins for weeks in order to make them out' (*Materials*, ii. 376). See *Journal*, p. 184. 'Yesterday a Roman urn with many coins apparently of different emperors was found in the Terrace ground. Unfortunately the men broke it and divided the coins not thinking them of any use as they said. However we recovered a good many' (Emily Tennyson to Mrs Gatty, *c.* 24 April, Sheffield Central Library).

[1] Probably the first two volumes of the third edition of Browning's *Poetical Works* (Chapman and Hall, 1863): (i) *Lyrics, Romances, Men and Women* (see *Tennyson in Lincoln*, i, No. 639); (ii) *Tragedies and Other Plays*.

[1] Robert Seymour Bridges (1844–1930: *DNB*), Poet Laureate in 1913, was at this time a schoolboy in the sixth form at Eton, where at 'speeches' he had recited a passage from *The Princess*, and thereafter received a gift of a portrait and an autograph of Tennyson. Drawing an easy conclusion, he wrote: 'I hope you will excuse my troubling you with my thanks, which I owe you the more, being an entire stranger. Had I known you personally I could hardly have wished a greater honour; as it is, I could have no greater' (Charles Tennyson, pp. 344–5).

11 *June* 1863

MONCURE DANIEL CONWAY'S VISIT TO FARRINGFORD[1]

Text. Conway, *Autobiography, Memories and Experiences*, ii. 29–32.

[11 June 1863]

My first experience of an old-fashioned English inn was in Tennyson's country. It was at Freshwater and from my tidy room in the 'Albion' I had a beautiful outlook over the bay. . . .

On arrival I sent from the inn my letter from Browning[2] and received an invitation from Mrs. Tennyson to dine at Farringford at eight. . . .

I was the only guest at Farringford. Mrs. Tennyson was attractive, and lighted up the table by her cordiality and pleasant voice. After dinner the poet took me up to his study, where he sat smoking his pipe—having given me a cigar—and talking in the frankest manner. . . .

It had been a stormy evening, and the night was of pitchy darkness when I started out, against invitations to remain, to go to the 'Albion.' Tennyson insisted on showing me a nearer way, but in the darkness got off his bearings. Bidding me walk close behind him, we went forward through the mud, when suddenly I found myself precipitated six or seven feet downward. Sitting in the mud, I called on the poet to pause, but it was too late; he was speedily seated beside me. This was seeing the Laureate of England in a new light, or rather, hearing him under a novel darkness. Covered with mud, groping about, he improved the odd occasion with such an amusing run of witticisms that I had to conclude that he had reached a situation which had discovered in him unexpected resources. His deep bass voice came through the congenial darkness like mirthful thunder, while he groped until he found a path. 'That this should have happened after dinner!' he exclaimed; 'do not mention this to the temperance folk.'

Next morning I was punctual to an appointment Tennyson had made to take me around his manor and his favourite cliffs. Mrs. Tennyson met me with the explanation of our fall; she had directed the gardener to make an addition to a walk in the garden which required a deep cut, of which Mr. Tennyson had not been informed. She expressed more regret than was necessary, but smiled at the drollery of her husband's account, and declared that the place should be named Conway Walk.

Tennyson was in every way different from the man I expected to see. The

---

[1] Moncure Daniel Conway (1832–1907: *DAB*), American preacher, author, reviewer, editor. Virginian by birth, Methodist by upbringing, Unitarian by choice (Harvard Divinity School, BD 1854), he moved to England in April 1863, partially financed by New England abolitionists, to lecture against slavery and bring about a favourable attitude toward the northern states. A friend of Emerson, Longfellow, Thoreau, and others, an early advocate of Browning's poetry in the United States and of Whitman's in England, he arrived in London with excellent references, and gained quick access to literary and political leaders. In 1864 he succeeded to the pulpit of William Johnson Fox, in South Place Chapel, Finsbury, a position he held for twenty years before returning home. See his *Autobiography*; Mary Elizabeth Burtes, *Moncure Conway: 1832–1907*; *DAB*; *Journal*, p. 87; and *The Swinburne Letters*, i. 207–8.

[2] Printed in Thomas J. Collins, 'The Brownings to the Tennysons', *Baylor Browning Interests*, No. 22 (May 1971), 29.

portrait published with his poems in America conveyed some of the expression around his eyes, but not the long head and the long face. Moreover, of all the eminent men I have met he was the one who could least be seen before he had spoken. His deep and blunt voice, and his fondness for strong Saxon words, such as would make a Tennysonian faint if met in one of his lines, his almost Quaker-like plainness of manner, albeit softened by the gentle eye and the healthy humanity of his thought, did not support my preconception that he was the drawing-room idealist. When in speaking of Robert Browning with high estimaton he yet wondered at 'a certain roughness' in his poems, it rather amused me; for Browning put the utmost daintiness—while Tennyson put all his roughness—into his talk. . . . In his library Tennyson put me in an easy chair, then went on telling good anecdotes—these not about his contemporaries, but concerning personages of a past generation. But I admired him most out on the cliff. When he had accompanied me along the sea on my way to the station, then turned and walked slowly back, I gave a look at him from a hundred yards distance, and he appeared to me the ideal Prospero summoning around him the beautiful forms that will never fade from his Isle.

Tennyson wrote me a letter in response to my book, 'The Sacred Anthology,'[3] a copy of which I sent him. He wished me to print an edition of smaller size, which one could carry on his walks. He was astonished to find that non-Christian peoples were so exalted in their religion and ethics, and no doubt startled to find how many ideas in his own poems had been anticipated by Oriental poets. . . .

EMILY SELLWOOD TENNYSON
to GEORGE FREDERICK WATTS

MS. University of Virginia.

FARRINGFORD, FRESHWATER, ISLE OF WIGHT, June 24, 1863

My dear Signor

'This is one of the great pictures that future generations will look at' was one of the exclamations which greeted yours on its arrival.[1]

I really can only feel ashamed when I think how much of your time and thought have been spent on me and when I know that it is a picture of myself and such an one that a lady (Lady Grant, Sir A's mother) said this morning she almost felt in sitting near it that I could speak to her.

I do not know how such a beautiful picture has come but you are a subtle alchemist, a great magician, that I do know.

His thanks he hopes to give in person tomorrow.

Ever most truly yours
Emily Tennyson

---

[3] *The Sacred Anthology: A Book of Ethical Scriptures* (1874).

[1] Reproduced in colour in *Journal* (frontispiece). The exclamation is doubtless the comment of Argyll (see *Journal*, p. 187).

26 June 1863   333

To WILLIAM COX BENNETT [?]

MS. Boston Public Library.

                                         June 26, 1863
Sir
I have pleasure in granting the permission you desire to insert 'The Brook,' 'The Charge of the Light Brigade,' and 'The Lord of Burleigh' in your poetical Reader providing you mean by The Brook that which is generally meant in such publications, the song in my Idyll of 'The Brook.'[1]
I have the honour to be, Sir,
                                     Your obedient servant
                                         A. Tennyson

To EMILY SELLWOOD TENNYSON

MS. Tennyson Research Centre.

                                   Sunday, June 28, 1863
Dearest
I had a very good journey up with Mrs. C[ameron], hardly sneezing at all, the rain of the day before having laid the dust. We got a coupe to ourselves, she being in the immoral habit of bribing the guard. Mrs. P[rinsep] would send all the way to Hendon this morning for Dr. J[ackson] to look at my leg, but he is in his bed with bronchitis and so I shall see Paget[1] tomorrow. Thackeray and his daughter[2] have just been to see me. Love to the boys and Edmund.
                                              Thine
                                              A. T.

[1] See below, p. 524 n.

[1] James Paget (1814–99; created baronet, 1871: *DNB*), surgeon and pathologist, one of the leading medical men of his day. He was appointed Surgeon-Extraordinary to the Queen in 1858, Serjeant-Surgeon-Extraordinary in 1867, and Serjeant-Surgeon in 1877. He had 'strong religious convictions', wrote a 'classical English', was prodigiously dignified and 'one of the best speakers in England', was painted by Millais and caricatured by Spy (*Vanity Fair*, 12 February 1876), fathered two bishops, and never charged Tennyson a fee (Charles Tennyson, p. 345). See G. W. E. Russell, *Portraits of the Seventies*, pp. 308–9.

[2] The novelist and his daughter Anne Isabella Thackeray (1837–1919), herself a novelist and essayist. After her father's death at the end of 1863, she, with her sister Harriet Marian (1840–75), who subsequently married Leslie Stephen (1832–1904), occupied a cottage in Freshwater lent them by Mrs Cameron. 'From that time until the poet's death', writes Charles Tennyson (p. 347), 'there was no more frequent or welcome visitor at his home than Annie Thackeray', and she often accompanied him on his walks. In 1877 she married her second cousin Richmond Thackeray Willoughy Ritchie (1854–1912: *DNB*), seventeen years her junior, a union flawed only by his brief love affair, later, with Lionel Tennyson's widow. Ritchie had a notable thirty-five-year career in the India Office (KCB 1907; Permanent Under-secretary of State for India, 1909). See Winifred Gérin's excellent book *Anne Thackeray Ritchie* (1981).

To EMILY SELLWOOD TENNYSON

Text. Materials, ii. 379.

June 29, [1863]

A French doctor,[1] a man of great and growing celebrity here, saw my leg last night, as he was going to dine here, so I thought he had better have a look at it and he said it did not matter, was very annoying and gave me some directions to follow. Dr. Jackson came this morning and saw it too and agreed with the Frenchman. Mrs. Prinsep is very civil and doctors me and bandages me day and night. (All owing to my being vaccinated.)[2]

LITTLE HOLLAND HOUSE, June 30, [1863]

I am not going to stir just at present from Little Holland House till my eczema leg is better. I am glad that Edmund Lushington relieves a little in the teaching of Lionel. My hay fever is certainly better.

To ANNE ISABELLA THACKERAY

MS. Armstrong Browning Library.

Wednesday, [1 July 1863]

My dear Annie Thackeray

I can't come 1st because my good hostess and nurse says that I ought not in my present state 2dly because there is a floating invitation sent out to divers friends of mine and acceptable until Monday.

Yours ever
A. Tennyson

---

[1] Henri Guéneau de Mussy (1814–92), physician throughout his life to the Orléans family, who came to England with Louis-Philippe in 1848; he had a substantial private practice, and was one of the 'few foreigners elected to the full fellowship of the Royal College of Physicians' (Boase). See *The Thackeray Letters*, ed. Ray, iv. 403 n.; *The George Eliot Letters*, ed. Haight, iv. 336, 383; and below, p. 336.

[2] Tennyson had been vaccinated on 19 May (*Journal*, p. 186). 'Mrs. Cameron was profoundly interested in keeping the poet well, and fit for work. One evening a friend who was dining with her mentioned that there was small-pox in the neighbourhood. Mrs. Cameron started. "Alfred Tennyson has not been vaccinated for twenty years," she said. "We must not lose a moment." She went at once in search of the village doctor, took him to Farringford, and made her way to Tennyson's study. He was busy and did not want to see her, but she pursued him from room to room. In the end he said: "Madam, if you will leave me I will do anything you like." He was vaccinated. The sequel was told me by Tennyson himself. The vaccine proved to be bad, and he was not really well again for six months, so Mrs. Cameron's intervention did not prove quite so fortunate as she had hoped' (Wilfred Ward, *Men and Matters*, p. 259). In another version, she 'followed him up to the smoking-room, where he had retreated and locked himself in. She hammered at the door, calling out "Alfred, you are a coward." Alfred reiterated, "Woman, go away, I will be vaccinated to-morrow." He kept his promise, but being done from a gouty baby, had eczema in his leg for two years' (A. G. C. Liddell, *Notes from the Life of an Ordinary Mortal*, pp. 313–14).

To EMILY SELLWOOD TENNYSON

Text. Materials, ii. 379.

July 2, 1863

The book lost was not *Ovid* Vol. II., but that *Lucretius* which Sellar gave me with his marks in it. Browning, William Rossetti and Mr. Bowman[1] were here last night and there was a very pleasant evening.

To THE DUCHESS OF ARGYLL

MS. Tennyson Research Centre.

Thursday, July 2, 1863

My dear Duchess

I will be ready for you at Little Holland House on Monday evening—7.15 and I will call upon you tomorrow about 1 o'clock except you send me word that you will be out.

Yours ever
A. Tennyson

To EMILY SELLWOOD TENNYSON

MS. Tennyson Research Centre.

LITTLE HOLLAND HOUSE, KENSINGTON, Friday, [3 July 1863]

Dearest

I am still here as you see. I am going to call on Clara today.[1] I have to dine with Milnes on the 10th. I am terribly afraid of the dinners, and shall avoid them as much as possible. I never got down to the House but the Duke[2] will take me whenever I like. I suppose about matters in general thou must do as seemest best to thee: I shall go up to see mother after I get to Palgrave's whither I go on Tuesday. 5, Yorkgate, Regent's Park, is I think the direction. Mrs. Brookfield dines here today. That is all the news except this. I saw the

---

[1] William Bowman (1816–92; created baronet, 1884: *DNB*), noted ophthalmic surgeon (see below, p. 000 n.). Next day Browning wrote Tennyson a dazzling letter on the 'enclitic δέ' in 'A Grammarian's Funeral', continuing the evening discussion (Thomas J. Collins, 'The Brownings to the Tennysons', *Baylor Browning Interests*, No. 22 (May 1871), 29–30).

[1] Clara Hinde Palmer (née D'Eyncourt). He wrote to her from Farringford on 20 June: 'I haven't the chance of coming to you, even if you could tolerate a smoker in your house which possibly you couldn't' (Maggs Bros. Catalogue, and Sotheby's Catalogue, 14 Dec. 1976, Lot 251). In another letter to her (Sotheby, same sale, Lot 252) on 25 July 1863, he regrets having missed her the other day: 'I had only moved to the York Baths [54 York Terrace, Regents Park] two doors off.'

[2] Argyll.

British Institution yesterday. One or two fine old portraits.[3] Watts is working away at me.[4] Love to all.

Thine × × × × ×
A. T.

EMILY SELLWOOD TENNYSON
to FREDERICK JAMES FURNIVALL

MS. Huntington Library.

FARRINGFORD, FRESHWATER, ISLE OF WIGHT, July 4, 1863

My dear Sir

I will forward the petition to Mr. Tennyson. He often says how many things he has to thank you for so I hope you will not believe him ungrateful because his thanks are not so often expressed to yourself as they ought to be were it not that it is impossible for him to write all that should be written.[1] Believe me,

Very truly yours
Emily Tennyson

F. J. Furnivall Esqre
3 Old Square
London, W. C.

To EMILY SELLWOOD TENNYSON

Text. Materials, ii. 379–80.

LITTLE HOLLAND HOUSE, July 4, [1863]

I am told by Dr. de Mussey[1] that the stocking I have been wearing is very bad for the leg.[2]

LITTLE HOLLAND HOUSE, July 6, [1863]

The weather is so hot that I am advised not to move into London, so I shall stop here till further notice.

---

[3] 'The British Institution opened in June for the Exhibition of pictures by Old Masters. The room devoted to the English school contained a tolerably complete collection of the works of Romney' (*Annual Register*, p. 365).

[4] Identified by Richard Ormond (*Early Victorian Portraits*, i. 447–8) as the portrait painted for William Bowman (see above, p. 335), of which the painting in the National Portrait Gallery (reproduced in ii, Plate 890), 'begun at the same time' and 'almost identical in pose, features, and composition', is a variant.

[1] See below, p. 338.

[1] Mussy, the famous 'French doctor' mentioned above, p. 334.

[2] See above, pp. 154, 173.

LITTLE HOLLAND HOUSE, July 9, [1863]

The Duchess of Sutherland's party at Chiswick [House] came off very well. Gladstone was there and Charles Howard. It is a very pretty place and there is the chamber in which Fox died. Canning, I believe, died there too. The Duchess asked me to a Prince's and Princess's croquet party next day but I did not go.

July 10, [1863]

I saw Paget to-day, and he is reckoned the first surgeon in London; he says that the hands will take longer than the leg, that the leg will heal itself if I hold it up in a week or so, but the hands in three. There is no danger of any kind, only need of patience, so I submit. He has had thousands of similar cases and he says those whose forefathers were gouty are liable to this. I am going with my foot still kept up to Palgrave's to-day.

To EMILY SELLWOOD TENNYSON

MS. Tennyson Research Centre.

July 13, [1863]

Dearest

I have written every day but one I think since I left. I fear that some of them have disappeared in the Yarmouth P.O. I shall therefore get Palgrave to direct this for me. I am still horizontal but otherwise well enough (saving the nerves which are still irritable). Do as thou wilt about evening parties only it will seem oddish to the neighbours that they are all asked when I am out.

Thine × × × × × ×
[A. T.]

I hope no one will pluck my wild Irises which I planted—if they want flowers there is the kitchen garden—nor break my new laurels etc. whose growth I have watched.

To EMILY SELLWOOD TENNYSON

MS. Tennyson Research Centre.

July 14, [1863]

Dearest

Don't bother thyself about me—I feel perfectly well—only tied by the leg—I shall not be home, I should think, by what the Doctors say for at least a month, though the leg is close upon healing, yet after the skin has joined [?]

I shall have to wait three weeks till the varicose starting can be cured.[1]

I don't quite like children croquetting on that lawn. I have a personal interest in every leaf about it.

Thine, dearest,
A.

EMILY SELLWOOD TENNYSON
to FREDERICK JAMES FURNIVALL

MS. Huntington Library.

FARRINGFORD, FRESHWATER, ISLE OF WIGHT, July 17, 1863

My dear Sir

Thank you for your kind wish to dedicate the book[1] to my husband. He accepts the dedication and with pleasure I am sure.

Very truly yours
Emily Tennyson

F. J. Furnivall Esqre
3 Old Square
Lincoln's Inn, W. C.

To ?

MS. University of Kentucky.

FARRINGFORD, FRESHWATER, ISLE OF WIGHT,[1] July 17, 1863

Sir

Your letter dated the 13th has only reached me to-day. I thank you for the sympathy which makes you feel that the request for the poems to be published in your Magazine is not one with which I can comply. I am, Sir,

Your obedient servant
A. Tennyson

---

[1] Browning wrote to a friend on 19 July: 'I cannot get Romola—spite of my repeated applications at Mudie's—and shall give up subscribing to him in consequence; his humbug is too much. I found Tennyson, reading it in bed last Thursday—he has got an eruption—suppressed hay fever or irregularly-acting vaccination, he thinks. I dined with him the week before, and found him very pleasant: he has poems ready,—one, in particular, called 'Enoch the Sailor', which I wish he would make haste and print' (*New Letters of Robert Browning*, ed. DeVane and Knickerbocker, p. 154).

[1] *Le Morte Arthur*, ed. by Furnivall from Harleian MS 2, 252, for the Early English Text Society (1864).

[1] Embossed. The letter is in Emily Tennyson's hand; apparently she sent it to London for the signature (in his hand).

To EMILY SELLWOOD TENNYSON

Text. *Materials*, ii. 380.

YORK GATE, July 20, [1863]

Of course I am not going to write poems on Lifeboats at bidding, nor can I.[1] I wonder she should ask me.

YORK GATE, July 22, [1863]

It will be better I think to exchange the greatest part [of the port],[2] though I must say I hate claret. I begin to doubt the use of my coming down to Farringford before I start for Harrogate.

To EMILY SELLWOOD TENNYSON

MS. Tennyson Research Centre.

[23 July 1863]

Dearest

Dr. Jackson thinks I had better not return to the Isle at present but go on straight to Harrogate. I don't know whether, all things considered, it would be better for you to go along with me or not. I purpose starting on Monday but I could wait later here if you could join me and Mrs. Prinsep offers her house to you: then whether it would be better in case you came to leave the children with the tutor at Farringford or to bring children and tutor[1] to be left at Grasby or to go all to Harrogate I don't know. If you come of course I could stop here till you could be ready a day or two later. Then, there is no absolute necessity for your coming. Think about these things and arrange as you think best. Of course it would be more comfortable to have you with me but I don't know what money I have in the Bank, and am half afraid to draw.

Thine
A. T. x x x x x

Let somebody pick off the seeds of the rhododendrons in the avenue that the plants may spread.

Expenses etc. have to be considered.

---

[1] Perhaps suggested (to Mrs Gatty? Mrs Cameron?) by J. Gilmore's article, 'The Ramsgate Life-boat: A Night in the Goodwin Sands', *Macmillan's Magazine*, iii (Apr. 1861), 487–98, noted in Journal (TRC) on 3 March 1862: 'A. reads the first of the nights in the Goodwin Sands in Macmillan. A true story of wonderful heroism.'

[2] Doctor's orders—for Harrogate sulphur and no port in the storm (see below, p. 340 n.).

[1] Mr. Butterworth—mentioned in *Journal*, pp. 189–90—was perhaps Charles Henry Butterworth (born *c.* 1843), scholar at Trinity College, BA 1866 (Foster), who filled in as tutor after Dakyns's departure.

To WILLIAM OR THOMAS FAIRBAIRN

MS. Bodleian.

July 24, 1863

My dear Fairbairn

How very kind an invitation you have sent me, and how sorry I am that I cannot accept it. I have been laid up here at Palgrave's and am ordered away to Harrogate by my doctors.

Always yours
A. Tennyson

To EMILY SELLWOOD TENNYSON

Text. Materials, ii. 381.

LONDON, July, [*c*. 24, 1863]

W. G. Clark whom I saw the other day said he would be on the look out for a tutor for us and added 'I have more opportunities than most men.'[1] Paget and Dr. Jackson attend me gratis every day very kindly.

EMILY SELLWOOD TENNYSON to MARGARET GATTY (extract)

MS. Boston Public Library.

CLIFTON HOUSE, QUEEN'S PARADE, HARROGATE, August 14, 1863

... You will be sorry to hear that Ally instead of being amongst any crowd where you were or were not was in his sickroom or in bed. In bed a fortnight with a gouty affection for which he is ordered here. Not gout nor in any way dangerous the doctors say but very tedious and very trying. We have been here a fortnight with no visible improvement but the doctor says he is better so we must hope he is. ....[1]

SAMUEL LAURENCE to JULIA MARGARET CAMERON (extract)

MS. Tennyson Research Centre (transcript).

August 22, 1863

I will take the freedom of asking you a favour. It is to ask Mrs. Tennyson if she will lend me that head in oil, that I did of her husband some years ago. Now that I can colour better, I might perhaps make one from it. I have had a

---

[1] See above, p. 202 n. He recommended Thomas Wilson, who began on 26 November (*Journal*, p. 191; see also *Memoir*, i. 511–12). See below, p. 345 n.

[1] On 31 August she wrote from Harrogate: 'Will Mr. Schonberg be so kind as to send four more bottles of the Amontillado to-day to Mr. Tennyson' (MS, Wellesley).

22 *August* 1863   341

commission (which are not plentiful with me now) these two years to do one,[1] and I thought for an old acquaintance he would sit, but he won't. Were I on the spot he should, without knowing it. The photographs of him that I have seen are not so good as to provoke me to buy one, and with all the great merit of that portrait by Watts, there is not his colour, or the robustness of his brains. It has delicacy of sentiment, but delicacy and strength unite in Tennyson, more than any man I know of, and it is to be seen in his look as much as in his works, but it is dangerous to criticize without incurring the suspicion of being illnatured, but I continue to look after my own deficiencies as much as ever, and after all see them with too friendly eyes, I daresay. I do admire Watts very much and am jealous that his work should not be all I wish.

To FREDERICK JAMES FURNIVALL

MS. Huntington Library.

FARRINGFORD, FRESHWATER, ISLE OF WIGHT, September 17, 1863

My dear Sir

I have read your extract with interest and would have returned it earlier had it not arrived here when I was from home. I have just returned.[1] Many thanks.

Yours very truly
A. Tennyson

To ?[1]

MS. University of Virginia.

September 24, 1863

Sir

I have but lately returned home after a long absence. I beg now to say that I have much pleasure in giving you the permission you require to insert a few lines of mine in your 'Wise Sayings'. I have the honour to be, Sir,

Your obedient servant
A. Tennyson

---

[1] For a Mr Blodgett, in the United States, 'who wishes to give to the Athenaeum Club a good likeness of Tennyson' (TRC, Laurence to Tennyson, 20 May 1860, quoting Mrs Laurence's letter, from New York, to himself). Identification of Laurence's portraits of Tennyson (see i. 235 n.) becomes more complex and elusive. 'Mr. Lawrence' went to Farringford for a 'crayon portrait' in March 1864 (see below, p. 360), but twenty years later yet another one was commissioned, and was apparently under way when Laurence died suddenly (see vol. iii, Macmillan to Hallam Tennyson, January 1884).

[1] On 14 September (Allingham's *Diary*, p. 87). The paper has been cut for the autograph: 'Many thanks . . . Tennyson' added in another hand.

[1] Unidentified, but possibly to George Routledge (see below, p. 379), publisher of *Wise Sayings of the Great and Good* (1864). In 1867 and again in 1875, though Tennyson is not in the 1875 edition, the only one we have seen.

To JAMES THOMAS FIELDS

MS. Yale.

FARRINGFORD, I. W., September 30, 1863

My dear Sir

I have to thank yourself and Mr. Ticknor for your draft for £100. As to my publishing this autumn it is more than problematical. When I do, I will endeavour to let you have the sheets as early as possible. With best remembrances to Mr. Ticknor, believe me, my dear Sir,

Yours very sincerely
A. Tennyson

EMILY SELLWOOD TENNYSON to MARGARET GATTY (extract)

MS. Boston Public Library.

October 1, 1863

It did not seem of so much use writing as I could only say we could not accept your kind invitation. We refused two others nearer Harrogate both to beautiful places but the cold and damp of Harrogate had proved so harmful to me that it was necessary we should get home as soon as the doctor would let him leave and not improbable that we should go abroad for a warmer climate than our own even. However, though we have had storm and rain since we came home he is a good deal better and I hope I shall be soon.

... We are busy making a little green-house outside the back door in the court-yard. We have turned the pantry door there and so made the front hall quite private. The servants are very glad of the prospect of looking on vines and roses and myrtles instead of flagstones and windows and bricks and safes only.

I found a most acceptable birthday gift in the shape of a lettered cabinet for letters. My work does not seem so hopeless now that my hoping[?] to have it arranged can satisfy itself. I thank the kind donor of the cabinet, Edmund Lushington, many a time and oft for this. ...

WILLIAM ALLINGHAM, *A DIARY*, pp. 87–9.[1]

Saturday, October 3, [1863]

Cross by 3 o'clock Boat, invited to Spend Sunday at Mrs. Clough's. ... Mrs. Clough tells me I am invited to go to the Tennysons with her to-night. (Hurrah!) We drove to Farringford, picking up on the way Mr. Pollock (afterwards Sir F. P.) and his son, a youth in spectacles. Drawing-room, tea, Mrs. Tennyson in white, I can sometimes scarcely hear her low tones. Mrs. Cameron, dark, short, sharp-eyed, one hears very distinctly. I wandered to

---

[1] Much of this is in *Memoir*, i. 512–14.

the book-table, where Tennyson joined me. He praises Worsley's *Odyssey*.[2] In a book of Latin versions from his own poetry he found some slips in Lord Lyttelton's Latin—'Cythera Venus,' etc.[3] 'Did I find Lymington very dull?' I told him that since coming there I had heard Cardinal Wiseman lecture (on 'Self-culture'), Spurgeon preach, and seen Tom Sayers spar.[4] 'More than I have,' he remarked. In taking leave he said, 'Come to-morrow!'

Sunday, October 4, [1863]

In the forenoon I walk over alone to Farringford; find Mrs. T., the two boys, and their tutor, Mr. Butterfield, fair-haired, modest-mannered.[5] T. at luncheon: 'John Wilson's *Life*[6]—leave such things alone! they're done for money.'—'Entozoa—germs were mingled in convict's food, for experiment; after his death the parasites were found stuck all over him inside. Fancy one feeding on your brain!'—'what do we know of the feelings of insects? nothing. They may feel more pain than we.' I think *not*.

T. takes me upstairs to his 'den' on the top-story, and higher, up a ladder to the leads. He often comes up here a-night to look at the heavens. One night he was watching shooting-stars and tumbled through the hatchway, falling on the floor below, a height of at least ten feet I should say. The ladder probably broke his fall and he was not hurt. I quoted 'A certain star shot madly from his sphere.'

T.—'I've never heard any Sea-Maid's music in Freshwater Bay, but I saw an old lady swimming one day.'[7]

The view of sea and land is delectable, stretching northward across the Solent up into the New Forest. Then we went down and walked about the grounds, looking at a cedar, a huge fern, an Irish yew. The dark yew in *Maud* 'sighing for Lebanon'[8] he got at Swainston,—Sir John Simeon's. In one place are some little arches half-covered with ivy, which I pretend to believe are meant for mock-ruins. This T. repudiates. He paused at a weed of goats-beard, saying, 'It shuts up at three.' Then we went down the garden, past a

---

[2] Philip Stanhope Worsley (1833–66: *DNB*), of an Isle of Wight family (at Gatcombe, but more recently at Shorwell), translator of *The Odyssey . . . in the Spenserian Stanza* (1861–2) and part of *The Iliad*. He died of tuberculosis in May 1866, and was buried in All Saints churchyard, Freshwater (*Journal*, p. 247).

[3] George William Lyttelton (1817–76: *DNB*), 4th Baron of Frankley (tutored by and friend of Brookfield), educator and classical scholar. His wife and Gladstone's were sisters, and he and Gladstone published *Translations* [from Greek and Latin] in 1861; 2nd edition, inscribed to Tennyson, July 1863—see *Tennyson in Lincoln*, i, No. 1462.

[4] Three champions. Nicholas Patrick Stephen Wiseman (1802–65: *DNB*), first Cardinal-Archbishop of Westminster in the restored Roman Catholic hierarchy, was a noted lecturer; Charles Haddon Spurgeon (1834–92: *DNB*), the 'most popular preacher of his day', held forth, from 1861 till his death, at the Metropolitan Tabernacle, London, which seated 6,000; Tom Sayers (1826–63: *DNB*), British boxing champion (1857), 'the most distinguished fighter of his day'.

[5] Butter*worth* (see above, p. 339 n.).

[6] Mary Gordon's *Christopher North, A Memoir of John Wilson* (2 vols., 1862).

[7] *A Midsummer Night's Dream*, II, ii. 152–4.

[8] 'Maud', I. 615–16—but a *cedar*. The 'Dark yew' is in *In Memoriam*, xxxiv. 4.

large tangled fig-tree growing in the open—'It's like a breaking wave,' says I. 'Not in the least,' says he. Such contradictions, *from him* are noway disagreeable: and so to the farmyard.

'Have you a particular feeling about a farmyard?' he asked, a special delight in it? I have. The first time I read Shakespeare was in a haystack.—*Othello*—I said, "This man's overrated." Boys can't understand Shakespeare, nor women. We spoke a little of the Shakespeare 'Ter-Centenary' next year.

'Most people pronounce "Arbutus" wrong, with the second syllable long. Clematis too, which should be Clē-matis.'[9]

In the porch, or somewhere near it, I noticed a dusty phial hanging with some dried brown stuff in it. 'It's a Lar,' he said, with a twinkle in his eyes. 'And what else is it?' I asked. 'An old bottle of Ipecacuanha.' I thought the woodwork of the windows a rather crude green: 'I don't know why you shouldn't like it,' he said. We looked at the great magnolia stretching up to the roof, then into the hall and saw some fossils. 'Man is so small!' he said, 'but a fly on the wheel.' Mrs. Clough was in the house and she and I now departed, T. coming with us as far as the little south postern opening on to the lane, afraid to go further. He said he was one day pursued full cry along the road by two fat women and sixteen children! Another day he saw a man's face, who had climbed on the outside fence and was looking over into the garden: 'I said to him, "It isn't at all pretty of you to be peeping there! You'd better come down"—and he did.' 'Was he like an educated man?' 'Yes—or half-educated.' In parting he said to me, 'We shall see you sometimes?'—which gladdened me.

To HENRY SAMUEL KING[1]

MS. British Library.

FARRINGFORD, FRESHWATER, ISLE OF WIGHT, [late November, 1863]

My dear Mr. King

As I shall probably not be able to see these again will you attend to the papers[2] and not let the Devils have their own way.

1. Attempts at etc.
2. Hexameters no worse than daring Germany gave us,[3] one stop and that

---

[9] See below, p. 349 and n.

[1] Henry Samuel King (1817–78), originally a bookseller in Brighton, became a partner (1863–8) with George Smith (1824–1901) in the agency, banking, and publishing business of Smith, Elder, and Co., 65 Cornhill (see above, p. 0000 n.). When the partnership was dissolved in 1868, King established his own firm, and in 1873 became Tennyson's publisher (Boase). See vol. iii, letter to King, 16 April 1873.

[2] The proofs of four experimental poems—'Attempts at Classical Metres in Quantity' (Ricks, pp. 1153–7): 'On Translations of Homer: Hexameters and Pentameters', 'Milton: Alcaics', 'Hendecasyllabics', and 'Specimens of a Translation of the Iliad in Blank Verse'—published in *Cornhill Magazine* in December, of which Thackeray was then the editor and Smith, Elder were the proprietors.

[3] Line 5: 'German hexameters he disliked even more than English. He once said—"'Was die Neugier nicht thut': What a beginning of an hexameter!" and "What a line 'Hab ich den Markt und die Strassen, doch nie so einsam gesehen!'"' [*Hermann und Dorothea*, ll. 1, 4] (*Memoir*, ii. 11).

only a comma in this line. The devil stuck in a negation, and said they *were* worse than the German ones.

3. Slight dash at the end of the 2d stanza in the Milton.[4] Note to be abolished.

4. In the Hendecasyllabics comma to be substituted for dash and another comma inserted lower down.

5. Destroy the heading of the Homeric translation and substitute the little bit of prose, putting Iliad 8 c. at the end.[5]

6. All my stops in the *new* copy of the Translation are as I wish them to be. I have not had time to write out the notes in the printed proof which you sent. Will you see them inserted?[6]

I am sorry to give you this trouble. It would be better for me to overlook them again—but it can't be helped.

Yours ever
A. Tennyson

You have bagged my MSS and you may keep them except that one of the *first* Homeric translation which I sent you.[7]

WILLIAM ALLINGHAM, *A DIARY*, p. 93.

Sunday, December 20, [1863]

I lunched at Farringford. We all helped in wheeling Mrs. Tennyson to the top of High Down. Then A. T., the Tutor[1] and myself walked to Totland's Bay, the talk all upon Classic Metres, of which he is full at present. I am invited for Christmas.

Tuesday, December 22, [1863]

Feel out of sorts and as it were stupefied; write to Mrs. Tennyson declining the Christmas invitation, which I was so glad to have! On the second day after, came a very kind note from Mrs. T. renewing the invitation, and on the 26th I went to Farringford. . . .

---

[4] Line 8, 'onset—'. The cancelled note is in *Memoir*, ii. 11).
[5] The 'little bit of prose' is printed in *Memoir*, ii. 15 (and Ricks, p. 1156).
[6] Ricks, p. 1156.
[7] Other experiments with Homer in blank verse: 'Achilles over the Trench' [*Iliad*, xviii. 202–24], first published in the *Nineteenth Century*, ii. (Aug. 1877), 1–2; and two fragments (Ricks, pp. 1157, 1779).

[1] Thomas Wilson (born 1841), tutor from November 1863 (see above, p. 340) to 11 November 1864 (*Journal*, p. 216), matriculated at Cambridge from Trinity in 1860, and went to the Inner Temple in 1866, and then to the Inns of Court (Venn). He is not listed in *Men-at-the-Bar* (1884), and probably died early. Even in 1863–4 he 'was not in good health, sometimes suffering from fits of melancholy' (*Memoir*, i. 512).

Saturday, December 26, [1863]

... At Farringford I find F. T. Palgrave. Tennyson, he, and I walk up High Down.

Dinner at six, the usual immediate move (with the wine) to Drawing-room, and talk all about Classic Metres, to which I naturally have little to contribute, nor can I see that the discussion throws much if any light on English metrical effects.

To THE DUCHESS OF ARGYLL

MS. Tennyson Research Centre.
FARRINGFORD, FRESHWATER, ISLE OF WIGHT, Saturday, December 26, 1863

My dear Duchess

I dare say 'Good Words' is a very meritorious and very popular publication[1] but you see my feeling is against writing in Magazines. 'Why then did you'—I know the argument against me, but what I put in the Cornhill were things sui generis, experiments which I wished to try with the public.

I rejoice with you about Sir John Lawrence's appointment.[2] I was introduced to him last summer by Mrs. Prinsep but she said such very pretty things about him before his face that he fairly turned round his back upon me from pure modesty. I am sorry to hear from you that his health was much tried in 57–58. Why—why won't they transfer their metropolis to some loftier or at least healthier site?

My boys and their Tutor celebrated the Stanleian nuptials with the waving of red flags and salvos of percussion-caps from the top of the house. The marriage in the old Abbey by gaslight I hear was very imposing—the bride a little tremulous in her replies—but all went off well.[3]

While you sit not under your vine and figtree[4] at Rosneath but round your Christmas one with your little ones, you will I doubt not even from that home-circle be able to spare a touch of sympathy for poor Annie Thackeray who has just lost her father and whose mother has been for years in an asylum. I suppose you must have known him. A man of most kindly nature,

---

[1] The Duchess had written on 21 December (TRC): 'I should make Norman Macleod extremely grateful if I could persuade you to send him something for "Good Words"—and I should like to please him, as I think him an excellent Man. He has *not* asked me to do this. You know it is the best of all the *Cheap* periodicals, and you should be glad to help it. They are printing 1,500,000—for next year!' For Macleod, see below, p. ooo n.

[2] Sir John Laird Mair Lawrence (1811–79: *DNB*), created baronet, 1858; Indian Civil servant, 1830–59, whose counsel and action resulted in the capture of Delhi from the mutineers in 1857. After serving in the India Office, 1859–62, he had just been appointed Viceroy of India (1863–9); he was created Baron Lawrence of the Punjaub and of Grately in 1869. As Viceroy, he would live at Calcutta.

[3] The wedding of Lady Augusta Bruce and Arthur Penrhyn Stanley on 22 December. See *Journal*, p. 192.

[4] 1 Kings 4:25. The Duchess had written from Rosneath on 21 December (TRC): 'We are very happy here tho' Scotland is not really the right place for Xmas. A great gathering of the Children makes it very bright to me, and they are as happy and busy as they can be preparing the Tree.'

with a heart of true flesh and blood. It was only his outer husk that was cynical and that only in his books—as far as I knew him. His loss has much saddened my Christmas to me.[5]

All good things to yourself and the Duke from me and mine.

Ever affectionately yours
A. Tennyson

WILLIAM ALLINGHAM, *A DIARY*, pp. 93-5.

FARRINGFORD, Sunday, December 27, [1863]

A. T. comes in to breakfast without greeting, which is sometimes his way. I play football with the two Boys. (Hallam is about eleven, Lionel about nine.) Then walk with A. T., Palgrave, H. and L. along High Down to the Needles. Lionel talks to me; he is odd, shy, sweet, and, as his mother says, *daimonisch*. Hallam has something of a shrewd satirical turn, but with great good nature. To the cliff edge, then returning we creep up long slopes of down and rest at the Beacon. . . . We talk of 'Christabel.' Race down. . . . After dinner more talk of 'Classic Metres': in the drawing-room, T. standing on the hearth-rug repeated with emphasis (perhaps apropos of metres) the following lines, in the following way:—

> Higgledy-piggledy, silver and gold,
> (There's—(*it's nothing very dreadful!*))
> There's a louse on my back
> Seven years old.
> He inches, he pinches,
> In every part,
> And if I could catch him
> I'd *tearr* out his *hearrt!*

The last line he gave with tragic fury. Prose often runs into rhyme. T. imitated the waiter in some old-fashioned tavern calling down to the kitchen —'Three gravies, two mocks, and a *pea*'! (soup understood). On 'pea' he raised the tone and prolonged it very comically.

FARRINGFORD, December 28 [1863]

A. T., Palgrave and I walk to Alum Bay and look at the coloured cliffs, smeary in effect, like something spilt. A. T. reproves P. for talking so fast and saying 'of—of—of—of,' etc. He also corrects me for my pronunciation (or so he asserts) of 'dew.' 'There's no *Jew* on the grass!' says he—'there may be *dew*, but that's quite another thing.' He quotes Tom Moore's 'delicious

---

[5] On Christmas Day they heard the news of Thackeray's death on the 24th (*Journal*, p. 192). Winifred Gérin's statements (*Anne Thackeray Ritchie*, p. 141) that 'they hurried to London to bring what consolation they could', and that Tennyson attended the funeral or burial on 30 December are not substantiated by any evidence known to us. (Thackeray's wife died in 1894).

night,' etc. (four lines), with a little grunt of disapprobation at the end.[1] Home at four. T. goes to have his hot bath. . . .

At dinner: Mr. and Mrs. Bradley of Marlborough, Mr. and Mrs. Butler of Harrow.[2]

In the drawing-room A. T., P., and the two Bs. all on 'Classic Metres.' T. setting the schoolmasters right more than once, I noticed. . . . I had the ladies all to myself, and we discoursed profoundly on 'poets and practical people,' 'benevolence true and false,' 'the gulf between certain people and others,' etc. Mrs. T. confessed herself tired of hearing about 'Classic Metres.' The company gone, T., P. and I went to Palgrave's room, where the poet read to us the 'Vision of Sin,' the 'Sea Fairies,' and part of the 'Lotos Eaters,'—a rich and solemn music, but not at all heavy. He will not admit that any one save himself can read aloud his poems properly. He suffered me to try a passage in the 'Lotos Eaters' and said 'You do it better than most people,' and then read it himself and went on some way further. . . .

After breakfast I took leave of Mrs. Tennyson and the boys. . . . When I went to T.'s room he said, 'Come whenever you like,' and as I went out by the garden he came after me and saw me through the gate. Truly friendly—a delightful visit!

---

[1] 'The Kiss', from Moore's *Poetical Works of Thomas Little, Esq.* (1801), omitted from nearly all editions, and possibly the same lines that, ten years later, Tennyson quoted to James Henry Mangles 'as equal to Ros[s]etti in obscenity' (*Tennyson at Aldworth*, ed. Knies, pp. 103, 105–6). See also *Memoir*, ii. 71.

> Give me, my love, that billing kiss
> I taught you one delicious night,
> When, turning epicures in bliss,
> We tried inventions of delight.
>
> Come, gently steal my lips along,
> And let your lips in murmurs move,—
> Ah, no!—again—that kiss was wrong,—
> How can you be so dull my love?
>
> 'Cease, cease!' the blushing girl replied—
> And in her milky arms she caught me—
> 'How can you thus your pupil chide;
> You know *'t was in the dark* you taught me!'

[2] Henry Montagu Butler (1833–1918: *DNB*), Trinity College and an Apostle, Headmaster of Harrow (1860–85), Dean of Gloucester (1885–6), Master of Trinity (1886–1918), with his first wife Georgina Isabella Elliot (d. 1883). They married 18 December 1861, a date that poses problems. The 'Mr. Butler' who called at Farringford in March 1856 (*Journal*, p. 62) was a brother, Arthur Gray Butler (1831–1909: *DNB*), who married in 1877. The 'Mr. and Mrs. Butler and Mr. Galton' who called in April 1859 *could* have been either another brother (George, with his wife) or, which seems more likely, a slip for Montagu Butler and his sister and brother-in-law Francis Galton (1822–1911; knighted, 1909: *DNB*), 'founder of the science of "eugenics"' and also a Trinity man. Butler first met Tennyson on an 'Easter walking tour' with Galton 'in or about 1859' (Edward Graham, *The Harrow Life of Henry Montagu Butler*, p. 327, and Butler's 'Recollections of Tennyson', in *Tennyson and His Friends*, p. 207.

THE BRADLEYS VISIT TENNYSON

MS. Marian Bradley's 'Diaries', British Library.

Wednesday, December 30, [1863]

A white evening. After dinner G[ranville] and I went alone to Farringford. (G. walked to the Needles before with A. T.) He recited to us in a rolling, swift manner and a most musical manner his 'Voyage'—says it is a great favorite of his. He next read to us his tragedy 'Edith' [Sir Aylmer *added above the line*].[1] It is a common enough story but the manner of treating it is essentially his own. The master touch makes unutterably sweet and noble thoughts. . . . The story is told with such exquisite grace and tenderness and refinement. He said as he read from time to time how incalculably difficult the story was to tell, the dry facts of it so prosaic in themselves. He often stopped to point out how hard he had found such and such a piece, how much thought and work it had cost him. One was the lawyer in his chambers at work. Another the pompous old Aylmer in his wrath. A 3rd the suicide. He said when he began 'Edith is the heroine, you have an Edith.'[2] He asked me several times if I understood things or recognized allusions. 1. the red in the chestnut blossom, 2. the maximum and minimum [glory] of a star. 3. the tented hop-fields in winter. 'I pride myself on that observation', he said, 'have you ever seen the hop-poles piled up like tents in the bare fields in winter?' There were some exquisite descriptions of cottages covered with creepers, he pointed out one about the Traveller's Joy.[3] The description of Edith with the babies is charming, the five pink beads on the little feet. Emily laughed and said, 'I knew you would be charmed with that.' The parting of the Lovers in the dark rainy night under the 'roaring pines' we asked for again. The sermon 'Lo your house is left unto you desolate' is wonderful. We are to hear the rest another time. His glorious profile as he sat in the high back chair reading was most striking, there are lines furrowed deeper and deeper from brow to chin. There is a look in his face like a brightly burning light, like an inward fire consuming his life.

To JAMES THOMAS KNOWLES [?][1]

MS. Tennyson Research Centre.

[December 1863 ?]

Sir

I have been considering your questions but I am not a God or a disembodied spirit that I should answer them. I can only say, that I sympathize with your

---

[1] 'The Voyage' (Ricks, p. 653) and 'Aylmer's Field' (Ricks, p. 1159) both appeared in *Enoch Arden* (1864).

[2] Edith Nicoll Bradley (later Ellison), author of *A Child's Recollections of Tennyson* (1906).

[3] 'Traveller's Joy' (in 'Aylmer's Field', l. 153) is *Clematis Vitalba* (*OED*); see above, p. 000. The other references are to 'Aylmer's Field' ll. 65, 72–3, 110, 147–64, 413–31 ('parting of the lovers'), 635–721 and 735–97 ('Lo your house').

[1] So conjectured by Priscilla Metcalf (*James Knowles*, p. 168 and n.).

grief, and if faith mean anything at all, it is trusting to those instincts or feelings or whatever they may be called which assure us of some life after this.

[A. Tennyson]

To JAMES HANNAY[1]

MS. Eleanor Witty (transcript by George W. Worth).

FARRINGFORD, FRESHWATER, ISLE OF WIGHT, January 21, 1864

Sir

I am much obliged to you for your memorial of my friend, Thackeray.[2] It is well and gracefully written. I particularly admire your likening the poetry in his nature to the Impluvium in the Roman house—like it indeed as much as I dislike the slang word, 'Cads'—for which I trust that you will substitute another when you reprint your essay.

Yours faithfully
[A.] Tennyson

KATHERINE MARY BRUCE[1] *to* ALFRED TENNYSON

Text. *Dear and Honoured Lady*, pp. 79–80.

January 21, 1864

Dear Sir

The Queen desires me to return from Her hearty thanks for the beautiful lines you have so promptly sent Her. Beautiful as they are, your tried kindness induces the Queen to let you know honestly that they do not quite express Her idea.

The Dean[2] may not have explained that the Mausoleum is divided into two parts—a lower chamber where the sarcophagus is placed—and a totally distinct upper chamber which is approached by a different path and encircled by a terrace where seats are placed and flowers grown in ornamental vases and where if the Duchess had lived it was her intention often to take tea, etc. In the centre of this Gallery, the statue will be placed under a cupola—the

---

[1] James Hannay (1827–72: *DNB*), journalist and novelist, editor of the *Edinburgh Evening Courant* (1860–4), author of two naval novels, *Singleton Fontenoy* (1850) and *Eustace Conyers* (1855), had known Thackeray since 1848. See *The Thackeray Letters*, ed. Ray, ii. 583 n.

[2] *A Brief Memoir of the Late Mr. Thackeray* (Edinburgh, 1864).

[1] Katherine Mary Bruce (d. 1869), a bedchamber woman-in-ordinary to Queen Victoria (1866), second daughter of Sir Michael Shaw-Stewart, 6th Baronet, was the wife of Major-General Robert Bruce (1813–62), of the Grenadier Guards, second son of the 7th Earl of Elgin, whom she married in 1848, and sister-in-law of Lady Augusta Bruce Stanley and Lady Charlotte Locker.

[2] The Dean of Windsor, Gerald Valerian Wellesley (1809–82: *DNB*), domestic chaplain to the Queen, wrote on 18 January (TRC) saying that the Queen would be 'very much pleased' if he 'would compose four lines for her, to be placed beneath the statue of the Duchess of Kent', her mother, in the Mausoleum at Frogmore, 'as soon as possible'. Tennyson had sent four lines beginning 'O blessing of thy child as she was thine', with which the Queen was *not* 'very much pleased' (see below, p. 351), *Dear and Honoured Lady*, pp. 79–80; *Journal*, pp. 193–4.

statue represents the Duchess standing in full evening costume and the Queen wishes to remember Her mother as she was in Life.

Your lines H. M. thinks would be most appropriate on the tomb itself. If you would write another verse taking for your motto 'Her children arise and call her blessed' which is more the sentiment the Queen wishes to express, Her Majesty would be extremely obliged to you—She desires me to apologise for again troubling you and believe me

Yours truly
Katherine M. Bruce

EMILY SELLWOOD TENNYSON
to MARGARET GATTY (extract)

MS. Boston Public Library.

January 24, 1864

... Alfred feels the cold very much and is not by any means well as I would have him.

I cannot but feel that a great and good spirit left us on Christmas eve though I could not read his books indeed never read more than The Newcomes and a Christmas Tale but he loved that which was to be loved and hated that which was to be hated and no doubt [persuaded] many to do the same. I only saw him three times I think but he was an old friend of Alfred though latterly one rarely seen or heard from.[1] His poor daughters are here in a cottage lent them by Mrs. Cameron.

KATHERINE MARY BRUCE *to* ALFRED TENNYSON

Text. *Dear and Honoured Lady*, p. 80; *Materials*, ii. 391.

OSBORNE, January 27, [1864]

Dear Sir

The Queen desires me to return you Her very sincere thanks for the beautiful lines you have sent Her—and for all the trouble you have taken to meet Her wishes.

I have by Her Majesty's command already sent to the Sculptor a copy of the lines beginning 'Long as the heart beats life, etc.' to be engraved on the pedestal of the statue. Her Majesty preferred this verse both from the expression 'Guardian-Mother mild' which she particularly admired, as so descriptive of the Duchess, and also because the Queen did not quite like Herself putting 'O blessing of thy Child *as she was thine*' under the image of her Mother. H. M. thought it too presuming.[1]

Again thanking you in Her Majesty's name, believe me

Yours truly
Katherine M. Bruce

---

[1] See above, p. 347.

[1] See above, p. 350. The sculptor was William Theed (1804–91: *DNB*).

To FREDERICK JAMES FURNIVALL

MS. Huntington Library.

FARRINGFORD, FRESHWATER, ISLE OF WIGHT, [31 January 1864]

Dear Sir

Many thanks for your handsome 2nd volume of the Graal which however I feel that I scarce deserve not having yet read the first.[1] Thanks also for the Prick of Conscience[2] if I did not thank you before: if I did not I ought to feel it: but I don't: so I suppose I did.

[Yours very truly
A. Tennyson][3]

To EMILY SELLWOOD TENNYSON

Text. Materials, ii. 392.

LONDON, February 9, 1864

Arrived all safe and found a fire and Spedding came in, and presently after the MSS poems 'Enoch Arden' etc. arrived. I have seen no one as yet.

February 10, 1864

I saw Evans yesterday and have given him 'Enoch' to print, not to publish, and I am going to give him the others.[1]

To EMILY SELLWOOD TENNYSON

Text. Materials, ii. 393–4.

LONDON, February [12, 1864][1]

I dined at Palgrave's yesterday and heard some of his brother's Arabian talk— very interesting. Gladstone came in for two hours and listened very

---

[1] See above, pp. 238, 268–9.

[2] Richard Rolle's *The Pricke of Conscience*, ed. Richard Morris (1863), and inscribed to Tennyson by Furnivall (*Tennyson in Lincoln*, i, No. 1899).

[3] Note by Furnivall: 'Signature given to —— 21 Jan. 1868.'

[1] On the 11th he dined with Frederick Pollock, Spedding, John Tyndall (1820–93: *DNB*)— the natural philosopher, popularizer of science, and Alpinist—and Sir John Frederick William Herschel (1792–1871)—the famous astronomer and favourite (since 1837) of Mrs Cameron (Pollock, *Personal Remembrances*, ii. 117).

[1] Date in *Materials*, iv. 296–7.

intently, and when he learnt Hallam's age he was very decided about the necessity of sending him to school instantly.[2]

TENNYSON AND WALTER WHITE

Text. *The Journals of Walter White*, pp. 155–6.

February 13, 1864.

Tennyson called on me this afternoon. I gave him two sorts of Hungarian wine to taste. He liked the Oedenberg.[1] I asked him about 'Enoch the Fisherman' which I had seen mentioned in the 'Reader.'[2] He answered that he had had a proof more than a year, could not yet make up his mind to publish. His friend Spedding liked it. He had been at Palgrave's the evening before; the Eastern Palgrave was there and talked of his travels, every one listening intently. Gladstone, Chancellor of the Exchequer, called in, and he listened with the others. Then the Laureate recited a ballad poem in the Lincolnshire dialect; an old farmer on his deathbed talks to his maid; will have his beer (yale); tells her what the Doctor and the Parson have been talking about.[3] He stayed an hour, and on departing, invited me to breakfast with him and Woolner at Spedding's.

February 14, 1864

At 9.30 to Spedding's. 60 Lincoln['s] Inn Fields. I was looking at the old engravings on the wall, when Tennyson entered and proposed a quarter of a mile's walk before breakfast, his usual practice, he said. So we walked up and

[2] Palgrave and Tennyson witnessed the signing of Browning's will on this occasion (*Memoir*, ii. 490–1). Thomas Knyvett Richmond (later Canon of Carlisle), son of George Richmond (1809–96: *DNB*) the portrait painter, arrived at 9.30; he wrote: 'I had heard that Browning was to be there, but was in no way prepared for the great assembly of wit. There were there, in order, Clifford [*sic*] Palgrave (the Eastern explorer), Tennyson, Dr. Ogle, Sir Francis Doyle, Francis T. Palgrave ('Golden Treasury'), Gladstone, Browning, Palgrave, Sir John Sim[e]on, and Woolner.... The talk when I entered was on the English education of boys, whether they ought to be taught Latin and Greek verse; to which all agreed.... Ogle and Sir Francis left ... and as they were going, says Tennyson, "I would not have my children smoke. It's all very well for a studious man, but it ruins an active man. I am sorry to hear the P. of W. smokes so. A King, even an English King, should be an active man." Then ensued a battle royal between Browning and Tennyson about John Forster's cutting Macready and being rude to Tennyson.... I shall never forget the evening. The grand head and shoulders, the tender yet powerful eyes of Tennyson. The sharpness and coxcombry of little Browning. The bad manners of Woolner and his horrid laugh. The grace of Gifford Palgrave. The tender power of Gladstone, and the odd, funny expression of Sir Francis Doyle' (A. M. W. Stirling, *The Richmond Papers*, pp. 175–7).

[1] Tennyson had weathered the Harrogate storm (see above, pp. 339, 340), but had not yet reached harbour. On 11 March 1864 Woolner wrote to Lady Trevelyan about this London visit: 'Tennyson was in town a short while back.... He was in capital spirits and unusually well, though I believe, the doctor forbidding him his usual allowance of port, the poor Bard had to content himself with sherry' (Raleigh Trevelyan, 'Thomas Woolner: Pre-Raphaelite Sculptor', *Apollo*, March 1978, p., 204).

[2] *The Reader: A Review of Literature, Science, and Art* (1863–7).

[3] 'Northern Farmer, Old Style' (Ricks, p. 1123).

down the north side of the Fields in the sunshine, he trying at times to outstrip me, but I told him I had learnt *tall* walking in America. As we returned to the house we saw some spilt milk on the pavement, and he would finger the congealed liquid to try whether it was really milk or chalk, and said he had once seen milk spilt on a doorstep evaporate and leave a layer of chalk! 'We should be mobbed,' he said, 'if this were a week day.' Soon after we remounted to Chambers, Spedding entered, a man with a Czechist's form of head, thoughtful-looking, and exact in his speech. Presently Woolner came and we sat down (Tennyson introduced me to Spedding as the 'author of Northumberland'). 'No, not exactly that, for "Northumberland" was created before he went there.' (It reminds me of 'The Heavens' by the author of 'The Earth and Sea,' one Mudie.)[4] There was no remarkable talk. After breakfast Tennyson and Woolner retired to smoke. Spedding and I talked till 12.30. . . . Then I went into the adjoining room to say good-bye to the smokers. Tennyson told a few good stories and invited me to Farringford.

To EMILY SELLWOOD TENNYSON

MS. Tennyson Research Centre.

Tuesday, [16 February 1864]

Dearest

Very likely 'tooth and nail' will go out.[1] Woolner and Spedding like the 2d poem.[2] Woolner says I never wrote anything more finished but he can't quite reconcile himself to the Indian, thinks the story does not *need* him though he grants that his objection very likely arises from the man not having been in the original tale. I have just given the Farmer and the Voyage to be printed.[3] The shirts arrived but truly I didn't feel the want of them as I get washed twice a week. Evans regrets that I did not send Enoch as a Christmas book. He would have printed it in an octavo he says at 4s.6 and I should make lots of cash. I suggested him the doing so now, as the poem would afterwards sell equally well in the smaller type. He will think of it.

Thine
A. T. x x x x x x

Love.

I am just going to hear Tyndall lecture on the sun.[4] My shaky hand on the direction is mimic for the P. O.

---

[4] Robert Mudie (1777–1842: *DNB*), author of 'about 90 volumes', including *The Elements: the Heavens, the Earth, the Air, the Sea*, published in 1837 (Allibone).

[1] Unidentified, but it suggests 'Boadicea' (l. 11?).

[2] 'Aylmer's Field' and, below, 'Northern Farmer, Old Style' and 'The Voyage' (Ricks, pp. 1159, 1123, 653). For 'the Indian' in 'Aylmer's Field', ll. 190–233, see below, p. 381 n.

[3] Interpolated here in *Materials*, ii. 392: 'I get a Turkish bath twice a week.'

[4] At the Royal Institution. Tyndall inscribed a copy of *Heat Considered as a Mode of Motion* (1863) to Tennyson on 14 February (*Tennyson in Lincoln*, i, No. 2245).

To EMILY SELLWOOD TENNYSON

MS. Tennyson Research Centre.

Wednesday [17 February 1864], 4 ¾ o'cl.

Dearest

Of course I'm vext about the c[*paper torn*] being clapt down at my gates. Certainly in that case I will not subscribe—it cannot be expected of me. I now shout up for Pri[t]chard's ⟨plan⟩ sale [?] and am thoroughly against Isaacson.[1]

Both of them ought to know that they are acting against me. I especially wonder at Pri[t]chard. I shan't be slow when I come back of telling them my mind about it. In the meantime tell them I as far as I am concerned and as far as my power lies will fight against them. I think you had better not *yet* get a valuer [?]; he may be very expensive and one may gain nothing by it. I saw Paddison[2] this morning but we did not talk much business: I only took him my Lincolnshire poem to see if he thought it good Lincolnshire—which he did with one exception I think. I saw Mother on Sunday looking very well.

Thine × × ×
A. T. ×

It's so dark I can't see what I've written.[3]

To EMILY SELLWOOD TENNYSON

MS. Tennyson Research Centre.

[19 February 1864][1]

Dearest

I dined at Gladstone's yesterday—Duke and Duchess there—Froude[2] and others—evening agreeable—but I can't abide the dinners. You were asked after by many and the boys too—'your two "beautiful" boys'—don't let'em

---

[1] Probably the proposed new road (see below, p. 374). John Frederick Isaacson (1801–86) was Rector of All Saints, Freshwater Parish Church (Venn; see below, p. 447 n.). Charles Pritchard (1809–93: *DNB*), astronomer, Savilian professor, Oxford, from 1870. In 1862 he had relinquished the headmastership of Clapham Grammar School (where he had taught George Grove and James T. Knowles), and settled with his family at Hurst Hill, Freshwater Parish, Isle of Wight. He was ordained in 1834. 'Farringford . . . was the nearest habitation in constant occupation, and between the poet and my father there grew up a very sincere friendship and regard. During my father's residence at Freshwater, he frequently occupied the pulpits of neighbouring churches, and occasionally acted as *locums tenens* for one of the clergy' (Ada Pritchard, *Charles Pritchard . . . Memoirs of His Life*, pp. 82, 90).

[2] Richard Paddison, solicitor (see above, p. 305).

[3] Evening of the 17th: 'Dined with Woolner, with whom Tennyson usually stayed at this time when in London. Met him, Spedding, F. Palgrave (with whom Tennyson used to stay). A. T. read to us "The Aylmers." and "The Lincolnshire Farmer", the names of which were not then definitely fixed' (Pollock, *Personal Remembrances*, ii. 118).

[1] Postmark.

[2] James Anthony Froude (1819–94: *DNB*), the historian, was editor of *Fraser's Magazine*, 1860–74. Later, as Carlyle's executor and biographer, he offended many, including Tennyson, who (Froude heard) accused him of selling his 'master for thirty pieces of silver', an accusation that Hallam Tennyson emphatically denied (20 March 1882, TRC).

see this. Now I'm beginning to be plagued, as you see, and I shall soon have to cut and run.

Thine
A. T. × × × × × ×

Mrs. L[ubbock]³ was introduced to me at Tyndall's lecture—an enthusiastic worshipper he described her—but I don't think I can go. Snowing here quite fast.

To EMILY SELLWOOD TENNYSON

MS. Tennyson Research Centre.

Saturday 19 or 20 [actually 20], [February 1864]

Dearest

I suppose I shall return some time early next week. Tyndall wants me to read Enoch at the Royal Institution where he gives his lectures, but I am hardly likely to do it. Spedding does not conceive there can be any offence in the Farmer—nor does Evans. Snow here today but not particularly cold. I have not yet answered the London Shakespearians: but I met Flower the Stratford Mayor in the street this morning and he asked me for an Ode—won't get it.¹

Thine
A. T. × × × × × ×

I shall not publish till May.

To EMILY SELLWOOD TENNYSON

Text. Materials, ii. 393–4.

LONDON, February 23, [1864]

I went yesterday to the Lubbocks and had a pleasant evening. She is a very nice creature with enthusiastic eyes—but she is not beyond bounds as some women are; and he is scientific and showed me a wonderful collection of flints, taken from mounds in Denmark. Tyndall took immense care of me yesterday.

---

³ The former Ellen Frances Hordern (d. 1879), first wife of John Lubbock (1834–1913; succeeded as 4th Baronet, 1865; created Baron Avebury, 1900: *DNB*), banker, scientist, MP for Maidstone, Kent, and then for University of London, and one of the founding members of the Metaphysical Society. See below and Horace G. Hutchinson, *Portraits of the Eighties,* pp. 133–44.

¹ Edward Fordham Flower (1805–83: *DNB*) was a highly successful brewer in Stratford-on-Avon, where he wsa four times mayor. He moved to London in 1873, and wrote several books on harnesses, bearing-reins, and gag-bits for horses in the interest of reducing their suffering. The Working Men's Shakespeare Committee planned a public demonstration and the planting of an oak at the foot of Primrose Hill, to mark the tercentenary of Shakespeare's birth on 23 April. See below, pp. 359, 361. Of the Ode, Tennyson said: 'They all look upon me as a boot-maker . . . and think that I can make a poem as a boot-maker does a pair of boots—to order' (*Materials,* ii. 397 n.).

LONDON, February 24, [1864]

I am getting on very well but have made no calls being much engaged with my sheets.[1] I missed Gifford Palgrave's Lecture at the 'Geographical' by going out to dine, I am told it was magnificent.

LONDON, February 26, [1864]

I have got all the things printed but I am going to keep them at present.

To THE DUCHESS OF ARGYLL
MS. Tennyson Research Centre.

60 LINCOLN'S INN FIELDS, Friday, [? 26 February 1864]

My dear Duchess

I have not gone today as I told your servant I should: I shall make another attempt to see you and the Duke on Sunday afternoon.* I only missed you—through the stupidity of my cabman who could not find the way—by two minutes.

Ever yours
A. Tennyson

*About 4 or a little later. If you will not be at home, will you send me a line to say so.[1]

To EMILY SELLWOOD TENNYSON
Text. *Materials*, ii. 394.

LONDON, February 28, [1864]

The Duke of Argyll has just been calling as I called and found them from home. I read him the 'Voyage.' He volunteered to come to Farringford again in the Spring. The other day I had a bath at the 'Old Hummums' and the waiter delivered me a letter written in 1861.

---

[1] Proof sheets of *Enoch Arden*, published in August.

[1] He dined at Woolner's. William Bell Scott (1811–90), the painter, dropping in, 'came upon a large party over their wine after dinner. Tennyson, Holman Hunt, the two Palgraves, Fairbairn, Spedding, and a lot more. It was a stroke of luck. Woolner you may imagine now goes in for the great style, with an unexceptionable white chocker to serve, and no end of visiting acquaintances. He says he must go out to everybody because they are his employers— different from a painter who almost never sells a picture in London to a private purchaser' (W. E. Fredeman, 'The Letters of Pictor Ignotus: William Bell Scott's Correspondence with Alice Boyd, 1859–1884', *Bulletin of the John Rylands University Library, Manchester*, lviii [Autumn 1975, Spring 1976], 21). Browning, invited, was already engaged: 'I never see enough of Tennyson, nor yet to talk with him about subjects we either of us value at three straws, I suppose: but I always enjoy smelling (even) his tobacco smoke' (Amy Woolner, *Thomas Woolner*, p. 244).

To JOHN FORSTER

MS. Tennyson Research Centre.

60 LINCOLN'S INN FIELDS, [29 February 1864][1]

My dear Forster

Doubtless I have felt myself much aggrieved—my grievance being it seems the same as yours—that I was dropt. Since it appears that we were both mistaken, let the mistake on both sides go by as a dream of the night and *nevermore* be mentioned.[2]

I hear that you are out of town, and likely to be so for some time and I myself leave town tomorrow, so that I have no chance of seeing you now, but believe me,

Yours as ever
A. Tennyson

EMILY SELLWOOD TENNYSON to CHARLES RICHARD WELD

MS. Tennyson Research Centre.

[? early March 1864]

My dear Charles

He thinks 'Manes'[1] for so it is in old books but he does not think it signifies which. We shall delight in watching the storm-glass but we never even dreamed of you giving us either yours or another. It is very good in you to give it. I congratulate you on the completion of the book. May it succeed to your heart's content.

Your affectionate sister-in-law
Emily Tennyson

To CHARLES RICHARD WELD

MS. Tennyson Research Centre.

[? early March 1864]

My dear Weld

Many thanks. I really didn't mean to beg it. I have no doubt it will be of great use and interest to us.

Ever yours
A. Tennyson

---

[1] Postmark.
[2] Apparently the tiff of 12 February, when Forster was 'rude to Tennyson': 'He asked Tennyson to dine, and T. said, "It's against my principles to dine out". *Forster*: "All your principles are eccentric", and this seemed to stick in the poet's gizzard' (A. M. W. Stirling, *The Richmond Papers*, p. 176). See above, p. 353 n., and below, p. 379.

[1] 'The deified souls of departed ancestors (as beneficent spirits)' (*OED*), probably for use in Weld's book *Last Winter in Rome* (1865; see *Tennyson in Lincoln*, i, No. 3404). Tennyson uses the word below, p. 362.

? early March 1864

To EDWARD FORDHAM FLOWER

MS. Shakespeare Birthplace Trust.

[? early March 1864]

Dear Sir

I gave you my answer to this request when I had the pleasure of meeting you in the street so suddenly. There are many others who will deem it an honour to be applied to, and really at present I am so knocked up or down by Influenza that I am incapable of a line.[1]

Yours truly
A. Tennyson

To FREDERICK JAMES FURNIVALL

MS. Huntington Library.

FARRINGFORD, FRESHWATER, ISLE OF WIGHT, March 2, 1864

My dear Sir

I will give you my guinea—my name too if you want it: but I do not much see the use of creating a presidentship.[1]

Yours very truly
A. Tennyson

I have only just now returned home and found your note.

To WILLIAM ROBERT GIBLIN[1]

MS. Yale.

FARRINGFORD, FRESHWATER, ISLE OF WIGHT, March 5, 1864

Sir

I regret that from illness and absence and other causes your letters have been so long without acknowledgement. Not knowing which photographs you have, my wife wishes me to send you this, which she considers most like the original.

Accept my sincerest thanks for all the kind things you say to me and believe me with every good wish

Truly yours
[A. Tennyson]

---

[1] See above, p. 356.

[1] Probably for the Early English Text Society, founded in 1864.

[1] William Robert Giblin (1840–87), Tasmanian Premier (1878, 1879–84), as well as Treasurer and from time to time Attorney-General and puisne judge of the Supreme Court (1885). He was admitted to the bar, and founded the Hobart Working Men's Club in 1864. 'He was also a founder and teacher of the Congregational Sunday School and helped in forming football teams to discourgae larrikinism' (*Australian Dictionary of Biography*). The letter is entirely in Emily Tennyson's hand and addressed by her: W. R. Gib*b*in Esqre | Stone Buildings | Hobart Town | Van Diemen's Land.

16 March 1864

To THE DUCHESS OF ARGYLL

MS. Tennyson Research Centre.

Wednesday, [16 March 1864]

My dear Duchess

Is this the photograph you allude to—one by Rejlander the Swede?[1] We think it a good one: the glass is unfortunately broken, but we have three or four left and if you like it, take it.

I am quite as indignant at Oxford as you are. She will have to sing her palinode I conjecture before many moons are over. We expect Mr. Jowett here on Monday, and though he is not one to be bowed down by half a score of universities railing at him I am sure he will be pleased with your indignation at the injustice done him.[2]

Ever yours
A. Tennyson

THE JOURNALS OF WALTER WHITE, pp. 157–8.

March 25, [1864]

At 9 a.m. by steamer to Yarmouth. . . . Walked hence to Farringford. Came to Tennyson's at ten, had an agreeable welcome. Introduced to Mr. Lawrance, who was taking a crayon portrait of the Poet. Then talk with Allingham, a rymer not unknown to fame. Then walk in plantations amid primroses and daffodils. At lunch introduced to Professor Jowett and Mr. Wilson, the tutor. Afternoon walk on the Downs. Dine at six.

Saturday, Sunday [26–7 March 1864]

Football with the boys and ramble with Allingham and the Laureate. In the evening I introduced the subject of pronunciation, with a view to learn what opinions were as to the subject. I contended that pho*to*graphy should be phot*ography* and the like. Sunday, to Freshwater Church with Professor Jowett and Hallam Tennyson. Afternoon, called on Henry Taylor, author of 'Philip van Artevelde,' and a walk to foot of cliffs by Watcomb Bay and on the Downs. After dinner, talk about Cosmology.

---

[1] Tennyson had been photographed several times by Oscar G. Rejlander (1813–75), fashionable with royalty and others—most recently in May 1863 (see *Journal*, pp. 184–5). (See also Wheatcroft, *The Tennyson Album*, pp. 88–9; Richard Ormond, *Early Victorian Portraits*, i. 454–5; and *Tennyson in Lincoln*, ii, Nos. 6032–51.)

[2] The last rumblings of the storm over *Essays and Reviews*. The prosecution of Jowett having failed, his remuneration as Professor of Greek, as a result of a vote before Convocation on 8 March, remained at £40 a year, where it rested until it was increased to £500 in 1865. (See Geoffrey Faber, *Jowett*, pp. 272–82, and *DNB*.) Allingham, at Farringford 'for an Easter holiday' 24–8 March, wrote: 'Professor Jowett was staying at a neighbouring house with two Oxford pupils, and came in to Tennyson's every day. One day T., J., and myself on the shore, throwing pebbles into the sea. Alas, I fear I have not set down anything of the conversation. This is usually the way when there is too much' (*Diary*, p. 97).

March 28, [1864]

After breakfast the poet showed me proofs of his forthcoming volume. I had only time to look at one or two little poems, and to see that there was one on 'Boadicea,' and at 11 a.m. I departed, walked to Yarmouth, and arrived in London at 6 p.m.

To GEORGE LINNAEUS BANKS[1]

MS. Shakespeare Institute, Birmingham.

FARRINGFORD, FRESHWATER, ISLE OF WIGHT, April 10, 1864

Sir

If this be, as you assure me it is, a genuine movement of the Working Classes, I would suggest that the honour of planting the Shakespeare oak should belong to one of themselves.

Let Alfred Shakespear rather than Alfred Tennyson plant the tree: then it will be doubly Shakespeare's oak and long may it live and flourish! Believe me, with all thanks,

Faithfully yours
A. Tennyson

Your letter only reached me this morning.

To ?

MS. Folger Shakespeare Library.

April 13, 1864

Sir

I beg to thank you for your kindness in forwarding me the invitation with which the Mayor of Birmingham has honoured me for the 23rd of April.[1] Will you say with my best thanks that it is not in my power to avail myself of it. I wish success to your Library. Its dedication on such a day seems to me most appropriate. I have the honour to be, Sir,

Your very obedient servant
A. Tennyson

[1] George Linnaeus Banks (1821–81: *DNB*), cabinet-maker by trade, amateur actor, orator, and editor (1848–64) of six newspapers, including the *Birmingham Mercury*. The author of poems and plays, he took a leading part in the Shakespeare tercentenary celebration. Samuel Phelps (1804–78: *DNB*), actor and theatre manager, 'performed the ceremonial office with an oak sapling that the Queen had donated for the occasion from Windsor Forest' (see *Annual Register*, pp. 64–7).

[1] For the tercentenary celebration a committee in Birmingham had undertaken to establish a collection of books on Shakespeare's life and writings that the city would then operate as a 'permanent, ever-increasing, and free' library (*Athenaeum*, 6 February, p. 196).

To MRS EDWARD FORDHAM FLOWER[1]

MS. Folger Shakespeare Library.

April 16, 1864

My dear Mrs. Flower

Three hundred thanks to yourself and your husband for your hospitable invitation to the Tercentenary at Stratford. If ever I mingled with pomp, pageant or festival I would come to yours, not only to do homage to the manes of Shakespeare but in memory of old days spent with kind friends in your neighbourhood.[2]

I trust that all will go well. To such of your family as may be with you on this occasion, and whom I know, give my best remembrances and believe me,

Always yours truly
A. Tennyson

To ARTHUR SEWELL[1]

MS. Indiana University.

FARRINGFORD, April 22, 1864

Dear Sir

You can publish the words with your music, if you will. All these songs have been set before more than once. Perhaps you are not aware of this.

Yours truly
A. Tennyson

2 songs from the Miller's Daughter
Break, break, break
The Poet's Song

Arthur Sewell Esq.

---

[1] Celina Greaves (1805–84: *DNB*), who married E. F. Flower in 1827.

[2] See i. 181. Even a festival-goer would have required stamina. The celebration at Stratford began with a banquet for some '700 ladies and gentlemen', lasting from 3 to 7.30 p.m., at which thirteen toasts were drunk, and was followed by 'a brilliant display of fireworks'. It included two sermons (one by R. C. Trench, Archbishop of Dublin), concerts, choral offerings, readings, performances of four of Shakespeare's plays, and concluded with 'a grand fancy ball' (*Annual Register*). The attendance, however, was not so large as expected, and the festival incurred 'a serious loss' (*Athenaeum*, 4 June, p. 77).

[1] Arthur Sewell (1841–?), son of Robert Burleigh Sewell, of Ashcliff, Bonchurch, IW (whose wife was the eldest daughter of George Turner Seymour, from whom Tennyson bought Farringford), was at this time an undergraduate 'choral scholar' at New College, Oxford, (BA 1866), and later was chaplain of the Order of St. John of Jerusalem (Foster; Montague Charles Owen, *The Sewells of the Isle of Wight*, p. 62). No Tennyson settings by him are listed in Gooch and Thatcher.

To JAMES PAGET

MS. Berg Collection.

FARRINGFORD, FRESHWATER, ISLE OF WIGHT, *April 25, 1864*

My dear Mr. Paget

H. B. Elliott (formerly Palgrave's servant) who waited upon me when I was under your care at Yorkgate[1] has asked me to give him a recommendation to yourself or some other medical man. I can bear honest testimony as to his being a very assiduous and tender sick-nurse. If (as the poor man is out of place) you could recommend him to any invalid who might require such an attendant, or put him into any situation whereby he might earn his bread you would add to my prior obligations to you.

I trust that you and yours are well. Believe me, dear Mr. Paget,

Always yours
A. Tennyson

P.S. I would not have troubled you except that I really believe the man would prove useful, and that I myself feel grateful to him, and bound to listen to his request.

To LOUIS CHARLES TENNYSON-D'EYNCOURT

Text. Charles Tennyson, *Alfred Tennyson*, p. 349.

[? early May 1864]

She had been hidden from me and my family for so many years—ever in fact since we left Lincolnshire—that the grave is only a deeper hiding.[1] Had she ever expressed a wish to see me or any of us, I or they would have gone to her immediately, but I don't suppose she did. Peace be with her! I remember her in her days of kindness when we lived near each other, and should have been glad to have seen her once again—and I don't know why I never volunteered to go to her—except, perhaps, that I knew her to be one of the most wayward and at times violent of human beings, and might possibly have been received very harshly. Still, I ought to have gone, I think.

To GIULIO [or JULIUS] TENNYSON (incomplete)

MS. Tennyson Research Centre.

FARRINGFORD, [? early May 1864]

My dear Giulio

(or Julius perhaps you prefer to be called—have it which way you like.) I

---

[1] See above, p. 333.

[1] Tennyson's aunt, Mary Tennyson Bourne (see i. 3 n.). She outlived her husband by fourteen years, which she spent in 'wandering about from one health resort to another, quarreling furiously and dramatically with landladies and companions and attacking her diseases, which, like all Tennysons, she believed to be many and severe, with "fierce medicines and strict regimen"' (*Background*, p. 34).

am glad you have got your lieutenancy and I trust you will do honour to it.[1] As for long letters I never write them to anyone. You want to know about Garibaldi.[2] Well he came over here and sat with me some three quarters of an hour and smoked his cigar in my little room upstairs which I dare say you remember and quoted Ugo Foscolo and wrote out for me some of his (Ugo's) verses which he particularly admired— from Dei Sepolcri—do you know the poem? Also we talked about Italy although I did not always understand him nor he me. He said 'I have a Campaign in me yet' but I hope he won't set about it yet, for I see but little chance for Italy at present. He is a man of noble presence and noble manners, a true gentleman it seems to me—

To THE DUKE OF ARGYLL

Text. Tennyson Research Centre (transcript); *Memoir,* ii. 3–4.

FARRINGFORD, [mid-] May, 1864

My dear Duke

'Did you hear him repeat any Italian poetry?' I did, for I had heard that he himself had made songs and hymns: and I asked him 'Are you a poet?' 'Yes' he said quite simply. Whereupon I spouted to him a bit of Manzoni's great ode,[1] that which Gladstone translated. I don't know whether he relished it but he began immediately to speak of Ugo Foscolo and quoted with great fervour a fragment of his Carme sui Sepolcri beginning with 'Il navigante che veleggio' etc. and ending with 'delle Parche in canto,' which verses he afterwards wrote out for me: and they certainly seem to be fine, whatever the rest of the poem may be.[2] I have not yet read it but mean to do so, for he sent me Foscolo's Poesie from London and in return I sent him the Idylls of the King which I do not suppose he will care for. What a noble human being! I expected to see a hero and I was not disappointed. One cannot exactly say of him exactly what Chaucer says of the ideal knight, 'As meke he was of port as is a maid,'[3] he is more majestic than meek and his manners have a certain divine simplicity in them such as I have never witnessed in a native of these islands—among men at least—and they are gentler than those of most young maidens I know. He came here and smoked his cigar in my little room and we had a half hour's talk in English, though I doubt whether he understood me perfectly and his meaning was often obscure to me. I ventured to give him

---

[1] Julius Tennyson, Frederick's eldest son, 'was reputed the strongest man in the British army' (*Background,* p. 104).

[2] For Garibaldi's visit, see *Annual Register,* pp. 44–58, *Journal,* pp. 196–8; and the next letter.

[1] 'Il Cinque Maggio' (1823), on the death of Napoleon, 5 May 1821, by Alessandro Manzoni (1785–1873), poet and novelist.

[2] Argyll had heard Garibaldi repeat from memory the whole of the 'Dei Sepolcri'—'a plaintive, cold, rather heathenish poem which is his great favorite. . . . He shocked Gladstone by showing comparatively little appreciation of Dante. . . . His horror of the Romish Priesthood, and his ignorance of religion in any better form, has divorced him from all definite belief: and in this way as well as in others, some of the best parts of Dante are a sealed book to Him' (15 May, TRC).

[3] Prologue to *The Canterbury Tales,* l. 69.

a little advice for I had heard from an officer here that [one] of his suite was anything but a gentleman and likely to get him involved: he denied that he came with any political purpose to England, merely to thank the English for their kindness to him and the interest they had taken in himself and all Italian matters and also to consult Ferguson[4] about his leg. Stretching this out he said 'There's a campaign in me yet.' When I asked if he returned through France he said 'he would never set foot on the soil of France again'. I happened to make use of this expression 'That fatal debt of gratitude owed by Italy to Napoleon.' 'Gratitude,' he said, 'hasn't he had his pay? his reward?[5] If Napoleon were dead I should be glad and if I were dead he would be glad.' These are slight chroniclings but I thought you would like to have them. He seemed especially taken with my two little boys.

As to sea blue birds, etc. defendant states—that he was walking one day in March by a deep banked brook and under the leafless bushes he saw the kingfisher flitting or fleeting underneath him and there came into his head and a fragment of an old Greek lyric poet

$$\mathrm{\dot{\alpha}\lambda\iota\pi\acute{o}\rho\phi\upsilon\rho o\varsigma\ \xi\acute{\iota}\alpha\rho o\varsigma\ \acute{o}\rho\nu\iota\varsigma^6}$$

'The sea-purple or sea-shining Bird of Spring,' spoken of as the Halcyon. Defendant cannot say whether the Greek Halcyon be the same as the British Kingfisher, but as he never saw the Kingfisher on this particular brook before March, he concludes that in that country at least, they go down to the sea during the hard weather and come up again with the spring, for what says old Belon.[7]

> Le Martinet-pescheur fait sa demeure
> En temps d'hiver au bord de l'océan
> Et en este sur la rivière en estan
> Et de poisson se repaist à toute heure.

You see he puts 'este' which I suppose stands for all the warmer weather. Was not the last letter in the 'Field' written by yourself?[8]

---

[4] Sir William Fergusson (1808–77; *DNB*), created 1st Baronet, 1866, perhaps the most eminent British surgeon at the time. As a part of the ministry's desire to reduce the number of Garibaldi's visits to some fifty provincial cities and towns, Palmerston wrote to the Queen: 'Mr. Fergusson, the surgeon, upon being consulted, gave a written opinion that the exertions of mind and body, which such visits would involve, would be more than the General in his weak state of health could bear' (Christopher Hibbert, *Garibaldi and His Enemies*, p. 347). In fact, Garibaldi was hustled out of the country, not only on account of his health, but also 'because of the endless jealousies and ill-blood that could be roused if he visited a town in Lancashire and omitted visiting some other in another county); and . . . all things considered, the sooner he returned to his home in Caprera the better' (Ronald Gower, *My Reminiscences*, p. 152). So he was taken by the Duchess Dowager of Sutherland (Gower's mother) on a visit to Cliveden and then dispatched.

[5] Nice and Savoy.   [6] Alcman, Fragment 26.

[7] Pierre Belon (1517–64), naturalist and writer, *Portraits d'oyseauz . . . Le tout enrichy de quatrains* (1557).

[8] Argyll, in his letter of 15 May, had alluded to 'a furious controversy' in *The Field* about the identity of the bird and the accuracy of Tennyson's reference in *In Memoriam* (xci): 'Flits by the sea-blue bird of March'. He quoted the last letter as saying, 'I know all about it—from

366   7 *May* 1864

Ever my dear Duke with all kind things from myself and wife to the Duchess

Yours
A. Tennyson

We are sorry not to have seen you at Farringford in the time of flowers, let us know when you can come. I hope the Queen is well and able to enjoy this fine weather.

To ?[1]

MS. University of Virginia.

FARRINGFORD, FRESHWATER, ISLE OF WIGHT, May 7, 1864

Sir

I am pillaged in such wholesale fashion without leave that I have been obliged to make restrictions. I have however pleasure in saying that you are at liberty to include 'New Year's Eve' and 'Lazarus' (The Brook I think is spoilt by being detached from its context) in your selection of School Poetry. I have the honour to be, Sir,

Your obedient servant
A. Tennyson

JOHN STUART BLACKIE[1]
to ELIZABETH WYLD BLACKIE (extract)

Text. *The Letters of John Stuart Blackie to His Wife*, ed. Archibald Stoddart Walker (Edinburgh and London: Blackwood), 1909), pp. 151–2.

FARRINGFORD, FRESHWATER, ISLE OF WIGHT, May 10, [1864]

Yesterday morning after breakfast I came here to this quiet, wooded and truly English little mansion. The lady of the house received me in the most gracious manner. She is of the genuine, sweet-blooded, sweet-voiced English style; pleasant expression; neatly dressed in black and white in a sort of loose

---

Tennyson himself. The Seablue Bird is a kingfisher', and added, 'my verdict is twofold. 1st that I don't know what connects the kingfisher with March. 2nd that if it be the kingfisher 'darts' would be better than 'flits' because the kingfisher goes past one like a flash of bluelightning. It is a wonderful flight.' Acceding to Argyll's observation but unwilling to change a line that had stood so long, Tennyson annotated it in the Eversley Edition: ' "Darts the sea-shining bird of May" would best suit the kingfisher.' Argyll stood mum about the authorship of the letter.

[1] Unidentified, but see above, p. 268, and below, p. 524; possibly, *Reading Book for Evening Schools Designed for the Use of the More Advanced Classes*, ed. C. Kegan Paul (1864).

[1] John Stuart Blackie (1809–95: *DNB*), Scottish professor and man of letters, was Professor of Greek at the University of Edinburgh (1852–82). Genial, gregarious, and resolutely eccentric, he wrote voluminously, and translated *Faust*, Aeschylus, and *The Iliad*. In 1842 he married Elizabeth Wyld; they had no children. The Tennysons' response to him was as favourable as his to them: 'We like the good, kind, wild man. . . . The Professor sings "The Genie with the Crooked Horn" and approves of our new carpet with its silver stars' (Journal). See also J. M. Barrie, *An Edinburgh Eleven*, ch. 3, and below, p. 410.

flowing, open, morning style. I at once saw that I was very welcome and felt quite at home. By this time it was five o'clock. Tennyson came down, shining from a hot bath which he had just been taking, quite in an easy, unaffected weighty style; a certain slow heaviness of motion belongs essentially to his character . . . : head Jovian: eye dark: face fresh: black flowing locks, like a Spanish ship captain or a captain of Italian brigands: something not at all common, and not the least English. We dined, talked and smoked together, and got on admirably. He reads Greek readily, and has been translating bits of Homer in blank verse. This morning we breakfasted at 9.30 and after breakfast walked about inspecting the beauties of the park and adjacent village: having a fine look-out through the trees to the sea both on the north and the south side of the island; quite an English scene: water, wood, and softly rounded green hills. . . .

ALFRED TENNYSON AND OTHERS
to THE VISCOUNT PALMERSTON

MS. Public Record Office, TI/6486B.

[May 1864]

The Right Honourable Viscount Palmerston K.G. etc. etc.
    First Lord of the Treasury
May it please your Lordship
    We beg leave to bring under your Lordship's notice the name of Mr. William Allingham, as in our opinion a fit and proper person to receive the grant of a literary pension from the Civil List.
    In addition to his contributions to periodical literature, Mr. Allingham's poems, chiefly on Irish subjects, are well-known, have gone through several editions, and been reprinted in America, and some of his songs and ballads (which are entirely free from politics or party-spirit) are in circulation among the peasantry of Ireland, as well as among the Irish in America and Australia.
    Mr. Allingham has been employed with credit in the Customs service in Ireland, in the class of Collectors and Controllers, during the last seventeen years. He was recently, at his own desire (involving a grave error of judgment) transferred to the London Customs establishment. His health and strength proving totally inadequate to the duties and anxieties of London, he has been obliged to obtain sick leave, with little prospect of being able to resume his present employment. He is most desirous, in accordance with the recommendation of his medical man, to retire to his native place, Ballyshannon, County Donegal. He has no private means, and the Retiring allowance from the Customs in the event of his case fulfilling the rules, would not exceed £22 a year.
    With reference not only to what Mr. Allingham has already done, but to that which may reasonably be expected from him in the fields of Anglo-Irish *belles-lettres*, and of Irish history and topography, in the event of his obtaining bodily and mental relief, and a modest support, we feel justified in

respectfully recommending him to your Lordship's consideration, and we believe that such a grant would be well received by the press and the public in Ireland, of all parties.[1]

Robert Browning
A. Tennyson
Jas. H. Todd, Senior Fellow and Librarian, Trinity College, Dublin
William Stokes, Regius Professor of Physics, T.C.D.
Richd. M. Milnes
Charles Graves, D.D., Senior Fellow, T.C.D. and President R. I. Academy
Charles Kingsley, Professor of Modern History, Cambridge
J. A. Froude
Tom Taylor
Arthur Helps
George L. Craik, Professor English Literature and History, Queens College, Belfast
John K. Ingram, Vice President, R. I. Academy
George Petrie, Vice President, R. I. Academy
Joseph Napier (Lord Chancellor of Ireland)
Saml. Ferguson (Q.C., Member R. I. Academy)

To ROBERT BROWNING

MS. Berg Collection.

FARRINGFORD, FRESHWATER, ISLE OF WIGHT, [31 May 1864]

Received—just now—(May 31st—64) gratefully—O imprudent poet, losing your five shillings and only winning my gratitude—for was I not about to order it this very day?[1]

Ever yours and always hoping that you will come and see me,

A. Tennyson

I have forgotten your direction and write my thanks through C[hapman] and H[all].

To JOHN STUART BLACKIE

MS. National Library of Scotland.

FARRINGFORD, FRESHWATER, ISLE OF WIGHT, June 2, 1864

My dear Sir

I have received your book and read it which is more than I do by many books which are sent me.[1] I agree with the most part of it thoroughly, but

---

[1] See above, p. 321. Allingham was awarded a Civil List pension of £60.

[1] *Dramatis Personae* (*Tennyson in Lincoln,* i, No. 635).

[1] *The Pronunciation of Greek: Accent and Quantity, A Philological Inquiry* (1852), inscribed to Tennyson on 25 May (*Tennyson in Lincoln,* i, No. 564).

I still think that to call 'primrose' an Iambus and 'celandine' an anapest is roaring madness ἀληθέυων εν αγάπη (to take your own motto) I prefer my bit of translation to your own.[2]

As to 'the gray metropolis of the North'[3] whenever you feel particularly riled (as the American phrase is) repeat three times

'The black metropolis of the South'

and that will be a comfort to you. With our kind regards.

Yours ever
A. Tennyson

To MARTIN FARQUHAR TUPPER

MS. University of Virginia.

FARRINGFORD, June 4, 1864

My dear Sir[1]

We are obliged to you for your 'seven-gabled' bee-hive-home and family group. You look very comfortable. I would send a photograph of my localities had I any one fit to send, but I have not. Some time or other perhaps I shall have the pleasure of making Mr. Evelyn's acquaintance. This is a fine day again after our raw weather of yesterday and I hope you and yours are enjoying it. Believe me,

Yours truly
Alfred Tennyson

To EMILY SELLWOOD TENNYSON

Text. Materials, ii, 397.

29, WELBECK STREET, LONDON, June 12, [1864]

I send 'Enoch'; two or three mistakes in it. Spedding likes it as well as when he heard me read it. I have not taken any steps toward the Shakespearians.[1]

---

[2] 'Speaking truth in love', Ephesians 4:15 (with a plural participle).
[3] 'The Daisy', l. 194.

[1] Replying to Tupper's letter of 3 June (TRC) enclosing a photograph, 'a small shadow of my poor old house; which, when Nathaniel Hawthorne was my guest langsyne [April 1856], was hailed as the veritable "House of Seven Gables" . . . and it is . . . the largest beehive in the kingdom'. Tupper enclosed also a 'shadow' of a family group of 'me and all my flock'—reproduced in Derek Hudson's excellent book, *Martin Tupper*, facing p. 177. William John Evelyn (1822–1908), of Wotton, Surrey, descendant of John Evelyn, the diarist, was a close friend of Tupper's (see *Landed Gentry*, *Who Was Who*, and Hudson's *Martin Tupper*).

[1] About the ode (see above, p. 356 and n.).

To SIR ARTHUR HALLAM ELTON[1]

MS. Lady Elton.

June 14, 1864

My dear Elton

I need not say that the photographs were very welcome and your kindness in sending them very pleasant to me.

Some day my wife and myself hope to be able to come to you, but this year we cannot. If Lady Elton and yourself ever come near this place it would give us great pleasure to welcome you here. Believe me,

Yours very truly
A. Tennyson

To EMILY SELLWOOD TENNYSON

MS. Tennyson Research Centre.

FARRINGFORD, FRESHWATER, ISLE OF WIGHT, [for LONDON]
[c. 15 June 1864]

Dearest

I got up without hayfever and the way was lightened by Val. Prinsep's anecdotes. I met a certain Mr. Day[1] on board who appears to have screwed a promise out of me that all the Foresters should march round my grounds on Coronation day the 28th. I am afraid that if they go up the glade they will damage the ferns etc. and Heard must contrive that they don't pass that way. They might come up the avenue and go round the lawn and so out again, I should think. It was rather a rash promise to give. I met Admiral Love[2] on the boat, who told me bad news of a railway to be brought from Newport and continued to Alum Bay: I am afraid they would go right through my grounds. I saw Paget this morning who says I have rheumatism in the shoulder and advises hot compress. He wants me to be an F. R. S. for the sake of the R. S. he says not for mine.[3]

The key of my portmanteau was forgotten but as the lock was broken in coming apparently it did not matter.

My best remembrances to your guest and her daughter. Get out into the fresh air with them as often as may be.

Thine × × × ×
A. T.

---

[1] Arthur Hallam Elton (1818–83), 7th Baronet of Clevedon Court, was Arthur Henry Hallam's first cousin and Jane Brookfield's brother. In 1841 he married Rhoda Susan Willis (d. 1873).

[1] Perhaps William James Day, a ship agent in Yarmouth, or possibly William Stuart Day, a merchant, ship and consular agent, and agent to the Hamburg Insurance Company, Castle Terrace, West Cowes (White's *Hampshire*, pp. 628, 617).

[2] Rear-Admiral Henry Ommanney Love, a resident and one of the chief burgesses of Yarmouth (White, p. 627).

[3] See below, p. 373. 'On 15 June Woolner's diary records: "Went with Tennyson to Hunt's pictures—at a gallery rented at 16 Hanover Street"' (Leonée Ormond, *Tennyson and Thomas Woolner*, p. 19).

To EMILY SELLWOOD TENNYSON

Text. Materials, ii. 398.

LONDON, June 17, [1864]

My only fear about the bit of land is that if I buy it I shall hurt the Prinseps. However, if their stables are likely to stare right into my premises, I suppose I must do it. Macmillan with whom I am going to dine to-day read my sheets and strongly advises immediate publication.

LONDON, June 18, [1864]

Just returned. A long hot waiting for Katherine and Margaret[1] at the National Gallery, nobody came. Val Prinsep says, his father and Watts have concluded the purchase but he says no doubt they will let me have it.[2]

To EMILY SELLWOOD TENNYSON

MS. Tennyson Research Centre.
FARRINGFORD, FRESHWATER, ISLE OF WIGHT, [for LONDON], Monday [20 June 1864]

Dearest

I hope my last didn't miss—Before I came to the 'forty' in thy note I said £50 rent for the chalk-pit, thinking it will be an annoyance.[1] I must leave it in thy hands to manage.

I dined with Simeon last night. Browning was there and very agreeable. Afterwards to the Cosmopolitan where I saw heaps of people.

If I publish now Payne says my Christmas account will be £2000.

Saw mother yesterday—looking very well and being very cheerful. Aunt Mary Anne[2] feeble but better than she has been. Pray get out every fine day in donkey-chair or otherwise. What about a Tutor?

Wilt thou send a copy of the printed Alcaics etc. from the Cornhill?[3]

Thine
A. T.

---

[1] Catherine Rawnsley and her daughter (*Journal*, p. 281).
[2] Thoby Prinsep and G. F. Watts, spending the summer on the Isle of Wight, bought land near Farringford for a house—where, in the event, Watts built The Briary in 1872–4. See below, p. 373.

[1] 'The best chalk pit of the place . . . on our land' (*Journal*, p. 67).
[2] Mary Anne Fytche (see i. 1 n.), living with Elizabeth Tennyson, at Rosemount, Hampstead.
[3] See above, p. 373.

To EMILY SELLWOOD TENNYSON

MS. Tennyson Research Centre.
FARRINGFORD, FRESHWATER, ISLE OF WIGHT, [for LONDON], [22 June 1864]
Dearest

Of course go to Aubrey house[1] but take care thou dost not catch cold. Lear is here and looks very bronzed: he has painted one very fine picture, 'Morn broadened on the borders of the dark' from a landscape near Rome.[2] I am almost afraid about that Greek letter that there was a first one—that this was a supplementary one—but I cannot say.

I am going to dine today with the Waughs[3] (the family of Woolner's betrothed) I ought to do it out of compliment to my host. I saw Lord Boyne yesterday—called there in consequence of Emma's writing to ask me to an evening party.[4] I am going to lunch there* tomorrow instead. Louie Simeon[5] is coming to drive me out at 4 ¼. Simeon was quite enthusiastic about the nurse so I have only put a line in—and it must go.

Thine × × × × × ×
A. T.

We have nearly got the new agreement with the Moxons made out. Paddison is doing it. He called here just now and harped on Miss Lee's lot.[6] My book will be out 2d week in July.

*Simeon drove me to the door and came in on Lord B's invitation to see his Hogarths, and got an invitation to Brancepeth besides. Emma was not at home.

---

[1] Aubrey House, Milford, near Lymington, bought by Henry Sellwood (or the Welds) 'in order to be within easy reach of us' (*Journal*, p. 201). 'We sent Heard first and then on his favourable report my sister Anne Weld and Agnes went with Mr. Wilson [the boys' tutor] to look at it. Nanny finds it much more humble than she expected but the nearness to ourselves and to connections of Mr. Weld and to the sea tempt her and as far as she goes she is resolved to buy, if, as she hears, the house and 7 acres are to be purchased for £900. The lowness of the rooms (8 feet 5 inches) is the greatest drawback, for though dilapidated she thinks some little outlay will repair' (Emily Tennyson to Mrs Gatty, 4 March, Boston Public Library). 'I trust her husband [Charles Weld, in Rome] will consent to the purchase and that all will be satisfactorily arranged though the fact of there being no land except the gardens may perhaps cause a difficulty by leaving the possibility of the view being built out' (as above, 7 March).
[2] Lear's illustration of 'A Dream of Fair Women', l. 265—at Civitella di Subiaco (*Later Letters of Edward Lear*, ed. Lady Strachey, p. 371).
[3] On 1 June, Woolner became engaged to (and on 6 September married) Alice Gertrude Waugh, daughter of George and Mary Waugh. (Holman Hunt married two of her sisters, in 1865 and 1875.)
[4] The 7th Viscount Boyne, married to Tennyson's cousin Emma (Russell)—see i. 23 n.
[5] Louisa Edith Simeon (d. 1895), daughter of Sir John Simeon; in October 1872 she married Richard Ward.
[6] Unidentified. White's *Hampshire* (1859) lists 'Misses Leigh' at Yarmouth.

To EMILY SELLWOOD TENNYSON

MS. Tennyson Research Centre.

Thursday, [23 June 1864]

Dearest

I must see the Prinseps if possible before I leave on this matter of the land.[1] I sent my sheets off to print yesterday and am to have them back on Saturday printed fair for publication.[2]

Can'st thou find out from Baxter's flower-book the name of the plant—the Latin name I mean—which I speak of 'as bearing the delicate fruit which looks a flower[3]—Rhamus something—skewer-wood Butcher's cleavers is the English name—I think.

Get out into the air as much as possible.

Thine × × × × × ×
A. T.

I have finally rejected the proposed F. R. S. You may like to see Paget's letter.[4]

To EMILY SELLWOOD TENNYSON

MS. Tennyson Research Centre.

[London, 24 June 1864]

Dearest

I went to Lord Boyne's. Gustavus and Lady Catherine were there and Mrs. Archer Clive (the authoress of Paul Ferroll) and Edwin D'Eyncourt came in: and all went off pleasantly.[1] And at night I dined at Palgrave's with Brookfield, Lord Houghton and Sir John Acton. In the evening came women and Lady Augusta, who was very agreeable and looking very well and asked after thee and the boys. I don't know what kind of attack thou hast, but if

---

[1] See above, p. 371.

[2] She was troubled about the title of the new volume; see *The Letters of Emily Tennyson*, pp. 180-2, and below, p. 377.

[3] 'A Dedication', ll. 12-13 (Ricks, p. 1184). See below, p. 375. It was glossed in the *Enoch Arden* volme as 'The fruit of the spindle-tree (*Euonymous Europeus*)'. William Baxter's *Phaenogamous Botany; or, Figures and Description of the Genera of British Flowering Plants* (6 vols., 1834-43; see *Tennyson in Lincoln*, i, No. 501).

[4] See above, p. 370. Paget's letter (20 June, TRC) said: 'It is very generally felt that you are one of the very few who, though not engaged in the pursuit of science, should be enrolled in the chief scientific community.' Emily Tennyson thought it 'might be worth while belonging to the Royal Society if it were only for the library' (*Letters*, p. 180).

[1] Gustavus Hamilton-Russell (see i. 90 n.) and his wife Lady Katherine Frances (d. 1903), daughter of the 2nd Earl of Eldon. Caroline Clive (1801-73: *DNB*), née Meysey-Wigley, novelist and verse-writer under the pen-name 'V', published *Paul Ferroll* in 1855—an effective and unusual novel whose hero, twice a murderer, is persuasively represented as a justified sinner. Sir John Acton (1834-1902: *DNB*), 8th Baronet and 1st Baron Acton (1869), historian and moralist; noted as a liberal Roman Catholic, vigorously and volubly opposed to the adoption of the dogma of papal infallibility; Regius Professor of Modern History at Cambridge, 1892-1902, and Honorary Fellow of All Souls (1891) and Trinity (1892). Tennyson and his older son called on Acton in 1880 in Tegernsee (*Memoir*, ii. 245).

better for it, it came for good. Col. Fisher could scarcely have the house for *half* the year without season prices I should think.² I see that Squire has corrupted the Road Commissioners—how taking the green from the side of the road to inclose it should improve its appearance, I am at a loss to understand.

Thine × × × ×
A.

Love to Anne and Agnes³

To EMILY SELLWOOD TENNYSON

MS. Tennyson Research Centre.
FARRINGFORD, FRESHWATER, ISLE OF WIGHT, [for LONDON], [25 June 1864]
Dearest

I have no doubt the air is fine which thou hast sent:¹ but what dost thou wish to be done with it? Shall I send it to Sterndale Bennett and take his opinion? My proofs are all come back reprinted and the book announced, I confess it inferior to my last but then I shall make money.² Gladstone is I believe coming here tonight and Woolner gives a party. Bowman called here this morning and after refusing I have finally agreed to become an F. R. S. as the President and all of them wish me particularly to do so.³

'Who live the noblest life' would be better than 'the most noble' for the metre.

I shall stop here till I have finished my corrections and return some time next week I expect.

Thine × × × × ×
A.

I read thine again. Shall I try and find out Sims Reeves?⁴

---

² Perhaps Edward Henry Fisher (1822–1910), Royal Artillery; Major-General, 1870; retired, 1880 (*Who Was Who* and *Whitaker's Naval and Military Directory*); possibly at this time Commandant of the Parkhurst Barracks, near Newport (see below, p. 376). For William Squire, see above, p. 200 and n. ³ Weld.

¹ 'The Song of the Alma River' (beginning 'Frenchman, a hand in thine'), of which the first stanza was Tennyson's. See *Memoir*, i. 380 n., and the next letter.

² *Enoch Arden and Other Poems*, published in August, was 'hailed with extraordinary enthusiasm, and for some time it was not easy to go into any drawing-room without finding the little green volume on the table, or to travel many miles in a railway carriage without seeing some traveller take it from his pocket' (*Annual Register*, p. 323). It 'sold 17,000 on the day of publication, 40,000 by November, and the whole first impression of 60,000 by the end of the year. Tennyson's half-yearly payment from Moxon for *Enoch Arden* in January 1865 was £6664 4s.2d., with £1400 17s. 8d. more coming in June 1865' (Hagen, *Tennyson and His Publishers*, p. 112; see also P. G. Scott, *Tennyson's 'Enoch Arden': A Victorian Best-Seller*, The Tennyson Society, Tennyson Research Centre, 1970.

³ As Paget's letter had said (see above, p. 373 n.). For William Bowman, see above, p. 335 n. The President was Major-General Edward Sabine (1788–1883: *DNB*). Tennyson was inducted into the Society 7 December 1865 (see below, p. 414).

⁴ John Sims Reeves (1818–1900: *DNB*), the foremost English tenor (he had been with Macready's company at the Drury Lane Theatre).

To EMILY SELLWOOD TENNYSON

MS. Tennyson Research Centre.

FARRINGFORD, FRESHWATER, ISLE OF WIGHT, [for LONDON,] [27 June 1864]

Dearest

I took thy song to Novelli yesterday—he is reported to be a great judge—he played it and pronounced it to be vigourous—broad and—English—three great merits, he said.[1] If thou wilt allow him to use thy name he will show it to Chap[p]ell, who will decide upon it. Santl[e]y not Sims Reeves he said should sing it: but without a name he says it would fall dead.[2] So at any rate I suppose thou wilt let thy name be *mentioned* at least to Chappel[l]. Words and Music by Mrs. A. T. no doubt would sell.

The Duke and Duchess have just called, both very agreeable. Gladstone dines here today tout seul with me and Woolner. Mrs. Prinsep has sent me a note saying she will do anything I wish—which *may* mean nothing.

I can't make out thy Rhamus *adea* or some such word. It is cramped so. Wilt thou write it clearer?

Thine × × × × ×
A. [T.]

I should think the sooner I had Plumbley's land the better.[3]

That lot for which Merwood gave (didn't give for he had no money) 225 ¾ of an acre Mr. P[ritchard?] gave £250 for.

To EMILY SELLWOOD TENNYSON

MS. Tennyson Research Centre.

[28 June 1864]

Dearest

Gladstone dined here yesterday and was very charming and simple. I asked him down to Farringford and he seemed quite delighted but doubted whether it be possible. The Duke and Duchess can't come this year. I have to decide upon a title today. 'Home Idylls' seems to me the best.[1] G[rann]y Forster has written asking me to dine with him on Friday.[2] So I suppose I must go. Gladstone said there would be a great night at the House either on

---

[1] A. H. Novelli, for whatever reason, changed his mind and wrote to Emily Tennyson 31 July (TRC) saying that her 'creation' had been 'placed . . . in the form needed for publication' by [Frederick] Lablache (1815–87: *DNB*). 'It would not do I fancy to publish the song as "edited by Alfred Tennyson".' 'The Song of the Alma River' was published in 1864 by Cramer (formerly Cramer, Beale, and Chappell): see *Letters of Emily Tennyson*, p. 182 n., and *Tennyson in Lincoln*, ii, Nos. 5316–18.

[2] William Chappell (1809–88: *DNB*), musical antiquary and publisher, New Bond Street (a member of Cramer, Beale, and Chappell, 1845–61); Charles Santley (1834–1922: *DNB*), baritone; knighted, 1907; his first wife was the daughter of John Mitchell Kemble.

[3] Probably Charles William Plumley, a farmer of Brooklands, in the Freshwater parish. See below, pp. 384, 386, and *Journal*, pp. 220, 224. (The proprietor of Plum*b*ly's Hotel was William Tooley Lambert (see White's *Hampshire*, p. 630).

[1] See *Letters of Emily Tennyson*, pp. 181–2. [2] See above, p. 358, and below, p. 379.

Thursday or Monday.[3] I think if the last I must stay over that, and then I am quite ready to come back. I don't think I shall go to Switzerland with the B[radley]s.[4] My arm is not much improved I think.

Do as thou thinkest best with the Col.[5] £80 I should think with power of underletting. As it seems best to thee.

Thine x x x x
A.

To ?

MS. Rosenbach Foundation.

29 WELBECK STREET, [late June 1864]

My dear Sir

Many thanks for your kind invitation: but even had I received it in time to have availed myself of it, I could not have come out to Chigwell. A man who comes to town for a day or two is immediately involved head over ears with innumerable engagements of one kind or other.

I think I must give up the Cornhill; though I have no doubt of the liberality of the proprietors.

Yours very truly
A. Tennyson

To EMILY SELLWOOD TENNYSON

Text. Materials, ii. 400.

LONDON, June 29, [1864]

The great night at the House is Monday so that I shall not be back in all probability till Tuesday and I may stop one day in the Forest.

WILLIAM ALLINGHAM, *A DIARY*, p. 102 (extract).

p. 102 (extract)

Thursday, June 30, [1864]

I walked through the Park to Woolner's in Welbeck Street, and found not only Woolner, but Tennyson there (up for some days), and also F. Palgrave.

---

[3] See below, pp. 377-8.   [4] See below, p. 378.
[5] 'The Upham Barrys had had the Terrace and have been enthusiastic in its praise. Colonel Fisher takes it now. I very busy getting the back stair-case altered and a groined arch made before A. returns. Mr. Wilson is so kind as to look after our people at Aubrey for me' (Journal, June or July). See above, p. 374, and below, p. 378.
'A few doors beyond Dimbola, nearest the downs, is "The Terrace", a little property bought, with the adjoining fields, by Lord Tennyson chiefly to prevent his beautiful view from Farringford being obstructed by other buildings' (V. C. Scott O'Connor, 'Tennyson and His Friends at Freshwater', *Century Magazine*, lv [Dec. 1877], 260).

Woolner is engaged to dine with Novello,[1] and I very gladly agree to stay and keep Tennyson company. T., P., and I walk in the Regent's Park, P. goes home. T. and I dine together. He has the proof sheets of a new book with him—some flitting notions of calling it 'Idylls of the Hearth'? 'Gladstone dined here on Monday'—Swinburne—Milnes—De Sade—Naked model—'the chastest thing I ever saw.'[2] T. said he must begin to correct his proofs, and with the word came the sound of a barrel-organ, bringing dismay! I took my leave, promising to quash the music, in which attempt I succeeded seeing the grinding man well out of the street. . . .

To EMILY SELLWOOD TENNYSON

Text. Materials, ii. 400

LONDON, June 30, [1864]

Gladstone had to apply especially in my interest to the Speaker to get me a place on Monday.[1] I now think of 'Enoch Arden etc.' as a title.[2]

To ARCHIBALD PEEL

MS. Edgar F. Shannon, Jr.

June 30, 1864

My dear Archie

Gladstone has got a place for me on Monday night. I am to be there before 4.30. Will you escort me, for I am unacquainted with the localities, and blinder than all beetles. I left a message for you with your man but perhaps he may forget to deliver it.

Ever yours
A. Tennyson

---

[1] A. H. Novelli, who lived at 12 St. Stephen Square, Westbourne Park, W.

[2] Tennyson was primed by Allingham, who, calling on Rossetti on 26 and 27 June, had seen him 'painting a very large young woman, almost a giantess, as "Venus Verticordia"', and also seen Rossetti's mistress, Fanny Cornforth: 'Then Swinburne came in, and soon began to recite—a parody on Browning was one thing' (*Diary*, pp. 100–1). In the painting 'Venus stands naked amongst a mass of honeysuckle and clusters of pink roses . . .' (Virginia Surtees, *Dante Gabriel Rossetti . . . A Catalogue Raisonné*, i. 99; reproduced, ii, Plate 248). Milnes had introduced Swinburne to the works of the Marquis de Sade in 1862, and Moxon (J. B. Payne) published both poets (see *The Swinburne Letters*, i. 46, 53–9, 143). The 'chastest thing' could in no wise refer to 'Venus Verticordia'.

[1] 'On Tennyson's behalf I have appealed to the Speaker [J. E. Denison, later Viscount Ossington] as I thought you would wish and he will treat the case as special and give him a place on Monday next' (Gladstone to Woolner, 28 June, in *Thomas Woolner*, p. 251). See *Journal*, p. 203.

[2] The very title she had wanted (see above, p. 373).

To GEORGE GRANVILLE BRADLEY

MS. Marian Bradley's 'Diaries', British Library.

[30 June 1864]

My dear Bradley
Can't go—too short a notice—but may all blessing go with you!

Yours ever
A. Tennyson

To EMILY SELLWOOD TENNYSON

MS. Tennyson Research Centre.

Friday, [1 July 1864]

Dearest
All right: no news.
Young Gladstone[1] is going to take me to the House on Monday.
Bradley just called.

Thine × × × × ×
A.

I send Lionel a fairy book.

To ARCHIBALD PEEL

MS. Indiana University.

[1 July 1864]

My dear Archie
Not hearing from you, and thinking you must be out of town, I have accepted the escort of young Gladstone to the House of Commons.

Ever yours
A. Tennyson

To EMILY SELLWOOD TENNYSON

MS. Tennyson Research Centre.

[2 July 1864]

Dearest
I am glad thou hast settled with Col. Fisher.[1] He has the house quite cheap enough. Paddison at last reports that the Commissioners are coming down to

---

[1] William Henry Gladstone (1840–91), the eldest son, in Parliament, 1865–85, and a junior lord of the treasury in his father's first ministry (1869–71). He died a lingering death of brain cancer. 'He had possessed great physical strength and had been an enthusiastic mountaineer. Although he had spent many years in Parliament and had held minor office, William Gladstone was without ambition, and he had given up a great amount of time to music. He was idolized by his mother' (Philip Magnus, *Gladstone, A Biography*, p. 377).

[1] See above, pp. 374, 376.

hear objections on the 25th.[2] Shall we be at home? Dined with Forster yesterday. He was very agreeable and made no allusions to our tiff.[3] Venables was there. I read Enoch and Mrs. Procter[4] came in the evening to hear me with two daughters. I am to meet Lord Strangford at dinner tomorrow at Palgrave's—he is I am told about the first Oriental scholar in England.[5] I shouldn't think Mr. Wilson[6] had any chance of getting into the House.

Thine × × × × ×
A.

To EMILY SELLWOOD TENNYSON

Text. Materials, ii. 401.

LONDON, July 5, [1864]

In the House Gladstone spoke with real passion. Dizzy never seemed to me to lose himself although he doubled up his fist in a sort of pseudo-rage.[1]

To GEORGE ROUTLEDGE[1]

MS. Routledge, Kegan Paul.

FARRINGFORD, July 27, 1864

Dear Sir

I beg to thank you for the cheque of £91 which I have received this

---

[2] 'The Commissioners came to decide the Eastern field question. Our flags up to show how we may be built out of the view for which we have fought so hard and paid so much but the Commissioners are inexorable' (*Journal*, p. 204).

[3] See above, pp. 353, 358.

[4] Mrs. Procter (see i. 274 n.) and, presumably, Agnes and Edith (Adelaide, the poetess, having died 2 February 1864).

[5] Percy Ellen Frederick William Smythe (1826–69: *DNB*), 8th Viscount Strangford of Ireland, and 3rd Baron Penshurst of the United Kingdom, was educated at Harrow and Merton College, Oxford, where he was a postmaster but left (1845) without a degree for a position in the embassy at Constantinople, and served there for a number of years as attaché, and latterly as Oriental secretary. A sound classical scholar, he learned Persian at public school and Arabic at university, had 'a considerable acquaintance with Celtic', and 'made a thorough study of Sanskrit'. He spoke Persian, Turkish, modern Greek, Afghan, Hindustani, and knew something of 'the Slavic tongues'. A frequent contributor to the *Pall Mall Gazette* and the *Saturday Review*, he was an authority on Eastern questions, and President of the Royal Asiatic Society when he died suddenly in January 1869. See the *Publisher's Circular*, xxxi (16 Jan. and 1 Feb. 1869), 6, 70 ('the finest Oriental scholar in Europe'). See also below, p. 512.

[6] Thomas Wilson, the boys' tutor.

[1] The Schleswig-Holstein question. See *Annual Register*, pp. 72–102, and *Journal*, p. 203.

[1] George Routledge (1812–88: *DNB*), the publisher, signed an 'agreement with Tennyson dated January 16, 1863, "to print and publish for their own use a further impression of the illustrated edition of his Poems in quarto (formerly published by Moxon) to consist of 5,000 copies, the publishers to pay a royalty of four shillings on every copy, reckoning thirteen as twelve, in conformity with their customary mode of selling their publications to the trade"; and to issue the book for sale to the public at not less than one guinea per copy' (F. A. Mumby, *The House of Routledge*, p. 80).

morning in second payment of my royalty on the Illustrated Edition of my Poems. Believe me, dear Sir,

Truly yours
A. Tennyson

To JAMES THOMAS FIELDS

MS. University of Virginia.

FARRINGFORD, September 14, 1864

Dear Mr. Fields

Many thanks for your Bill of Exchange which I would have acknowledged on the instant had I not been on a continental tour from which I have just returned.[1] I and my wife and boys have been into wild Brittany and had to rough it rather, also into parts of Normandy, and on coming back I find yours among a whole monticule of letters and poems on my drawing room table. I will look among my old papers and see if I can light upon any MSS and if I succeed I will dispatch it to Trubner and Co.[2] for you.

My wife's best remembrances to yourself and Mrs. Fields. Shall we ever see you here again? Believe me,

Always truly yours
A. Tennyson

To BARON BERNHARD VON TAUCHNITZ

Text. Der Verlag Bernhard Tauchnitz, pp. 121–2.

FARRINGFORD, FRESHWATER, ISLE OF WIGHT, September 14, 1864

I am grieved that I was not at home when your letter arrived; and that I have missed the opportunity of being introduced to your son. In fact I have only just returned from a continental tour. If your son be still in England I need not say that I shall be happy to see him.[1] With respect to my new volume Messrs. Williams and Norgate[2] write to me asking what sum I require for granting you permission to print it in Germany. I think I had better leave this matter altogether in your hands.

---

[1] The tour of Brittany, 6 August–9 September, is described in *Journal*, pp. 205–14.

[2] Nicholas Trübner (1817–84: *DNB*), the chief proprietor of Trübner and Co., scholar, author, publisher, who in the 1850s visited the United States and established connections with 'leading American writers and publishers', issued in 1855 his *Bibliographical Guide to American Literature* (expanded in 1859), and at this time was London agent for Ticknor and Fields (Austin, *Fields of the Atlantic Monthly*, p. 31).

[1] Tauchnitz himself was at Farringford in early November (*Journal*, p. 216), and Tennyson met the son some time later (see below, p. 491).

[2] Tauchnitz's London agent (see above, p. 247 n.).

22 *October* 1864

To WILLIAM COX BENNETT

MS. British Library.

[22 October 1864]

My dear Sir

Look at this pile which on my return from abroad I find heaped on my table. I ought to have thanked you before for your generous lines—but look at the pile—some three feet high[1]—and let that apologize for my silence—and believe me, though penny post maddened,

Yours ever
A. Tennyson[2]

To SIR IVOR BERTIE GUEST[1]

MS. Tennyson Research Centre.

FARRINGFORD, October 24, 1864

Dear Sir Ivor

Many thanks for your proffered hospitality. Some day we hope to avail

---

[1] Drawing of pyramid on left-hand side of page (reproduced in Schooling, 'The Handwriting of Alfred Tennyson', *Strand Magazine*, viii [1894], 604); both slopes of the pyramid labelled 'Letters for Autographs'; peak of left slope labelled 'Anonymous insolent letters'; of right slope, 'Letters asking explanation of particular passages'; apex, 'Letters from America, Australia, from Monomaniacs etc.'; below apex in horizontal divisions, 'Begging letters of all kinds'; next level down, 'Subscriptions asked for church buildings, Baptist chapels, Wesleyan etc.'; next, 'Newspapers gracious or malignant—Magazines etc.'. Then, in four blocks descending to base of left slope of pyramid: (1) 'Printed circulars of poems asking for subscriptions'; (2) 'Presentation copies of poems'; (3) 'Printed proofsheets of poems'; (4) 'MSS poems'. The rest of the lower half of the pyramid is filled with four rows of blocks, each containing 'do'; the blocks in the bottom row, at the base, each have 'do' twice.' See below, p. 391.

[2] None the less, he was visited that evening by Frederick Pollock (who had taken a house at Ventnor in 1855 but in 1864 settled at Easton Farm, Freshwater): 'Evening at Ffarringford [Pollock's wicked spelling]. Tennyson read "Boadicea" and "The Lincolnshire Farmer". The latter gains immensely by his giving the words their proper accent, and by the enormous sense of humour thrown into it by his voice and manner in reading it. I asked Tennyson which he preferred of the two poems, "Enoch Arden" and "Aylmer's Field". He replied "Enoch Arden", which he thought was very perfect and a beautiful story. "Aylmer's Field" had given him more trouble than anything he ever did. At one time he had to put it aside altogether for six months, the story was so intractable, and it was so difficult to deal with modern manners and conversation. The Indian relative was introduced solely for the sake of the dagger, which was to be the instrument of the lover's suicide' (Pollock, *Personal Reminiscences*, ii. 126). The dagger, however, produced its own benefits (see below, p. 397 and n.).

[1] Sir Ivor Bertie Guest (1835–1914), 2nd Baronet created Baron Wimbourne of Canford Magna, four miles from Wimbourne, in Dorsetshire, in 1880. He was the eldest of the ten children of Lady Charlotte Schreiber (1812–95: *DNB*), translator (as Lady Charlotte Guest) of *Mabinogion* (see above, p. 156 n.), and collector of old china, fans, and playing cards. Her first husband having died in 1852, she married Charles Schreiber (1826–84), a wealthy manufacturer, in 1855. She was the daughter of the 9th Earl of Lindsey and his second wife, Susannah Elizabeth Layard, of Uffington Hall, Lincs., and Tennyson knew her at least as early as October 1857 (*Journal*, p. 103), when they met at Mrs Cameron's, at Ashburton Cottage.

ourselves of it: not at present: for our boys I believe are to have another tutor[2] at home and do not go to Bailey Gate till Easter. Believe me,

Yours respectfully
A. Tennyson

THOMAS WOOLNER to EMILY SELLWOOD TENNYSON

Text. Amy Woolner, *Thomas Woolner*, p. 257.

29, WELBECK STREET, W., November 17, 1864

My dear Mrs. Tennyson

The Bard's room is all prepared and he can enter at will.

A thousand thanks! the cheque came safely to hand. I had been looking out but was not satisfied with what I saw, but now I have got a glorious silver mug, 90 years old and there will be engraved upon it 'Given by Alfred and Emily Tennyson to Thomas Woolner Sep: 6, 1864'—my wedding day. I shall look quite splendid.[1]

I will tell the Bard what I think of your projects for the 6*d*. Numbers.[2]

Alice[3] has returned to me again, having been absent a week with her mother.... She is very pleased at the notion of having to look after the Bard and make him snug....

Most truly yours
Thos. Woolner

---

[2] 'I believe we must send the boys to a private Tutor near Wimbourne, Mr. Paul of Baillie. Our good Tutor Mr. Wilson has been there these three months. We have been hoping for his return but now he is ordered abroad for the winter. It seems as if it were a duty to send them away now. It is so difficult to get a proper Tutor and then when one does he has so soon to go' (Emily Tennyson to Mrs Gatty, 13 October). On the 26th she wrote again: 'Mr. Paul does not wish to have the boys till Easter and has undertaken to provide us with a Tutor meanwhile. At present I have no help with them by way of Tutor unless when Ally steps in' (Boston Public Library).

The reason for the postponement was her reluctance to cut the boys' 'beautiful golden hair' before spring for fear of their catching colds (see below, p. 388, and *Journal*, pp. 216–24). For Paul, see below, p. 386 and n. The new tutor, Mr Lipscombe, came on 11 November 1864 and stayed until 2 May, when he left to become a master at Winchester (*Journal*, pp. 216, 224). See below, p. 396 n.

[1] 'We hope that in consideration of our being so far away from town, you have chosen a tankard or gold bracelets or whatever you will by way of memorial of our good wishes' (Emily Tennyson to Woolner, 4 November, in *Thomas Woolner*, p. 257).

[2] The result, published in January 1865 in Moxon's Miniature Poets series, and dedicated to the 'Working men of England', was *A Selection from the Works of Alfred Tennyson* in an octavo volume, but also 'Issued in eight Parts, each Part consisting of two sheets, thirty-two pages. The sheets were "stabbed", and furnished with mauve-coloured paper wrappers. The published price was Sixpence a Part' (Wise, *Bibliography*, i. 179). See Charles Tennyson, p. 354; below, p. 383, and *Letters*, p. 188.

[3] His wife.

To EMILY SELLWOOD TENNYSON

Text. Materials, ii. 407.

29 WELBECK STREET, November 19, [1864]

We had a good passage. Mr. and Mrs. Bowen[1] were on board going to Winchester and very pleasant. I found the Woolners expecting me and I am installed in my old apartment at the top of the house.

THE JOURNALS OF WALTER WHITE, pp. 158-9.

November 20, [1864]

Going out at 1 p.m. met Tennyson in the courtyard. Turned back, gave him lunch and opened a bottle of Oedenberg for which he asked. Told me he had sold more than 40,000 of 'Enoch Arden' and cleared more than £5000, that he had abusive letters from people who blame him for accepting so much profit. Talked of his project of sixpenny numbers: said P[a]yne, Moxon's manager, expects to sell 50,000 copies. If this expectation be not disappointed the profit will be £10,000.[1] Talked about the encroachment of buildings around Far[r]ingford, and the villas and hotel that are to be built at Alum Bay, sides of his land.[2] I suggested his buying an estate of heathland, ninety acres including a hill, one of the Devil's jumps, at Chart near Haslemere, which was in the market for £1500. He seemed to like the notion but started objections. He then proposed a walk, and I proposed the Zoological Gardens. We called for Woolner, who gave me to taste a new kind of Spanish wine, Ampurdan. As we walked about the Gardens, Tennyson said, as we looked at the white peacock sitting crouching and with loose feathers looking somewhat strange in the damp air, that people had written to ask him what he meant by 'Now dro[o]ps the milkwhite peacock like a ghost,'[3] and Woolner broke out, 'Why, don't they know that a mass of white always looks ghost-

---

[1] Charles Synge Christopher Bowen (1835-94: *DNB*), knighted, 1879, and created life peer as Baron Bowen (1893), and his wife, Emily Frances (d. 1897), née Rendel, whom he had married in 1862. Educated at Rugby and Balliol, where, still an undergraduate, he was elected a fellow, and where he began a lifelong friendship with Jowett. He was called to the bar in 1861, and had joined the Western circuit. In due course he became a distinguished judge, and was caricatured by Spy in *Vanity Fair*, 12 March 1892. His father was Rector of St. Thomas's in Winchester.

[1] See above, p. 382 and n. 'The *Selections* brought Tennyson *in toto* £2210 4s. 2d. in 1865, and over £3500 in 1866' (Hagen, *Tennyson and His Publishers*, p. 114).

[2] Edward Lear visited the Tennysons in October, and, in his hostess' accents, wrote to a friend: 'I found all that quiet part of the Island fast spoiling, and how they can stay there I can't imagine. Not only is there an enormous monster Hotel [Stark's] growing up in sight—but a tracing of the foundations of 300 houses—a vast new road—and finally a proposed railway—cutting thro' John Simeon and A. T.'s grounds from end to end. Add to this, Pattledom has taken entire possession of the place—Camerons and Princeps building everywhere: Watts in a cottage (not Mrs. W.), and Guests, Schreibers, Pollocks, and myriads more buzzing everywhere' (*The Later Letters of Edward Lear*, ed. Lady Strachey, p. 47).

[3] *The Princess*, vii. 165.

like in the dusk?' We met Bence-Jones,[4] to whom I introduced the Poet, and he (B. J.) took occasion to beg him to give a recitation at the Royal Institution.

November 21, [1864]

Tennyson called to enquire about the estate at Haslemere.

To EMILY SELLWOOD TENNYSON
Text. Materials, ii. 407.

29 WELBECK STREET, November 21, [1864]

There was a young surgeon a Mr. Barwell[1] (accounted a very rising man) dining here yesterday). Gladstone is coming to dine with me today at Palgrave's. I want the sheets back, as the book should be out before Christmas.[2]

To EMILY SELLWOOD TENNYSON
MS. Tennyson Research Centre.

Wednesday, [23 November 1864]

Dearest

Just as I expected about Plumbley—he is not a man to do business with. I call his conduct abominable. He knew (for I told him) what value I set on the trees: he will now tell me they were cut down contrary to his orders. I have done with him.[1] I walked home with Gladstone last night. He again inquired about the boys and asked their ages and exprest his wish that they might go to school. I asked him to come to us and he said with great earnestness, 'I will take the very earliest opportunity' and I told him how much thou wert interested in many things which interested him. He is a very noble fellow and perfectly unaffected but that is small praise.

Tyndal[l] sends his express love to the boys.

Thine × × × × × ×
[A.]

---

[4] Henry Bence Jones (1814–73: *DNB*), physician and chemist, educated at Harrow and Trinity, Cambridge, was physician to St. George's Hospital, 1846–62, FRCP 1849, and Secretary to the Royal Institution, from 1860 until his death.

[1] Perhaps Richard Barwell, 'Demonstrator of Anatomy at St. Thomas's Hospital', and author of several works on skeletal subjects (Allibone).

[2] For *Selections*, see above, p. 382 n.

[1] See above, p. 375, 376 n., and below, p. 386.

To EMILY SELLWOOD TENNYSON

Text. Materials, ii. 407–8.

November 24, [1864]

I am sorry I missed Mr. J. A. Symonds.[1] I shall not be able to get down to see the Haslemere property as the agent is going into Devonshire next week.

November [25 ?, 1864]

I went last night to Moxon's and found a circle who made me read the 'Farmer' and 'Morte d'Arthur,' then I returned to Woolner's and found the two Confederates, men of the finest gentlemanship, perfectly simple and noble-mannered.[2]

November 26, [1864]

It appears I cannot get all the sheets printed till Tuesday. I have not yet been to Hampstead but I must go to mother's. I met a lot of men at Palgrave's last night, and tomorrow I dine at the Conservative Club in St. James' Street and am going to read 'Maud' to a circle of eight or nine.

November 27, [1864]

It all went off very well. I went to Hampstead. Mother exceedingly well and bright looking, Aunt M. A.[3] also quite recovered, Arthur and his wife there. Tilly and Mrs. A. came with me down through Hampstead. The first heard a man say as I passed 'there goes a Shakespeare-looking fellow.'

---

[1] John Addington Symonds (1840–93: *DNB*), historian, poet, literary critic, translator, was educated at Harrow and Balliol (BA 1862), where he was a protégé of Jowett. On 10 November he married Catherine North, and, after a fortnight at Brighton, they continued their honeymoon on the Isle of Wight, where, with letters from Jowett and Henry Graham Dakyns, by then a tutor at Clifton College, they called at Farringford on 23 November. See P. G. Scott's fine article 'John Addington Symonds and the Reaction against Tennyson', *Tennyson Research Bulletin*, ii (Nov. 1974), 85–95, and *The Letters of John Addington Symonds*, ed. Schueller and Peters, i. 506–14.

[2] Walker Fearn, for whom, see below, p. 408 n., and John Reuben Thompson (see above, p. 17 n.), who was in London, on the staff of *The Index*, as an official propagandist for the Confederacy. On 24 November he wrote in his diary: 'Spent in the evening at the home of Mr. Woolner, sculptor, in Cavendish Square, with Alfred Tennyson, the poet laureate, a quiet simple-mannered man who smoked a pipe and drank hot punch with us (Fearn and myself). He talked much of the American war, which he deplored, and of the Yankees, whom he detested (James Grant Wilson,' 'John R. Thompson and His London Diary, 1864–5', *The Criterion*, November 1891, p. 13).

[3] Aunt Mary Anne Fytche, Arthur Tennyson, and his first wife, Harriet (née West; d. 1881), whom he married in June 1860, and Matilda Tennyson.

28 November 1864

To EMILY SELLWOOD TENNYSON

MS. Yale.

Monday, [28 November 1864]

Dearest

They must have the statue—though statues a[t] £6 a head are not likely to be chef d'oeuvres. Pretty sort of thing it's likely to be. I don't want any choice of prophets. I don't want anybody to point out *the* one which I gave—Woolner laughs at the price.[1] There are 90 acres at Haslemere to be sold for £1500. Walter White says they were offered to him. Land I should think poor enough but scenery he says splendid. They lie on the side of a healthy hill. Shall I go and look at them.

I feel more and more against buying Plumbley's 56 acres.[2] If I make something like what I expect by summer I really think the best thing would be to buy India Government shares—at 5 per cent. Bradley has some. There is an income for life—and they are safe as the state itself.

I don't altogether approve of an *unexpurgated* D[on] Q[uixote] for L[ionel]. There are some wanton tales of intrigue in it very unfit for such young boys—if I recollect right.

Decide as thou wilt about [?] the stabling.[3]

I am going to have a new photograph taken for my people's edition—to be always lithographed.[4] Publishers say that will sell 2000 more.

Thine × × × ×
A.

To CHARLES KEGAN PAUL[1]

MS. Library of Congress.

[*c.* 30 November 1864]

Dear Mr. Paul

I am summoned out on unavoidable business. If I chance not to be in at 5 o'clock I shall be very soon after. So please wait if you can wait.

A. T.

---

[1] 'Statue on each side of Altar in Freshwater Church' (written in an unidentified hand on facing page).
[2] See above, pp. 375–6, 384.
[3] The Prinseps's new stables (see above, p. 371 and n.).
[4] 'Taken by the London Stereoscopic Company, *Nov. 28th*, 1864' (Wise, *Bibliography*, i. 180).

[1] Charles Kegan Paul (1828–1902: *DNB*), clergyman, author, publisher. Educated at Eton and Oxford, and in every sense an *enfant du siècle*, he became at the university a friend of Charles Kingsley, and through him associated with F. D. Maurice, Thomas Hughes, J. M. Ludlow, and other Christian Socialists. After curacies in Oxfordshire (and by now 'broadly high church'), he was chaplain at Eton (1853–62) and Vicar of Sturminster Marshall, an Eton living, where he took pupils and dabbled, in turn, with mesmerism, vegetarianism, and Positivism. Eventually losing sympathy with the Church of England, he gave up his living in 1874 and moved to London, where he wrote *William Godwin, His Friends and Contemporaries* (1876), his most important book. A reader for Henry S. King (and like a Farfrae to King's Henchard), he acquired King's business in 1877, establishing himself as C. Kegan Paul and Co., at 1 Paternoster Square, and succeeded King as Tennyson's publisher (1877–80). His firm, with the

To EMILY SELLWOOD TENNYSON

Text. *Materials*, ii. 408.

December 1, [1864]

I have sent off my sheets today, but I am to see them once more. I don't think I can be back before Friday.

To JAMES KENWARD[1]

Text. *Materials*, iii. 67–8.

FARRINGFORD, December 19, 1864

Dear Sir
  I am grieved to learn that the widow and daughters of the Rev. John Williams Ap Ithel are in such poor circumstances, and have not yet succeeded in obtaining a pension.[2] The author of the *Ecclesiastical History of the Cymry*, the translator of the *Gododin*, a man so famous in old British History and Archaeology ought I should think to be sufficiently known to entitle his family to Lord Palmerston's consideration but I daresay he will do what he can when he can. You know a Premier has so many claims upon him and it is but a limited fund out of which these pensions are granted.

Yours very truly
A. Tennyson

addition of Alfred Trench (son of R. C. Trench), became Kegan Paul, Trench and Co. (1881), then Kegan Paul, Trench, Trubner and Co. (1883), and, after financial reverses, was eventually swallowed up by Routledge (see above, p. 379 and n.). Paul converted to Roman Catholicism in 1890. See also Hagen's excellent discussion in *Tennyson and His Publishers*, pp. 139–57.

[1] James Kenward (dates unknown) was a poet, antiquary, Celtophil—and (apparently) Welshman. Later he lived at Smethwick, near Birmingham. His publications, as listed in Allibone and the British Library *Catalogue* date from 1854 to 1885 (or 1902?). See *Dictionary of Welsh Biography* (1959), ed. Lloyd and Jenkins.

[2] The Revd John Williams Ab Ithel (1811–62: *DNB*), Welsh antiquary and indefatigable (though uncritical) writer on Druidic tradition and bardic lore, educated at Jesus College, Oxford (BA 1835). 'His first curacy was at Llanfor, where he married Elizabeth Lloyd Williams (his vicar's niece) and where in 1836 he published his first book' (*Dictionary of Welsh Biography*)— information that clears him of the slur in *DNB*, perhaps unintentional but certainly careless, of having married only weeks before his death. He was perpetual curate of Newquis near Mold 1843–9, then Rector of Llan ym Mowddwy 1849–62, and for the last few months of his life Rector of Llan Enddwyn near Barmouth. He published *Ecclesiastical Antiquities of the Cymry* (1844) and an edition of the *Gododin* (Llandovery, 1852: see above, p. 156 n. and 168). He founded the Cambrian Archaeological Association (1846) and the Cambrian Institute (1851), and edited (or co-edited) several antiquarian journals. (Kenward wrote a memoir of him in seven numbers of the *Cambrian Journal*, concluding in December 1864—published separately in 1871).

To MESSRS TICKNOR AND FIELDS

MS. Harvard.

FARRINGFORD, FRESHWATER, ISLE OF WIGHT, December 20, 1864

Gentlemen

As far as in me lay I constituted your house my sole publisher in America; and since by paying for early copies of the proof-sheets, and by other occasional remittances, you may be said to have bought the right to be so, I cannot but call it (to say the least of it) exceedingly unhandsome for any other American publisher to poach on what is, as it were, your Manor. I have the honour to be, Gentlemen,

Your obedient servant,
A. Tennyson

Your letter though dated the 5th has only arrived today.

To THE DUCHESS OF ARGYLL

MS. Tennyson Research Centre.

FARRINGFORD, FRESHWATER, ISLE OF WIGHT, December 26, 1864

My dear Duchess

We are shocked to hear that you have been so unwell: I live so out of the world that I have never heard of this nor of the birth of another little daughter[1]—and I never look at Births in the papers. Certainly Lord Carlisle's death must leave the sense of an aching void in your house. I never saw him I think but once at your villa on Camden Hill and I then thought what an exceedingly pleasant man he was, and how well worth knowing more of, he seemed to me as loveable as Charles Howard, whom I always like better every time I light upon him.[2]

Thanks for your kind enquiries. My boys are still at home. They were going to a Tutor's over the water near Wimborne who has a few pupils but my wife sent their photographs beforehand and asked whether they could come in their long hair and he said they couldn't, and she did not like to cut it off in mid-winter for fear they should take cold as they have worn it long all their lives—and the result was, that they do not go till Easter which for their sakes I trust may be a warm one. She wrote to you the other day and I suppose the letters crost.

The Royal Society of Edinburgh have just made me an Hon. Member of their Society. If the Duke had anything to do with this move of theirs pray

---

[1] On 21 December the Duchess had written that she had been 'more ill than ever before after the birth of a little daughter on the 11th of November' (TRC)—Constance Harriet Campbell (1864–1922).

[2] George William Frederick Howard (1802–64), 7th Earl of Carlisle, the eldest brother of the Duchess's mother, statesman, speaker, and writer, Lord-Lieutenant of Ireland (1855–8, 1859–64), had died on 5 December. The Duchess had written in the same letter that his illness was a 'great trial', since he 'became almost speechless', which he 'felt . . . acutely, tho' it never caused a moment of irritation. It had been such a happy, and happy-making life. It was hard to bear this heavy cloud at the close' (TRC). For Charles Howard, younger brother (whom the Tennysons had met in October 1857), see above, p. 308 and n.

thank him for me. I hope he is quite well. I suppose he is from your not saying anything about his health.

I am glad that your son likes Cambridge.[3] It is a much better place for a young man to move in, than when I was young.

Ever, my dear Duchess, yours,
A. Tennyson

To LEWIS FYTCHE

MS. Tennyson Research Centre.
FARRINGFORD, FRESHWATER, ISLE OF WIGHT, December 26, 1864

My dear Lewis

Your letter has been mislaid and sought for but remains unfound. And among the myriads of letters which I get my memory sometimes gets entangled and confused so that I cannot tell whether you asked any particular question or made any particular request. Never mind. A happy Christmas to you and yours.

Your affectionate cousin
A. Tennyson

P. S. My wife reminds me that there was an invitation in your letter. Many thanks. Our love.

EMILY SELLWOOD TENNYSON
to MARGARET GATTY (extract)

MS. Boston Public Library.
FARRINGFORD, FRESHWATER, ISLE OF WIGHT, [late December 1864]

Our expected guests could not come for Christmas-day but Ally was so cheerful we needed nothing else to make us so.

We have just heard that a railway is likely to knock down our old house with its fine staircase and stately oak carvings[1] and two branches of one threaten this our present home. So the railways have taken a spite at us it seems.[2]

We are talking of 'Devil's Jumps' not far from a home I had and lived [in] with my Father in Surrey only one talks in such a way as not believing, not daring to believe we shall ever be driven from this that has grown so dear in spite of ever-increasing vexations of land to be bought to keep away or to shut out brick boxes. . . .[3]

---

[3] The Marquis of Lorne, at Trinity College.

[1] Chapel House, Twickenham.

[2] 'Mr. Bird comes about the railways and is glad to get A.'s vote against them' (*Journal*, p. 218). See below, p. 396.

[3] 'He called again with Mr. Woolner and proposed to meet me at Haslemere with Mrs. Tennyson and go and look at the land, which, being heath and having a hill and a brook on it, has charms for both of them' (*Journals of Walter White*, p. 159).

To FREDERICK LOCKER

Text. Memoir, i. 488–9; Materials, ii. 372–3.

FARRINGFORD, January 31, 1863 [for 1865][1]

Dear Mr. Locker

I am glad that your young lady approves of my little book. Why wouldn't you let me give it to her?

As to this canard of a Baronetcy, I remember the same foolish rumour arising some years ago, and with some little trouble I put it down, or it died down of itself. In this instance the notice had been out in the *Athenaeum* several days before I heard of it, but I answered the first letter which alluded to it by declaring that the rumour was *wholly* unfounded; so that as no Baronetcy has been offered, there is less reason for considering your friendly pros and cons as to acceptance or refusal; if it had, I trust that I should have had grace and loyalty enough to think more of the Queen's feelings than my own in this matter.[2] I mean whichever way I answered. Both myself and my wife have been somewhat vexed and annoyed by all this chatter.

Kind regards to Lady Charlotte. I shall be glad to see you here, whenever you like to come our way. Froude promised me he would come in January, but January is breathing his last to-day.

Yours very truly
Alfred Tennyson

Your letter only arrived yesterday, though dated the 28th.

To JAMES THOMAS FIELDS

MS. University of Virginia.

FARRINGFORD, February 3, 1865

My dear Mr. Fields

Many thanks for the promised cheque. As we are not at war *yet* I am at a loss to understand how you never received proofs of the selections[1] which my publisher Mr. Payne (Moxon and Co.) duly sent off to you before publication here. I will write to him today and tell him to forward the book to you.

---

[1] Both *Memoir* and *Materials* misdate this letter 1863; the abridgement printed in *An Appendix to the Rowfant Librray*, p. 169, is dated correctly. It replies to Locker's letter of 28 January (incomplete draft in Armstrong Browning Librray). The 'young lady' was his daughter Eleanor Mary Bertha Locker, who married first (1878) Lionel Tennyson, father of Sir Charles Bruce Locker Tennyson, and secondly (1888) Augustine Birrell (1850–1933), and died in 1915 (*DNB*, *Peerage*).

[2] 'Sir Alfred Tennyson, Bart. is—we believe—the new style of the Poet Laureate. The Queen has tendered this choice honour to the great poet,—an offering from the heart, not to be denied, not to be postponed—and the great poet has accepted Her Majesty's gift in the spirit in which it was offered to his acceptance. Sir Alfred is the first Laureate who has been actually created a baronet' (*Athenaeum*, 14 January, p. 55). The next week the *Athenaeum* (p. 90) quoted a correspondent ('Caesariensis') who asserted that the report of an offer of a baronetcy to Tennyson possessed a 'solid foundation in fact', but added that, although 'for the moment' the matter of the baronetcy was 'delayed', Her Majesty's favour would 'end in the Laureate becoming Sir Alfred Tennyson, Bart'. See also *Journal*, p. 219.

[1] See above, p. 382 and n.

Perhaps also (as you do not mention the receipt of it) you never had my letter asserting your claim to the sole right of republishing my poems on your side of the water, as far as it was in my power.[2]

I will send you 'Break, Break' in a day or two; haven't I written it for you before? And I will also look out for some bit of old MSS for you. All good wishes to you and yours and believe me

Yours very truly
A. Tennyson

CHARLES TENNYSON TURNER to ALFRED TENNYSON

Text. Materials, i. 39 n.

February 6, 1865

I cannot however suppose that his casting our little book (with names disentangled) on the waters of its and our advanced life can signify one jot as to your or my reputation, or vendibility. Mine being small, it cannot injure it, and yours so big! It seems to me a mere trifle.[1]

To DRUMMOND RAWNSLEY

MS. Mrs. H. D. Rawnsley (who made the transcript).

FARRINGFORD, February 17, 1865

My dear Drummond

I send you a £10 cheque. You should not be hurt but rather pity us for our worse than Egyptian plague of letters, books, MSS. etc. not from England alone but from the colonies, U. S., even France, Italy, Germany—nay Liberia and the negroes: and the demands for churches, chapels, hospitals,

---

[2] Above, p. 388.

[1] Messrs Jackson, at Louth, publishers of *Poems by Two Brothers* (see i. 8–14) had unearthed the MS, and (according to Hallam Tennyson's note containing this letter), 'My uncle Charles wrote to my father . . . urging him not to mind if Jackson divulged the authorship of some of the poems, for he could not be certain of all from the manuscript'. In the event, Hallam Tennyson said (*Memoir*, i. 22): 'It fell to me to publish the second edition, sixty[-six] years after the publication of the first, and to endeavour to initial the poems.' See also Wise's *Bibliography*, i. 4.

So much for the record. The truth is uglier: Jackson blackmailed and Tennyson paid, as revealed by a copy (TRC) of a letter from Allen Nicol and Allen, 88 Queen Street St, Cheapside, to Payne on 16 January: 'Alfred Tennyson and Messrs. Jackson of Louth | Mr. Thomas Jackson has called on us with reference to the "Poems by Two Brothers". He says there are not any copies out and for sale—there are none left except a few in their own hands for personal use in their own families. | Mr. Jackson evidently intends, if he can, to make a purse out of the matter—he says he is now ready to put a New Edition to press. He has no doubts he can sell *at least 10,000* copies. That would yield him a profit of 2/ per copy which would be £1000 and he would rather publish the Book than take that sum. However he is anxious not to do anything contrary to Mr. Tennyson's wishes and is open to an offer based on such terms, *as a matter of business*, as may be thought reasonable, tho' [the] 20 or 50£ we hinted at, he treated as quite out of the question. What will Mr. Tennyson do? | Yrs very truly | (signed) Allen Nicol and Allen' | J. B. Payne Esqre.

schools—horseleeches all crying Give, give—are more than the Marquis of Westminster could satisfy.[1]

Hurt? when we are both dead of pennypost softening of the brain you will have to sprinkle a repentant tear over our ashes and believe in us as of old.

A. Tennyson

To THE DUKE OF ARGYLL

Text. Memoir, ii. 20.

FARRINGFORD, February 17, 1865

My dear Duke

Before answering definitely, I should like to know something about expenses. 'The Club'?[1] It is either my fault or my misfortune that I have never heard of it. I suppose one has not to pay some 25 guineas entrance and some 7 ditto a year, because then, I would not say that the game is not worth the candle, but that the candle is too dear for me. Does one only pay for one's dinner when eaten, or how is it?

Ever yours not ungratefully
A. Tennyson

I have ascertained that weasels *have* a hunting-cry.[2]

To THE DUKE OF ARGYLL

Text. Tennyson Research Centre (transcript); *Memoir*, ii. 20.

FARRINGFORD, February 20, 1865

My dear Duke

Propose me: I agree: yours be the shame if I'm blackballed!!![1]

---

[1] See above, p. 381.

[1] Argyll had written (15 February, TRC): 'You must have heard of "The Club", founded by Sam: Johnson, Reynolds, Gibbon etc. It is a Club which dines together on every second Tuesday during the London Season. It contains eminent men of all callings—Literary, Scientific, Political etc., but not Political men as *such*—only if they have some flavour of literature about them. It is a very pleasant Society somewhere about 30 in all. But seldom more than 12 or 14 actually attend, sometimes not more than 4 or 5. Dinner punctually at 7.30 and nobody waited for. Well, I think this said Society would be very much pleased if they could get you to join them, and I now write to ask you whether if elected you would accept the membership and companionship . . . .'

To Tennyson's inquiry, he replied (18 February, TRC) that expenses were 'not so heavy . . . as you might imagine. . . . I think I am correct when I tell you that the Entrance Fee is £5—(not one fourth of the value of 5 lines from your pen) and each time one dines one pays 21s. one guinea for one's dinner.' He added that at the beginning of the year to replenish the exchequer there was sometimes a subscription required of 1 or 2 pounds. On The Club, see also *Memoirs . . . of Henry Reeve*, ii. 67–8.

[2] See the next letter about the very beautiful conclusion to 'Aylmer's Field'.

[1] On 14 March, along with the Duc d'Aumale, Froude, and Stanley, Tennyson was elected to The Club. Besides the entrance fee of £5, he had to pay a subscription of £2 (see Argyll's letter, 15 March, TRC, misdated in *Memoir*, ii. 21, and also below, p. 000.

20 *February* 1865 393

Weasels.

I have not heard of any weasels crying in the chase after a *mouse*. Nor where it is a *solitary* hunter of *anything*. But I am assured by those who have heard them that when they join in the chase after *great* game such as a rabbit (even though there should be no more than two), they not unfrequently utter their faint hunting-cry. I suppose the size of their victim excites them.[2]

I never see 'The Field.' Would it be worth while writing thereto on this matter?[3]

Yours ever
A. Tennyson

I hope the Duchess is quite well again.

To EMILY SELLWOOD TENNYSON

Text. Memoir, ii. 18.

ROSEMOUNT, HAMPSTEAD, February 21, 1865

Mother had gone before I came, she went at 10 p.m., age 84.[1]

I dare not see her. I shall have to stop over the funeral. She did not ask for me especially, which is one comfort.

HAMPSTEAD, February 25, 1865.

I am going to put up at Arthur's.[2] We are all I think *pretty* cheerful. I hope Woolner will make himself quite at home (at Farringford) and have an attic for smoking, for he enjoys his pipe.

---

[2] Argyll had written on 18 February (TRC) concerning 'Aylmer's Field', ll. 13–14: 'ANENT the Weasel. I am certain that it has no hunting cry which is uttered ALWAYS when hunting. Because on more than one occasion I have seen a weasel pass me in full pursuit of a Field Mouse, and on none of these occasions did the weasel utter a cry. On one of these I was much interested, for I was lying in concealment watching for Wild Pigeons when a Field Mouse came running past me, going straight over every obstacle, as hard as it could run. After the space of about a minute up came the Weasel following the track with perfect accuracy, evidently following the scent. Now this is just the occasion when a Hound would be in FULL CRY. But the Weasel ran upon the hot scent in perfect silence. Of course they may SOMETIMES cry. But I am satisfied they don't *give tongue* as a habit in hunting.'

[3] Through the naturalist Francis Trevelyan Buckland (1826–80), who was a staff contributor to *The Field*, Argyll obtained a report from a clergyman 'very learned' on the subject, 'that weasels do utter a cry *sometimes when in packs*, and when close upon their victim' (11 March, TRC). In the Eversley Edition (ii. 361) Tennyson defended his original reading: 'The Duke of Argyll says of them that in hunting rabbits, in packs, they give a "faint hunting cry".'

[1] See *Journal*, pp. 220–1 (where the dates vary slightly from these).
[2] Arthur Tennyson.

To EMILY SELLWOOD TENNYSON

MS. Tennyson Research Centre.

Monday, [27 February 1865], 11 a.m.

Dearest

I am very sorry that I missed the Post on Saturday. I went to London with Arthur and the post goes so early here for the country at 4 ½ or thereabouts, but as Louie[1] wrote I hope thou hadst no anxiety. We are going to the funeral today—[*a few words excised*]. The departure of so blessed a being almost whose last words were, when asked how she felt, 'very quiet' seems to have no sting in it and she declared that she had no pain.[2] We all of us hate the pompous funeral we have to join in, black plumes, black coaches and nonsense. We should like all to go in white and gold rather—but convention is against us. I will write again if I have time after the funeral.

Thine x x x x
A. T.

I shall be back I expect in a day or two. I [*a few words excised*]

To EMILY SELLWOOD TENNYSON

MS. Tennyson Research Centre.

[27 February 1865]

Dearest

All has gone off very quietly—a funeral came before us and a funeral followed. I could have wished for the country churchyard. No more just now.

Thine x x x
A. T.

EMILY SELLWOOD TENNYSON to JAMES THOMAS FIELDS

MS. Huntington Library.

March 7, 1865

Dear Mr. Fields

My husband sends you this with kind regards.[1] He is at this moment looking for a fragment. He has been away from home or it would doubtless have been found in time for the next mail. He is extremely annoyed that neither of the two copies of The Specimens[2] sent to you should have reached you. He has requested Messrs. Moxon to forward you a third.

---

[1] Louisa Tennyson Turner (Emily Tennyson's sister).
[2] Tennyson said to the clergyman conducting the service: 'I hope you will not think that I have spoken in exaggerated terms of my beloved mother, but indeed she was the beautifullest thing God Almighty ever did make' (*Background*, p. 95).

[1] 'Break, break, break' (see above, p. 391).
[2] Perhaps a slip for *Selections* (see above, p. 382 n.).

With very kind remembrances for Mrs. Fields. Believe me,
Very truly yours
Emily Tennyson

I feel certain he copied Break Break for you before. It must have missed also? There is now no book-post to America we hear. The books were sent by carrier. The bill arrived safety. Mr. Tennyson's best thanks.

To ALGERNON CHARLES SWINBURNE

MS. Berg Collection.

FARRINGFORD, [March 1865]

My dear Sir

Accept my congratulations on the success of your Greek play.[1] I had some strong objections to parts but these I think have been modified by a reperusal and at any rate I dare say you would not care to hear them. Here however is one. Is it *fair* for a Greek chorus to abuse the Deity something in the style of the Hebrew prophets?

Altogether it is many a day since I have read anything so fine—for it is not only carefully written, but has both strength and splendour, and shows moreover that you have a fine metrical invention which I envy you.

Yours very truly
A. Tennyson

To THE DUKE OF ARGYLL

Text. Tennyson Research Centre.

FARRINGFORD, March 16, 1865

My dear Duke

Along with yours I have received Dean Milman's intimation of the honour done me, and will send the £7 when I know the banker's name.[1]

Thanks for the solution of the natural history question which you have procured for me[2]—and for yours and the Duchess's enquiries.

I think I am rather in a low way at present—but perhaps my spirits may grow with the growing year.

Yours ever
A. Tennyson

---

[1] *Atalanta in Calydon* (published in the first half of March). Tennyson's opinion (elsewhere) was the same and not the same: 'Ally's verdict about the Swinburne Poem is that it is extremely fine but that his objections to it are as deep as heaven and hell' (Emily Tennyson to Woolner, 28 March, TRC).

[1] Election to The Club: see above, p. 392 n. and *Memoir*, i. 21 n. Henry Hart Milman was chairman for the evening.

[2] The hunting cry of weasels (see above, p. 393 and n.).

To THE DUKE OF ARGYLL

Text. Tennyson Research Centre (transcript).

March 21, 1865

My dear Duke

We shall be very glad to see [you] both at Easter—only I must let you know when we shall have to be away with the two boys—for we have to take them over the water to their first school some time in Easter.[1]

I should have written to you yesterday but my whole afternoon was taken up about a railway with which they threaten us here, the terminus of which is to be at Freshwater Gate, so may be this will be your last visit to me here for assuredly I shall not stay if they do bring this terminus close by me—almost *everyone* is against it here, and if they accomplish their design, I shall consider I am living under a worse and more senseless despotism than any continental one: if we are to have a railway surely the terminus ought to be in the centre of the place not all of a side—but I see no necessity for one at all.[2]

I hear you are a great man of business on Committees—perhaps you would say a word for Freshwater against this vicious 'Western Section.'

Yours always
A. Tennyson

To JOHN MURRAY[1]

MS. Dr. W. Baker.

April 4, 1865

Mr. Alfred Tennyson presents his compliments to Mr. Murray and regrets that circumstances have so long delayed his thanks for the very interesting Guide Book of Surrey and Hampshire which Mr. Murray has been so kind as to give him.

To JOHN SULLIVAN[1]

MS. University of Virginia.

April 5, 1865

Sir

I am obliged to you for the Poems which you have been so kind as to send me. I cannot pretend to criticize those in Norman French. I am honoured by

---

[1] To Charles Kegan Paul's (see above, pp. 382 n., 386).

[2] 'We hear from Mr. Estcourt that the threatened railway with a terminal at the bay is to be stopt at Hock Hill or Pound Green' (*Journal*, p. 221).

[1] John Murray (1808–92: *DNB*), the well-known publisher.

[1] Addressed: John Sullivan Esqre | Notary Public | Jersey—probably the versifier and translator of numerous works into French listed in the *Catalogue of the British Library* with dates of publication 1866–92.

your wish to translate Poems of mine. They are at your service. I have the honour to be, Sir,

Your very obedient servant
A. Tennyson

To THE FLORENTINES

MS. Tennyson Research Centre.

[May 8, 1865]

Sir

Pray pardon me for having neglected to answer your first letter. I suppose that a severe family loss which happened about the time when this arrived, put it out of my head. You only asked for 'due versi' and I have taken you at your word and sent you something like a Greek epigram, which you are at liberty to insert or reject as you will.[1] I have the honour to be, Sir,

Your most obedient Servant
A. Tennyson

To CHARLES HAY CAMERON[1]

Text. Materials, iii. 12–13.

FARRINGFORD, May 15, 1865

My dear Mr. Cameron

I well remember your coming here to dine one day and that we had a very pleasant talk and smoke together, and I was glad to be reminded of that past hour by your present of the dagger. It is exceedingly curious and interesting and I have shut up your letter thereanent in the scabbard with it that its history may be patent to everyone who draws it for examination.

Your good father has not been so well lately or in such good spirits as I would wish him to be. The necessity of selling his Ceylon estates and just now the death of his friend Mr. P.,[2] by his own hand, has weighed heavily upon him, but at present he seems to be recovering his elasticity—but I need not tell you all this as I dare say you hear regularly from home, nor need I say that I shall be most happy to see you here once more whenever you return to England—a wish in which my wife joins. You will hardly know my

---

[1] 'To Dante (Written at the Request of the Florentines)' (Ricks, p. 1191): 'Last evening, in answer to a letter from Florence asking for lines on Dante, he made six and sent them off to-day in honour of Dante's six hundredth centenary' (*Memoir*, ii. 22; see also 255–6).

[1] Charles Hay Cameron (b. 1848), son of Julia Margaret and Charles Hay Cameron, was a 'coffee planter at Glencairn, Dikoya Valley, Ceylon', and never married (Helmut Gernsheim, *Julia Margaret Cameron*, p., 21; date of birth in Colin Ford, *Julia Margaret Cameron*, p. 144; a photograph *c.* 1890 on p. 18).

[2] 'The Bard's Dagger arrives from Mr. Charles Cameron. A tremendous looking weapon' (Journal, 9 May). See above, p. 381 n. According to *Materials*, iii. 12, Cameron was in Surat, India, and the dagger was an 'Indian Bard's'.

[3] Unidentified.

two little ones again, I fancy. They have shot up so much. Believe me, dear Mr. Cameron,

Yours ever
A. Tennyson

ALFRED AND EMILY SELLWOOD TENNYSON
to AUBREY DE VERE

Text. Memoir, ii. 22–3.

FARRINGFORD, May 15, 1865

My dear Aubrey

The death of my good friend Stephen has not taken me in any way by surprise.[1] I had even expected to hear of it some weeks ago. Death is, I should hope, to most of us a 'deliverance,' and to him especially, suffering as he did continually from these attacks, it must have been a 'great' one. I have had such dear and near losses this year that—I do not say I can on that account sympathise more fully with his wife and children, but I do most fully feel for and with them: and tell them so whenever an opportunity occurs. I hope they are all well, and you also.

Ever yours
A. Tennyson

P. S. He was one of the five of his friends I knew before our marriage, and the third (the other two Arthur Hallam and Henry Lushington) who has left us. No new friends can be like the old to him or to any, I suppose, and few of the old were so dear to him as he. May I too say all that is kind and sympathising. How does his father bear his loss? It seems a long time since we met.

Ever yours
Emily Tennyson

DEREK HUDSON, *MUNBY MAN OF TWO WORLDS, THE LIFE AND TIMES OF A. J. MUNBY*,[1] p. 208.

YARMOUTH, May 23, 1865

At 4.30 by steamer (3 or 4 times a day) across Solent to Lymington, Hants. Dirty weather, sea and down hung with mist. On board with us went Tennyson and (I suppose) his wife. T. about 5 feet 8, largely made, hands big and muscular: wore old careless dress, tall wideawake, camlet cloak, loose blue trousers, frock coat and open shirt front—no gloves. Long wild curling

---

[1] Stephen Spring Rice, Aubrey de Vere's first cousin, died on 9 May aboard the steam vessel *Tripoli*, returning from Gibraltar. He was survived by his wife (who died 23 March 1869) and ten children (see i. 96 n. and *Peerage*).

[1] Arthur Joseph Munby (1828–1910: *DNB*), Trinity College, Cambridge (BA 1851), and perhaps the strangest of her sons, poet and civil servant: he held the ecclesiastical commissioner's office, 1858–88, and wrote six volumes of poetry, 1852–1909.

hair: beard thin on cheeks, full round wild [?] lips and chin. Complexion sallow, finely cut acquiline nose, veined: mouth grave and subtle in expression, face deeply lined: eyes hidden by blue spectacles. Voice deep and slow: gait stooping and heavy, almost aged. I watched him talking with a fat parson: round him other parsons, tourists, sailors; and his face supreme in manliness and mental power.

To ?

MS. New York University Libraries.

HAMPSTEAD, June 5, 1865

My dear Sir

I am extremely sorry that I should have been again absent from home when you proposed calling to see the coins.[1] I also much regret having been prevented from answering your letter before.

Another time I trust I shall be more fortunate. Believe me, dear Sir,

Truly yours
A. Tennyson

To SIR JOHN SIMEON

MS. Syracuse University.

June 15, 1865

My dear Sir John

Please to put my name on your committee. I would it were not merely a name! However let us hope that the greatest of all triumphs for yourself awaits you—a personal triumph. Not because people agree with you but in spite of all disagreement. I hope we shall prove ourselves sensible that you are the man who has had the best interests of the Island most at heart and has worked hardest to promote them.[1]

We know you have no time for visiting now but make us your home at any time of any day should this be convenient. With our love

Ever yours affectionately
A. Tennyson

To LEWIS FYTCHE

MS. Tennyson Research Centre.

FARRINGFORD, June 17, 1865

My dear Lewis

You will think I have forgotten you and your kind invitation to Thorpe Hall: but the fact is I have such bundles of letters to answer that my best friends often have to wait for an answer. There never was such a plague

---

[1] See above, p. 329.

[1] Simeon was elected to Parliament in July.

invented for a literary man as the penny post, which lays him open to the importunities and impertinences of all the world: moreover I have been marvellously unwell with hayfever and at this present [moment] can hardly see to write from itching and irritability in the eyes. What shall I say of the deaths of our good mothers—nothing—to quote a line of my own—

> Comfort thyself: what comfort is in me?[1]

And as to visiting you we never or hardly ever visit anywhere. What we do at this time of year is to rush abroad for a couple of months and so escape the season when the cockneys come trampling over my grounds and staring into the windows.

I trust that yourself and your wife and your young are all flourishing. Poor Albert. What a shock to him his arrival in England will be![2] Believe me, my dear Lewis,

Always affectionately yours
A. Tennyson

To FREDERIC WILLIAM FARRAR

MS. University of Virginia.

FARRINGFORD, June 21, 1865

Sir

I have this morning received your essay on the Origin of Languages, and beg leave to thank you for it.[1] Believe me

Yours faithfully
A. Tennyson

To THE DUKE OF ARGYLL

Text. Tennyson Research Centre (transcript).

June 24, 1865

My dear Duke

I did come up to town in order to be present at the Royal Society on June 5th.

Hay I don't care for, but the dust and stew of an express train brings on with me the very worst and most maddening phases of hay-fever. The result of my journey was among other inconveniences a swelled mouth which made all dining impossible and London intolerable. So being advised to return to the country, back I went in the cool of an evening to Winchester and next day

---

[1] 'Morte d'Arthur', l. 243.
[2] The arrival of Albert Fytche from India, to find that his mother has died.

[1] Farrar was now a master at Harrow (see above, p. 35 n.). His *Origin of Languages* was first published in 1860, and in 1865 he published *Chapters on Language*. With the former Darwin was so impressed that in 1866 he proposed Farrar 'for the Fellowship of the Royal Society, to which he was duly elected' (Reginald Farrar, *Life of Farrar*, pp. 106–8).

made an easy stage home again in the evening—and here I have been ever since.

Now I think of making another attempt next week and when I reach town I will let you know. If a wet day would intervene and lay the dust I would start at once.

Thanks for your offer of a bed at Argyll Lodge but I shall not need it, though I should wish you to introduce me to 'The Club'—if I can go.[1] With best regards to the Duchess from us both, believe me

Ever yours
A. Tennyson

The boys have got properly 'hogged' and uglified, but seem very comfortable.[2]

WILLIAM ALLINGHAM, *A DIARY*, pp. 117–19.

Saturday, June 24, [1865]

After Custom-House, steamer to Island. Farringford, hid my bag—find some people in the hay-field and Mrs. Cameron photographing everybody like mad.

Went to house: A. T. says, 'Are you come to stay?' I confess the bag and we go to fetch it. Mrs. Cameron focuses me, but it proves a failure and I decline further operations. She thinks it a great honour to be done by her. Dress for dinner. Mr. King, the publisher, at dinner and Mrs. King. Talk of Ireland,—Petrie[1] and other men, of whom A. T. hardly knows the existence. The cholera. T.'s den at top of house; smoking,—Public Schools, Charterhouse, etc., effect of a few bad boys on the rest—Tupper—Swinburne. The Kings take leave, are at the Albion Hotel. I sit reading and A. T. comes down to me.

Farringford, Sunday, June 25, [1865]

Fine—at breakfast A. T. with his letters, one from D. of Argyll.[2] Swinburne—Venables. Out and meet the Kings—Mrs. Cameron. Return to Farringford. Dinner (which is at 6.30 always). Sitting at claret in the drawing-room we see the evening sunlight on the landscape. I go to the top of the house alone; have a strong sense of being in Tennyson's green summer, ruddy light in the sky.

---

[1] Argyll's letter (22 June, TRC), pointing out that the last dinner of the season for The Club was scheduled for 4 July, said: 'Now it would be desirable, *if possible*, not to let the Session in which you were elected pass, without your making *one* appearance,' and added, 'on this as well as on other grounds I should like very much to see you there, and if it could be arranged, I should like to go with you to the Club'.

[2] Their hair was cut—see above, pp. 382 and n., 388.

[1] George Petrie (1798–1866: *DNB*), Irish antiquary and artist.

[2] Part of Argyll's letter (24 June, TRC) was manifestly about Swinburne: 'I saw Venables at the Athenaeum yesterday, who told me of some new poetical luminary appearing above the horizon—that you had looked at Him—pronounced his light genuine. I must get Him, tho' I don't like dramatic poems much. Venables spoke of his lyrics as specially good.'

When I came down to drawing-room found A. T. with a book in his hand; the Kings expectant. He accosted me, 'Allingham, would it disgust you if I read "Maud"? Would you expire?'

I gave a satisfactory reply and he accordingly read 'Maud' all through, with some additions recently made. His interpolated remarks very amusing.

'This is what was called namby-pamby!' —'That's wonderfully fine!'— 'That was very hard to read; could you have read it? I don't think so.' . . .

Upstairs, talk of Poe. I praise Emerson, to which T. rather demurs, but says little. By and by he asks me to lend him Emerson's books, which I will gladly do. I feel his naturalness much.

Monday, June 26, [1865]

Cloudy. Farringford. A. T. last night intended to come across with me and let me show him some places. Now, at breakfast time, he can't make up his mind.

The Queen is liberal minded, she thinks Churchmen are in the way to ruin the Church by bigotry—likes droll stories—story of great fire and little fire to burn doll—when T. visited her she curtseyed very low in receiving him—was there anything particular in this?[3]

Another Majesty, Dowager Queen Emma of the Sandwich Islands, is expected soon on a visit to Farringford.[4]

To LADY FRANKLIN

MS. Colorado College Library.

Tuesday morning, [4 July 1865][1]

Dear Lady Franklin

Woolner and myself will have great pleasure in coming to you on Saturday, i.e. if I am not quite knocked up with London ways. I write on the only bit of paper I can light on—my host being engaged in his studio I don't like to disturb him.

Affectionately yours
A. Tennyson

THE JOURNALS OF WALTER WHITE, p. 160.

July 9, 1865

To breakfast at Woolner's, Tennyson, Spedding, and Mr. Pollock. We had talk about spelling, about a universal language, about Bell of Edinburgh's mode of writing sounds of any language so that any one ignorant of the

---

[3] See *Journal*, pp. 185–6.   [4] See below, p. 405.
[1] Endorsed: Recd. 4th July 1865.

language can pronounce the sounds.[1] Then when pipes were lit the Laureate read us a poem. Another Northern Farmer, who had made money and enlarged his farm and is proud thereof; and mounted on his horse 'property' expostulates with his son, who wants to marry the pretty but penniless daughter of the curate.[2] After that Macmillan and Lawrence and Arthur Hughes and Fenn came in. The latter talked about getting Gustave Doré to illustrate an edition of the Poems.[3]

To OLDLING, OSBORNE AND CO. [?][1]

MS. University of Kansas.

FARRINGFORD, FRESHWATER, ISLE OF WIGHT, July 29, 1865

Gentlemen

I beg to enclose a cheque from Messrs. Routledge[2] and the Treasury Certificates for July requesting that you will kindly acknowledge them. Also that you will pay for me to the account of The Revd C. Kegan Paul of Bailie eighty-nine pounds seven shillings and sixpence, £89. 7. 6, into the National Provincial Bank at Wimborne.

May I likewise request that you will do me the favour to make up my Banking Book and return it. I am, Gentlemen,

Your very obedient servant
A. Tennyson[3]

WILLIAM ALLINGHAM, *A DIARY*, pp. 118–19.

Saturday, July 29, [1865]

To Farringford. After dinner T. spoke of boys catching butterflies.

'Why cut short their lives?—What are we? We are the merest moths. Look at that hill' (pointing to the one before the large window), 'it's four hundred

---

[1] Alexander Melville Bell (1819–1905: *DAB*), teacher and prolific writer on speech, elocution, and phonetics, was the author of *Visible Speech: Every Language Universally Legible, Exactly as Spoken, Accomplished by Means of Self-Interpreting Physiological Symbols, Based on a Discovery of the Exact Physiological Relation of Sounds* (1864; revised 1865; 1867, etc.), father of Alexander Graham Bell (1847–1922: *DNB*), inventor of the telephone.

[2] 'Northern Farmer, New Style' (Ricks, p. 1189).

[3] Probably Samuel Laurence (also misspelt above, p. 340); Arthur Hughes (1832–1915: *DNB*), the Pre-Raphaelite painter, illustrated 'Enoch Arden' in 1866 (see below, p. 428); George Manville Fenn (1831–1909: *DNB*), novelist, editor of *Cassell's Magazine* and proprietor of *Once a Week*, with some Lincolnshire background, including a wife from there—the boys' books for which he is famous began in 1867. For Doré, see below, p. 452.

[1] Bankers, 20 Clement's Lane, Lombard Street, EC, but temporarily at 29 Gracechurch Street, EC (*P.O. London Directory*). Tennyson wrote a check on this bank on 10 February 1863 (see above, p. 282).

[2] Royalty on the Illustrated Edition (see above, p. 379).

[3] With some clerks' notations at the end—e.g. 'Cash 124-4'—of which the relevance is not obvious.

millions of years old;—think of that! Let the moths have their little lives.'

Speaking of the Colonies, he said, 'England ought to keep her colonies and draw them closer. She ought to have their representatives sitting in London, either in or in connection with the Imperial Parliament.'

Tennyson is always well at sea. 'To own a ship, a large steam-yacht,' he said, 'and go round the world—that's my notion of glory.'

Of the Norwegian waterfalls he said, 'I never was satisfied with water before. On the voyage out, standing at the door of the deck cabin, I saw a moving hill of water pass the side of the ship. I got on the top of the cabin, and saw the sea like a mountainous country, all hill and valley, with foam for snow on the summits;—the finest thing I ever saw.'[1]

Tennyson loathes the necessity, which he fancied himself under, of writing for money. 'The fine thing would be to have a good hereditary estate and a love of literature.' Of the expenses of land-owning he said, 'it costs £100 an acre, and brings in nothing yet.'

T. said he had read part of Carlyle's *Frederick* till he came to, '*they* did not strive to build the lofty rhyme,' and then flung the book into a corner.[2]

He read some extracts in the *Spectator* about poetry, and referred to Carlyle's contemptuous way of speaking of poets, saying, 'We are all tadpoles in a pool, one a little larger or smaller than others!' How differently Goethe would have spoken of this minor poet: 'he was useful in his own time and degree.'[3] See MS. in 'Minor Poets.'

'I was at an hotel in Covent Garden, and went out one morning for a walk in the Piazza. A man met me, tolerably well-dressed but battered-looking. I never saw him before that I know of. He pulled off his hat and said "Beg pardon, Mr. Tennyson, might I say a word to you?" I stopped. "I've been drunk for three days and I want to make a solemn promise to you, Mr. Tennyson, that I won't do so any more." I said that was a good resolve, and I hoped he would keep it. He said, "I promise you I will, Mr. Tennyson," and added, "Might I shake your hand?" I shook hands with him, and he thanked me and went on his way.'

---

[1] See above, p. 205, 207.

[2] 'Lycidas', l. 10—a telling revelation: Tennyson read fewer than a hundred (of more than 3,400) pages, balking in Book ii, ch. 6, at the discussion of the Teutsch Ritterdom (Teutonic Order), unmistakably the knights of the Round Table overcoming the heathen (Prussian) hordes and building Camelot. A few pagers later (if he had retrieved the volume even briefly) he would have noticed Carlyle's citation, pointless unless pointed, of a single line from a medieval minne-song: '*Ich wünsch ich wäre tot*, I wish that I were dead' (*Frederick the Great*, ii. 8)—unmistakably suggesting 'Mariana', which Carlyle despised (James Pope-Hennessy, *Monckton Milnes, the Flight of Youth*, p. 59).

[3] Possibly an allusion to (though not a quotation from) Carlyle's essay 'Corn Law Rhymes'.

EMILY SELLWOOD TENNYSON
to MRS JAMES THOMAS FIELDS

MS. Huntington Library.

FARRINGFORD, October 5, 1865

My dear Mrs. Fields

I found the kind gift of the Farringford Edition[1] on my return from Germany where we have all been for a little time making our way by Waterloo, Treves, and Weimar to Dresden and returning by Brunswick and Hanover and Aix la Chapelle. A journey which only wanted a little more health and strength to have made it very delightful. As it was much of it had a very lively interest (lifefull if there were such a word) for all.[2]

The various interests by which you are now surrounded must be almost overpowering.

What will your country emerge after this fiery trial?[3] A question of deepest interest for the whole world. One which Mr. Fields leads us to hope you may answer for yourself by word of mouth, but which the event alone can answer fully. Will it be soon or must we yet wait long?[4]

Our latest guest had made me meditate on the movement of the age. Queen Emma—who could think that that calm and sweetly dignified lady is so near the days of Captain Cook![5]

Our boys came home to see her but they are again gone to their private Tutor's at Baillie near Wimbourne. A sad blank they leave you will not doubt.

My husband is not very strong, still much better than he was two years ago. We trust you are both well.

With very kind remembrances from us both believe me

Very truly yours
Emily Tennyson

There I stupidly wandered off in mind to many places and in imagination to the Field of Waterloo and Goethe's study before I had begged you to give my best thanks for the very pretty edition and for the kindness in dedicating it to myself; the thanks seemed so to belong to the mere [?] acknowledgement of the gift, I suppose. Am I wrong in asking that the dedication might be to Mrs. Alfred Tennyson when it is reprinted. In England Mrs. Emily Tennyson would mean his unmarried elderly sister and you see I am bound not quietly to give up the honour meant for me and may the error in the Exhibition Ode Part for Art be corrected.[6]

---

[1] *Poems* (2 vols., Ticknor and Fields, Boston, 1865; *Tennyson in Lincoln*, ii, No. 3609).

[2] For accounts of this trip of 9 August–12 September 1865, see *Journal*, pp. 229–34, and *Memoir*, ii. 24–7.

[3] The American Civil War had ended in April.

[4] Till November 1866, when the Fieldses visited again (see *Journal*, p. 255).

[5] Emma, Dowager Queen of Hawaii (1836–85), widow of Kamehameha IV (1834–63), her half-brother, visited the Isle of Wight in September–October (see *Journal*, pp. 234–6; *Memoir*, ii. 27–8). Captain James Cook (1729–79: *DNB*), the explorer and discoverer of the Sandwich Islands, was murdered there by natives in 1779.

[6] See above, p. 305.

To ROBERT BROWNING

MS. Berg Collection.

FARRINGFORD, October 11, 1865

My dear Browning

Very welcome is the nosegay, not only for 'the *love* in the gift'—which make me who am physically the most unbumptious of men and authors—proud: but also for its own very peculiar flowerage and beautification, for which I think I have as high a respect as any man in Britain.[1] I stick it into my buttonhole and feel Bulwer's cork heels added to my boots.[2]

My wife always remembers you—and another. I too when last at Paris took a long look at the Hotel Douvres[3] thinking of the former time.

Ever yours affectionately
A. Tennyson

To RICHARD OWEN

MS. Berg Collection.

FARRINGFORD, [October, 18]65[1]

My dear Owen

I suppose when you say 'quantity' like most English people you mean accent. 'embryonic' would be the accent though the *syllable* is a short one, embryŏnic not embryōnic. As for 'embryonal' I never heard of such a word, but if there be such, it may be a moot point whether you laid the accent on the first syllable, or the one before the last: for there is a word 'embryonate' (being in the state of an embryo) which I find accented on the first: embryonal would be certainly wrong: but except you really want the two words for some scientific distinction, it would be better to stick to 'embryonic'.

I and my wife are grieved to hear that you have overtasked your muscular powers in your Highland holiday. Pray for your own and your friends' sake obey your doctors (you scarce have a better and kindlier than Paget) and cease to work for awhile that you may work better hereafter. We cannot afford to lose your brains. Not at least till all our lizards are dug out, and this

---

[1] *A Selection from the Works of Robert Browning* (second of Moxon's Miniature Poets, 1865). See the accompanying letter in *Memoir*, ii. 28. The prefatory note to the volume (now at Boston University—Kelley and Coley, *The Browning Collections*, C541) reads: 'It is the wish of Messrs. Chapman and Hall, who now publish my poems, that a little gathering from the lightest of these should be tied together after the pretty device of my old publishers, Messrs. Moxon. Not a single piece here belongs to the selection already issued by the former gentlemen, which was, perhaps, a fair sample of the ground's ordinary growth; this, such as it may prove, contentedly looks pale beside the wonderful flower-show of my illustrious predecessor—dare I say? my dear friend: who will take it, all except the love in the gift, at a mere nosegay's worth. R. B. London, March 21, 1865.'

[2] See i. 147–8 n., and Ricks, pp. 736–9.

[3] Where in 1851 Emily Tennyson had first met the Brownings (see *Memoir*, ii. 16, and *Journal*, p. 26).

---

[1] Possibly September, but October seems implied in *The Life of Richard Owen*, ii. 162–3.

stretch of red cliff which I see from my attic windows no longer needs an interpreter. Believe me,

Ever truly yours
A. Tennyson

To RICHARD OWEN

MS. Gordon Ray.

October 26, 1865

My dear Owen[1]
I have just lighted on your old world lizard-bones among the modern eggs on my breakfast table, and beg with all thanks, to subscribe myself

always
Geologically, diapsically
Plesiosaurically
and
Palaeontographically

Yours
A. Tennyson

To JOHN REUBEN THOMPSON

MS. University of Virginia.

November 1, 1865

Dear Mr. Thompson
I find that I have mistaken your meaning. I understood from your letter that you were coming to Freshwater and more that you would be here or hereabouts for two or three days: so, as I never am over-fond of writing letters I thought I will thank him in person for his present when he calls: but you never did call nor can I find out that you have been at either of the Hotels. So I take it, you changed your mind and went back to London. However let me thank [you] now for your Tobacco which was pronounced by some friends staying here as super-excellent.

I need not add that if ever you do come my way I shall be most happy to welcome you.

I never see Blackwood's Magazine, but would most willingly read the

---

[1] In July 1865 Owen came to Farringford, and he and Tennyson went to Brightstone (Brixton), and 'spread out their luncheon on Mr. Fox's lawn. They looked at the great dragon which was new to the Professor, and quite answered his expectation' (*Materials*, iii. 15; *Memoir*, ii. 23; *Journal*, pp. 228–9). Owen came again in January 1866, and said he 'had half a chance to look over the Rev. Mr. Fox's fossils at Brixton'; a note adds that 'Fox discovered the *Poikilopleuron* and other interesting fossil Dinosaurs' (*The Life of Richard Owen*, ii. 169). In 1897 V. C. Scott O'Connor reported seeing under the porch at Farringford 'some fossil remains of a huge lizard, dug up in Freshwater Bay and brought here in Tennyson's lifetime. "My father was deeply interested in geology", was Lord Tennyson's comment when he drew my attention to them' (*Century Magazine*, lv [Dec. 1897], 250).

'Memoirs of the Confederate War for Independence' which you are good enough to offer to send me, particularly as you tell me that the most spirited and *truthful* account of that heroic struggle is to be found there.[1]

Present my best regards to the gallant Captain Fearn[2] when you see him and believe me

Yous very truly
A. Tennyson

To THE VISCOUNTESS BOYNE

MS. Viscount Boyne.

FARRINGFORD, ISLE OF WIGHT, November 8, 1865

My dear Emma

I have not heard of my Aunt's kind intentions toward me, and I thank you for your affectionate thought in telling it to me. I need not say that the remembrance is very precious to me perhaps all the more for having been so made and recorded.[1]

We hope very soon to have better news of you. Matilda has been suffering from rheumatism. She settles here as well as can be expected considering the recent past.[2] My wife adds her best wishes to mine and with my kind regards to Lord Boyne, believe me

Your affectionate cousin
A. Tennyson

---

[1] In February 1865, 'Heros Van [sic] Borcke, who had served as chief of staff to General J. E. B. Stuart, arrived in London with his notes on the war. Van Borcke wanted to publish these notes in the form of a book-length memoir, for the English were eager to read about the war. He doubted his own abilities as a writer, however, so he hired Thompson, with whom he was already acquainted, to ghost-write the book for him. On July 15, he noted in his diary, "fifty-six closely written pages of Van Borcke's Journal" which he had written during the week were sent off to *Blackwood's*. On August 31, he received fourteen pounds as his share for Part One of the Memoirs, which were being published serially in *Blackwood's* over a ten-month period. Thompson received about seventy dollars a month for his work, but no recognition. When the book was published in October 1866, as *Memoirs of the Confederate War for Independence* by Heros Van Borcke, Thompson's name was not mentioned' (Gerald Garmon, *John Reuben Thompson*, pp. 123–4. See also James R. Belcher, Jr., and Ronald L. Heinemann, 'Heros von Borcke, Knight Errant of the Confederacy', *Virginia Cavalcade*, xxxv, No. 2 (Autumn 1985), 87–95).

[2] Walker Fearn (1832–99: *DAB*), of Mobile, Alabama, a diplomatic representative for the Confederacy, whom Tennyson had met in November 1864 at Woolner's (see above, p. 385 n., and *Journal*, pp. 221–4). (Later President Cleveland appointed Fearn Minister-Resident and Consul-General to Greece, Roumania, and Serbia.)

[1] Tennyson's favourite aunt, Elizabeth Russell, who had made gifts of money to him from his youth upward (e.g., see i. 69, 333), now remembers him in her will. The Tennysons last saw her in July, in Cheltenham: 'We got lodgings near Aunt Russell's, 20 Lansdowne Crescent. She looks peaceful and beautiful in spite of a painful kind of paralysis. A. and I have each long talks alone with her and one day he refreshed her spirit by telling her of Primeval Dragons and particularly of that found not far from Farringford which Professor Owen is coming to see' (Journal; *Journal*, p. 227).

[2] 'Two of our bedrooms are now taken up by our sister Matilda Tennyson and her maid their home being at present with us' (Emily Tennyson to Mrs Gatty, 24 November, Boston Public Library).

I send you a photograph of your Godson Lionel by Rejlander. Unfortunately the plate is broken—so this is the last I have but one.

To HENRY DICKFORD WOODFALL[1]

MS. Rowland Collins.

November 9, 1865

My dear Mr. Woodfall

Thank you much for your volume which I received this morning and will treasure as a memorial of you and therefore of our pleasant bit of touring together. It was nearly I think the *most* pleasant of all my little outings, though we had I recollect one Sunday to dine on brown paper. I trust that your journey to Nice will set you up again, but Nice I have heard is not always genial so you will have to take care of yourself even there.

With my wife's remembrances to you and mine to your brother (as I gather from the Maidstone postmark that you are still with him), I am

Yours always
A. Tennyson

To GEORGE FRANCIS ARMSTRONG[1]

MS. The Queen's University of Belfast.

FARRINGFORD, FRESHWATER, ISLE OF WIGHT, November 14, 1865

Sir

I have just received the volume of your brother's poems. The preface is full of interest. The poems I have not yet looked into. I am with thanks for the gift.

Your obedient servant
A. Tennyson

---

[1] Henry Dickwood Woodfall Esq., 18 Dean's Yard, Westminster (*P.O. London Directory*)—presumably son of George Woodfall and brother of Col. Woodfall (1810 [or 1811]–67), both of Maidstone (Boase; Venn; *Gentleman's Magazine*, March 1863 and May 1867). See above, p. 205. The volume is unidentified.

[1] George Francis Armstrong, later Savage-Armstrong (1845–1906), afterwards Professor of History and English Literature at Queen's College, Cork, and himself a poet, was the younger brother of Edmund John Armstrong (1841–65), a promising Irish poet, who died on 25 February 1865, before he had completed his undergraduate studies at Trinity College, Dublin. His friends had arranged for the publication of *Poems by the Late Edmund J. Armstrong* (Moxon, 1865), with a prefatory memoir by G. A. Chadwick. G. F. Armstrong edited *The Poetical Works, Essays and Sketches*, and *Life and Letters* of his brother, all in 1877 (*DNB*, Allibone). See also Henry Taylor's review of these three works, 'The Remains of Edmund J. Armstrong', *Edinburgh Review*, cxlviii (July 1878), 57–80, and his letter to George Armstrong, 8 January 1878, in *Correspondence of Henry Taylor*, ed. Dowden, pp. 379–80. See also *Tennyson in Lincoln*, i, Nos. 442–5.

To ALGERNON CHARLES SWINBURNE

MS. John S. Mayfield.

November 21, 1865

My dear Sir
 Here is a Chastelard just arrived[1]—I know not, if it came from you or Payne for there is no inscription—but if from you, many thanks.

Yours truly
A. Tennyson

To ARTHUR PENRHYN STANLEY

Text. Facsimile in John Wilson, Catalogue 54, May 1984.

November 24, 1865

My dear Stanley
 Your 2d series of the Jewish Church has come to me, but, there being no inscription, I am not sure whether you or your publisher has sent it. I flatter myself in thinking that it is from you, and am with all thanks

Ever yours
A. Tennyson

Kind remembrances to Lady Augusta from both of us.

To EMILY SELLWOOD TENNYSON

Text. Materials, iii. 25.

LONDON, December 2, 1865

 The steamer was not at Yarmouth, she lost her way in the mist and went back to Lymington. We took a boat with four rowers, and missed the train by ten minutes. Allingham met me; I went to his rooms for a while, and then we had a long rambling walk to Brockenhurst from which the train started at 5.35, landing us at Waterloo at 10.7 Singularly London was quite clear, though the country was misty all the way up.

EMILY SELLWOOD TENNYSON
to JOHN STUART BLACKIE

MS. National Library of Scotland.

FARRINGFORD, December 2, 1865

Dear Professor Blackie
 My husband is from home but I can answer for him that he is not engaged

---

[1] And just published, by Moxon

in translating the Iliad and I do not think he is likely to be. All success to your translation!¹

Our boys have been with a private tutor near Wimbourne since May 24. We hope to have them home for Christmas. The house is dreary without them I need not say. Believe me

Very sincerely yours
Emily Tennyson

To EMILY SELLWOOD TENNYSON

MS. Tennyson Research Centre.

Monday, December 4, 1865

Dearest

I called yesterday on Lady Franklin and found that she had already departed for the east. Queen Emma was to go either today or tomorrow Mrs. Thomasson¹ told me—so I will call today. Yesterday I called also with W[oolner] on Froude and then we all walked to Carlyle's. Mrs. C. seemed feeble but was very glad to see me. Then Carlyle walked a mile or two with us and was agreeable and amusing as usual. Payne has got himself into a mess I think which is a pity. I will go and see him and state my opinion of the matter friendly to him.² I dine at W[alter] White's on Thursday and Prof. Sharpey is to introduce me to the R[oyal] S[ociety].³

Thine × × × × ×
A. T.

To JAMES MACLEHOSE¹

MS. University of Virginia.

December 4, 1865

Sir

Your letter of the 29th November has only reached me this morning owing to my absence from home.

---

¹ A welcome answer to an interested inquiry, for Blackie's *Homer and the Iliad, A Translation in Ballad Metre*, three volumes of translation and notes, with an introductory volume of ten Dissertations, rejected by Longmans, Macmillan, Murray, and others, was published in 1866 by Edmondston and Douglas in Scotland 'on condition that they should be guaranteed against loss'—a proviso that cost Blackie £200 (Stoddart, *John Stuart Blackie*, pp. 13–28). Matthew Arnold wrote to his sister that Blackie was 'as capable of translating Homer as of making the Apollo Belvedere' (*The Complete Works of Matthew Arnold*, ed. R. H. Super: *On the Classical Tradition*, p. 252).

¹ Probably the wife of Thomas Thomasson (1808–76: *DNB*), the wealthy Quaker manufacturer and political economist.

² Not clear, but see the next letter.

³ William Sharpey (1802–80: *DNB*), Professor of Anatomy and Physiology, University of London, Secretary of the Royal Society.

¹ James MacLehose (1811–85), bookseller and publisher in Glasgow. The nature of the misunderstanding is not clear.

I regret most sincerely to learn the misunderstanding which has taken place betwixt yourself and Messrs. Moxon and Co. I think you will see that I am not a fit person to attempt to pronounce a judgement on the details of this misunderstanding: but I should be glad to hear that friendly relations have been resumed. I have the honour to be, Sir,

Your obedient Servant
A. Tennyson

To EMILY SELLWOOD TENNYSON

MS. Tennyson Research Centre.

Tuesday, [5 December 1865]

Dearest

I called on Queen Emma twice yesterday—first time I forgot to thank her for the book[1]—so I called again having previously written her a little note in case she should not be at home—however she was at home and I gave her the note too—which was colder than I felt—for I was a little hampered with court European forms. She was rather sad, I thought—and had a cough which she said she caught that morning when she went with Hallam up the down before breakfast.[2] Hoapili had a cough too caught he said in Lincolnshire but Mrs. H. was very well.[3] Our Queen had been very kind and cordial to Q[ueen] E[mma] and had given her a rich gold bracelet with a superb onyx and a portrait of herself and a lock of her hair. Q[ueen] E[mma] was off for the continent this morning at 8 o'clock.

The great man Gladstone is coming to dine with me here on Friday: a ⟨great⟩ compliment but how he can find time from the mighty press of business amazes me.

I go over to Palgrave's tomorrow (Wednesday). Thou dost not mention having received my last.

Thine × × × ×
A.

To ?

MS. University of Virginia.

[5 December 1865]

a true feeling in them and must have somewhat soothed the Queen in her great sorrow. I called upon her again yesterday having in my previous visit

---

[1] *The Book of Common Prayer*, translated into Hawaiian by Queen Emma's late husband, Kamehameha IV (see *Journal*, p. 239, and the next letter below).
[2] *Journal*, p. 236.
[3] Mr and Mrs Hoapili (the 'huge native' and his wife), who accompanied Queen Emma (*Journal*, p. 235).

forgotten to thank her for her gift of the Prayerbook in Hawaiian. She seemed rather sad, poor soul, and sorry to leave us. Believe me,

Yours very truly
A. Tennyson

To EMILY SELLWOOD TENNYSON

MS. Tennyson Research Centre; *Memoir,* ii. 30; draft *Materials,* v. 41.

[29 WELBECK STREET,] [6 December 1865]

[I am very sorry to hear about Lionel stammering. I hope it is only work and weather.][1]

[I go to Palgrave's to-day,] 5 York Gate, Regents Park. I dined there yesterday and met Joseph Hooker[2] who told me my tropical island was all right; but Arthur Hughes in his illustrations has made it all wrong, putting a herd of antelopes upon it which never occur in Polynesia. I saw Payne and have written a letter to Maclehose which I hope will serve as a mediator.

Thine × × ×
A. T.

To EMILY SELLWOOD TENNYSON

MS. Tennyson Research Centre.

5 YORK GATE, Thursday, December 7, 1865

Dearest

I am installed here having come from Woolner's last night where I dined with Mr. Jenner[1] who has ordered my bust from W. and who is going to leave it to the National Portrait Gallery—an amiable and reverential man he seems. I called on the Guests yesterday for Schreiber saw me walking in the Green Park and shouted out to me through the rails as he was riding down the street and begged me to call.[2] Enid was in and he: Lady C[harlotte] was out. I found fault with the Palgraves' tea and Mrs. P. begged me to ask (she always changing her tea-dealers) about Ridgway's tea—what kind it was and how much [it] was and how much we gave for it.

---

[1] Bracketed words from *Memoir,* ii. 30.

[2] Joseph Dalton Hooker (1817–1911: *DNB*), naturalist and botanist, an intimate of Charles Darwin, with whom he collaborated in researches into the origin of species, was Assistant Director of Kew Gardens (1855–65) and had recently succeeded his father as Director. He was a prolific writer on flora, was knighted in 1877, and received the OM in 1907. See below, p. 464.

[1] Charles Jenner, of Easter Duddingston, a brother of Sir William Jenner (1815–98: *DNB*), physician to the Queen and the Prince of Wales, commissioned Woolner to carve a replica of his bust of Tennyson, done for Trinity College (1857), which, in 1893, he gave to Hallam Tennyson to place at the grave in Westminster Abbey (*Woolner,* p. 180—see also pp. 129, 267—and *Memoir,* ii. 30 n.).

[2] See above, p. 381.

I must go and call on Forster today. I saw old Procter yesterday better than he was but very feeble. Mrs. P. is in Glo[uce]stershire.

> Thine × × × ×
> A. T.

Ellen's marriage comes under the head of 'Miracles' I think.[3]

To EMILY SELLWOOD TENNYSON

Text. Materials, iii. 27.

YORK GATE, December 8, [1865]

I was inducted into the Royal Society last night, after dining with W. White whither Woolner accompanied me. We had a merry dinner with lots of anecdotes; there were very few people, and I went through it without nervousness.[1] I walked across the park to see Forster yesterday, and got wet through, all in vain, for he was at his office. He sent me a very pretty letter this morning. The poor man is slowly recovering from his first fit of the gout.

To ELLEN TENNYSON D'EYNCOURT

MS. Lincolnshire Archives Office.

December 8, 1865

My dear Ellen

Your letter has been forwarded to me here in town where I am staying at 5 York Gate, Regents Park, having come up for the purpose of being inducted into the Royal Society of which I am a fellow.

It is good news that you tell me of your approching bridals.[1] Let me say that I am happy in your happiness,[2] for I trust that a life of happiness awaits you—and believe me

> Affectionately yours
> A. Tennyson

---

[3] Ellen Tennyson d'Eyncourt, Tennyson's first cousin, married Henry Mill Bunbury of Marlston House, Berks., on 13 February 1866 (*Landed Gentry*). See i. 62 n. and below.

[1] 'Tennyson, Woolner, and Dr. Sharpey dined with me. We had merry stories and grave and cheerful talk. At 8.30 to the evening meeting [of the Royal Society], at which the Bard was admitted and Prof. R. Grant of Glasgow. At the end of Cayley's paper on the 'Ischirnhausen's Transformation', Tennyson and Woolner went back to the dining room for a smoke. Then at the close of meeting to the Lower Library for tea and talk. Attracted by the portrait of Copernicus; and then I showed them Galileo. The former they thought imaginative and grand, the latter has the painful look of one in mental sufferings. Woolner told me the Chancellor of Exchequer (Gladstone) is to dine at his house to-morrow, as Tennyson says, 'to meet the poor Poet'' (*Journals of Walter White*, pp. 160–1). Robert Grant (1814–82) was an astronomer, Arthur Cayley (1821–95) a mathematician (*DNB*).

[1] They attended her wedding (Charles Tennyson Turner's 'Memorandum Book for 1866', TRC; transcribed by Roger Evans).

[2] Keats's 'Ode to a Nightingale', l. 6.

8 December 1865

LETTERS AND PAPERS OF JOHN ADDINGTON SYMONDS, ed. Horatio F. Brown (London: John Murray, 1923), pp. 1–10.[1]

December 8, 1865

My father came to us this afternoon. He is going to dine with Woolner, to meet Tennyson, Gladstone and Holman Hunt. I am to go in the evening at 9.30.

When I arrived at Woolner's, the maid said she supposed I was 'for the gentlemen.' On my replying 'Yes,' she showed me into the dining-room, where they were finishing dessert. Woolner sat of course at the bottom of the table, Tennyson on his left, my father on his right hand. Gladstone sat next Tennyson and Hunt next my father. I relapsed into an arm-chair between Woolner and my father.

The conversation continued. They were talking about the Jamaica business—Gladstone bearing hard on Eyre,[2] Tennyson excusing any cruelty in the case of putting down a savage mob. Gladstone had been reading official papers on the business all the morning and said, with an expression of intense gravity, just after I had entered, 'And that evidence wrung from a poor black boy with a revolver at his head!' He said this in an orator's tone, pity mingled with indignation, the pressure of the lips, the inclination of the head, the lifting of the eyes to heaven, all marking the man's moral earnestness. He has a face like a lion's; his head is small above it, though the forehead is broad and massive, something like Trajan's in its proportion to the features. Character, far more than intellect, strikes me in his physiognomy, and there is a remarkable duplicity of expression—iron, vice-like resolution combined with a subtle, mobile ingeniousness.

Tennyson did not argue. He kept asserting various prejudices and convictions. 'We are too tender to savages; we are more tender to a black than to ourselves.' 'Niggers are tigers; niggers are tigers,' in *obbligato, sotto voce*, to Gladstone's declamation. 'But the Englishman is a cruel man—he is a strong man,' put in Gladstone. My father illustrated this by stories of the Indian

---

[1] First printed in Symonds's 'Recollections of Lord Tennyson. An Evening at Thomas Woolner's', *Century Magazine*, xlvi (May 1893), 32–7; also in *The Letters of John Addington Symonds*, ed. Schueller and Peters, i. 591–7. Four months earlier, in August 1865, Woolner was at Clifton sculpting a bust of Symonds's father, Dr John Addington Symonds (1807–71: *DNB*), a prominent physician and a cultivated writer, and the son, eavesdropping 'through an open door', recorded Woolner's gossip: 'Woolner is doing a bust of my father. . . . Tennyson is a great friend of his, and so is Browning. Browning tells him that he writes straight down, and never looks again at what he writes. Tennyson composes in his head, and never writes down until he is about to publish. Tennyson has composed as much as he has ever published and lost it again, owing to this habit. In particular, he once wrote a Lancelot, and now only a few lines or words come back upon his memory. Tennyson says form is immortal, instancing the short poems of Catullus. Browning hopes to live by force of thought, and is careless about form. Tennyson, Palgrave, and Woolner went to Tintagel. The poet there conceived four idylls about men, answering to his four idylls about women. Jowett put them out of his head by wondering whether the subjects could be properly treated. Tennyson makes mistakes about the poets he admires. He once wrote to [Philip James] Bailey [see i. 263 n., 266, 283], and said he was a wren singing in a hedge, while the author of 'Festus' was an eagle soaring above him' (Horatio F. Brown, *John Addington Symonds, A Biography*, 2nd edn., 1903, pp. 186–7).

[2] See below, p. 429 n.

Mutiny. 'That's not like Oriental cruelty,' said Tennyson; 'but I could not kill a cat, not the tomcat who scratches and miawls over his disgusting amours, and keeps me awake,' thrown in with an indefinable impatience and rasping hatred. Gladstone looked glum and irate at this speech, thinking probably of Eyre. Then they turned to the insufficiency of evidence as yet in Eyre's case, and to other instances of his hasty butchery—the woman he hung, though [mercy] recommended by court-martial, because women had shown savageness in mutilating a corpse. 'Because *women*, not *the woman*— and that, too, after being recommended to mercy *by court-martial*, and he holding the Queen's commission!' said Gladstone with the same hostile emphasis. The question of his personal courage came up. That, said Gladstone, did not prove his capability of remaining cool under and dealing with such special circumstances. Anecdotes about sudden panics were related. Tennyson said to my father, 'As far as I know my own temperament, I could stand any sudden thing, but give me an hour to reflect, and I should go here and go there, and all would be confused. If the fiery gulf of Curtius opened in the City, I would leap at once into it on horseback. But if I had to reflect on it, no—especially the thought of death—nothing can be weighed against that. It is the moral question, not the fear, which would perplex me. I have not got the English courage. I could not wait six hours in a square expecting a battery's fire.' Then stories of martial severity were told. My father repeated the anecdote of Bosquet in the Malakoff.[3] Gladstone said Cialdini had shot a soldier for being without his regimental jacket.[4] Tennyson put in, *sotto voce*, 'If they shot paupers, perhaps they wouldn't tear up their clothes,' and laughed very grimly.

Frank Palgrave here came in, a little man in morning dress, with short beard and moustache, well-cut features, and a slight cast in his eye, an impatient, unsatisfied look and some self-assertion in his manner. He directed the conversation to the subject of newspapers. Tennyson all the while kept drinking glasses of port and glowering round the room through his spectacles. His moustache hides the play of his mouth, but as far as I could see, that feature is as grim as the rest. He has cheek-bones carved out of iron. His head is domed, quite the reverse of Gladstone's—like an Elizabethan head, strong in the coronal, narrow in the frontal regions, but very finely moulded. It is like what Connington's head seems trying to be.[5]

---

[3] Pierre François Bosquet (1810–61), Marshal of France and senator, who distinguished himself in the Crimean War at Alma, Inkerman, and in the final attack on Sevastopol, where he commanded the assault troops on the Malakoff and was severely wounded. Upon witnessing the charge of the Light Brigade, he was quoted as saying, 'C'est très magnifique, mais ce n'est pas la guerre' (*The Times*, leader, 13 November 1854, and Cecil Woodham Smith, *The Reason Why*, p. 247).

[4] Enrico Cialdini (1881–92), Italian general, politician, and diplomat. He had stopped Garibaldi at Aspromonte in 1862.

[5] John Conington (1825–69: *DNB*), classical scholar, Corpus Professor of Latin at Oxford, 1854–69. A friend and confidant at Oxford of John Addington Symonds, when an undergraduate, Conington was responsible for Symonds's telling his father of the homosexuality of Dr Charles J. Vaughan (1816–97: *DNB*), Headmaster of Harrow, which led to his enforced resignation in 1859 (Phyllis Grosskurth, *John Addington Symonds*, pp. 33–40). (Vaughan was Stanley's brother-in-law and a friend of the Tennysons.)

8 December 1865

Something brought up the franchise. Tennyson said, 'That's what we're coming to when we get your Reform Bill, Mr. Gladstone; not that I know anything about it.' 'No more does any man in England,' said Gladstone, taking him up quickly with a twinkling laugh, then adding, 'But I'm sorry to see you getting nervous.' 'Oh, I think a state in which every man would have a vote is the ideal. I always thought it might be realized in England, if anywhere, with our constitutional history. But how to do it?' This was the mere reflector. The man of practice said nothing. Soon after came coffee. Tennyson grew impatient, moved his great gaunt body about, and finally was left to smoke a pipe. It is hard to fix the difference between the two men, both with their strong provincial accent—Gladstone with his rich flexible voice, Tennyson with his deep drawl rising into an impatient falsetto when put out: Gladstone arguing, Tennyson putting in a prejudice; Gladstone asserting rashly, Tennyson denying with a bald negative; Gladstone full of facts, Tennyson relying on impressions; both of them humorous, but the one polished and delicate in repartee, the other broad and coarse and grotesque. Gladstone's hands are white and not remarkable. Tennyson's are huge, unwieldy, fit for moulding clay or dough. Gladstone is in some sort a man of the world; Tennyson a child, and treated by him like a child.

Woolner played the host well, with great simplicity. His manner was agreeably subdued. Palgrave rasped a little. Hunt was silent. My father made a good third to the two great people. I was like a man hearing a concerto; Gladstone first violin, my father second violin, Tennyson violoncello, Woolner bass viol, Palgrave viola, and, perhaps, Hunt a second but very subordinate viola.

When we left the dining-room we found Mrs. Woolner and her sister, Miss Waugh (engaged to Holman Hunt),[6] in the drawing-room. Both of these ladies are graceful. They affect the simplicity of pre-Raphaelite nature, and dress without crinoline very elegantly. Miss Waugh, though called 'the goddess,' is nowise unapproachable. She talked of Japanese fans like a common mortal. Mrs. Woolner is a pretty little maidenly creature who seems to have walked out of a missal margin.

Woolner gave Gladstone a MS. book, containing translations of the 'Iliad' by Tennyson, to read. Gladstone read it by himself till Tennyson appeared. Then Woolner went to him and said, 'You will read your translation, won't you? And Palgrave, 'Come you! A shout in the trench!' 'No, I shan't,' said Tennyson, standing in the room, with a pettish voice, and jerking his arms and body from the hips. 'No, I shan't read it. It's only a little thing. Must be judged by comparison with the Greek. Can only be appreciated by the difficulties overcome.' Then seeing the MS. in Gladstone's hand, 'This isn't fair; no, this isn't fair.' He took it away, and nothing would pacify him. 'I meant to read it to Mr. Gladstone and Dr. Symonds.' My father urged him to no purpose, told him he would be φωνοῦντα συνετοῖσιν[7] but he cried, 'Yes, you and Gladstone, but the rest don't understand it.' 'Here's my son, an Oxford first-class man.' 'Oh, I should be afraid of him.' Then my father

---

[6] See above, p. 372 and n., and *Woolner*, p. 159.
[7] 'Speaking to an intelligent audience'.

talked soothingly in an admirable low voice to him such as those who have to deal with fractious people would do well to acquire. He talked to him of his poems—'Mariana in the Moated Grange.' This took them to the Lincolnshire flats—as impressive in their extent of plain as mountain heights. My father tried to analyse the physical conditions of ideas of size. But Tennyson preferred fixing his mind on the ideas themselves. 'I do not know whether to think the universe great or little. When I think about it, it seems now one and now the other. What makes its greatness? Not one sun or one set of suns, or is it the whole together?' Then to illustrate his sense of size he pictured a journey through space like Jean Paul Richer's,[8] leaving first one galaxy or spot of light behind him, then another, and so on through infinity. Then about matter. Its incognisability puzzled him. 'I cannot form the least notion of a brick. I don't know what it is. It's no use talking about atoms, extension, colour, weight. I cannot penetrate the brick. But I have far more distinct ideas of God, of love and such emotions. I can sympathise with God in my poor way. The human soul seems to me always in some way, how we do not know, identical with God. That's the value of prayer. Prayer is like opening a sluice between the great ocean and our little channels.' Then of eternity and creation: 'Huxley[9] says we may have come from monkeys. That makes no difference to me. If it is God's way of creation, He sees the whole, past, present, and future, as one' (entering on an elaborate statement of eternity *à la* Sir Thomas Browne).[10] Then of morality: 'I cannot but think moral good is the crown of man. But what is it without immortality? Let us eat and drink, for to-morrow we die. If I knew the world were coming to an end in six hours, would I give my money to a starving beggar: No, if I did not believe myself immortal.[11] I have sometimes thought men of sin might destroy their immortality. The eternity of punishment is quite incredible. Christ's words were parables to suit the sense of the times.' Further of morality: 'There are some young men who try to do away with morality. They say. "We won't be moral." Comte, I believe, and perhaps Mr. Grote too, deny that immortality has anything to do with being moral.'[12] Then from material to moral difficulties: 'Why do mosquitoes exist? I believe that after God had made His world the devil began and added something.' (Cat and mouse—leopards.) My father raised moral evil—morbid art.) The conversation turned on Swinburne for the moment, and then dropped.

In all this metaphysical vagueness about matter, morals, the existence of evil, and the evidences of God there was something almost childish. Such points pass with most men for settled as insoluble after a time. But Tennyson has a perfect simplicity about him which recognises the real greatness of such

---

[8] In Richter's *Lebens des Quintus Fixlein* (1796), translated by Carlyle.

[9] Thomas Henry Huxley (1825–95: *DNB*), the famous scientist and guardian of science, friend of Tyndall, Hooker, and Darwin, who later, in the Metaphysical Society, came to know Tennyson personally (*Journal*, p. 334; *Memoir*, ii. 143), and wrote a poem on him in 1892 for the *Nineteenth Century* (Priscilla Metcalf, *James Knowles*, p. 339).

[10] In the last chapter of *Hydrotaphia, or Urn-Burial* (1658).

[11] See 'A Voice Spake Out of the Skies' (Ricks, p. 1193), and below, p. 477.

[12] Philosophical radicals both (and friends)—Auguste Comte (1798–1857), the French positivist philosopher, and George Grote (1794–1871: *DNB*), the historian of Greece (12 vols., 1846–56).

questions, and regards them as always worthy of consideration. He treats them with profound moral earnestness. His 'In Memoriam' and 'Two Voices' illustrate this habit. There is nothing original or startling—on the contrary, a general commonplaceness, about his metaphysics; yet, so far as they go, they express real agitating questions—express, in a poet's language, what most men feel and think about.

A move was made into the dining-room. Tennyson had consented to read his translations to Gladstone and my father. I followed them and sat unperceived behind them. He began by reading in a deep bass growl the passage of Achilles shouting in the trench.[13] Gladstone continually interrupted him with small points about words. He has a combative, House of Commons mannerism, which gives him the appearance of thinking too much about himself. It was always to air some theory of his own that he broke Tennyson's recital; and he seemed listening only in order to catch something up. Tennyson invited criticism.

Tennyson was sorely puzzled about the variations in Homeric readings and interpretations. 'They change year after year. What we used to think right in my days I am told is all wrong. What is a poor translator to do?' But he piqued himself very much on his exact renderings. 'These lines are word for word. You could not have a closer translation: one poet could not express another better. There! those are good lines.' Gladstone would object, 'But you will say Jove and Greeks: can't we have Zeus and Achæans?' 'But the sound of Jove! Jove is much softer than Zeus—Zeus—Zeus.' 'Well, Mr. Worsley[14] gives us Achæans.' 'Mr. Worsley has chosen a convenient long metre; he can give you Achæans, and a great deal else.' Much was said about the proper means of getting a certain pause, how to give equivalent suggestive sounds, and so on.

Some of the points which rose between the recitations I will put down.

Τανύπεπλος.—My father asked why Gladstone translated this 'round-limbed.' He answered that he had the notion of 'lateral extension' of the robe, since a long trailing dress was not Achæan, but Ionian. Homer talks of the Ionians, ἑλκεχίτωνες. Tennyson did not heed this supersubtle rendering, but said, 'Ah! there's nothing more romantic than the image of these women floating along the streets of Troy with their long dresses flying out behind them. Windy Troy! I dare say it was not windier than other places, but it stood high, open to the air. As a schoolboy, I used to see them. A boy of course imagines something like a modern town.'

Φυσίζοος αἶα.—My father instanced this as a curious fixed epithet, and incongruous for a burial-field of battle. Gladstone objected it was not a common epithet. He and Tennyson agreed in the pathos which it strikes by way of contrast with death. The exactness of Homer's epithets—not nearly so fixed and formal as supposed.

Γλαυκῶπις.—Tennyson translated this 'grey-eyed,' in the Shakespearean meaning of 'blue-eyed.'[15] Gladstone said it ought to be 'bright-eyed.' Homer

---

[13] His translation in blank verse of the *Iliad*, xviii. 202–31, 'Achilles over the Trench' (Ricks, p. 1157), read aloud in December 1864 (*Journal*, p. 218) but not published until 1877.

[14] See above, p. 343 and n.   [15] *The Tempest*, I. ii. 269.

knew nothing about colours: the human eye had not yet learned to distinguish colours. Question raised whether it were not that the nomenclature of colours had not yet been perfected. Gladstone preferred to think that the sense itself had not been educated to perceive colours.[16] [No green in Homer—χλωρηὶς ἀηδών means truly 'the nightingale that loves the greenwood.' But this is a rare instance, & the idea of greenness is not predominant. (Query whether this has not reference to the colour of the bird itself. Scholiast says ἡ ἐν χλωροῖς διατρίβωσα: L[iddell] and S[cott] add 'but wrongly.') Again πορφύρεος means simply dark—brown or blue—even ἰοειδής is applied to sheep. (Query what ἴον really meant—a violet? or some other flower?) There was of course some probability in this argument; but Gladstone overworked it, & denied that even Egyptians understood colour, who, however, in frescoes at least as old as Homer, as my father suggested, evince a most accurate sense of colour. (e.g. the negroes, Nubians and Assyrians; black, red, and yellow; under Rameses—even complexions finely distinguished: the different colours of the Lotos etc. On the other hand they paint some skins of men blue.)] It seemed as if Gladstone were a champion in the medieval schools, throwing down theses and defending them for pure argument-sake, not for any real love of truth—a dangerous quality in a statesman, and apt to make him an untrustworthy debater.

Καλλίτριχες ἵπποι.—Tennyson translated 'beauteous horses.' He thought it meant sleek, etc.; might have said 'fair-haired,' but wanted same quality of sound which 'beauteous' had. Gladstone said, what had occurred to me, that καλλίτριχες was meant as a picturesque epithet, to describe the flowing mane of the horses as they stopped suddenly and turned, affrighted by the shout of Achilles. This seemed supersubtle.

[ηὖδε φθέγγατο Tennyson had made the first *spake* and the second *shouted*. Gladstone said, I think rightly that it ought to have been V. V.][17]

Other points—

(1.) Gladstone said Virgil had misrepresented Homer intentionally; had used him, but altered, so that we could gain nothing from reading Homer in Virgil's light.

(2.) His deep meaning. Gladstone thought a special significance might be found in the list of Thetis' nymphs. They have pure Greek names, whereas Nereus was an old non-Hellenic Pelasgic god. Homer, Hellenising Thetis, the mother of his Greek hero Achilles, invents a train of pure Greek ladies for her. He never mentions Nereus by name, calls him 'the old man,' keeps him in the background. Is not this supersubtle? He was angry with Lord Derby for cutting up these names.[18]

(3.) 'Lord Derby's, not blank verse; prose divided into five beats.' Said to

---

[16] Bracketed insertion, here and below, from *The Letters of John Addington Symonds*, ed. Schueller and Peters, i. 597.

[17] *Iliad*, xviii. 217, 218; in Tennyson's translation, ll. 17 ('shouted'), 18 ('called').

[18] Edward George Geoffrey Smith Stanley (1799–1869: *DNB*), 14th Earl of Derby; classicist; and Prime Minister, 1852, 1858–9, 1866–8; published *The Iliad of Homer Rendered into Blank Verse* (2 vols.) in 1864 (privately printed, 1862).

have been improvised as the mood seized him; and wondered at by some people accordingly.

(4.) Could it be got into hexameters? Tennyson repeated some quantitative hexameters, 'beastly bad,' which he had made.[19] English people could not understand quantity. 'I showed'em to a man, Allingham; he wanted to scan'em; couldn't see they had quantity.' Gladstone observed that modern Greek readings of Homer must be all wrong. We have lost accent, which was not emphasis, but arsis and thesis of voice. At end of word, *e.g.*, the grave becomes the acute, and the voice is raised. There are three parts in pronunciation: time, emphasis, and pitch.

Palgrave suggested a translation of Homer into Biblical prose. He began it. Jowett dissuaded him, saying he thought he had not enough command of English. (How like Jowett!) 'Rather disparaging to you,' said Tennyson.

Tennyson said he had read out in Old English to his wife the 'Odyssey.' 'And it struck me I did it very well.'

(5.) Real difficulty of translation. No two languages hit each other off. Both have some words 'like shot silk'[20] (Tennyson's metaphor, good). These cannot be rendered. We can never *quite* appreciate another nation's poetry on this account. Gave as an instance the end of 'Enoch Arden,' 'Calling of the sea,'[21] a phrase well known to sailors, for a clear night with a sea-sound on the shore in calm. A German translator rendered it 'Geschrei,' which suggested storm, etc., wrongly. He meant a big voice of the sea, but coming through the calm. (The Venetian sailors, however, say 'Chiama il mare.')

Gladstone, just before we parted, said he always slept well. He had only twice been kept awake by the exertion of a great speech in the House. On both occasions the recollection that he had made a misquotation haunted him.

At about one we broke up. Gladstone went off first. My father and I walked round the studio, then shook hands with Tennyson and got home.

To EMILY SELLWOOD TENNYSON

MS. Tennyson Research Centre; *Memoir*, ii. 30.

December 9, 1865

Dearest

Yesterday at Woolner's—Gladstone, Holman Hunt, and a Dr. Symmons [*sic*] and his son—[Dr. S. is a] famous physician of Bristol who had come all the way to dine with Gladstone and myself. I liked him much. The great man was infinitely agreeable and delivered himself very eloquently and freely on Homer, etc. I asked him to speak to Lord Russell about increasing Allingham's little pension which he promised to do—he spoke too about

---

[19] Ricks, pp. 1153–4.
[20] 'Poetry is like shot-silk with many glancing colours. Every reader must find his own interpretation according to his ability, and according to his sympathy with the poet' (*Memoir*, ii. 127).
[21] 'Enoch Arden', l. 904.

Jamaica, and seems, though he suspends his judgement, to think that Eyre has been so terribly in the wrong that he may have to be tried for his life.

I have not yet learnt about the Bank. I told Payne to pay my money into it which he has done—£1100.

I am sorry that Tilly feels rheumatic with us: she wants acclimatizing.

Thine × × ×
A. T.

To EMILY SELLWOOD TENNYSON

Text. Materials, iii. 28; draft *Materials*, vi. 43.

YORK GATE, December 11, [1865]

I started off to Simeon's, nobody at home. The servant said he was possibly at Lord Colville's a few doors off.[1] I went, he was not there. Lady Simeon was there, she said that in an hour he would be at Mr. Cameron's in May Fair, so after some time I walked with her there, but then we had another hour to wait. At last he came in, and told me with respect to the juryship that if I didn't attend, and if they couldn't make up a jury without me, I should probably have to pay £5 or £10, but I certainly shall not go, for the case might last two or three days [and living at Southampton would cost some £3 or £4]. It is very tiresome. The Dean of St. Paul's[2] and the Stanleys are coming tonight and some others. I have almost made up my mind to take Lady Franklin's house Gore Lodge.

To EMILY SELLWOOD TENNYSON

MS. Tennyson Research Centre.

[12 December 1865][1]

Dearest

I had two telegrams from Mr. Estcourt yesterday—the last of which said 'You need not attend.' Whether I have anything to pay I know not. I suppose Crozier must have the turf though how in that case I am to stave off others it is hard to say.[2] Dean Milman was very agreeable yesterday. The Stanleys did

---

[1] Baron (later Viscount) Colville of Culross (1818–1903), 42 Eaton Place, was the brother of Lady Simeon, 72 Eaton Place. They walked to 43 Hertford Street, Mayfair, residence of Hugh Cameron (*P.O. London Directory*)—either the Scottish painter (1835–1918: *Who Was Who*), or, more probably, Hugh Thomas Cameron (b. 1831: *Men-at-the-Bar*), son of Hugh Innes Cameron, also Scottish and a London banker.

[2] Henry Hart Milman (see i. 3 n.); Stanley was Dean of Westminster.

[1] Postmark.

[2] Rear-Admiral Richard Crozier (1803–80), of West Hill, Yarmouth, IW, retired as Admiral on half-pay in 1870; his widow, the former Julia Stone, died in 1883. He was succeeded by his son, Richard Pearson Crozier (b. 1842), who retired as Lieut.-Col., 31st East Surrey Regiment, in 1883; lent his yacht, the *Assegai*, to Tennyson in 1891 and 1892 (see vol. iii); and died childless in 1911. The Admiral's younger brother, Captain William Pearson Crozier, RN, of Marina, Freshwater, IW, died unmarried in 1868 (*Landed Gentry*, Boase, *Whitaker's Naval and Military Directory*, Walford's *County Families*, White's *Hampshire*).

not come. Browning was here. I go tonight to a gathering at Payne's.[3] I am glad that L[ionel] seems better.

Thine × × ×
A. T.

Sir John Lubbock has just sent me his Prehistoric Times which I shall find greatly interesting.[4] I dine at the Deanery (St. Paul's) tomorrow.

To EMILY SELLWOOD TENNYSON

MS. Tennyson Research Centre.

Wednesday, [13 December 1865][1]

Dearest

I went to Payne's last night and found a large party, Martin Tupper, H. Dixon, Arthur Hughes, and others.[2] I like old Tupper much, a very worthy man. We had oysters and stout at 11, and I came back past 12.

The Palgraves go into the country on Monday and I leave this house, but whether I shall get beyond Winchester the first day is, I should think doubtful.

Thine × × × ×
A. T.

I don't much like Lionel's sporting propensities but then you know man is naturally a beast of prey.

---

[3] See the next letter.
[4] For Lubbock, see above, p. 356 n. and below, p. 526 n.; his *Pre-historic Times* (1865), inscribed is in *Tennyson in Lincoln*, i, No. 1436.

[1] Postmark.
[2] William Hepworth Dixon (1821–79: *DNB*), historian, traveller, novelist, and editor of the *Athenaeum*, 1853–69. Other guests were Lord Houghton, Palgrave, G. H. Lewes, and (conspicuously) Swinburne, who was accused of tipsiness by Houghton (see *The Swinburne Letters*, i. 143). Edmund Yates (1831–94: *DNB*), the novelist and journalist, also present, said that Hughes's illustrations of 'Enoch Arden' were 'submitted to the Laureate, who approved of them all with one exception. "This is not right," he said in his deep voice. "There came so loud a calling of the sea." The man cannot have lived by the sea; he does not know what a "calling" means. It is anything but a great upheaval such as is here represented' (*Edmund Yates: His Recollections and Experiences*, ii. 166; see also *Memoir*, ii. 8). This *soirée* may have been the occasion of the excellent epigram by Martin Tupper, who had recently moved from Hatchard to Payne (Derek Hudson, *Martin Tupper*, p. 249):

> Though nothing is meeter, this baffles all measure,—
> That Moxon's the mainspring of poets is plain,
> And poetry's mainspring all know to be pleasure
> Yet Moxon's own mainspring is nothing but Payne!

To EMILY SELLWOOD TENNYSON

MS. Tennyson Research Centre.

Thursday, [14 December 1865]

Dearest

Dined at Milman's yesterday—took 3 glasses of his port which was too fat and has given me a bit of a headache this morning—but otherwise I am better than in the country for I take more exercise. Milman told me that Her Majesty's household do not serve on juries and if ever I am asked again so to do to state this, Her M. being supposed to be always requiring their services.

I called on Tyndall yesterday and had a long chat with him about mind and matter etc. He is coming to see me tonight at Woolner's where I dine and meet Dr. Woolley, the Australian,[1] and Froude.

I have to write to Gladstone about Allingham. Farewell.

Thine × × × ×
A. T.

To WILLIAM EWART GLADSTONE

MS. British Library.

[14 December 1865]

My dear Mr. Gladstone

As you were kind enough to say that you would forward to Lord Russell Mr. Allingham's application for an increase of pension together with my petition that it might be taken into consideration I send you A's letter to myself, wherein he sets forth at full what his claims are and why he wishes them to be attended to.

As I said to you at the time the man has a true spirit of song in him—I have no doubt of it—and my opinion I am happy to say is confirmed by Carlyle in his letter to A. which I only do not forward because from A's letter it does not appear that I am at full liberty to do so.

Carlyle also mentions some work of Allingham's (—I have not seen it myself—it is probably some preface to his projected work on Ireland—) in these flattering terms.

—Your pleasant and excellent Historical Introduction might, if its modesty would permit, boast itself to be the very best ever written perhaps anywhere for such a purpose. I have read it with real entertainment and instruction on my own behalf and with real satisfaction on yours—so clear, so brief, definite, graphic; and a fine genially human tone in it.

I think you will agree with me that this testimonial from one who is a great name in Britain and who has won his own laurels chiefly in the field of History, does go some way in establishing a case for Allingham.

And for myself I really believe that if he were set free as he says by his pension being raised to the amount required—he might do good to Ireland

---

[1] John Woolley (1816–66: *DNB*), an old friend of A. P. Stanley's at Oxford, was chosen as first Principal of Sydney University in 1852; he was drowned at sea while returning to Australia in January.

and through Ireland to England by accomplishing a work which under his present circumstances seems all but impossible.

I may add that I have known him for years, that he is very industrious, and in his life sober and moral—his age somewhere between 40 and 50. Believe me, my dear Mr. Gladstone,

Ever sincerely yours
A. Tennyson

To EMILY SELLWOOD TENNYSON

MS. Tennyson Research Centre.

Friday, [15 December 1865]

Dearest

A great gathering last night at Woolner's. Dr. Woolley seems altogether of the higher class of men. Thompson the Confederate was there and Browning and innumerable anecdotes were told.[1]

Today I dine here—nobody asked—at my request.

Thine × × × ×
A. T.

To EMILY SELLWOOD TENNYSON

Text. Materials, iii. 29.

December 16, [1865]

I saw Spedding yesterday. Browning has given me a book of selections from his wife's Poems for my wife.[1]

---

[1] 'A pleasant evening at Mr. Thomas Woolner's where I met Tennyson, Robert Browning, Mr. Palgrave, Professor Tyndall, and others. Leaving the ladies in the drawing-room at eleven o'clock, we the "bards" and the rest of the company adjourned to the dining-room, where we found wines, etc., with pipes and cigars, and spend two hours in general conversation. Tennyson was always spoken of by his friends, I observed, as "the bard". The talk was of dreams, murders, cannibalism, stammering, Charles Lamb, epitaphs, etc. Tennyson said his most frequent nightmare was the sensation of losing all physical power. He mentioned that Mr. Hallam had once declared that, of our popular fallacies, he thought the belief that "murder will out" the greatest; and in confirmation of this opinion he (Tennyson) brought up the case of a servant girl being found murdered, some years ago, on a doorstep at Mornington Crescent, when he lived there, concerning whose murder nothing was ever discovered. The poet also told us of the first murder that made a deep impression on him as the child, an old man and his wife killed with a knife by their nephews for their money, in the lonely fens of Lincolnshire, within sound of the sea, and the assassin carrying off only three shillings and sixpence, so immediately was he paralyzed by remorse' (James Grant Wilson, 'John R. Thompson and His London Diary', *The Criterion*, November 1901, p. 23).

[1] *A Selection from the Poetry of Elizabeth Barrett Browning* (1866; *Tennyson in Lincoln*, i, No. 3300). That night, wrote Walter White, 'Tennyson, Woolner, and Cresy dined with me. The Bard spoke of a man who persists in writing to him, addressing the letters to *Miss* Tennyson, and reproaching him sorely with having made £5000 by "Enoch Arden". He said he often gets letters of enquiry as to the meaning of passages of his poems, "as if", he continued, "I could remember.

To MARTIN FARQUHAR TUPPER

MS. University of Illinois.

[*c.* 17 December 1865]

My dear Sir

I have received your Essay[1] and though I have not read it yet with attention I see what it is about, and I ask you whether you don't think that Ovid knew he was rhyming in innumerable pentameters.

Thanks. I can't come by Albury for alas the while a huge dinner party awaits me at home. Believe me

Yours very truly
A. Tennyson

I know my Alcaics were not exactly after the Horatian model but was Horace exact to his Greek model? Was I not at liberty to modify them to suit the genius of the English language? I will look at your Essay again, but I have so little time here.[2]

To LADY AUGUSTA (BRUCE) STANLEY

MS. Robert Taylor.

5 YORK GATE, REGENTS PARK, N. W., [mid-December 1865]

Dear Lady Augusta

I have not the slightest notion where I shall be on Friday—possibly at Oxford, possibly at Paris, or back again in I. W.[1] So, with many thanks, and not without regret, I must decline your kind invitation. Believe me

Yours truly
A. Tennyson

I knew what I meant when it was fermenting in my brain, but how am I to tell now what I meant then?" At twenty minutes to twelve we found ourselves talking of free will and necessity, and then the party broke up' (*The Journals*, p. 161).

[1] 'Rhyme and Reason', in *Watch Tower*, No. 2, a church periodical (Hudson, *Martin Tupper*, pp. 243-4, 333).

[2] On 29 December, Emily Tennyson wrote to Tupper (University of Illinois): 'I find this among my husband's papers brought from Town and send it hoping that you will forgive its not having been sent before....'

[1] He returned to Farringford on 19 December. 'I have not had much opportunity of talking to Alfred since he returned on Tuesday. He came home to a dinner party and I think if I do not hear what has befallen on the first day I have not much chance afterwards for on the second he seems as if he had never been away' (Emily Tennyson to Mrs Gatty, 21 December, Boston Public Library). Jowett arrived on Christmas Eve, and she wrote in her Journal next day: 'A. T. read us some *Lucretius*. Mr. Jowett read aloud on the last nights of the old year, *Revelation, Daniel, Isaiah*, 53rd Chapter. Also the *Vision of Er* out of Plato's *Republic*' [x. 614B–621D] (*Materials*, iii. 29).

To ?

Text. Sotheby's Catalogue, 30 May, 1961, Lot 527.

FARRINGFORD, [? late December 1865]

My dear Sir

The little 'murmur of applause' among the F. R. S.'s is a greater compliment than the roar of the Undergraduate when I was D. C. L.'d at Oxford, which sounded like the sea on the shingle. Thanks for your sympathy in this matter and believe me,

Yours
A. Tennyson

I would have answered earlier but for the bother of innumerable letters.

To HENRY SAMUEL KING

MS. New York University Libraries.

December 29, 1865

My dear Mr. King

The Bearer Mr. C. R. Weld my wife's brother-in-law wishes much to be introduced to you. He is just starting for Florence (to spend the winter there) and possibly, if you liked it, might contribute something 'thereanent' to your Cornhill; but of this he has not spoken to me.

We trust that Mrs. King is quite strong again. With best wishes for you both. Believe me

Ever truly yours
A. Tennyson

To FRANCIS TURNER PALGRAVE

Text. Memoir, ii. 33 n.

[c. 31 December 1865]

What a season! The wind is roaring here like thunder, and all my ilexes rolling and whitening. Indeed we have had whole weeks of wind.[1]

To MESSRS TICKNOR AND FIELDS

Text. Materials, iii. 30.

FARRINGFORD, January 5, 1866

Dear Sirs

I have received your cheque for £100 and beg to thank you for it.

I have also read the correspondence between yourselves and my publishers, and am much grieved at the tone of their letters, which seems to me wholly uncalled for. I will write to them on the subject and hear what they have to

---

[1] He wrote '1865–1866' (Ricks, p. 1192): see below, p. 478.

say for themselves—then I will communicate with you again.[1] Meantime, believe me, my dear Sirs,

> Yours very truly
> A. Tennyson

I ought to add that the illustrated 'Enoch Arden' is theirs not mine except for my royalty on it.[2]

To JAMES BERTRAND PAYNE

MS. Huntington Library.

FARRINGFORD, January 8, 1866

My dear Mr. Payne

Messrs. Ticknor and Fields have sent me the whole of your mutual correspondence. I confess I am much annoyed by the receipt of these American letters. Why *should* you call them impertinent, ignorant, unbusinesslike, tricky? Even admitting them to be wrong I am quite sure you are much more likely to convince them of it by quiet courteous words than by the language you use towards them. Pray grant me the favour never to use such again when I or my works are in question. Out of regard for your own interest as well as mine I feel bound to say this. I may add that Mr. and Mrs. Fields are friends of mine and have visited here. Believe me

> Very truly yours
> A. Tennyson

Messrs. Ticknor and Fields have in this year remitted me £250; and I myself have no wish to break off relations with them. Enoch Arden (the illustrated one) is of course yours to do as you please with.

I enclose the letter to Mrs. Bruce to be sent with the Queen's Book.[1]

To THE DUCHESS OF ARGYLL

MS. Tennyson Research Centre.

FARRINGFORD, January 11, 1866

My dear Duchess

We reciprocate your good wishes for 1866 and are glad to hear that you have had so pleasant a Christmas with all your young ones in Inveraray.

I envy your eldest boy his voyage to Jamaica. I have always had a longing to visit the island and see once in my life a little tropical scenery. I once had a

---

[1] See the next letter. 'Ticknor and Fields sold eleven thousand copies of their first edition of the *Idylls* in the first month after its publication, and the editions of *Enoch Arden* were too numerous and their sale too rapid for accurate recording' (John Olin Eidson, *Tennyson in America*, p. 148).

[2] 'Both Ticknor and Fields and another Boston publisher, J. E. Tilton, published editions of *Enoch Arden* in 1864. Houghton Mifflin ... lists 40,000 copies of the Ticknor and Fields edition as printed during the first year' (Eidson, p. 250).

[1] Probably *Enoch Arden*, illustrated by Arthur Hughes (Moxon, 1866).

very kind invitation from poor Eyre whom everybody according to the fashion of our pleasant world is yelling against before his case comes to trial.[1]

I, my wife and two boys took a little trip to Trèves this autumn through Brussels—stopping four days at Waterloo: then going on to Dresden chiefly to see the picture gallery.[2] We are not disappointed at the Raphael Madonna, which appeared to her the only painting she had seen worthy of the subject. I thought it would have been still finer if the feet had not been seen—if they had been rolled up in clouds. I got rather a shock in the Grunes Gewolbe. The learned Herr Professor was showing us through the armoury, and stopt at a suit that had been made for Edward 4 of England, and suddenly turned before all the party, addressed me as Herr Tennyson, and made a long speech of which I did not understand a tenth and concluded with a low bow. I made him another not without wrath in my heart, and then he asked for an autograph. As I never enter my name on the Hotel-books except when just going to leave I am at a loss to know how he found me out.

As to the storm we seem to have had one storm for weeks. Today is our first really quiet one for I know not how long. All yesterday the great North opened his mouth and bellowed like a wild beast till I really thought the roof would have blown off. We have no two hundred-year old beeches to lose but down came an old arbutus and a very fine Scotch fir.[3] There is no snow as yet here but I see [it] lying thinly on St. Catherine's which closes our view seawards.

It is possible we may take Lady Franklin's house[4] for February and March if my wife can stand the cold journey to London. At present she cannot stir out of the doors.

Give my love to your good mother—we are sorry to learn that she has been so ailing. And with best remembrances to the Duke believe me

Yours affectionately
A. Tennyson

To ?

MS. Lincoln City Library.

FARRINGFORD, January 17, 1866

Gentlemen

I have forwarded your letter to my Publishers who will communicate with you on the subject of the American copies. I have the honour to be, Gentlemen,

Your obedient servant
A. Tennyson

---

[1] Edward John Eyre (1815–1901: *DNB*), Governor of Jamaica, whose rigour in suppressing a native rebellion in October 1865 excited and divided England. 'Eyre was a pupil at the Louth Grammar School soon after Tennyson had left' (Henry J. Jennings, *Lord Tennyson*, p. 188). See below, p. 443, and Bernard Semmel, *Democracy versus Empire* (1969), first published 1962 as *The Governor Eyre Controversy*, and in 1963 as *Jamaican Blood and Victorian Conscience*, and Geoffrey Dalton, *The Hero as Murderer: The Wife of Edward John Eyre* (1967).
[2] See *Memoir*, ii. 24–7, and *Journal*, pp. 229–34.
[3] The Duchess had written (5 January, TRC): 'One of our 200 year old beeches is down.'
[4] Upper Gore Lodge, Kensington.

To HENRY GLASSFORD BELL

Text. James Lowe, Catalogue 12 (1980? 79?), Lot 162.

FRESHWATER, ISLE OF WIGHT, January 28, 1866

Mr. Alfred Tennyson presents his compliments to Mr. Glassford Bell and begs to thank him for his book just received and regrets that he was away from home when Mr. Bell called some years ago. . . .[1]

To JAMES THOMAS KNOWLES[1]

MS. Gordon Ray.

FARRINGFORD, January 31, 1866

My dear Sir

I have received your Photograph from Raffaelle and much admire it and am very grateful; but yet—fie upon 'but yet'—says Cleopatra in Shakespeare[2]—I would request you not to send me any other present. You are laying a heap of obligations upon me which I cannot return and as I am not your enemy 'the coals of fire'[3] can be no object to you. Believe me,

Yours very truly
A. Tennyson

J. T. Knowles Esqr.

To JAMES KENWARD[1]

MS. Brotherton Collection.

FARRINGFORD, February 5, 1866

My dear Sir

I am much obliged to you for the first volume of 'Barddas' which I have not yet seen, but which will arrive in due time from Moxon's.[2]

I am sorry that the pension has not yet been given to the descendants of Ap Ithel. I am afraid (so great a delay has intervened between the asking and the granting) that the chance of it is not very great. You see that I am not so 'hopeful' as yourself about it.

I envy you your visit to Villemarqué.[3] When I was in Brittany stopping at Auray, I think—I asked the landlord how far off he lived, and I found it was some 14 or 15 miles—a long way to post—and it was not certain whether he

---

[1] See above, p. 219. His book is *Romances and Minor Poems* (London, 1866).

[1] See above, p. 288 n. [2] *Antony and Cleopatra*, II. v. 51. [3] Proverbs 25:22.

[1] See above, p. 387 n.

[2] *Barddas; or, A Collection of Original Documents Illustrative of the Theology, Wisdom, and Usages of the Bardo-Druidic System of the Isle of Britain*, with translations and notes by the Rev. John Williams (2 vols., Llandover, 1862).

[3] Theodore Hersart de La Villemarqué (1815–95): see above, p. 90 n. The Tennysons were in Auray in mid-August 1864 (*Journal*, p. 208). Two articles by La Villemarqué were Matthew Arnold's source for 'Tristram and Iseult'.

were at home or not. Believe me, dear Sir, in great haste (for (substitute 'letters' for 'bairns') I am like 'the old woman who lived in a shoe')

Yours truly
A. Tennyson

To LOUIS TENNYSON D'EYNCOURT

MS. University of Newcastle-upon-Tyne.

FARRINGFORD, February 5, 1866

My dear Louis

I have received Mrs. Roscoe's ballad with the illustrations which seem to be very creditable for an amateur—I trust she will not be offended by this limitation.[1]

We have taken part of a farm-house in Hants on the mainland[2] whither to fly now and then for the sake of a drier air, and also it must be confessed to take refuge occasionally from cockneys or lion-hunters for some other reasons —and this move I suppose has been more or less misrepresented by the newspapers.

My wife (thank you for your enquiries) has been kept to the house by cough and cold for about two months—and the boys have colds too but nothing to signify.

I trust that your own family are flourishing. Believe me with love

Your affectionate cousin
A. Tennyson

To THE DUCHESS OF ARGYLL

MS. Tennyson Research Centre.

UPPER GORE LODGE,[1] Tuesday, February 13, 1866

Dear Duchess

Could you and the Duke look in upon us Thursday evening any time after 9 o'clock? I saw him this morning, and was glad to see him.

Ever affectionately yours
A. Tennyson

P. S. There will be a *very small* gathering.

---

[1] Unidentified, but possibly Maria Fletcher Roscoe (1798–1885), author of *Vittoria Colonna* (1868) 'and many tales for children' (Boase).

[2] Stoatley Farm (see below, p. 445).

[1] Lady Franklin's house (see above, p. 429). Brookfield's diary, 13 [for 15] February: 'We dined with Alfred and Mrs. Tennyson, Spedding and Venables. After dinner an evening party! Duke and Duchess of Argyle, Lady Boyne, Mrs. Gladstone, the Lockyers, etc. Spedding and Venables and myself staid behind to smoke with Alfred.' On 17 February: 'To Lady Stanley of Alderley, where there was a great crowd. Standing close together were to be seen Alfred Tennyson, Browning, Houghton, and Carlyle, and by way of a not less remarkable group, Lord Shaftesbury and Sir Alexander Cockburn' (*The Cambridge 'Apostles'*, pp. 79–80).

To THE DUKE OF ARGYLL

MS. Tennyson Research Centre.

February 27, 1866

My dear Duke

I am very sorry, but I had engaged myself without remembering the Club-day.[1] I hope your little ones are going on well, ⟨especially⟩ Lady Edith. Our love to the Duchess.

Always yours
A. Tennyson

To SIR JOHN SIMEON

MS. Syracuse University.

[? March 1866]

My dear Simeon

Tell Lord Dunraven[1] that I grant the Lady's request.* I am grieved to hear that Mary[2] does not improve. I myself have got influenza and feel utterly sapless and dry and despondent.

But ever yours
A. Tennyson

*though I must say I never heard of a woman's opinion ab[out] our lives coming to anything.

To ELEANOR EDEN[1]

MS. University of Chicago.

March 5, 1866

My dear Miss Eden

I find that I really cannot go to Froude's—lumbago and headache and sore throat are all mine this morning, though the first is undoubtedly better.[2]

---

[1] See above, p. 392 n. A list of the thirty-four members of the Club is in Henry Reeve's *Memoirs*, ii. 133–4.

[1] Edward Richard Wyndham-Quin (1812–71), 3rd Earl of Dunraven and Mountearl. He had a mother and four daughters living who could qualify (technically) as 'the Lady'.

[2] Mary Jane Simeon (d. 1905), the second daughter.

[1] Eleanor Eden (1826–79), writer, daughter of the 3rd Baron Auckland, Lord Bishop of Bath and Wells, and niece of Emily Eden (1797–1869: *DNB*), the novelist and travel-writer. She died unmarried. See below, p. 454.

[2] He felt better by nightfall. John Reuben Thompson's diary, 5 March: 'In the evening went to Lady Franklin's to see Tennyson. He was ill with a severe cold, but received me cordially. I met there Mr. Woolner, Dr. Baker, who has discovered the source of the Nile, Macmillan the publisher, Lady Florence Cooper, and other prominent persons.' Tennyson had left his card on Thompson on 22 February, and on 1 March Thompson wrote in his diary: 'In the afternoon called on Mr. Tennyson (saw both the poet and his wife, a very sweet woman)' (James Grant Wilson, 'Thompson's London Diary. Third Paper', *The Criterion*, November 1901, p. 24).

I read your novel through at one stretch and found it very pleasant reading.[3]
Will you come over this morning and see us?

Ever yours
A. Tennyson

To CUTHBERT EDWARD ELLISON

MS. Sudely Castle, Winchcombe, Glos.

March 12, 1866

My dear Ellison
 I wish I could: but my influenza which succeeded lumbago absolutely prohibits my going out in the evening.[1]
 I now think of getting away as soon as I am able to move.

Ever yours
A. Tennyson

To CATHERINE GLADSTONE

MS. University of British Columbia.

March 14, 1866

My dear Mrs. Gladstone
 I wish I could come to you this afternoon but influenza is mightier than I am—neither do I think that I shall be equal to dining with you on Wednesday: in fact as soon as I and my wife can move we shall get away from town.
 Our best and kindest remembrances to Mr. Gladstone.

Ever yours
A. Tennyson

To LORD HOUGHTON (RICHARD MONCKTON MILNES)

MS. Tennyson Research Centre.

[c. 14 March 1866]

My dear Houghton
 I wish I could—but while this influenza lasts it is an impossibility.

Ever yours
A. Tennyson

---

[3] Probably *False and True* (1859).

[1] 'Mar. 13: Emily and Alfred wrote. Alfred is ill of sore throat and lumbago and had to receive sev[era]l people and Japanese Noble in his cloak [*2 words illegible*]' (Charles Tennyson Turner's 'Memorandum Book for 1866', TRC; transcribed by Roger Evans).

To SIR ANTHONY CONINGHAM STERLING[1]

MS. University of Kansas.

March 14, 1866

My dear Sir Anthony

I have been hoping, spite of influenza, that I should be able to join your party tonight—but now I must give it up—not without great unwillingness—for I have always heard that your dinners are among the most agreeable in town. Believe me,

Yours truly
A. Tennyson

To THE DUKE OF ARGYLL

Text. Tennyson Research Centre (transcript).

April 20, 1866

My dear Duke

The son's sonnet is, I think, creditable to him both as regards feeling and execution, only the third line is a little lazy 'Nor after long life'—'didst thou die' seems to be wanted here. I read and am grieved to hear of his illness in the Times but he is it seems all right again now. I know nothing of politics here except from the newspapers, but I suppose the Bill is looking up as they say since I left town and that you are not going to Switzerland as you threatened.[1]

I see that Mr. Lowe did me the honour of quoting me the other night. If anyone of your side wished to make his speech culminate in a quotation which may be a prophecy he might possibly produce an effect by quoting the last two stanzas of my address to the Queen in the preface to my poems—

> And statesmen at her councils met
> Who knew the season when etc.[2]

which really would seem a propos.

Ever, my dear Duke, yours
A. Tennyson

---

[1] Sir Anthony Coningham Sterling (1805–71: *DNB*), John Sterling's brother, had seen active service in the Crimea and, as Military Secretary, in India during the Mutiny. The Tennysons met him at Swainston in 1862 (*Journal*, p. 168).

[1] The Second Reform Bill (extending the franchise). Debate had begun on 12 April. The speech of Robert Lowe (1811–92, later Viscount Sherbrooke: *DNB*), opposing his own party's measures, is summarized in the *Annual Register*, pp. 125–8. Russell's government fell in mid-June, Lord Derby's succeeded, and the Bill, brought forward by Disraeli in a far more radical form, was passed in August 1867. (Matthew Arnold's *Culture and Anarchy* is the most visible *literary* result). Lowe's citation of 'Lancelot and Elaine', ll. 871–2 ('His honour rooted in dishonour stood . . .') was picked up in a speech by the Marquis of Huntington reported in *The Times*, 13 April, p. 8.

[2] 'To the Queen', 1852, ll. 29–30 (Ricks, p. 990).

To ?

MS. University of Virginia.

FARRINGFORD, April 28, 1866

Gentlemen

I have pleasure in placing my name at the disposal of the Committee of the Loan Exhibition though I fear that I have little or nothing worth lending. I have the honour to be, Gentlemen,

Your obedient servant
A. Tennyson

ALFRED AND HALLAM TENNYSON *to* EMILY SELLWOOD TENNYSON

MS. Tennyson Research Centre.

READING, [1 May 1866][1]

Waiting here all night.

A. T.

Very wet day. Keep up spirits.

H. T.

To EMILY SELLWOOD TENNYSON

MS. Tennyson Research Centre.

THE LODGE, MARLBOROUGH COLLEGE, [2 May 1866]

Dearest

We are arrived and chilled to the bones. I am sure it would have been madness for you to come. Mrs. B[(radley] says she is grieved not to see you but 'almost hoped' you wouldn't come. Now, I write this today which cannot get to Farringford till the day after tomorrow. I don't know whether Barrett has written. I think except the weather alters it would be much better not to move at all at present. I can't get an answer till the day of your proposed visit to London has gone by. I can't get your answer till ⟨Friday⟩ Saturday [?] afternoon [?]. You might telegraph and I might meet you at Basingstoke: but I very strongly advise you to think of yourself rather than Barrett and not move at all if this weather continues which is too much even for me.

Thine
A. T. × × × × ×

---

[1] Postmark. 'Today I was to have gone with A. to take our Hallam to Marlborough but could not. My cough is so bad and the weather so bitterly cold that A. will not let me go. They write to me from Reading. A. and Hallam pleased with Marlborough and the Forest. Poor A. two days on the road home because of changes of which he was not made aware and Sunday [t]rains and no boat from Lymington' (*Journal*, pp. 246–7). *Materials*, ii. 246–7, prints accounts of the visit by 'one of the masters' of Marlborough and by Mrs Bradley.

My hand is so numbed I can hardly write. They press me very much to remain.

If you telegraphed in accordance to my suggestion after receiving this, I don't think there would be time for me to receive the telegraph and get to Basingstoke on Thursday. There are nearly five hours journey between this and Basingstoke, and telegraphs are often very lingering besides.

Was not Thursday the day on which you proposed going to Barrett's?[1]

To BASIL MONTAGU PICKERING[1]

MS. Harvard.

May 14, 1866[2]

Sir

I have no letter with the Proof sheets sent me from R[ichard] H[erne] S[hepherd], but I conclude that they are sent to me with a view to ascertain my wish with regard to their publication.

While giving all due thanks for the kind intention of the Compiler, I must acknowledge that it will be entirely against my desire that they are published, if published, having myself an infinite dislike to the sort of book about anyone and finding moreover in this many mis-statements both as to facts and as to the Poems attributed to me.

May I request that you will make my sentiments known to R. H. S. and let me have an answer as soon as possible. I have the honour to be, Sir,

Your obedient servant
A. Tennyson

To GEORGE MACDONALD[1]

MS. Yale.

May 15, 1866

Dear Mr. MacDonald

I have just returned home and found your very pretty looking little

---

[1] Tennyson left Marlborough on 5 May (*Materials*, iii. 41); then 'A. takes me to London about my health', apparently on or about 10 May, and they returned to Farringford on the 12th (*Journal*, p. 247).

[1] Basil Montagu Pickering (1836–78: *DNB*), publisher and rare book dealer.
[2] The letter (in Emily Tennyson's hand, except the signature) is headed by her: 'Copy of letter to Mr. Pickering. Will you keep this please.' The reference is to Pickering's publication (1866) of *Tennysoniana: Notes Biliographical and Critical on Early Poems of Alfred and C. Tennyson*, anonymous, but by Richard Herne Shepherd (1842–95: *DNB*), bibliographer, editor, and literary 'pirate' (see *Tennyson in Lincoln*, i, No. 2029). See below, p. 000, and Wise's *Bibliography of Tennyson*, ii. 7–21.

[1] George MacDonald (1824–1905: *DNB*), Scottish poet and novelist, whose best-known novel, *At the Back of the North Wind*, appeared in 1871. See 19 March 1875 to Frederick Locker, vol. iii.

Tauchnitz.[2] I commenced reading it and am already half-in-love with the little girl. Many thanks. Believe me

Yours very truly
A. Tennyson

To EMILY SELLWOOD TENNYSON

MS. Tennyson Research Centre.

FARRINGFORD, FRESHWATER, ISLE OF WIGHT, May 29, 1866

Dearest

I send this to Barrett's as I can't be certain where you have taken refuge. I send some of the letters that have come, your Father's and Hallam's. There is likewise one from Chapman. I feel very anxious about you. Mrs. W[oolner] gets on very well by herself. I take my book after dinner and she hers. I will say no more, thinking to hear from thee tomorrow morning.

Thine × × × ×
A. T.

Remember to send for me if *at all* wanted. Quite hot here today and the bees in my windows as loud as ever.

To ?

MS. Indiana University.

May 29, 1866

Dear Sir

I have received your Gladstoniad[1] which seems spirited. I do not keep photographs for distribution. Some people think the best is that by Elliot and Fry. Miss Ivy must do as she chooses. I had rather not be consulted in the matter.

Yours very truly
A. Tennyson

To ?

MS. Boston Public Library.

June 3, 1866

My dear Sir

Everything in the Yankee's letter is an invention or a misstatement.[1] 'A porch completely festooned with woodbines,' there is not a leaf of woodbine anywhere about it. 'Ancient oaks threw their spreading branches *completely over the broad approach to the house*': a complete fiction. 'Wide level lawns extended on either side': there is not a bit of level ground anywhere near the

---

[2] *Alec Forbes of Howglen* (Tauchnitz, 1865).

[1] Unidentified.

[1] Unidentified.

house. 'A Butler': I don't keep a Butler: he saw the boy.[2] 'A cabinet with a collection gathered by himself.' I didn't gather a single specimen. I am *'perhaps 5 feet 9 if I hold myself up.'* I am 6 feet. 'His gait is feeble.' I dare say I had corns. And so on. You may judge whether [there] be any truth in the conversation as reported. Fancy my 'clasping hands' with such a fellow 'on all aesthetical subjects'—and fancy his carrying away 'pictures'—'plentifully mixt with grey' he says my hair is. I haven't a grey hair in my head, nor has he an eye in his. I will admit no more Yankees into my house until they learn to reverence the hearth.

As to verses I do not venture to pronounce upon them. I have reams of them every week and am totally 'distraught' with them.

I trust your tour will bring you health and pleasure. Believe me

Yours very truly
A. Tennyson

To BRADBURY AND EVANS

MS. Punch Office, 23–27 Tudor Street.

FARRINGFORD, FRESHWATER, ISLE OF WIGHT, June 11, 1866

My dear Sirs

I myself have no manner or matter of complaint against you, nor did I know that the plates were withdrawn.[1] I will write to Mr. Payne and send you what he says. Believe me,

Yours very truly
A. Tennyson

To WILLIAM FREDERICK POLLOCK

Text. Frederick Pollock, *Personal Remembrances*, ii. 152.

[*c.* 13 June 1866]

Dear P.

Can't come.

A.T.[1]

EMILY SELLWOOD TENNYSON *to* JOHN REUBEN THOMPSON

MS. New York Public Library.

FARRINGFORD, FRESHWATER, ISLE OF WIGHT, June 27, 1866

My dear Sir

We shall be very glad to see you when Mr. Payne comes. I think he will

---

[2] His name was Butler (*The Letters of Emily Tennyson*, pp. 208–9).

[1] Of the Illustrated Edition of *Enoch Arden*?

[1] To an Apostles' dinner. The note is probably Tennyson's shortest poem.

come on Saturday next.[1] Believe me with my husband's kind regards.

Very truly yours
Emily Tennyson

ANNE GILCHRIST to WILLIAM HAINES (extract)

Text. *Anne Gilchrist, Her Life and Writings*, ed. H. H. Gilchrist, pp. 161–5.

BROOKBANK, HASLEMERE, September 16, 1866

I was sitting under the yew tree yesterday, when Fanny [the maidservant] came to me and put a card into my hand. And whose name do you think was on that card? . . . It was 'Mr. Alfred Tennyson.' He looks older than I expected, because of course the portraits one was early familiar with have stood still in one's mind as the image to be associated with that great name. But he is to my thinking far nobler looking now; every inch a king; features are massive, eyes very grave and penetrating, hair long, still very dark, and, though getting thin, falls in such a way as to give a peculiar beauty to the mystic head. Mrs. Tennyson a sweet graceful woman with singularly winning gentle manners, but she looks *painfully* fragile and wan.

They said they should like to see the 'Jumps,' the 90 acres to be sold for £1,400; beyond the Punch Bowl, if I could tell their driver the exact spot. I felt the most useful thing to do would be to introduce Mr. Simmons, and sent over for him; but, alas! he was just gone to Churt, so then I ran over and had a consultation with Mrs. Simmons, and she proposed having the pony put to an driving me over with them (accompanying their fly), that we might find Mr. Simmons and then proceed to the 'Jumps,' and that we did.

But what you will be most anxious to hear is all that he said. Mrs. Tennyson having mentioned that they had just come over from Petersfield, and that they had been there to see a clergyman who takes pupils with an idea of placing their boys with him. When Giddy [a child of seven] came into the room [Tennyson] called her to him, asked her her name, kissed her, stroked her sturdy legs, made Mrs. Tennyson feel them, and then set her on

---

[1] Thompson's Diary: 'June 30—With Bertrand Payne, of Moxon and Company, by railway from Waterloo Station to Lymington, and thence by ferry to Yarmouth, where we took a carriage for Farringford, the residence of Alfred Tennyson. Were cordially received by the poet. A nephew of Sir Robert Peel, and son of the present General Peel, had been a fellow-passenger of ours from London, and preceded us to Farringford. A lovelier spot it would be difficult to find. An irregular Gothic cottage, surrounded by beautiful trees, the ilex and the elm, and exquisite turf, and with cool glimpses of the sea from almost every window, abundant roses and a thrifty magnolia growing over the wall (nailed up like apricots), and almost total exclusion from the world without—all was charming. Books everywhere inside, engravings and photographs, a few paintings, some casts and statuettes. Dinner at seven. Mrs. Tennyson, a most gentle lady in evidently feeble health, with remains of rare maidenly beauty, the poet's sister no longer young, two boys, Hallam and Lionel, these were the family. After dinner, which was excellent and simple—soup, salmon, roast mutton, duck, peas, pudding, tarts, fruit, cherries and strawberries —the gentlemen adjourned to the top of the house, where, in Tennyson's sanctum, we had pipes and tobacco—Virginia and other varieties—with pleasant talk till two o'clock or thereabouts' (James Grant Wilson, 'John R. Thompson and His London Diary', *The Criterion*, November 1901), p. 30).

his knee, and talked to her all the while I was over at the Simmons' arranging matters. Afterwards when we were walking up a hill together he said, 'I admire that little girl of yours. It isn't everyone that admires that very solid kind of development of flesh and blood. But I do. Old Tom Campbell used to say that children should be like bulbs—plenty of substance in them for the flower to grow out of by-and-by.' Tennyson asked me how many children I had; and when I said 'four,' answered quite hastily, 'quite enough! quite enough!' At which I was not a little amused.

By the time we reached Churt a heavy shower came on, so we all took shelter in Mr. Simmons' little farmhouse there.

In course of conversation, Tennyson repeated a good story, which a Southern American had recently told him. . . .

As soon as the shower cleared off we (fly, pony-chaise and Mr. Simmons on horse-back) went to the piece of ground in question—the Jumps. Tennyson was by no means favourably impressed with it, and indeed it struck me as one of the barest, most desolate looking spots to be found hereabouts, though it is not without a certain bleak grandeur; but it is just outside and beyond all the beauty: 'Very dear at the money,' he said emphatically, and 'what is the use of a number of acres if they will not grow anything?' . . .

Tennyson then said he should like to see the Punch Bowl: while we were driving thither, one of the most tremendous rain storms I ever saw swallowed up the country behind us, a magnificent effect it was. I think Tennyson was much impressed with the grandeur of the views from the top of Hind-head, though he saw them under decidedly unfavourable circumstances.[1] . . .

I will only add, that when we parted he thanked the Simmonses and myself very cordially and pleasantly—said he should like another day here when he could find the opportunity. And though we certainly saw nothing to suit him this time I do not despair of our doing so by and by. It *was* a happy day! . . . One feels, somehow singularly happy and free from constraint in his presence—a sense of a beneficent, generous, nobly humane nature being combined with his intellectual greatness.

To FRANCIS TURNER PALGRAVE

MS. John Whale.

October 3, 1866

Dear Palgrave

I am grieved that we could not meet you at the White Hart, Salisbury. We were on that day at Petersfield and due that very day at home where my wife's father was expected. We had been going to Switzerland and had taken out duly £100 of circular notes but whether frightened by the cholera or by the weather, we never got beyond British bounds, and as to weather, Tyndall who has been to Switzerland tells me he had hardly a fair day—that his tour was as good as none—so we had an escape.

[1] See below, pp. 444–6.

The Rector of Trevena is I suppose the identical person who once modestly proposed to me to write an ode on the opening of his schools, and was indignant either that I did not comply with his request or that I did not answer his letter. You may tell him that I never laureatize except for the Queen and at her exprest desire, and then not willingly—no, you needn't tell him that, but you may easily find excuses for me, diplomatic as you are.

We shall be charmed to see you and your wife, whenever you like to come. In the middle of this month we shall be away from home but afterwards here till the year closes. I don't know whether you are in Yorkshire or the Regent's Park. I send this at a venture to the latter.

Ever yours
A. Tennyson

DANTE GABRIEL ROSSETTI to ALFRED TENNYSON

MS. Yale.

16 CHEYNE WALK, October 6, 1866

My dear Tennyson

This letter does not come with the least intention of troubling you for an answer, which it does not need, but it is necessary I should write it.

Edward Jones told me today what when he lately saw you, you were speaking of the qualities which displease you in Swinburne's poetry, and after attributing their origin in one respect correctly, you added that you supposed they might be also owing to his intimacy with me.

As no one delights more keenly in his genius than I do, I also have a right to say that no one has more strenuously combatted its wayward exercise in certain instances, to the extent of having repeatedly begged him not to read me certain portions of his writings when in M. S. I remember that in a conversation I had with you when returning from Mr. Procter's some months ago, I stated this; though not then in denial to reports of which I then knew nothing, and which seem to have more weight with you than my statement. So let me now say distinctly that any assertion to the contrary is either ignorant gossip or lying slander.

The attacks on Swinburne in the press have been for the most part coarse and stupid; and it is only to a very few, such as yourself, that I should at this moment say anything which could by any possibility be misconstrued as taking part against him. I trust to your not so construing it; but having made such efforts as I could before his book appeared, in what I thought his interest, I cannot now myself submit to misrepresentation in a quarter where I should much regret it.

I am, my dear Tennyson,

Yours very truly
D. G. Rossetti

A. Tennyson Esq.

To A. HARBOTTLE ESTCOURT

Text. Materials, iii. 50.

October [8], 1866

My dear Sir

Let me say how much my wife and I are grieved at your loss—a loss not yours only, but our own and that of all who have been fortunate enough to have had your brother as a friend and adviser.[1] We must trust that Mrs. Estcourt and the children bear this sorrow as well as you can expect.

Most truly yours
A. Tennyson

To JAMES HUNT[1]

MS. Huntington Library.

FARRINGFORD, I.W., October 9, 1866

My dear Sir

I have been intending to write to you for some time past to know how Lionel gets on and whether you can fix a probable time for his return.[2] His last letter informed us that he had been in bed for a week with a bad headache. As this never occurred to him before we feel anxious about him and should be much obliged to you if you would let us know exactly what the matter is. Believe me, my dear Sir,

Yours very truly
A. Tennyson

To GEORGE GROVE

MS. Rowland Collins.

October 11, 1866

My dear Grove

I have got your Heine and am much obliged to you for him and I am

---

[1] Charles Wyatt Estcourt. 'You will, I know, be sorry to hear that Mr. Estcourt is dead after an illness of two or three weeks. He caught cold in driving from Yarmouth. He has left a wife and eight children. I think you know he is a great loss to us; and Sir John Simeon still greater. He is very much grieved' (Emily Tennyson to Lionel, 19 October, TRC).

[1] James Hunt (1833–69: *DNB*), ethnologist and speech therapist, had a clinic at Ore House (a name the boys must have had fun with), near Hastings, where Lionel had gone on 17 (not 7) August (*Memoir*, ii. 39; *Materials*, iii. 48; *Journal*, p. 70) on account of his stammering. Hunt had treated Charles Kingsley and also Charles Dodgson, who said, 'I think so little of him as a gentleman that it might be disagreeable for a lady to be in the house' (*The Letters of Lewis Carroll*, ed. Cohen, i. 54; see also i. 42 n.). In this connection, see *The Swinburne Letters*, i. 288 n.

[2] 'Papa is writing to Dr. Hunt to inquire about you. . . . I really think you had better come home as soon as Dr. Hunt pronounces you could for it does not seem to me that you are by any means as well as usual at Ore House' (Emily Tennyson to Lionel, 9 October, TRC). Lionel remained at Hunt's at least until April 1867 (Emily Tennyson to Lionel, 24 April 1867, TRC).

considering your proposition.¹ I think I shall be in town sometime this month or next: but if with respect to Payne's proposal—whatever it may be—you wish to have my opinion earlier, write to me here, and I will give it my best attention—or come yourself.²

Ever yours
A. Tennyson

Couldn't you come next Saturday and stay over Sunday?

To ALEXANDER HAMILTON HUME[1]

Text. Memoir, ii. 40–1.

[*c.* 23 October 1866]

Sir

I thank you and the Committee for the honour done to me.

I sent my small subscription as a tribute to the nobleness of the man, and as a protest against the spirit in which a servant of the State, who has saved to us one of the Islands of the Empire, and many English lives, seems to be hunted down.

But my entering my name on your committee might be looked upon as a pledge that I approve of all the measures of Governor Eyre. I cannot assert that I do this, neither would I say that he has erred, my knowledge of the circumstances not being sufficient.

In the meantime, the outbreak of our Indian Mutiny remains as a warning to all but madmen against want of vigour and swift decisiveness.

I have the honour to be

Your most obedient servant
A. Tennyson

---

[1] In reply to a letter from Grove, 5 October (*Memoir*, ii. 40), asking Tennyson to compose a song cycle modelled on Heine. The result was 'The Window or, The Song of the Wrens' (Ricks, p. 1196). See below, pp. 444, 447, 468, 556.

[2] Grove's letter (complete in *Materials*, iii. 49) concludes: 'Is there any chance of your being in town soon? If so and if you could give me an hour, I should be very grateful as I want to consult you on a proposition which Payne has made to me and about which I am very much divided. You were so good to me at the beginning of the year that I am bold enough to wish to ask you about this. I would come any reasonable distance to see you.' Grove was at Farringford on 16–17 October (*Journal*, p. 253; Graves, *Life and Letters of Grove*, p. 133).

[1] Alexander Hamilton Hume (1797–1873: *DNB*), Australian explorer: 'When the Eyre Defence Committee had been formed in early August, the self-appointed secretary of the new Committee, . . . an Australian living in London . . . , without having any idea of what had happened in Jamaica, had determined to support the man who had won fame as an explorer of his native country' (Bernard Semmel, *Democracy versus Empire*, p. 110). See above, p. 429, and *Journal*, pp. 253–4. J. M. Ludlow published a long letter deploring Tennyson's subscription in the *Spectator*, xxxix (3 Nov. 1866), 1225–6.

To W. W. BENNETT [?][1]

MS. University of Kentucky.

October 23, 1866

Dear Sir

I shall be glad to see you when I return. At present I and my wife are going away perhaps for three weeks.

With respect to your proposed work I have long ago thought that if such a thing were well done it might be good for the country. Nevertheless I cannot pledge myself to help you in it. Believe me,

Yours very truly
A. Tennyson

W. W. Bennett, Esq.

GEORGE GROVE to OLGA VON GLEHN (extract)

Text. Charles L. Graves, *The Life and Letters of Sir George Grove,* pp. 133–4.

October 28, 1866

Last week I went down to Freshwater and had a charming afternoon and evening with Tennyson. He was at his very best, and made a much deeper and more favourable impression on me than ever before. I had proposed to him to write a *Liederkreis* for Sullivan to set to music and Millais to illustrate, and he had caught the idea at once and had done three songs out of seven—very charming songs and very good for music.[1] Sullivan went down with me, and pleased both Mr. and Mrs. Tennyson extremely. In the evening we had as much music as we could on a *very tinkling* piano, very much out of tune, and then retired to his room at the top of the house where he read us the three songs, a long ballad, and several other things, and talked till two o'clock in a very fine way about the things which I always get around to sooner or later—death and the next world, and God and man.

THE JOURNALS OF WALTER WHITE, p. 162.

November 5, 1866

Talk with Mrs. Gilchrist about the lands at which Tennyson is to look. At one o'clock to the station; met the Poet and Mrs. Tennyson and Payne. After lunch a walk to the Hill Copse, commanding a glorious view towards Little Hill, and all the diversified landscape between. Heavy misty rain. The Poet was pleased with the place and made up his mind to buy it. He would like the spring better were it a rush of water. The firwood on hilltop and expanse of wild heath to rear charmed him.

---

[1] *Sic,* but probably W. C. Bennett (see below, p. 449), projecting his *Proposals for and Contributions to a Ballad History of England and the States Sprung from Her* (1868).

[1] See above, pp. 442–3.

To THE DUKE OF ARGYLL

Text. Tennyson Research Centre (transcript).

STOATLEY FARM, HASLEMERE, November 8, 1866[1]

My dear Duke

I shall be very glad to read your book, which I suppose is waiting for me at Farringford.[2] We are at present lodging at a farm house in the neighbourhood of Haslemere. My wife has always had a fancy for the sandy soil and heather-scented air of this part of England and we are intending to buy a few acres and build a little home here—whither we may escape when the cockneys are running over my lawns at Freshwater. I am sorry that I did not see the Marquis, but I will call for the calumet when I go to town. It is odd that the Americans always send me pipes or tobacco, as if I cared for nothing else in the world; and their tobacco is not my tobacco, nor their pipes my pipes; bird's eye and a Milo-cutty being more according to my fancy than costlier things. I don't however mean to undervalue Longfellow's gift.[3] I envy you your journey. I have been along the Corniche as you may read in my little poem 'The Daisy.' I don't suppose that Europe, or Asia perhaps, has a more splendid piece of coast scenery—but at this time of year you will hardly see it in perfection. Perhaps however if the Autumn tints remain they may more than make up for the loss of the opulence of summer which seemed to satiate heart and eye when I looked from the hill above Nice over rock and ruin and down-streaming vineyard to the many-coloured Mediterranean. We did not get further than Florence—Rome is only a dream to me and not a very distinct one.

Are you going with your wicked Protestant eyes to see the Fall of the Beast?[4] Mine and my wife's love to the Duchess and all joy to you both. You must feel like the starling that has got out,[5] and the sweets of office out-sweetened by the sweets of out of office.[6] Hallam is at Marlborough and flourishing, Lionel with Dr. Hunt near Hastings. Lady Edith is, we trust, quite recovered and enjoying her visit.

Ever yours
A. Tennyson

To ANNE GILCHRIST

MS. Harvard.

November 16, 1866

My dear Mrs. Gilchrist

We have arrived safety; my wife is better though still suffering from

---

[1] Dated 1867 in transcript and in *Memoir*, ii. 46.
[2] *The Reign of Law* (see Appendix C).
[3] See below, p. 448.
[4] This sentence (omitted in *Memoir*) apparently refers to Emperor Napoleon's withdrawal of French troops from Rome, leaving 'the Pope to maintain himself as a temporal Sovereign without the aid of a foreign Power' (*Annual Register*, p. 206).
[5] Lawrence Sterne, 'The Passport. The Hotel at Paris', in *A Sentimental Journey*.
[6] See above, p. 434 n.

inflamed eyes: I fear it will be some days before she is able to write. She desires to say this and to send her love.

We slept at Winchester and had plenty of money. We have very grateful recollections of your kindness.[1] Believe me,

Ever yours
[Signature cut off]

To GEORGE STOVIN VENABLES

MS. National Library of Wales.

FARRINGFORD, ISLE OF WIGHT, November 17, 1866

My dear Venables

We have just returned home from a short sojourn in Surrey and found your letter here. We heard of you and your loss[1] from F. Lushington and others and I need not say sympathized with you, who are so old a friend.

My wife is unable to write for one of her eyes is blind with an inflammation caught by going into a cold farmhouse where we had taken lodgings and where the fires took three or four hours to light on the evening of our arrival there.

I have no manner of wish to be the Oxford Poetry Professor, but you can put this of course a little more graciously to those who asked whether I had.

My wife begs me to thank you for your invitation to Llysdinam and to say that she hopes some day to come to you there—though indeed the Welsh climate does not very well agree with her. Believe me

Ever yours
A. Tennyson

We have good news of both the boys.

To BENEDICT LAWRENCE CHAPMAN

MS. Indiana University.

FARRINGFORD, ISLE OF WIGHT, November 18, 1866

My dear Chapman

My wife and I have just returned from a short tour into Surrey, she I am sorry to say with an inflammation of the right eye, so that she can neither read and [sic] write. Many thanks for your note and the Banking Book and to

---

[1] See *Journal*, pp. 254–5. As the first entry in December the Journal (TRC) says: 'Mr. Simmons arranges the agreement about Greyshott and we choose papers and Mrs. Gilchrist sees the workmen about them.'

[1] The death of his brother, Joseph Henry Venables (b. 1813), a barrister-at-law, on 15 September (Venables's Diaries, National Library of Wales; *Landed Gentry*).

Mr. Kent[1] for his services: we shall like to know what we owe him besides thanks.

Her best remembrances and believe me,

Ever yours
A. Tennyson

WILLIAM ALLINGHAM, *A DIARY*, pp. 145–6.

Wednesday, November 21, 1866

Farringford. Breakfast. Letter for Tennyson from Poets sending specimens of their work, and autograph seekers.[1] T. says, 'I should like to sneak about and get a cup of tea by myself.' At which Mrs. T. smiles sweetly on us. T. added, in a matter-of-fact way, 'I breakfasted alone for a quarter of a century.' Mrs. T. asks me to stay, but go to Lymington I must, so hurry off to Yarmouth, running part of the way, to catch steamer. Cross again in the afternoon, and walk to Farringford. Dinner. Parson F.[2] defends Church and state. Parson's wife angry and shows it.

Drawing-room.—T. on the death of children, without any reference to orthodox phrases or notions. Mrs. F., driven out of her wits almost, declares what he says to be 'mere chop-logic.' After this he goes upstairs leaving us silent and the parson's wife enraged.

T. and I upstrairs—'Swinburne—he has a metrical swing. W. M. Rossetti's pamphlet.'[3]

You shocked Mrs. F.'

'Can't help it.'

Thursday, November 22, 1866

Farringford. After breakfast T. reads a number of Songs of his under the general title of *The Window*, or, *The Loves of the Wrens*,[4] prefacing it by the remark, 'They're quite silly.'

These songs were privately printed some little time ago at the press of Sir Ivor Guest. Arthur Sullivan saw a copy and managed to get a promise from T. to allow him to set them to music and publish them, all together, on some

---

[1] Unidentified (but see below, p. 470).

[1] On 19 November he had sent four autographs to Mr. Mossman, a Lincolnshire friend of Charles Tennyson Turner, who had 'made apologies' two weeks earlier 'abt A's autograph' (Charles Tennyson Turner's 'Memorandum Books for 1866', TRC; transcribed by Roger Evans).

[2] If 'F' is accurate, the parson would be Randle Henry Feilden (1802–75), Rector of St. Lawrence, IW, 1848–52, unbeneficed 1853–4 (*Landed Gentry*, Venn), and listed in White's *Hampshire* (1859) as living at Thorncliff, Bonchurch, IW. If misleading, the parson was probably John Frederick Isaacson, Rector of All Saints, the Freshwater parish church (see above, p. 355).

[3] 'Swinburne's Poems and Ballads, A Criticism' (Moxon, 1866).

[4] See above, p. 443.

half-profit arrangement. T. repented of this and tried hard to back out. Some lines in them one remembers like a nursery rhyme—

> When the winds are up in the morning,
> Vine, vine and eglantine,
> Rose, rose and clematis
> Kiss, kiss!

There are naivetes and niaiseries—

> You are small, am I so tall?
> Cannot we come together?
> Why?
>
> For it's easy to find a rhyme—
> It's ay, ay, ay, ay!

In reading this, T. jumped round most comically, like a cock-pigeon. He is the only person I ever saw who can do the most ludicrous things without any loss of dignity.

Reading the lines—

> After-loves of maids and men
> Are but meats cook'd up again,

he remarked, 'That's very like Shakespeare.'

To HENRY WADSWORTH LONGFELLOW

MS. Bowdoin College.

FARRINGFORD, FRESHWATER, ISLE OF WIGHT, November 27, 1866

My dear Mr. Longfellow

I had desired to smoke the pipe of peace before writing to you but it seems that it cannot be: so lest I should appear ungrateful I will delay acknowledging it no longer.

The Marquis of Lorne wished to deliver it to me in person but he could not come at the time I named for his visit and afterwards I went from home. Since then I have been always expecting to see him, but now it seems he has gone to Berlin and the other day the Duke of Argyll wrote to me from France saying that the pipe was left for me at his house in London, but since I cannot at present make a pilgrimage thither to claim it, it is better before it is actually in my hand, to tell you how grateful I am and how much I shall value it as your gift—and let me hope that a day may come when we may smoke it together.[1] We English and Americans should all be brothers as none others among the nations can be, and some of us come what ay will always be so I trust.[2]

---

[1] See above, p. 445.
[2] Longfellow quoted this sentence in a letter to Charles Sumner 1 January 1867 (*The Letters of Henry Wadsworth Longfellow*, ed. Andrew Hilen, v. 108). Tennyson claimed the pipe in June 1867 (*Journal*, p. 263).

I was very sorry to have missed seeing your son.[3] If he have not left England, or if he returns through it, I may hope to see him yet. Believe me,
Always yours
A. Tennyson

To CHARLES ELLIS

MS. Washington University Libraries.

Christmas Eve, 1866

My dear Sir

Once more accept my thanks for your Christmas gift of choice wines, which are not only welcome for their own sake, but doubly so as being proofs of your kindliness. I cannot quite make out from your letter whether you called here or no when you were in the Island last year. If you did I am most sorry that I was not at home. I shall always be glad to see you.
Ever yours
A. Tennyson

EMILY SELLWOOD TENNYSON to WILLIAM COX BENNETT

MS. University of Kentucky.

FARRINGFORD, December 30, 1866

Dear Sir

My husband bids me thank you for your kindness in sending him 'Our Glory Roll.'[1] We hope that you will be able to come to us on the 7th of January. Believe me,
Truly yours
Emily Tennyson

To SIR IVOR BERTIE GUEST[1]

MS. Tennyson Research Centre.

FARRINGFORD, I.W., January 8, 1867

My dear Sir Ivor

Your book[2] is a very handsome one and does credit to your printing-press, and the skill of the compositors: if you have kept the types standing (and I

---

[3] Charles Appleton Longfellow had been at West Cowes, IW, in August (Longfellow's *Letters*, v. 79–80).

[1] *Our Glory-roll and Other National Poems*. His visit is noted in *Journal*, p. 257.

[1] See below, pp. 468–9. On the Canford Manor press, see T. J. Wise's *Bibliography*, i. 181.
[2] *Enid, an Idyll*, privately printed at Canford Manor, Dorset, along with his mother's *Geraint*, translated from *Mabinogion*. See *Tennyson in Lincoln*, ii, Nos. 4009–10. The errata are in 'Geraint and Enid', l. 213, and 'The Marriage of Geraint', l. 842.

mention this that the book may be quite perfect) you might correct two errata—one p. 46

    Having less etc.

instead of

    Less having etc.

the other p. 37

    Remembering how that first

instead of

    Remembering how first etc.

Our best remembrances to all your household and believe me, with thanks,
Very truly yours
A. Tennyson

To MISS DE MONTMORENCY DAUBENY[1]

MS. Indiana University.

FARRINGFORD, January 15, 1867

Mr. Alfred Tennyson presents his compliments to Miss de Montmorency Daubeny and regrets that he must refer her to Messrs. Moxon (his publishers) for an answer respecting her illumination of The Lord of Burleigh.

WILLIAM ALLINGHAM, *A DIARY*, pp. 149–50.

Friday, January 24 [for 25], 1867]

Lymington. Fine and vernal. Ferry to steamer—delightful colours of earth, sky, and sea, a bloom upon the landscape. From the Solent see the woody background of Lymington recede, the Island approach with a welcome; a boat with red sails passes in the sunshine. I feel tranquilly happy. Yarmouth, send two bottles of whisky to A. T. by Lambert's driver. Walk to Farringford, field-path, warm. Drawing-room. Mrs. T. (looking ill), Miss T.,[1] T. He and I walk on the downs; very friendly talk. I said I felt happy to-day, but he—'I'm not at all happy—very unhappy.' He spoke of immortality and virtue,—Man's pettiness.—'Sometimes I have a kind of hope.' His anxiety has always been great to get some real insight into the nature and prospects of the Human Race. He asks every person that seems in the least likely to help him in this, reads every book. When *Vestiges of Creation* appeared he gathered from the talk about it that it came nearer to an explanation than anything before it. T. got the volume, and (he said to me), 'I trembled as I cut the leaves.' But alas, neither was satisfaction there.[2]

---

[1] Unidentified

[1] Matilda Tennyson.   [2] See i. 230 and n.

Plato: T. says he has not really got anything from him. Aeschylus is great; he quoted from a Chorus in the *Agamemnon*.

Women in towns, dangers to health, horrible diseases, quack-doctors, etc. T. would have a strict Contagious Diseases Act in force everywhere.

We go through kitchen garden, lane and gate to the road as usual, where we take leave after some talk upon Christ and the People. T. loves the spirit of Christianity, hates many of the dogmas.

Friday, February 1, 1867

Tennyson is unhappy from his uncertainty regarding the condition and destiny of man. . . .

Saturday February 2, 1867

T. and Lionel just starting for a walk; we took the green road at foot of downs. T. had in his pocket a volume, or pamphlet of Edwin Waugh's *Lancashire Songs*, and when we paused he read, 'Coam whoam to thy children and me,' with praise.[3] We went to the end of the downs overlooking the Needles. T. spoke of Campbell'—his vanity—'has written fine things'. . . .

Sunday, February 3, 1867

Walk with T. to Brook Bay, ship ashore, the *Fannie Larabee* of Bath, large, three masts, good model. There are people on the shore, but T. doesn't seem to mind. We walked to next point and saw a steamer ashore at Atherfield; then turned up to downs and came back by a path slanting along the cliff side, like a frightful dream rather, my head being lightish. T. tells of people who have fallen over, and at one place is a monumental stone to commemorate such an accident. I said (walking close behind him) 'suppose I were to slip and catch hold of you, and we both rolled down together,' on which T. stopped and said, 'you'd better go on first.'

We talked of Dryden, Campbell, etc. T. told me he was prevented from doing his Arthur Epic, in twelve books, by John Sterling's Review of 'Morte d'Arthur' in the *Quarterly*.[4] 'I had it all in my mind, could have done it without any trouble. The King is the complete man, the Knights are the passions.' Home a little late for dinner. Afterwards T. rose to leave the room. Matilda (I think) asked, 'Where are you going?'

'To read the Scriptures.'

Later in the drawing-room he read aloud some of the Goethe's lyrics.

To JAMES THOMAS FIELDS (incomplete)

MS. Berg Collection.

February 11, 1867

My dear Mr. Fields

I fear that I have been a little dilatory in not acknowledging earlier your

---

[3] Edwin Waugh (1817–80: *DNB*), 'the Lancashire Burns'. *Lancashire Songs* appeared in 1863.
[4] See i. 99 n.

draft of one hundred pounds. Accept my thanks. I have not any book coming out this season.

Thanks for your kind invitation to my two boys, but they are too young to accept it and now both at school. We have heard of your coming to England but I suppose there was no foundation for the report.

My wife desires her best remembrances to Mrs. Fields—to which pray add mine and believe me

Very truly yours
A. Tennyson

P. S. I see that you have printed the International ode[1] with two mistakes: you copied it from the Times and did not see my letter to the Times about it.

'Earth's invention stored' it should be:
I should never have written so unmusically as
    ntions st——

'Part divine' should be 'Art divine.' The story goes that the man who pirated it for the Times when it was being printed with the music mistook the P of piano for a P of the text;

To GUSTAVE DORÉ[1]

MS. Huntington Library.

FARRINGFORD, ISLE OF WIGHT, [c. 16 February 1867]

Permettez, Monsieur, que je vous fasse part du grand plaisir que m'ont fait les Illustrations de mes Idylles déjà accomplies. Je n'en ai vu que les quatres apportées ici par M. Payne, et quant à elles il me semble que leur beauté morne et noble accorde parfaitement avec le génie des vieilles légendes, et M. Payne m'écrit qu'il y en a d'autres encore plus ravissantes, qu'enfin on ne peut mieux.

J'aurais voulu vous assurer à l'instant combien je me sentais heureux d'avoir trouvé un tel interprète, mais je craignais vous importuner de mon méchant Français.

Aujourd'hui M. Payne me fait espérer qu'une telle assurance ne vous déplairait point.

Puissent ces illustrations relever encore une renommé si éminente! Ce qui sera pour moi un plaisir de plus.

Veuillez, Monsieur, agréer la haute considération de votre très humble Serviteur.

A. Tennyson

---

[1] See above, pp. 281, 292.

[1] Gustave Doré (1832–83), French artist and one of the most famous illustrators who ever lived. With the thirty-six Doré illustrations of the *Idylls of the King* in 1868, Tennyson (whose French in this letter is not altogether idiomatic) joined the company of Balzac, Dante, Cervantes, the Bible, and Milton.

SARTOR RESARTUS: BAYARD TAYLOR VISITS TENNYSON, 21 FEBRUARY 1867

Text. Taylor to E. C. Stedman, 11 March 1867, in Marie Hansen-Taylor and Horace E. Scudder, *Life and Letters of Bayard Taylor*, ii. 471–3.

We landed at Southampton in heavenly May weather, and I determined to visit Farringford before going on to London. So I wrote at once to Tennyson, proposing a visit of an hour or two.[1] Next morning came a friendly reply from Mrs. T., saying there was a room ready for us, and we must make a longer visit. M[arie] and I crossed to Cowes and Newport, and took a 'fly' to Farringford, distant twelve miles; a glorious drive across the Isle of Wight, between ivied hedges and past gardens of laurel and laurustinus in blossom. Green meadows, cowslips, daisies, and hyacinths,—think of that for February 21st! I found Farringford wonderfully improved: the little park is a gem of gardening art. The magnificent Roman ilexes in front of the house are finer than any I saw in Italy. We arrived about three o'clock, and were ushered into the drawing-room. The house has been refurnished, and a great many pictures and statues added since I was there. In a minute in came Tennyson, cordial as an old friend, followed by his wife. In Tennyson himself I could see no particular change. He did not seem older than when I saw him last. We walked through the park and garden; then M. returned to the house, while he and I went up on the downs, and walked for miles along the chalk cliffs above the sea. He was delightfully free and confidential, and I wish I could write to you much of what he said; but it was so inwrought with high philosophy and broad views of life that a fragment here and there would not fairly represent him. He showed me all his newly acquired territory; among the rest, a great stretch of wheat-fields bought for him by 'Enoch Arden.' We dined at six in a quaint room hung with pictures, and then went to the drawing-room for dessert. Tennyson and I retired to his study at the top of the house, lit pipes, and talked of poetry. He asked me if I could read his 'Boadicea.' I thought I could. 'Read it, and let me see!' said he. 'I would rather hear you read it!' I answered. Thereupon he did so, chanting the lumbering lines with great unction. I spoke of the idyl of Guinevere as being perhaps his finest poem, and said that I could not read it aloud without my voice breaking down at certain passages. 'Why, I can read it and keep my voice!' he exclaimed triumphantly. This I doubted, and we agreed to try, after we went down to our wives. But the first thing he did was to produce a magnum of wonderful sherry, thirty years old, which had been sent to him by a poetic wine-dealer. Such wine I never tasted. 'It was meant to be drunk by Cleopatra, or Catherine of Russia,' said Tennyson. We had two glasses apiece, when he said, 'To-night you shall help me drink one of the few bottles of my Waterloo —1815.' The bottle was brought, and after another glass all round Tennyson took up the 'Idyl[l]s of the King.' His reading is a strange, monotonous chant, with unexpected falling inflections, which I cannot describe, but can imitate exactly. It is very impressive. In spite of myself I became very much

---

[1] Taylor to Tennyson, 6 January 1867 (TRC).

excited as he went on. Finally, when King Arthur forgives the Queen, Tennyson's voice fairly broke. I found tears on my cheeks, and M. and Mrs. Tennyson were crying, one on either side of me. He made an effort and went on to the end, closing grandly. 'How can you say,' I asked (referring to previous conversation), 'that you have no surety of permanent fame? This poem will only die with the language in which it is written.' Mrs. Tennyson started up from her couch. 'It is true!' she exclaimed. 'I have told Alfred the same thing.'

After that we went up the garret to smoke and talk. Tennyson read the 'Hylas' of Theocritus in Greek, his own 'Northern Farmer,' and Andrew Marvell's 'Coy Mistress.' . . . We parted at two o'clock, and met again at nine in the breakfast room. I had arranged to leave at noon, so there were only three hours left, but I had them with him on the lawn and in the nook under the roof. . . . Tennyson said at parting, 'The gates are always open to you.' His manner was altogether more cordial and intimate than at my first visit. He took up the acquaintance where it first broke off, and had forgotten no word (neither had I) of our conversation ten years ago. When I spoke of certain things in his poetry which I specially valued, he said more than once, 'But the critics blame me for just that. It is only now and then a man like yourself who sees what I meant to do.' He is very sensitive to criticism, I find, but perhaps not more than the rest of us; only one sees it more clearly in another. Our talk was to me delightful; it was as free and frank as if you had been in his place. . . . I felt, when I left Farringford, that I had a friend's right to return again.[2]

ALFRED AND EMILY SELLWOOD TENNYSON *to* ELEANOR EDEN

MS. Berg Collection.

FARRINGFORD, February 27, 1867

Dear Lena Eden

I have this morning received your 'Dumbleton Co⟨ttage⟩mmons'[1] and return my best thanks, and give you my promise that I will read it, and hope I shall like it as well as I did the other two. As I am a married man and an old, I trust that the Dedication will breed no scandal.

My wife's kindest regards to yourself and your Aunt.[2]

Always yours
A. Tennyson

---

[2] But by a quirk of fate he lost the right. This letter 'fell into the hands of a newspaper correspondent, who kept it long enough to copy the portion relating to Mr. Tennyson, and then, without asking leave of the author, the recipient, or conscience, printed it as a lively piece of literary gossip. Bayard Taylor heard nothing of the publication until he learned it in a roundabout way from Mr. Tennyson himself' (Hansen-Taylor and Scudder, ii. 474–5 n.). See below, p. 514.

[1] Her novel (2 vols., 1867) inscribed to Tennyson (*Tennyson in Lincoln*, i, No. 889), preceded by *Easton and Its Inhabitants: Sketches of Life in a Provincial Town* (1858) and *False and True* (1859).

[2] Emily Eden (see above, p. 432 n.).

I am going to write and tell you when we are settled in the Farmhouse. You will come to see us will you not? Perhaps in a fortnight, but I am not sure.

Yours affectionately
E. T.

ALFRED AND EMILY SELLWOOD TENNYSON to SIR JOHN SIMEON

MS. Syracuse University.

MARLBOROUGH COLLEGE, [? 3 March] 186[7]

My dear Simeon

He is better today. Yesterday we thought he was going for the pulse stopt and he was seized with a coups des nerfs. We telegraphed for Dr. Symonds of Bristol who gave us good hopes that he is past the worst and will recover—it was an attack of pneumonia with low symptoms.[1] In great haste

Yours ever
A. T.

My kindest love and thanks to dear Lady Simeon for all her loving sympathy, to you both. We may hope that he will be restored to us now. Mr. and Mrs. Bradley say that they never knew till now all Ally's greatness, so thoughtful for everyone, so kind and calm.

To LIONEL TENNYSON

MS. Tennyson Research Centre.

[c. 5 March 1867]

My dear Lionel

I have been just writing to Dr. Hunt to prevent your running such long paper-chases. Everyone here (all the Masters) exclaim against it as ruining and breaking up the constitution. Arthur Bradley is knocked up at this moment from having run only 5 miles and you say you have run ⟨fifte⟩ 16. You must not do it.[1] We have left Hallam a little more comfortable tonight.

Your affectionate father
A. Tennyson

---

[1] See *Memoir*, ii. 42; *Journal*, pp. 259–61; *Letters of Emily Tennyson*, pp. 210–13.

[1] 'Paper chases are supposed to have done Arthur [Bradley] so much harm that he is not allowed to work his brain at all now. One of Mrs. Bradley's brothers, a big strong broad-shouldered young man, died in consumption from them and Mr. Bradley says that he ruined his own health by them. Even Rugby is growing weary of them, we hear, owing to all the mischief they have done' (Emily Tennyson to Lionel, 23 March, TRC).

To LAURA BARKER TAYLOR

MS. Duke University.

MARLBOROUGH COLLEGE, [mid-]March 1867

My dear Mrs. Taylor

Take the song and welcome—it has been set before I believe more than once, but that perhaps will not deter you from publishing your own setting.[1]

We are here, for Hallam our eldest has had and still suffers from a very dangerous attack of pneumonia. My love to your husband.

Yours ever
A. Tennyson

To FRANCIS TURNER PALGRAVE

Text. Materials, iii. 55–7.

March 23, 1867

Dear Palgrave

I suppose I may come up to Town some time after we are settled in our farm house[1] where I have taken rooms for ourselves and three servants for two years, and can have them for six if I choose. We go there in about a week more or less: there will one room for a guest.

I don't give the name of the place because I wish it to be kept secret: I am not flying from the cockneys here to tumble in among the cockneys there I hope: though some of my friends assert that it will be so, and that there will be more cockneys and of a worse kind, but I don't believe them, for the house is quite solitary and five miles from town or village. You ask whether Doré's illustrations are a success financially.[2] I don't know; they couldn't anyway be a great success to me since I think Payne told me that I was only to receive two shillings or so a volume and that after £3,000 had been cleared, the original outlay. I liked the first four I saw very much though they were not quite true to the text, but the rest not so well, one I hate, that where the dead lady is stuck up in a chair, with her eyes open, as if her father had forgotten to close them, or as if she had opened them again, for they are closed in the voyage down the river. On the whole I am against illustrators, except one could do with them as old Mr. Rogers did, have them to breakfast twice a week and explain your own views to them over and over again. Arthur Hughes would not have made such a mull of his tropical isle if he had only condescended to submit his design to me, or even to ask me a question or two, to be sure, poor fellow, he was hurried by Payne. What's become of Payne, do you know? I can't get a word of answer from him when I write.

---

[1] Probably 'Ask me no more'. See Gooch and Thatcher, p. 600, where it is listed with 'Sweet and low'. See above, p. 33 n. (Three earlier settings are recorded of the former, many of 'Sweet and low'.)

[1] Grayshott (see above, p. 446 n.).

[2] 'Sales were excellent. Though priced at one, three and five guineas, these were "the books most looked for in each year of the issue"' (Hagen, *Tennyson and His Publishers*, p. 113, citing Joseph Shaylor, *The Fascination of Books*, p. 53).

My wife (thanks for your enquiries) had been shut up in the house for nearly three months with cough and cold. The Queen sent her an invitation to go with me to Osborne but I was obliged to make her excuses and went alone,[3] and found Her Majesty quite jolly, for the time at least, whatever she may be in private. You say that you expect another little one in June, ought I to congratulate you or condole? Love to Mrs. Palgrave from both. Believe me,

> Yours ever
> A. Tennyson

WILLIAM ALLINGHAM, *A DIARY*, p. 151.

FARRINGFORD, Wednesday April 3, 1867

Tennyson and I busied ourselves in the shrubberies, transplanting primroses with spade, knife, and wheelbarrow. After dinner T. concocts an experimental punch with whisky and claret—not successful. Talks of Publishers, anon of higher things. He said, 'I feel myself to be a centre—can't believe I shall die. Sometimes I have doubts, of a morning. Time and Space appear thus by reason of our boundedness.'

We spoke of Swedenborg, animals, etc., all with the friendliest sympathy and mutual understanding. T. is the most delightful man in the world to converse with, even when he disagrees.

To JAMES RIPLEY OSGOOD[1]

MS. Buffalo and Erie County Public Library.

FARRINGFORD, April 4, 1867

Dear Sir

I am not in the habit of inserting poems in the English Magazines, and why should I in the American?—particularly as in this unhappy condition of international Copyright law the English Magazines would immediately pirate any thing of mine in yours. I cannot at all say when I shall publish a new volume. It has at present to be uncertain.

---

[3] In mid-January (*Journal*, p. 258; *The Letters of Emily Tennyson*, pp. 208–9).

[1] James Ripley Osgood (1836–92), American publisher. He 'had been a clerk in the firm [of Ticknor and Fields] since 1858', and, having been groomed for the job by Fields, became a junior partner in October 1868, and 'head of the new James R. Osgood and Company in 1871 upon Fields's retirement' (James C. Austin, *Fields of the Atlantic Monthly*, pp. 38, 421). Osgood may have been soliciting a poem for the *Atlantic Monthly*, *North American Review*, or *Every Saturday*, all of which were owned by Ticknor and Fields, or possibly for *Putman's Magazine*, revived in 1868. In the event, 'The Victim' (Ricks, pp. 1194–6) appeared in *Good Words* in January 1868, and in February in the *Atlantic*; and 'Lucretius' appeared simultaneously in *Macmillan's Magazine* and *Every Saturday* in May 1868 (see below, pp. 475–6).

Pray give my best remembrances to Mr. Fields on your return[2] and believe me,

Yours faithfully
A. Tennyson

To JAMES BERTRAND PAYNE

MS. Tennyson Research Centre.

FARRINGFORD, April 17, 1867

My dear Mr. Payne

You drew your own inferences from what I say and wrong ones. I never accused you of trying to overreach me. I merely asked a question or two—growlingly, perhaps. Certainly the £74.2 inserted as omitted, without a word of apology or explanation seemed to be a liberty; and you must recollect that in the accounts of your house some few years ago there was an absolute error to a much greater amount: which proves that you are not always so accurate as you suppose. Here, for instance, in your last to me you speak of the advertisements in -66 as amounting to 29.8. I make them out from the accounts you have sent me in the sheets of the year -66—thus

	66	
Gen'l adv. June 30		£13. 8
do		
Adv. to this date June 30		12. 11. 3
G'l adv. Dec. 31		16.
Adv. to this date Dec. 31		14. 17
		56. 16. 3

Again, the £74, of which you and Mr. Jones[1] according to your letter, seem to know nothing, though it is charged against me, as you have by this time seen.

I mentioned the fact of Mrs. Tennyson's not having been able to look over the accounts—to explain how it was that no notice had been taken of the 15 per cent before.

The duplicate of the rider has not been found. Are you sure that you gave me one? It is any way strange that the whole affair should so utterly have passed from my mind, and stranger if I ever possessed this tangible proof of the transaction.

I remember the 15 per cent on the Selections and nothing more. I have always thought that your New Selection was to be from dead not living authors, therefore Mrs. Steele's letter came upon me as a surprise—however if you still think it expedient to make such a selection I do not say that I shall deny Mrs. Steele's request.[2]

---

[2] The envelope is addressed to James R. Osgood Esqre | Tavistock Hotel | Covent Garden | W. C.

[1] Presumably, Payne's manager or accountant (see the next letter).
[2] Unidentified, but see below, p. 459.

I neither affirmed not denied anything about the dividend. I implied that it was satisfactory as of course it is though there are certain things in the account not equally so. I have always said to everyone as I have said to yourself that I never had so good a dividend as since the affairs were in your hands but I cannot see why this should in any way close my mouth if I see anything which seems to me wrong or if there be anything which I cannot understand.

Yours very truly
A. Tennyson

P. S. I said nothing in my last about arrangements with individuals respecting the poems. I merely said that I could not accept anything from Govt. nor I think can I directly or indirectly.

Therefore if you do not return the £50 let it belong wholly to the firm.

To JAMES BERTRAND PAYNE

MS. Haverford College.

FARRINGFORD, FRESHWATER, ISLE OF WIGHT, April 18, 1867

My dear Mr. Payne

Mr. Jones's apology is sufficient and I am very glad to receive it. What can I desire more than to find that all your accounts are strictly correct.

As to that wretched volume[1] of course if it can be put a stop to let it at once. What a couple of snobs! I don't want to be at much expense about it, but you will take the best advice.

A. Tennyson

To MRS STEELE[1]

MS. Syracuse University.

FARRINGFORD, FRESHWATER, ISLE OF WIGHT, April 20, 1867

Madam

You are at liberty or rather I should say will you tell Lady Wood[2] with my compliments that she is at liberty to make the extracts from my books for which she asks

> 'Sir Launcelot and Queen Guinevere'
> 'Come not'
> 'The Poet's Song'
> 'The Departure'

---

[1] Unidentified, but see the next letter.

[1] Unidentified, but see the two letters preceding.

[2] Emma Carolina Wood (née Mitchell; d. 1879), widow of The Revd Sir John Page Wood, 2nd Baronet (older brother of Baron Hatherley), Vicar of Cressing, Sussex. (Their youngest daughter was Katherine O'Shea, later Parnell.) The volume was *Leaves from the Poets' Laurels* (Moxon's Miniature Poets, 1869), with 'Come not', 'Will', and selections from *Maud*, 'The Palace of Art', 'The Gardener's Daughter', and 'Enoch Arden'.

and those portions of 'The Palace of Art,' 'The Two Voices,' 'Love and Duty,' and 'The Gardener's Daughter' marked in your book which I return and any short extract, not exceeding a few lines, from my other Poems. I have the honour to be, Madam,

Your obedient servant
A. Tennyson

In Memoriam is an anonymous work and not to be meddled with.

To THE DUCHESS OF ARGYLL
MS. Tennyson Research Centre.

GREYSHOTT HALL, HEADLEY, LIPHOOK, May 11, 1867

My dear Duchess

I came home tonight (Saturday), home to Greyshott Hall that is, from which place it takes a letter two days to get to London so that I suppose you have a chance of receiving this before you leave for Scotland.

Your note to me [and] my wife is in London. I was there three or four days always intending to go down to Argyll Lodge, but the charms of the Academy, Museum etc. occupied my few days and I always thought 'Well, I am coming up again in a week or so and I will call then'—so I have missed any opportunity of seeing you for which I am really sorry.

I cannot say where I shall be at the end of the month: but I or my wife will write and tell the Marquis where we are then.

In the meantime I have written to thank Longfellow: my love to the Duke—

Yours affectionately
A. Tennyson

To JAMES HUNT
MS. University of Virginia.

GREYSHOTT, HEADLEY, LIPHOOK, May 12, 1867,

My dear Sir

I ought to have written to you before but I have been on the move.

Lionel's utterance seems to us much better than it was at Christmas; and his health has improved in this air since he rejoined us; and as he has lost so much time in his education we think it would be better for him not to return to Ore House unless there be a relapse.

We hope you will approve of this arrangement. We are much indebted to you for the pains you have bestowed on our boy and to Mrs. Hunt for all her kindness to him. Believe me, with our kind regards,

Very truly yours
A. Tennyson

To JOHN STUART BLACKIE

MS. Morgan Library.

GREYSHOTT HALL, May 13, 1867

My dear Professor

I dare say you have published your lecture by this time: if not you are quite at liberty to quote me about the a-s and the i-s.[1]

A greater fault than the mispronunciation of these two is the false quantity which boys indulge in, e.g. such lines as these fine ones in the Georgic[2] a modern boy would pronounce

η
Fluctus ut in medio coepit quum albescere ponto

as in sign
Longius ex altoque s*i*num trahit utque volutus

ω
Ad terras immane *so*nat per saxa nec[que] ipso

as in miner
Monte minor procumbit—

horrible misquantities and a boy if taught properly would in Latin learn his quantities if he gave the vowels properly as he read.

I have been flitting—or would, as I said, have answered before.

Yours very truly
A. Tennyson

Her kind regards.

To JAMES THOMAS FIELDS

MS. Massachusetts Historical Society.

GREYSTOCK [sic] HALL, HEADLEY, LIPHOOK, June 5, 1867

My dear Mr. Fields

I have to acknowledge the receipt of your bill for £200 and am very glad that the Diamond Edition[1] has turned out so profitable. It is not without errors: in the very last line 'morning' for 'morn' which offends my ear and there still remains (I think for I have not the book with me here) in the Inaugural Ode 'invention*s s*tored' which offends my ear still more, 'stion*s* stor' *sto* is horrible not to mention that 'Invention' is the less prosaic.

I will think of your proposal which seems to me very liberal.

I am rejoiced that your house is (as you say) going in strongly for an International Copyright. I am sure that England and America would profit if

---

[1] 'Music of Speech in the Greek and Latin Languages', a lecture delivered in the Royal Institution this month (Anne M. Stoddard, *John Stuart Blackie*, ii. 33).

[2] *Georgics*, ii. 237 ff. See *Tennyson and His Friends*, p. 94.

[1] *Poetical Works* (Boston: Ticknor and Fields, 1867, 1868—*Tennyson in Lincoln*, i, No. 3610.) 'Morning' for 'morn' was in 'Specimen of a Translation of the Iliad in Blank Verse', variant reading, and 'inventions stored' in 'Ode Sung at the Opening of the International Exhibition', l. 2. See above, pp. 305–6.

such a measure were carried. Believe me, with best remembrances to Mrs. Fields,

Very truly yours
A. Tennyson

I ought to have answered you before but I have not been at home lately and there has been some delay in forwarding my letters.

EMILY SELLWOOD TENNYSON
to MARGARET GATTY (extract)

MS. Boston Public Library.

GREYSHOTT HALL, June 10, 1867

We have not yet received a plot of land in this neighbourhood as we had hoped to have done.

Until yesterday he has had but the lightest touch of hay-fever. He was walking about five hours yesterday and this I fear brought it on for he has been very unwell since and now that we have no longer the inducement to remain here that we had so long as he was well I *trust* that we may soon be going home for this undrained house is very trying to me who am shut up in it so much. They have been driving out a good deal for we have the pony-carriage here and two swift ponies instead of the old ones. The heathy wilds all about are delightful now and will be more so soon.

To HENRY WADSWORTH LONGFELLOW[1]

MS. Harvard.

GREYSHOTT HALL, HEADLEY, LIPHOOK, June 12, 1867

My dear Mr. Longfellow

As you see, I am not, nor have been for some weeks, at home; or I should have received and answered your kind letter earlier—indeed, I fled hither not only for the sake of pure air and solitude but to escape for a while both the cockneys, who are far too rife in my seawatering place, and letters which at times almost overwhelm me.

I shall be charmed to receive your translation, though in my heart I believe that translations of Poets are all but impossible, and that to transfer the Commedia successfully into English is beyond the power of the greatest poet living.

Very likely the book is waiting for me at Farringford, and I will treasure it as a memorial of you for though as I said I do not believe that translations are possible, I can scarce doubt but that yours will have grace and closeness enough to enhance your American and European reputation. I hope I may

---

[1] In reply to Longfellow's letter of 24 May 1867 *Memoir*, i. 444; date supplied in *The Letters of Longfellow*, v. 139).

see your son on his return. Whether I shall be in the Isle is problematical: but by enquiring at my publisher's, 4 Dover Street, Piccadilly, he will learn my whereabouts and may at least save himself the trouble of a bootless journey.[2]

Lonely as this place is we are only an hour and a half from London. We have lodgings in a farmhouse high up on a brown moorland (which however I am told is for three months a perfect glory of heathblossom) and if he came, while we were here, we would make him as comfortable as we could. Believe me, my dear Mr. Longfellow, with great regard,

Always yours
A. Tennyson

To MR TENNYSON OF CHESTER[1]

Text. Memoir, ii. 45.

June 13, 1867

Dear Sir

I have not been at home for many weeks or your kindly letter would not have remained so long without an answer, notwithstanding the multitude of letters, which really make it impossible for me to answer all. You have paid me a great compliment, nay, it is more than a compliment—in naming your son after me.

I wish him a useful and happy career, and only hope that he will take a better model than his namesake to shape his life by.

It is doubtless a pleasure to know that I have had sometimes the power to cheer the soldier, whose life of devotion to his country I honour; and few things in the world ought to gratify me so deeply as the assurance that anything I may have written has had an influence for good. Believe me, dear sir,

Yours truly
A. Tennyson

To ?

MS. Tennyson Research Centre.

FARRINGFORD, July 13, 1867

Sir

As one of Her Majesty's Household I claim exemption from serving on juries. I have the honour to be Sir

Your obedient servant
A. Tennyson

---

[2] See above, p. 449. He had been in Russia with his 'half-uncle', Nathan Appleton.

[1] 'An unknown correspondent ... who had named his child "Alfred"' (*Memoir*, ii. 45).

17 *July* 1867

WILLIAM ALLINGHAM, *A DIARY*, pp. 154-9.

Wednesday, July 17, 1867

Lymington. Fine; hurry to steamer. Excursion to visit the French Fleet at Spithead. At Yarmouth a large Tennyson party comes on board—A. T., his brother Charles and Mrs. Charles, Hallam and Lionel, two daughters of Fredk. Tennyson, from Jersey,[1] and Matilda T. A. T. and I collogue. At Cowes a bustle: The Queen embarking in her steam-yacht.

We see the fleet at Spithead, 'like Milan Cathedral.' Rain comes on. The Queen having reached the French Fleet—Ironclads, huge, black, ugly,—royal salutes thunder, the yards are manned, but we can see very little for the thick weather. Ryde Pier, Tennyson and I land, among others; the ladies ill and draggled. Pier Hotel. A. T., Charles T., and I go up High Street and out into a field beyond, where we sit on a balk of wood, looking at some cows grazing, and A. T. smoking. He quotes a sonnet of his brother's about elms and calls it *daimonisch*.[2] We return by lower road and all go aboard again, where A. T., Sir Andrew Hammond[3] and I dine. The weather still thick with frequent showers; some want to turn homeward without running through the Fleet, etc., as arranged. Captain Cribb will do whatever the passengers wish,— whereupon a debate below. In an interval of silence a deep voice is heard grumbling out—'I know it's not the least use my saying anything, but I'm for going back.' This was A. T., but the majority were plainly for going on, and soon we steamed in the rain close to the dark sullen row of huge Ironclads. Then fireworks, and we turned homewards. We nestled down near the boiler, A. T., Lionel, W. A., and the rest—chatted, asked riddles, and so we reached Yarmouth, where they landed and I was left lonely again.

To FRANCES HARRIET (HENSLOW) HOOKER[1]

MS. Jerry N. Showalter.

August 11, 1867

My dear Mrs. Hooker

Dr. Hooker is far more likely than myself to know whether the C[onvolvulus] grandiflora is found in the South Polynesian islands. Ellis in his Polynesian Researches[2] talks of the brilliant *pink* blossoms of the conv[olvulus] so 'roses' might seem to be the word required: but it would be ⟨better⟩

---

[1] Elise and Emilia (*Journal*, p. 264).

[2] Perhaps 'A Photograph on the Red Gold, Jersey, 1867', in Charles Tennyson Turner's *A Hundred Sonnets*, selected by Charles Tennyson and John Betjeman (1960), p. 40.

[3] Captain (or Vice-Admiral) Sir Andrew Snape Hamond, RN (1811-74), 3rd Baronet, of Norton Lodge, Freshwater. See above, p. 150 n.

[1] Frances Harriet (Henslow) Hooker (d. 1874), first wife of Joseph Hooker (see above, p. 413 n.).

[2] William Ellis, *Polynesian Researches* (1829; *Tennyson in Lincoln*, i, No. 904); 'Enoch Arden', l. 572: 'The lustre of the long convolvuluses'.

safer for Prof. Selwyn[3] to translate simply 'the lustre' 'Flore——nitido'. In some of the earlier lines which I saw there is it seems to me an error

Turba senum ae juvenum

for 'great and small.'[4] Believe me

Yours very truly
A. Tennyson

WILLIAM ALLINGHAM, *A DIARY*, pp. 156–9.

Friday, August 23, 1867

Very fine. Steamer 11.40 to Yarmouth. Tennyson on the quay, also his brother Frederick and two daughters. A. T. is going to Lyme Regis alone.

'I have wanted to see the Cobb there ever since I first read *Persuasion*. Will you come?'

Can I possibly? Yes, I will!

We cross to Lymington. I rush up and make hasty arrangements at Custom-House and lodgings; then off go A. T. and I, second class, to Dorchester. A. T. smokes. (T. is a great novel reader, very fond of Scott, but perhaps Miss Austen is his prime favourite.) . . .

Once safely *incognito* T. delights in talking to people, but touch his personality and he shuts up like an oyster. Ringwood, Wimborne, Poole harbour, Wareham (mounds), Dorchester. Walk in the warm afternoon, through stubblefields and reapers at work, to the grand old Keltic fortress now called 'Maiden Castle,' view the great green mounds, and lie on a slope looking over the autumnal landscape. Then descend and return, finding corn-flowers and 'Succory to match the sky.' Shall we stay to-night at Dorchester? T. vacillates, at last agrees. We go to the 'Antelope,' rooms not good—out, and into the Museum, up a backyard,—British antiquities, Roman pottery, etc. High Street, at its foot a clear little river, *the Frome*. A tipsy cobbler accosts us. Riverside walk through meadows. County Jail looks like a pleasant residence. Return by back street to the 'Antelope,' which produces a pint of good port at dinner. The twilight being fine I propose that we should visit William Barnes, whom T. personally knows, and whose Poems in the Dorset dialect T. knows and likes. I show the way to Came Vicarage, where I had enjoyed hospitality from a Saturday to a Monday a year or two before. The cottage-parsonage lies in a hollow among trees about a mile from Dorchester, separated from the public road by a little grass-plot and shrubbery. We find the gate by starlight and reach the house door between 9 and 10 o'clock. The worthy old Poet-Vicar is truly delighted to see us, especially such a guest as T. (whose poetry, he used to say, has a 'heart-tone' in it). . . .

---

[3] William Selwyn (1806–75: *DNB*), Lady Margaret Professor at Cambridge, translated 'Enoch Arden' into Latin verse. He sent Tennyson 'a larger copy of Enochus', with a letter in January 1868 (TRC), from Ely, where he was a canon residentiary.

[4] Line 63.

Saturday, August 25 [for 24], 1867

Dorchester—To Maiden Newton—Bridport. We start off to walk to Lyme Regis, leaving bag to come by carrier. Uphill, view sea, down to Chidiock, pretty village, old church, flowery houses. We push on (as like two tramps as need be) along the dusty road to Martin's Lake, sea on one hand, shore hills on the other. Down a long hill to Charmouth, where we have beer and cheese in a little inn, then Tennyson smokes in the porch and chats to the waitress. She says she is from the Isle of Wight. 'So am I,' says T.,—'what part?' 'From Cowes,' says the girl. 'I come from Freshwater,' says T., which surprises me, —but he revels in the feeling of anonymosity. We see Lyme below us and take a field-path.

Down into Lyme Regis, narrow old streets, modest little Marine Parade. 'The Cups' receives us in the fair plump good-humoured person of a House-Keeper Barmaid. T. gets a good bedroom and I a tolerable one; we go into a garden sloping down-hill and out by some back steps to a Mrs. Porter's, where the F. Palgraves are lodging—not in.

Back to 'The Cups' and order dinner; then by myself up steep street to top of town, pleasant, view of shore and headlands, little white town far off. Dinner. Then T. and I out and sit on bench facing the sea, talking with friendly openness. Marriage,—'How can I hope to marry? Some sweet good woman would take me, *if I could find her.*' T. says, 'O yes,' adding, 'I used to rage against the social conditions that made marriage so difficult.'

Sunday, August 25, 1867

Lyme Regis. Very fine. T. up first and at my door. He has been on the Cobb, and eats a hearty breakfast. We go down to the Cobb, enjoying the sea, the breeze, the coast-view of Portland, etc., and while we sit on the wall I read to him, out of *Persuasion*, the passage where Louisa Musgrave hurts her ankle. Palgrave comes, and we three (after Manor House and some talk of Charham) take a field-path that brings us to Devonshire Hedge and past that boundary into Devon. Lovely fields, an undercliff with tumbled heaps of verdure, honeysuckle, hawthorn and higher trees. Rocks peeping through the sward, in which I peculiarly delight, reminding me of the West of Ireland. I quote—

Bowery hollows crowned with summer sea.[1]

T. (as usual), 'You don't say it properly'—and repeats it in his own sonorous manner, lingering with solemn sweetness on every vowel sound,—a peculiar *incomplete* cadence at the end. He modulates his cadences with notable subtlety. A delightful place. We climb to the top, find flat fields, and down again. Stile and path—agrimony—we sit on a bank, talk of Morris, Ned Jones, Swinburne, etc. Whitechapel Rock. Then return by winding paths to the town. Miss

---

[1] 'Morte d'Arthur', l. 263.

Austen, Scott, novel writing. P. counsels me to write a novel. Inn, dinner, fat waitress, port. In the coffee-room a gentleman, who joins in conversation—High Church, etc., State of England,—and speaks well but guardedly. T. talks freely—human instincts, Comte, etc.

We go to Palgrave's, who says, 'thought you were not coming'. They smoke. When T. and I are walking back to the Inn he takes my arm, and by and by asks me *not* to go back to Lymington. I (alas!) have to reply that I must. 'Well then,' says T., 'arrange your business there and come back.' I doubted if I could. 'Is it money?' says he,—'I'll pay your expenses.' Most delicious! that the man whose company I love best should care about mine. Most mortifying! for I am tied by the leg.

To JAMES BERTRAND PAYNE

Text. Materials, iii. 71–2.

September 26, 1867

My dear Mr. Payne

I am glad that you can assure me that the house of Moxon and Co. is in a 'perfectly sound financial condition,' only, I do not quite understand what you subjoin 'as far as I know,' surely you either know it or not. With respect to the report, I may tell you that for more than half a year I have been in the habit of receiving anonymous letters, and of hearing statements from various people, to the effect that the house of Moxon and Co. was in a most precarious condition, and would not last till Christmas.

I did not choose to bother you with these, but when it came to a rumour that your house had actually failed I considered that my best and handsomest course was to apply directly to yourself, to ascertain the real state of things.

You must excuse my declining to give the name; since it was a feeling of friendliness to myself and no unfriendliness to you that made me acquainted with the rumour. Believe me,

Yours very truly
A. Tennyson

P. S. Seeing that I have stuck to the house of Moxon from the beginning through evil report and good report, and really have been and am the main pillar of it, it seems to me (and I say it with all kindliness) that you cannot but feel that it is not only due to me but also your duty to yourself that I should be fully informed of the state of affairs: and with this view, and in accordance with your offer that you can afford me reasonable proof of your financial soundness, I propose deputing a friend in whom I have confidence to confer with you respecting our mutual business relations.

To ANDREAS MUNCH[1]

Text. Nils Erik Enkvist, *British and American Literary Letters in Scandinavian Public Collections* (Abo: Abo Akademi, 1964), p. 107.

FARRINGFORD, October 2, 1867

Dear Sir

I have received your translation of Enoch Arden and had I been at home would have thanked you for it sooner. I know no Norse; nevertheless, without either Grammar or Dictionary, by comparing it with the original, I have succeeded in making out most of it. Ignorant as I am of your language, does it not seem presumptuous in me to declare it a good translation? Yet so it *seems* to me. Pray forgive me—of course I have no right to pronounce even a favourable criticism—I feel very sensible of the compliment done to me by dressing me out in the Old tongue, and beg you to believe me,

Truly yours
A. Tennyson

To FREDERICK JAMES FURNIVALL

MS. Huntington Library.

FARRINGFORD, October 2, 1867

My dear Mr. Furnivall

Thank you for your Percy[1] and believe me,

Yours always
A. Tennyson

Will you kindly receive for me the two years subscription due for the early English Text Society.

A. T.

F. J. Furnivall Esqre
3 Old Square, Lincolns Inn W. C.
London

To ENID GUEST[1]

MS. Tennyson Research Centre.

October [8], 1867

My dear Enid

I send you a few little songs to print—a song-cycle—I think the Germans call it. Mr. Grove of the Crystal Palace begged me to write such a form for

---

[1] 'Andreas Munch (1811–84), Norwegian poet, translated Tennyson's *Enoch Arden* (1866) and *Idyller on Kong Arthur (1876)* . . . ' (Enkvist, p. 107 n.).

[1] *Bishop Percy's Folio Manuscript: Loose and Humorous Songs* (1867), ed. J. W. Hales and Furnivall; this was followed by *Ballads and Romances* (3 vols., 1867–8).

[1] Mary Enid Evelyn Guest (*c.* 1837–1912), daughter of Lady Charlotte Schreiber and sister of Sir Ivor Guest (see above, pp. 449, 381 n.). In 1869 she married her cousin Austen Henry Layard.

A. Sullivan to set to music.[2] They are nothing in themselves and only will become something when they are set. Perhaps when they are printed I will furnish Sir Ivor with a short preface.

Ever yours
A. Tennyson

(My wife's love)[3]

To SIR IVOR BERTIE GUEST

MS. Tennyson Research Centre.

October 11, 1867

Dear Sir Ivor
   Splendidly printed. I expect publisher's Bill for—

	£	s	p
Corrections	2.	2.	0

Ever yours
A. Tennyson

To SIR IVOR BERTIE GUEST

MS. Tennyson Research Centre.

October 21, 1867

Dear Sir Ivor
   Will you wait for the proof a day or two longer. I have a good deal to do just at this present.
   The sheets were torn accidentally in opening. What 'hidden meaning' could there be?

Yours ever
A. Tennyson

---

[2] 'The Window or, The Loves [later 'Song'] of the Wrens' (see above, p. 443 n.).

[3] Allingham's *Diary*, p. 163 on this date: 'To Farringford, and walk with A. T. to near Alum Bay. He thinks "England is going down"—"Christianity becoming extinct? There's something miraculous in man." "There is more in Christianity than people now think." Publisher P[ayne] and rumours of insolvency, etc.' See above, p. 467.

To CHARLES KENT[1]

MS. Huntington Library.

[22 October 1867][2]

Sir

I have never yet attended any public dinner—it is not my fashion; but if you merely wish my name to appear in your list of stewards as a mark of respect to my friend Charles Dickens, I am willing that it should and have the honour to be

Your obedient Servant
A. Tennyson

To SIR IVOR BERTIE GUEST

MS. Tennyson Research Centre.

FARRINGFORD, October 25, 1867

Dear Sir Ivor

It appears from the papers that the 'Wrens' have fallen into ill repute: I don't mean the songs but the *word*.[1] However let that remain as it is in the solitude of Canford Manor. I don't suppose that half the songs will be published:[2] and I know that I may depend on your secrecy. Let me see the proofs once more if it doesn't bore you. Believe me,

Yours ever
A. Tennyson

To THE DUCHESS OF ARGYLL

MS. Tennyson Research Centre.

November 4, 1867

My dear Duchess

You need not have thanked me for you know I was ungracious enough to refuse you—and as to Dr. MacLeod—(though there was such a pathos in his letter enclosed to me by Strahan that it bore me down) I gave in to his wish against the grain:[1] perhaps indeed for that I ought to be thanked more not

---

[1] William Charles Mark Kent (1823–1902: *DNB*), editor and proprietor of the *Sun*, 1853–71, and, as an intimate friend of Dickens, 'Hon. Secretary of Charles Dickens Dinner Committee' (as the envelope is addressed), the farewell banquet given on 2 November at the Freemason's Hall before Dickens's departure for America: 'Almost all the notables of the literary, dramatic, and artistic world were among an assembly numbering close to four hundred and fifty' (see Edgar Johnson, *Charles Dickens, His Tragedy and Triumph*, ii. 1074–5).

[2] Postmark.

---

[1] The meaning of this is opaque.

[2] Published in December 1870 (dated 1871), with Arthur Sullivan's music (Ricks, p. 1196).

---

[1] Norman Macleod (1812–72: *DNB*), Scottish divine, chaplain to the Queen, Moderator of the Church of Scotland (1869–70), was the editor of *Good Words*, which published 'The Victim' in January—for £700 (Charles Tennyson, p. 374; Donald Macleod, *Norman Macleod, D. D.*). Touting *Good Words*, for which the Duke had 'written a good deal' and which paid him 'very well' and 'is read by thousands', the Duchess (3 October, TRC) urged Tennyson to make Macleod 'happy' before he left on a mission to India by giving him 'a few lines' for publication. See *Journal*, p. 267, and below, p. 504.

less—but as far as you are concerned—I can't see that you owe me anything but objurgation.

Now I am

Afraid to think what I have done[2]

for my one answer to all applicants is no longer usable.

I am very glad to hear so good an account of the good Duchess your mother. I hope she will go on improving. Pray give her my affectionate remembrance and believe me,

Yours always
A. Tennyson

To ENID GUEST

MS. Tennyson Research Centre.

November 5, 1867

My dear Enid

I send back the ballad: it is intended for Norman Macleod's magazine.[1] I don't like the word 'shrieking' in the last stanza and I have tried all sorts of words in vain. 'Crying' would be better but the 'cry' occurs just before. 'Wailing' is not high-pitched enough, 'saying' still less. Can you or Lady C[harlotte] find me a word? You have not sent the Dedication.[2] If it is not to your taste pray leave it out.

Yours ever
A. Tennyson

EMILY SELLWOOD TENNYSON to ENID GUEST

MS. Tennyson Research Centre.

FARRINGFORD, November 15, 1867

My dear Enid

Ally omitted one sheet yesterday. I trust that you have not been stopt by this. I ought to have answered your question as to how many copies he would

---

[2] *Macbeth*, II. ii. 51.

[1] 'The Victim', privately printed at Canford Manor (*Tennyson in Lincoln*, ii, Nos. 4311–14). 'You asked me to find out from Miss [Charlotte] Yonge where she had found the story in the 59th page of her book "Golden Deeds". She has written twice about it, and here is all that can be found out. "It is in an appendix to collected editions of Mrs. Hemans' life and works, where she had made notes of subjects from history suitable to write poems upon, unluckily without saying where they came from. I (Miss Yonge) have watched for this story for years. . . . I will write to the friend who owns the copy of Mrs. Hemans' from which I took it"' (W. P. Warburton to Tennyson, 6 June 1865, TRC). 'Shrieking' was retained in l. 7.

[2] To 'The Window': 'These little songs, whose almost sole merit—at least till they are wedded to music—is that they are so excellently printed, I dedicate to the printer' (quoted in Henry J. Jennings, *Lord Tennyson, A Biographical Sketch*, p. 192).

like to have. He does not care to have more than three or four himself but would of course wish each of those of you who wish for one to have one.

Your very affectionate
Emily Tennyson

EMILY SELLWOOD TENNYSON to ENID GUEST

MS. Tennyson Research Centre.

FARRINGFORD, November 20, 1867

My dear Enid

Ally says, will you send by return the manuscripts if you have not the sheets printed for him as he wants to take them to town with him perhaps on Monday.

Your very affectionate
E. T.

To DAVID GRIFFITH [?][1]

MS. John S. Mayfield.

FARRINGFORD, November 22, 1867

Dear Sir

I thank you for your book and your kind words. Believe me,

Yours truly
A. Tennyson

WILLIAM ALLINGHAM, *A DIARY*, p. 166.

Monday, November 25, 1867

Fine gray day; Mrs. Clough has written to say she is coming, I meet her at 11.17 train and cross with her to Island: with her, her little Blanche Athena, dark-eyed, pleasant, sweet little mouth. At Yarmouth the Tennyson carriage. Farringford, luncheon. A. T. on 'the Fenians.' Prince Consort's Book, the Queen's autograph inscription—

Alfred Tennyson, Esq.,

Who so truly admired and appreciated the character of her beloved Husband.

Victoria R.[1]

---

[1] David Griffith, a Unitarian minister (Allibone), whose book of sermons *The Continuity of Religious Development* (1867) was inscribed: 'To Alfred Tennyson this volume is offered in grateful acknowledgement of untold joy, strength and peace, won from the perusal of his works, 2, Loxham Villas, Cheltenham, November, 1867, (*Tennyson in Lincoln*, i, No. 1069).

[1] 'The Queen's Book arrived for A. with an inscription in her own hand. The second precious heirloom of the kind. Anxious accounts in the papers of Fenians and the Abyssinian expedition' (Journal, 17 November 1867). The book was Charles Grey's *Biography of the Prince Consort* (privately printed, 1866: *Tennyson in Lincoln*, i, No. 1068), also issued by Smith, Elder in 1866 and 1867.

To JAMES KENWARD

Text. Materials, iii. 68–9.

FARRINGFORD, December 10, 1867

My dear Sir

I thank you for the Poems and M. Villemarqué's translation which however I fear I shall scarce be able to make out even with the help of the original. I doubt not that the last congress must have been very interesting but at this distance of time I could scarcely pledge myself to be present at the next even though Mr. Villemarqué himself were to invite me. I have looked into the *Barddas* more than once and though I was aware of much that was in it, found some things quite new to me. Writing in a hurry I find I had begun on the sheet wrong side upwards which forgive, and believe me,

Yours truly
A. Tennyson

To WILLIAM BRADBURY

MS. Huntington Library.

December 24, 1867

Dear Sir

It is quite correctly printed and I expect will bring upon me more spiteful letters.[1] It is no particular letter to which I allude: *I have had dozens of them* from one quarter or another.

Though you are kind enough to say that I may make my own changes I must leave all that to yourself and Mr. Evans. Believe me,

Yours truly
A. Tennyson

WILLIAM ALLINGHAM, *A DIARY*, pp. 167–9.

Tuesday, December 24, 1867

Steamer.... To Farringford with Parry.[1] I introduce him to Mrs. Tennyson. He soon retires. A. T. comes in with Sir John Simeon.... dine at Farringford, no guests. T. rages against the Fenians—'Kelts are all mad furious fools!'

Irish landscape—'I saw wonderful things there—twenty different showers at once on a great expanse—a vast yellow cloud with a little bit of rainbow stuck on one corner' (T. swept his arm round for the cloud and then gave a nick in the air with his thumb for the bit of rainbow)—I wish I could bring

---

[1] 'The Spiteful Letter' (Ricks, p. 1218), in *Once a Week* (published by Bradbury and Evans), 4 January 1868.

[1] Charles Hubert Hastings Parry (1848–1914: *DNB*), an undergraduate at Exeter College, Oxford. Later, he won fame as a historian of music, composer, and Director of the Royal College of Music; he was knighted in 1898, and made a baronet in 1902. In January 1892, as will be seen in volume iii, he visited the Tennysons at Farringford, and wrote memorably about his stay.

these things in! I was travelling in Kerry through a great black landscape—bogs. A lady beside me asked how I liked the country; I said, it might be greener; to which she replied indignantly, "And where then would the poor man cut his bit of turf?"' . . .

Friday, December 27, 1867

. . . Farringford. T. in his big cloak on lawn.

'Poe on metres—he knows nothing about them.'

Tauchnitz—T.'s poems smuggled in; T. complained; Treasury letter, 'the public complain of much searching.' Boys at football. . . . To Farringford. Dine in study—jokes and puns—after dinner, pleasant talk.

T.—'We remember Summer walks in Winter, Winter in Summer.'

Treads newspaper into metre.

T. says: 'Boys become beasts for a time—no conscience: I don't know what it means.

'I hate publishing! The Americans forced me into it again. I had my things nice and right, but when I found they were going to publish the old forms I said, By Jove, that won't do!—My whole living is from the sale of my books.'

He went upstairs by himself. When he came down again spoke of Greek Poetry,—'The *Odyssey* the most delightful book in the world. Blank verse is the only English metre to translate Homer in, and even that will not do. Lofty Scriptural prose would be best.'

Of Latin Poetry he said, 'Virgil's is the most finished of any; Catullus is exquisite; Lucretius wonderful, but much of him hard and tiresome to read, and very obscure.' . . .

Saturday, December 28, 1867

. . . To Farringford. At dinner Mr. Clark[2] talks of Rome, Greece, foreign travel (pleasant life). T. denounces publisher P[ayne].[3] Says he is trying Hebrew.

'Do you (to Clark) know any Hebrew?'

C.—'Only the letters.'

T.—'Exactly! the priests can't read their own sacred books.'

C. (rather disconcerted). 'The New Testament I can, more or less.' (One

Monday, December 30, 1867

Dine at Farringford. T. discourses on 'Maud': I make him laugh by misquoting lines about the shell, thus—

> 'Did he stand at his own front-door
> With a diamond stud in his frill?'[4]

---

[2] See above, pp. 202 and n., 340 and n.

[3] In a letter to Payne on 24 December Emily Tennyson thanks him for 'one of the cheeses of happy memory', and adds 'a postscript about an "astonishing revelation" just received from Moxon' (Sotheby's Catalogue, 20 May 1975, Lot 395).

[4] 'Maud', II. ii. 16–17.

To ?

MS. Columbia University Libraries.

FARRINGFORD, FRESHWATER, ISLE OF WIGHT, January 1, 1868

Dear Sir

I am much obliged to you for your pipe. I have got however so used to my Milos, that I fear I shall scarce take kindly to yours, though I doubt not that it well deserves the name you have given it.

Yours truly
A. Tennyson

To ENID GUEST

MS. Tennyson Research Centre.

FARRINGFORD, FRESHWATER, ISLE OF WIGHT, January 2, 1868

My dear Enid

The books look very pretty, bound, and worthy.[1] My thanks—take them therefore, Sir Ivor and yourself. I only hope that the binder is to be depended upon. All wishes of the time to you and yours! from us both.

A. T.

To LEWIS FYTCHE

MS. Tennyson Research Centre.

FARRINGFORD, FRESHWATER, ISLE OF WIGHT, January 3, 1868

My dear Lewis

All good wishes of the season to yourself and wife and little daughter from me and mine! But as to coming this year en famille I fear that will be impossible.

I am glad to find that Albert[1] has distinguished himself so much in the East—he has sent me two newspapers.

It's cold enough *here*. What must it be at Risley Hall, Derby? 15 below zero. The 'unknown cousins' send 'love and kisses' in return to little Mary. And believe me, dear Lewis,

Your affectionate cousin
A. Tennyson

GEORGE GROVE *to* GEORGE GRANVILLE BRADLEY (extract)

Text. Charles A. Graves, *The Life and Letters of Sir George Grove*, pp. 155–6.

January 8, 1868

... on Thursday I made a shift to go to Farringford, where I passed Friday

---

[1] 'The Window' (see above, p. 469 n.), and *Tennyson in Lincoln*, ii, No. 4325.

[1] Albert Fytche, his brother (see i. 165 n.).

in great contentment, coming back on Saturday. A. T. was very charming. He did not say a word I wished unsaid; and he said a great many I would fain remember. He is working hard at Hebrew, and thinks the Psalms and Isaiah the finest poetry there is. Moreover, he was very religious and *Christian* in all his talk about life and politics, etc. He has been pleased to promise me *Lucretius* for *Macmillan*. The subject is not pleasant, but it is a grand poem: *one of the grandest of all his works*.[1] ... Also I hope that you will see in our February number a poem by him called *Wages*, more characteristic and more lofty (though shorter) than either of those in *Good Words* or *Once a Week*.[2]

They are expecting you there in ten days or so. The boys please me much. Hallam is growing very manly: and with plenty of humour. . . .

To ALEXANDER MACMILLAN

MS. Yale.

FARRINGFORD, FRESHWATER, ISLE OF WIGHT, January 8, 1868

My dear Mr. Macmillan

Many thanks for yours.[1] Perhaps I may be able to add another little poem to 'Wages'—can't say: but I leave you free to reject Lucretius after you have seen it if you don't like it.[2]

Ever yours in great haste
A. Tennyson

To MRS FAULKNER[1]

MS. University of Pennsylvania.

FARRINGFORD, FRESHWATER, ISLE OF WIGHT, January 10, 1868

Mr. Tennyson presents his compliments to Mrs. Faulkner and has pleasure in saying that she is at liberty to quote the passages required for her book of Flowers, the name of which Mr. Tennyson feels is best left to herself.

---

[1] Grove, now editor of *Macmillan's Magazine*, had been seeking a poem from Tennyson and, piqued by the advertisement of one to appear in *Good Words* in January, arranged to go to Farringford on 1 January; but the day was bitter cold, and he was 'fairly floored' with lumbago. See E. F. Shannon, Jr., 'The Publication of Tennyson's "Lucretius"', *Studies in Bibliography*, xxxiv (1981), 146–86, for a full account of the circumstances leading to the publication of 'Lucretius'.

[2] 'The Victim' and 'On a Spiteful Letter'. 'Wages' (Ricks, p. 1205) appeared in *Macmillan's Magazine* in February.

[1] Macmillan had written on 6 January to confirm Grove's verbal terms—£300 for 'Lucretius', £50 for 'Wages'. He also said he would try to prevent newspaper piracies of 'Lucretius', but doubted that anything could be done about so short a poem as 'Wages'. He offered to make arrangements with Ticknor and Fields about American publication of 'Lucretius', expressing no objection to Tennyson's profiting so long as the poem did not appear first in the United States.

[2] Macmillan was a prude, and Tennyson knew it. 'Mr. Macmillan is far more inexorable against any shade of heterodoxy in morals than in religion,' Mrs Gilchrist wrote in 1862 (H. H. Gilchrist, *Anne Gilchrist and Her Writings*, p. 128). See below, pp. 482–3.

[1] Unidentified.

To GEORGE GROVE *or* ALEXANDER MACMILLAN

MS. Tennyson Research Centre.

[12 or 13 January 1868]

My dear Grove, or Macmillan

God spake out of the skies
To a good man and a wise,
'The world and all within it
Will only last a minute.'
Then a beggar began to cry
'I must eat, or I must die.'
'Is it worth his while to eat,
Or mine to give him meat?'
And the world and all within it
Were nothing the next minute.[1]

This is the first poem which if you like it you may put in before 'Wages'. Of course I want nothing more in the way of money. But with respect to the Lucretius I am staggered by what I hear from good authority. That if I publish in a serial I virtually give up my copyright and anyone has a right to republish me. Really if this be so I must decline giving it to your Magazine however unwillingly.[2] Believe me, respected friends,

Yours ever
A. Tennyson

If you prefer the first reading in Wages pray keep it.[3]

To WILLIAM HEPWORTH THOMPSON

MS. Trinity College.

[*c*. 15 January 1868]

A smoking room! If I put pipe to mouth *there* should I not see gray Elohim ascending out of the earth—him whom we capped among the walks in golden youth—and hear a voice—Why hast thou disquieted me to bring me up?

---

[1] 'A Voice spake out of the skies' (Ricks, p. 1193) was first published in *The Death of Oenone* (1892). Macmillan evidently found its agnosticism too disquieting, even as a gift and in conjunction with the stalwart hope of 'Wages'—a 'very noble and true idea fitly expressed', as he wrote to Tennyson on 11 January (Shannon, 'The Publication of "Lucretius"', p. 150). See above, p. 418, n. 11.

[2] Macmillan accordingly prefaced the poem with a note declaring that extracts 'Must be confined to moderate length, and that the reproduction of either the whole or the major part of "Lucretius" will be an infringement of the law of copyright'. *Lloyd's Weekly Newspaper*, 10 May, p. 8, paying him in his own coin, refused to make *any* quotation: 'We will take not a single hair from the tail of their expensive Pegasus.'

[3] Macmillan thought 'flying by' (l. 2) 'too *light* a sound in the middle of the line', but the original reading was not restored. See below, p. 480.

I happened to say to Clarke[1] that from old far-away undergraduate recollections of the unapproachable and august seclusion of Trinity College, Cambridge, I should feel more blown out with glory by spending a night under your roof, than by having lived Sultanlike for a week in Buckingham palace. Now, you see, I was not proposing a visit to you, but speaking as after wine and over a pipe, and falling into a trance with my eyes open.[2]

At the same time your invitation and that of Mrs. Thompson (to whom present all my best thanks) is so kindly and hearty that I may—I can't say when at this moment—try to realize this vision—and if I do I will let you know some time beforehand.[3] Meantime, my dear T, I am

Yours ever
A. Tennyson

My wife's best regards.

To JAMES THOMAS FIELDS

MS. Morgan Library.

FARRINGFORD, FRESHWATER, ISLE OF WIGHT, January 17, 1868

My dear Mr. Fields

Many thanks for your new-year's gift and honorarium. I send you a small poem written you see when.[1] I shall send it also to Mr. Strahan for March. I should think though you say that you require any article for your Magazine to be forwarded two months in advance of publication here, you could easily make room in your March number for so minute a piece.

I have a longer poem somewhere about 270–80 lines—the death of Lucretius —which is going into Macmillan's Magazine. If you and he could arrange together so that it should not come out till April, so [?] it might appear synchronously on both sides [of] the water. I am writing to the Editor today and I dare say he will consent.

Trübner and Co. write to me in a sort of rapturous amaze at your liberality to Charles Dickens: but I think Macmillan may be said to march pari passu along with you.

My wife sends her best remembrances and all good new-year and Xmas wishes to yourself and Mrs. Fields. Believe me

Yours always
A. Tennyson

---

[1] See above, p. 202 n.

[2] And with stirrings of 'Timbuctoo', 'Recollections of Arabian Nights', 'Morte d'Arthur', and *In Memoriam*, 87.

[3] He went on 9 February (see *Journal*, pp. 270–1, and below, p. 480).

[1] '1865–1866' (see above, p. 427). Fields published it in *Every Saturday*, 22 February 1868, p. 256.

Wages

Glory of warrior, glory of orator, glory of song,
   Paid with a voice flying by to be lost on an endless sea—
Glory of Virtue to fight, struggle, to right the wrong—
   Nay, but she aim'd not at glory, no lover of glory she—
Give her the glory of going on, and still to be.

2

The wages of Sin is death; if the wgaes of Virtue be dust,
   Would she have heart to endure for the life of the worm and the fly?
She desires no isles of the blest, no quiet seats of the just,
   To rest in a golden grove, or to bask in a summer sky:
Give her the wages of going on, and not to die.

This will appear in the February Macmillan: if too late for your Atlantic, at any rate it will serve for an autograph for Mrs. Fields, to whom present it with my regards.

To GEORGE GROVE

MS. Berg Collection.

               FARRINGFORD, FRESHWATER, ISLE OF WIGHT, [17 January 1868]

My dear Grove

   The lawyer's opinion has not arrived but if it can be depended on there would seem no good reason why Lucretius should not appear in Macmillan's.[1] In that case (I send you Ticknor and Fields letter) perhaps it would be as well not to let it appear before April, as that would accommodate the American publishers. Then it should be printed first and sent to me to correct, and afterwards dispatched to Boston.[2] The firm has been immensely liberal to Dickens giving him £2000 for some slight essays in their publications and I suppose would also give me something.

   The passage in that foolish book of Büchner's (and we have looked all over the book to find it) wouldn't do as a motto.[3]

                                                       Yours always
                                                       A. Tennyson

---

[1] Macmillan to Grove, 17 January: 'I hope you got Hopgood's written opinion which you might forward to Tennyson. I can't see the least difficulty in arranging matters so as to prevent the annoyance he anticipates' (Shannon, 'The Publication of "Lucretius"', p. 157). See above, p. 477.

[2] It was published in *Every Saturday* on 2 May (see below, p. 484 n.).

[3] Louis Büchner, *Force and Matter: Empirico-Philosophical Studies, Intelligently Rendered*, ed. J. Frederick Colingwood (1864), a translation of Friedrich Karl Christian Ludwig Büchner's *Kraft und Stoff* (*Tennyson in Lincoln*, i, No. 654), of which the thesis was atheistic materialism and which, moreover, devoted one chapter ('Personal Continuance') to disproving personal immortality and another ('The Soul of Brutes') to denying 'any *essential* difference . . . between the animal and human brain'. For the 'motto', many passages qualify—e.g. Jouvencel's observation (p. 38): 'There is neither chance nor miracle; there exist but phenomena governed by laws.'

I think 'flying by' is the best reading: fame goes clanging overhead like a great bird—fainter and fainter,[4] till the cry dies away.

My wife is copying Lucretius as there is only one MSS it is thought better not to trust that to the post. There are a few slight errors in the copy—*she* says she does not think it will shock people.[5]

To WILLIAM PARSONS WARBURTON

Text. Memoir, ii. 53.

January 21, 1868

My dear Warburton

No Ginsburg[1] yet; and I looked rather reckoningly for it every morning. What is the publisher's name? will you write again? or shall I tell mine to get it for me? I flatter myself that I have hit upon something like the right sound of the Y [= Hebrew letter]. I can produce a sound in the throat (for is it not a gutteral?) something between a *y* and a *g*, and easily melting into a vowel, where the Y [same Hebrew letter] is supposed to be soft.

Ever yours
A. Tennyson

To FRANCES ELIZABETH THOMPSON[1]

MS. Trinity College.

29 WELBECK STREET, February 13, 1868

My dear Vice-Chancelloress

I hope you did not scold Manockjee Cursetjee much.[2] I sent his father who had asked me for a poem (the subject—education of Indian girls in the English fashion) three £3 instead, and since the father never answered, I suppose the son called on me to render 'the beggarly thanks.'[3]

I forgot to ask the Master for my Lucretius. Will you tell him to send it by return of post? I want to leave it with Macmillan.[4]

---

[4] See above, p. 477.
[5] It shocked Macmillan. See below, pp. 481 n., 483.

[1] Christian David Ginsburg, *Coheleth, commonly called The Book of Ecclesiastes*, translated from Hebrew (1861). See Warburton's letter to Tennyson in *Memoir*, ii. 53, to which this one is a reply. Four additional letters are in TRC.

[1] Née Selwyn, widow of George Peacock, she married W. H. Thompson in 1866 soon after he succeeded Whewell as Master of Trinity. Thompson was Vice-Chancellor 1867–8.

[2] Manockjee Cursetjee (1848–?), whose father, of the same name, was a judge of a small cause court in Bombay and a writer on legal subjects, and had called on Tennyson in May 1866 (*Journal*, p. 247). The son took a BA degree (Christ Church) in 1867, was a student at Lincoln's Inn, and was called to the bar in 1869 (Foster, *Men-at-the-Bar*).

[3] 'And when a man thanks me heartily, methinks I have given him a penny, and he renders me the beggarly thanks' (*As You Like It*, II. v. 27–30).

[4] Probably the galley proof of 'Lucretius', with autograph corrections, now in TRC (*Tennyson in Lincoln*, ii, No. 4130).

I had a very pleasant time with you which I shall always remember.[5]
Believe me,
Yours ever
A. Tennyson

To ALEXANDER MACMILLAN

MS. W. S. G. Macmillan.

Shrove Tuesday, [25 February] 1868

My dear Mr. Macmillan
I had rather if you have no objection see my Lucretius once again. If you don't publish before May—(have you decided upon it) there will be ample time to send it out to Fields.[1] Payne has put me into a great perplexity by advertising the Standard Edition in his tremendous style—before any agreement was signed and before I had made up my mind as to whether I would have one at all. I expect now that if I do not publish this edition (and I have little desire to do it) the sale of the old one will fall off in expectation of this.[2]
Yours ever
A. Tennyson

I left in the Oread—do you wish her out?[3]

[5] R. C. Jebb (see below, p. 492 n.) met Tennyson on 9 February or (8?). His letter, dated 9 February 1867, was manifestly written in 1868: 'We had a very pleasant party at the Lodge last night. To begin with, the Poet Laureate, Woolner, the sculptor, the Public Orator, Cope, Munro, Sidgwick, and I. It was surely a party that one might feel proud of having been asked to; at least I might, and did, very. Tennyson is exactly like his photographs—I mean quite as shaggy. His long black hair is very thin now; he is bald on the crown; and it falls as from a tonsure about his ears. He looks older than I should have expected; his accent is decidedly Lincolnshire, and this was one of the things that surprised me. It is impossible not to like him, and not to understand that he is a man of genius. I do not mean to say that one would have found it out from his talk to-night if one did not know it before; only, that given the fact of his genius, his personality makes it more intelligible; you see its workings. Tennyson had a tremendous argument with Munro about a Latin passage. It was great fun to see them' (Caroline Jebb, *Life and Letters of Sir Richard Claverhouse Jebb*, 1907, pp. 93–4).

[1] See below, p. 484.

[2] The 'Standard Edition', never issued, must have been mere bluster. Payne's 'tremendous style': 'Messrs. Moxon and Co. furnish further particulars respecting the Standard Edition of the works of Alfred Tennyson, Poet Laureate. This most important work, which will contain many new productions, will at the same time embody the author's latest corrections of his published writings. The edition will be published in four handsome crown 8vo volumes, to sell at 10s. 6d. per volume. This series will be cheaper than the existing seven volumes, especially when the new poems are taken into consideration. As an enormous circulation of Vol. One (which will appear in the middle of April) may be anticipated, orders should be sent in as soon as possible, so as to enable the Publishers to issue to all simultaneously, without those delays which in the case of popular volumes are so vexatious both to the bookseller and customer. Vols. 2, 3, and 4 will succeed vol. 1 bi-monthly' (*Publishers' Circular*, xxxi [2 Mar. 1868], 116–17).

[3] He certainly did, and tactfully (perhaps mendaciously) ascribed the same wish to Grove. Tennyson drafted a denatured alternative to ll. 188–91, omitting every erotic detail from the amorous sun to the 'budded bosom-peaks', and on 27 February Macmillan wrote: 'Grove seems to prefer the shorter description of the Oread. On the whole the balance of taste seems in favour of it' (Shannon, 'The Publication of "Lucretius"', p. 162). The comedy, however, was not finished: see below pp. 482–3.

482   *? late February* 1868

To WILLIAM HEPWORTH THOMPSON

MS. New York University Libraries.

FARRINGFORD, FRESHWATER, ISLE OF WIGHT, [? late February 1868]

My dear Thompson

'The grave and reverend body' owe no thanks to *me*. The specimen was admired by Hallam and bought by him of Keeping[1] with his own money— tips—which one or other friend or relative had given him from time to time. Keeping told him that there was no such specimen of the Planorbis in the Cambridge Museum, whereupon he gave it to that institution not quite perhaps without a pang; ample compensation for which however has been made by the thanks inclosed in your note.

Ever yours, with best regards to the V. C.

A. Tennyson

GEORGE GROVE *to* ALFRED TENNYSON

MS. Tennyson Research Centre.

MACMILLAN'S MAGAZINE, LOWER SYDENHAM, March 2, 1868

Dear Mr. Tennyson

Enclosed is Lucretius in his last stage with the alternative version of the *Oread*.[1] I have put a query or two at some places where the punctuation seemed to me wrong, which you will pardon with your usual clemency. For the public perhaps the new Oread is the best—though I confess I love the old one—only I find fault with the 'who' ('who this way runs')—I can't read it without an emphasis on the who, and then I am obliged to make a question of it 'who this way runs before the rest?'

'Vast and filthy hand' I prefer hand*s* as it was in the original MS.

'But who was he' etc. This seems to me very abrupt, to spring from nothing that has gone before (my ignorance doubtless), and the very '*but*' itself helps the feeling.

'Nymph and Faun' I prefer Nymph*s* and Faun*s*. Is the singular ever used in the case of animate or intelligent creatures? 'into oak and ash'—I should not mind—but the other displeases me a little.

'Dash them afresh'[2] the *sh* seems to me to go badly with that in afre*sh*— and the dash has a rude sound of collision, not like the operation of nature or of atomic nature: would not 'force' or 'thrust' be better.

'Care not thou' is not an improvement— the *idea* is better than the old one, but the words are awkward I think—on the whole I like the two last lines better as they stood before.

I know the Poem now pretty well: and every time I say it to myself like it

---

[1] Henry Keeping; see above, pp. 285 n., 328. 'Planorbis' is 'A genus of fresh-water snails (pond-snails) characterized by a flat rounded spiral shell' (*OED*), perhaps the 'lovely shell' of 'Maud', II. 49).

[1] See above, p. 481.   [2] The only suggestion not brushed off by Tennyson.

better and see more force in it. Please do some Old Testament subjects in the same way. My kindest regards to Mrs. Tennyson.

Yours ever
G. Grove

1865–6 is LOVELY—and so full of life—a trifle—but WHAT A TRIFLE.[3]

To GEORGE GROVE

MS. Berg Collection.

FARRINGFORD, FRESHWATER, ISLE OF WIGHT, March 3, 1868

My dear Grove

                To peer behind the laurels

is to me the least decorous passage in the poem. I have altered it

                —do I wish—
           What? that the bush were leafless, or etc.

then

           I know you careless, yet behold, to you

'backward instead of backwards[1]
I never put an unnecesary S. Hand for hands is the printers not mine.

    Pray let this be sent off by the next American mail, I believe, on Thursday or Fields will say it has come too late. With respect to the Oread please yourself but send the full passage to America. They are not so squeamish as we are.[2]

Yours, my dear Grove, in great haste
A. Tennyson

Kypris for Kupris   anew for afresh

BENJAMIN JOWETT *to* ALFRED TENNYSON

Text. Evelyn Abbott and Lewis Campbell, *The Life and Letters of Benjamin Jowett* (2nd edn.), i. 428.

March 8, 1868

My dear Tennyson

    Will you look at the enclosed letter which, though long, is not unamusing, and will you see whether you can write a few lines addressed to Sellar or

---

[3] '1865–1866' (Ricks, p. 1192) was published in *Good Words* in March.

[1] 'Lucretius', ll. 205–6, 208, 221.

[2] 'We' is tactful, for even Emily Tennyson did 'not think it will shock people' (see above, p. 479). Fields, not 'squeamish', printed the unexpurgated text, and Tennyson himself reverted to it in the *Holy Grail* volume.

Professor Fraser[1] (who is an excellent man) which might be of service? I would not ask you to do such a thing for anyone but Grant, and there is no reason why you should do it at all if you think that you can't or would rather not, as I have not spoken to them. But I am sure that a 'pithy' word from you would have effect, and if you don't mind it had better be addressed to Professor Fraser, as he is not supposed to be a friend of Grant's.

I hope that you are well and have 'thoughts which voluntary move harmonious numbers':[2] I heard of you in London, where you were reported to be looking 'quite youthful.'

Don't write any more in Magazines if you can help: indeed it is a goodnatured mistake and will do you harm. The Magazine-writers say, 'Art thou become as one of us?' etc.[3]

With most kind regards to Mrs. Tennyson and the boys, believe me, dear Tennyson,

Ever yours
B. Jowett

To JAMES THOMAS FIELDS

MS. Wellesley College.

FARRINGFORD, FRESHWATER, ISLE OF WIGHT, March 10, 1868

My dear Mr. Fields

The Editor of Macmillan's Magazine tells me that according to my request he has forwarded to you Lucretius.[1] I find a misprint in the proofs sent to me 'windy *W*alls' instead of 'Halls of Heaven'—pray correct it when you insert the piece in your May number. Believe me

Yours very truly
A. Tennyson

---

[1] Alexander Campbell Fraser (1819–1914: *DNB*), Professor of Logic and Metaphysics at Edinburgh University, where Sellar was Professor of Latin, and Alexander Grant became Principal (1868–94).
[2] *Paradise Lost*, iii. 37–8.
[3] Genesis 3:22.

[1] It was not forwarded to Fields until 17 March, however, and Fields replied: 'Tennyson's "Lucretius" did not reach us in time for our May Atlantic. We printed it in our "Every Saturday", and it was immediately cribbed all over the country and printed in magazines and newspapers. It was a great disappointment to us not to have it for the Atlantic, but we did the next best thing left us and put it into the weekly' (Shannon, 'The Publication of "Lucretius"', p. 168).

To EDWARD CAMPBELL TAINSH[1]

MS. Robert Taylor.

FARRINGFORD, FRESHWATER, ISLE OF WIGHT, March 24, 1868

My dear Sir

I have waited that I might have leisure to look at your book before writing to you. It is of course difficult to criticize a critique on oneself, but at all events it is not difficult but on the contrary very pleasant to express to a kindly critic the thanks which are so justly due to him.

There are naturally some points in which you are mistaken, and others in which we do not agree. For instance by

'Those wild eyes'

is intended the Pacific Islanders—wild having a sense of 'barbarian' in it. I should never have ventured to use so vague a periphrasis for 'sailors.' Again

'bar of Michael Angelo'

does not mean 'meeting eyebrows' but that broad bar of frontal bone over the eyes—for which he was remarkable.[2]

There are several of these little errors, and I have no time today to explain them. Two words about Enoch Arden. A friend of mine told me that he heard his own parish-bells in the midst of an eastern desert, not knowing at the time that it was Sunday.[3] He accounted for it to me by stating that there was a ringing in his ears which his old associations moulded unconsciously with the sound he heard. There is nothing really supernatural mechanically or otherwise in Enoch Arden's hearing bells: though the author most probably did intend the passage to tell upon the reader mystically.

2. The costly funeral is all poor Annie could do for him after he was gone—entirely introduced for her sake and in my opinion, quite necessary to the perfection of the Poem.

I hate writing even so little about my own compositions.[4] So pray believe me

Yours very truly
A. Tennyson

Under 'a' palmtree is the printer's mistake, not mine.

[1] Edward Campbell Tainsh (1834–1919) published *A Study of the Works of Alfred Tennyson* in 1868; 2nd edn., revised and corrected, 1869; New Edition Completed and Largely Rewritten, 1893. He also wrote several novels and a Prize Essay, 'The Best Means of Making the Schoolmaster's Function More Efficient than It Has Been in Preventing Misery and Crime' (Edinburgh, 1858). See Kenneth Walter Cameron, 'Tennyson to Edward Campbell Tainsh', *The Emerson Society Quarterly*, No. 19 (Second Quarter 1960), 29–35.

[2] *In Memoriam*, xxxvi. 15, lxxxvi. 40.

[3] Identified in *Memoir*, ii. 8, as Tennyson's old friend Arthur William Kinglake (1809–91: *DNB*), author of *Eothen* (1844) and *A History of the Invasion of the Crimea* (8 vols., 1863–87).

[4] When Tainsh wrote later for more information for the second edition, Emily Tennyson replied (11 November 1868): 'Mr. Tennyson has this morning left home possibly for some time. I write for him to say that it was Henry Fitz Maurice Hallam, Arthur Hallam's brother, who died at Siena. It is true that Julia Hallam the wife of Colonel Lennard is still alIve. She is the youngest daughter. I fear it will not be possible for Mr. Tennyson to devote sufficient time to your book at present for the criticism you ask' (Cameron, pp. 34–5).

To WILLIAM KIRBY[1]

Text. Lorne Pierce, *Alfred, Lord Tennyson and William Kirby*, p. 39.

FARRINGFORD, FRESHWATER, ISLE OF WIGHT, March 28, 1868

Dear Sir

Your National Song reached me at a time when it was impossible for me to acknowledge it.

I beg you, therefore, not to attribute my silence to any want of interest in Canada. Most heartily do I echo both the watchword of the song, and its burden and I have the honour to be,

Your very obedient servant
A. Tennyson

EMILY SELLWOOD TENNYSON to JOHN STUART BLACKIE[1]

MS. National Library of Scotland.

FARRINGFORD, FRESHWATER, ISLE OF WIGHT, April 1, 1868

My dear Professor

You may think how annoying these things are to us. I wrote immediately to Mr. Howard[2] saying that he was very welcome to the Poems, also to Mr. Payne asking him to remit the fine. To which he replied that it had nothing to do with Mr. Tennyson's poems, whose copyright was his own, but that it had reference to Hood's Song of the Shirt which is the property of the firm. I have asked Mr. Payne to state explicitly that this is the case.

Many thanks for the good news of the apparently favourable disposition toward Sir Alexander Grant.[3] Much as one desires to have him here one feels rather guilty towards India even in the wish that he should leave the great work which one believes that he is doing there.

---

[1] William Kirby (1817–1906, born in Hull, migrated with his family to the United States in 1832, the year of the First Reform Bill (a date both causative and symbolic), and then, repudiating rampant republicanism, moved to Canada, where he remained, more royalist than the Queen, more loyalist than her first minister, more Tory than Walter Scott (his great original), more Anglican than Fielding's Parson Thwackum. His excellent historical novel *The Golden Dog* (1877) is still in print. His National Song 'Canadians Forever' (printed in Pierce, pp. 37–8) concludes:

> Then deck Victoria's regal throne
> With may flowers and the maple tree;
> And one for all and all for one,
> The watchword of her Empire be,
>   And heart and hand
>   United stand
> Confederate and great, and free,
>   Canadians forever"!
> No foe shall dissever
> Our glorious Dominion—
> God bless it forever.

[1] See above, p. 366.
[2] Unidentified, but see 'Edinburgh pirates', below, p. 490.
[3] See above, p. 484.

My husband's very kind regards. You know that I am his secretary so you will forgive him for not writing himself. Believe me, my dear Professor,

Very truly yours
Emily Tennyson

JAMES BERTRAND PAYNE
to EMILY SELLWOOD TENNYSON

MS. Hughenden Manor.

April 7, 1868

My dear Madam

I directed one of my clerks to write to the Guernsey bookseller, one Stephen Barbet, and pay 10/- for *the whole of Mr. Tennyson's works*! He has this morning sent Tauchnitz' edition in five volumes for that sum. It is now pretty evident why there is and has been a falling off in the general sales for the last three or four years. I have heard it estimated that Tauchnitz sells from 35,000 to 50,000 sets of Mr. Tennyson's works through the book-post in England annually; and I, myself, have no doubt the quantity is not overstated. I do sincerely hope Mr. Tennyson will let no feelings of mistaken kindness prevent his triturating this Barbet in the mortar of the law, and thus make of him a seasonable example. It will be also as well to make especial application to Mr. D'Israeli (who, as a literary man, will sympathise with any author who suffers from such hardship) to prevent the bookpost being abused in this fashion; no doubt, such an application would receive attention.[1] I am, my dear Madam,

Yours very truly
J. Bertrand Payne

WILLIAM ALLINGHAM, *A DIARY*, pp. 175-6.

Friday, April 10, 1868

Good Friday . . . To Farringford by field-path, Miss T[hackeray], Fitzjames S[tephen] and I . . . they go in—I flee. Luncheon at Miss T's. We find A. T. and walk to the Beacon; meet one stranger, at sight of whom A. T. nearly turns back.

Lincolnshire stories. Preachers: 'Coom in your rags, coom in your filth, Jesus'll take ye. Jesus won't refuse ye.' 'Time has two ends, and the Law cooms down wi' a *bang*!' 'Glory' a very favourite word.

Lincolnshire manners. 'One of my brothers met a man in the lane near our house and said in a friendly voice, 'Good-night!' to which the man replied, 'Good night—and *dom* you!' I asked a man one day, 'Do you know what o'clock it is?' he answered, 'Noa! and I don't want to.'

Grace said by a Dissenting Minister according to the nature of the feast.

[1] See below, p. 488.

If a poor one, he snivelled and sneered in a thin voice, 'O Lord, bless these *miserable* creatures to our use,' etc.; if a good spread, he rolled out in unctuous tones: 'We desire to thank Thee, O Lord, for all these mercies Thou hast provided for us.'

To BENJAMIN DISRAELI

MS. Hughenden Manor.

FARRINGFORD, FRESHWATER, ISLE OF WIGHT, April 13, 1868

private

My dear Sir

I had the pleasure of being introduced to you many years ago at the door of the House of Commons and you were kind enough to give me an order for the House. I dare say you have forgotten the circumstance, but pray pardon me if on the strength of that introduction I venture to bring under your notice, with a view to some remedy, a heavy grievance under which myself and doubtless other authors are now labouring.

Thousands of copies of my books are yearly imported into Great Britain by means of the Book-Post, and also by Travellers who are not subjected to the Customs' examinations as strictly as formerly. They are not even asked a question. My belief in your sympathy for the wrongs of a class to which you yourself belong must plead as my excuse for troubling you with this matter amid your vast businesses.

I beg leave to enclose a letter (though a somewhat heady one) from my publisher to Mrs. Tennyson, as a proof that I do not complain without reason.[1]

It has been suggested to me that some regulation might be made by Order in Council which would in a measure remedy this evil as far at least as the post goes. Might it not be rendered illegal to send a volume by post without the name of author and publisher being inscribed outside, the sender of the book being made liable to a penalty of £50 or 100 should he put a false name on the cover. Throwing myself on your better judgement, I am, my dear Sir,[2]

Yours faithfully
A. Tennyson

To THE PRIVY COUNCIL (fragment; draft)

MS. Tennyson Research Centre.

[*c*. 13 April 1868]

My Lords

My publisher informs me and the decrease in my receipts confirms what he says that I am being 'mercilessly plundered' by the importation of foreign editions of my works. I see by the papers that the Paris edition, at 10 fr., is selling at the rate of 5000 volumes a month, and I am informed that this

---

[1] See above, p. 487, and Disraeli's reply in *Memoir*, ii. 54.

[2] In a draft of this letter (TRC), this paragraph is rewritten in Emily Tennyson's hand.

edition especially (not to mention German and American ones) are not only smuggled in with passengers' baggage but sent likewise in great numbers by the international book-post.

As these practices are thoroughly illegal might I venture to suggest to your Lordships that some more stringent regulations be adopted toward their prevention.

JAMES BERTRAND PAYNE to ALFRED TENNYSON

MS. Yale.

DOVER STREET, April 17, 1868

My dear Mr. Tennyson

I beg to submit the account of the sales of your books up to Xmas last, and I shall be much gratified to learn that you find them correct and satisfactory to yourself. You should have had them a little earlier, but I am only just out of bed from a very severe attack of my old enemy—gastric affections—which weakens and depresses me beyond expression.

The only item which remains for your final decision is the question of the royalty on the illustrated Idylls. I have nearly exhausted the 7th thousand of Elaine and have sold in round numbers 3,000 each of Vivien and Guinevere. My own opinion[is] that the 2/. royalty on each Idyll after I had sold 6,000 of each, seems to me to be fair, because I made the offer when the success of the whole edition was a remote contingency, and in the end I am persuaded you will make more now by this plan than by my buying the text at your ordinary rate of profit. As, however, my earnest desire in all matters of business between us is to carry out and further your own wishes and views without regard to myself, pray let me know your choice, and I will act accordingly.[1] You will see the respective balances by comparing the account with the schedule lettered A. If it will be any convenience to have the whole or any portion of the £1500 before June it will please me much to oblige you.

I hope something may be done to deter the Guernsey bookseller from inundating the country with the Tauchnitz editions of your books.[2] If you find nothing legal will be effectual, there can be no surer method of protecting yourself than by at once bringing out the new edition, so revised as to make the present volumes obsolete, and to permit me to register them all over Europe where reciprocal treaties on the copyright question are made with Gt. Britain. You would soon perceive the benefit of this in more ways than one.

Mr. White told me the other day the first stone of your new house was soon to be laid. If the design includes a keystone over the principal Entrance, you should let me present you with one of the far-famed Jersey granites, sculptured with your arms, which on this sparkling stone would look splendid.

I have been so anxious to act in conformity with Mrs. Tennyson's suggestions

---

[1] Note by Emily Tennyson: 'It however having been previously arranged that a royalty equal to the profits of the ordinary edition should be paid. ET'.

[2] See above, p. 487.

touching the Edinburgh pirates, that I have given instructions to my solicitors to be as lenient as possible under the circumstances.[3]

Mrs. Moxon desires to be very kindly remembered to yourself and Mrs. Tennyson, and, I am,

Yours very truly
J. Bertrand Payne

To BENJAMIN DISRAELI

MS. Hughenden Manor.

J. KNOWLES'S, CLAPHAM COMMON, April 25, 1868

Dear Mr. D'Israeli

Pray accept my best thanks for the instant attention you have paid to this small matter of mine. I never quite believed my Publisher's statistics, but he has pressed this topic upon me so constantly, and I myself have met with so many who confessed that they had foreign editions of my poems, that I thought it a sort of duty to myself and other authors to make this application: and though the result appears to be nil, I do not the less feel an obligation to you; and am quite as much pleased to know that it is owing to the author of that charming lovestory, Henrietta Temple,[1] as to the Prime Minister of England. Believe me,

Ever yours truly
A. Tennyson

To BARON BERNHARD VON TAUCHNITZ (draft)

MS. Tennyson Research Centre (draft); *Memoir*, ii. 55.

FARRINGFORD, FRESHWATER, ISLE OF WIGHT, April 29, 1868[1]

My dear Sir

I pray your pardon for not having answered you earlier. I scarce know by what carelessness, or fatality, I have omitted till now to acknowledge yours of February 25th but finding your letter lately at the bottom of my pocket, I was struck with my own ungraciousness, and as I say—pardon my negligence.

I am quite aware that I made rather a bad bargain with you, in selling the continental copyright for so small a sum, and my Publisher affirms (whether rightly or not) that I lose annually some hundreds of pounds by this transaction, but I am also aware that the royalty you offer me now is all of your free Grace, and that I have no claim upon you. I can only hope that my accepting this offer will not be made a pretext by sellers (of course I am not including

---

[3] See above, p. 486.

[1] In 1890 'He looked through *Henrietta Temple* again. He had told Disraeli that the "silly sooth" of love was given perfectly there' (*Memoir*, ii. 371).

[1] As from Farringford. Tennyson had left home on 22 April to lay the foundation stone of Aldworth (*Journal*, p. 274), and went thence to stay with Knowles at Clapham Common, where Frederick Pollock saw him on the 26th and (with Tyndall) dined with him on the 30th (Tennyson having lunched with Mrs Pollock on the 27th).

yourself) and buyers for introducing more copies into England. Accept my thanks therefore. Believe me, my dear Sir,

Yours very truly
A. Tennyson

I hope your son I had the pleasure of seeing once at Farringford is well and prospering. ⟨Please to send the Christmas account to the address at the head of this letter.⟩

To WILLIAM EDWARD HARTPOLE LECKY[1]

MS. Koninklijke Bibliotheek, The Hague.

[c. 1 May 1868]

Dear Mr. Lecky

Can you dine with me today at Mr. Knowles' house, Church Buildings, Clapham Common and then we can arrange about your coming to see me.

Yours ever
A. Tennyson

dinner at 7 o'clock

To THE DUCHESS OF ARGYLL

MS. Tennyson Research Centre.

FARRINGFORD, FRESHWATER, ISLE OF WIGHT, [? early May 1868]

My dear Duchess

There is no need of any 'word of advice' from me. The whole country is so small and easily seen, and I think there is hardly anything to be seen but the sea and the coast: and any landlord and landlady will be too happy to give you any information. Land's End of course you will go to and Tintagel where, when I was there, the people were as charmingly simple as in the days of King Arthur—though I found they had begun to be corrupted at Boscastle —Kynance cove too with the serpentine rocks and the Lizard should be visited—I think on the whole Tintagel from a certain weirdness about it took my fancy most.[1]

The initiatory sentence in your note looks as if it involved a little reproach

---

[1] William Edward Hartpole Lecky (1838–1903: *DNB*) won fame with his *History of the Rise and Influence of the Spirit of Rationalism in Europe* (2 vols., 1865), and won still more fame, while still young, with his *History of European Morals from Augustus to Charlemagne* (2 vols., 1869), of which Tennyson said: 'It is a wonderful book for a young man to have written, a great book for any man to have written, and proves that he has genius, true genius' (*A Memoir of W. E. H. Lecky*, by his wife, 1909, p. 58). These were followed by his *History of England in the Eighteenth Century* (8 vols., 1878–90), *Democracy and Liberty* (2 vols., 1896), and others. He married Elizabeth von Dedem, Lady-in-Waiting to Queen Sophia of the Netherlands, became a privy councillor, was awarded honorary degrees and the Order of Merit, and was painted by Watts, photographed by Mrs Cameron, caricatured by Spy in *Vanity Fair*, and died childless. See his 'Reminiscences of Tennyson' in *Memoir*, ii. 200–7; *Tennyson in Lincoln*, ii, Nos. 1374–7; *Tennyson and His Friends*, p. 229; *Journal*; Allingham's *Diary*.

[1] See i. 289, and above, pp. 465–7.

—but I asure you that I always, or all but always, come down to Argyll Lodge when I am in town, but I am hardly ever in town. When my house near Hazlemere is built[2] I shall hope to see you oftener. I am *very heartily* glad to hear of your good Mother's improved health.[3] Believe me,

Always yours affectionately
A. Tennyson

To WILLIAM MORRIS[1]

MS. Formerly owned by Sydney Carlisle Cockerell (who suplied the transcript).

FARRINGFORD, May 9, 1868

Dear Mr. Morris

Many thanks for your new book and for your kind regards. If I like the Paradise as well as I did the Jason I shall find it a rich gift.

Yours truly
A. Tennyson

EMILY SELLWOOD TENNYSON
to ALEXANDER MACMILLAN (extract)

MS. British Library.

FARRINGFORD, FRESHWATER, ISLE OF WIGHT, May 12, 1868

Dear Mr. Macmillan[1]

It is very kind in you sending the favourable reviews. Unless there be anything you particularly wish him to see perhaps he has now seen enough when he has seen the Jebb you mention.[2] Those three you name are decidedly

---

[2] The foundation stone was laid on 23 April, Shakespeare's birthday (*Memoir*, ii. 54; *Journal*, p. 274).   [3] The Duchess of Sutherland died on 27 October.

[1] William Morris (1834–96), having sent Tennyson a copy of *The Defence of Guenevere* in February 1858 (*Journal*, p. 109) and *The Life and Death of Jason* in 1867 ('He tried to read Morris's *Jason*, but said "No go" ' (*Tennyson and His Friends*, p. 117), now sends the first volume of *The Earthly Paradise*. (See *Tennyson in Lincoln*, i, Nos. 1644–6.) They must have met (Allingham was a close friend of both), but no meeting appears to be on record.

[1] In reply to Macmillan's letter of 11 May: 'I hope I am not boring you in sending notices that appear in the papers about "Lucretius." It is a habit we have in regard to our books generally, but some authors—I don't blame them—dislike all these pattings on the head, or slappings in the face, from men whose praise or blame often is equally worthless. The *Pall Mall*, *Spectator*, and *Punch* are about the best. Would Mr. Tennyson care to look at Mr. Jebb's article on the poem and the subject? It seems to me very delicately done' (Shannon, 'The Publication of "Lucretius"', pp. 170–1).

[2] Richard Claverhouse Jebb (1841–1905: *DNB*), educated at Charterhouse and Trinity (BA 1862), where he was Fellow and Lecturer 1863–75, was later Professor of Greek at Glasgow (1875–88), succeeding Edmund Lushington, and Regius Professor of Greek at Cambridge (1889–1905); he was knighted in 1900, and awarded the Order of Merit in 1904. Himself an Apostle, he had met Tennyson at a party at the Master's Lodge in February (see above, p. 481 n.). They became friends and in 1889 Tennyson dedicated 'Demeter and Pesephone' to him, with an introductory poem 'To Professor Jebb' (Ricks, p. 1372). Jebb's article 'On Mr. Tennyson's "Lucretius"' appeared in *Macmillan's Magazine* in June, pp. 97–103. The 'most impertinent' review was in the *Nation*, vi (30 Apr. 1868), 352–3. Of the *Cosmopolitan*, a weekly, no copy for 2 or 9 May is recorded in British or American libraries.

the best, I think. 'The Nation,' the most impertinent I have seen as a whole I have fortunately been able to hide from him. The beginning of the Cosmopolitan, equally impertinent, he saw. . . .

[P.S.] He seems to enjoy his Clapham visits, thank you.[3] We shall be very anxious to know that you are not a loser by Lucretius.[4]

To FRANCISQUE XAVIER MICHEL

MS. Harvard.

FARRINGFORD, FRESHWATER, ISLE OF WIGHT, [25 June 1868][1]

My dear Sir

I have just returned home and found your letter of the 23rd. I am not 'prevenu' against you by anybody, though I think I know whom you mean by 'mauvais drole.'

I have a Norse, a Dutch, and a German translation of Enoch Arden—and you wish to add a French one. Well—so be it: though I warn you that you will find it a task of great difficulty.[2] Believe me

Yours very truly
A. Tennyson

I did not go to the Queen's Ball.[3] The names of all who are invited are inserted in the newspapers as if they had been present.

To HENRY WADSWORTH LONGFELLOW

MS. Harvard.

FARRINGFORD, FRESHWATER, ISLE OF WIGHT, June 26, 1868

Dear Mr. Longfellow

I should like so very much to see you before you leave England.[1] I came back here yesterday and have to leave again on the 6th or 8th of July. Not knowing your plans I—and perhaps too boldly—ask you and yours to come to us early next week lest you should not be able to visit us when we return in

---

[3] To J. T. Knowles.

[4] 'Tennyson's *Lucretius* has more than sustained its great reputation. The last number of *Macmillan's Magazine* has already reached a third edition in consequence of its appearance' (*The Nonconformist*, 20 May 1868, p. 511).

[1] Postmark.

[2] No such translation is recorded by Michel (1809–87), professor at Bordeaux; but he did the original four *Idylls* (Hachette, illustrated Doré, 1867–9)—see Bowden, *Tennyson in France*, pp. 60–6.

[3] On 15 May at Buckingham Place: 'a party of upwards of 1,700 was invited' (*The Times*, 16 May 1868, p. 5).

[1] Late July.

the autumn; but whether now or then you will be most welcome. Believe me,
Yours always
A. Tennyson

I don't know your locality but I have been told to direct to Captain Ferguson's.[2]

To LORD HOUGHTON (RICHARD MONCKTON MILNES)

MS. Trinity College.

FARRINGFORD, FRESHWATER, ISLE OF WIGHT, [? c. 27 June 1868]

My dear Houghton

I should have delighted to have met your Princess*[1] but unhappily we had left town before your invitation arrived.

Yours ever
A. Tennyson

*and also to have lunched with *you*

To HENRY WADSWORTH LONGFELLOW

MS. Harvard.

FARRINGFORD, FRESHWATER, ISLE OF WIGHT, July 1, 1868

My dear Mr. Longfellow

I suppose you have not received my note sent through Captain Ferguson of Carlyle.* I had asked you, if possible, to come here before the 8th for I have to leave home about then: I have just learnt that you are at the Langham Hotel,[1] and propose coming on the Isle of Wight. Would you tell me when, for I would fain be here to bid you welcome.

Yours always
A. Tennyson

*Carlisle. I am so used to the old name that I spelt it in the old manner inadvertently.

To HENRY WADSWORTH LONGFELLOW

MS. Harvard.

FARRINGFORD, FRESHWATER, ISLE OF WIGHT, July 3, 1868

My dear Mr. Longfellow

I am grieved that I cannot meet you at Macmillan's; but would you, if you

---

[2] 'Robert Ferguson (d. 1898, aged eighty-one), a partner in the firm of Ferguson Brothers, silesia manufacturers of Carlisle, England, had called on Longfellow on September 27 [1865].' His brother-in-law, Edwin Guest, Master of Caius College, was Longfellow's host on 16 June when Cambridge awarded him an honorary LLD. (*The Letters of Longfellow*, iv. 434; v. 240–1).

[1] Princess Christine, mother of Princess Alexandra.

[1] Portland Place, London; address sent by the Duchess of Argyll (29 June, TRC), who said: 'He wishes very much to see you.'

know, tell me the *date* of your visit to the island? if you still keep your purpose of coming here, I will postpone my leaving for a few days in order to receive you.[1]

Yours ever
A. Tennyson

LONGFELLOW'S VISIT TO TENNYSON, 15 JULY 1868

Text. Anne Longfellow Pierce,[1] 'A visit to Farringford', *Boston University Studies in English*, i (1955), 96–8.

Thursday, A. M., July 16, [1868]

A short drive through the narrow winding roads of Freshwater, between stone walls overhung with ivy, or hedges of sweet briar, or a mixture of thorns, eglantine, privet, ivy and all growing things combined, brought us to the simple gate of Farringford—a long winding avenue through fine tall trees led us with many turns to the house of Tennyson—we entered, under the arches of the piazza, covered with ivy and honeysuckles, a simple rambling mansion, plainly furnished but the walls covered with pictures—the whole length of the stairway hung with photographs of places and persons, hung one above the other in rows like steps. A mask of Dante, with red velvet back and sort of cowl, among them in a conspicuous place—at the foot—the large Dante, with the impression of the nail near it, and a bust of Dante on the table—a narrow passage led us through the breakfast room to the Drawing room full of every day comfort—table with books, newspapers, and writing materials stood in the centre—sofa, couches and a variety of armchairs offered attractive seats—the only window in the room, a large oriel making a deep recess opposite the fire place, looked out upon the lawn through two very large shade trees, of Elm, I believe, to the two pines—a border of sweet and bright flowers under the window and continued all around the somewhat irregular house—A small mask of Shakspear over the book shelves in the wall at the end of the room—with endless and various small things, in photo and painted, around the walls—a low red screen standing beside one of the couches was covered with photos—one the figure of a beautiful dark haired boy, Hallam the eldest son, among them. Each side of the book shelves a small recessed arch, in one a low organ, in the other an etarge with books and little things—picture over each, a room of comfort and refinement.

Here we were recd. with most friendly cordiality by the wife of Tennyson, a very lovely and attractive lady, exceedingly delicate looking in health—dressed in blk silk deeply trimmed with crape—with a most simple bit of white lace edged with silk gimp falling from the front of her head back, and down to her shoulders—plain blk hair tied behind at the neck with a broad

---

[1] Longfellow's reply, 6 July, is in his *Letters*, v. 247. In the event, he left London on 13 or 14 July.

[1] Longfellow's sister. He was accompanied by two sisters, a brother-in-law, a brother, three daughters, a son and daughter-in-law.

blk ribbon the ends trimmed with crape—A spinster sister of the Poet's, dispeptic and angular, was not so attractive.

Summoned to the Dining room to lunch, a most attractive room only one window, a large oriel filling nearly one end—opposite to this a bouffet— opposite the fire place on the side of the room a large side board in full blast of usefulness—over it hung an oil Holy Family—all the pictures in the room were in oils, except a large print of the Queen and Prince Albert framed together—of which T. said 'there's a hateful picture hanging there, but as the Queen presented it to me I felt obliged to hang it up.' On one side o₁ the window was a beautiful picture of two handsome youths, with frills round their necks, portraits of Hallam and Lionel the sons—or as the father said, 'those are my boys when they were girls,' a very charming picture, faces handsome and fine in coloring—on the other side of the window was a lovely portrait of Mrs.T. by the same artist, the name I forget.[2] In front of the window grows a very large Ilex, or Italian Oak, almost if not quite as fine as the one we saw on the grounds at Wilton, at Lady Herbert's.

All the appointments of the lunch were exceedingly simple and refined— mutton of his 'own raising' etc. etc. exquisitely nice in cooking, and dessert.

Our first introduction to Mr. T. was very informal as we were seated and had begun our lunch before the gentlemen came in—our names were all pronounced and he graciously shook hands with each one on our side of the table as he passed down to take his seat.

EMILY SELLWOOD TENNYSON
to HENRY WADSWORTH LONGFELLOW

Text. Harvard (transcript by Henry Dana).

FARRINGFORD, FRESHWATER, ISLE OF WIGHT, July 17, 1868

My dear Mr. Longfellow

Will you kindly tell our boys what would be agreeable to you?[1] We are entirely at your command (as all England is for that matter judging from our little corner). Are your plans irrevocably fixed? or will you allow us the pleasure of taking you tomorrow for luncheon at Swainston either to return

---

[2] Watts, who, in fact, had detained Longfellow in London: 'I fear I shall have to stay another week, as Mr. Watts wishes to paint my portrait, which I am only too happy to have him do' (Longfellow to Tennyson, 6 July, in the former's *Letters*, v. 246). Apparently, however, he did not do it.

[1] The Longfellow party apparently put up first in the neighbourhood of Farringford (probably, at Plumbly's Hotel), and then on the 18th certainly moved on to Henry Ribbands' Bonchurch Hotel. It is not easy to reconcile all the dates in Emily Tennyson's *Journal* (reprinted from *Materials*, iii. 82–3) with this letter and the accounts flanking it here. The *Journal* seems to merge the events of 16 and 17 (and possibly 18) July under the 16th. The 'afternoon tea' took place on the 17th, and, apparently on the next day, before going to Bonchurch, Longfellow visited Sir John Simeon at Swainston, and was taken by Tennyson to Mrs Cameron's studio for the famous photograph. Tennyson is reported to have said: 'I will leave you now, Longfellow. You will have to do whatever she tells you. I will come back soon and see what is left of you' (quoted in Helmut Gernsheim, *Julia Margret Cameron*, p. 35). See *Journal*, pp. 277–8; Longfellow's *Letters*, v. 249–55.

here or on your way if needs must elsewhere? A verbal answer if you please as the servant waits from Swainston.

Yours very sincerely
Emily Tennyson

LONGFELLOW'S VISIT TO TENNYSON, 17 July 1868: TINY COTTON *to* AGNES JONES[1]

Text. Morgan Library (transcript ? by Agnes Jones).

July 18, 1868

I must send you a scrap about our day at Farringford yesterday and our introduction there to Longfellow.—Yesterday in conjunction with all Freshwater we were bidden in the morning to 'afternoon tea' and Longfellow at 5 P. M. We went and there found an assembled multitude among whom angelic Mrs. Tennyson was floating in her most etherial manner. The Hero soon appeared on the ground with Tennyson and at first was introduced only to a few gentlemen. Busy tea was going on under the shady trees—*my* cup of pride and pleasure was full because Mrs. Tennyson at the first request vacated her seat to me. I poured out for everybody. It was very pleasant work, consisting simply in turning the tap of a silver kettle in which the tea had been made—the gentlemen handed about cups as fast as I could fill them, and the ladies were seated on shawls and rugs of the brightest hues which looked at a little distance like parterres of flowers. Then by and by Lizzie and I grew a little jealous because the knot of gentlemen absorbing both poets kept all wit and wisdom to themselves and only allowed us glimpses of their amused faces such as we could catch from the background and a distance. So, Tennyson passing by, we hailed him with acclamations of displeasure. He was charming and so delightfully shy and *naive* with it! protesting it wasn't his fault and held out his hand to me saying 'Come, I'll introduce you to him or anybody who wishes!' *I* hung fire (of course) but a moment after Mrs. Tennyson in the most beautiful manner made it all right by putting her arm within Longfellow's and telling him 'the ladies were dying to shake hands with him' (a kind but slight mistake as regarded some of them) and she took him round the lawn with an appropriate word to each. She told Liz and Sissie this morning she could not possibly have done it to an Englishman but to an American it would not be objectionable.

He was very agreeable and most affable, has rather—perhaps I ought to say a *very* venerable appearance with his large white whiskers and beard and long white hair, but his face was, to my thinking, by no means an unfathomable one. Tender and true it was all on the surface. There was a great gulf

---

[1] Tiny Cotton was the daughter of Benjamin T. Cotton, wealthy landowner, who lived at Afton House, 'on the eastern side of the river Yar, about two miles South of Yarmouth', with 'a finely wooded lawn descending to the water' (White's *Hampshire*, p. 629). She is mentioned frequently in Emily Tennyson's *Journal*, and married Captain Speedy (see below, p. 499 n.) in December 1868 (*Journal*, p. 284).

fixed between his smooth countenance and the furrowed lines of our bard.[2] When he had gone thro' his ceremonious ordeal with great good grace he subsided into a chair at the end of the row saying in the most good tempered way—'There, now give me a chair and I'll be perfectly happy,' and he instantly began rallying some young ladies on the English croquet mania. I was not near him. Then moved, I did not hear him speak at all beyond a word or two, and in the large concourse of people it was impossible that beyond commonplaces and politeness anything should go on. Besides I fear I am unappreciative of 'our privilege.' To me it was a far greater pleasure to pour out Tennyson's own tea and rally him about the sugar I put in than to shake hands with the Long *man* (he is tall but that wasn't a pun.) I fear I have nothing else to tell about it and that has been stupid enough.
[Note by ?Agnes Jones:]

I have also had a letter from Miss Cotton speaking of her 'over-full month.' She says of Mrs. Tennyson, referring to several meetings there, the Tennysons having stayed at home on purpose to see the Grants (Miss C's cousins), 'Dear Mrs. Tennyson has been more lovely in spirit and in person than ever. There certainly is an angelic halo about her. I never saw her to greater perfection than when she was taking round Longfellow to be introduced separately to about 40 people on their lawn all assembled for afternoon tea 'to view the lion.' Her graceful dignity and genial courtesy entirely obliterated the faintest idea of stuffiness and caused an additional mantle of goodwill to fall upon the hero who performed his part with all possible kindness.

EMILY SELLWOOD TENNYSON *to* HENRY WADSWORTH LONGFELLOW

Text. Harvard (transcript by Henry Dana).

FARRINGFORD, FRESHWATER, ISLE OF WIGHT, July 18, 1868

My dear Mr. Longfellow

I thank you for your kindness in having called on our tenant Mr. Freeman. My boy owes you an apology for not having presented my humble petition that you do so, in due form. I trust your kindness too much not to be sure that you will pardon the apparent liberty which came only of his shyness. With kindest remembrances,

Most sincerely yours
Emily Tennyson

WILLIAM ALLINGHAM, *A DIARY*, pp. 182–3.

Monday, July 20, 1868

Hot. Tennyson and Mrs. T. on the steamer, I with them to Brockenhurst. 'To London, the dentist; then Scotland.' T. said of Longfellow, 'A very gentlemanly man: seemed very tired. We had ten at luncheon. They slept

---
[2] Longfellow was tw. years older than Tennyson.

at the hotel, stayed two days. Little King Theodore of Abyssinia now at Farringford with Captain Speedy.[1]

'Longfellow—I didn't compliment him—told him I didn't like his hexameters: he rather defended them.'

We spoke of Swedenborg: T. says his Hell is more striking than his Heaven; praises Hinton's book on Man and Nature.[2] The up-train; T. shakes my hand warmly. It is always a real happiness to see him.

EMILY SELLWOOD TENNYSON'S JOURNAL

Text. Materials, iii. 84–5; Memoir, iii. 56–7.

July 20, [1868]

To town, where our hospitable friend Mr. Barrett[1] took us in. Then to Eton to enter Lionel there. . . .

July 23, [1868]

To Ross, and the next day to Goodrich Castle.

July 25, [1868]

We drove to Tintern. . . . A. T. told me that it was here he thought of 'Tears, idle tears'.

To Chepstow, thence to the Castle of Caerphilly. John Price[2] arrived at the station with a farm cart, a leathern chair was hoisted on to this and I drove seated in this to the village. The Castle fine but not so fine as we had expected.

From Caerphilly we went through Cardiff to Bath, and next day attended service at the Abbey. We stayed at Bellevue (Mrs. Weld's).

August 8, [1868]

Back at Farringford. Mr. Gassiot, the electrician, Mr. Allingham, and Dr.

---

[1] Alamayu (Alamayahu), son of Emperor Theodore of Abyssinia (who had died, a suicide, in April in a confrontation with the British), was brought to England by Captain Tristram Charles Sawyer Speedy. They were of course photographed by Mrs Cameron: see Allingham's *Diary*, p. 185, and *Victorian Photographs of Famous Men and Fair Women*, Plates 34, 41. The entry in the *Rugby School Register*, iii. 8, reads: 'Simyen Alamayu, only legitimate son of the late Theodore, King of Abyssinia, and Teruwark, Princess of Simyen, Queen of Abyssinia; since March 4, 1872, ward under the British Government of Dr. Jex-Blake, School House, Rugby, aged 13, April 23. Left 1877. Sandhurst, 1878. Died at Headingly, near Leeds, November 14, 1879, and was buried in St. George's Chapel, Windsor, November 21. The coffin bore the following inscription:— Prince Alamayu, | Of Abyssinia | Born April 23rd, 1861, | Died November 14th, 1879. | A Memorial Tablet was placed in the School Chapel in 1880.'

[2] Either *Man and His Dwelling Place. An Essay towards the Interpretation of Nature* (1859; *Tennyson in Lincoln*, i, No. 1149) or *Life in Nature* (1862), articles reprinted from the *Cornhill Magazine*. For Hinton, see below, p. 520 n.

[1] Henry John Barrett. [2] Unidentified.

Hooker arrived.[3] Dr. Hooker said that he had nowhere seen finer tobacco plants than ours in the kitchen garden.

WILLIAM ALLINGHAM, *A DIARY*, pp. 184–5.

August 10, 1868

... He [Joseph Hooker] comes with me to Farringford, where we find A. T. on the lawn, sitting at a small table with books and tobacco. Walk round garden, the three of us. Dr. H. giving the names of various plants as we go along. 'Kuyphofia,' etc. Tobacco plant about seven feet high—'never saw so fine a one in the tropics.'

August 11, 1868

... Dr. Hooker and I to Plum[b]ley's Hotel (where he is put up); T. and Hallam come in, and T. calls me 'an ass' for not taking a bed at Farringford. I to little shop—and then to Farringford. After dinner come in Mr. Erasmus Darwin, brother of Charles, an old bachelor and invalid, living in London; Mrs. Darwin, and second Miss Darwin;[1] also Captain Speedy, six feet and a half high, who has pleasant manners. He talks of Abyssinia—the churches there, religion, slaughter of animals, the Trinity. The Hindoos and Beloochs 'wept for Theodore.'

Little Alamayu (means 'I have seen the world') Theodore's son, is here at Freshwater in Speedy's charge, by the Queen's wish. The little prince has a native attendant, a young man who is devoted to him. Speedy the other day overheard them amusing themselves by mimicking English people. Attendant comes up in the character of an English lady, shakes hand—'How you do?'

Alamayu replied—'How you do?'

Attendant.—'How you like this country?'

Little Prince.—'Ver' mush.'

Attendant.—'Ah! you like ver' mush'—and so on.

T. complains of hotel charges, especially in England.

I say—'They ought to let you go free, as a Poet.'

T.—'They charge me double! and I can't be anonymous (turning to Mrs. Cameron) by reason of your confounded photographs. The party breaks up about twelve, 'an orgie,' T. calls it. He comes out with me and we wander some distance. Jupiter and a half-moon in the sky; talk of immortality. I go

---

[3] John Paul Gassiot (1797–1877), science writer: 'His work was almost entirely concerned with the phenomena of electricity' (*DNB*). But as a wine merchant (Martinez, Gassiot, and Co., London and Oporto) he may have advised Tennyson about port.

[1] Erasmus Alvey Darwin (1804–81), though an old friend of the Carlyles (see i. 214 n.), was interested primarily in art and literature, and was 'Distinguished by a great charm of manner and a strong sense of humour' (Peile, *Biographical Register of Christ's College*). Other members of the family present, were Mrs Charles Darwin, née Wedgwood (d. 1896), and Elizabeth Darwin (d. 1926). Henrietta (Darwin) Litchfield, the older surviving sister, wrote: 'Tennyson came several times to call on my parents, but he did not greatly charm either my father or my mother' (Emma Darwin, *A Century of Family Letters*, ii. 190).

back with him and find the door locked! He rings and says 'My wife will come,' but a servant woman comes. Nobody guessed he was out.

August 12, 1868

Freshwater. Pack bag, to Farringford. Breakfast in the study, the boys pleasant; Lionel back from bathing; A. T., letter from America for autograph. Mrs. T., 'Lionel going to Eton.' She dislikes Darwin's theory. I sit in study: A. T. teaching Hallam Latin—Catiline.

Charles Darwin expected, but comes not. Has been himself called 'The Missing Link.' Luncheon. Then T. and I walk into croquet-ground talking of Christianity.

'What I want,' he said, 'is an assurance of immortality.'

For my part I believe in God: can say no more.

To FRANCISQUE XAVIER MICHEL

MS. Harvard.

FARRINGFORD, FRESHWATER, ISLE OF WIGHT, August 12, 1868

My dear Sir

I have again been out on a short tour and on coming home here found your letter.

The French passage which you send me and call French of 'Stratford atte Bow' never issued from this house. You have apparently misread it: what you read 'au long' is 'le long,' 'presque,' 'jusque,' etc. etc.

The passage you send does not represent the original. There is no question of Arthur. The father of the little nun looks back and sees all the Capes to the westward ⟨as far as he can see⟩ and to the sunset, each with a beacon-fire at the top and the phosphoric light of the sea at the base: perhaps you have been somewhat misled by 'his' the old English form for 'it's.'[1] Believe me, my dear Sir,

Yours very truly
A. Tennyson

To JAMES THOMAS KNOWLES

Text. Gordon Ray (photocopy).

AT THE SAXON STANDARD [i.e. WHITE HORSE], HAZELMERE, [20 or 21 August 1868][1]

'Idylls of the King' implies something more and other than mere legends of Arthur: else why did I not name the book Idylls of King *Arthur*?

It should have been clearer to my readers that in the very title there is an allusion to the King within us.

[1] 'Guinevere', ll. 232–40.

[1] 'Mr. Lear comes and A. goes to Greenhill [*i.e.* Aldworth]; he will not let me go with him because of the torrents of rain' (Journal, TRC, 20 August 1868).

After you were gone it struck me that you might touch upon this in your preface.[2]

A. Tennyson

To ?

MS. Rowland Collins.

FARRINGFORD, FRESHWATER, ISLE OF WIGHT, August 28, 1868

Sir

I regret that I am unable to answer your inquiries except by telling you that someone has I believe lately written a History of the Poets Laureate so that I should think it would scarcely be worth your while to undertake the task you name. I have the honour to be, Sir,

Your obedient servant
A. Tennyson

To FRANCIS TURNER PALGRAVE

MS. John Whale.

FARRINGFORD, FRESHWATER, ISLE OF WIGHT, August 31, 1868

Dear Palgrave

I don't think I can come your way this year. I have to take Lionel to Eton (we have entered him there) on the 21st for his preparatory examination. I hope he will pass, for he is not without talent, though at times incredibly careless in genders and quantities. After that—(I have promised Knowles to pay him a visit at a house he has taken in the neighbourhood of Ipswich)—I shall leave Eton for Suffolk: but if I cannot come to you I hope you and yours will come on here before you return to town.

Congratulate Gifford from me and my wife on his approaching happiness. He has been (Gifford-like) very quick about it all. You may tell him that Coggie Ferrier was here the other day, and I told her about his engagement, and as she neither turned away her head nor coloured, nor gave the slightest sign of emotion, I suppose he might not have succeeded in that quarter had he attempted. At any rate it was not a 'veni, vici' case.[1]

I don't know that you ought to have shown my little lyric to anybody. How could Ivor Guest have come across it? Well, it doesn't matter much—let him have it to print if he like: but, please, hereafter, if I give you any little unpublished piece keep it to yourself. I can't find your letter and forget whether you asked any other question.

---

[2] To the third edition (1868) of Knowles's *The Legends of King Arthur* (see *Tennyson in Lincoln*, i, No. 1338 and above, p. 288), in which Knowles wrote: 'The very title "Idylls of the King" implies something more and other than mere legends of Arthur, and contains an allusion to the king within us; else why was not the book named "Idylls of King Arthur"?'

[1] In 1868 he married Katherine Simpson. 'Coggie' was probably Elizabeth Anne Ferrier, Alexander Grant's sister-in-law.

Pray give my kindest regards to your wife, and let me hope that you will accept my invitation.

Yours ever
A. Tennyson

To ?

Text. Tennyson Research Centre (transcript).

FARRINGFORD, FRESHWATER, ISLE OF WIGHT, September 9, 1868

Madam

I regret that absence from home and other causes have prevented me from thanking you for your little volume of poems so very meritorious under the circumstances you name.

I think that if the clergyman of your parish would certify facts, some of them might have a chance of being accepted by one or two good magazines (possibly by Good Words for instance). 'The Shop' I consider the best and I should advise you to try this first. You would be much more likely to make money in this way, I think, than by attempting to publish them as a volume. I am, Madam,

Your obedient servant
A. Tennyson

WILLIAM ALLINGHAM, *A DIARY*, p. 187.

September 20, 1868

To Farringford. —Tennyson.—Is writing his 'San Grail'.

'I'm spoiling it. Will you take a turn?'—then we talk on Hinton's book,[1] and on his brother Charles's Sonnets.[2] 'All is not chemistry and matter.' . . .

T. said he had a rich cousin who drank hard and talked loud.[3] 'He used to quote Byron to me—

Over the waters of the dark blue sea—[4]

and so forth, adding, "Poets have some sense." ' He offered to lend me Castle B—— for our wedding month—'will you come down to B——? then you may go to Hell!'

A. T. then went upstairs and dulness set in.

---

[1] See above, p. 499 n.
[2] *Small Tableaux* (Macmillan, 1868).
[3] William Russell, brother of Emma Russell, who inherited Brancepeth Castle on his death.
[4] *The Corsair*, i. 1 ('O'er the glad waters . . . ').

To FRANCISQUE XAVIER MICHEL

Text. Materials, iii. 352–3. *MS.* Yale (draft).

[early October 1868][1]

My dear Sir

'A nine days' wonder' is equivalent to 'La merveille d'un jour' in your tongue.

It raged—this flame for talking—'like fire in stubble.'[2]

'Battle-writhen' is an old form of the participle from the word 'to writhe, twist.' Here it means, sinews that had become hard and knotted in frequent battle.

I wish you would put back the old romance word 'Elaine.' It comes from the old French 'Sir Launcelot' I believe; why need it be modernised into 'Helene?'

Will you pardon me if I tell you that your translation (as far as I can judge) is a little too modern. I should have liked a slight touch of archaism in the language but for that it is a good translation.

My wife has been hard at work at your proof sheets all today and part of yesterday and she seems to me to have improved them. I hope you will agree with me. These alterations we meekly suggest for some of them may not be perfect French. They may, however, give you a notion of what we mean. 'Sur le tapis' for instance is not a phrase that seems dignified enough.[3]

You shall have the proofs in a day or two. I do not know if they are to be published immediately.

Yours very truly
A. Tennyson

EMILY SELLWOOD TENNYSON to MARGARET GATTY (extract)

MS. Boston Public Library.

FARRINGFORD, FRESHWATER, ISLE OF WIGHT, October 7, 1868

My dear Mrs. Gatty

It is not pleasant to say no—especially to one who is always so kind as you are but what else can he say? In an evil hour if we look only to the consequences to himself, he yielded to the entreaties of friends that he would do what he could to relieve Mr. Norman Macleod's mind of anxiety during his Indian mission,[1] then his friend Mr. Grove would be hurt if refused,[2] then his printers must have something and so he heaped up abuse to himself by giving such little things as he had by him,[3] and then another friend for charity[4] but you will quite understand that this is very different from writing

---

[1] *Journal*, 30 September (p. 281): 'Francisque Michel's proofs, alas!'
[2] 'Lancelot and Elaine', l. 735; 'battle-writhen', l. 812.   [3] For 'on the wolfskin', l. 808.

[1] 'The Victim' (see above, p. 471).   [2] 'Lucretius' and 'Wages' (see above, p. 476).
[3] 'The Spiteful Letter' (see above, p. 473).
[4] '1865–1866'? (see above, p. 483), but possibly 'The Window' or another Canford Manor printing.

something at their request. This, to save his life he could not do worthily unless the fit were upon him. So please take in all kindness what is written in all kindness though a refusal.

To WILLIAM EWART GLADSTONE

MS. British Library.
                FARRINGFORD, FRESHWATER, ISLE OF WIGHT, October 13, 1868
My dear Mr. Gladstone
    The enclosed has been sent to me—possibly to you also: if not, read it now. It seems to me a terrible cry.[1]
    I don't much believe in the accuracy of the Irishman generally—but I wish you who enlightened us formerly on the Neapolitan prisons[2] to consider whether here too there be not a grievous wrong to be righted.
                                                        Yours ever
                                                      A. Tennyson

To JOHN STUART BLACKIE

MS. National Library of Scotland.
                FARRINGFORD, FRESHWATER, ISLE OF WIGHT, November 6, 1868
My dear Professor
    With all thanks to all I must absolutely decline.[1]
                                                     Yours very truly
                                                      A. Tennyson

To EMILY SELLWOOD TENNYSON

Text. *Materials*, iii. 90–1.
                                            Saturday, November 14, [1868]

    I came home too late last night for the country post. I had been calling on Lear, and sitting there waiting for Mr. Knowles which delayed me. I and Mr. Knowles had an interview with Arnold White[1] yesterday, and things as

---

[1] 'Oct. 10th. A. wrote to Mr. Gladstone about the alleged bad treatment of the Fenians in prison, enclosing *Lays of a Convict*' (*Memoir*, ii. 58).
[2] *Two Letters to the Earl of Aberdeen on the State Prosecution of the Neapolitan Government* (1851) and *An Examination of the Official Reply of the Neapolitan Government* (1852).

[1] Probably an invitation to further in some way the use of conversation in the teaching of Greek and Latin; see Anna M. Stoddart, *John Stuart Blackie*, ii. 43–5.

[1] Arnold William White (1830–93; knighted, 1887), Tennyson's solicitor (and the Queen's), of the firm of Arnold and Henry White (later White, Broughton, and White), Great Marlborough Street (Boase).

far as I am concerned seem to be unsatisfactory, but W[hite] described ——— [? Payne] as being extremely sour.²

Strahan³ dined here yesterday and has not the least doubt that he can make the £4000 per annum⁴ (which he has promised me) remunerative to himself, quite laughs at all the warnings which White and I give him. I have sent him the 'Grail' to be *printed*, and I will send a copy when it comes. I read it last night to Strahan and Pritchard who professed themselves delighted. Strahan asserts that he makes a clear profit of £7000 a year by *Good Words* alone, and that my business would bring no end of grist to his mill. I am grieved for the poor old shepherd (losing his wife).⁵ Jowett's letter is very kind, but I do not like Lionel's going by rail alone to Oxford. If I were to go for a few days to Paris, Pritchard and Woolner seem inclined to go with me; but there is nothing decided on yet.⁶ Woolner and Mrs. W. dine here today and we can talk it over. Nothing can be kinder than the Knowleses.

To SIR JOHN SIMEON

MS. Syracuse University.

J. KNOWLES', THE HOLLIES, CLAPHAM COMMON, [17 November 1868]

My dear Simeon

I have this morning (Tuesday) got yours of Sunday.

---

² W. M. Rossetti, who saw Payne on 5 November, also found him sour: 'I find he has (*valeat quantum*) an unfavourable impression as to the character of Tennyson, and runs him down even as a poet: he regards him as selfish, narrow in money-matters, not of lively affections; he is punctilious in paying his score in company, and expecting his companions to pay theirs' (*Rossetti Papers*, p. 331).

³ Alexander Strahan (b. 1836 or 1837), who was Tennyson's publisher for about three years, founded *Good Words* in 1860 ('such literature as will not ignobly interest nor frivolously amuse, but convey the wisest instruction in the pleasantest manner') and also the *Sunday Magazine* (1864), *Argosy* (1865), *Contemporary Review* (1866), and *Good Words for the Young* (1869)—all inspirational in nature. 'Unfortunately', wrote Frank Arthur Mumby (*Publishing and Bookselling*, p. 228), 'his financial gifts were not as shrewd as his literary judgment, and he was at length forced to acknowledge defeat. With all his unbusinesslike habits Strahan seems to have been a lovable character.' Mumby was wrong. Strahan's pietism led him to back Robert Buchanan against Rossetti and Swinburne (see *The Swinburne Letters*, iii. 90), and to ditch Knowles as editor of the *Contemporary Review* (see Priscilla Metcalf, *James Knowles*, pp. 268–75), an action that produced a far better rival magazine, *The Nineteenth Century*. (He wrote twelve essays, 'Twenty Years of a Publisher's Life', consisting of 'Reminiscences of Well-known Writers' with whom he had been associated—Norman Macleod, Dean Alford, Kingsley, Wilberforce, and others—in *The Day of Rest*, January–December, 1881.)

Arnold White wrote to Macmillan on 14 November (TRC) that Strahan had 'spontaneously renewed an offer which he made some time ago (before Mr. Tennyson had decided to leave Messrs. Moxon) and Mr. Tennyson feels that it would be ungracious in him not to accept the offer thus made'. Emily Tennyson said (*Journal*, p. 288) that 'Strahan has offered to publish A. T. for nothing but that A. T. would not allow'.

⁴ Charles Tennyson (p. 376) and Robert Martin (pp. 477, 502) say £5,000; Joseph Shaylor (*Sixty Years a Bookman*, p. 89) says £4,500; William Garden Blaikie (cited by Mumby, p. 228) !4,000. See below, p. 512.

⁵ John Paul—pictured in Andrew Wheatcroft's *Tennyson Album*, p. 106. See *The Letters of Emily Tennyson*, p. 226.

⁶ Only Frederick Locker went with him, 2–12 December; see the account in *Memoir*, ii. 66–7.

I cannot say whether I shall be able to come down in time to vote on Monday. I must finish the business (an important one to me) which brought me here and I am moreover somewhat laid up with headaches and lumbago: if this last were to get worse in the next few days I shouldn't be able to move: however if at the last you are so pressed as to feel the want of even one vote telegraph to me and I will come if possible.

In the meantime I send you a letter which may help you possibly if it come in time more than my vote. You *may make any use of it* you choose: though I dare say B[enjamin] C[otton] and Co. will call me an atheist on the strength of it—an assertion which may be backed by the fact of my never going to old Isaacson's church.

Yours ever affectionately
A. Tennyson

To SIR JOHN SIMEON

MS. Syracuse University.

THE HOLLIES, CLAPHAM COMMON, November 17, 1868

My dear Sir John

I return you the voting-paper duly signed, whereby you will see that I intend to give you my vote; but in case the business that brought me to town should unavoidably detain me I take this occasion to say that I should think it quite a misfortune for us if you are not again returned as our member.

It is in my opinion no small advantage to the House of Commons to have a liberal Catholic Christian among them who may stand up in his place and refute the bigotries both of Roman and Protestant.

I cannot but trust that your well-earned popularity will carry you successfully through the present Election in spite of this invasion of the '*Over-ers*'[1] as we call them in the island. Believe me, my dear Sir John,

Yours ever
A. Tennyson

To ALICE WOOLNER

MS. Tennyson Research Centre.

Tuesday, [? 17 November 1868]

Dear Alice Woolner

Knowles wants you and Woolner to come and dine here on Friday. Won't that do as well?

Yours ever
A. Tennyson

---

[1] 'Not born natives' (*OED*). Simeon was re-elected. (See above, p. ooo).

? 17 November 1868

To MRS FRANCIS TURNER PALGRAVE[1]

MS. Brotherton Collection.

FARRINGFORD, FRESHWATER, ISLE OF WIGHT, [? for THE HOLLIES, CLAPHAM COMMON] [?17 November 1868]

My dear Mrs. Palgrave

I cannot come to you at present. I write from bed, having lumbago and cold (I suppose).[2]

Yours always
A. Tennyson

I will let you know when I can come.

To EMILY SELLWOOD TENNYSON

Text. Materials, iii. 91.

LONDON, November 20, [1868]

Called on Lady Franklin and Sophy Cracroft yesterday, very kind and agreeable and offered me a bed in their house, but I have promised myself to Palgrave, and if I do not hear from Simeon tomorrow that I am wanted, I shall go over there. Then I went to Miss Eden's[1] where we tried to move a table mesmerically. Browning came in and returned with me and Knowles to dinner, where again I read the 'Grail,' and Browning said it was my 'best and highest.' B. is coming again tonight to read part of his new poem, also Macmillan.

To EMILY SELLWOOD TENNYSON

Text. Memoir, ii. 59.

November 21, [1868]

I do not think I can possibly come down while this business is yet pending, for it is not yet finished.[1] In the meantime I have written to Pritchard (who is on the election committee on the other side—Conservative) to pair off with me; and, if he be not going to vote, to get Mr. Cotton, who is I suppose against Simeon, to pair off with me.

Browning read his Preface to us last night,[2] full of strange vigour and remarkable in many ways; doubtful whether it can ever be popular.

---

[1] Cecil Grenville Milnes Palgrave (d. 1890), daughter of James Milnes Gaskell.
[2] He had them again (or still) on 28 November, when his trip to Paris was postponed (*Memoir,* ii. 66).

[1] Emily Eden (see above, p. 432 n.), aunt of Eleanor Eden and sister of George Eden (1784–1849), 1st Earl of Auckland and Governor-General of India (1835–41), whither Emily Eden had accompanied him.

[1] Leaving Moxon and Co. for Strahan.
[2] Book 1 of *The Ring and the Book.* Volume 1 was published 21 November; Volume 4 27 February 1869 (see below, p. 000).

I am not going as yet to Palgrave's? if I go, it will be on Monday afternoon, but I rather want to come home again as soon as I can to work at the other 'Idylls of the King.'

To EMILY SELLWOOD TENNYSON

Text. Memoir, ii. 59.

[5 YORK GATE,] November 23, [1868]

I have sent the whole of 'The Lover's Tale' to the press,[1] and am to have it back on Thursday. I stop here till Friday morning, when Gifford Palgrave comes with his bride. The agreement (with Strahan)[2] is now all ready for signature. Woolner is out in the country, doing Darwin's bust.

To BENJAMIN JOWETT

MS. University of Kansas.

November 26, 1868

My dear Jowett

I am much obliged but I am altogether uncertain about my movements: my *present belief is that I am going almost immediately to Paris with Locker. So don't expect me.

Ever yours
A. Tennyson

*3 p.m.

To ALEXANDER STRAHAN

MS. Liverpool City Libraries.

[THE HOLLIES, CLAPHAM COMMON] [? 30 November 1868]

Dear Mr. Strahan

Send me, please, the fourth part of The Lover's Tale, the part which I gave you to print last week.[1] My friend here wishes to see it, and I should like to have it today.

Yours
A. Tennyson

---

[1] The 'trial edition' (Wise, *A Bibliography*, i. 53). See Ricks, pp. 299–300.
[2] Square brackets in *Memoir* (1899), p. 466.

[1] 'Part iv ['The Golden Supper', Ricks, p. 338] does not appear until the trial edition of 1868, and was presumably written then' (Ricks, p. 300).

To THE DUCHESS OF ARGYLL

MS. Tennyson Research Centre.

91 VICTORIA STREET,[1] December 16, 1868

My dear Duchess

I am very grateful to you for not having misconstrued my silence into want of sympathy with yourself or of regret for Her.[2] Indeed, I may say that though I had seen but little of her, I myself had an affection for her—nothing of course as measured by yours, but still as far as it went a quite true feeling; but, altogether I thought, rightly or wrongly, that there are some sorrows in whose presence all expressions of sympathy must at first fall flat—even if they be not half-resented as an intrusion. But if I erred in this you have already forgiven me and I say no more.

I was with my friend Frederick Locker in Paris when your letter arrived, and it has been forwarded to me here. I am sorry that I have to leave town on the very day you come; but I hope to see you some time in the Spring, when, possibly, the sense of your great loss may be somewhat less poignant, and the child's health, I trust, full[y] re-established.

Present my best wishes and congratulations to Lady Edith and believe me
Ever yours affectionately
A. Tennyson

To FRANCIS TURNER PALGRAVE

Text. Memoir, ii. 61–2; *Materials,* iii. 95–6.

FARRINGFORD, [for HEADON HALL, ALUM BAY], December 24, 1868

My dear Palgrave

You distress me when you tell me that, without leave given by me, you showed my poem to Max Müller:[1] not that I care about Max Müller's seeing it, but I do care for your not considering it a sacred deposit. Pray do so in future; otherwise I shall see some boy in some Magazine making a lame imitation of it, which a clever boy could do in twenty minutes—and, though his work would be worth nothing, it would take away the bloom and freshness from mine.

I can't conceive how the Grail M. M. mentions can well be treated by a poet of the 13th century from a similar point of view to mine, who write in the 19th, but, if so, I am rather sorry for it, as I rather piqued myself on my originality of treatment.

If Max Müller will give you or me the name of the book, which contains all the Mediaeval literature about the Grail, I will order it of the London Library; though, if it be in German prose, I fear I shan't have the patience to wade through a tenth of it.

The 'Grail' is not likely to be published for a year or two, and certainly not along with the other thing which you hate so much (too much it seems to

---

[1] Frederick Locker's.   [2] Her mother, the Duchess of Sutherland, died 27 October.

[1] 'The Holy Grail'—in reply to Palgrave's letter of 23 December (TRC).

me). I shall write three or four more of the 'Idylls,' and link them together as well as I may. Jowett comes on Saturday, and I will give him your message. The boys are both here and well, not at Farringford, which is getting scoured and cleaned, but at a house at Alum Bay (Headon Hall) where Nature in winter at least, seems always in a rage.[2]

Please attend to my request about the 'Grail' and the 'Lover's Tale,' and show them to no one, or if you can't depend upon yourself, forward them to me.

Always yours
A. Tennyson

But of course you can depend upon yourself, even in [a] genial hour of pipe and grog. As for your advice, to make the whole thing larger, I will think of it but at present I do not see my way.

To SIR JOHN SIMEON

Text. draft Materials, iv. 86.

[c. 29 December 1868]

My dear Simeon

I wrote a very careful letter some time ago to Lord Russell praying that the pension of Allingham might be increased in order (as he then said his intention was) that he might be at leisure to devote his life to a history of Ireland. . . . In great haste

Yours affectionately
A. Tennyson

To CHARLES EDWARD COCKIN[1]

Text. Memoir, ii. 61.

FARRINGFORD, December 31, 1868

Sir

I never saw the lines before: and the coincidence is strange enough, and until I saw the signature I fully believed them to be a hoax.[2]

Yours faithfully
A. Tennyson

---

[2] *Cymbeline*, IV. ii. 259. They stayed there from 18 to 28 December because one of the maids had typhoid fever (see below, p. 520, and *Journal*, pp. 284–5).

[1] Charles Edward Cockin (b. 1844), BA Oxford (Wadham) 1866, became Rector of Lea, Lincs., in 1874 (Foster).

[2] Cockin's letter (*Memoir*, ii. 60–1) asks whether some verses (by Joshua Sylvester) in *The Divine Weekes and Workes* of Du Bartas 'suggested the two last stanzas in the song in "The Miller's Daughter" '.

To MESSRS STRAHAN AND CO.

MS. Greater London Record Office and Library.

FARRINGFORD, December 31, 1868

Dear Sirs

Although in the Agreement between us dated this day it is expressed that you are to pay me £4300 per annum: during the continuance of the agreement yet it is perfectly understood between us that in the event of Mrs. Moxon dying during the continuance of this agreement, I am not, after the happening of such event, to call upon you to pay me more than £4000 per annum: (except in respect of additional works as provided in the agreement). But so long as the £4300 is payable I am to have the free and uncontrolled disposal of the whole of that amount.[1] I am, Dear Sirs,

Yours truly
A. Tennyson[2]

To Messrs. Strahan and Co.

EMILY SELLWOOD AND ALFRED TENNYSON to THE VISCOUNTESS STRANGFORD[1]

MS. Mark L. Reed.

FARRINGFORD, FRESHWATER, ISLE OF WIGHT, January 12, 1869

You dear lonely one. You must indeed be desolate. We both feel with all our hearts that yours is no common loss. Last night he asked me whether I would not write. I said I cannot. I should feel it an intrusion on such a sorrow.

Someday God will give you a little comfort in the consciousness of what you were to him in all the blessed memories of the past and the hopes of the future but now I know it seems almost cruel to speak of comfort. Yet I know too that that that 'noble lovely face.' will be a continued presence with you of which nothing and no one can rob you, nor I must believe of the assurance that your lives are ever one in God and this will be a sweetness in the desolation.

Forgive me—of what avail are my poor words. Only the living and loving God can comfort you. When you can, do let us hear of or from you. I beg him to add his own little word and you know how true a one it is, for you saw

---

[1] See above, p. 506 n.
[2] In this legal document only the signature is in Tennyson's hand.

[1] Emily Anne Beaufort (d. 1877) married the 8th Viscount Strangford in 1862 (see above, p. 379 n.), and it was a marriage of true *minds*. He was a notable scholar in poor health, she 'a woman of great physical energy and intellectual refinement' who had travelled extensively in Egypt and the Middle East. She published *Egyptian Sepulchres and Syrian Tombs* (2 vols.) in 1861—Strangford reviewed it and married her—and *The Eastern Shores of the Adriatic* in 1863, and *A Visit to Montenegro* in 1864. After Lord Strangford's sudden death (see *Journal*, p. 286), she took extensive training to become a nurse, and devoted the rest of her life to that calling (*DNB*).

what pleasure he took in being with your beloved while you were here. With affectionate sympathy,

Yours
Emily Tennyson

I knew him but little it is true, but the little I did know made me wish to know him more—he was (and not for his learning alone) very interesting to me.

Ever yours in all sympathy
A. Tennyson

To ISABEL HEWLETT KNOWLES

MS. University of Virginia.

FARRINGFORD, FRESHWATER, ISLE OF WIGHT, January 12, 1869

My dear Mrs. Knowles
I posted a telegram today to you, and another to Mr. Knowles at Raymond Buildings to say that I was *not* coming up, as I had got notice from Mr. White that I was not as yet wanted. I trust you and he got them in time.

But I can't feel easy at present and must come up. So if nothing happens to hinder me I shall come tomorrow. I shall most likely hear from you tomorrow morning as to whether you can accommodate me.

If I do not (by the bye I made a mistake in my last to your husband—I meant Vauxhall Station when I wrote Clapham) I shall make a dash upon you from Vauxhall and take my chance.

Ever yours
A. Tennyson

To FREDERICK LOCKER

MS. Armstrong Browning Library.

[mid-January 1869]

My dear Locker
Won't you store this from the Daily Telegraph among your curiosities?[1]
Fancy 'Antient Pistol F.R.S.L., Editor of the Idylls,' closing in a blaze of glory, sealskin jacket and all, in a Bude light!!![2]
Love to Lady C.

Ever yours
A. T.

---

[1] The *Daily Telegraph*, 4 January, p. 5, said: 'Messrs Strahan and Co. . . . announced that on, and after, the 15th of this month the Poet Laureate's works will be published by their house', and also that 'the Moxon connection . . . has closed in a blaze of glory' with the edition of the *Idylls* illustrated by Doré; it referred to 'J. Bertrand Payne, F.R.S.L., editor of the Idylls of the King'.

[2] See below, p. 523. Pistol is described 'the foul-mouth'dst rogue in England' in 2 *Henry IV*, II. iv. 77–8.

Payne has stopt my 'Times'. He used to pay for it and put it with his account: and none has come now for four days.

To JAMES THOMAS FIELDS

MS. New York Public Library; Huntington Library.[1]

FARRINGFORD, FRESHWATER, ISLE OF WIGHT, [mid- or late January 1869]

Dear Mr. Fields

I have received your cheque for £500, and herewith enclose a more formal receipt.

If you visit England this year I shall be most happy to see you here if I be at home for I believe you are a man with some reverence for the hearth, not like Mr. Bayard Taylor who being received with open arms (for he called himself a friend of Thackeray) saw in me not a man but a paragraph, and even out of that made a parody.[2]

With best remembrances to Mrs. Fields, believe me,

Yours very sincerely
A. Tennyson

To [? ALEXANDER STRAHAN]

MS. University of Kansas.

[18 January 1869]

Preparatory to an article by Payne on my avarice and want of pity to Mrs. M[oxon] (*great* poet put in to seem not Payne)

exactly 500 in excess etc.

exactly £2300 would be much nearer the mark

but £800 was the account of the summer before last but the 'exactly' must have come from P[ayne]. Who else was to know?

---

[1] The greeting and first sentence (NYPL) are in Tennyson's hand. Of the remainder (Huntington), the second sentence, through 'for the hearth', and the closing ('With best . . . A. Tennyson') are added in pencil; the words 'not like . . . parody' are in Tennyson's hand.

[2] See above, p. 453. Fields wrote to Taylor, 23 February 1869, quoting this sentence (James C. Austin, *Fields of the Atlantic Monthly*, p. 398; Taylor wrote to Fields, 26 February (TRC), explaining what had happened; Fields wrote again to Taylor on 1 March (Austin, pp. 398–9), advising him to print an explanation in the New York *Tribune*, and Taylor wrote to Tennyson, 2 March (TRC), enclosing Stedman's letter of explanation to himself (27 February, TRC).

exactly 500!!!

I have just come in and find in the Publishers Circular[1]

A. T.

To FREDERICK LOCKER

MS. Armstrong Browning Library.

Monday, January 19 [for 18], 1869

My dear Locker

I am advised by my lawyer not to speak *at present* of my reasons for parting from Moxon and Co.

Some part of them at any rate may be conjectured from Mr. Payne's proposal to Mr. Mortimer Collins for whose letter I am much obliged to yourself and him.[1]

Ever yours
A. Tennyson

---

[1] These notes, with the several letters following, reflect passages in three issues of *The Publishers' Circular*. From 6 January, p. 6: 'The Laureate will greatly benefit by the removal of his agency from Messrs. Moxon to Messrs. Strahan. The *Telegraph* informed us that the latter have agreed to pay our great poet £4,000 per annum for two years; the sum, we believe, is £4,500, exactly £500 in excess of the sum paid yearly by the former house. However we may regret the loss to the widow of Mr. Moxon, himself a poet, we cannot affect surprise. We have, therefore, now no exclusively poetical publishers such as we had in those high and palmy days when "my Murray" monopolised one great poet, and the "gentle publisher, himself a bard," was surrounded by almost all others worthy of the name.' From 1 February, p. 70: 'We adverted in our last number to a paragraph that appeared in the *Daily Telegraph* and other journals relative to the alleged arrangements between the poet-laureate and his publishers; we are authorized to say that the statements referred to have been hazarded on entirely erroneous information, alike unjust to Mr. Tennyson and the Messrs. Strahan and Co.' From 15 February, p. 97: 'We observe with some regret that Mr. Strahan complains in a letter which he has published in a contemporary that he had no opportunity given him of suggesting any alteration in the paragraph in our last Circular relative to Mr. Tennyson's arrangements with his publishers. It is, however, due to ourselves to state that a proof of our paragraph was with due courtesy submitted to Mr. Strahan on Saturday; but owing to his absence, we presume, returned only on Monday morning *after* the copies of the Circular had been despatched by the early mail. It remains only for us to add, that which we hope will be unnecessary to the majority of our readers, that in adopting from what we believed an excellent source the original paragraph in these pages, the Editor had not the slightest intention of conveying any inference unfavourable to the Laureate, who has, he is informed and believes, treated both his past and present publishers with distinguished consideration and kindness.'

[1] Mortimer Collins (1827–76: *DNB*), journalist and hack novelist, was solicited by Payne to attack Tennyson (see below, p. 524). He was a friend of Locker, who wrote to Tennyson on 29 July (Yale): 'I met Mr. Collins in the street yesterday. I had not seen him since he wrote me that letter about Payne. He told me that he had not seen Payne since that time, and indeed that his application to M. C. to write against you was made by letter. I am quite sure that Collins is not naturally hostile to you, but I daresay that he would fight as a mercenary under any banner.' For another view of Collins, even lower than Tennyson's, see *The Swinburne Letters*, ii. 167–8.

To JAMES THOMAS KNOWLES

MS. Duke University.

[20 January 1869]

My dear Knowles

Strahan is going to reply to the malignant and insidious passage in the Publisher's Circular.[1] 'We are not surprised etc.' as if my avarice were a well known thing. I have told him to consult you before sending his answer. I myself am amazed that so respectable a publication should have endured [?] to print such an article.

Has White seen it? It seems to me that Mrs. M[oxon] and her son are running it very hard against me. Whatever she does *not* know she must know what my receipts are—and for such a paragraph she is, as head of the house, responsible, and should be told so. I had a great mind to write to her but I forebore out of respect to Arnold White; but it is intolerable that she to whom I meant to behave with all kindness should treat me in this fashion.

Is such an article actionable? I don't say if it were I would bring the action.

Ever yours
A. Tennyson

To [? ALEXANDER STRAHAN]

MS. Rowland Collins.

January 20, 1869

My dear Sir
Will you answer the enclosed?
Have you seen Payne's two lies in the Publisher's Circular?[1]

Yours very truly
A. Tennyson

EMILY SELLWOOD TENNYSON to JAMES THOMAS KNOWLES

MS. Duke University.

FARRINGFORD, January 22, 1869

My dear Mr. Knowles

I did not write as usual to tell of his arrival because he wrote himself and as to my thanks for your goodness I hope you believe that they are as unwearied as that goodness.

I entirely agree with Mr. Arnold White and yourself as to the expediency of silence. I am afraid that he gets more nervous here than with you; but I am trying to persuade him to work at his Idyll and then I know he will feel the worry less. With kindest remembrances to you both,

Most sincerely yours
Emily Tennyson

---

[1] See the two letters preceding.

[1] See above, p. 514.

? late January 1869

To FREDERICK LOCKER (incomplete)

MS. Tennyson Research Centre.

FARRINGFORD, FRESHWATER, ISLE OF WIGHT, [? late January 1869]

My dear Locker

It had been my wish to part kindly from Mr. Payne, were it only for the sake of Mrs. Moxon: but it appears that he will not have it so. For Mrs. Moxon's sake I have borne with a great deal from this man which I would not have put up with from any other publisher. The general insolence ⟨and superhuman pomposity⟩ of the man, his unscrupulous use of my name in extracting money from publishers (one case in particular where he got £70 from a publisher for the reprint of an American book with a poem of mine in it, which £70 he never gave any account of to me—how many more cases of the kind there may be I know not[)]—the case of Hachette and Co. where he is manifestly proved to be no other than a trickster[1]—his total carelessness to all my feelings and wishes.

To THE DUCHESS OF ARGYLL

MS. Tennyson Research Centre.

January 27, [1869]

My dear Duchess

I called on you on Saturday and was grieved not to find you at home; and I called on the Duke at the India House on Monday and he was not there: I wished to speak with him on a matter which I dare say has been submitted to him since. I saw Lady Augusta Stanley before I left, and she promised the Dean should propose it to him. We make our petition to him that he would consent to be the President of our new club, to be called The Metaphysic[al] and Theological Club or by some such name.[1] In our meetings all the questions which agitate and perplex this 19th century are to be freely discussed and handled by men of all religious and metaphysical shades of

---

[1] Not clear. We have seen a letter (23 January 1866, probably to Payne) in which Tennyson alludes to the 'Agreement' between himself and 'Mr. Hatchett[e]' of which he cannot find the duplicate. See below, p. 525.

[1] The Metaphysical Society originated in a discussion on 13 November 1868 at Knowles's when Tennyson read 'The Holy Grail' (see above, p. 506), and was 'dissolved' twelve years later on 16 November 1880. 'We can surmise that the intellectual stimulus came from Pritchard, the spiritual inspiration from Tennyson, and the practical, social impetus from Knowles,' writes Priscilla Metcalf (*James Knowles*, p. 213), in the best brief account of the society. She quotes Knowles: 'While King Arthur was being so much and so frequently discussed between us the mystical meanings of the Poem led to almost endless talk on speculative metaphysical subjects— God—the Soul—free will—Necessity—Matter and spirit—and all the circle of Metaphysical enquiry. Tennyson said how good it would be if such subjects could be argued and debated by capable men in the manner and with the machinery of the learned Societies. "Modern Science" he said "ought surely to have taught us how to separate light from heat—and men ought to be able now-a-days to keep their tempers—even while they discuss theology." I said that if he and Mr. Pritchard would join such a society—I would endeavour to get it up in London.' See also *Memoir*, ii. 166–72; Wilfred Ward, *William George Ward and the Catholic Revival*, ch. 12, and, for a full discussion, Alan Willard Brown's excellent book, *The Metaphysical Society, Victorian Minds in Crisis, 1869–1880*.

opnion, and when they quarrel, as perhaps they are not unlikely to do, he is to keep us in order.

I hope he will consent.[2]

Ever yours
A. Tennyson

We shall perhaps have the physical men also among us, Tyndall, Huxley, etc.

To [? MESSRS STRAHAN AND CO.]

Text. Materials, iii. 267.[1]

FARRINGFORD, FRESHWATER, ISLE OF WIGHT, [? February 1869]

Gentlemen

My former volumes having through the negligence of my former publishers (Moxon) been left unprotected, Baron Tauchnitz unasked gave me a certain sum for his edition of my works and a small percentage on their sale, therefore, though I do not doubt you could make a better bargain for me, I feel in honour bound to Tauchnitz. With this exception I shall feel obliged if you will make any arrangements for my foreign rights that you may think well.

Mr. Arnold White has the document which you sent me and which must be altered in accordance with this letter.

A. T.

To MARTIN FARQUHAR TUPPER

MS. Buffalo and Erie County Public Library.

FARRINGFORD, FRESHWATER, ISLE OF WIGHT, [c. 10 February 1869]

My dear Sir

At your request I send

For

Brantz Mayer[1]
from
A. Tennyson

Many thanks for your good wishes and believe me,

Yours very truly
A. Tennyson

---

[2] He declined, in a letter of 20 February (*Materials*, iii. 104; MS, TRC).

[1] Under an implied date of *c*. May 1878 and headed: 'From Alfred Tennyson to Kegan, Paul and Co. (who had taken on all the publishing business of Messrs Henry King).

[1] Brantz Mayer (1809–79), American lawyer, author, antiquary and, from 1863, paymaster in the US Army (Allibone). The letter is inscribed: 'Addressed to me, at Albury,—as asked of Tennyson for Brantz Mayer of Baltimore, Feb. 10, 1869. Martin F. Tupper.' Tupper had probably met Mayer in his first American tour in 1851.

EMILY SELLWOOD TENNYSON
to WILLIAM EWART GLADSTONE

MS. British Library.

FARRINGFORD, FRESHWATER, ISLE OF WIGHT, February 14, 1869

Dear Mr. Gladstone

You listen so patiently to all, please listen to me one moment while I tell you what the proposal of the Agricultural Association has helped to put into my head.

Is it not possible to throw land and all money produce whether of mechanic skill or of brain into one great mass to be taxed and rated and tithed equally for general purposes leaving the special to be specially dealt with (such as lighting of cities).

Money in this case would take rank with land in its form of interest not of principal (3 £ [?] pr 100) which, I think, might solve many difficulties. (Perhaps my thoughts have been often before thought.) The whole country to be divided into districts, each district to be under the charge of a steward, a gentleman of standing and education to be as irremoveable as the Judges who shall register, collect, administer somewhat after the theory of some native Indian administrators I think.

Pardon me and do not of course waste one moment in answering me. With all most earnest wishes that you may have wisdom given you to rule this great land, for great I still believe it, thank God, believe me with much reverence[1]

Very truly yours
Emily Tennyson

To ROBERT BROWNING

MS. Wellesley.

March 2, 1869

My dear Browning

I am very pleased to have your four books from yourself.[1] Wonderful books and sui generis, and with so much subtlety, learning and vigour, such exquisite touches of human tenderness and divine love in them, that perhaps it is a presumption in me to speak of them at all till I have made a more

---

[1] Docketed: 'Mrs. Tennyson. Wishes *all* land and money produce to be taxed in the lump, and the country to be divided into districts under a steward, etc.' Gladstone's dexterous reply (*Materials*, iii. 103): 'Taxation and all that belongs to it form a rather painful chapter in human affairs. For good nine years and over I had to pore over that chapter night and day. I am now in a measure emancipated from that and inducted into another and more varied servitude. But the best answer I can make to your note is to claim upon the strength of it that you should within no long time give me an opportunity of conversing upon it with you by a visit to or better still a sojourn in London.'

[1] *The Ring and the Book* (see above, p. 508).

careful study of them than as yet I have had a chance of doing. Meanwhile believe me

Yours always and thankfully
A. Tennyson

EMILY SELLWOOD TENNYSON
to MARGARET GATTY (extract)

MS. Boston Public Library.

FARRINGFORD, March 5, 1869

... Ally sends many thanks for the book. He has read some of it and finds it interesting. It is sad to have his widowed brother and his five little ones in one of our houses and my widowed sister and her Agnes here with us and to think that there is also a gap in another home of the family:[1] the Lushingtons having lost their middle daughter at about nineteen from the very typhoid fever which drove us from our home for Christmas, a servant having had it for six weeks and it not being thought right that Ally and the boys should come to the house fresh for he having to go away at the beginning I kept him away.[2] Perhaps I have told you all this before.

He is talking of going away altogether from Farringford having been so much annoyed by the conduct of the people on the occasion of a furze screen being fired on the 5th of November in our belt. I don't mean their conduct to himself but their swearing and forswearing and their behaviour to our good Heard who is so annoyed that he had resolved on leaving and Ally says he cannot stay without him.[3] ...

To JAMES HINTON[1]

MS. Robert Taylor.

FARRINGFORD, March 17, 1869

My dear Sir

I shall be very glad to make your acquaintance when I come to town.

---

[1] Horatio Tennyson's wife, Charlotte Maria Elwes, died 31 October 1868, Charles Weld 15 February 1869 (*Journal*, p. 287), Emily Lushington (daughter of Cecilia and Edmund) in December 1868 (*Journal*, p. 285).

[2] See above, p. 511.

[3] The furze-brake was damaged by fire on Guy Fawkes day. Heard was the gardener (*Journal*) and manager of the farm (*Letters of Emily Tennyson*, p. 161).

---

[1] James Hinton (1822–75: *DNB*), an aural surgeon and philosopher, was a sort of secular Teilhard de Chardin of Victorian England, and thus in some measure a mirror image of what Tennyson found so attractive in scientists like Pritchard, Herschel, Lockyer—the reconcilers of science and religion. Hinton, though an ineffectual angel and humanist, was the most original and appealing of them all. He was one of the nuclear members of the Metaphysical Society ('at the wish of the Poet Laureate', according to Ellice Hopkins, editor of Hinton's *Life and Letters*, p. 256); and Ruskin, who knew him there, wrote of him in *Fors Clavigera* (Letter 75 as one 'who could have taught us much'. His best-known books are *Man and His Dwelling Place* (1859), *Life in*

I have more than once thought of calling upon you but being an utter stranger did not venture to do so.

Yours very truly
A. Tennyson

I have been away or would have answered before.[2]

J. Hinton Esq.

To JAMES THOMAS KNOWLES

MS. Yale.

[c. 4 April 1869]

My dear K.

This is an extract from my brother-in-law's letter to his brother[1] who forwarded it to me.* I have today sent it to Strahan asking for an explanation. I believed that I had his word of honour that he would not print it: the poem:[2] but if he has done so, what am I to think of him?

We think it better on the whole not to come up to town till toward the conclusion of the month.

I send the extract to you because you remember the circumstances of the printing but if you chance to see Strahan you need not say that the letter was my brother-in-law's.

*What permission has Strahan or has he any permission to send about in print to whomsoever he thinks good the new unpublished Idyl? Yesterday these facts came to my knowledge told me by A who heard it from B who met C in Glasgow. I know all 3 but I doubt if A. T. ever saw B. C to B—'Have you seen Tennyson's new Idyl?' B greatly surprised to C—'Why have you?' C—O yes—etc. the explanation being that Strahan had it in print and sent copies to his friends whom he thought worthy to read it. I have no doubt that my reporter spoke accurately.

Nature (1862, essays reprinted from the *Cornhill Magazine*), and *The Mystery of Pain* (1866). See *Tennyson in Lincoln*, i, No. 1149–50. A. W. Brown (*The Metaphysical Society*, pp. 123–5) observes that Hinton 'made a noble impression on his friends and colleagues in the society', and that Hinton 'can properly be considered as the first of that long line of thinkers and psychologists who have asserted the centrality of the sexual impulse in human life'. He advocated polygyny (though not at the Society) and almost certainly practised it.

[2] Tennyson had been invited to meet Hinton by Lord Hatherley (*Materials*, iii. 102), but this letter is in reply to Hinton's to Tennyson of 12 March 1869 (TRC), inviting him for an evening's conversation when next in London.

[1] Edmund to Franklin Lushington, who came to Farringford on 3 April (*Journal*, p. 290). The Tennysons left on the 19th for Haslemere, where they met Knowles, who went with Tennyson 'to Town after dinner'. On the 21st 'Lionel and I go to "The Hollies." Mr. Knowles kindly meets us in a brougham at Vauxhall Station. Mr. Knowles and A. go to the first dinner of The Metaphysical Club' (Journal).

[2] 'The Holy Grail'.

522   19 *April* 1869

To COLONEL ALFRED BATE RICHARDS[1]

Text. [Richard Herne Shepherd], *Tennysoniana*, 2nd edn. (London: Pickering, 1879), pp. 116–17.

FARRINGFORD, FRESHWATER, ISLE OF WIGHT, April 19, 1867 [for 1869][2]

I most heartily congratulate you on your having been able to do so much for your country; and I hope that you will not cease from your labours until it is the law of the land that every man child in it shall be trained to the use of arms. I have the honour to be

Yours faithfully
A. Tennyson

To THE DUKE OF ARGYLL

Text. Tennyson Research Centre (transcript).

THE HOLLIES, CLAPHAM COMMON, Wednesday, April 21, 1869

My dear Duke

We dine today (that is, the Metaphysical and Physiological Club) at Willis' rooms. The dinner hour is 7 and I have been requested to ask you to dine along with us for the sake of your society only: there is to be no Chairman, and we meet [at] a round table of the καλοκαγαθος.

Ever yours
A. Tennyson

This is only drawing a bow at a venture,[1] but we may chance to hit you—

To [? FREDERICK LOCKER] (incomplete)[1]

MS. Harvard.

[*c.* 1 May 1869]

... at Marlborough. When in London I was not in London proper but down at Clapham Common and driving into town every day and all day long buying furniture etc. for my Hazlemere house till I was half dead of fatigue.[2] I thought of you and of calling on you more than once but I had no time.

---

[1] Alfred Bate Richards (1820–76), dramatist, poet, journalist, and in 1855 first editor of the *Daily Telegraph*. He was the 'onlie begetter' of the Volunteer Rifle Corps in April–May 1859, and 'held his commission [as head of the Corps] till 1869, when a testimonial was presented to him in recognition of his efforts (*DNB*, which quotes this letter). See above, p. 223 n.

[2] Printed in *Memoir*, i. 436, under an implied date of 1859; in Walter E. Wace (pseudonym of W. R. Nicoll), *Alfred Tennyson, His Life and Work* (1881), pp. 79–80, probably from *Tennysoniana* and with the same date.

[1] 1 Kings 22:34.

[1] And the page is torn; omissions are conjecturally supplied in brackets.

[2] 'To dine at Knowles. Tennyson and Mrs. T. there, and Mrs. Knowles, Bard and wife in town to buy furniture for their new house at Haslemere. Had a pleasant evening' (*Journals of Walter White*, p. 166). See *Journal*, p. 291, and Priscilla Metcalf, *James Knowles*, pp. 206–7.

I shall be in town again in three or four weeks time I believe and then I will make amends to myself and you by looking in upon you. The one night when I was in London I was at a Royal Society meeting where I met (I forget whom) Pollock I think, who told me [? of you. There too] I saw standing among the savants and the foremost that happy mixture of ass, rogue, and peacock the so-called Captain Bertrand Payne, who has lately bribed his bully to write me down in Temple Bar, by way of spiting me and spoiling Strahan's bargain.[3]

> Ancient Pistol, Peacock Payne
> Brute in manner, rogue in grain,
> How you squeezed me, peacock Payne!
> Scared was I and out I ran
> And found by Paul's an honest man.
> Peace be with you, peacock Payne,
> I have left you, you remain
> Ancient Pistol, sealskin Payne.[4]

To WILLIAM RALSTON SHEDDEN-RALSTON[1]

Text. M. P. Alexeyev, 'William Ralston and Russian Writers of the Later Nineteenth Century', *Oxford Slavonic Papers*, xi (1964), 88.

FRESHWATER, I. W., May 2, 1869

My dear Sir

I have returned from a visit to Marlborough and found your Krilof's fables on my table. I have read a few of them and find them good and pithy beyond the wont of fables. Thanks. As for sending me Russian translations I fear that would be utterly fruitless at present seeing that I have got [*sic for* yet] to learn my ABC in Russian, but your rough notes I should not be ungrateful for, whenever you may have put them in order.

One French translation (that of M. Michel) I have seen but it is lame and tame. Believe me,

Yours very truly
A. Tennyson

---

[3] The anonymous article in *Temple Bar*, xxvi (May 1869), 179–94 (reprinted, with alterations, in *The Poetry of the Period*, 1870, and in *The Critical Heritage*), was in fact by Alfred Austin (1835–1913), who, *faute de mieux*, succeeded Tennyson as Poet Laureate and who was not bribed by Payne but motivated by pleasure, though he came to think the article written with 'excessive vigour'. Austin confessed his authorship to Locker (in the course of a game of croquet), and Tennyson taxed him with it when they first met, fifteen years later, in the summer of 1884 (see Austin's *Autobiography*, ii. 1–2, 219–27).

[4] Ricks, p. 1229. See above, p. 513.

[1] William Ralston Shedden-Ralston (1828–89: *DNB*), critic, translator, folklorist, who worked in the Department of Printed Books in the British Museum and taught himself Russian. His translation of *Krilof and His Fables* appeared in 1868. In May 1871 he visited Farringford, and in June, with Turgenev, Aldworth. See *Journal*, pp. 321, 324–5, and Patrick Waddington's excellent book *Turgenev and England*, pp. 198–205.

To WILLIAM COX BENNETT

MS. Rosenbach Foundation.

FARRINGFORD, FRESHWATER, ISLE OF WIGHT, May 10, 1869

My dear Sir

I see that April 20 is the date of your letter: I was away when it came and this and the book only turned up yesterday—nay the book only this morning. All success to it and may the people interest themselves in it and old England![1] You know you are welcome to my 'Light Brigade' whenever you want it for your other volume.[2]

I see than Ancient Pistol, my ex-publisher,* has been attacking me through his bully in Temple Bar: I hope he feels easier for it. Believe me,

Yours truly
A. Tennyson

*and I see too your kind words in the Dispatch.[3]

To WILLIAM COX BENNETT

MS. Indiana University.

FARRINGFORD, FRESHWATER, ISLE OF WIGHT, [18 May 1869][1]

My dear Sir

One word: the writer in Temple Bar is a wholly unknown writer. I saw Payne's letter to a chum of his (Mortimer Colins who sent the letter on to a friend of mine: and he, for it was not marked private, showed it to me). Payne wanted M. C. to publish a whole volume against me, 'slashing' (he advised) 'make him out a third-rate poet.' Payne I suppose would have fee'd him with something of that which he has been getting out of me: but M. C. would not write the volume and Payne got another.[2]

It is not worth your while to answer his attack nor mine to notice it. Strahan says that it can't possibly do any harm: but I am obliged to you for your proposed defence. Non ragioniam di lor ma guarda e passa.

Yours very truly
A. Tennyson

---

[1] See above, p. 444.
[2] *School Book of Poetry* (1870: Allibone), apparently Bennett's part of 'The consecutive narrative series of reading books, by C. Morell, edited by J. F. Morell, to which is added a selection of the best English poetry edited by W. C. Bennett, nos. 1–5' (1870: *New CBEL*, iii, col. 508).
[3] Untraced.

[1] The date is from the legend under the facsimile of the second paragraph published in J. Holt Schooling, 'The Handwriting of Lord Tennyson', *Strand Magazine*, viii (1893), 606.
[2] See above, pp. 523, 515.

To DRUMMOND RAWNSLEY

MS. Harvard.

[May 1869]

My dear Drummond

Your clown's letter is capital and we were all (i.e. wife, Anna Weld and Agnes and myself) charmed with it. I hope when you come south I shall be at home to receive you, either here, or at my new home near Hazelmere 800 feet above the sea.

I wish you or Booth[1] would before I publish another edition write out for me in the dialect which lives about you my 'Northern Farmer' and send it me. Will you? and I shall be

Yours gratefully
A. Tennyson

Private

I have left my old publisher because he was a rogue as proved by the issue of the case Hatchet [*for* Hachette] v. Moxon[2]—he was also in the habit of extorting large sums from unfortunate people who inserted poems of mine in their books, and giving no account of these sums to me. He is now employing his bullies in the Magazines to write me down—if he can.

To LORD HOUGHTON (RICHARD MONCKTON MILNES)

MS. Trinity College.

FARRINGFORD, FRESHWATER, ISLE OF WIGHT, May 21, 1869

My dear Houghton

In reply to your question I may say that, though my boy was not cured of stammering by Dr. Hunt,[1] this was made very much less remarkable by the treatment and that he came back with a very well developed chest and straight back—and nothing has ailed him since—and sometimes in dry weather he does not stammer at all.

I think it might be worth your while to try Hunt. I have not tried anyone else—but before Lionel went to Hunt's I took the advice of Dr. Johnson of Savile Row[2] who, as far as I recollect, approved of Hunt's system.

Yours ever
A. Tennyson

---

[1] Probably Augustus Booth (see i. 311 n.). [2] Mentioned above, p. 517 n.

[1] See above, p. 442 n. The inquiry was probably for his son Robert Offley Ashburton Milnes (1858–1945: *DNB*), later Marquis of Crewe, whom his wife described as 'in speech, a quiet pleasant voice, but with at times, in public, prolonged moments—almost minutes—of hesitation while he fastidiously chose the right word' (Margaret Crewe, Foreword to James Pope-Hennessy, *Lord Crewe, 1858–1945, The Likeness of a Liberal*, p. x).

[2] Sir George Johnson (1815–96: *DNB*), 11 Savile Row.

EMILY SELLWOOD TENNYSON
to JAMES THOMAS FIELDS

MS. Huntington Library.

FARRINGFORD, FRESHWATER, ISLE OF WIGHT, May 21, 1869

Dear Mr. Fields

We are shocked that in the interlacing of letters and telegrams there should have been a misunderstanding.

We feared from Mrs. Fields' note that you were too unwell to come at present and we therefore waited to fix a more distant time than this week. Pray forgive the mistake and come to us on Monday next if agreeable to you and prevail on Miss Lowell to accompany you.[1]

If you will leave by the eleven o'clock train from Waterloo we will send a carriage to meet you by the 3 o'clock boat.

Believe me with our very kind regards.

Very truly yours
Emily Tennyson

To JAMES THOMAS KNOWLES

Text. Memoir, ii. 168; Priscilla Metcalf, *James Knowles*, p. 222.

[30 or 31 May 1869]

I am not coming up for your meeting, i.e. I believe so, today, and your request that you may read the poem at that meeting abashes me. If you are to read it, it ought to be stated surely that I have but ceded to your strongly expressed desire. Hutton can have a copy of it if he choose; but an I had known that such as he wanted it, I would have looked at it again before I let it go. But it wants to be read in a big voice. Can you make yours big enough?[1]

To EMILY SELLWOOD TENNYSON

MS. Tennyson Research Centre.

5 YORK GATE, REGENT'S PARK, [8 June 1869]

Dearest

Knowles has written to thee appointing Friday for Blackdown: I take it that thou wilt come up on Thursday to look after the furniture at Guildford then next day might join us there in the train which starts from Waterloo on Friday 11.30. But how about the beds? If thou wouldst like to come up here

---

[1] They came on 25 May, with Mabel Lowell, daughter of James Russell Lowell (*Journal*, p. 293).

[1] 'The Higher Pantheism' (Ricks, p. 1204). 'The first regular meeting of the [Metaphysical] Society was held on Wednesday, June 2, 1869, at the Deanery, Westminster, with Sir John Lubbock in the chair. Tennyson's poem . . . was read by Mr. Knowles [Hon. Secretary] in the poet's absence . . .' (A. W. Brown, *The Metaphysical Society*, p. 27). Richard Holt Hutton (1826–97), journalist, theologian, critic, and 'joint-editor and part proprietor of the "Spectator"' (*DNB*), read a paper at this meeting. (The last two sentences are from Metcalf.)

to this house on *Tuesday* and Wednesday—there is a bed but Mrs. P[algrave] apologizes for the smallness of the room. I don't think that would matter much. Then on Thursday thou couldst go down to Guil[d]ford. And I perhaps too, if I can get off an engagement. Otherwise I doubt whether there will be time before Sunday for thee to choose beds. As now we shall not get into the house till perhaps the middle of July (i.e. if I go to Switzerland) you might perhaps to save fatigue take some other time for the beds. Do as it seems best.

I dined at Simeon's yesterday—a pleasant party.

Thine × × × ×
[A. T.]

Locker will go with me to S[witzerlan]d and very likely Palgrave also.

To JAMES THOMAS KNOWLES

MS. Rowland L. Collins.

FARRINGFORD, FRESHWATER, ISLE OF WIGHT, [for London, 8 June 1869]

My dear Knowles

I am not going to call on Lord Egmont:[1] he says the matter requires 'deep consideration' and who am I to break in upon his profound contemplation of the scarce-possible little bit of road?

But my heels suffer this hot weather from the boots I am wearing, and the old ones are not sent. Will you prick the man with his own awl? I was to have had them on Monday.

Yours ever
A. T.

To FREDERICK LOCKER

MS. Armstrong Browning Library.

[? *c.* 10 June 1869]

Dear L

I am not going to move out all day.

A. T.

To FREDERICK LOCKER

MS. Armstrong Browning Library.

Saturday, [12 June 1869]

My dear Locker

We will go by the Brussels route, we might possibly be detained at Paris

---

[1] George James Perceval (1794–1874), 6th Earl of Egmont. Tennyson 'had forgotten that there was no make-up road across the moor from Haslemere [to Aldworth]. He now found that none could be made without leave of the Lord of the Manor, Lord Egmont, who was not at all disposed to help' (Charles Tennyson, p. 380). See *Letters of Emily Tennyson*, pp. 238–9, 245, 261–2.

which seems ready to break out into fire.[1] 8.45 we will meet at Charing Cross or rather at 8.30.

Yours etc.
A. T.

To STENTON EARDLEY[1]

MS. Abel Berland.

Saturday, [12 June 1869]

Dear Mr. Eardley

We go down on Sunday evening to Dover, and we cross from Dover at 10.45 on Monday. It may be as well to avoid Paris just at present as we might possibly be detained there if a row breaks out. Therefore let the Brussels route be taken.

Yours truly
A. Tennyson

To STENTON EARDLEY

MS. University of Chicago.

5 YORK GATE, REGENT PARK, Sunday, June 13, 1869

Dear Mr. Eardley

We have *finally* decided to go by Boulogne to Paris. The boat goes from Folkstone at 12.30 p.m. and you will have to meet us tomorrow *morning* on Folkstone quay *at that time*.

Yours truly
A. Tennyson

A friend has volunteered to go to Streatham and deliver this into your hand.[1]

---

[1] 'Some serious disturbances took place during the elections, which were not concluded before the early part of June, and in several parts of Paris crowds of men traversed the streets, shouting, "Vive la Republique! Vive la *Lanterne*! (meaning M.Rochefort's newspaper) and singing the "Marseillaise Hymn"' (*Annual Register*, p. 220).

[1] Stenton Eardley (1823–?83: Venn), Vicar of Emmanual Church, Streatham, Surrey, and 'a perfect enthusiast for mountains' (*Journal*, p. 293). 'Tennyson and the Rev. Stenton Eardley spent a month together in Switzerland, and once, when rambling over the mountains, the poet was seen by his companion on his hands and knees intently looking at something in the grass. "Look here", he exclaimed, "I can see the colour of the flower through the creature's wings." The creature was a dragon fly, and the flower an Alpine rose' (J. Cuming Walters, *Tennyson: Poet, Philosopher, Idealist*, p. 252).

[1] Endorsed: 'I was the "friend" here spoken of. Mr. Tennyson asked me to go over to Streatham to arrange with Mr. Eardley about their Swiss trip. | Arthur Locker | Clifton Villas Highgate Hill, N. | June 14th 1869.' Arthur Locker (1828–93: *DNB*), novelist and journalist, was Frederick's younger brother.

TENNYSON IN SWITZERLAND

Text. 'A. T.'s Diary. Switzerland, June–July 1869', *Materials*, iii. 109–10.

Sun. June. 13th. From London to Folkestone.
Mon. 14th. From Folkestone to Paris, slept at an hotel near the station.
Tues. 15th. Came to Basle, Rhine muddy, slept at Trois Rois.
Wed. 16th. To Neuhausen (Swetter Hof).
Thurs. 17th. Enst—went up mid-cataract crag—dined at Schloss-Laufen—came to Zurich.
Fri. 18th. Left Zurich for Berne then to Interlaken.[1]
Sat. 19th. Left Interlaken—came to Lauterbrunnen—walked up to Murren.
Sun. 20th. Snow. Fine opening of the mountains in the evening.
Mon. 21st. Snow all day long.
Tues. 22nd. Rain nearly day. Walked out twice.
Wed. 23rd. Fine. Walked after lunch to Schmadrabach. (Delighted in the evenings, astonishing.)[2]
Thurs. 24th. Returned from Schmadrabach. After walked in the fields. Ants and arnica.
Fri. 25th. Walked to Lauterbrunnen. View of snowy mountains up through the valley. Rode to Wengern Alp Hotel.
Sat. 26th. Walked from Wengern Alp Hotel all down to Grindelwald. Adler Inn.
Sun. 27th. Rested mainly.
Mon. 28th. Walked up to the upper Grindelwald glacier: sat watching the avalanches come down like the Lauterbrunnen fall over a great rock. The Shreck Horn meets the Viescheshat one. Innumerable little clear streams rushing down to form the rivers of Europe. Bluest water. Holes in ice. Path of broken snow.
Tues. 29th. A little up the fields over Grindelwald. Drove in rain to Interlaken. Embarked and arrived at Griessbach. Delicious place. Falls lighted.
Wed. 30th. Climbed up to the crags over the waterfall. Rough walk.
Thurs. July 1st. Lovely view this morning from my bedroom window. Garden in foreground with trees and pines. Both lake and mountains. Took boat across the lake to Brienz. Carriage to Lucerne. Rich wide valleys. Came to L.
Fri. 2nd. Cloud on Pilatus. Didn't climb it. Took boat. Storm on lake.
Sat. 3rd. Wet morning. Came to Strasburg.

---

[1] At Interlaken, Locker wrote to Emily Tennyson, and Tennyson scribbled on the letter: 'All well; I wrote today from Berne. Thine ×××××' (TRC). See Locker's account of the Swiss trip in *Memoir*, ii. 69–78.

[2] From Murren, Locker wrote to Emily Tennyson on the 23rd, saying that Tennyson had written nearly every day: 'It has snowed or pour'd all and every day since we have been here and if today had not been fine I really think we should have given up this place in despair.... Mr. Tennyson gets up about 6.30, has breakfast at 7. We have luncheon at 1 and dinner at 7, and he goes to bed soon after 10 o'clock. I think he is quite well, and he has not complained in any way' (TRC).

Sun. 4th. Went to cathedral.³
Mon. 5th. Came to Nancy. Place Stanislas. Walked in La Pépinière. Front of Musée Lorraine. New church very good. Came to Rheims.
Tues. 6th. Cathedral. Front wonderfully rich. Rose window perfect.
Wed. 7th. Climbed to the top of the cathedral. Came to Paris.
Thurs. 8th. Called on Doré (about illustrated 'Idylls'). Not at home.⁴
Fri. 9th. Sainte Chapelle and Louvre.

Reminiscences of Journey.

'The last cloud clinging to the peak when all the mists have risen.' 'Snow and peak through cloud unbelievably high.' 'The top of the Jungfrau rich saffron colour at dawn, the faded moon beside it.' 'The vision over the valley of Schmadrabach.' 'Splendour of sunlit clouds passing over the shadowed peak of the Eiger.'

To FREDERICK LOCKER

MS. Armstrong Browning Library.

August 6, 1869

My dear Locker

I am rather shocked at receiving your magnificent M. Antonio and Guercino: I feel myself (as compared with you, who know so much more of these matters) unworthy to be the possessor, at least blameworthy in accepting them. Nevertheless I do accept them, and value them not only as they are beautiful, but as memorials of your friendship.¹

We have got into our new house, which is very charming. Nothing in it pleases me more than the bath, a perennial stream which falls through the house, and where I take three baths a day.²

I hope that presently when we get things a little arranged you will come and see us.

Yours ever
A. Tennyson

---

³ Locker's account in *Materials*, iii. 126, adds here: 'As we were swiftly borne along through France, we passed a pretty and very rural looking village, half hid away in a cleft on the side of a hill, the white-washed cottages clustering round the primitive grey church spire. Tennyson remarked: "That village is all the world to its inhabitants; and swindling, and lust, and cruelty are going on there, all day long." '

⁴ But they met Doré on the 10th (*Memoir*, ii. 77), and on the 12th, Frederick Pollock 'Dined with Frederick Locker in Victoria Street, to meet Tennyson, just returned from a tour in Switzerland with him' (*Personal Remembrances*, ii. 208).

¹ 'After the journey, Mr. Locker gave us a drawing by Guercino and a print by Marc Antonio of Mary standing over the dead body of Christ' (Emily Tennyson in *Memoir*, ii. 81).

² 'At the end, looking out over the porch, was the bathroom, a great feature of the design, where Tennyson used (while the pleasure was still new and strange, for there was no bathroom at Farringford) to take three baths a day, carrying the water in a large jug afterwards, when the weather was dry, to throw from one of the southern first-floor windows on to the newly sown lawn—"an innocent sight" my grandmother charmingly called the process' (Charles Tennyson, *Aldworth, Summer Home of Alfred Lord Tennyson*, The Tennyson Society, TRC, 1977, p. 8). See also Charles Tennyson, p. 382.

To GEORGE GROVE

Text. Charles L. Graves, *The Life and Letters of Sir George Grove*, p. 174.

BLACK HORSE COPSE, BLACKDOWN, August 12, [1869]

My dear Grove

I am in a house 800 feet above the sea—no roads and no post—or I would have thanked you earlier for your proposed glass of Locker and Co. to be drunk in my honour on the 8th—[a] day which I always feel inclined to pass like a Trappist without speaking—or to keep it sitting in sackcloth and ashes. . . . all health and enjoyment to you on the top of Etna.[1]

Ever yours
A. Tennyson

To WILLIAM EWART GLADSTONE

MS. British Library.

BLACK HORSE COPSE, BLACKDOWN, HASLEMERE, August 12, 1869

My dear Mr. Gladstone

I am requested by Mr. Bennett,[1] a worthy man and poet—whom indeed I believe you know—to give you my opinion of his qualifications for an Assistant Commissionership under the New Endowed Schools Act; and I have pleasure in stating that as far as I understand the matter he must be well suited for the office both by literary ability and by his long acquaintance with the wants of the middle and lower classes in the way of education, and by his incessant and arduous labours in attempting to supply them. He has furnished me with details but I am loath to occupy your time and moreover in all probability you know more of him than I do: be this as it may, I cannot but hope that he may be successful in his application.

His letter followed me here where I have been busy in getting into a new house, built on the top of a mountain 1.30 from London, where I should be charmed to see you but to which as yet there is no post, so that some time has gone by since Mr. Bennett wrote.

I trust that you have now perfectly recovered your health and strength, and that your daughter is also convalescent. Believe me,

Always yours
A. Tennyson

[1] The last sentence ('all health . . . Etna') is from the galley proofs of a few pages (TRC) of Grove's *Life and Letters*.

[1] William Cox Bennett—and no doubt a *quid pro quo*: 'In 1868 he proposed Gladstone to the liberals of their borough as their candidate, and assisted to secure his return by very strenuous exertions. He was a member of the London council of the Education League' (*DNB*).

To THE DUKE OF ARGYLL

Text. *Memoir*, ii. 81–2.

ALDWORTH, August 17, 1869

My dear Duke

I apologise in the first place for troubling you with this letter rather than Gladstone, but I wrote to him lately in behalf of another petitioner, and am loth to intrude on him again so soon: moreover I thought that, being yourself a geologist, you were more likely to be interested in the writer of the letter. However that may be, Mr. Fox is a very worthy man, and poor, and has been for many years curate at Brixton near me in the Isle of Wight, whose sole delight, always and excepting that which he takes in the discharge of his clerical duties, lies in exploring on our coast; and it would break his heart I believe to be separated from the localities of his favourite study.[1] If the government would give him this living, they would make him happy for life: for the worth and value of his contributions to geology, Owen will answer.

I will say no more, and what I have said comes I fear too late: for I have been living here in my new house near Haslemere, to which as yet there is no post, and all my letters arrive irregularly, and so his was delayed in reaching me: still, if the living be not already promised, I should be grateful if you could help him to it.

I do not know where you are at present, but I direct this to Inverary. With best remembrances to your Duchess, believe me,

Always yours
A. Tennyson

To EDWIN THOMAS BOOTH[1]

MS. Library of Congress.

BLACKDOWN, HASLEMERE, September 9, 1869[2]

Dear Sir

I have just heard from Mr. Arthur Matthison[3] of the success that has attended your production of 'Enoch Arden' at your Theatre in New York and I have received Mr. Winter's critique upon it.

I think it is hardly necessary for me to say how much gratified I am by the

---

[1] See *Memoir*, ii. 23; *Journal*, p. 321. Fox is not listed in White's *Hampshire* (1857), but 'Mrs. Fox' is mentioned in *Journal*, p. 151, in 1860. See above, p. 407 n.

[1] Edwin Thomas Booth (1833–93), tragedian and producer, and brother of John Wilkes Booth (1838–65), who shot Lincoln. Booth's reply is in TRC.

[2] The letter is written in an unidentified hand; only the signature is Tennyson's.

[3] Arthur Matthison (1826–83: Boase), English journalist, playwright, vocalist, lecturer, and actor, adapted 'Enoch Arden' for stage production, in Boston, New York (opening 21 June), and Philadelphia—in five acts, with music, songs, and a morris dance. A letter from Matthison, 24 June 1869 (TRC), suggested that Tennyson write to Booth, and enclosed a newspaper with 'the critique of Mr. Wm. Winter [1836–1917] (of the Tribune), one of the most accomplished critics here', a copy of Matthison's adaptation, a 'little book' of 37 pages (*Tennyson in Lincoln*, ii, No. 393; Wise, *Bibliography*, i. 176–7), and a programme of the performance.

account of the success which has attended your spirited efforts in bringing out this Drama.
I am, Sir,
Your obliged and faithful servant
A. Tennyson

Edwin Booth, Esq.
23rd Street
New York

To HARRY C. BURRICHTER[1]

Text. Memoir, ii. 91.

September 9, 1869

Dear Sir
You have done me the honour in associating my name with your institution, and you have my hearty good wishes for its success. Will the following Welsh motto be of any service to you? I have it in encaustic tiles on the pavement of my entrance hall: 'Y Gwir yn erbyn y byd.' (The truth against the world.) A very old British apophthegm, and I think a noble one, and which may serve your purpose either in Welsh or English. Your letter arrived when I was away from England, or would have been earlier answered. Believe me,
Yours truly
A. Tennyson

EMILY SELLWOOD AND ALFRED TENNYSON
to ALEXANDER STRAHAN

MS. Macalester College.

BLACKDOWN, October 5, 1869

My dear Sir
Mr. Tennyson is as you will easily believe very indignant at this book of Moxon's or rather Mr. Payne's.[1] Did you perceive that he has virtually printed The Window, an unpublished poem? The only one of the Poems at which Mr. Tennyson h[as] looked is indeed [? given] whole. Is it not possible to prohibit the sale of the book on this score?
The Portrait is very like an Irish beggar. Believe me,
Very truly yours
Emily Tennyson

---

[1] Secretary of the Tennyson Literary Association in Philadelphia—named only in *The Critic*, xxii (July–Dec. 1892), 289 (reprinted from the Philadelphia *Ledger*), though the letter appeared also in *Materials*, iii. 139; *Notes and Queries*, 30 October 1869; *Daily News*, 22 October 1869; and Henry J. Jennings, *Lord Tennyson, A Biographical Study*, p. 197.

[1] Brightwell's *Concordance to the Entire Works of Alfred Tennyson* (Moxon, 1869; *Tennyson in Lincoln*, ii, No. 4390). The frontispiece is 'Facsimiled from a Photograph by W. Jeffrey Esq. of Gt. Russell St.'. See *Journal*, pp. 167, 174; Wheatcroft's *Tennyson Album*, p. 83; and Richard Ormond, *Early Victorian Portraits*, i. 455. See also next letter.

Pray ask Mr. Arnold White whether the book as containing the *whole of certain unpublished poems* of mine viz. The Window cannot be stopt. The allusion—obscure enough in the preface—to the date alludes doubtless to some misrepresen[tation] of Payne's.

A question arises whether it would be worth while to state publicly that the Book is published altogether without my sanction. In fact I think it makes me ridiculous—if it be not understood that it is Moxon and Co.'s doing and that I am thoroughly against it.

Yours very truly
A. Tennyson

To DANIEL BARRON BRIGHTWELL[1]

MS. British Library.

BLACKDOWN, HASLEMERE, October 12, 1869

Sir

Your letter has just reached me. I thank you for the kindness of your expressions and for your offer of the Concordance; it has been sent to me.

I may tell you that this book is published altogether without my sanction or knowledge. I first heard of it and that lately from Mr. Strahan.

The obscure passage in your preface[2] (if the words be your own and not dictated by another) would seem to imply that I had given my consent to the publication of such a work: something else perhaps they imply—I know not what.

But you have done—and, I would fain hope, also at the dictation of another—a thing thoroughly illegal. You have made a concordance of certain little songs of mine privately printed—and have made it in such a manner that anyone with 20 minutes['] labour can put them together.[3]

If I did not see in this act rather my ex-publisher than yourself I should not now have been answering your letter.

As to the fac-simile or fac-dissimile—the caricature at the beginning of your book, it is equally disgraceful to publisher and engraver, and will I am afraid annoy my good honest friend Jeffrey[4] seeing it is as like me as I am to—Ancient Pistol. Believe me, Sir,

Yours faithfully
A. Tennyson

[1] Daniel Barron Brightwell (1834–99), remains as obscure as even Tennyson could have wished. The *British Library Catalogue of Printed Books* lists one other title by him, '*Forms of Latin Parsing* [A card]', 1861.

[2] 'A plan of the work was first submitted to Messrs. Moxon in the spring of 1868, and received from them the most prompt and courteous consideration. A specimen which had been prepared met with their approval, and I was requested by them to undertake the completion of the scheme. This date, which under ordinary circumstances would have been a matter of trivial importance, may possibly, in the light of more recent events, possess a certain interest.'

[3] And someone did—with Brightwell's collusion (see next letter).

[4] William Jeffrey, photographer, at 114 Great Russell St. (*P.O. London Directory*).

FREDERICK LOCKER to ALFRED TENNYSON

MS. Yale.

October 17, 1869

My dear Tennyson

When I got home last night I found a parcel from Wilson[1] containing your copy of the 'Loves of the Wrens,' and the one I told him to buy. It consists of 16 pages, just the size of the enclosed, it is rather ill printed, on Common White Paper, and appears to be word for word like Sir I. Guest's. Your name does not appear. Wilson gave 30/ for it. The man said it was given him, and if he (Wilson) did not buy it then and there, he could not get it at all. He made rather a mystery of it. I learnt all this from Wilson to whom I went this morning, and I told him that I should write and tell you all, and that on Monday (tomorrow) morning I should take the book to Mr. Tennyson's lawyer, and he would decide what course should be pursued—[*illegible*] of course, I should suppose he would at once insist on knowing where the book came from, and he (Wilson) said if the lawyer wrote he should be happy to help him in every way in his power, but he would rather do it through the lawyer than through me. I will go to Mr. [Arnold] White tomorrow morning and tell him all I am telling you.

Wilson does not think it is Payne's doing, as he says half a dozen could not have been so sold without its coming to your ears. There is no printer's name on the tract, and nothing in fact whereby to trace it. I will write tomorrow and tell you what A. W. says. So you see I did not bring you up to town with a mare's nest!

It looks very like Hotten, but I hardly think he would venture, where did he get it, unless he got it from the Concordance.[2] If I were you I would write a line to Sir I. Guest and to Millais and Sullivan. I think it is as well that they should now be published. How delightful it would be if we could trace them to Ancient Pistol.

I hope you got home all right—we are very sad without you, and hope you have forgotten the steak.

---

[1] Probably Effingham Wilson's son, William Wilson ('who was with his father for twenty-five years, [and] still continues the business under the old name'—*The Bookseller*, 1 July 1868, pp. 459–60), publisher and stationer, at 11 Royal Exchange (*City of London Directory*, 1884).

[2] 'For cool impudence Mr. Herne Shepherd's confession of the means he adopted in order to obtain the text of the (then unpublished) *Window* will take a lot of beating. A copy of the private folio edition, printed at Canford Manor, had been entrusted to Mr. Barron Brightwell . . . upon his giving an undertaking not to supply to anyone a transcript of the Verses. The references to the lines given in the *Concordance* "I was able,' writes Mr. Shepherd, "with some labour and effort to piece together, and with the compiler's aid, who supplied the *lacunae* (though he had promised not to give anyone a copy), I was able to secure what was substantially the complete text of the twelve songs, as privately printed at Canford Manor, more than a year before the appearance of the published edition. I printed a few copies privately, as a little pamphlet of sixteen pages, uniform in size with Moxon's editions of the poet's other works, and in December, 1870, I wrote two anticipatory notices which appeared in *The Echo*, some days or weeks before the publication of the volume containing Mr. Arthur Sullivan's music, much to the indignation of the publisher, the printers, and I suppose of the Author"' (quoted in T. J. Wise's *Bibliography*, iii. 8, from Richard Herne Shepherd's *Bibliography of Tennyson* (1895), pp. 45–6.

My hands are so cold that I can hardly write. I would send you the pamphlet but I think it important that A. W. should see it.

I left a brown sock in your room, so guard the one you have and we will bring them together again. My best to Mrs. Tennyson

Yours ever
F. Locker

Perhaps you had better do nothing till you hear what A. W. says.

To MARGARET OLIPHANT OLIPHANT[1]

MS. University of California at Los Angeles.

BLACKDOWN, HASLEMERE, October 18, 1869

Madam

I forwarded your request to Mr. Strahan because to him properly belongs the right over my published poems. What he says of my objection to having any part of In Memoriam published to music is perfectly correct. Those portions which you have seen so published have been granted to the solicitations of friends not to be refused, as this is now granted to Mr. Carlyle's and would, I have no doubt, have been granted to your own, had I the privilege of your friendship.

Pardon my seeming discourtesy and believe me,

Your faithful servant
A. Tennyson

To EMILY SELLWOOD TENNYSON

MS. Tennyson Research Centre.

Thursday, [11 November 1869][1]

Dearest

Nothing to tell except that I called on the Lockers who were out yesterday —but L. called here this morning. I saw too the new Holborn viaduct[2]— most of the granite pillars are already cracked from false pitching and because the weight falls unequally from above: some [?] beast, some clerk of

---

[1] Margaret Oliphant Oliphant (1828–97: *DNB*), Scottish novelist and historical writer, friend of the Carlyles, and author of a life of their friend Edward Irving. Carlyle had introduced her to the Tennysons in a letter on 9 October: 'Mrs. Oliphant, whose Note this accompanies, is an old and esteemed Friend in this house; distinguished in literature (*Life of Edwd Irving*, etc.) and, what is best of all, a highly amiable, rational, and worthy Lady. Be pleased to answer her needful little Inquiry, and oblige withal | Yrs ever truly | T. Carlyle' (Sanders, p. 217; *Memoir*, ii. 237). For the setting by J. Frederick Bridge (*DNB*), Mrs. Oliphant's friend (for whom she was interceding), organist at Holy Trinity Church, Windsor, of 'The time draws near the birth of Christ', see Gooch and Thatcher, p. 549.

[1] Postmark.

[2] The Queen had come to London from Windsor on 6 November for the opening of Blackfriars Bridge and the Holborn Viaduct (*Annual Register*, pp. 121–7). The cracks were reported in *The Times*, 12 November, p. 7.

the works, hadn't seen to it. I have written to Hallam to learn the name of the play.

Thine
× × × × × A.

To ALEXANDER STRAHAN

MS. Abel Berland.

December 2, 1869

My dear Sir
Let Mr. Eardley (the Bearer) have any or all my books which he asks for.
A. Tennyson

A. Strahan Esq.

To SMITH, PAYNE, SMITH[1]

MS. University of Virginia.
FARRINGFORD, FRESHWATER, ISLE OF WIGHT, December 11, 1869

Gentlemen
Your letter is a perfect mystery to me. I have never been 'interested (as you say you have reason to believe) in the receipt of subscriptions for the creation of a Shakespeare monument' nor have I ever withdrawn small sums, which you say were paid into your house in 1864 toward such a subscription; nor can I consent to take charge of 'the small amount further' which you tell me you have received. I have the honour to be, Gentlemen,
Your obedient Servant
A. Tennyson

To FREDERICK JAMES FURNIVALL

MS. Huntington Library.
FARRINGFORD, FRESHWATER, ISLE OF WIGHT, [14 December 1869][1]

My dear Sir
Thanks for your Brunne.[2] I am afraid that Arthur is past help for he has not only past away with his 'grievous wound'[3] but has to suffer another grievous wound from the misconceptions of the Press, who will never see what he means: but Arthur in these days is mystic or nothing.
Yours very truly
A. Tennyson

---

[1] Smith, Payne, Smith, bankers, 1 Lombard St, EC (*P.O. London Directory*).

[1] Postmark.
[2] Furnivall's edition of Robert of Brunne's *Handlynge Synne* was inscribed to Tennyson on 11 January 1862 (*Tennyson in Lincoln*, i, No. 1499).
[3] 'The Passing of Arthur', l. 450, in *The Holy Grail and Other Poems*, just published.

14 *December* 1869

I have ordered a copy to be sent you.

F. J. Furnivall
3 St. George's Square
Primrose Hill, London, N. W.

To DRUMMOND RAWNSLEY

MS. Harvard.

FARRINGFORD, FRESHWATER, ISLE OF WIGHT, [14 December 1869][1]

My dear Drummond

I read the beginning of your friend's volume[2] at Blackdown and quite agree with his views as to intellect and thumb-worship. I don't think I should close so fully in what follows—I can't tell: in our 'flitting' the book got locked up among the rest and I shall not see it again till March or April.

In return for your gift I send you my new volume. Arthur is mystic and no mere British Prince as I dare say you will find out.

Yours affectionately
A. Tennyson

Pray apologize for me to Catherine. I did not answer her but did what she wished, writing my thanks for Dr. L. Beale.[3]

To WILLIAM COX BENNETT

MS. Abel Berland.

FARRINGFORD, December 22, 1869

My dear Sir

Thank you for the music you make in my behalf and the criticisms which you have sent me: it isn't every bird who sings so prettily in an Author's ear.[1]

Yours very truly
A. Tennyson

To GERALD MASSEY

MS. Cornell University.

January 3, 1870

Dear Mr. Massey

I thank you for your new Poems[1] and I send an inscribed copy of The Holy

---

[1] Postmark.   [2] Unidentified.

[3] Lionel Smith Beale (1828–1906: *DNB*), physician, microscopist, and philosopher; author of *Life Theories. Their Influence upon Religious Thought* (1870–1), *The Mystery of Life* (1871: *Tennyson in Lincoln*, i, No. 503), and *Our Morality* (1887).

[1] Two poems by Bennett addressed to Tennyson are inserted in a volume inscribed to him in 1877: *Tennyson in Lincoln*, i, No. 509.

[1] *A Tale of Eternity and Other Poems* (1870).

Grail according to your desire. I have been waiting for it or I should have answered your note before.

I am by no means sure of being at home on the 26th of February but if you will kindly give me an opportunity of communicating with you immediately before I will let you know whether I am or not.

As to telling you what I think of your book, I am sorry that I cannot promise to do much of that, having, as I think you know, been obliged to decline all or nearly all criticism.

My wife begs to thank you for your inquiries. Believe me,
Faithfully yours
A. Tennyson

To JAMES THOMAS KNOWLES

MS. Yale.

FARRINGFORD, FRESHWATER, ISLE OF WIGHT, January 11, 1870

My dear Knowles

Is not Strahan bound to pay over to me £4300 on the first of January? I can't make out that he has and we are at our wit's end how to meet the Christmas bills for furnishing the new house—such bills some of them—Maples for instance charging £150 for putting up blinds.[1]

I have written somewhat sharply to Strahan. I am so weary of publishers. Routledge has not paid either.

We had very bad accounts of the water coming into Blackdown house from Kingshot[2] and thereupon I sent Heard over who confirmed them. I trust you will have made all right. Heard thought that a stopcock should be put in the kitchen basement to prevent the water rising into the house when we are away, and the pipes (when we are away) bursting in the frost as it appears some have. Will you give orders for such a cock if it seem right to you?

Your letter to the Spectator is the best and indeed might be called the only true critique on the Idylls.[3] It is very succinctly and clearly written and I like it so much that I sent it by the Dean of Westminster, who was here the other day to the Queen along with the Idylls.

Have you heard of Payne's last American dodge?[4]

Yours ever
A. Tennyson

---

[1] John Maple and Co., upholsterers, Tottenham Court Road (then as now).

[2] Unidentified.

[3] In anticipation of the *Holy Grail* volume (1870, issued 10 December 1869), Tennyson, during the summer of 1869, had given the MSS of 'Pelleas and Ettarre' and 'The Coming of Arthur' to Knowles to make notes towards an article, which took the form of a letter: 'Tennyson's Arthurian Poem', *Spectator*, 1 January 1870, pp. 15–17. See Metcalf, *Knowles*, pp. 232 n., 256–7.

[4] Not absolutely clear, but in a 1952 catalogue cutting, Tennyson, in a letter, expresses regret at '*the dishonourable conduct* of Harper and Co. with regard to my work'. See below, p. 556.

If you see Strahan *row* him! I see that heavy Smith has had a Quarterly 'Holy Grail'—nice mess he'll make of it![5]

To JAMES SPEDDING

MS. Tennyson Research Centre.

ISLE OF WIGHT, January 19, 1870

My dear James

Send me the box—please—not without your new volume[1]—hither. I shall be grateful for both. I am glad that you find anything to approve of in the Holy Grail. I don't think I have yet finished the Arthurian legends, otherwise I might consider your Job-theme. Strange that I quite forget our conversation thereupon

Where is Westbourne Terrace? if I had ever clearly made out I should assuredly have called. I have often when in town past by the old 60,[2] the vedovo sito[3] with a groan, and thinking of you as no longer the comeatable, runupableto, smokeable with J. S. of old but as a family man, far in the west, sitting cigarless among many nieces, clean and forlorn, but I hope to see you in Somewhere in '70 for I have taken chambers in Victoria Street for three years,[4] though they are not yet furnished.

Where is the difficulty of that line in the Flower?[5] it is rather rough certainly, but had you followed the clue of 'little flower' in the preceding line you would not have stumbled over this, which is accentual anapaest—

> What you are—root and all—

rough, doubtless. Believe me,

Yours ever
A. Tennyson

To COTSFORD BURDON[1]

MS. Joanna Richardson.

FARRINGFORD, FRESHWATER, ISLE OF WIGHT, January 28, 1870

My dear Sir

Many thanks for your interest in my affairs and your proffered hospitality. I will write to you definitively before the meeting.

---

[5] Reviewed in the *Quarterly* (cxxviii [Jan. 1870], 1–17), not by Goldwin Smith but by J. R. Mozley (1840–1931: *DNB*), Professor of Mathematics, Owens College, Manchester (*Wellesley Index*).

[1] *The Letters and the Life of Francis Bacon*, vol. 5 (1869) (vol. 12 of *Works*).
[2] Lincoln's Inn Fields.   [3] 'Widowed region', *Purgatorio*, i. 26.
[4] Albert Mansions—furnished for him by Lady Charlotte Locker (*Journal*, p. 304).
[5] 'Flower in the crannied wall' (Ricks, p. 1193).

[1] Cotsford Burdon (b. 1815), of Parkhurst House, Haslemere, equity draftsman and conveyancer and an Aldworth neighbour; see *Journal*, pp. 296, 298 (etc.); *Tennyson at Aldworth*, ed. Earl A. Knies, p. 41 n.; Foster; *Men-at-the Bar*; *Landed Gentry*; and below, p. 541.

Meantime with mine and my wife's best remembrances to Mrs. Burdon, believe me,

Yours very truly
A. Tennyson

To JAMES THOMAS FIELDS

MS. Harvard.

[30 January 1870]

Dear Mr. Fields

I suppose the foregoing will answer the purpose. Many thanks. I am glad that you enjoyed your visit.

There is only one drawback to the pleasure I find in entertaining my kinsmen from over the water—and *there* you are not guilty, as has been proven.

Ever yours
A. Tennyson

To [? MR. ALBERY][1]

MS. University of Virginia.

FARRINGFORD, FRESHWATER, ISLE OF WIGHT, February 1, 1870

My dear Sir

The accompanying note I think need not be shown to Mr. Tallant [?][2] except he will agree to the terms. If he *then* want confirmation of my proposal given under my own hand let him see it.

Mr. Simmons[3] in a letter to my wife says (she wrote to him not being quite sure as to what we had already agreed upon) 'I will attend the meeting on your part if Mr. Burdon thinks it well for me to do so.' She had told him that you had kindly promised to act for us.

Yours very truly
A. Tennyson

To LEWIS FYTCHE

MS. Tennyson Research Centre.

FARRINGFORD, FRESHWATER, ISLE OF WIGHT, February 14, 1870

My dear Lewis

I shall be glad to see you and your wife and Lilly May at Blackdown whenever we are there and you like to come. It is too cold there in the winter for us to stay—so we come to Farringford till the warmer days: but it can

---

[1] Unidentified, but see below, p. 542 and n.

[2] Unidentified (and possibly Talbot, also unidentified).

[3] James Simmons, Haslemere magistrate, friend and neighbour of Mrs Gilchrist (see above, pp. 439, 446 n.). The 'meeting' was about an access road to Aldworth. See above, p. 527 and below, p. 545.

scarce be colder I think anywhere than here at present where the ground is hardbaked with frost and the bitter east [wind] has been blowing for a week.

Lionel left us a few days ago for Eton but Hallam is not yet gone back to Marlborough. I am glad to hear that you are all well. With my wife's best regards, I am dear Lewis,

Your affectionate cousin
A. Tennyson

I find that inadvertently I have written on two sheets.

To WILLIAM KIRBY

Text. Lorne Pierce, *Alfred, Lord Tennyson and William Kirby*, p. 40.

FARRINGFORD, FRESHWATER, ISLE OF WIGHT, February 21, 1870

Sir

I thank you for your Poem[1] and be assured that as a son of the same Empire as yourself I feel a personal pride and delight in the great deeds it records and that with all earnestness I re-echo your last words and say

'one for evermore!'

I have the honour to be

Your very obedient servant
A. Tennyson

To [? Cotsford Burdon][1]

MS. University of California at Berkeley.[2]

FARRINGFORD, February 26, 1870

My dear Sir

Will you kindly send this to Mr. Carter[3] or not as you judge it right. We trust that you have both borne the fierce cold well. With very kind remembrances believe me,

Very truly yours
A. Tennyson

Is the notice legal coming as late as it does? I shall get Mr. Albery to appear for me if it be allowable supposing you answer that I ought to appeal.

---

[1] *The U. E.: A Tale of Upper Canada*, a 'long poem', printed and bound by Kirby himself, ending with 'England's proud Empire, one for evermore' (Pierce, p. 40 n.).

[1] See above, p. 540.
[2] All but the signature is in Emily Tennyson's hand.
[3] Carter was presumably Lord Egmont's agent, Albery the Tennysons'. See *The Letters of Emily Tennyson*, pp. 261–2.

WILLIAM ISBISTER to ALFRED TENNYSON (extract)

MS. Yale.

February 28, 1870

My dear Sir

I had purposed coming to you tonight myself, to explain matters, but I find it will be quite impossible as I must see the Chairman of the Board of Inland Revenue tomorrow morning anent this Glasgow smuggling.[1] Mr. Strahan has been in Glasgow since Thursday last and we have succeeded in buying copies of the American Editions at four different shops. We wanted the Board of Customs to take the matter up but they refuse and the Board of Inland Revenue is not much better as you will see from a letter of Mr. Strahan's I enclose.[2] . . .

EMILY TENNYSON to CHARLES LUTWIDGE DODGSON

MS. Yale.

[c. 5 March 1870]

Dear Sir

It is useless troubling Mr. Tennyson with a request which will only revive the annoyance he has already had on the subject and add to it.

No doubt 'The Window' is circulated by means of the same unscrupulous person whose breach of confidence placed 'The Lover's Tale' in your hands.[1]

---

[1] 'The flow of pirated volumes from America cut into Tennyson's income. In particular, in Scotland certain Glasgow booksellers were dealing briskly in American Tennyson editions. Early in 1870 the White firm decided to start civil proceedings to stop them. An injunction was obtained in the Edinburgh County session; and then when "one of them (Forrester) continued this trade, Tennyson and Strahan sued him and recovered £500 damages"' (Hagen, p. 131). See also Henry Jennings, *Lord Tennyson*, pp. 194–5. For Isbister, see Hagen, p. 134.

[2] Strahan's letter of 26 February (Yale), complaining of 'red-tape roundabout circumlocution', said 'we can get on without either of the Boards [Customs and Excise] but our purpose would be so much better served were we able to announce that the seizure was made by the Board of Customs. . . . You should enter all Tennyson's books at Stationer's Hall in our name on Monday morning, as this must be done before we proceed a step. Of course we will raise a civil action against the Forresters when the Custom House business is done, for injuries to our property. We must get £200 or £300 from them. The Fiscal recommends this.'

---

[1] Dodgson wrote on 3 March: 'There is a certain unpublished poem of yours called "The Window" which it seems was printed for private circulation only. However it has been transcribed, and is probably in many hands in the form of MS. A friend, who had a MS copy given to him, has in his turn presented me with one. I have not even read it yet, and shall do so with much greater pleasure when I know that you do not object to my possessing it. What I plead for is first, that you will make me comfortable in possessing this copy by giving your consent to my preserving it—secondly, the further permission to *show* it to my friends. I can hardly go so far as to ask for leave to give away copies of it to friends, though I should esteem such a permission as a great favour.

'Some while ago, as you may remember, I had a copy lent me of your "Lover's Life", and a young lady, a cousin of mine, took a MS copy of it. I wrote to you about it, and in accordance with your wish prevailed on her (very reluctantly, I need hardly say) to destroy the MS. I am not aware of any other copies of *that* poem in circulation—but *this* seems to me a different case. MS copies of "The Window" are already in circulation, and this fact is unaffected by *my* possessing, or not possessing, a copy for my own enjoyment. Hoping you will kindly say you do

It would be well that whatever may be done by such people a gentleman should understand that when an author does not give his works to the public he has his own reasons for it.

Yours truly
Emily Tennyson

To JOHN WHITE[1]

Text. Memoir, ii. 97.

FARRINGFORD, March 8, 1870

Dear Sir

Your present has rather amazed me, though not unpleasantly: so I accept it with thanks, and I will sit by the 'blue light' gratefully, and hope for you that *your* light may be no longer 'low,' and if you ever come my way I shall be glad to see you.

Yours faithfully
A. Tennyson

To EMILY SELLWOOD TENNYSON

MS. Tennyson Research Centre.

[LONDON] [21 March 1870]

Dearest

I can't get waited on here which is a nuisance—ring the bell 20 times and nobody comes. Knowles recommends me to hire a call-boy to sit at the top of the stairs and run up and down at 1.6 a week. Perhaps I shall.[1] I have seen nobody yet but Palgrave, Locker and Woolner. As for Dodgson's letter I shall take my time to answer it.[2]

Thine
A.

---

not object to my—first reading—and secondly preserving the MS that has been given to me, and with kind remembrances to Mrs. Tennyson and your sons' (*The Letters of Lewis Carroll*, ed. Cohen, i. 150–2). To Emily Tennyson's reproof, Dodgson replied firmly. Tennyson answered with equal *hauteur* (see below), though of this letter only a fragment has turned up, and Dodgson riposted wittily (*Letters*, i. 151–3). See also Appendix D.

[1] John White was a shipbuilder, Medina Docks, West Cowes (White's *Hampshire*). Tennyson 'received from a stranger, Mr. John White of Cowes, a melancholy letter and a present of a cartload of wood—old oak from one of the broken up men-of-war' (*Memoir*, ii. 97).

[1] 'Pray get a call boy', she wrote next day. 'I cannot bear to think of thee all alone with no one to supply thy very few and simple wants' (*Letters of Emily Tennyson*, p. 252). She wrote every day, or nearly so, sending him fresh butter, eggs, biscuits, sheets, table cloths, plates, knives, and a hamper of wines and seltzer water, not prepaid, 'thinking they would be safer unpaid' (16 March, TRC). 'I fear thy visit to Blackdown was a very wretched one from what Heard says. (I gave orders that I hoped would have insured thy comfort.)' (19 March, TRC).

[2] See above, p. 543. Only a fragment of Tennyson's letter survives: 'no answer to that request reached her, whereupon I was naturally disgusted and believed that whether I liked it or not, you were resolved' (Helmut Gernsheim, 'Photographs of Tennyson', *TLS*, 21 July 1950, p. 460).

To EMILY SELLWOOD TENNYSON

MS. Tennyson Research Centre.

[LONDON,] Wednesday, [23 March 1870]

Dearest

I met Simeon just now and he told me that he has spoken to Walpole, who was much interested in the subject of the Blackdown road and has promised to do all he can with Lord Egmont: he (S) is going to call here tomorrow and hear all about it from me.[1]

I haven't quite shaken off my cold yet and not been out to dinner anywhere but I am going today to Woolner's.

Thine × × × ×

[A. T.]

Don't expect to hear everyday. I am glad the boys are working. Things appear to be telling heavily against Payne. Routledge is particularly fiery—and no wonder.

To EMILY SELLWOOD TENNYSON

MS. Tennyson Research Centre.

[LONDON,] [28 March 1870]

Dearest

The dinner went off very well though two pretty glasses got broken by the clumsiness of a waiter.[1] Carlyle could not see us at night being poorly but I walked with him in the morning instead.[2]

Rejlander is near me and I have been photographed in 3 or 4 different poses by him for Routledge's illustrated Edition.

---

[1] See above, p. 541. Spencer Horatio Walpole (1806–98: *DNB*), MP and Derby's Home Secretary in 1852, 1858–9, and 1866–7, was a grandson of the 2nd Earl of Egmont and a cousin of George James Perceval, the 6th Earl (see above, p. 527).

[1] Of the dinner Emily Tennyson wrote on 25 March (TRC): 'I have been thinking if there is anything I could send thee to help the dinner. And I have come to the conclusion that certainly at some restaurateur's or the other thou canst do better than could be done by cooking things here to have them re-cooked there.' And she wrote again on 29 March (TRC): 'Are the pretty glasses those called "Venetian" in the bills. I am sorry thou hast found [?] broken.' Next day Tennyson dined with Houghton, who had written to his aunts on 27 March: 'I have the honour of entertaining Tennyson at dinner to-morrow. He insists on dining at 7, and on having some old port. I have brought some from Fryston . . .' (Reid, *Life . . . of Richard Monckton Milnes*, ii. 221).

[2] 'I had a *second* night of insomnia, and a weary walk yesterday seeking out Alfred Tennyson's London Lodgings,—upon which I felt bound to "leave a card"; he having called here last Sunday on very good-natured terms, and borne me ditto company on my walk. Good-natured, almost kind; but rather dull to me! He looks healthy yet, and rather hopeful; a stout man of 60,—with only one deep wrinkle, *crow* wrinkle, just under the cheek bones.—I was lucky enough (for my then mood, lucky) to find nobody; nothing required but a *card*' (Carlyle to his brother John, 2 April, in Sanders, p. 218).

11 *April* 1870

I am grieved for the Franklins and Hallam did well to write.[3]

Thine x x x x
[A.]

My cold doesn't go, though it gets no worse.

To JANE OCTAVIA BROOKFIELD

MS. Morgan Library.

FARRINGFORD, FRESHWATER, ISLE OF WIGHT, April 11, 1870

My dear Jane

I beg your pardon for not answering immediately. When I got home there was half-a-yard's depth of letters and yours got confounded in the heap.

However Strahan has been written to, and I can only trust that he will do something for you.[1] Believe me,

Yours affectionately
A. Tennyson

We hope you will come to see us when we get to Blackdown.

To JAMES THOMAS KNOWLES

MS. Boston Public Library.

April 15, 1870

My dear Knowles

I got to the station a full ¼ hour before the time, but the whole place was 'fourmillante'. I never saw such confusion before at any terminus here or abroad. I stood and bawled ineffectually for porters till at last I took my portmanteau in hand and flung it into the truck of one of them, and told him to label [it] Lymington which he promised to do: then I rushed to the ticket office where I waited among the multitudes and only got my ticket after the time was up: ran out again, the whole platform seething and buzzing, could not find my luggage: at the very last saw it being wheeled trainward, at the bottom of a heap of boxes, asked whether it was labelled Lymington, bewildered porter knew nothing about it—train began to move. I caught hold of an open door, and was pulled in by two passengers. When I came to Brockenhurst no luggage for me: guard intimated that he had noticed just such a portmanteau as the one I described labelled Southampton Junction, accordingly I telegraphed up the line: then took an open boat and steered under the moon (previously warning my two boatmen that I couldn't see an inch before my nose) to Yarmouth—thence took a fly and home about 10. And this morning sent a cart from Farringford to meet the earliest boat and

---

[3] The son of Col. (later, Major-General and CB) Charles Trigance Franklin (1822–95), Royal Artillery, in the Isle of Wight and then in India, died at Marlborough. See *Letters of Emily Tennyson*, p. 254, *Journal*, p. 305, and Walford's *County Families* (1904).

[1] Probably for the novel, *Influence*, published by Chapman and Hall in 1871, by her daughter-in-law, Olive (Mrs. Arthur Brookfield). See *Tennyson in Lincoln*, i, No. 3419.

recovered my luggage at last. You see not only the Easter holydaymakers made the train double its ordinary length but the Prince and Princess of Wales with all their footmen and family came along with us and made confusion worse confounded.[1]

But the worst of all this is that I had, or believe I had, in the breast pocket of my coat an open letter to my wife which I had written that morning, when I was intending not to go home till Saturday: it was not signed by me but was directed to her, and described our little party, and expresst my hope that Hopwood[2] would so tackle Payne that I should not be subpoenaed. Now when I got into the train this letter was gone; and my fear is that in pulling out my purse which was in the same pocket as the letter it dropt to the ground among the feet of the crowd and will appear in The Queen's M.[3] or some other place a few day's hence.

It is just possible that I lost it in the Victoria-Station Restaurant where I took a plate of soup. I forget the names of the restaurateurs something like ⟨Poole⟩ Spiers and Ford[4] I think—two monosyllables. Would you mind asking there whether a letter was found? Another faint hope I have that I *may* have burnt it before starting. Another faint hope that I may have thrown it into one of the top drawers of that chest of ditto in my bedroom.

My wife will write about the papers for the rooms.

I enclose a letter from Canada, thinking that if no names were mentioned part of it might be published in the Spectator and do some good.[5]

Ever yours
A. Tennyson

To JAMES THOMAS KNOWLES

MS. New York Public Library.

FARRINGFORD, FRESHWATER, ISLE OF WIGHT, [? *c.* 18 April 1870]

My dear Knowles

I see no harm in your sending the Canadian letter to the Spectator under the conditions you mention and not giving the name of the writer—for I have not his leave.

Of course in due time I should like to see the Ethics of Spinoza. Likewise get for me the Epic of Arthur in the Edinburgh.[1] I saw it named in the advertisement, and thought that very likely it was semi-abuse. But if [it] goes

---

[1] *Paradise Lost*, ii. 996.

[2] *Sic*, but probably a slip for John Hopgood (d. 1902), Knowles's (also Macmillan's and later Henry James's) solicitor (Metcalf, *Knowles*, p. 65 n.).

[3] *The Queen's Messenger; a Weekly Gazette of Politics and Literature* (which began and ended in 1869).

[4] Spiers and Pond.

[5] From William Kirby, printed in the *Spectator*, 6 May 1870, and included in Lorne Pierce, *Alfred, Lord Tennyson and William Kirby*, pp. 41–3: Canadian separation would mean 'immediate annexation to the United States, and the transfer of the maritime supremacy of the world from England to her most implacable enemy and rival'.

---

[1] *Edinburgh Review*, cxxxi (Apr. 1870), 502–39, by Margaret Oliphant (*Wellesley Index*). See Tennyson's grudging letter above, p. 536 and n.

on the other tack pray send it—and also my key which locks up the cellar etc. I suppose so careful a man as yourself didn't leave it in the lock. My cold is as bad as ever it was.

Ever yours
A. Tennyson

Heard who has just come back from Black Down reports very favourably of my floor and says he felt when pacing it as if he were walking on solid earth rather than on boards.

To WILLIAM KIRBY

Text. Lorne Pierce, *Alfred, Lord Tennyson and William Kirby*, p. 41.

April 28, 1870

Sir

Will you forgive me for having requested the Editor of the Spectator to insert portions of your letter in his paper without of course giving your name. The subject is one which I have at heart as much as yourself I think—and it seemed to me that your words might do good.

Believe me with full sympathy

Yours
A. Tennyson

To ELLEN (TENNYSON D'EYNCOURT) BUNBURY

MS. Walter Tennyson D'Eyncourt.

FARRINGFORD, FRESHWATER, ISLE OF WIGHT, May 2, 1870

My dear Ellen

You have sent me sad, sudden, strange news—strange indeed to me who thought the handwriting on the envelope was *hers*, or might be hers, for there was a likeness—and I opened it and found she was gone![1] I do not know how Lord Boyne bears it: I fear he suffers dreadfully; nor do I know whether I ought to write to him in his first grief—whether I should do harm or good: yet as it might seem unkind or neglectful if I did not write, I send a little note with such word of comfort as I could give—and this you may read to him or not as it seems best to you, and your husband.

Pray give mine and my wife's kindest regards to Gustavus and let us know presently how Lord Boyne goes on. Believe me, dear Ellen,

Your affectionate Cousin
A. Tennyson

[1] The death of the Viscountess Boyne (Emma Russell) on 29 April.

To WALTER JONES[1]

Text. Memoir, ii. 98–9.

June, 1870

Sir

First let me thank the Committee and yourself for the honour you have desired to confer upon me, which, however, I feel obliged to decline accepting; for I am neither a diner out, nor a speaker after dinner, nor could without violence to the truth be called a man of business. I should be but a *roi faineant*, which I don't wish to be—the square man in the round hole—, but, if you wish for the square man in the square hole, I am sure Lord Houghton would be proud to serve your cause as President.[2]

At the same time, with the permission of your committee, I should be happy to be one of your Vice-Presidents by the side of my friend Longfellow. I have the honour to be, Sir,

Your obedient servant
A. Tennyson

To LORD HOUGHTON (RICHARD MONCKTON MILNES)

MS. Trinity College.

June 10, 1870

My dear Houghton

I want to talk with you on a little matter tomorrow at 5 o'clock: I told Locker to write to you; and I hope you have the letter.[1]

Ever yours
A. Tennyson

---

[1] Presumably Secretary of the Newsvendors' Benevolent and Provident Institution, at whose annual dinner on 5 April Dickens had presided (*The Times*, 6 April, p. 12).

[2] Houghton was the once and future (first and continuing) president of the Newspaper Press Fund, 'to provide for the working journalists . . . in seasons of distress or of bereavement' (T. Wemyss Reid, *Life of Lord Houghton*, ii. 465).

---

[1] The date could be 16 but is probably 10, and the letter must refer to the death of Dickens on 9 June. Locker 'was staying with Tennyson at Aldworth, and heard of Dickens's sudden death' (*My Confidences*, p. 327), and Dean Stanley wrote to Houghton 'to find out whether the public demand for an Abbey burial was fervent enough to override the novelist's own directions for a simple burial in Kent. *The Times* article which called for Dickens's funeral in the Abbey was inspired and perhaps written by Lord Houghton' (James Pope-Hennessy, *Monckton Milnes, The Flight of Youth*, p. 216; see also Reid's *Life*, ii. 229–30). Alternatively, Tennyson could have been preparing for his nomination of Houghton for membership in the Metaphysical Society; Houghton was proposed on 13 December but not elected (Allan Willard Brown, *The Metaphysical Society*, p. 28 n.).

To EMILY SELLWOOD TENNYSON

MS. Tennyson Research Centre.

20 WELBECK STREET, June 18, 1870, 2 o'clock

Dearest

I have just been buying some pictures for the dining room from Woolner: so if the great mirror come don't put it up there.

Thine
× × × × [A. T.]

To THOMAS WOOLNER

MS. Wellesley.

ALDWORTH, BLACKDOWN, HASLEMERE [for LONDON], June 18, 1870

My dear Woolner

I feel almost certain that I told somebody yesterday that I should be at home to him on Sunday.[1] So—I have decided not to move out of town.

Ever yours
A. Tennyson

To EMILY SELLWOOD TENNYSON

MS. Tennyson Research Centre.

[21 June 1870]

Dearest

I shall be down in time for lunch tomorrow *if possible*—if not in time for dinner.

Thine × × × ×
[A.]

---

[1] Unidentified. On Friday, 17 June, he was at home to others: 'Called by invitation to see Tennyson, staying just at present with his architect Knowles at 16, Albert Buildings, Westminster. He looks well and brisk, hardly older than when I saw him last—I daresay four or five years ago. His younger son has a *slight* tendency to verse-writing. He expressed to me admiration of some of Gabriel's poems, to others he objects, also to a rhyme here and there, as 'water' and 'clear'. Saw here Lecky, Leyland, and Mrs. Procter, whom I had never met before' (*The Diary of William Michael Rossetti*, ed. Odette Bornand, pp. 13–14). 'Leyland' was Charles Godfrey Leland (1824–1903), author of dialect poems gathered in 1914 as *Hans Breitmann's Ballads*, who was introduced by Strahan: 'I think so highly of him that I am going to take the great liberty of bringing him with me to your tea-drinking this afternoon' (Strahan to Tennyson, 17 June, TRC). Leland met there 'Lady Charlotte Locker and Miss Jean Ingelow' (*Memories*, p. 391), but said later that he didn't think much of Tennyson as a conversationalist: 'he tried three times to talk to me but made a poor fist of it' (Elizabeth Robins Pennell, *Charles Godfrey Leland*, i. 401).

To CATHERINE DOROTHEA COLVILLE SIMEON

Text. Materials, iii. 155.

ALDWORTH, June 27, 1870

My dear Lady Simeon

My wife opened your letter before I came down and I never saw the direction and though I read your letter I (I don't know how) fancied it was for her, and when she told me she had written to you my mistake was confirmed, only yesterday she asked me whether I had answered you and I was grieved to think I might have seemed to neglect you in your great grief, of course nothing could be more grateful to me than some memorial of my much-loved and ever honoured friend, the only man on earth, I verily believe, to whom I could, and have more than once opened my heart, and he has also given me in many a conversation at Farringford in my little attic his utter confidence.[1] I knew none like him[2] for tenderness and generosity, not to mention his other noble qualities, and he was the very Prince of Courtesy; but I need not tell you this, anything, little book, or whatever you will choose and send me or bring when you come and do pray come on the 4th July, and we will be all alone, and Louie will come when she will and you can spare her. Believe me,

Always affectionately yours
A. Tennyson

To CHARLOTTE BURTON

Text. Materials, i. 311.

ALDWORTH, BLACKDOWN, HASLEMERE, July 12, 1870

My dear Mrs. Burton

I was on my way into Lincolnshire to see you and other friends once again, to shake you by the hand, and roam over the old places; but I am unfortunately laid up with a bad leg which postpones my journey; and still more unfortunate in that I hear from Drummond Rawnsley that you are going away on the 13th for some time, for how long he does not say: perhaps if I come a little later in the year I may have the pleasure of seeing you at home, and renewing our acquaintance now broken by an interval of twenty years. I trust that you and yours are all well and flourishing and that I may find you so when I come, believe me in the mean time,

Ever yours truly
A. Tennyson

[1] Simeon died in Fribourg on 21 May, and on the 31st Tennyson went 'to Swainston for the funeral. "All dreadfully sad and trying and seeming all the sadder that the sun shone and the roses bloomed profusely. A great many people there"' (*Journal,* p. 306, double quotes in MS Journal, indicating a quotation from a letter—*Memoir,* ii. 98). 'Prince of Courtesy' is from 'In the Garden at Swainston' (Ricks, p. 219), l. 10, written on the occasion. Emily Tennyson wrote to Venables on 2 June (National Library of Wales): 'You know how sad we have been of late in the loss of our friend and yours. The island has lost one of its greatest charms to us. The day (the 31st) at Swainston was very dreadful as you may think but I will not say any more on the subject.' See Charles Tennyson, p. 389.

[2] Echoing 'Maud', I. 600.

To EMILY SELLWOOD TENNYSON

MS. Tennyson Research Centre.

ALDWORTH, BLACKDOWN, HASLEMERE [for LONDON], July 16, 1870

Dearest

Thou hast done quite right as to Lady Simeon's request: and the road business I suppose has been as well managed as could be. I write from bed whence I arise about 4 o'clock. A certain Dr. Brown [?][1] is attending me at Paget's request—a very gentlemanly man. Paget said that if I were in Bartholomew's hospital I might be cured in 10 days but here in not less than a fortnight. Dr. B. thinks he shall effect a cure in less time than either.

Thine
[A.] × × × × ×

A thunder shower this morning and cataracts of rain.

That beast—Napoleon! was there ever such a 'causus belli' since the middle ages?[2] if even then. Locker saw Lord Boyne yesterday who said he feared we should be dragged into it.

To EMILY SELLWOOD TENNYSON

MS. Tennyson Research Centre.

ALDWORTH, BLACKDOWN, HASLEMERE [for LONDON, 18 July 1870]

Dearest

The brooch arrived a day or two back—it seems Oriental—Locker calls it a pretty thing. Should I forward it or bring it when I come? A man has undertaken to do the urns [?] (K[nowles] says) very cheap for the honour of doing them. I don't much trust such offers: however K. is going to design one for me to see.

The leg goes on very well—all but healed the Doctor says—nevertheless I shall [have] to be some more days in bed. Lord S[tratford] de Redcliffe[1] is to call today and I'm afraid the bed looks rather dirty.

Thine × × × ×
[A.]

Napoleon said not very long ago to Delane the Times Editor[2] 'When I *do* move I shall move with such rapidité and ferocité that the world will be astonished.'

---

[1] Unidentified.

[2] He had called out the reserves—and he declared war on the 19th. His ambassador, Count Benedetti, had demanded that the king of Prussia, at Ems, withdraw the nomination of a Hohenzollern prince to the Spanish throne, and the king's account of the demand became Bismarck's famous Ems telegram (about which the truth was not made public till 1894).

[1] Stratford Canning (1786–1880: *DNB*), 1st Viscount Stratford de Redcliffe, diplomat, was brought to Tennyson by Locker, whose account of the visit is in *Memoir*, ii. 79.

[2] John Thaddeus Delane (see above, p. 305 n.).

To PERCY TENNYSON[1]

MS. University of Virginia

August 1, 1870

My dear Percy

Uncle Alfred thanks you for your kind little note and wishes you many happy returns of the day and that you may always be 'good Percy' whether little or big.

Uncle's leg is better than it was a week or two ago but no[t] so well as it was on Saturday. Uncle is afraid he has walked too much but he has been lying down a long time and now is rather tired of it. There has been a great deal of noise in the skies here too. Uncle thinks it means 'Give unto the Lord O ye mighty, give unto the Lord glory and strength'[2] and a great deal more besides.

Uncle Alfred and Aunt Emmie hope that you will have a very happy tea with Lillie and Polly and they send their love to Papa and brother and sisters and to the dear Bernie too.

           Your affectionate uncle
           A. Tennyson

Cousin Hallam's eye is quite well but he is afraid he must not throw away the ball. Aunt Emmy's love to the dear Bernie and she is very thankful to have better news of her sister and Agnes. She cannot write today.

To ?

MS. Robert Taylor.

August 8, 1870

My dear Sir

You ask me who first wrote in the metre of In Memoriam. Had you put this query to me any time during the composition of the above I should have answered 'Myself' for though there is no particular invention in the form, seeing that [it] may be regarded as only a quatrain of the sonnet shortened, I knew then of none other who had used it: subsequently I found a poem in B. Jonson and just the other day while looking over a new book, 'Hunt's History of Religious Thought in England,' I came upon a couple of stanzas

---

[1] Horatio Tennyson's fifth child (born 1865). Though only four—Cecilia, Maud, Violet, Bertram—are allowed him in *Background to Genius*, p. 133, Percy is named in *Journal*, p. 285, and in a letter from Farringford on 8 February [1874?] Matilda Tennyson wrote to Mrs Craik: 'I am in the midst of relations here, Horatio, his wife, and five children are living here at present' (MS Arthur Houghton, Jr.).

[2] Psalm 29:1.

by Lord Herbert of Cherbury in this metre. Rossetti's little note might as well I think have been spared.[1]

My son who is here desires me to give his best remembrances and for myself believe me

Yours very truly
A. Tennyson

To SAMUEL WARD[1]

MS. Rowland Collins.

September 26, 1870

My dear Sir

I thank for your kind letter. It is not possible for me to come up to town now but if you can any day come to me here it will give my wife and myself much pleasure to see you. At present we cannot offer you a bed on account of a pressure of guests but when we have one to spare we will let you know. We are only two hours from town. Our station is Haslemere. Unfortunately we have not the French 'Come into the Garden Maud' here. Believe me,

Very truly yours
A. Tennyson

To JULIA CAMERON NORMAN[1]

MS. Duke.

October 3, 1870

My dear Julia

I am persistently required to write to somebody on behalf of my nephew Eustace Jesse[2] whose parents want a nomination for him to a Bank of

---

[1] An early draft of this letter is in TRC (see also *Memoir*, i. 305). John Hunt's *Religious Thought in England from the Reformation to the End of the Last Century* appeared in three volumes in 1870–3. Rossetti's note, appended to 'My Sister's Sleep' (written in 1847, first published in 1850) in *Poems*, 1870, was cancelled in 1881. Tennyson thought, none the less, that Rossetti had taken the 'metre from him, for [the] poem [*In Memoriam*] had been read and quoted years before published' (*Tennyson at Aldworth, The Diary of James Henry Mangles*, ed. Knies, p. 113). See vol. iii, letter to Knowles, 23 April 1876. Moreover, in *Poems* (1842) Tennyson had published in the *In Memoriam* stanza 'You ask me why' and 'Love thou thy land' (Ricks, pp. 489, 613).

[1] Samuel Ward (1814–84: *DAB*), American lobbyist, financier, author, and adventurer, well known in London. He wrote *Lyrical Recreations* (1865; *Tennyson in Lincoln*, i, No. 2294), and was caricatured by Spy in *Vanity Fair*, 10 January 1880.

[1] In January 1859 Julia Hay Cameron (d. 1873) married Charles Loyd Norman (1833–89), son of George Warde Norman (1793–1882: *DNB*), of Bromley Common, Kent, a director of the Bank of England 1821–72 (*Landed Gentry*, s.v. Cameron of Lochiel, Norman of the Rookery).

[2] Richard Eustace Russell Jesse, later (1875) Eustace Tennyson d'Eyncourt Jesse (1853–?), second son of Emily and Richard Jesse, entered Queen's College, Oxford, in 1875; took a BA, University College, Durham, in 1878: and 'held various curacies 1878–85, rector of Kirkley St. Peter, Suffolk, 1875' (Foster). He married Edith Louisa James, of the Elms, Croydon (b. 1866) in 1886, and was the father of Fryn Tennyson Jesse (d. 1958). He was the author of 'Notes on the 22nd Article', 'Prayers for the Departed, Purgatory' (Jesse Family Tree, TRC).

England clerkship. It is in vain I assure them that I do not know a single Director. I am only told that at least I must know somebody who knows one and this I cannot deny if the 'George Norman Esqre' on the list is your Father-in-law.

Forgive me if I pass my trouble on to you and say, will you mention the lad's name to him if you think you can do so. He is a good lad, I believe, and I shall be much obliged to you if you will befriend him.

Our very kind regards to your husband and our love to yourself and to Mr. Cameron if still with you.

Yours affectionately
A. Tennyson

EMILY SELLWOOD TENNYSON
to HALLAM TENNYSON

MS. Tennyson Research Centre.

October 21, 1870

Beloved

We have a bright day after all the storms and I think that Papa is going to the gardeners at Milford for we are alone for the first days for I know not how long. Happily moreover the d'Eyncourts and Mr. Garden cannot come before Thursday next as Papa is tired of guests and does not feel in spirits for them, this long confinement having tired him so much.

He hears such bad things of the state of morals in London that this helps to depress him. He feels sure that without any talk of tower-of-Siloam judgements, God's laws of the world doom those who lose faith in Him and give themselves up to the world, the flesh and the Devil, to such baseness of soul that even common courage forsakes them. The result as it seems now of the literature of France and echoes of this, one would fear, are poisoning the springs of life in England. What a great work must there be before every Englishman.

I did not remember to tell thee that two of Mr. Mornington's brothers called, the clergyman and the Marlborough one. The last sent thee his love. They are neither of them so prepossessing as our Mr. Mornington.[1]

Dr. Isaac was very kind and advised new remedies for Papa which I pray God may restore him. Not that his health is bad, I trust, except that he is a little lowered by want of air and freedom.

Did I tell you of the fever Tiny has had? Mr. Cotton gives a better account of her today. Robert comes from India soon and Ben is gone to town for the winter with his children.

I will add any news that may be in the papers today. At present I do not remember anything fresh in any way except the discovery of a kind of

---

[1] Unidentified, but see *Journal*, pp. 267, 276, 303.

crocodile in a Lancashire cave, a beast four or five feet long. It was killed. God bless thee, own darling. Our best love.

Thy loving Mother
Emily Tennyson

I have a most touching letter from Lady Simeon saying how good it has been for Louy to have been here and thanking thee for thy kindness to her nephew, who she says is as happy as a king at Marlborough. [*illegible*] wants to leave at once now but as he talks of compensation perhaps things will not be arranged as his idea of it and ours may differ too much.

To ALEXANDER STRAHAN

Text. Herbert Sullivan and Newman Flower, *Sir Arthur Sullivan, His Life, Letters, and Diaries*, p. 84.

[c. 5 November 1870]

'He that sweareth to his neighbour and disappointeth him not'[1]—so I must consent to the publication of the songs,[2] however much against my inclination and my judgment, and that I may meet your wishes as to the time of publication, I must also consent to their being published this Xmas, however much more against my inclination and judgment—provided, as I stated yesterday that the fact of their having been written four years ago, and of their being published by yourself, be mentioned in the preface, also that no one but Millais shall illustrate them.

Yours very truly
A. Tennyson

To ARTHUR O'SHAUGHNESSY[1]

MS. Brotherton Collection.

[7 November 1870]

Sir

Your inscription bears the date of October but I have only just now

---

[1] '... shall dwell in thy tabernacle ... or rest upon thy holy hill' (*Book of Common Prayer*, Psalm 15).

[2] 'The Window or, The Song of the Wrens' (see p. 443), published by Strahan, with Arthur Sullivan's music and without illustrations. The songs had been pirated in the United States. See above, p. 539, and also Henry Jennings, *Lord Tennyson*, pp. 192–4, and *Journal*, p. 312.

[1] Arthur William Edgar O'Shaughnessy (1844–81: *DNB*), poet and herpetologist (British Museum). He published four volumes of poetry, of which the first, here acknowledged, was *Epic of Women* (1870). His best known poem, 'Ode' (We are the music makers, | And we are the dreamers of dreams') was in *Music and Moonlight* (1874), which shows his Pre-Raphaelite and Swinburnian affinities. See *The Swinburne Letters*, ii. 255, and W. D. Paden, 'Arthur O'Shaughnessy: the Ancestry of a Victorian Poet', *Bulletin of the John Rylands Library*, xlvi (Mar.

received your volume, and have as yet had no time to give it any attention. Pray however accept my thanks in the mean time and believe me,

Yours faithfully
A. Tennyson

Arthur O'Shaughnessy, Esq.

To SAMUEL REYNOLDS HOLE[1]

Text. The Works of Tennyson (Eversley Edition), vii. 376–7.

[? early December 1870]

The Book of Roses was heartily welcomed by me: I do not worship the yellow but the Rosy Roses—rosy means red, not yellow—and the homage of my youth was given to what I must ever look up to as the Queen of roses—the Provence—but then you as a great Rose master may not agree with me. I never see my Queen of Roses anywhere now. We have just been planting a garden of Roses, and were glad to find that out of our native wit we had associated the berberis with them as you advise.

To ARTHUR SULLIVAN

Text. Herbert Sullivan and Newman Flower, *Sir Arthur Sullivan, His Life, Letters, and Diaries,* p. 85

[December 1870]

Dear Mr. Sullivan

I have been some time in answering your note because I have been asking several friends who had already seen my little preface to the Songs of the Wrens, what their impression of it was.[1] They had all failed to see in it the slightest kind of unfriendly allusion to yourself, and only took it as an expression of my own regret at the unappropriateness of the time of publication, and even that my words were not worthy of your music.

1964), 429–47). Rossetti wrote a good-natured limerick on him (*Rossetti Papers*, p. 496):

> There's the Irishman Arthur O'Shaughnessy—
> On the chess board of poets a pawn is he:
>   Though bishop or king
>   Would be rather the thing
> To the fancy of Arthur O'Shaughnessy.

---

[1] Samuel Reynolds Hole (1818–1904: *DNB*), author and, from 1887, Dean of Rochester, was a man of enormous energy and varied interests (hunting, fishing, gardening). His *Book about Roses: How to Grow and Show Them* (1869) went into many editions, and on 28 November (TRC) he sent a copy of the third to Tennyson. In one of his three books of recollections, *The Memories of Dean Hole* (1894), p. 94, he speaks of 'letters from the Laureate, in one of which he crowns me as "the Rose-King", placing me on a "throne of purple sublimity"'. Hole replied (TRC) to this letter on 9 December, and to another on the 15th.

[1] Ricks, p. 1197. Sullivan was hurt by the last sentence: 'I am sorry that my four-year-old puppet should have to dance at all in the dark shadow of these days [of the Franco-Prussian War]; but the music is now completed and I am bound by my promise.'

You may feel certain that there was and is no intention on my part to give the public any other impression; and you can, if you choose, let all your chaffing friends of the Club know that you have this under my hand and seal.

A. Tennyson

APPENDIX A

11 August 1852 to Julia Margaret Cameron

Julia Margaret Cameron (1815–79), a free spirit, is important in the history of photography, and refreshing in Tennyson's life; her husband, Charles Hay Cameron (1795–1880), a jurist, was a notable Civil Servant in Ceylon and India. She was one of the celebrated Pattle sisters.

'It is worth looking at the ramifications of the Pattle family. . . . The seven surviving daughters of James and Adeline Pattle: were Adeline (1812–1836) who married Colin Mackenzie (later General); Julia Margaret . . . ; Sarah (1816–1887) who married Henry Thoby Prinsep, an official in the East India Company [see above, p. 173 and n.]; Maria (1818–1892) who married Dr John Jackson; Louisa (1821–1873) who married H. V. Bayley; Virginia (1827–1910) who married Lord Eastnor (later Earl Somers); Sophia (1829–1911) who married Sir John Dalrymple.

'Sarah Prinsep's daughter Alice married Charles Gurney and had two daughters, Laura and Rachel. Laura (Queenie) married Sir Thomas Troubridge and Rachel the Earl of Dudley. Laura Troubridge [see vol. iii] had a son Ernest, who married Una Taylor, who later married John Radcliffe Hall and wrote *The Well of Loneliness*.

'Maria Jackson [see above, p. 284] had three daughters, Adeline, who married Henry Halford Vaughan, Mary who married Herbert Fisher, and Julia, who married first Herbert Duckworth and second Leslie Stephen. . . . The two daughters of Julia's marriage to Sir Leslie Stephen . . . were Vanessa, later the wife of Clive Bell, and Virginia, who became the wife of Leonard Woolf; the two sons were Thoby and Adrian Stephen' (Editor's Note, *Victorian Photographs of Famous Men and Fair Women by Julia Margaret Cameron*, with introductions by Virginia Woolf and Roger Fry, expanded and revised edition, edited by Tristram Powell, Boston, 1973, p. 21).

The Camerons at this time lived at East Sheen, not far from the Tennysons and, more to the point, Henry Taylor, whom she adored, and whose *Autobiography* abounds with information and anecdotes about her. In 1860 she bought two houses near the Tennysons at Farringford, connected them with a castellated tower, and called the result Dimbola. See *The Cameron Collection, an Album of Photographs by Julia Margaret Cameron Presented to Sir John Herschel*, ed. Colin Ford (London, 1975). See also Laura Troubridge, *Memories and Reflections*, ch. 1–2, for a charming account of the Gurneys, Pattles, Prinseps, Camerons, and Tennyson.

APPENDIX B

25 August 1855 to George Granville Bradley

The 'gifted X' is probably Archer Thompson Gurney (see above, p. 119 n.). No review of 'Maud' by him has been identified, but none is called for. Gurney's special detestation was the 'Spasmodics', whom he had ridiculed in *A Satire for the Ages, The Transcendentalists* (1853: see *Tennyson in Lincoln*, i, No. 1082), and in a revision of the poem in 1855 he identified Tennyson with the Spasmodic school, especially of course 'Maud'. We cite the following lines from the second edition (pp. 2–4, 36–7):

>   Thee, Tennyson, despite thy genius real,
>   Thee we must thank for this *intense* 'Ideal;'
>   To thee we owe these tenebrific strains,
>   This glut of nonsense, this sad lack of brains,
>   This mystical parade, insane pretence,
>   That never, never deviates into sense.
>
>   'Tis true, thy Muse pure feeling's deeps has traced,
>   With all the gifts of tenderness is graced,
>   An undisputed tragic power possesses,
>   And yet is rich in music and caresses,
>   Owns every charm to poet could belong,
>   Except the natural melody of song,
>   But, O! thine imitators—O, the crew
>   That bray hoarse echoes, critic-laurell'd too!
>   Thy strains oracular bred these men's ravings:
>   And then the hapless hyperbolic cravings,
>   Which all the sons of mediocrity,
>   The *criticlings*, have haply stolen from thee.
>
>   Ah, thou hast much to answer for, poor Bard!
>   But then, thy penance, that to bear were hard.
>   . . . . . .
>   Alack, ill satisfied with such renown,
>   Thyself hast lept the murk abysses down,
>   Hast proved thy own faint soul by humbug awed
>   In the grim rubbish of a thing called 'Maud.'
>   We mourn thy crime, still more thy weakness rue,
>   And groan, 'The Laureate's transcendental too.'
>   . . . . . .
>   But seems it harsh, perchance, to hunt the hare,
>   While the red lion snuffs the forest air?
>   Should I pursue an Alexander's track,
>   While Alfred glares his calm defiance back?
>   Ah, Alfred, Alfred, gentlest child of song,
>   Rich in meek ditties, in bland pastorals strong,
>   Is't thou who savage rhymes hast pished and pshawed?
>   Is't thou who wrot'st this rude barbaric 'Maud?'
>   . . . . . .

This fierce mock-passion, aim'd at boys' applause,
These hideous rhymes, these leafless hips and haws
This Locksley-hall-man with a wider scope,
Whose soul's desert were verily a rope,
This puling maundering over harmless flow'rs,
Which rose and lily strips of Nature's dow'rs,
And last, this sanguine cry for blood, red blood,
To wash away the deep-encrusted mud
Alike from century and thy hero's soul—
What call'st thou this? Is't not—a nameless whole?
And thou could'st fling it on the world, unawed
By wholesome dread, this shapeless mooney 'Maud!'

APPENDIX C

12 May 1857 to the Duchess of Argyll

More letters survive from Tennyson to the Duke and Duchess of Argyll than to anyone else except his wife. George Douglas Campbell (1823–1900: *DNB*), his older brother having died two years earlier, succeeded as 8th Duke of Argyll in 1847. His great interests were religion, politics, and science, which were to him aspects of one majestic moral principle ('One God, one law, one element'), as set forth in his books *The Reign of Law* (1867) and *The Unity of Nature* (1884). His politics can hardly be discriminated from Tennyson's. (See Tennyson's poem 'To the Duke of Argyll', Ricks, p. 1298.) In religion they had a spacious meeting ground in the traditional commonplaces of Protestantism, and Argyll's science, though far outstripping Tennyson's, was so circular that he comes up behind. As a natural scientist, in fact, he compares with Layard as an archaeologist, Bradley as a theologian, Martin Tupper as a poet; but as an *orator* he ranked with Bright, Gladstone (with whom be broke over Home Rule), and Disraeli (whom he could not abide).

Physically, as well as intellectually, he was a very short man who made a very tall impression. 'His hair was as vividly red as that of his namesake Rob Roy, and was brushed straight back and up from a truly intellectual brow. His manner suggested a combination of the Highland chief with the University Professor. . . . A quality not easily distinguished from arrogance showed itself in the Duke's social bearing. He never seemed to realize that his associates were in any sense his equals. As a professor, he harangued and expounded and laid down the law. As a chieftain, he summoned one guest to his side and then in turn dismissed him to make way for another. He spoke as the Elder of the Kirk when he rebuked episcopacy; as the President of the Geological Society when he reproved Evolution; and as the hoary Whig when he preached the sanctity of property to the socialistic and inexperienced Gladstone, who was fourteen years his senior' (G. W. E. Russell, *Portraits of the Seventies*, pp. 73–4).

Like his father, he married three times. In 1844 he married Lady Elizabeth Georgiana Leveson-Gower (d. 25 May 1878), eldest daughter of the 2nd Duke of Sutherland, by whom he had five sons and seven daughters; in 1881 he married Amelia Maria Claughton, who died in 1894; and in 1895 Ina Erskine MacNeill, who died in 1925. The Marquis of Lorne (1845–1914, later 9th Duke of Argyll: *DNB*), the eldest son, broke with tradition in three ways—he married once, married royalty (Princess Louise, in 1871), and they separated (Jeremy Maas, *The Victorian World in Photographs*, p. 207. See *DNB* and Argyll's *Autobiography and Memoirs*, ed. by the Dowager Duchess of Argyll.

APPENDIX D

[early August 1857] to William Fairbairn

At Tent Lodge, a 'pretty little villa [on the Marshalls' grounds] on Coniston Water', [see i. 332] where they had spent part of their honeymoon, they seem to have suffered from colds, and on 13 August 'Mrs. Marshall has sent Mr. Bywater to him [Tennyson] and he not being at home Dr. Davey came'. On 24 August, Tennyson having proposed a trip to Furness Abbey, 'Kind Miss Bulford walks in the heat to the Beavers to bring Mrs. Marshall thence', and the latter met them in the Barouche. They returned by train to Broughton. In the next week they took drives, and Tennyson read to his wife Christian Ginsberg's new translation of *The Song of Songs*, and she noticed that '[. . .] of beams slant down the [. . .] and show us green nooks where all seemed brown before. Mr. and Mrs. Marshall and Mr. Venables arrive at Mr. James Marshall's. They come to us after morning church. The gentlemen lunch with us and A. dines'. On 4 September 'He goes to Miss Heathcote's over the [. . .]. She kindly asked us a short time ago but we could not. 5th. He returns and with him Mr. William Spring Rice'.

Charles Lutwidge Dodgson (1832–98: *DNB*), not yet famous, called on 18 September, dined on the 21st, and on the 28th 'photographed virtually everyone present' (*The Letters of Lewis Carroll*, ed. Morton N. Cohen, i. 34–5 and n.).

They had to postpone their scheduled visit to the Monteiths, at Carstairs in Lanarkshire, having given insufficient notice; so, leaving Tent Lodge on 29 September, they spent a night at Carlisle, and next day, passing through a 'Dreary rain' in Glasgow, 'We go to the Tontyne [Tontine Hotel], Greenock. Very comfortable it is'. At Inverary (population a few hundred) on 3 October they learned that the Duke of Argyll was at Balmoral, the Duchess at Dunrobin, Sutherlandshire, the palatial seat of her parents, the Duke and Duchess of Sutherland, and they therefore put up at an inn, probably the Argyll Arms. Lord Lorne, age thirteen, with his tutor called next day, begging them to move to the Castle, but they held out and holed up in the inn. On the 7th, 'After luncheon we came by Lord Lorne's invitation to stay at the castle' (*Materials*, ii. 190; this must be the visit to the 'castle of a certain distinguished nobleman' described in Charles K. Tuckerman's *Personal Recollections of Notable People at Home and Abroad*, pp. 26–8). In the early evening a white owl knocked at the window, and soon after, the Duchess (with her daughter and uncle Charles Howard), who had hired a special steamer in order to come more quickly, knocked at the door. On the 8th Tennyson went to bed with a cold, and the Duchess, Emily Tennyson, and William George Howard, another uncle, went out for a drive. On the 11th, 'Miss Howard and Captain Howard come', and on the 12th the Tennysons drove 'with them, Mr. Charles Howard, and the Duchess'. They remained at Argyll Castle until 13 October, and, after an overnight stop at the Queen's Hotel in Glasgow, arrived on the 14th at Carstairs, where they stayed two days. From there they left by train on the 16th, and spent three nights with the James Garth Marshalls at Headingly, Yorkshire, where the great Marshall fortune was amassed and where they 'went over the [worsted and flax] mills belonging to the Marshalls' (*Materials*, ii. 190); thence to Peterborough and, on the 20th, and no doubt gratefully, 'We reach Park House and leave again, he on the 27th with Edmund and Cissy, I on the 28th' for Ashburton Cottage, Addiscombe Farm, Croydon. Then, on 4 November, 'We joyfully return to our own darling home. Day rainy at first. Mrs. Cameron runs after and comes with us to London. Clear as we cross. Rosy streaks as we near home at sunset. The children lavish all manner of tender words on their home' (all citations from Journal).

APPENDIX E

24 September 1861 Baron Dufferin and Clandeboye to Alfred Tennyson

Frederick Temple Hamilton-Temple Blackwood (1826–1902: *DNB*), diplomat and administrator, succeeding his father as 5th Baron (Irish peerage) in 1841, was created baron in the peerage of the United Kingdom in 1850, earl in 1871 and Marquis of Dufferin and Ava in 1881. He held many important posts, including crucial ambassadorships, and was Governor-General of Canada in 1872, and, more to the point (as will be seen in volume iii), of India in 1884–8. Tennyson created his love of poetry ('I not only did not care for poetry . . . but absolutely disliked it'). He sought Tennyson's acquaintance by letter, with his book *Letters from High Latitudes*, in February 1858 (*Memoir*, i. 427), and later proposed yachting to Cowes in September to realize it (TRC). Harold Nicolson, Dufferin's nephew, wrote a very readable book on him, *Helen's Tower* (1937), which views him, to some extent, as a rather Byronic figure (see p. 119).

Dufferin was an only child. His mother, to whom the *Letters* were addressed, was Helen Selina Sheridan (1807–67), granddaughter of the dramatist (and sister of Caroline Norton); and 'almost legendary' was the 'love which existed between her and her son' (Nicolson, p. 58). The figure-head of his ship was a bronze effigy of her by Marochetti, making a gap in nature—'the well-known lovely face, with its golden hair, and smile that might charm all malice from the elements, beaming like a happy omen above our bows' (Letter 4). Dufferin married (finally) on 23 October 1862, ten days after his mother married her patient suitor of twenty years, Lord Gifford (1822–62, son of the 8th Marquis of Tweeddale), then gravely ill—circumstances that allow Nicolson to purr at his silkiest (p. 58): 'With that fine scrupulousness of the Victorian epoch she first ascertained from his doctors that there was small chance of his recovery and no chance whatsoever of his producing an heir. She then consented to marry him; and his aching frame was transported to her own bright home in Highgate. They were married in the bedroom. The letter which, on that occasion, she wrote to her enraged father-in-law, Lord Tweeddale, is a masterpiece of dignity. Eight weeks later Gifford died.' An equally 'fine scrupulousness' requires the editors to record another passage (p. 103): 'Even Mr. W. H. Auden—not always the tenderest of our English poets—refers to it [*Letters from High Latitudes*] in his *Letters from Iceland* almost in a tone of comradeship. In fact it is a gay book, high-spirited, witty and alert.' See above, p. 317.

APPENDIX F

? early October 1861 to Baron Dufferin and Clandeboye

Tennyson sent *three* versions of 'Helen's Tower' to Dufferin, who acknowledged them on 8 October (*Materials*, ii. 337–8, and Alfred Lyall, *The Life of the Marquis of Dufferin and Ava*, i. 144–5) and also wrote to Emily Tennyson (TRC) on the same day (Tennyson's transcripts, 'scratches', and all that follows in these notes are in Dufferin's hand in TRC).

[A]

[i] Fullest form

> Helen's tower here I stand
> Dominant over sea and land
> Son's love built me and I hold
> Mother's love engrav'n in gold.
> Spare me, tempest! whirlwind, spare
> Me that guard the mother's prayer.
> Smite not hissing thunderstone
> The pious labour of the son.
> Yet the thunderstone will smite
> Blast will blow and frost will bite   [10]
> For love is in and out of time
> And I am mortal stone and lime
> But if my girdle were as strong
> As either love, to last as long,
> I should keep my crown entire
> To and thro' the doomsday fire,
> And be found of angel eyes
> In earth's recurring paradise.

[ii] 2d form [*deletes ll. 5–10*]

[iii] Shortest form (wh. I rather prefer) [*deletes ll. 5–12 from 'Fullest form'*]

[B: *variant readings and comments*]

[i. 4:] 'if it is not engrav'n on the gold—inscribed or inframed would do'. [iii. 2, for Dominant:] 'Far-looking'; [iii. 4, 5] 'A [Son's love]', 'A [Mother's love]'; [iii. 5] 'What stone is the tower built of? I should prefer for instance some such reading as this—

> if my granite zone were strong
> would my marble were as strong
> zone of flint

[iii. 10, 'recurring Paradise':] The fancy of some poets and theologians that Paradise is to be the renovated earth, as, I dare say, you know.

Appendix F 567

[C]

[*Another transcription of '2d form', with Tennyson's letter at the bottom of the page and with minor variants headed:*] '5th [March 1862 | D[ufferin] L[odge]. The one I prefer'.

INDEX OF CORRESPONDENTS

Albert, Prince, 257
Albery, ? Mr, 541
Alice, Princess, 289, 291, 293
Allibone, Samuel Austin, 225
Allingham, William, 18, 55, 84, 107, 162, 376
Argyll, Duchess of, 177, 178, 181, 183, 188, 191, 195, 196, 207, 215, 221, 227, 259, 260, 269, 272, 275, 291, 294, 302, 303, 316, 318, 322, 323, 328, 335, 346, 357, 360, 388, 460, 491, 510, 517, 522, 532
Argyll, Duke of, 196, 222, 233, 236, 244, 252, 256, 282, 295, 297, 298, 301, 304, 309, 364, 392, 395, 396, 400, 432, 434, 445
Armstrong, George Francis, 409
Ashburton, Lady, 138
Auldjo, John, 259

Baines, Benjamin, 79, 161, 163, 165
Banks, George Linnaeus, 361
Barnard, Mr, 30
Barnes, William, 271
Barrett, George, 280
Barry, Sir Redmond, 320
Bell, Henry Glassford, 430
Bellew, John Chippendale Montesquieu, 322
Bennett, William Cox, 129, 214, 333, 381, 449
Bennett, William Sterndale, 292, 301
Bennett, ? W. W., 444
Blackie, Elizabeth Wyld, 366
Blackie, John Stuart, 366, 368, 410, 461, 486, 505
Blewitt, Octavian, 312
Booth, Edwin Thomas, 532
Borcke, Heros von, 408n
Boyne, Viscountess, 408
Bradbury, William, 473
Bradbury and Evans, 209, 438
Bradley, George Granville, 122, 124, 378, 475
Bridges, Robert Seymour, 330
Brightwell, Daniel Barron, 534
Brimley, George, 136
Brookfield, Jane Octavia, 19, 46, 113, 546
Brookfield, William Henry, 19, 26
Browning, Elizabeth Barrett, 36, 37, 39
Browning, Robert, 280, 368, 406, 519
Bruce, Lady Augusta, 304, 310, 327
Bruce, Katherine Mary, 350, 351
Bunbury, Ellen (Tennyson d'Eyncourt), 548
Burdon, Cotsford, 540, 542 (?)
Burrichter, Harry, 533

Burton, Charlotte, 551

Cameron, Charles Hay, 397
Cameron, Julia Margaret, 37, 82, 319, 340
Carlyle, Jane Welsh, 28
Cator, Julia (Hallam), 223
Chapman, Benedict Lawrence, 59, 65, 116, 119, 446
(?) Chapman and Hall, 330
Chatelain, Jean Baptiste François Ernest, Chevalier de, 128
Child, Francis James, 166
Chisholm, Caroline, 57
Cholmondeley, Mr, 203
Clifton, Mr, 6, 7
Clough, Arthur Hugh, 162, 164, 166, 167, 276
Clough, Blanche, 276
Cockin, Charles Edward, 511
Colam, John, 325
Colquhoun, Ludovic, 52
Cotton, Tiny, 497
Cowell, Elizabeth, 56, 81
Cox, Mr, 8

Davey, Margaret, 86
De Montmorency Daubeny, Miss, 450
De Vere, Aubrey, 40, 96, 398
Dempster, William Richardson, 163, 164, 170
D'Eyncourt, Ellen Tennyson, 414
D'Eyncourt, Louis Charles Tennyson, 300, 431
Disraeli, Benjamin, 488, 490
Dodgson, Charles Lutwidge, 543
Donne, William Bodham, 78
Doré, Gustave, 452
Doyle, Richard, 168
Dufferin and Clandeboye, Baron, 278, 280, 313

Eardley, Stenton, 528
Eden, Eleanor, 432, 454
Ellis, Charles, 73, 449
Ellison, Cuthbert Edward, 433
Elmhirst, Sophia (Rawnsley), 2, 4, 5, 29, 39, 62, 92
Elton, Sir Arthur Hallam, 370
Estcourt, Arthur Harbottle, 442

Fairbairn, ? Thomas, 340
Fairbairn, William, 187, 340 (?)

Index of Correspondents

Farrar, Frederic William, 35, 400
Faulkner, Mrs, 476
Fenwick, Isabella, 96
Ferrier, James Frederick, 103
Fields, James Thomas, 152, 227, 229, 232, 233, 234, 260, 342, 380, 390, 394, 451, 461, 478, 484, 514, 526, 541
Fields, Mrs James Thomas, 237, 405
FitzGerald, Edward, 56
Fitzgerald, Mrs, 50
Florentines, the, 397
Flower, Edward Fordham, 359
Flower, Mrs Edward Fordham, 362
Flowers, George French, 58, 72
Forster, John, 2, 11, 13, 16, 27, 37, 41, 42, 44, 46, 49, 85, 92, 97, 100, 101, 102, 117, 118, 119, 121, 174, 175, 209, 358
Fox, William Johnson, 134
Franklin, Lady Jane, 47, 402
(?) Freiligrath, Ferdinand, 182
Fulford, William, 142
Furnivall, Frederick James, 79, 98, 238, 268, 336, 338, 341, 352, 359, 468, 537
Fytche, Lewis, 93, 114, 123, 208, 287, 323, 389, 399, 475, 541
Fytche, Mary Anne, 81

Gatty, Alfred, 255, 285
Gatty, Margaret, 192, 225, 285, 288, 340, 342, 351, 389, 462, 504, 520
Giblin, William Robert, 359
Gilchrist, Anne, 439, 445
Gladstone, Catherine, 433
Gladstone, William Ewart, 230, 255, 316, 317, 424, 505, 519, 531
Glehn, Olga von, 444
Grant, Sir Alexander, 234
(?) Griffith, David, 472
Grove, George, 91, 442, 444, 475, 477, 479, 482, 483, 531
Guest, Enid, 468, 471, 472, 475
Guest, Sir Ivor Bertie, 381, 449, 469, 470
Gurney, Archer Thompson, 137

Haines, William, 439
Hall, Anna Maria, 272
Hallam, Henry, 39, 44, 46, 58, 70, 174
Hannay, James, 350
Harrison, Robert, 320
Hawker, Robert Stephen, 120, 237
Hayward, Miss, 41, 42
Helps, Arthur, 196
Hill, Richard, 65
Hinton, James, 520
Hodgson, Anne, 208
Hole, Samuel Reynolds, 557
Hooker, Frances Harriet (Henslow), 464

Houghton, Lord, see Milnes, Richard Monkton
Hume, Alexander Hamilton, 443
Hunt, James, 442, 460
Hunt, Leigh, 192

Isbister, William, 543

Jackson, Maria (Pattle), 284, 293
Jerrold, Mrs, 260
Jesse, Matilda, 18
Jones, Agnes, 497
Jones, Walter, 549
Jowett, Benjamin, 197, 198, 483, 509

Kane, Elisha Kent, 165, 166
Kent, Charles, 470
Kenward, James, 387, 430, 473
Ker, Alan, 75, 148
King, Henry Samuel, 344, 427
King, John W., 214
Kingsley, Charles, 63, 76, 253
Kirby, William, 486, 542, 548
Knowles, Isabel Hewlett, 513
Knowles, James Thomas 288, 349, 430, 501, 516, 521, 526, 527, 539, 546, 547

Langford, John Alfred, 124
Latham, Robert Gordon, 270
Laurence, Samuel, 340
Lear, Edward, 111, 273
Lecky, William Edward Hartpole, 491
Leighton, William Allport, 247
Locker, Frederick, 193, 390, 513, 515, 517, 522, 527, 530, 535
Longfellow, Henry Wadsworth, 93, 234, 448, 462, 493, 494, 496, 498
Lord Chamberlain, 323
Lushington, Cecilia, 38
Lushington, Edmund, 14, 38, 94, 113, 123, 321
Lushington, Franklin, 26, 38, 78
Lushington, Henry, 38, 74

MacDonald, George, 436
MacLehose, James, 411
Macmillan, Alexander, 242, 246, 249, 253, 476, 477, 481, 492
Mann, Robert James, 127, 131, 139, 145, 147, 160, 167, 170, 182, 193, 211
Mann, Mrs Robert James, 211
Marshall, James Garth, 188
Marshall, Mary A., 12
Massey, Gerald, 87, 114, 121, 538
Michel, Francisque Xavier, 493, 501, 504
Milnes, Richard Monckton (Lord Houghton),

Index of Correspondents 571

22, 41, 43, 44, 60, 64, 248, 254, 307, 433, 494, 525, 549
Monteagle, Lord, 16
Monteith, Robert, 15, 64, 71
Morris, William, 492
Moultrie, John, 44
Moxon, Edward, 1, 48, 52, 76, 79, 98, 116, 120, 195
Moxon, William, 203
Munch, Andreas, 468
Mundy, Charles Henry [Massingberd-], 95
Murray, John, 396

Norman, Julia Cameron, 554
Novelli, Augustus Henry, 256

Odling, Osborne and Co., 403
Oliphant, Margaret Oliphant, 536
Osgood, James Ripley, 457
O'Shaughnessy, Arthur, 556
Owen, Richard, 406, 407

Paget, James, 363
Palgrave, Francis Turner, 27, 200, 212, 230, 427, 440, 456, 502, 510
Palgrave, Mrs Francis Turner, 508
Palmer, Clara (Tennyson d'Eyncourt), 90
Palmerston, Viscount, 367
Parker, John William, 80, 99, 161, 196, 199
Patmore, Coventry, 20, 24, 86, 99, 154, 164, 189, 312, 313
Patmore, Emily Augusta, 14, 38
Paul, Charles Kegan, 286
Payne, James Bertrand, 428, 459, 467, 487, 489
Peel, Archibald, 377, 378
Philpot, William B., 122
Phipps, Charles Beaumont (later Sir), 190, 191, 290, 295
Pickering, Basil Montagu, 436
Pittis, Francis, 149
Plackett, A., 169
Pollock, William Frederick, 29, 438
Prinsep, Sarah Monckton, 220
Privy Council, 498

Ratcliff, J. C., 311
Rawnsley, Catherine, 36, 81, 110
Rawnsley, Drummond, 43, 45, 391, 525, 538
Rawnsley, Thomas Hardwicke, 24, 221
Rawnsley, Mrs Thomas Hardwicke, 24
Read, Thomas Buchanan, 167
Repton, George Herbert, 56
Rice, *see* Spring Rice
Richards, Col. Alfred Bate, 522
Rogers, Samuel, 17
Rossetti, Dante Gabriel, 441

Rossetti, Frances, 207
Rossetti, William Michael, 207
Routledge, George, 379
Russell, Elizabeth, 36, 45, 50, 83, 88, 149, 155

Saunders, John, 96
Schofield, Mrs, 61
Scott, Robert, 112
Sellar, William Young, 69, 152
Sewell, Arthur, 362
Sharpe, Samuel, 12
Shedden-Ralston, William Ralston, 523
Silas, Edward, 325
Simeon, Catherine Dorothea Colville, 551
Simeon, Sir John, 103, 146, 264, 399, 432, 455, 506, 507, 511
Smith, George, 248
Smith, Payne, Smith (bankers), 537
Southey, Reginald, 171
Spedding, James, 25, 29, 30, 64, 154, 540
Spring Rice, Stephen, 321
Stanford, Edward, 8
Stanley, Arthur Penrhyn, 410
Stanley, Lady Augusta (Bruce), 426
Steele, Mrs, 459
Stephenson, Appleby, 60, 75
Sterling, Sir Anthony Coningham, 434
Strahan, Alexander, 509, 514 (?), 516 (?), 533, 536, 556
Strahan and Co., Messrs, 512, 518
Strangford, Viscountess, 512
Suckling and Co., 302
Sullivan, Arthur, 557
Sullivan, John, 396
Sutherland, Duchess Dowager of, 309
Swinburne, Algernon Charles, 395, 410
Symington, Andrew James, 312

Tainsh, Edward Campbell, 485
Tauchnitz, Baron Christian Bernhard von, 246, 247, 254, 380, 490
Taylor, Henry, 12, 51, 311, 319
Taylor, Laura Barker, 456
Taylor, Theodosia Alice, 311
Taylor, Tom, 33, 51
Tennyson, Emily Sellwood, letters from, 24, 36, 53, 59, 61, 116, 123, 188, 215, 223, 234, 237, 253, 255, 285, 332, 358, 398, 405, 410, 438, 449, 454, 455, 471–2, 486, 496, 498, 512, 516, 519, 533, 543, 555;
to Duchess of Argyll, 207, 322, 323, 328;
to Fields, 227, 229, 232–3, 394;
to Forster, 92, 100–1, 118, 121, 142, 208, 209;
to Furnivall, 238, 336, 338;
to Fytche, 208, 287, 323;
to Gatty, M., 225, 285, 288, 340, 342, 351,

Tennyson, Emily Sellwood (*cont.*):
389, 462, 520;
to Macmillan, 249, 253, 492;
to Tuckerman, 107, 132, 250;
to Venables, 11, 129, 144, 148, 150, 180, 213, 224
Tennyson, Emily Sellwood, letters to, 19, 25, 27, 28, 175, 214, 242, 301, 313, 382, 487;
from Alfred, 1, 2, 6, 8, 20–1, 23, 31–3, 34, 49, 51, 58, 60, 62, 66–9, 70, 71, 72, 74, 89–90, 94–5, 110, 125–6, 128–9, 139–41, 143–4, 153, 159–60, 171, 173, 174, 175, 176, 177, 199, 200–2, 204, 211, 216, 218, 220–1, 226, 227, 228, 229, 230, 231–2, 238–41, 262, 285, 286, 305–9, 316, 333–40, 352, 354–6, 357, 369–76, 377, 378–9, 383–6, 387, 393–4, 410, 411–14, 421–4, 425, 435, 437, 508–9, 526, 536, 544–5, 550, 552
Tennyson, Frederick, 53
Tennyson, Giulio (or Julius), 363
Tennyson, Hallam, 172, 174, 217, 228, 263, 324, 435, 555
Tennyson, Lionel, 172, 455
Tennyson, Percy, 553
Tennyson, Mr, of Chester, 463
Tennyson d'Eyncourt, *see* D'Eyncourt
Thackeray, Anne Isabella, 172, 334
Thackeray, William Makepeace, 19, 181, 245
Thompson, Frances Elizabeth, 480

Thompson, John Reuben, 17, 407, 438
Thompson, William Hepworth, 296, 477, 482
Ticknor, William Davis, 133
Ticknor and Fields, 146, 212, 388, 427
Trench, Richard Chenevix, 63
Trevelyan, Lady, 205
Tuckerman, Frederick Goddard, 104, 106, 107, 108, 113, 132, 250
Tuckerman, Sophia May, 109
Tupper, Martin Farquhar, 27, 369, 426, 518
Turner, Charles Tennyson, 391

Venables, George Stovin, 11, 61, 76, 77, 105, 129, 139, 144, 148, 150, 168, 180, 213, 224, 446
Villiers, Mrs Edward Earnest, 299

Warburton, William Parsons, 480
Ward, Samuel, 554
Watts, George Frederick, 332
Weld, Anne, 13, 15, 81, 82, 173
Weld, Charles Richard, 22, 30, 115, 131, 134, 153, 182, 203, 223, 358
White, John, 544
White, Walter, 286
Wightwick, George, 189
Woodfall, Henry Dickford, 409
Woolner, Alice, 507
Woolner, Thomas, 10, 205, 215, 312, 382, 550

INDEX

Entries are mainly confined to people associated with the Tennyson circle; places where the Tennysons lived or visited on holiday; and publications by Tennyson. Married women are entered under their maiden names (and cross-referenced) until they are married.

A general, comprehensive index covering all three volumes will be included in the third volume.

Acton, Sir John, 373 and n
Alamayu, King of Abyssinia, 499 and n, 500
Albert, Prince, 149, 264, 297; visits Farringford, 150–1; death, 289–95; memorial, 296, 299 and n
Albery, Mr, 542
Alexandra, Princess of Wales, 322n, 324n
Alfred, Prince, 326
Alice, Princess, 289n, 292n, 295, 300, 303, 304, 326
'All along the valley', 329
Allibone, Samuel Austin, 225n
Allingham, Helen (née Paterson), 18n
Allingham, William, 5n, 360, 377n, 410, 421, 499; diary, 18n, 342–4, 345–6, 347–8, 403–4, 447–8, 450–1, 457, 464, 465–7, 469n, 472, 473–4, 487–8, 503; pension for, 321, 367–8, 421, 424–5
Amps, Mr, 249n
Anderson, Dr, 38, 40
Ansell, Edmund, 213n
Appleton & Co., 146
Arabin, Richard, 286
Archibald, Mr, 48
Argyll, Duchess of (Lady Elizabeth Georgiana Leveson-Gower), 177, 218, 219, 229, 284n, 291n, 308, 319n, 562, 563; children, 20, 208, 269, 317 and n, 388 and n, 389 and n, 448, 562, 563
Argyll, Duke of, 177, 179, 218, 219, 228, 229, 269n, 284n, 291n, 279n, 298n, 301n, 305n, 335, 357, 365n–6n, 562; children, see under Argyll, Duchess of; and 'The Club', 392n, 401 and n; as Privy Seal, 317 and n; on weasel, 393n
Armstrong, George Francis (later Savage-Armstrong), 409n
Arnold, Matthew, 124
Arthur, Prince, 326
Ashburton, Lady, 138n–9n, 140, 142, 153, 168 and n
Ashburton, Lord, 135n, 140, 168, 206
'Ask me no more', 456 and n
Auldjo, John and Caroline (née Hammet), 259n

Austin, Alfred, 523n
Austin, Wilfred Stanton Jr., 179n
'Aylmer's Field', 284n, 349 and n, 354n, 355n, 381n
Aytoun, William Edmonstoune, 53, 236n

Bacon, Charles, 251n
Bailey, Philip James, 415n
Baines, Benjamin, 77, 78
Banks, George Linnaeus, 361n
Barbet, Stephen, 487
Baring, Louisa, 141 and n
Barnes, William, 271n
Barrett, Henry John, 58, 60, 110, 129, 205 and n
Barry, Sir Charles, 250 and n
Barry, Edward Middleton, 250 and n
Barry, Sir Redmond, 320n
Barwell, ? Richard, 384 and n
Bayley, H. V. and Louisa (née Pattle), 559
Beale, Lionel Smith, 538 and n
Beatrice, Princess, 303, 304, 325, 326, 327
Beaufort, Emily (later Strangford), 512n
Beauvau, Prince Charles-Juste de, 324n
Beckford, ? William, 244 and n
Belgrave, Anne, 153
Bell, Alexander Graham, 403n
Bell, Alexander Melville, 403n
Bell, Clive, 559
Bell, Henry Glassford, 219 and n, 430
Bell, Robert, 153 and n, 161
Bell, Vanessa (née Stephen), 559
Bellew, J. C. M., 322n
Belon, Pierre, 365 and n
Bence Jones, Henry, 384 and n
Bennett, William Cox, 129, 531 and n
Bennett, William Sterndale, 282 and n, 306, 323, 374
Biddulph, Thomas Myddleton, 301n, 302
Birrell, Augustine and Eleanor Mary (née Locker), 390n
Blackie, John Stuart, 366n
Blackwood, Frederick Temple Hamilton-Temple, see Dufferin, Lord
Blewitt, Octavian, 312n, 313

Bliss, Mrs J. Worthington (née Lindsay), 33 and n
Blodgett, Mr, 341n
'Boadicea', 271, 283, 354n, 361, 453
Boggs, George, 317n
Bolton, Mr and Miss, 48
Bonewitz, Maria Volckmann, 51n
Booth, Augustus, 525 and n
Booth, Edwin Thomas, 532n
Booth, Mary (later Richardson), 251n
Bosquet, Pierre François, 416 and n
Boufflers, Chevalier de, 324n
Bourne, Mary Tennyson (aunt), 363 and n
Bowen, Charles Synge Christopher (later Sir), 383 and n
Bowen, Emily Frances (née Rendel), 383 and n
Bowman, William, 335 and n, 336n, 374
Boyne, Viscount, 372 and n, 373, 552
Boyne, Viscountess (Emma Russell), 45, 84, 88, 372 and n, 548 and n
Bradbury, William, 209 and n
Bradbury and Evans, 247 and n
Bradley, Arthur, 455 and n
Bradley, Edith Nicoll (later Ellison), 349
Bradley, George Granville, 35n, 123n, 348, 349
Bradley, Marian (née Philpot), 123n, 292n, 348, 349, 435
'Break, break,', 193n, 391
Bridges, Robert Seymour, 330n
Bright, John, 135n, 145, 147
Brightwell, Daniel Barron, 534n, 535n
Brimley, George, 136n, 243
British Quarterly Review, 131
'Brook, The', 250n, 333
Brooke, James (Rajah of Sarawak), 217 and n, 256-7n
Brookfield, Jane Octavia, 46, 47, 141, 142, 239n, 335
Brookfield, Olive, 546n
Brookfield, William Henry, 46, 47, 141n, 238, 239 and n, 373
? Brown, Dr, 552
Brown, Maria (later Peel), 143 and n
Browne, Sir Thomas, 418
Browning, Robert, 34, 39, 116, 128, 286, 331, 332, 335, 338n, 368, 371, 425; at Hallam Tennyson's christening, 48; poetry of, 252, 330, 406n, 415n, 508; will signed, 353n
Browning, Elizabeth Barrett, 34, 48, 116, 128, 168n, 425n; death 286n
Bruce, Lady Augusta (later Stanley), 303 and n, 310n, 325, 327, 329, 346n
Bruce, Katherine Mary, 350n
Bruce, Maj-Gen. Robert, 350n
Brunne, Robert of, 537 and n

Büchner, Louis, 479 and n
Buckland, Francis Trevelyan, 393n
Bulford, Miss, 563
Bunbury, Ellen (née Tennyson d'Eyncourt), 414n
Bunbury, Henry Hill, 414n
Bunsen, Christian Karl Josias, Baron von, 177 and n, 197, 269 and n
Burnard, Neville Northey, 214 and n
Burrichter, Harry C., 533n
Butler, Arthur Gray, 348n
Butler, George, 348n
Butler, Georgina Isabella (née Elliot), 348 and n
Butler, Henry Montagu, 348 and n
Butterworth, Charles Henry, 339n, 343
Byrne, George Grey, 226 and n, 227

Cain, Mr, 3-4
Cambridge, visit to, 241-2
Cameron, Charles Hay, 48, 129, 178, 397n, 559
Cameron, ? Hugh (b. 1835), 422 and n
Cameron, Hugh Thomas (b. 1813), 422 and n
Cameron, Julia Hay (later Norman), 554n
Cameron, Julia Margaret (née Pattle), 48, 129, 173, 175, 178, 204, 206, 215, 237, 258, 334, 401, 559
Campbell, George Douglas, *see* Argyll, Duke of
Campbell, Tom, 440
Canning, Stratford (Lord Stratford de Redcliffe), 552 and n
Carlisle, Lord (George William Howard), 388n
Carlyle, Jane Welsh, 46, 140, 142
Carlyle, Thomas, 46, 140, 141n, 142, 404 and n, 424, 545 and n
Carroll, Lewis, 276n
Carter, Mr, 542
Cator, Eleanor, 58
Cator, John Farnaby (later Lennard), 39
Cator, Julia (daughter of Julia Hallam Cator), 58, 60
Cator, Julia Hallam (later Lennard), 39, 58-9, 62
Cavendish, Lord Frederick Charles, 314 and n
Cavendish, William, 314n
Chapman, Benedict Lawrence, 67, 74, 77, 117, 120
Chapman, Edward, 285n
Chapman, Frederic, 285n
Chapman and Hall, 368
Chappell, William, 375 and n
'Charge of the Light Brigade, The', 100 and n, 101, 102, 114, 116n, 121, 133, 134 and n, 333, 524; copies sent to Crimea, 117-18n, 132-3

Index

Charlesworth, Elizabeth (later Cowell), 56n
Chawner, Rosa, 92 and n, 216
Cherbury, Lord Herbert of, 554
Chisholm, Caroline, 57n
'Christabel', 347
Christine, Princess, 494 and n
Cialdini, Enrico, 416 and n
'Circumstance', 108n
Clarendon, Lord, 299
'Claribel', 108n
Clark, William George, 202 and n, 340, 474 and n, 478
Classical metres, experimental poems with, 344n, 345n
Claughton, Amelia Maria (later Duchess of Argyll), 562
Clifton, Mr, 4, 5, 8
Clinton, Henry Pelham (Duke of Newcastle), 70 and n
Clive, Caroline (née Meysey-Wigley), 373 and n
Clough, Arthur Hugh, 162n, 216, 276; death 286 and n
Clough, ? Mrs Blanche, 342, 344, 472
Cobden, Richard, 135n
Cockbin, Charles Edward, 511n
Colam, John, 325n
Colburn, Eliza (née Crosbie, later Forster), 176 and n
Collins, Mortimer, 515 and n, 524
Colquhoun, Ludovic, 65, 66, 67, 70
Colville of Culross, Baron, 422 and n
'Come not', 459 and n
Comte, Auguste, 418 and n
Conington, John, 416 and n
Constitutional Press, 225
Conway, Moncure Daniel, 331n
Cookesley, William Gifford, 248 and n, 254
Copley, John Singleton, 230n
Cornforth, Fanny, 377n
Cornhill Magazine, 249 and n, 252, 253, 346, 376
Cornwall, visit to, 262–7
Cotton, Benjamin T., 497n, 508
Cotton, Tiny, 497n, 498, 555
Cowell, Edward Byles and Elizabeth (née Charlesworth), 56n
Cox, Mr, 11
Cracroft, Sophia (Sophy), 47 and n, 508
Cracroft, Thomas, 133n
Cracroft-Amcotts, Colonel Robert, 133n
Craig, Mr, 226
Craik, George L., 368
Creswick, Thomas, 89 and n
Crewe, Annabella Hungerford (later Milnes), 144 and n
Crewe, Marquis of (Robert Milnes), 525n

Crosbie, Eliza Ann (later Colburn and Forster, 176 and n
Cross, Elizabeth Dennistoun (Zibbie), 69n, 165
Crowe, Mr, 205
Crozier, Julia (née Stone), 422n
Crozier, Rear-Admiral Richard, 422 and n
Crozier, Lieut.-Col. Richard Pearson, 422n
Crozier, Capt. William Pearson, 422n

Daily Express, 127
Daily Telegraph, 300, 513 and n
'Daisy, The', 369 and n
Dakyns, Henry Graham, 276 and n, 277–8, 385n
Dallas, Eneas Sweetland, 125n
Dalrymple, Sir John, 559
Dalrymple, Lady Sophia (née Pattle), 227, 559
Damant, Caroline (later Wightwick), 189
Darwin, Elizabeth, 500 and n
Darwin, Erasmus Alvey, 500 and n
Darwin, Mrs Charles (née Wedgwood), 500 and n
D'Aumale, Duc, 218 and n
Davey, Mary, 80 and n, 99
Davies, Thomas, 151, 213n
Davy, Dr John, 10
Day, ? William James, 370 and n
Day, ? William Stuart, 370 and n
De Vere, Aubrey 48, 87, 154, 200, 289, 319
De Vere, Stephen Edward, 151 and n
De Vere, Sir Vere Edmond, 41
'Dedication, A', 373n
Delane, John Thaddeus, 305n, 552 and n
Dempster, William Richardson, 163n
Derby, Lord, *see* Stanley, Edward
Derbyshire, visit to, 314–16
D'Eyncourt, Clara, *see* Palmer, Clara
D'Eyncourt, Edwin (cousin), 373
Dickens, Charles 20, 46, 185, 478, 479; death, 549n
Disraeli, Benjamin (D'Israeli), 379, 487
Dixon, William Hepworth, 423 and n
Dobell, Emily (née Fordham), 271n
Dobell, John, 271
? Dobell, Sydney, 104n, 271
Dobson, Mr, 21
Dodgson, Charles Lutwidge, 543n, 544
Doré, Gustave, 452n
Dore, John, 161
D'Orsay, Count, 20
Dorset, 95, 372
Doyle, Sir Francis, 353n
Doyle, Richard, 64, 146, 169n, 175
Drake, Bernard, 99

Duckworth, Herbert and Julia (née Jackson), 559
Dudley, Earl and Countess (née Rachel Gurney), 559
Duff Gordon, Sir Alexander and Lady, 48, 313, 317, 294, 295, 317, 565–6
Dunraven, Lord (Wyndham-Quin), 432n
'Dying Swan, The', 52

Eardley, Stenton, 528n, 537
Eastnor, Lady (Virginia Pattle), 559
Eastnor, Lord (later Earl Somers), 559
Eden, Eleanor, 432n
Eden, Emily, 432n, 454 and n, 508 and n
Eden, George, 508n
Edinburgh News and Literary Chronicle, 121 and n, 127, 131
Edinburgh Review, 233
Edwards, Charles, 158 and n
Eglinton, Earl of, *see* Montgomerie
Egmont, Lord, *see* Percival
'1865–1866', 483 and n
'Elegiacs', 108n
Ellice, Edward, 142n
Elliot, Georgina Isabella (later Butler), 348 and n
Elliott, H. B., 363
Elliott, Margaret, 271
Ellis, Charles, 167
Ellison, Cuthbert Edward, 6
Ellison, Edith Nicoll (née Bradley), 349n
Elmhirst, Revd Edward, 62
Elton, Lady Rhoda Susan (née Willis), 370n
Elton, Sir Arthur Hallam, 370n
Emma, Dowager Queen of Sandwich Islands, 402, 405 and n, 411, 412–13
'Enid', 152, 156, 175
Enid and Nimuë: the True and the False, 179 and n, 180, 181 and n, 235
'Enoch Arden' ('Enoch the Fisherman'), 284n, 297 and n, 338, 352, 356, 357 and n, 377, 381n, 485, 532; earnings from, 374n, 383, 428 and n, 453; illustrated, 403n; opinions of, 314, 353; readings of, 311, 369, 374n, 379; translated, 421, 465 and n, 468, 493
Estcourt, Arthur Harbottle, 147n
Estcourt, Charles Wyatt, 147 and n, 442 and n
Evans, Frederick Mullett, 209 and n, 231, 322 and n, 354
Evelyn, William John, 369 and n
Examiner, 23, 26, 100, 102, 117n, 127
Eyre, Edward John, 415, 416, 422, 429 and n

Fairbairn, Dorothy (née Mar), 184n, 187n
Fairbairn, Thomas, 187n, 305 and n
Fairbairn, William, 184n, 187n, 206, 257n, 563

Farrar, Frederic William, 35n, 400n
Farringford House, 74 *et seq.*
Faucit, Helena (later Martin), 226 and n
Fearn, Capt. Walker, 385n, 408 and n
Fechter, Charles Albert, 322 and n
? Feilden, Randle Henry, 447 and n
Fenn, George Manville, 403 and n
Fenwick, Isabella, 96n
Fenwick, Capt. (later Admiral) William Henry, 150
Ferguson, Robert, 494n
Ferguson, Samuel, 368
Ferguson, Sir William, 365 and n
Ferrier, Elizabeth Anne (Coggie), 502 and n
Ferrier, James Frederick, 103n
Field, The, 22, 23
Fields, James Thomas, 133, 237, 250, 481
Fields, Mrs James Thomas, 153, 250
Fisher, Col. Edward Henry, 374 and n, 376 and n, 378
Fisher, Herbert, 559
Fisher, Mary (née Jackson), 559
FitzGerald, Edward, 144
Fletcher, Mary (later Richardson), 251n
Flower, Celina (née Greaves), 362n
Flower, Edward Fordham, 356 and n
'Flower in the Crannied Wall', 540 and n
Foley, John Henry, 296 and n
Foote, Samuel, 269 and n
Forster, Eliza Ann (née Crosbie and formerly Colburn), 176 and n
Forster, John, 19, 23, 25, 127, 175, 176, 209, 358n, 375, 379
Foscolo, Ugo, 364
Fox, Caroline, 266
Fox, Mr, 532
Fox, Revd Mr, 407n
Fox, Robert (b. 1845), 266n
Fox, Robert Barclay (b. 1817), 266n
Fox, William Johnson, 134n
France, visits to, 276–8, 380
Franklin, Col. (later Maj.-Gen.) Charles Trigance, 546 and n
Franklin, Lady Jane, 47n, 411, 429, 508
Franklin, Sir John, 13n, 110n, 251n
Fraser, Alexander Campbell, 484 and n
Fraser's Magazine, 22
Freshwater, *see* Farringford House
Froude, James Anthony, 217, 355 and n, 368, 390, 411
Furnivall, Frederick James, 79n
Fytche, Albert (cousin), 287n, 400 and n, 475 and n
Fytche, John (uncle), 114 and n
Fytche, Lewis (cousin), 81, 153
Fytche, Mary Anne (aunt), 371 and n, 385 and n

Index

Galton, Francis, 348n
Gandy, Mrs, 61, 174
Garden, Francis, 54, 79, 216
'Gardener's Daughter, The', 236n, 460
Garibaldi, 269, 364–5 and n
Garrick, David, 187 and n
Gaskell, Cecil (later Palgrave), 508n
Gaskell, James Milnes, 508n
Gaskell, William, 187 and n
Gassiot, John Paul, 499
Gatty, Alfred, 211n, 255n
Gatty, Margaret, 192n-3n, 224, 255 and n, 256n
Giblin, William Robert, 359n
Gifford, Katherine (née Simpson), 502
Gilchrist, Anne, 444
? Gillian, Miss, 57
? Gillies, Miss, 57
Ginsburg, Christian David, 480 and n
Gladstone, William Ewart, 135n, 229, 304, 307, 308, 337, 352–3, 374, 375, 412; 'Great Budget', 255n; writings, 318n; on boys' schooling, 353, 384; arranges visit to House of Commons, 377 and n; at Woolner's, 451–21
Glastonbury, 94–5
'God Save the Queen', extra verses for, 190–2
Godley, John Robert, 286 and n
Goldsmith, *see* Lyndhurst, Lady
Good Words, 346
Grant, Sir Alexander, 95 and n, 191, 197, 486
Granville, Lord, 292 and n
Graves, Charles, 368
Greaves, Celina (later Flower), 362n
Gregory, William, 54 and n
Grenville, William Wyndham (Baron), 308 and n
Grey, Sir George, 8
Greyshott Hall, 460–3
Griffith, David, 472n
Grigsby, Mr, 11
Grosvenor, Lady Constance Gertrude (née Leveson-Gower), 308 and n
Grosvenor, Hugh Lupus, 308n
Grote, George, 418 and n
Grove, Florence Craufurd, 238 and n, 239, 240
Grove, George, 91n, 476n 504
Guest, Lady Charlotte (later Schreiber), 381n
Guest, Sir Ivor Bertie, 381n, 447, 502, 535
Guest, Mary Enid Evelyn (later Layard), 413, 468n
'Guinevere', 200n, 206, 208, 220 and n, 228, 230, 233, 235, 237n, 250, 265, 297, 310n, 453, 489, 501 and n
Guizot, François Pierre Guillaume, 252 and n, 327, 329

Gully, Anne, 65 and n
Gunter, Thomas, 48 and n
Gurney, Alice (née Prinsep), 559
Gurney, Anna, 267 and n
Gurney, Archer Thompson, 119n, 120, 560
Gurney, Charles, 559
Gurney, Laura (later Troubridge), 559
Gurney, Rachel (later Dudley), 559

Hall, Anna Maria, 27n
Hallam, Arthur Henry, 40, 94, 277, 290n
Hallam, Henry, 47, 48, 90, 177, 223, 230, 266
Hallam, Henry FitzMaurice, 485n
Hallam, Julia (later Lennard), 485n
Hamilton-Russell, Gustavus, 373 and n
Hamilton-Russell, Lady Katherine Frances, 373 and n
Hammet, Caroline (later Auldjo), 259n
Hammond, Sir Andrew Snape, 464 and n
Hampshire, 125–6, 274–6, 343
'Hands All Round', 25 and n, 26n, 27, 236 and n
Hannay, James, 350n
Harrison, Robert, 320n
Haslemere, 445, 531–6, 550–2
Hatch, Edwin, 194n
Hawker, Revd Robert Stephen, 120, 237n
Hawthorne, Nathaniel, 369n; journal of, 183–4
Hayward, Abraham, 41n
Heard, Charles, 287n, 370, 372n, 520 and n, 539, 548
Heath, Dunbar Isidore, 54 and n
Heathcote, Margaret, 116 and n, 213, 563
Hegel, G. W. F., 197, 198
'Helen's Tower', 279 and n, 280, 294, 566–7
Helena, Princess, 326
Helps, Arthur, 153 and n, 368
Hengstenberg, Ernest Wilhelm, 54 and n
Herschel, Sir John Frederick William, 125 and n, 352n
Hill, Richard, 65n
Hinton, James, 520n
Hoapili, Mr and Mrs, 412 and n
Hodges, J. Sydney Willis, 265n
Hodges, S., 266
Hodgson, Shadworth Hollway, 208n
Hole, Samuel Reynolds, 557n
Hollway, Anne (later Hodgson), 208n–9n
Hollway, John Palmer, 208n
'Holy Grail' ('San Graal') 268, 269, 503, 506, 508, 510–11, 517n, 521, 539–40
'Home Idylls', 375
Hooker, Frances Harriet (Henslow), 464n
Hooker, Joseph Dalton, 413 and n, 464n, 500
Hopgood, John, 547 and n

Hordern, Ellen Frances (later Lubbock), 356 and n
Horsley, John Callcott, 89 and n
Houghton, Lord, see Milnes, Richard Monckton
(?) Howard, Mr, 486 and n
Howard, Charles Wentworth George, 229n, 308 and n, 337, 388, 563
Howard, Capt. (later Admiral) Edward Granville George, 229n
Howard, George William Frederick (Lord Carlisle), 388n
Howard, Harriet Elizabeth Georgiana, see Sutherland, Duchess of
Howard, Henry Francis, 244n
Howard, Henry George, 244 and n
Howard, Mary Matilda Georgiana (Lady Taunton), 308 and n
Howard, William George, 229 and n, 563
Hudson, Derek, 398
Hudson, George, 32
Hughes, Arthur, 403 and n, 413, 423, 456
Hughes, Thomas, 218 and n
Hume, Alexander Hamilton, 443n
Hunt, Dr James, 442n, 445, 525
Hunt, William Holman, 89 and n, 200–1, 206, 262, 265, 415, 417
Hutton, Mr, 526
Huxley, Thomas Henry, 418 and n

Idylls of the King ('King Arthur'), 212 and n, 215 and n, 216, 237, 261, 267, 313, 364, 428n, 451, 501, 509; illustrations, 452 and n, 489; opinions on, 233, 245n, 246 and n, 250, 257, 271, 290n, 297 and n, 501, 502n, 539; Prince Albert and dedication, 257n, 258, 290, 291 and n, 292n, 293 and n, 294 and n, 295; readings, 217n, 453–4; Smith's offer for, 249n; title page, 232
Illustrated Edition ('Moxon Tennyson'), 79 and n, 89n, 146, 180 and n, 192, 210–11, 299
'In Memoriam', 108–9, 130, 243, 266, 290 and n, 297n, 298 and n, 365n, 460, 536; metre of, 553
'In the Valley of Cauteretz', 309n, 327 and n
Inchbold, John William, 263 and n
Inglefield, Edward Augustus, 55 and n, 62
Inglis, Henry, 71 and n
Ingram, John K., 368
Ireland, Mr, 185
Isaac, Dr, 555
Isaacson, John Frederick, 355 and n, 447 and n
Italy, visits to, 19, 26,

Jackson, Adeline (later Vaughan), 559

Jackson, Dr John, 280 and n, 281, 333, 334, 340, 559
Jackson, Julia (later Duckworth and Stephen), 559
Jackson, Maria (née Pattle), 284n, 559
Jackson, Mary (later Fisher), 559
Jackson, Thomas, 391n
James, Edith (later Jesse), 554n
Jebb, Richard Claverhouse, 481n, 492 and n
Jeffrey, William, 534 and n
Jenner, Charles, 413 and n
Jerrold, Douglas William, 260n
Jerrold, Mrs, 260n
Jerrold, William Blanchard, 260n
Jesse, Arthur Henry Hallam (nephew), 254 and n, 255
Jesse, Edith Louisa (née James), 554n
Jesse, Edward, 32
Jesse, Eustace Tennyson d'Eyncourt, 554n
Jesse, Fryn Tennyson, 554n
Jesse, Richard Eustace Russell, 554 and n
Jewsbury, Frank, 187 and n
João Carlos, Oliviera e Daun (Duke of Saldanha), 240n
Johnson, Sir George, 525 and n
Jolly, Emily, 271n
Jones, Mr (accountant?), 458, 459
Jones, Agnes, 497
Jones, Edward, 441
Jones, Walter, 549n
Jowett, Benjamin, 122, 139, 271, 360 and n, 421, 506

Kane, Elisha Kent, 165n
Keeping, Henry, 284 and n, 328, 482 and n
Kent, Duchess of, 327 and n, 350–1
Kent, Mr, 447
Kent, William Charles Mark, 470n
Kent, visit to, 62–3, 236–7
Kenward, James, 387n
Ker, Alan, 21, 23, 70, 71n
Ker, Dr Buchanan, 21n, 24
Ker, Mary (sister, née Tennyson), 21, 24, 28, 159, 264
King, Henry Samuel, 344n
King, John W., 214n
Kingsley, Mrs Charles, 250
Kingsley, Revd Charles, 79, 219, 250 and n, 368
Kirby, William, 486n, 547n
Knowles, James Thomas, 288n, 505, 506, 508

Labouchere, Henry (Baron Taunton), 308n
'Lady Clara Vere de Vere', 318
'Lady Clare', 1
Lambert, William Tooley, 200 and n, 375n

'Lancelot and Elaine' (Maid of Astolat'), 218 and n, 233, 504 and n
Landor, Walter Savage, 27
Landseer, Sir Edwin, 89 and n
Langford, John Alfred, 124n
Lansdowne, Lord, 218 and n
Latham, Robert Gordon, 270n
Lathrop, Rose Hawthorne, 186
Laurence, Samuel, 74, 254, 267, 341n, 360, 403 and n
La Villemarqué, Théodore Hersart, Vicomte de, 90n, 430 and n, 473
Lawrence, Abbott, 27
Lawrence, Sir John Laird Mair, 346 and n
Layavd, Austen Henry, 147, 468n
Layard, Mary Enid (née Guest), 468n
Le Marchant, Sir Denis, 255
Leacock, Mrs (?), 147
Leader, Mrs Dora (née Gillicuddy), 18 and n
Lear, Edward, 62, 64, 111 and n, 122, 123, 206, 372 and n, 383n
Lecky, William Edward Hartpole, 491n
Lee, John Edward, 159 and n, 160
Lee, Miss, 372
Lennard, Julia (née Hallam, later Cator), 39, 485n
Leopold, Prince, 326
Leveson-Gower, Constance (later Lady Grosvenor), 308 and n
Leveson-Gower, Lady Elizabeth Georgiana, *see* Argyll, Duchess of
Leveson-Gower, Granville Gower, 292n
Levison, Georgy, 162, 163
Lewes, George Henry, 423n
Lincolnshire, visits to, 34, 183, 185n
Lindsay, M. (later Bliss), 33 and n
Lipscombe, Mr, 382n
Litchfield, Henrietta (Darwin), 500n
Livingstone, David, 191 and n
Lloyd, John, 158 and n, 160
Locker, Eleanor Mary (later Tennyson and Birrell), 35n, 390n
Locker, Frederick, 193n, 510, 529n, 530n
'Locksley Hall', 105, 197n, 261
London: life in, 1–7, 10, 12–49, 56–65; major visits to, 89–90, 128–9, 171–7, 216–21, 226–32, 280–4, 305–9, 334–9, 352–8 383–7, 410–26, 506–10, 526–7
'Long as the heart beats life', 351
Longfellow, Charles Appleton, 449 and n
Longfellow, Henry Wadsworth, 93n, 496n, 497–8
'Lord of Burleigh, The', 333
Lorne, Marquis of, 389 and n, 448, 562, 563
'Lotos-Eaters, The', 348
Louis, Prince (Grand Duke of Hesse), 289n, 326

Louis Napoleon, 20, 47n, 236 and n
Louis Philippe d'Orléans, Henri Eugène, 218n
Louisa (Louise), Princess, 326, 562
Love, Rear-Admiral Henry Ommanney, 370 and n
'Love and Duty', 107
'Lover's Tale, The', 509, 511, 543
Lowe, Robert (later Viscount Sherbrooke), 434 and n
Lowell, Mabel, 526 and n
? Lubbe, Mr, 202
Lubbock, Ellen Frances (née Hordern), 356 and n
Lubbock, Sir John, 356n, 423
'Lucretius', 457n, 476, 477 and n, 478, 479–80, 481, 482, 483, 484 and n, 492n, 493, 504n
Ludlow, John Malcolm Forbes, 76 and n
Lushington, Cecilia (sister Cissy, née Tennyson), 23, 103n, 213n
Lushington, Edmund Henry, 130 and n, 141, 151n, 213n
Lushington, Edmund Law, 15, 48, 50, 62, 63, 110, 130n, 151, 213n, 219, 276, 334, 521 and n
Lushington, Ellen, 116n, 117, 130
Lushington, Emily, 116n, 117, 130, 520 and n
Lushington, Franklin, 49, 59, 90, 111n, 122, 273n, 521 and n
Lushington, Henry, 77, 78n, 116, 123, 130n, 145n, 213n
Lushington, Louisa Sophia, 94n, 123 and n, 213n
Lushington, Maria Catherine, 94, 116n, 130 and n, 213n
Lushington, Judge Stephen, 315 and n
Lushington, Mrs Stephen Rumbold, 213n
Lushington, Tom, 168
Lushington, Vernon, 177 and n, 206–7
Lushington, William Bryan, 216 and n
Lyall, Alfred, 566
Lyndhurst, Lady (née Goldsmith), 230 and n, 231
Lyttelton, George William, 343 and n
Lytton, Mr, 236n

Macaulay, Hannah More (later Trevelyan), 317 and n
Macaulay, Thomas Babington, 233 and n, 236, 244; death, 252 and n, 259
McClintock, Capt. (later Admiral Sir), Francis Leopold, 251 and n
MacDonald, George, 436n
MacGillicuddy, Dora (later Leader), 18 and n
Mackintosh, Robert James, 70 and n
Mackenzie, Adeline (née Pattle), 559
Mackenzie, Colin (later General), 559

Mackenzie, Lord Thomas, 219 and n
Maclean, Revd Hippisley, 34
MacLehose, James, 411n, 413
Macleod, Dr Norman, 470 and n, 471, 504
Maclise, Daniel, 89n, 211
Macmillan, Alexander, 241, 242n, 253n, 371, 476
Macmillan, Daniel, 242–3, 248
Macmillan's Magazine, 484
MacNeill, Ina Erskine (later Duchess of Argyll), 562
Macready, William Charles, 2
Manchester, visit to, 183–7
Mangles, James Henry, 348n
Mann, Dr Robert James, 73 and n, 110, 182n
Manzoni, Alessandro, 364 and n
Mar, Dorothy (later Fairbairn), 187n
Marochetti, Carlo, 296 and n, 565
Marshall, Mrs Henry, 68
Marshall, James Garth, 12–13, 16, 17, 32, 48, 179, 563–4
Marshall, Mary Alice (née Spring Rice), 13, 16, 17, 40, 43, 48, 83, 188 and n, 189
Marshall, Victor, 48 and n
Martin, Theodore and Helena (née Faucit), 226 and n
Massey, Gerald, 87n
Masson, David, 242 and n
Mathilde (nurse), 219, 224 and n
Matthison, Arthur, 532 and n
Maud, 104, 113 and n, 116n, 120, 122, 127, 132, 134, 145–6 and n, 236, 343; earnings from, 144 and n; opinions of, 119 and n, 121 and n, 124, 127, 133, 136 and n, 137–8, 147 and n, 155n, 554, 560; readings of, 128, 135, 141 and n, 178, 235, 402, 474
Maurice, John Frederick Denison, 47 and n, 48, 243
Max Müller, Friedrich, 246 and n, 510
'May Queen, The', 195, 318
Mayall, John Jabez Edwin, 115 and n, 303
Mayer, Brantz, 518 and n
'Merlin', 152, 154, 155n
'Merlin and Vivien', 147, 148 and n, 180n
Merwood, ? Jeremiah, 72 and n, 194, 287n
Metcalf, Thomas, 17
Meysey-Wigley, Caroline (later Clive), 373 and n
'Michael', 311
Mildmay, Ven. Carey Anthony St John-, 306 and n
Mildmay, Caroline Waldegrave, 306 and n
Millais, John Everett, 89 and n, 175, 176, 444, 556
Millar, Matilda or Martha, 3
Milman, Dean Henry Hart, 144 and n, 212 and n, 395 and n, 422 and n, 424

Milnes, Mrs (cook), 3(?), 23, 48
Milnes, Annabella Hungerford (née Crewe), 144 and n
Milnes, Richard Monckton (Lord Houghton), 64, 144 and n, 314, 335, 368, 373, 423n, 549n
Milnes, Robert Offley Ashburton, 525n
Mitchell, Emma (later Wood), 459 and n
Monsell, William, 151 and n
Monteagle, Lord, 8, 321
Monteith, Robert, 67, 216
Monteith, Mrs Robert, 65, 67
Montgomerie, Archibald Wilson (Earl of Eglinton), 75 and n
Moore, Tom, 347
Morgan, Kate Maria (later Lushington), 213, 281
Morier, James Justinian, 282n
Morier, Robert Burnet David, 48 and n, 175 and n
Morning Chronicle, 22, 23
(?) Mornington, Mr, 555
Morris, Mowbray, 60 and n
Morris, William, 492n
'Morte d'Arthur', 166, 193n, 385, 297 and n, 400 and n, 451, 466 and n
Moultrie, John, 43 and n
Moxon, Edward (and Company), 15, 28, 49, 50, 52, 63, 74, 77n, 89
Moxon, William (and Company), 108, 113, 117, 118, 119, 161, 201, 203, 237, 372, 481n; finances, 108, 201, 467; *Illustrated Edition*, 79 and n, 89 and n, 146, 180 and n, 192; disagreement with, 209, 412; illness and death, 196, 199 and n, 515n
Moxon, Mrs William, 512, 515n, 516, 517
Mudie, Robert, 354 and n
Mulready, William, 89 and n
Mumby, Frank Arthur, 506n
Munby, Arthur Joseph, 398 and n
Munch, Andreas, 468n
Murch, Mr and Mrs, 205
Murray, John, 396n
Murray, Mrs, 152
Murrow, Thomas, 233 and n
Mussy, Henri Guéneau de, 334n 336
'My Lords', 21

Napier, Joseph, 368
Napoleon, 445n, 552
Newcastle, Duke of, 70 and n
Nicolson, Harold, 565
(?) Ninnie, 93 and n
Norman, Charles Loyd, 554n
Norman, George, 554n, 555
Norman, Julia Hay (née Cameron), 554n
Normanby, Lord, 34

North, Catherine (later Symonds), 385n
'Northern Farmer' ('Farmer') 354 and n, 355n, 356, 385, 525
'Northern Farmer, New Style', 403n, 454
Norton, Brinsley and wife, 226 and n
Norway, visit to, 204–5, 207, 250
Novelli, Augustus Henry, 256n, 375 and n, 377 and n
Nutt, Mr, 247

'O blessing of thy child', 350n, 351
O'Brien, William Smith, 289 and n
O'Connor, V. C. Scott, 407n
'Ode on the Death of Duke of Wellington', 48, 51, 52–3, 56, 58, 279 and n
'Ode Sung at Opening of International Exhibition' ('International Ode') 281 and n, 283, 284, 289 and n, 301–2, 305 and n, 306, 307n, 312, 452, 461
Ogle, Dr, 353n
'Old Woman, The' ('The Grandmother'), 230n
Oliphant, Margaret Oliphant, 536n
Orme, Charles E., 129 and n
Osgood, James Ripley, 457n
O'Shaughnessy, Arthur William Edgar, 556n, 557n
Owen, Richard, 32, 407n, 532
Owen, Mrs W. H., 134n
'Owl, The', 325

Paddison, Richard, 305 and n, 355 and n, 372, 378
Paget, James, 333 and n, 337, 340, 370, 373 and n, 552
'Palace of Art, The', 460
Palgrave, Cecil Grenville Milnes (née Gaskell), 508n
Palgrave, Sir Francis (born Cohen), 27n
Palgrave, Francis Turner, 27n, 107, 151, 153, 217, 337, 342, 347, 352–3, 376, 412, 413; at Hallam Tennyson's christening, 48; visits Cornwall, 266, 267, 268n; visits Derbyshire and Yorkshire, 314–15; visits Scotland, 67, 68; visits Spain, 238, 239, 241 and n; writings, 202; at Woolner's, 416, 417
Palgrave, William Gifford, 262 and n, 352–3n, 357, 502, 509
Palmer, Clara Hinde (née Tennyson d'Eyncourt—cousin), 90n, 335 and n
Palmer, John Hinde, 90n, 91
Palmerston, Lord, 321, 387
Parish, Dr Henry, 38
Parker, John William, 80n, 153 and n, 197
Parry, Charles Hubert Hastings, 473 and n
Paterson, Helen (later Allingham), 18n

Patmore, Coventry, 18n, 25, 26, 108, 131n, 154, 233n
Patmore, Emily Augusta, 24, 25, 87, 164, 312n
Pattle, James and Adeline: daughters of, 559
Paul, Revd. C. Kegan, 382n, 386n–7n, 403
Payne, James Bertrand ('Ancient Pistol'), 383, 390, 422, 456, 481, 486, 506 and n, 515; disagreement with, 513, 516–17, 523, 524, 533, 534–5, 539
Peach, Charles, 7
Peacock, Frances Elizabeth (née Selwyn), 480n
Peacock, George, 480n
Peel, Archibald, 54, 85 and n, 177
Peel, Edmund, 73
Peel, Maria (née Brown), 143 and n
Peel, Miss, 48
Pelham-Clinton, Robert Renebald, 308n
'Penny-Wise, The' ('The Poem of Arm'), 22 and n
Perceval, George James (Lord Egmont), 527 and n, 545
(?) Perring, Mr, 200 and n
Petrie, George, 368, 401 and n
Petty-FitzMaurice, Henry (Lord Lansdowne), 218 and n
Philips, Samuel, 53 and n
Philpot, Marian, see Bradley, Marian
Phipps, Col. Charles Beaumont 191–2, 290n, 291, 295n
Pickering, Basil Montagu, 436n
Pierce, Anne Longfellow, 495 and n
Pittis, Francis, 149n
Plato, 197, 198
Plumley (Plumbley), Charles William, 375 and n, 384, 386
'Poem of Arm, The', see 'Penny Wise, The'
'Poet's Song, The', 459
Pollock, Sir Frederick (d. 1870), 29n
Pollock, Sir Frederick (d. 1937), 29n
Pollock, Sir William Frederick, 29 and n, 202, 352n, 381n, 342
'Portrait, The', 533
Portugal, visit to, 239–40, 244, 250
Price, John, 499
Price, Thomas, 156n
Princess Royal, see Victoria Adelaide
Princess of Wales, see Alexandra
'Princess, The', 1, 63, 210 and n, 211, 330n, 383n
Prinsep, Alice (later Gurney), 559
Prinsep, Henry Thoby, 173, and n, 371 and n, 373, 559
Prinsep, Sarah Monckton (née Pattle), 173 and n, 175, 201, 204, 206, 221, 231, 237, 333, 334, 559

Prinsep, Valentine Cameron, 227 and n, 262, 265 and n, 370, 371
Pritchard, Charles, 355 and n, 375, 506, 508
Procter, Agnes, 379 and n
Procter, Anne, 379 and n, 414
Procter, Bryan Waller, 414
Procter, Edith, 379 and n
Putnam's Monthly Magazine, 132n

Quillinans, 65

Radcliffe Hall, John, 559
Ralph, John, 179n
Rashdall, John, 23-4
Rawnsley, Alfred Edward, 53
Rawnsley, Catherine (Kate), 4-5, 9, 16, 29, 43, 45, 48, 53, 371 and n
Rawnsley, Drummond, 16, 48, 53, 551
Rawnsley, Margaret, 371 and n
Rawnsley, Willingham Franklin, 29
Read, Thomas Buchanan, 167n
Redcliffe, Lord Stratford de (Canning), 552 and n
Reeves, *see* Sims Reeves
Rejlander, Oscar G., 360 and n, 545
Rendel, Emily (later Bowen), 383 and n
Repton, George Herbert, 56n, 57
'Reticence', 191 and n
Richards, Alfred Bate, 522n
Richardson, Mary (née Booth), 251n
Richardson, Mary (née Fletcher), 251n
Richardson, Sir John, 251n
Richmond, Thomas Knyvett, 353n
Richter, Jean Paul, 418
'Rifle-Clubs!!!' ('The War'), 20-1, 25, 223n
'Riflemen Form!', 223 and n
'Ring out wild bells', 243
Ritchie, Anne Isabella (née Thackeray), 333 and n
Ritchie, Richmond Thackeray Willoughby, 333n
'Rivulet, The', 260
Robert, Henry, 70
Robertson, Frederick William, 328 and n
Robertson, James Craigie, 216 and n
Rogers, Samuel, 5, 10, 59
Rogers, William Henry, 274 and n
Rolle, Richard, 352n
Roscoe, Maria Fletcher, 431 and n
Rossetti, Dante Gabriel, 89n
Rossetti, William Michael, 204, 335, 377n, 506n, 554 and n, 557
Routledge, George, 341n, 379 and n, 387n, 403
Russell, Elizabeth, 155n, 408 and n
Russell, Emma, *see* Boyne, Viscountess
Russell, Lady John, 5

Russell, Lord John, 5n, 511

Sabine, Maj.-Gen. Edward, 374n
Saldanha, Duke of, 240 and n
Sandford, Francis Richard, 281 and n
Santley, Charles (later Sir), 375 and n
Sartoris, Adelaide (née Kemble), 200 and n, 227
Saunders, John, 96n
Savage-Armstrong, George Francis, 409n
Sayers, Tom, 343 and n
Schreiber, Charles, 381n, 413
Schreiber, Lady Charlotte, 381n
Schroeter, Gottlieb Heinrich von, 97 and n
Scoones, Revd William Dalton, 48 and n
Scotland, visit to, 65-71, 188, 201
Scott, George Gilbert, 299n
Scott, Robert, 112n
Scott, Sir Walter, 316 and n
Scott, William Bell, 357n
'Sea Dreams, an Idyll', 191 and n, 245, 246 and n, 253n
'Sea Fairies, The', 348
Seaford, 49-56
Sellar, William Young, 67 and n, 68, 69, 151, 321 and n
Sellar, Mrs William Young, 69
Sellway, Mrs, 82
Sellwood, Anne, *see* Weld, Anne
Sellwood, Henry, 35 and n, 60 and n, 372n
Selwyn, Frances Elizabeth (later Peacock and Thompson), 480n
Selwyn, William, 465 and n
Sewell, Arthur, 362n
Sewell, Elizabeth Missing, 170n
Sewell, Ellen Mary, 170 and n, 171
Seymour, Revd George Turner, 72 and n, 74, 132, 148, 151
Shafto, Rosa (Baring), 92 and n
Sharpey, William, 411 and n
Shedden-Ralston, William Ralston, 523n
Shepherd, Richard Herne, 436, 535n
Sherbrooke, Viscount (Robert Lowe), 434 and n
Sheridan, Helen Selina, 565
Shiel, Mrs, 18
Shorter, Thomas, 268
Simeon, Charles, 216 and n
Simeon, Lady Catherine Dorothea, 422 and n
Simeon, Lady Jane Maria, 144, 263, 264
Simeon, Louisa Edith (later Ward), 319 (?), 372 and n
Simeon, Mary Jane, 432 and n
Simeon, Sir John, 97 and n, 144, 135, 154, 189, 263, 264, 343, 371, 372; death, 551 and n
Simmons, James, 541 and n
Simpson, Katherine (née Gifford), 502

Index

Sims Reeves, John, 374 and n, 375
'Sir Lancelot and Queen Guinevere', 459
Skipworth, Miss, 287
Smith, Adam, 63
Smith, Elder and Co., 237, 245 and n, 249n 254, 344n
Smith, George, 245 and n, 249n, 252, 344n
Smith, Goldwin, 140 and n
Smith, ? Henry, 187n
Smith, John Stores, 187n
Smythe, Percy Ellen Frederick, see Strangford, Lord
'Song of the Alma River, The', 374n, 375n
'Song—The Owl', 108n
Southampton, 139, 238
Southey, Reginald, 171n
Spedding, James, 55, 100, 142, 305, 352n, 353, 354, 369
Speedy, Capt. Tristram Charles Sawyer, 497, 499 and n, 500n
Speedy, Mrs, 497n
'Spirit Haunts, A' ('Song'), 108n
'Spiteful Letter, On a', 473n, 476n
'Splendour falls on castle walls, The' ('Bugle Song'), 153 and n
Spring Rice, Charles, 48
Spring Rice, Mary Alice, see Marshall, Mary Alice
Spring Rice, Stephen, 17, 48, 398 and n
Spring Rice, William, 563
Spurgeon, Charles Haddon, 343 and n
Squire, William, 200 and n, 216, 306, 307, 374
Stanfield, Clarkson, 89n
Stanford, Edward, 3 and n, 6, 9, 61
Stanley, Arthur Penrhyn, 346n
Stanley, Lady Augusta (née Bruce), 346n, 373, 517
Stanley, Edward George Geoffrey Smith (Earl of Derby), 420 and n
Stanley, Edward John, 8, 12
Stephen, Adrian, 559
Stephen, Julia (née Jackson), 559
Stephen, Sir Leslie, 333n, 559
Stephen, Thoby, 559
Stephen, Vanessa (later Bell), 559
Stephen, Virginia (later Woolf), 559
Stephens, John Lloyd, 144 and n
Stephens, Thomas, 151 and n
Stephenson, Mrs, 65
Sterling, Sir Anthony Coningham, 434n
Sterling, John, 267, 451
Stirling, Mary Ann (Fanny), 51
Stokes, William, 368
Stone, Julia (later Crozier), 422n
Strahan, Alexander, 470, 506 and n, 509, 515n, 516, 536, 539–40, 543 and n
Strand Magazine, 381n

Strangford, Emily Anne (née Beaufort), Lady, 512n
Strangford, Lord (Percy Smythe), 379 and n, 512 and n
Sudhoff, Karl, 327n, 329
Sullivan, Arthur, 444, 447, 469, 557n
Sullivan, John, 396n
Sumner, Charles, 183 and n, 250, 317 and n
Sunday at Home, The, 324
Sutherland, Duchess of (Harriet Howard), 201 and n, 229, 270, 272, 283n, 284, 291n, 300, 337
Sutherland, Duke of, 272n
'Sweet and Low', 33, 456n
Swinburne, Algernon Charles, 194 and n, 271n, 320, 401 and n, 423n, 441
Switzerland, visit to, 529–30
Syme, James, 69 and n
Symington, Andrew James, 312n
Symonds, Catherine (née North), 385n
Symonds, Dr John Addington, 415 and n, 416–21
Symonds, John Addington (son of Dr John Addington), 385 and n, 415 and n, 416n, 420n

Tainsh, Edward Campbell, 485n
Talfourd, Thomas Noon, 85(?)
Tauchnitz, Baron Christian Bernhard von, 246n, 247n, 380n, 437, 487, 489, 518
Taunton, Lady Mary (Howard), 308 and n
Taunton, Lord (Labouchere), 308n
Taylor, Bayard, 181n, 182, 191, 207, 453–4, 514
Taylor, Henry (later Sir), 5, 48, 53, 116, 258 and n, 559
Taylor, Mrs Henry, 19, 37, 48, 82
Taylor, Tom, 33, 48, 90, 140, 142, 144, 146, 196, 368
Taylor, Mrs Tom, 33, 140, 142, 144, 146
Taylor, Una (later Troubridge), 559
'Tears, idle tears', 499
Temple, Frederick, 110, 112
Temple Bar, 523, 524
Tennyson, Alfred (described), 184, 185, 332, 439, 497
Tennyson, Arthur (brother), 54, 385 and n, 393
Tennyson, Cecilia (sister), see Lushington, Cecilia
Tennyson, Charlotte Maria Elwes, 520n
Tennyson, Eleanor Mary (née Locker), 35n, 390n
Tennyson, Elise, 464 and n, 465
Tennyson, Elizabeth Fytche (mother), 21, 24, 72, 114, 209, 371; death, 393–4
Tennyson, Emilia, 464 and n, 465

Tennyson, Emily Sellwood (wife) 4, 9, 26, 234; death of first child, 13-14, 15-16; births of sons, *see under* Tennyson, Hallam and Tennyson, Lionel; described, 170n, 186, 207, 267, 270, 331, 366, 439 and n, 495, 498; journal, 156-9, 160

Tennyson, Frederick (brother), 54n, 86, 281, 464, 465

Tennyson, Giulio (nephew, Julius), 54 and n, 281, 364n

Tennyson, Hallam (son), 36n, 445, 495, 496; birth, 36-43; christening, 44-8; and Lionel's birth, 82, 86; childhood, 55, 56, 67, 68, 103, 133, 141, 163, 172n, 174 and n, 198, 235, 250, 288, 347; illness 455-6; father dreams about, 201; on visit to Queen, 325-6; memoirs, 391n

Tennyson, Harriet (née West), 385 and n

Tennyson, Horatio (brother), 209, 520 and n, 553n

Tennyson, Lionel (son), 386, 409, 413, 423, 442 and n, 445; birth, 81-2, 85, 86; christening, 92; childhood, 92, 106, 133, 174n, 198, 219, 235, 250, 275, 278, 288, 334, 347; Eton examination, 502, 506, 542; stammering, 525; marriage, 35n

Tennyson, Mary (sister), *see* Ker, Mary

Tennyson, Matilda (sister, Tilly), 48, 50, 209, 385 and n, 408n

Tennyson, Percy, 553n

Terry, Ellen, 220n

Thackeray, Anne Isabella (later Ritchie), 319, 333 and n, 346

Thackeray William Makepeace, 5n, 198, 245, 248, 252, 333 and n, 350; death, 346, 347n

Thackeray, Mrs William Makepeace, 347n

Theed, William, 351n

'Third of February, 1852, The', 21n, 26n

Thomasson, Thomas, 411 and n

Thompson, Frances Elizabeth (née Selwyn), 480n

Thompson, John Reuben, 17n, 385n, 408n, 425 and n, 432n

Thompson, William Hepworth, 480n

Ticknor and Fields, 133n, 428 and n, 479

Ticknor, Reed and Fields, 105, 428

Tilton, J. E., 428

Times, The, 23, 53, 100n, 125n, 127, 131, 300, 305, 317

'Tithonus', 248 252, 253

'To the Queen', 434 and n

Todd, James A., 368

Townshend, John Robert, 323n

Tregarthen, Capt., 264

Trench, Richard Chenevix, 79, 140

Trevelyan, Charles Edward, 314n

Trevelyan, Lady Hannah (née Macaulay), 267n 270n, 317 and n

Trollope, Edward, 222 and n

Troubridge, Ernest, 559

Troubridge, Lady Laura (née Gurney), 559

Troubridge, Sir Thomas, 559

Troubridge, Una (née Taylor), 559

Trübner, Nicholas, 247, 380 and n

Tuckerman, Frederick Goddard, 104n, 109n

Tuckerman, Dr Samuel, 104n, 109 and n

Tuckerman, Sophia May, 109n

Tupper, Martin Farquhar, 27n-8n, 59, 104n(?), 241n, 423

Turner, Charles Tennyson, 48

Turner, Louisa Tennyson (Louie), 48, 394 and n

Tweedie, Alexander, 205 and n (?)

Twickenham, Chapel House, 3-7, 10, 12-49, 56-65, 147

'Two Voices, The', 460

Tyndall, John, 35n, 424

'Ulysses', 248, 252

Vaughan, Adeline (née Jackson), 559

Vaughan, Dr Charles J., 416n

Vaughan, Henry Halford, 559

Venables, Edmund, 230 and n

Venables, George Stovin, 5, 6, 9, 12, 33, 48, 74, 130, 140, 141, 146, 159, 379

Venables, Joseph Henry, 446 and n

Venables, Revd Richard (d. 1858), 168n

Venables, Revd Richard Lister (d. 1894), 159 and n

Verrochio, Andrea del, 205n

'Victim, The', 457n, 471 and n, 476n, 504n

Victoria Adelaide Mary Louisa, Princess Royal, 190 and n, 191, 195, 297 and n, 298, 300, 325

Victoria, Queen, 10, 16, 17, 142, 288-9, 310n-11n, 323; visit expected, 150-1; extra verses for national anthem, 190-2; and Prince Albert's death, 289-95, 297n, 298; memorial to mother, 350-1; Tennyson's visit, 301 and n, 302, 304, 325-9, 402, 457; and Queen Emma, 412

Vincent, Henry, 31

'Vision of Sin, The', 348

'Vivien', 489

'Voice spake out of the skies, A', 477 and n

'Voyage, The', 349n, 354 and n, 357

'Wages', 476 and n, 477 and n, 479, 504n

Wales, visit to, 156-60, 499

Walker, William Sydney, 43, 44

Walpole, Spencer Horatio, 545 and n

'War, The', *see* 'Rifle-Clubs!!!'

Warburton, Eliot, 22 and n

Warburton, William Parsons, 274 and n
Ward, Louisa Edith (née Simeon), 372n
Ward, Richard, 372n
Ward, Samuel, 554n
Warninglid, 8–9
Watkins, Herbert, 276n
Watts, George Frederick, 204, 208, 217n, 220 and n, 221 and n, 231, 247, 336, 341
Waugh, Alice Gertrude (later Woolner), 372n
Waugh, Edwin, 451 and n
Waugh, Fanny (later Hunt), 417
Waugh, George, 372 and n
Waugh, Mary, 372 and n
Wedgwood, Emma (later Darwin), 500 and n
Wegg-Prosser (earlier Haggitt), Richard, 151 and n
'Welcome to Alexandra, A', 322 and n, 323 and n
Weld, Agnes Grace, 30, 34, 48, 115 and n, 135
Weld, Anne (née Sellwood), 6n, 30, 48, 202
Weld, Charles Richard, 3, 4, 13n, 23, 48, 59, 82, 90, 93, 139, 141, 166–7, 209, 210, 273 and n, 427; death, 520n
Weld, Frederick Aloysius, 171 and n
Weld, Isaac, 115 and n
Wellesley, Gerald Valerian, 350 and n
Wellington, Duke of, 10, 43 and n, 48, 51; *see also* 'Ode on the Death etc.'
West, Harriet (later Tennyson), 385 and n
Whewell, William, 84
White, Arnold William, 505 and n, 506n, 516, 518, 534
White, James, 42
White, John, 544n
White, Walter, 216, 217n, 309n, 386, 411, 489; journals of, 261, 353–4, 360–1, 383–4, 414n, 425n–6n
Wight, Isle of, *see* Farringford
Wightwick, Caroline (née Damant), 189
Williams and Norgate, 246, 380
Williams Ap Ithel, Elizabeth Lloyd, 387n
Williams Ap Ithel, Revd John, 168, 387 and n
Williams, Ebenezer [Eliezer], 157
Williams, Elizabeth (later Williams Ap Ithel), 387n
Williams, Sydney, 246n

Willis, Rhoda (later Elton, Lady), 370n
Willmott, Revd Robert Aris, 125 and n, 127, 131
Wilson, Mrs, 16
Wilson, Thomas, 345n, 360, 379, 382n
Wilson, William, 535 and n
'Window, The' ('The Loves of the Wrens'), 444, 468, 469n, 470, 471 and n, 475, 480, 504n, 556 and n, 557; music for, 447, 469; pirated edition, 533–4, 535, 543 and n; readings of, 447–8
Wiseman, Cardinal Nicholas Patrick Stephen, 343
Wolff, Dr Joseph, 255 and n, 256n
Wood, Lady Emma Carolina (née Mitchell), 459 and n
Wood, Revd Sir John Page, 459n
Woodfall, Henry Dickwood, 205, 409n
Woodford, John, 306 and n
Woodford, John Lord, 306 and n, 307
Woolf, Leonard and Virginia (née Stephen), 559
Woolley, John, 424 and n, 425
Woolner, Alice (née Waugh), 372n 382
Woolner, Thomas, 200, 218, 251, 262, 267, 311, 353n, 354, 357n, 374, 382, 383, 402, 506; design for Wordsworth monument, 31 and n; medallions by, 55 and n; in Manchester, 184, 185, 187; and Tennyson portrait, 217n; recommended by Tennyson, 251, 299, 304; marriage, 372n; Symonds visits, 414–21
Wordsworth, William, 10, 31 and n, 162 and n
Worsley, Philip Stanhope, 343 and n, 419
'Wrens', *see* 'Window, The'
Wright, Harnet, 4
Wyndham-Quin, Edward Richard (Earl of Dunraven), 432 and n

Yates, Edmund, 423n
Yonge, Charlotte, 471n
Yorkshire, visits to, 31–5, 65, 314–16, 340, 342

Zeller, Caecilie, 310n